TIM BLANNING

The Pursuit of Glory

Europe 1648–1815

PENGUIN BOOKS

For Nicky, Tom, Lucy and Molly

PENGUIN BOOKS

Published by the Penguin Group
Penguin Books Ltd, 80 Strand, London WC2R ORL, England
Penguin Group (USA) Inc., 375 Hudson Street, New York, New York 10014, USA
Penguin Group (Canada), 90 Eglinton Avenue East, Suite 700, Toronto, Ontario, Canada M4P 2Y3
(a division of Pearson Penguin Canada Inc.)
Penguin Ireland, 25 St Stephen's Green, Dublin 2, Ireland
(a division of Penguin Books Ltd)
Penguin Group (Australia), 250 Camberwell Road, Camberwell, Victoria 3124, Australia
(a division of Pearson Australia Group Pty Ltd)
Penguin Books India Pvt Ltd, 11 Community Centre, Panchsheel Park, New Delhi – 110 017, India
Penguin Group (NZ), 67 Apollo Drive, Rosedale, North Shore 0632, New Zealand
(a division of Pearson New Zealand Ltd)
Penguin Books (South Africa) (Pty) Ltd, 24 Sturdee Avenue, Rosebank, Johannesburg 2196, South Africa

Penguin Books Ltd, Registered Offices: 80 Strand, London WC2R ORL, England

www.penguin.com

First published by Allen Lane 2007
Published in Penguin Books 2008
004

Copyright © Tim Blanning, 2007
All rights reserved

The moral right of the author has been asserted

Typeset by Rowland Phototypesetting Ltd, Bury St Edmunds, Suffolk
Printed in England by Clays Ltd, St Ives plc

978-0-140-16667-5

www.greenpenguin.co.uk

ALWAYS LEARNING   **PEARSON**

THE PENGUIN HISTORY OF EUROPE

GENERAL EDITOR: DAVID CANNADINE

THE PURSUIT OF GLORY

'Europe's early-modern history viewed from an Olympian height – a grand, gripping and all-encompassing read' *Sunday Times*

'A triumphant success . . . Blanning brings to his period knowledge, experience, sound judgment and a colourful narrative style' *Economist*

'One of the most impressive general histories to have appeared for many decades . . . a big – though colossally complicated – story. It is good, then, to see it told so colossally well' *Sunday Telegraph*

'An exciting, well-written and judicious book' *BBC History Magazine*

'Magisterial' *Financial Times*

'Excellent . . . a surefooted guide to the complexities of diplomatic manoeuvring and armed conflict' *Guardian*

'History writing at its best – authoritative, fresh, crammed with incident and ideas and eminently readable' *Sunday Herald*

THE PENGUIN HISTORY OF EUROPE

ABOUT THE AUTHOR

Tim Blanning is Professor of Modern European History at the University of Cambridge and a Fellow of Sidney Sussex College, Cambridge. He is also a Fellow of the British Academy. His books include *The Culture of Power and the Power of Culture*, *The French Revolutionary Wars, 1787–1802*, *The Origins of the French Revolutionary Wars*, *The French Revolution: Class War or Culture Clash?*, *The French Revolution in Germany*, *Joseph II* and *Reform and Revolution in Mainz*.

Contents

Part One: Life and Death

Part Two: Power

Part Three: Religion and Culture

List of Illustrations

Photographic acknowledgements are given in parentheses.

1. A section of new road from Valencia to Barcelona, eighteenth-century engraving. Private collection.
2. Francisco da Goya y Lucientes, *Highwaymen Attacking a Coach*, 1787. Private collection. (Giraudon/Bridgeman Art Library)
3. Pierre Mignard, *Louis XIV at Maastricht*, 1673. Galleria Sabauda, Turin. (Scala, Florence)
4. Pierre Patel le Père, View of the château de Versailles, 1668. Châteaux de Versailles et de Trianon, Versailles. (Copyright © Photo RMN – Gérard Blot)
5. The burning of Heidelberg by the French in 1689, woodcut from a pamphlet published by J. J. Felsecker (Nuremberg, 1690). Germanisches Nationalmuseum, Nuremberg. (BPK, Berlin)
6. Johann Bernhard Fischer von Erlach's design for a new palace at Schönbrunn, engraving by Johann Adam Delsenbach, *c*.1695. (akg-images)
7. School of Adam Frans van der Meulen, Louis XIV hunting near Fontainebleau, second half of the seventeenth century. Châteaux de Versailles et de Trianon, Versailles. (akg-images/VISIOARS)
8. Fox-tossing at the Electoral Palace, Dresden, 1678, engraving from Gabriel Tzschimmer, *Die Durchlauchtigste Zusammenkunfft* (Nuremberg, 1680).
9. A hunt at Neckargemünd in 1758 organized for the Elector Karl Theodor of the Palatinate. Kurpfälzisch Museum, Heidelberg.
10. Palazzo di Caserta, engraving by Carlo Nolli from *Dichiarazione dei Disegni del Reale Palazzo di Caserta*, published by Luigi Vanvitelli, 1756. (The Stapleton Collection/Bridgeman Art Library)

Maps

Map 1: Europe in the era of Louis XIV

Map 2: Europe in the eighteenth century

N

NORWAY
Christiani

SCOTLAND

IRELAND
Dublin

North
Sea

DENMARK
Copenhagen

East Friesland
Holstein
MECKLENBR

GREAT
BRITAIN

WALES
ENGLAND
London

Amsterdam

UTD. PROVINCES

Hanover

P
Berli

Cleves
Berg
Jülich

SAXONY

ATLANTIC
OCEAN

Austrian
Netherlands

HOLY ROMA

Paris

Seine

Palatinate

Upper
Palatinate

Rhine
BADEN
WÜRTTEM-
BERG

Loire

Mainz

BAVARIA

FRANCE

Rhône

Montbéliard

SWITZERLAND

Tyrol

SAVOY

Milan

Piedmont

Milan

VENIC

PORTUGAL

Ven-
aissin

PARMA
GENOA
LUCCA

MODENA

TUSCANY

PAPAL
STATES

Lisbon

Madrid

SPAIN

CORSICA

Rome

SPAIN

Balearic Is.

SARDINIA

TWO SICILI

Mediterranean Sea

—— Boundary of the Holy Roman Empire

| 0 | 100 | 200 | 300 | 400 | 500 mls |

| 0 | 200 | 400 | 600 | 800 km |

Map 3: Europe in 1809

N

KINGDOM OF NORWAY AND DENMARK

SCOTLAND

IRELAND

North Sea

Copenhagen

HELIGOLAND (Gr. Br)

Lübeck

GREAT BRITAIN

WALES

ENGLAND

Bremen

Hamburg

WESTPHALIA

Berlin

London

Antwerp

Brussels

Leipzig 1813 ✕

Auerstädt 1806 ✕

SAX

ATLANTIC OCEAN

Seine

Amiens

Waterloo 1815

Jena 1806 ✕

CONFEDERATION OF THE RHINE

Paris

Lunéville

WÜRTTEMBERG

Loire

Rhine

BADEN

BAVARIA

FRANCE

Rhône

Zurich

SWITZERLAND

ILLYRIAN

Milan

Po

KINGDOM OF ITALY

Marengo 1800 ✕

Genoa

Marseilles

Lisbon

Madrid

CORSICA

Elba

PORTUGAL

SPAIN

Rome

Naples

Trafalgar 1805 ✕

SARDINIA

GIBRALTAR (Gr. Br)

KINGDOM OF NAPLES

Mediterranean Sea

✕ Major battles

| 0 | 100 | 200 | 300 | 400 | 500 mls |

| 0 | 200 | 400 | 600 | 800 km |

MALTA (Gr. Br)

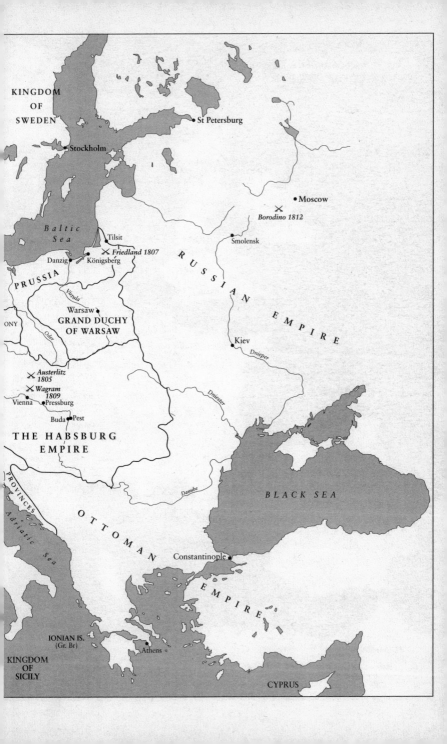

Map 4: Europe in 1815

N

NORWAY
Christiania

SCOTLAND

North
Sea

IRELAND
Dublin

DENMARK
Copenhagen

GREAT
BRITAIN

WALES
ENGLAND
London   Amsterdam   HANOVER

ATLANTIC
OCEAN

Brussels   UNITED NETHERLANDS   WEST-
                                          PHALIA   SAXONY   K. of
                                                                      SAXONY

LUX.   BOH

Paris   Seine   BADEN   BAVARIA

Loire
                Rhône   WÜRTTEM-
                                           BERG

FRANCE   SWITZERLAND   ILLYRIA

                SAVOY   Milan
                             LOMBARDY-VENETIA

PORTUGAL   PIEDMONT   PARMA

Lisbon   MONACO   MOD   SAN
                                          LUCCA   MARINO
        Madrid   TUSCANY
                ANDORRA   PAPAL
                                          STATES
SPAIN   CORSICA   Rome

                Balearic Is.   K. OF THE TWO SICILIES

                                          SARDINIA

        M e d i t e r r a n e a n   S e a

——— Boundary of German Confederation

0   100   200   300   400   500 mls

0   200   400   600   800 km

Map 5: The Holy Roman Empire and the Habsburg Monarchy in the eighteenth century

Baltic

North Sea

UNITED PROVINCES

(HOLLAND)

AUST. NETHERLANDS (BELGIUM)

Brussels
Liège

Osnabrück
Münster
MÜNSTER
Essen
Cologne
COLOGNE
Bonn

HANOVER

Hildesheim
Paderborn
Göttingen

PRUSSIA
•Berlin

SAXONY
Leipzig• •Hubertusburg
Dresden•

Wetzlar
Fulda
Frankfurt•

TRIER

Luxemburg
Trier•
BAR

Mainz•

Würzburg •Bamberg

Prague•

BOHEMIA

LORRAINE

PALATINATE
Speyer•

MAINZ

ANSBACH

Strassburg•

WÜRTTEM-BERG

Regensburg•

BAVARIA
Augsburg•

Passau•
Linz•

VORLANDE
St Blasien•
Basle•

SWABIA

INNVIERTEL (1779)

Munich•

UPPER AUSTRIA

FRANCE

Constance•
VORARLBERG

Salzburg•

Innsbruck•

SALZBURG

STYRIA

SWISS CONFEDERATION

TYROL

CARINTHIA

PIEDMONT
(K. OF SARDINIA)

Milan•
Pavia•
LOMBARDY

VENICE
•Verona
Mantua•

Gorizia•

CARNIOLA

Parma•

Venice•

GENOA

Modena•
•Bologna

Adriatic Sea

San Remo•

Lucca•
Florence•

Mediterranean Sea

TUSCANY

PAPAL STATES

CORSICA

—	Generally accepted boundary of the Empire (Reich)
	Principal ecclesiastical states
	Prussian gains by partition of Poland in 1772
	Prussia from the 1740s
	The Monarchy from the 1740s
	The Monarchy's gains in the 1770s
	Military frontier regions

0   100   200 mls
0   100   200   300 km

Sea

Danzig•

EAST PRUSSIA

Vistula

Warsaw•

P O L A N D

S I L E S I A

Breslau•

•Neisse

SILESIA

•Wieliczka

Teschen•

Lemberg•

G A L I C I A
(1772)

Olmütz•

MORAVIA

ZIPS
(1770)

Dniester

Sereth

Shrutz

Brünn•

LOWER

•Melk

Vienna•

•Pressburg

AUSTRIA

Danube

•Vác

Buda•

•Pest

H U N G A R Y

BUKOVINA
(1775)

Pruth

M O L D A V I A

T R A N S Y L V A N I A

Hermannstadt•

•Temesvár

B Á N Á T

W A L L A C H I A

Carlstadt•

SLAVONIA

Belgrade•

Old Orsova•

LITTLE

•Passarowitz

WALLACHIA

CROATIA

Save

Danube

B O S N I A

O T T O M A N

DALMATIA

S E R B I A

E M P I R E

MONTENEGRO

Preface

In the course of the many years it has taken to prepare and write this book, I have incurred many debts. Not the least of them is to my editor at Penguin, Simon Winder, who has always been as supportive as he has been patient. I owe a very great deal to the generations of students at Cambridge I have been fortunate enough to teach and learn from. This particular acknowledgement goes well beyond conventional courtesy, for it is only when thinking about what I might say to them, and then improvising it in the lecture- or seminar-room, and seeking to deal with their criticisms, that any worthwhile ideas have come my way. Another activity conducive to creative thought is walking the dog, from home to the Faculty in the morning, out into the fields west of Cambridge at lunchtime and back home in the evening. For that reason, I have included Molly the Dalmatian among the dedicatees of this book. Although usually dozing, she has been present on her favourite armchair in the window-alcove of my office while every word of this book has been written. The Faculty of History has provided me with the ideal working environment, not least because it contains the largest dedicated history library in the country, and is only a couple of minutes away from one of the great libraries of the world, in the shape of the University Library. To the staffs of both libraries, especially Dr Linda Washington of the Seeley Historical Library, I express my warm appreciation. Of the very numerous colleagues, in and outside Cambridge, who have helped me in all sorts of ways, I single out for special thanks Chris Clark, Brendan Simms, Heinz Duchhardt, Charles Blanning, Ivan Valdez Bubnov, Eirwen Nicholson, Emma Griffin, David Brading, Robert Tombs, Robert Evans, Jo Whaley, Roderick Swanston, Martin Randall, Peter Dickson, Simon Dixon, Uwe Puschner, Ulrike Paul, Hagen Schulze, Munro Price, Bill Doyle, Julian Swann, Peter Wilson, Maiken Umbach and Jonathan Steinberg. I owe a special debt to Derek Beales and Hamish Scott, who heroically read my typescript and saved me from many sins of omission and commission. Not long after I began writing, my son Tom was born, to be joined three years later by Lucy. Although their arrival slowed progress appreciably, they also provided the necessary impetus to get me through the sticky periods. I could not have finished at all if my wife, Nicky, had not shouldered most of the burdens of parenthood, leaving me with just the pleasures. So it is right that her name should appear first on the list of dedicatees, just as she is first in my heart.

Tim Blanning
Cambridge, July 2006

Introduction

Every history of Europe has to start at some arbitrary date, unless of course an attempt is being made to cover everything since the emergence of *Homo sapiens*. But some dates are more arbitrary than others. Unfortunately, within the same period a date can mean something for one kind of human activity but very little for another. Seventeen eighty-nine, for example, has a thunderous resonance for politics but barely registers a bat's squeak for music or the visual arts. Sixteen forty-eight is of that kind. It looks like a sensible starting point because it was in that year that the Peace of Westphalia was concluded, bringing to an end a war that had lasted thirty years and had inflicted more devastation on Europe than any previous conflict. Moreover, it settled at least two major issues, for the independence of the Dutch Republic from Spain was recognized, and the structure of German-speaking Europe was settled for a century and a half. More important still was what lay behind those two settlements: the recognition that confessional pluralism had come to stay. Both Catholic and Protestant zealots would continue to dream dreams of the triumph of their true faiths, but the stalemate recognized in 1648 was never seriously threatened.

So this volume's initial date can be justified, but it must also be recognized that the Westphalian settlement left as much unfinished business as it concluded. The war between Spain and France sputtered on until the Peace of the Pyrenees in 1659, and perhaps did not really end until the Bourbon inheritance of Spain was given international recognition in 1714. In the north and the east, the situation continued to be fluid, as Swedish supremacy was contested by first one power and then another in a confusing series of wars that did not end until the Peace of Nystad in 1721. What were to become the two dominant forces in international politics were the 'Second Hundred Years War' between

England and France, which did not begin until 1688, and the expansion of Russia, which did not begin until 1695. If anything, the direction being taken by domestic politics was even more uncertain. It was in 1648 that the French civil wars – the *Frondes* – began and in 1649 that a republic was proclaimed in England, following the execution of Charles I. The very different resolutions of those conflicts had to await the beginning of Louis XIV's 'sole reign' in 1661 and the 'Glorious Revolution' of 1688 respectively.

There were loose ends in 1648 and there were to be loose ends in 1815. In the chapters that follow, the threads are spun together to provide a guide through the labyrinth that seeks to be coherent without being schematic. If there is no master-narrative of the kind advanced by Hegel or Marx – or even the Whig historians – there are certainly lines of development to be identified. In politics, the most striking of these was the relentless march of the state to hegemony. By 1815 in most parts of Europe the claims of the state to a monopoly of legislation and allegiance within its borders were established in fact if not in law. Although there was a rich multiplicity of constitutional forms, ranging from democracy to autocracy, behind them all lay the sovereignty of an abstraction – the state. Political structures unable to achieve that 'monopoly of legitimate force' (Max Weber) that lies at the heart of the state, such as Poland and the Holy Roman Empire, became easy prey for rivals who had read the signs of the times more accurately. Part and parcel of this development was secularization, which in Catholic countries involved the exclusion of any form of papal interference and everywhere dictated the subordination of Church to State. But the blood that ran through the veins of the state was thin and tepid. To motivate its members, the transfusion of something more inspiring was needed. Increasingly, that was found in nationalism, a secular religion with the ability to unleash devotion and hatred just as fierce as anything experienced during the religious conflicts of an earlier period.

Successful states also needed to adapt to social change. Only those which succeeded in integrating their elites could flourish. This might be achieved through a court, as in Louis XIV's Versailles project; or through a representative assembly, such as the English Parliament; or through a service nobility, as in Prussia and Russia; or through a combination of all three, as in the Habsburg Monarchy. In every case, there proved to be an inbuilt tendency to that ossification that seems to be inseparable from political institutions. Even the unusually adaptable British solution was experiencing a hardening of the arteries by 1815. Whatever their social complexion, all European states had to come to terms with the emergence of a new kind of cultural space – the public sphere. Situated between the private world of the family and the official world of the state, the public sphere was a forum in which previously isolated individuals could come together to exchange information, ideas and criticism. Whether communicating with each other at long range by subscribing to the same periodicals, or meeting face to face in a coffee-house or in one of the new voluntary associations, such as a reading club or Masonic lodge, the public acquired a collective weight far greater than the sum of its individual members. It was from the public sphere that a new source of authority emerged to challenge the opinion-makers of the old regime: public opinion. The timing of this transition naturally varied across Europe. First in the field were Britain and the Dutch Republic, for they had in common relatively high rates of literacy and urbanization and enjoyed a relatively liberal censorship regime. *Mutatis mutandis*, at the other extreme and at the other end of Europe, it is next to impossible to find anything resembling a public sphere or public opinion in Russia before the nineteenth century. As we shall see, when managed effectively, public opinion could be a source of extra resources and extra authority for a state. Where it was ignored, misunderstood or alienated, as it was in France, the result could be revolutionary change.

The forces that created the public sphere derived most fundamentally from the expansion of Europe both at home and abroad. After the acute problems of the first half of the seventeenth century caused by war, recession, plague and famine, recovery was slow, fitful and patchy, but gradually the indicators began to point upwards: rising population, higher agricultural productivity, expanding trade and manufacturing, increasing urbanization and a resumption of colonial expansion. By the second quarter of the eighteenth century, the process began to consolidate and accelerate, although still punctuated by setbacks. Of special importance were the improvements in physical communications that are discussed in the first chapter. The benefits were spread unequally. First in the queue was the state, whose appetite for more taxation to sustain the ever-increasing armed forces reached out to grasp both the rich man in his castle and the poor man at his gate. Next came the landowners, happily taking advantage of the 'price scissors' that opened up between the increasing sums they received for their agricultural produce and the relatively declining cost of the manufactured goods they purchased. With the price of land trebling and the prestige attached to landownership undiminished, the enterprising could flourish mightily. A key group were the tenant-farmers, to whom credit for most of the agricultural innovations of the period must be given. Also blooming were the financiers, especially those who managed to get involved in state financing, and the merchants, especially those involved in the colonial trades. Enterprising manufacturers able to work outside the restrictive practices of the guilds could enjoy a double benefit from both the growth of the labour supply and the consumer revolution that gathered strength as the eighteenth century progressed.

In short, the economic expansion of the eighteenth century produced a large and growing class of beneficiaries. Perhaps best placed to make the most of the century's opportunities was a grandee who owned large estates rich in mineral resources, served by good communications and located in industrializing regions, and – perhaps most important of all – who was blessed with the necessary intellectual and personal qualities to become an entrepreneur. In an ideal world, he – and he would need to be a 'he' too, for women were subject to all manner of discrimination – would also marry into a family engaged in government finance, investment banking and overseas commerce. He would need a conscience robust enough to allow him to forget the involuntary services performed by the seven million slaves transported from Africa to the Caribbean during the course of the century. He would also be well-advised to be an Englishman and thus relatively immune to the sudden visits from Nemesis in the shape of war or revolution, to which his continental colleagues were so prone, especially after 1789.

But the benefits were spread very unevenly. Geographically, there was a sharp gradient from the commercial north-west of Europe, where significant industrialization was well underway by 1815, to the underdeveloped east, where one could travel for weeks without encountering anything resembling a town and where, if material and social conditions had changed at all, they had changed for the worse. Here servitude, illiteracy, poverty and low life expectancy were still the norm in 1815, as they had been in 1648. Even in the west the economic expansion could not absorb the rapidly growing population. The inelasticity of food production drove up prices, while the inelasticity of industry pushed down wages. The result was impoverishment for that large proportion of the population that was not self-sufficient. A new kind of poverty emerged, not a sudden affliction by famine, plague or war but a permanent state of malnutrition and underemployment. It was also a vicious circle, for the undernourished were not so wretched as to be unable to produce the children who perpetuated their misery. They were also increasingly at the mercy of market forces, as capitalism eroded the traditional society of orders and its values.

It is tempting to adopt a rationalist teleology to chart the progress of the new values. 'The age of reason' or 'the age of enlightenment' are labels for the period so popular as to be almost clichés. But behind every cliché there must stand a core of truth. This period did indeed witness a degree of rationalism and secularization unprecedented in European history. It saw the publication of Newton's *Principia*, Locke's *An Essay Concerning Human Understanding*, Hume's *A Treatise of Human Nature*, Montesquieu's *The Spirit of the Laws* and Diderot and d'Alembert's *Encyclopédie*, just to mention a few of the crucial texts that eroded the traditional theocentric view of the universe. Yet just as good a case could be made for calling it 'the age of faith', for it was marked by a number of powerful religious revivals, including Jansenism, Pietism and Methodism, and religious literature had never been more popular. Nor was there any tapering off as the eighteenth century progressed, as the great Romantic revolution demonstrated. As will be argued in Chapter 10, it makes more sense to conceptualize cultural developments not as a linear progression from faith to reason but as a dialectical encounter between a culture of feeling and a culture of reason. The most profound exploration of this existential conflict was undertaken by Goethe in *Faust*, the gigantic poem of more than 12,000 lines that occupied him off and on for most of his adult life and from which the following lines can serve as an epigraph for this book:

> Two souls, alas, dwell within my breast, and their
> Division tears my life in two.
> One loves the world, it clutches her, it binds
> Itself to her, clinging with furious lust;
> The other longs to soar beyond the dust
> Into the realm of high ancestral minds.

PART ONE

Life and Death

I

Communications

Communication is central to human existence. Apart from basic physical functions such as eating and defecating, waking and sleeping, nothing is more central. Whether the form it takes is symbolic, as in speech, or physical, as in travel, it is communication between people and people, or between people and places, that weaves the social fabric. That is why communication provides the best point of entry to the past. A time-traveller from today arriving in the seventeenth century would find no aspect of everyday life more alien to modern experience. Coming from a world which can be circumnavigated by air in less than two days, the shock at finding oneself anchored in glutinous immobility would be profound. Only with great effort, expense and time could even modest distances be traversed. Moreover, instead of being comforted en route by the presence of universal symbols, logos and language, the traveller would quickly encounter incomprehensible dialects and patois. As we shall see, it was from problems of communication, both physical and symbolic, that many of the distinctive features of the old regime derived.

ROADS

For most Europeans in the seventeenth and eighteenth centuries, it was the condition of the roads which dictated the pace of communications and the degree of mobility. Almost everywhere the 'roads' were tracks, with no foundations or drainage and consequently deeply pitted by wheel-ruts. They were muddy quagmires when it rained and dust bowls when the sun shone: 'more like a retreat of wild beasts and reptiles, than the footsteps of man', in the view of an English observer writing about the early eighteenth century. Even the main highways would count for forest tracks today. The roads of Europe were essentially those of the Roman Empire – after fourteen hundred years of neglect. Whether in Galway or Galicia, the average speed for the great majority of travellers rarely exceeded walking pace. Indeed, for most people the average speed could only be walking pace, for the good reason that this was the only way they could afford to move from place to place: 'on Shanks' pony', '*en el coche de San Fernando*', '*auf Schusters Rappen*', etc. In the weary words of the Scottish poet Robert Fergusson in 1774,

> And auld shanks-naig wad tire, I dread,
> To pace to Berwick.

Travelling by horse-drawn coach was more exclusive, a little faster, but much more expensive and arguably more gruelling, as a contribution to *The London Magazine* entitled 'The Miseries of a Stage-Coach' in 1743 made clear. After recounting the various discomforts of a journey from London to York, which included beginning at three o'clock in the morning, bumping and jolting along uneven roads, and having to put up with fellow passengers who variously smelt of garlic, broke wind, snored, talked incessantly, blasphemed and complained, the author concluded,

> If, of stages the boasted convenients be sung –
> May I travel a foot, though it be on a crutch.

Journeys were seldom hastened by the routing of roads along the shortest distance from point to point. The sinuous, time- and effort-consuming nature of English roads was legendary. Although this meandering caused travellers inconvenience, one foreign observer, Pierre Jean Grosley, when travelling from Dover to London in 1771, saw it as a symptom of political virtue:

The high roads are very far from being exactly rectilineal; not but that there are engineers in England skilful enough to draw a right line across a field; but, besides that the dearness of land requires some caution, property in England is a thing sacred, which the laws protect from all encroachment, not only from engineers, inspectors, and other people of that stamp, but even from the king himself; add to this, that, as we shall find in the Article of gardens, the right line is not to the taste of the English.

Conditions on the continent were no better, rather the contrary. Arthur Young found the post-chaise which bore him from Calais to

Paris in 1787 to be much worse and even more expensive than its English equivalent. Nowhere did suspensions cushioned by springs become common before 1800. Dutch coaches were notoriously uncomfortable: an English visitor took one look at the vehicle which was to carry him from Hoorn to Enkhuizen and declined to get aboard. He allowed his luggage to be put in but preferred to walk the 13 miles (21 km). If he had walked on into the Holy Roman Empire, he would have found no respite. In the view of James Boswell, the typical German coach was a 'barbarity', as it was 'just a large cart, mounted on very high wheels, which jolts prodigiously. It has no covering and three or four deal boards laid across it serve as seats.' His verdict was confirmed by the Russian Nikolai Karamzin, who recorded in 1789: 'The Prussian "stagecoach", so-called, bears no resemblance whatever to a coach. It is nothing but a long covered wagon with two benches, and with neither straps nor springs.' Its slowness and unreliability were also notorious; one contemporary complained that the best way of learning the need to be patient, apart from marriage, was travelling around Germany. It was no better south of the Alps, where Arthur Young described the carriages as 'wretched, open, crazy, jolting, dirty dung-carts', adding, 'to step at once from an agreeable society into an Italian *voiture* is a kind of malady which does not agree with my nerves'. Travelling on the King's business was no guarantee of comfort or speed, as Louis XIV's special envoy, Nicolas Mesnager, found when he went to Madrid in 1708. From Bayonne he reported to Versailles that his journey had already taken nine days, due to the poor state of the roads and the disorder of the staging system. In terms of distance, he was already more than halfway to his destination, but he estimated that he would be another fortnight on the road, so difficult was it to obtain mules.

Four or six draught animals were needed to pull a coach and they had to be changed every 6 to 12 miles (10 to 20 km), depending on the condition of the roads. In England it was calculated that one horse was needed for every mile (1.6 km) of a journey on a well-maintained turnpike road. So, for the 185 miles (300 km) from Manchester to London, 185 horses had to be kept stabled and fed to deal with the seventeen changes required by the stagecoaches which travelled the route. Those horses in turn required an army of coachmen, postillions, guards, grooms, ostlers and stable-boys to keep them running. As a coach could carry no more than ten passengers, fares were correspondingly high and out of reach of the mass of the population. A journey from Augsburg to Innsbruck by stagecoach, although little more than 60 miles (100 km) as the crow flies, would have cost an unskilled labourer more than a month's wages just for the fare. On the very eve of the coming of the railway, after significant improvements to roads and carriages had brought the cost down appreciably, a stagecoach journey from Paris to Bordeaux was still costing the equivalent of a clerk's monthly wages. Writing in the middle of the nineteenth century, the German social historian Karl Biedermann estimated that travelling had been fourteen times more expensive two generations earlier. Only the introduction of a steam locomotive able to pull a train carrying hundreds of people could create economies of scale and thus democratize travel.

Yet although the coming of the railways in the second quarter of the nineteenth century certainly did represent a revolution in transportation, it should not be allowed to overshadow the very real progress that had been made in the previous century or so. France led the way with an early initiative promoted by Jean-Baptiste Colbert, Louis XIV's chief minister for domestic affairs. One of his first measures, after securing the disgrace of his rival Fouquet in 1661, was to centralize responsibility for the maintenance of roads. In 1669 special 'commissioners for bridges and highways' were appointed to serve alongside the 'intendants', the most powerful provincial officials. As a first step towards their upgrading, all roads were classified either as 'royal roads' (*chemins royaux*) with a width of between 23 and 33 feet (7–10 m), or secondary roads (*chemins vicinaux*) or side-roads (*chemins de traverse*). Following Colbert's death in 1683, the project faltered and then became bogged down in a general relaxation of central control. By the end of the century it was reported from Flanders that the supposedly paved 'royal road' from Lille to Dunkirk was now impassable at several points, obliging merchants to send their goods from the coast by water to Ypres and then to employ double the usual number of horses to drag their carts along the muddy track that led to Lille. In general, Pierre Léon has concluded, the situation in 1700 was no better than it had been in 1660.

Significant improvement did not come until the 1740s, when the service was reorganized and a special academy established to train engineers in the art of road-building. The growing interest of the French state can be charted in the amount of money it was prepared to make available. Pierre Léon's figures demonstrate that the budget specified by

Colbert in 1668 envisaged only 0.8 per cent of national expenditure, although pressure of war in the 1670s did not allow even that target to be reached. From an average annual expenditure of 771,200 *livres* between 1683 and 1700 there was a sharp increase in the following reign to 3,000,000 *livres* for 1715–36, to more than 4,000,000 in 1770, 6,900,000 in 1780 and 9,445,000 in 1786, representing a 213-per-cent increase in the course of the century. The cumulative effect of greater expertise and investment was to create arterial roads capable of carrying passenger transport much more quickly and reliably than in the past. This is one improvement that can be quantified: in 1650 two weeks were needed to travel from Paris to Toulouse, by 1782 that had been cut by more than half; in 1664 it took ten or eleven days to travel from Paris to Lyon, a century later just six days; in the seventeenth century it had taken at least three days to cover the 60-odd miles (100 km) from Paris to Rouen, on the eve of the Revolution it could be managed in thirty-six hours. Perhaps the most spectacular reduction was in the time needed for the route to Bordeaux, which shrank from fifteen days in 1660 to five-and-a-half in 1789. According to Daniel Roche, there was not a city in France in 1789 that could not be reached in a fortnight. In 1786 the duc de Croÿ left Calais at 5.30 in the morning and reached Paris in time for a late supper at 8 p.m., having travelled 170 miles (280 km) at an average speed of almost 12 mph (20 kph).

Such a dramatic acceleration in the pace of travel was perhaps the *Ancien Régime*'s most impressive domestic achievement. It was given its most durable visual tribute by Joseph Vernet, in his magnificent painting of 1774 entitled *The Construction of a Highway* (now in the Louvre). In the foreground a group of workmen are creating a broad paved road, supervised by a foreman who is pictured reporting to a group of engineers on horseback, dressed in smart blue uniforms with gold facings; the road winds its way along an embankment cut out of the side of a hill towards a three-span bridge, itself under construction with the assistance of two large cranes; the ultimate destination is a hill-top town, overlooked by a large windmill. The entire painting speaks of hostile nature tamed by human ingenuity and labour.

There is also literary evidence in abundance. The sharp eye and mordant pen of Arthur Young found much in France to criticize, but the roads excited his enthusiasm: the road from Calais to Boulogne was 'excellent'; the road from Limoges to La Ville-au-Brun was 'truly noble';

the road to Montauban 'finely made and mended with gravel'; the roads in Roussillon 'made with all the solidity and magnificence that distinguishes the highways of France ... stupendous works ... These ways are superb even to a folly ... There is a bridge of a single arch, and a causeway to it, truly magnificent; we have not an idea of what such a road is in England'; and so on.

Yet the glamour generated by rapid passenger traffic from Paris to the provinces concealed several tenacious problems. Freight continued to move at its earlier lethargic pace of 2–2½ mph (3–4 kph). The cloth of Laval in Mayenne still took two good weeks to reach the ports of Brittany and Normandy and three to four weeks to reach Lille. Even along the new arterial routes from the capital, the improvement registered by passenger traffic was not replicated by freight, which needed three weeks in 1715 to travel from Paris to Lyon and only five or six days fewer in 1787. Along the lateral roads linking one provincial town with another there was no perceptible change: a journey from Amiens to Lyon lasted between twenty-five and thirty days in 1787, just as it had done in 1701. Adam Smith identified the problem in *The Wealth of Nations* (1776):

In France the great post-roads, the roads which make the communication between the principal towns of the kingdom, are in general kept in good order; and in some provinces are even a good deal superior to the greater part of the turnpike roads of England. But what we call cross-roads, that is, the far greater part of the roads in the country, are entirely neglected, and are in many places absolutely impassable for any heavy carriage. In some places, it is even dangerous to travel on horseback, and mules are the only conveyance which can safely be trusted.

He added that it was typical of the French system that a minister would lavish attention on a road likely to catch the eye of a court grandee and excite his praise and favour, but would neglect less glamorous but more useful projects. Even Arthur Young's praise for the excellence of French roads was tempered by the repeated observation that there was very little traffic on them. Travelling around Paris, he wrote of the roads: 'it is a desert compared with those around London. In ten miles we met not one stage or diligence; only two *messageries*, and very few chaises; not a tenth of what would have been met had we been leaving London at the same hour.' After the praise of the roads in Roussillon quoted above, he observed, 'In 36 miles, I have met one cabriolet, half-a-dozen carts, and some old women with asses. For what all this waste of treasure?'

Young's comments are put in perspective, and given indirect authority, by a very different account of conditions on the roads around London recorded by a French traveller, the naturalist and geologist Barthélemy Faujas de Saint Fond, just three years earlier, in 1784. As he travelled around the southern perimeter of London, visiting fellow scientists, he anticipated Young's compliment to his own country by commenting that the English road was 'as carefully made and as smooth as the avenue of a public promenade' but, unlike Young, he was overwhelmed by the amount of traffic:

The road was, at this time [Sunday evening], covered with numerous cavalcades of men and women, with many servants in their train. Carriages of every kind, most of them very elegant, but all of them substantial and commodious, and many of them with superb equipages, succeeded each other without interruption, and with such rapidity, that the whole picture looked like magic: it certainly showed a degree of wealth and extent of population, of which one has no notion in France. All was life, movement and rapidity; and, by a contrast only to be seen here, all was calm, silent and orderly.

His impression was confirmed by the Russian traveller Nikolai Karamzin, just off the boat from France: 'everywhere great numbers of coaches, chaises, and horsemen, and crowds of well-dressed people, for those who travel to and from London or the villages and country houses drive on the highroad; everywhere inns with saddle horses and cabriolets for hire. In short the road from Dover to London is like the main street of a populous city.'

This contrast between two contemporary experiences offers a salutary warning against seeing the construction of good roads as a sufficient route to modernity. Only a tiny proportion of the French population could travel in post-chaises up and down the 'royal routes'. According to Pierre Goubert, most peasants – i.e. most of the population – lived out their lives within a radius of only 4 to 5 miles (6 to 8 km), that is to say the area which encompassed their family, the weekly market, the notary and the seigneurial court and which they traversed on foot. They had been doing that in 1660, and they were still doing it in 1815. France covered such a huge area (more than four times the size of England), and included such diverse regions so difficult to access before the motor car, that the King's Highways could make little impression on the economy and society in general.

As Faujas de Saint Fond noticed, by the late eighteenth century the situation was different in Great Britain. Distances between major centres were shorter, the terrain was more co-operative, commercial incentives were stronger, and capital was more plentiful. Together with an instinctive aversion to initiatives directed and financed by the centre, this combination pointed to a different solution to the problem of road construction and maintenance. Since 1555 every parish had been obliged to provide labour and tools for the maintenance of the roads which passed through it. As the 'surveyor' appointed to supervise the work was not paid for his trouble, was not allowed to decline to serve and could be fined for negligence, such work as was actually undertaken was performed slowly, grudgingly and inadequately. John Billingsley recorded in his *Survey of Somerset* of 1798: 'Whenever a farmer is called forth to perform statute labour, he goes to it with reluctance and considers it a legal burden from which he derives no benefit. His servants and his horses seem to partake of the torpor of the master. The utmost exertion of the surveyor cannot rouse them, and the labour performed is scarcely half what it ought to be.'

Another contemporary source estimated that 'more work could be done with three hired teams than five statute teams, and more with five hired labourers than twenty others'. Recognizing the productivity gap between forced and paid labour, the General Highway Acts of 1766 and 1773 allowed parishioners to commute their duty into a cash payment. By that time, however, another method had been found. This was the 'turnpike', a word which originally designated just a barrier across a road to keep marauders out. As a place where a toll was to be paid, the word was first used in legislation of 1695, which began a new age of road improvement. It was underpinned by the profit motive. An entrepreneur secured an Act of Parliament authorizing him to levy a fee on traffic passing along a certain stretch of road, in return for maintaining it in good condition. For the first – but by no means the last – time we encounter here a striking feature of the British state: in terms of actual implementation of legislation, it was appreciably more effective than many of the 'absolutisms' of continental Europe. This was due to the substantial overlap between the national law-makers (Members of Parliament) and the local law-enforcers (Justices of the Peace). So, although there was vigorous, and often violent, opposition to the introduction of road tolls, the Turnpike Acts were made to stick. The beneficial effects were quickly felt.

As Defoe makes clear, the main beneficiaries were country gentlemen, who could now travel up to London much more rapidly and comfortably, to sit in Parliament, where they could pass more Turnpike Acts. This they did with relish: there were 25 Turnpike Acts in the 1730s, 37 in the 1740s, 170 in the 1750s, and 170 again in the 1760s. In 1750 143 Turnpike Trusts administered 3,500 miles (5,600 km), by 1770 500 Trusts administered 15,000 miles (24,000 km). This amounted to the construction of a national road network in the space of a couple of generations. The Turnpike Trusts were kept up to the mark less by statutory obligation than by pressure from their customers. What the latter wanted was speed, and that was what they got, as the time taken to travel between the major centres of the British Isles halved and halved again in the course of the century. A newspaper advertisement of 1754 proclaimed: 'however incredible it may appear, this coach will actually arrive in London four days after leaving Manchester'. Thirty years later, competition had cut even that 'incredible' figure in half. The following table shows the number of hours taken to travel from London to the provinces.

Table 1. Travel times from London 1700–1800 (in hours)

	1700	1750	1800
Bath	50	40	16
Edinburgh	256	150	60
Exeter	240	120	32
Manchester	90	65	33

It was a change too radical not to be noticed. In Richard Graves' novel *Columella*, for example, the eponymous hero 'observed, that the most remarkable phaenomenon which he had taken notice of these late years, in his retirement, was the surprising improvement in the art of locomotion, or conveyance from one place to another. "Who would have believed, thirty years ago," says he, "that a young man would come thirty miles in a carriage to dinner, and perhaps return at night? or indeed, who would have said, that coaches would go daily between

London and Bath, in about twelve hours; which, twenty years ago, was reckoned three good days journey?"' The most spectacular acceleration was achieved in moving people and – as we shall see later – post, but freight too could benefit. Much larger and more heavily laden wagons could pass along the improved roads: in the 1740s three-ton loads were permitted, by 1765 that had been doubled. The improved surfaces meant that fewer draught animals per ton were required. Writing in 1767, Henry Homer claimed that 'the carriage of grain, coal, merchandise etc. is in general conducted with little more than half the number of horses with which it formerly was'. By 1776, Matthew Pickford was advertising a delivery service from London to Manchester, departing daily (except Sundays) and using a 'fly wagon' of his own invention. The journey took four-and-a-half days, reduced to thirty-six hours by 1815.

The turnpikes brought speed and mobility into a society previously characterized by their opposites. This was a culture-shock which many found upsetting – especially when the lower orders started to move out of their villages, on to the roads and into the towns, picking up insubordinate habits on the way. John Byng complained bitterly in 1781: 'I wish with all my heart that half the turnpike roads of the kingdom were plough'd up, which have imported London manners and depopulated the country – I meet milkmaids on the road, with the dress and looks of Strand misses; and must think that every line of Goldsmith's *Deserted Village* contains melancholy truths.' The reference to Goldsmith's poem of 1770 is revealing, for it is an elegy for a lost world of rural innocence and harmony, from which the forces of modernization have banished the inhabitants to urban anomie and vice.

Among other disagreeable side-effects of the transport revolution to make contemporaries wonder whether it was all worth it were crime and congestion. Just as computers can solve crimes, but also allow more crimes to be committed, so did better roads both improve social control and create new opportunities for criminals. Turnpikes were places where hard cash had to be paid, so were frequently robbed. The more travellers there were on the roads, the more highwaymen appeared to make them stand and deliver. The legends surrounding Dick Turpin, hanged at the Knavesmire outside York in 1739, and his mare Black Bess, epitomized the new career opportunities offered by better roads. As those roads now made it worthwhile to keep a private carriage, towns came to be plagued by traffic jams, especially London, where about a third of the

20,000 carriages paying tax in 1762 were kept. Faujas de Saint Fond revealed both phenomena when he recorded that he had been reluctant to leave Sir Joseph Banks' house at seven in the evening, because that was a time when highwaymen were known to be very active. However, he was assured that, as it was a Sunday, there would be safety in numbers, as so many Londoners would be returning home in their carriages from day-trips to the country.

His reluctance to set forth would have been incomparably greater if his host had lived in Lisbon, Almería or Palermo, not to mention Warsaw or Moscow. Broadly speaking, there was a north–south and east–west gradient in the condition and security of Europe's roads. Where good roads were to be found on the southern periphery, they were determined more by military or representational needs than by economic considerations. Arriving at Lisbon in 1772, Richard Twiss found a fine paved road from the capital to the royal residence at Cintra and to the fortress of St Julian at the mouth of the Tagus. When he set out for Porto, however, he soon encountered roads so defective that his two-wheeled chaise had to be supported on each side by a servant, to prevent it overturning, and he himself was obliged to walk for most of the way. The sight of severed heads of highwaymen, displayed on pikes at the roadside, did nothing to improve morale. Travelling on towards the Spanish frontier, Twiss gave this graphic account of the rigours of Iberian travel:

We passed the river Mondego over a bridge of three arches. Two oxen were added to the chaise to assist the mules in dragging it up. When we arrived at the top, we let the mules rest an hour, and afterwards passed over a bridge of a single arch: then the road became excessively dangerous, over loose rocks, deep clay, and slippery precipices. The mules frequently fell down, the traces broke, it rained hard, and was quite dark when we arrived at Vinhosa, where we put up at the worst inn I ever entered before or since. There was only one room, which was full of people. They had kindled a large fire of wet wood in the middle of it; and, as there was no chimney, the smoke was left to find its way out of the windows and door. I got some straw, placed it on the top of a large chest, and rolling myself up in my cloak, fell directly asleep with all my cloaths [sic] on, my head being half out of a window to avoid suffocation.

After his Portuguese experiences, Twiss was in the mood to be more generous to what he found in Spain. He was especially impressed by the road from San Ildefonso to Madrid, wide enough to accommodate five carriages abreast and, at the pass over the Sierra de Guadarrama, the first turnpike he had seen since he left England. The 30-mile (50-km) journey from the Escorial to Madrid could be completed in four hours with the help of relays of mules pulling four-wheeled post-chaises. Twiss conferred on this latter service the ultimate compliment of comparability with speeds achieved back home. However, he was not the only traveller to notice that these flagship roads had been built to facilitate the peregrinations of the royal family and the court: to El Pardo in January, on to Aranjuez in April, back to Madrid in June, to San Ildefonso in July, to the Escorial in October and back to Madrid in November. In other words, most of what could be spared from the budget for road construction was devoted to the topmost echelons of the elite. A French traveller, the chevalier de Bourgoing, found the road from Aranjuez to Madrid was 'as fine as any in Europe . . . no road could be more straight, solid or better formed', but felt obliged to add that it had yet to regenerate the economy of the region as a whole. When the intendant of the province of Cuenca complained in 1769 about the ruinous state of the road to Madrid, he was told: 'there is no money allocated to the repair of these roads at the moment'.

That rebuff was issued fifty years after the first Bourbon King of Spain, Philip V, had issued a long ordinance envisaging a radial network to link the capital to the four corners of the kingdom. A second legislative milestone was Charles III's ordinance of 1767, which ordered the construction of 'royal roads', the first paved highways since Roman times. There was certainly some improvement. By the end of the eighteenth century, it was possible to travel in a stagecoach from Madrid to Barcelona or Cadiz, for example. One distinguished economic historian, Jaime Vicens Vives, has claimed that the highway network totalled 6,000 miles (10,000 km) by 1800, but one must wonder whether 'highway' has any meaning in this context. There is just too much contemporary evidence to suggest that moving people around Spain was still very difficult and that moving freight was often impossible. Even the optimistic Bourgoing, ever eager to laud the achievements of the Bourbons, conceded that rain made the roads in Andalucia simply impassable. Further north, the intendant of Burgos reported, 'the roads that I have seen could not be worse; it only needs a few drops of rain and they are impassable'. In 1774 José Cadalso's fictional Moroccan commented,

'Since the roads are so bad in the majority of the provinces of your country, it is not surprising that carriages frequently break down, that mules stumble and travellers lose days.' Another problem was the ever-present danger from highwaymen. They were of course common to every European country, but Spain had a particularly bad reputation. Certainly it was a Spaniard – Goya – who produced what is surely the greatest picture of highway robbery ever painted.

So long as the Spanish state's meagre resources were spent on radial routes, especially those which led to royal palaces, there could be no national economy. As John Lynch has pointed out, there was no 'Spanish economy', just 'an archipelago, islands of local production and con-sumption, isolated from each other by centuries of internal tariffs, self-sufficiency, poor roads and meagre transport'. As natural produce, raw materials and manufactures could usually be transported only on the backs of mules and donkeys, the radius of any local economy was corres-pondingly short. For example, the price of wheat in Almería was twice what it was at Guadix, just 50 miles (80 km) away. So the population followed the examples of the other coastal towns and imported grain from France, Italy or even Africa. At the other end of Spain, the Basques bought their grain from France 'because although it is cheaper in Castile, they do not bring it in because of the distance and the bad roads'.

The situation in Italy was more varied but essentially similar. So overpopulated has the Mediterranean coastline become in modern times that a powerful effort of the imagination is required to return to an era when it was largely uninhabited. Arriving at Toulon in September 1789, Arthur Young found to his astonishment that there was no regular coach service to Italy: 'to a person accustomed to the infinity of machines that fly about England in all directions, this must appear hardly credible. Such great cities in France have not the hundredth part of connection and communication with each other that much inferior places enjoy with us: a sure proof of their deficiency in consumption, activity and animation.' So he was obliged to travel by boat as far as 'Cavalero' (Cavalaire sur Mer), where he hoped to be able to arrange transport. However, there were no mules to be had for love or money, so the obliging captain sent three members of his crew to haul his luggage to a village 10 miles (16 km) further on. Here too he was disappointed and *faute de mieux* hired an old lady and her donkey to carry his possessions, while he (and the old lady) walked.

For all his Anglocentric prejudices, Young was too fair-minded and objective an observer not to find things to praise in Italy. Especially in the north there were stretches of highway capable of carrying wheeled carriages in most weathers. If that achievement seems modest, it was of recent origin. It was not until the reign of Victor Amadeus III (1773–96) that a carriageway was built over the Colle di Tenda to link Piedmont with the Kingdom's transalpine possessions in the County of Nice. Further east, it was during the second half of the eighteenth century that the Austrian Habsburgs created a link between Trieste and Vienna, by means of a road which was praised by Count Graneri as 'excellent, wide, and safe, although with steep and exhausting gradients . . . despite the distances that have to be covered, the natural obstacles, the seasonal problems of ice and snow, and the north wind which always blows, the traffic on this route is huge (*immenso*) and continuous'. In another Habsburg territory, Tuscany, the abbé Dupaty found the road from Leghorn to Florence 'magnificent', although he added that on leaving Siena 'the reign of nature and of Leopold seems here to terminate'. By that he meant, of course, that he was leaving a state flourishing under the enlightened Grand Duke Leopold and was entering the temporal possessions of the Pope, a byword for backwardness: 'On these roads, which in ancient times were thronged by kings and nations from every corner of the universe, over which rolled triumphal cars, in which the Roman armies raised clouds of dust, and where the traveller met Caesar, Cicero, and Augustus; I met only with pilgrims and with beggars.'

Across the Straits of Messina in Sicily, land routes were even more primitive. Apart from a few miles of paved roads around the capital, Palermo, the only way of getting about by land was along mule tracks or *trazzere*, the sheep runs used by herdsmen. The distance from Trápani in the west to Messina in the east is about 200 miles (350 km), but it was a journey which usually took three weeks by land. Indeed, when the rains came, Messina was often inaccessible from other parts of the island, except by sea. An English traveller, the Reverend Thomas Brand, recorded in 1792: 'For about 16 miles from Palermo the road is excellent, thanks to a bishop of great wealth and public spirit – beyond it is rugged and precipice or mud. There is not a wheel in the whole country, the roads are mere paths for a single mule.' One of the most distinguished historians of Sicily in the period, Denis Mack Smith, has commented that 'a proper network of highways would have done more to change economics, politics and even morals than any other reform'. This was recognized by the government, which in the 1770s commissioned a military engineer to plan a highway from Palermo to Catania. His task proved hopeless, as both towns and noble landowners lobbied to bring the road their way. It was cynically suggested by one observer that the route could be deduced from the names of the landowners serving on the advisory commission. So the eighteenth century ended, as it began, 'without Sicily having any roads worthy of the name' (Mack Smith).

Whether it is contemporaries such as Arthur Young or the abbé Dupaty (and their comments could be replicated at will) or modern historians such as Paolo Macry or Denis Mack Smith (ditto), there is an important sense in which their contemptuous censure of Italian roads is inadequate. The Piedmontese merchant who waited patiently by a river, waiting for the flood waters to subside, or the Sicilian peasant who took his olives to market on the back of a donkey, had never been to England. They had never seen the turnpikes or the stagecoaches that were halving journey times and creating a national market. *They did not know that they were backward.* And is 'backward' anyway an appropriate concept to employ, when assessing seventeenth- and eighteenth-century conditions? If it can be agreed at once that a national road network would have greatly enhanced productivity, material prosperity, life expectancy and brought many other economic and social benefits, it can also be permitted to question whether that is the whole story. Looking past the snobbery of Arthur Young or the nostalgia of Oliver Goldsmith in the extracts quoted above, their doubts about the mobility of modernity can perhaps find a sympathetic resonance in the frenetic, congested, alienated world of the twenty-first century.

If the critics of the state of the roads in southern Europe had tried to travel to the continent's eastern periphery, they would have had plenty of time in which to think of even more punishing epithets. Even the best of Russia's arterial highways were constructed from tree trunks covered in sand or gravel, and became virtually impassable when it rained. That was true of Peter the Great's major achievement in this sector – a straight highway from St Petersburg to Moscow, begun in 1718. On good days, a speed of less than walking pace was all that could be achieved by wheeled vehicles. There were no metalled roads constructed anywhere in the vast Russian Empire during this period. In his epic *A Journey from St Petersburg to Moscow*, Aleksandr Nikolaevich Radishchev recorded:

'When I set out from Petersburg, I flattered myself that I was going on the best of roads. Such it was considered to be by everyone who had travelled on it in the wake of the Emperor. Such indeed it had once been, but only for a short time. The dirt, which covered the road and made it smooth in dry weather, turned it into a muddy bog under the softening rains of summer, and made it impassable.'

Similar complaints about conditions in the Holy Roman Empire can be found throughout the century, although there is also some evidence of improvement. At least some of the principalities began to lay down regulations as to how the major roads should be maintained: Baden in 1733, Württemberg in 1737, Hessen-Kassel in 1746, the Electorate of Trier in 1753, the Westphalian territories of the Electorate of Cologne in 1769, Saxony Weimar in 1779, Electoral Saxony in 1781 and Bavaria in 1790. Conspicuously absent from this list was Prussia, where it was alleged that Frederick the Great took the view that the longer travellers were obliged to spend in his dominions, the more money they would be obliged to inject into the local economy. In 1816 in all the territories west of the River Elbe, there were still only just over 185 miles (300 km) of highway. This was one department in which the Austrians were undeniably superior to their northern rivals, for Charles VI (1711–40) and his daughter Maria Theresa (1740–80) spent a good deal of time and effort constructing a radial system of highways from Vienna to Prague, Linz, Trieste and Pressburg (Bratislava). Other routes singled out for special praise were Aachen–Cologne, Mülheim–Düsseldorf and Bruchsal–Augsburg–Salzburg–Innsbruck. There were even contemporaries who did more than moan about the discomfort of travel. In 1784 the prolific writer Friedrich Carl von Moser looked back nostalgically to his youth when the pace of travel had been so much more leisurely. He thought it had suited the phlegmatic Germans to take their time; it was their more febrile French neighbours who were condemned to high-speed thinking, marching, shooting, hunting, eating, walking and travelling. But now all that had spread eastwards, Moser lamented. Recently he had been transported along one of the new highways (*Chausseen*) so quickly 'that I almost lost my ability to hear and see'.

WATERWAYS

The forces of friction that slowed the progress of carts and coaches were greatly reduced if the vehicle could be moved from land to water, for here there were tides and currents to be enlisted and winds to be harnessed by sails. Freed from bone-shaking discomfort and endemic hazards, waterborne travellers could glide to their destinations in boats or barges large enough to allow creature comforts (not least of which was the opportunity to keep one's distance from fellow passengers) and economies of scale. That was the theory. Practice was often less agreeable. The Straits of Dover are only 21 miles (34 km) wide, but for most passengers the distance could seem a very long way indeed. Embarking on his Grand Tour in 1777, George Ayscough made good progress from London, arriving in Dover at 4 a.m. after a journey of just nine hours. After breakfasting well but unwisely, the party joined the packet-boat which set sail for France at 8 a.m. After four hours of misery, during which every passenger was seasick, Calais hove into view. Alas, the tide was out, so the packet-boat had to beat up and down the coast. Eventually, a six-oared tender came out to collect the passengers and their luggage, but the seas were running so high that the transfer could be effected only with great difficulty and danger. After a protracted and terrifying final lap, with the tender in constant danger of foundering, Ayscough and his party reached shore feeling more dead than alive – only to be besieged by an army of 'ragamuffins' hoping to carry their luggage. This was not an uncommon experience; Arthur Young recorded laconically in his diary on 5 June 1789: 'Passage to Calais; 14 hours for reflection in a vehicle that does not allow one power to reflect.' Another grand tourist, Edward Wright, had the opposite experience. He returned across the Straits in five uneventful hours – but had been kept waiting for a favourable wind at Calais for four days. It could have been worse: in 1772, Richard Twiss waited at Falmouth for eighteen days before the winds relented and allowed the packet-boat to set sail for Lisbon.

That was the problem with sea travel: time and tide might wait for no man, but man often had to wait for time and tide. Passage from Nantes, on the west coast of France, to Danzig, in the eastern Baltic, could take as few as 18 days if conditions were just right, averaged about a month, but could be extended to 100 or even 150 days in winter, if the wind went round to the east and ships were obliged to take refuge in port. So one of the main characteristics of modern travel – the timetable – was conspicuously absent. For the eighteenth-century traveller, an incalculable amount of time was spent waiting for winds that never seemed to blow and ships that never seemed to come. It was the inland waterways which pointed the way forward, at least in terms of predictability. By 1789 there were regular services by 'water carriage' (*coche d'eau*) from Paris, leaving at 6 a.m. in summer and 7 a.m. in winter to Sens (Mondays), Montargis and Briare (Tuesdays and Thursdays), Auxerre on the Yonne (Wednesdays and Saturdays) and Nogent (Sundays). Given reasonable weather, there can have been no more pleasant way to travel.

It was in the Low Countries, however, that the plethora of both natural and man-made waterways made something approaching a modern passenger-transport system possible. The Dutch economic historian Jan de Vries has reconstructed a journey undertaken in the mid-seventeenth century from Dunkirk, in what was then the Spanish Netherlands, to Amsterdam in the Dutch Republic. As women travelled very seldom and never alone, it can be assumed that the traveller was male. Starting at dawn, as was usually the case, a passenger-carrying barge (*trekschuit*), pulled by a horse, took him along the newly constructed canal to Plasschendaele, near Ostende. After transferring to another barge on the other side of the sluice, he arrived at Bruges in time for a late supper, having travelled 42 miles (67 km) during the day. On the following day he embarked at 11 a.m. on a barge bound for Ghent. This was now barge travel *de luxe* on what was described by the English tourist Thomas Nugent as 'the most remarkable boat of the kind in all Europe; for it is a perfect tavern divided into several apartments, with a very good ordinary [meal] at dinner of six or seven dishes, and all sorts of wines at moderate prices'. Pulled by four horses, it took just eight hours to cover the 27 miles (44 km) to Ghent. From here he could have continued by barge and sailing ship to Rotterdam, but it was quicker and more predictable for him to resort to a conventional coach to travel on to Antwerp. There he caught one of the daily sailings to Dordrecht, a distance of 58 miles (93 km), which took about twenty-four hours. Now he encountered some uncertainty, as the departure of the four sailing vessels which plied between Dordrecht and Rotterdam was dependent on the tides. However, the city employed a town-crier to ensure that potential customers did not miss the sailings, so he managed to catch the last sailing and reached Rotterdam at the end of his fourth day on the road, or rather waterway. On the following day he could once again benefit from fixed timetables. He took the 5 a.m. barge, the first departure of a scheduled service which left every hour on the hour for Delft, changed there for Leiden, where he changed again, finally reaching Amsterdam at 6.15 in the evening.

However complex this journey may seem, it was relatively quick, comfortable and cheap. De Vries estimates that anywhere else in western Europe it would have cost at least three times as much to travel a comparable distance. The reputation of the Dutch passenger-barges spread far and wide: travelling west for the first time, Nikolai Karamzin was told by two Germans he met in Courland (Latvia), 'Anyone who wants to learn about the world should go to Holland. The people there live wonderfully and they all go about in boats!' Just as important symbolically was the regularity, punctuality and predictability. Traditionally, it was not only ships that set sail at approximate times, for coaches too departed 'in the morning' or 'in the evening'. The precise timetable of the Dutch passenger-boats was unusual enough to attract comment from visitors. The Englishman William Bromley, for example, recorded with a mixture of amazement and admiration in 1702: 'The hour for the Boat coming in, and going out, is so punctually observed, that upon the Ringing of a Bell it goes off, without staying for any person whatsoever.' This was part of a more general move away from what Walter Benjamin called the 'Messianic' concept of time, which had prevailed throughout the Middle Ages and well into the early modern period. It was characterized by a lack of awareness of the passage of historical time but a belief in the 'simultaneity of past and future in an instantaneous present'. So there seemed nothing odd about, say, Hieronymus Bosch depicting New Testament characters as if they were living in fifteenth-century Brabant, or Paolo Veronese depicting the same scenes as if they were occurring in sixteenth-century Venice. Alternatively, it has been suggested by Aaron Gurevich and others that perceptions of time ceased to be cyclical and became linear, so that the dominant metaphor became 'time's arrow' rather than 'fortune's wheel', in other words directional rather than endlessly repetitive.

Both symptom and cause was the growing popularity of clocks and watches. Together with developments such as the Dutch timetables, this encouraged a new sense of time – 'homogeneous, empty time' – perceived as diachronic and capable of measurement by calendar and timepiece. Once established, the idea that 'time is money' meant that coach or barge companies with an attitude of 'We'll start when I feel like it' were doomed. Travelling by passenger-barge in the Dutch Republic in 1670, Sir William Temple wrote: 'by this easie way of travelling, an industrious man loses no time from his business, for he writes or eats, or sleeps while he goes; whereas the time of labouring or industrious men is the greatest native commodity of any country'. This shift also had important cultural implications, as the notion of a 'time budget' increasingly divided the day into work and recreation and led to the separation of the arts from everyday activities. As we shall see in a later chapter, this helped the emergence not just of the autonomy of art but also of its sacralization.

This excursion may seem to have taken us a long way from horse-drawn passenger-barges plodding slowly, quietly but purposefully along the Dutch canals, but it is always as well to remember that physical communication and symbolic communication are intimately linked. Not the least important of the ties bonding them was simple prosperity. So far we have considered waterways only as a means of carrying passenger traffic. Of equal if not greater importance was their role in transporting objects. So defective were the roads that anything heavy was very expensive to transport along them, due to the number of draught animals that had to be employed. Many 'roads' were so narrow or so soft-surfaced that wheeled vehicles could not be used at all, so pack-horses or pack-mules had to be employed, each capable of carrying a maximum weight of an eighth of a ton (130 kg). Where conditions allowed, a wagon pulled by a single horse could manage about five times that amount. On a top-grade 'Macadam' road, such as was to be found only in the late eighteenth century, and then only rarely, it might manage as much as two tons. Even in this best-case scenario, however, the commodity being moved would have to be of high value if the profit margin were not to evaporate very quickly as transport costs whittled away at it.

Yet, if the freight could be off-loaded from the back of the pack-horse or the back of the wagon to a barge, the situation changed dramatically. Now the single horse could pull thirty tons, if the barge were on a river, and fifty tons if it were on a straighter and more tranquil canal. This was obvious and well known. Towards the end of the seventeenth century, the French fortifications expert and technocrat Marshal Vauban stated confidently: 'a boat of reasonable size, in good water, can by itself, with six men and four horses . . . take the load that 200 men and 400 horses would have the utmost difficulty in hauling over ordinary roads'. The same sort of figures applied to seagoing transportation. In 1670 an English author estimated that a small boat of thirty tons could carry as much from London to Bristol as a hundred horses overland. Another English observer, Sir Robert Southwell, quantified the cost benefit: in his view, sea carriage was twenty times cheaper than wheeled carriage. The chief beneficiaries of this discrepancy were dealers in commodities that were high in bulk but low in value. A single individual could carry a fortune in diamonds in his pocket, but a fleet of barges – or an army of wagons – would be needed to transport the equivalent value in coal or grain.

But not every European country was equally well-endowed with navigable waterways. Indeed, there was a steep north-west to south-east gradient. No part of the British Isles is more than 100 miles (160 km) from the sea, while the Low Countries are as much water as land. Moreover, the estuaries of the Thames, Severn, Mersey and Humber in the former, and the Rhine delta in the latter, cut deep into their respective countries. The French economic historian Maurice Aymard has estimated that the Dutch Republic was the only country in Europe where water transport was appreciably greater than land transport, in terms of tonnage carried. In England it was about 50-50; in Germany the ratio was 1:5, but in France it was 1:10. The contrast between these last two may seem surprising, but a glance at the map will reveal the reason. Germany has a relatively short coastline relative to its size, but is crossed at regular intervals by navigable rivers running roughly south-east to north-west, namely the Rhine, together with its numerous tributaries (Neckar, Main, Nahe, Moselle-Saar, Ruhr), the Weser, the Elbe, the Oder and the Vistula. In the south, the Danube rises in the Black Forest, is navigable by the time it reaches Ulm and picks up numerous tributaries, most notably the Inn, which flows in at Passau and more than doubles the volume of water.

Nature has endowed France with a more generous coastline but only three rivers of comparable potential. The most celebrated, the Seine, was also especially difficult to navigate in early modern conditions on account of its meandering course. Thanks to Alpine influence on its flow, the Rhône was prone to run too fast in spring and too slowly in summer, indeed it was unusable for around three months of the year. By far the most important French river was the Loire, which flows north-west from south of Lyon to Orléans and then across to the Atlantic at Nantes. Yet here too, uneven flows and sandbanks prevented its full exploitation. Nature needed a helping hand. Two major seventeenth-century enterprises showed that the necessary imagination, capital and political will could be mustered when potential rewards were great enough. In 1642 a major new canal was completed, thirty-eight years after construction began, linking the Loire with Paris via the Loing and the Seine, rising 128 feet (39 m) from Briare on the Loire before falling 266 feet (81 m) to the Loing at Montargis. Between 1682 and 1692 the duc d'Orléans added a second Loire–Loing canal, mainly to bring out timber from his forests. Together the two canals generated so much traffic that the Loing could not cope and an additional waterway had to be added alongside it until the confluence with the Seine. This complex certainly eased the capital's notorious supply problems, but the pace of transport was still very slow. The need to struggle with the Loire's capricious currents and other natural obstacles meant that shipments from Nantes to Paris could take six to eight months to cover a distance of less than 250 miles (400 km). As Roger Price has observed, the fact that this route was still preferred to transport overland bears eloquent testimony to the unsatisfactory state of French roads.

The other major project was the Canal du Midi, also known as the Languedoc Canal, which linked the Atlantic to the Mediterranean, and which has been hailed by one historian of world canals (Charles Hadfield) as 'the greatest canal so far built west of China, and Europe's finest seventeenth-century engineering work, perhaps her greatest since Roman days'. When it was completed in 1681 after just fifteen years of construction by an army of 10,000 workers, it stretched for 150 miles (240 km) and boasted 101 locks, including a dramatic eight-rise 'staircase' at Béziers, three major aqueducts, the first canal tunnel in Europe, the world's first artificial reservoir for canal supply and a dedicated canal port at Sète on the Mediterranean. Well might Corneille write a poem to celebrate 'The joining of two seas', which saved navigators a detour of 2,000 miles (3,200 km), and Voltaire hail the canal as 'glorious for its utility, its vastness and the difficulties of its construction'. A century after its completion, travellers were still enthusing; on his way to Spain in 1786, Joseph Townsend recorded:

The next day we dined at Béziers, a city into which the canal of Languedoc is constantly conveying the wealth which flows from agriculture. Here the corn, the wine, the brandy, the olives and the oil of a country formerly beyond the reach of commerce, find a ready market; and from hence all that tract of country is supplied, at a small expense of carriage, with the productions of distant nations.

Arthur Young added his encomium the following year: 'This is the best sight I have seen in France. Here Louis XIV thou art truly great! Here, with a generous and benignant hand, thou dispensest ease and wealth to the people!' Significantly, this great work was not originally a govern-ment project. The initiative came from Pierre-Paul Riquet, who owned an estate on the canal's route and dreamt of 'a highway from the western to the eastern sea' which would also help him to get his produce to market. Fortunately, his *mémoire* on the subject reached the desk of Colbert, Louis XIV's right-hand minister, who ordered first a feasibility study, and then gave his support to the full scheme. Of the colossal sums required, 7,500,000 *livres* came from central funds and 6,000,000 *livres* from the estates of Languedoc, while 2,000,000 were raised by Riquet personally.

Riquet died bankrupt six months before his grand project was com-pleted. His fate symbolized the end, not the beginning, of a 'canal age' in France. After a century of relative inactivity, the pace began to pick up again only during the reign of Louis XVI, but none of the three major projects had been completed by 1789. Only 31 miles (50 km) of the Canal de Bourgogne, designed to link Paris with the Mediterranean, had been completed by 1793. It was not until 1810 and the opening of the Saint-Quentin canal that France returned to the forefront of European canal-building. Elsewhere, there was a good deal more activity. In the Dutch Republic, where plentiful water supplies and flat terrain depressed construction costs but population density elevated demand, there was a veritable 'canal fever' (de Vries) during the middle decades of the seventeenth century. In Brandenburg too, the plethora of slow-moving, easily navigable rivers facilitated construction of a canal network, although there was not the same urban density. In the 1660s, Frederick William the Great Elector (1640–88) reconstructed a 25-mile (40-km) canal to link the River Spree to the Oder and thus to attract Silesian trade through Berlin and on to the North Sea via Hamburg. This was a project funded by the Elector personally, as were the cranes, docks and other ancillaries in Berlin. Hailed by one historian (Günther Vogler) as 'the first great deed by a German prince in the field of economics', the Müllroser canal initiated the rise of Berlin to economic predominance in north-eastern Germany. Further development under his son Frederick (1688–1713), Elector of Brandenburg and the first 'King in Prussia' after his assumption of the royal title in 1701, meant that by the early eighteenth century, three of the great German rivers – the Weser, the Elbe and the Oder – were linked by canals.

As the population of western and southern Europe grew, so did the demand for the grain of eastern Europe. So the economic encouragement for further improvement continued. Frederick the Great was well aware of the utility of canals, as he explained in his 'Political Testament' of 1752. During the early years of his reign, the building of the Plauen canal provided a short cut across the large curve of the lower Havel, while the refurbished Finow canal improved the link between the second of Berlin's rivers, the Havel, and the Oder. Among other things, it allowed greatly accelerated communication between Magdeburg on the Elbe and Stettin at the mouth of the Oder. Frederick claimed that the transport of bulk goods such as salt to East Prussia, Pomerania and Silesia now took a week less than in the past, while raw materials from Russia such as leather could be imported to Stettin, sent down the canals and rivers to Magdeburg, where they were turned into finished goods and exported to the rest of Germany. The Bromberg canal, built between 1772 and 1775, pushed the Prussian network significantly further east by linking the Oder to the Vistula, thus completing a chain of inland waterways which stretched from East Prussia to the North Sea. For the very far-sighted, developments towards the end of Frederick's long reign pointed to far greater sources of prosperity and power for the Prussian state. In 1772 he authorized a Dutch company to ship coal down the River Ruhr to a small port at the junction with the Rhine. It was then known simply as the 'Homberg Wharf', but eventually, renamed 'Ruhrort', it was to become the biggest inland port and the outlet of the most industrialized region in Europe. When Frederick the Great died in 1786, his state contained no less than 85 per cent of the 620 miles (1,000 km) of artificial waterways in the Holy Roman Empire. Yet it possessed not one single stretch of paved highway. Well might the journalist Schubart urge visitors to lift their gaze from the execrable roads to the magnificent waterways.

Great Britain, by contrast, was slow to take up canal-building on the French, Dutch or even Prussian scale. Partly this was due to the alternative natural waterways available. The tonnage of shipping travelling round the long coastline increased by two-thirds during the seventeenth century. There was a simultaneous extension in the length of navigable rivers by the construction of locks, dredging and the clearance of obstacles. The distance increased from about 700 miles (1,120 km) in 1660 to 900 (1,440) in 1700 and 1,100 (1,760) in the 1720s, or by almost 60 per cent in just over half a century. By 1650 substantial barges were going up the Thames as far as Oxford and a generation later the Severn had been made navigable to Welshpool. Yet coastal and riverine traffic was not without its problems. Loss from vermin and water penetration were permanent afflictions, while periodic naval warfare, first with the Dutch and then with the French, made the small, defenceless coasters easy pickings for the privateers. They could join protected convoys, but only at the cost of long delays until an economical number of ships had been assembled.

Rivers too had their limitations, the most serious being their inability to adapt their direction to changing human needs. That could only be accomplished by canals. The 'canal age' began in Great Britain a good century after 'canal fever' had gripped the Dutch. The model here was the Duke of Bridgewater's canal, opened in 1761 to bring coal from his mines at Worsley to rapidly expanding Manchester. Its well-publicized success encouraged a host of similar projects. The grand scheme of Bridgewater's engineer, James Brindley, was the 'Grand Trunk', which linked the Mersey to the Trent at Wilden Ferry and thus joined the west and east coasts of England. Among other things, this opened the Midlands and its manufactures to ports and export markets. Further links to the Thames and the Severn meant that by the end of the eighteenth century there was no part of the kingdom without easy access to what was now a national system of inland waterways. Nor was England the only one of the three kingdoms to benefit: by 1790 Scotland was crossed from the Forth to the Clyde, and by 1804 Ireland was crossed from Dublin to Shannon. This happened so rapidly that it was very much a perceived change, inspiring a sense of triumphalism in overcoming natural obstacles in the pursuit of prosperity. Travelling from Chester to London in 1780, Thomas Pennant was awestruck when he encountered the Grand Trunk aqueduct at Stonefield:

Parallel to my road runs that magnificent enterprize the canal, for the junction of the eastern and western oceans; designed to give to each side of the kingdom an easy share in the commodities of both. In other countries, the nature of the land permits a ready execution of these designs. Egypt and Holland are levelled to the workman's hands. Our aspiring genius scoffs at obstructions, and difficulties serve but to whet our ardour; our acqueducts pass over our once-admired rivers, now despised for the purpose of navigation: we fill vallies, we penetrate mountains. How would the prophet have been treated who, forty years ago, should have predicted, that a vessel of twenty-five tons would be seen sailing over Stonefield? Yet such is the case at present.

Three other major European initiatives in canal-building should be noted. The most fruitful was launched by Denmark in 1777, to cross the isthmus between the North Sea and the Baltic. Using a combination of the River Eider, navigable to Rendsburg, and a canal on to Kiel, the passage was complete by 1785, when the new waterway was declared open to 'all the nations of Europe'. In the first year of operation, 453 ships travelled along it, growing to 1,072 by 1789. The other two major projects were undertaken in Spain, providing further evidence of the vitality of economic enterprise there. In 1770 construction began on a major canal bypassing the unnavigable stretch of the Ebro from Tudela to Saragossa, thus opening up Navarre and the north to the Mediterranean. Among other things, this 50-mile (85-km) canal boasted an impressive aqueduct a mile (1.6 km) long to take it high across the Jalón valley. Even the hypercritical Joseph Townsend was impressed by the work he saw underway at Saragossa in 1786. Nothing could be more perfect than the locks and wharves being built by 3,000 soldiers and peasants, he recorded, although he added sourly that English canals could do the same job much more cheaply and efficiently because they were much narrower and shallower, 'but such contemptible canals would not suit the ambition of a Spaniard, nor coincide with his ideas of grandeur'. A second canal planned to run from Segovia to the Bay of Biscay made good progress during the same period, but was curtailed by the wars of the French Revolution.

Elsewhere in Europe, a combination of difficult terrain and a shortage of capital, technological expertise and government interest ensured that the availability of water transport was determined by the caprice of nature in granting or withholding appropriate rivers. In Portugal, the

Tagus could be navigated for only a few miles above Lisbon before rocks and cataracts barred the way. In the late seventeenth century, a company of Dutch engineers had submitted a proposal for making it navigable to Madrid via the Mançanares, but were rebuffed with the complacent observation that 'if God had been willing to have these two rivers navigable, he did not want the assistance of men to render them so'. Not least of the problems of the Habsburg Monarchy in modernizing its economy was the lack of a waterway network. Apart from the short stretch at Wiener-Neustadt and a few very minor enterprises, there were no canals. The map suggests that nature had made human effort unnecessary by providing the Danube, the greatest of all Europe's rivers, which enters the territory in the north-west and flows broad and deep for more than 600 miles (1,000 km) before exiting in the south-east. Unfortunately, on the great Hungarian plain the Danube was made unnavigable to all intents and purposes by being flanked by extensive swamps. These were caused by spring floods regularly breaking the river's banks and made the main stream inaccessible to heavy goods for most of the year. The Magyar nobility lacked both the ambition and the resources to undertake the drainage and canalization required to overcome these obstacles.

The same constraints operated even more powerfully in Russia. Of the various requirements for canal construction, only one was in plentiful supply – labour. Even so, water transport was relatively of greater importance here than anywhere else in Europe, due to the enormous distances and the unhelpful location of the country's natural resources and outlets: the bread-basket is to the south of the most populated regions, the largest iron-ore deposits are on the eastern slopes of the Urals, most of the timber is in the north, while the best ports are on the western or southern periphery. Consequently, according to Arcadius Kahan, the number working on the inland waterways almost quadrupled in the course of the eighteenth century, from 60,000 to 220,000. By the end of that century, Russia had gained access to the northern shore of the Black Sea and complete control of the Sea of Azov. Catherine the Great's annexation of the Crimea in 1783 and successful defence of her prize during the war against the Turks of 1787–91 brought control of the four great south-flowing rivers of eastern Europe: the Dniester, the Bug, the Dnieper and the Don. Within a few years, existing ports had been expanded and new ones created, as a long economic development began which was to reorientate the Russian economy from north to south. In 1786 there were eighty vessels on the Black Sea flying the Russian flag; ten years later that number had doubled. But this was more than an economic shift. It was also a geopolitical turning-point comparable in importance with Great Britain's defeat of France in the struggle for control of the world overseas, for Russia now regarded both the Balkans and the Mediterranean as vital zones of interest. From it came Russia's entry into the wars of the French Revolution in 1798 and the collapse of the First Republic; the Crimean War of the 1850s and the expulsion of Austria from Italy and Germany; and, arguably at least, the First World War too.

If that forward projection seems fanciful, more specific examples of the interaction between waterways and power politics can be found. Frederick the Great, for example, was well aware that annexing Silesia in 1740 also gave him control of the River Oder and therefore both economic and strategic domination of the region. Not the least attractive feature of the first partition of Poland in 1772 was the consideration that Prussia now controlled the lower reaches of the Vistula. As Frederick recorded with satisfaction in his *Memoirs from the Peace of Hubertusburg to the Partition of Poland*, his new acquisition gave him control of the Polish grain trade and consequently 'the Prussian states no longer had any thing to fear, either from dearth or famine'.

CUSTOMS AND TOLLS

One important advantage enjoyed by the transport industry in the British Isles was the absence of internal customs barriers or tolls (apart from turnpikes). In most of Europe they were ubiquitous. Especially in rural areas where cash was hard to come by, transient merchants were tempting targets. When they crossed a frontier, entered a town, forded a river, passed over a bridge, ascended a mountain pass, or whatever, there was often someone exacting a fee. For example, the Rhine is one of the world's great natural waterways. Even after the coming of the railway and the Autobahn, it is still thronged with barges. Yet under the old regime, nature's gift was spurned by human avarice. Between Basle and Rotterdam, there were no fewer than thirty-eight customs posts, administered by nineteen different authorities. The Elector of the Palatinate owned seven of them, the Elector of Cologne had five. So the cost of a load of 200 sacks of salt was 400 *talers* in Cologne but had risen to 712 *talers* by the time it reached Frankfurt am Main, with customs dues accounting for three-quarters of the increase. Nor does that take into account the amount of time wasted by being forced to stop every few miles for a load to be inspected, valued and taxed. This situation was not peculiar to western Germany: there were thirty-five customs posts on the Elbe between Pirna and Hamburg. Given the fragmentation of authority in the Holy Roman Empire and the tenacity of political and confessional rivalry, there was little if any prospect of a customs union. On the contrary: in 1777, for example, a dispute between the Landgrave of Hessen-Kassel and the City of Cologne brought all shipping on the Rhine to a standstill for three months.

Political unity was no guarantee of commercial liberty. In the Habsburg Monarchy, not only were there tolls separating one province from another, there were also tolls within each province, owned by the sovereign, by the Estates, monasteries, towns and even by private individuals. As the senior provincial officials were often major beneficiaries of the current system, there was precious little enthusiasm for reform. It required the application of the iron will of Joseph II and his enlightened bureaucrats to abolish the worst anomalies and introduce a measure of standardization. In 1775 he abolished all internal tolls in the western half of his dominions (the Austrian Hereditary Lands, Bohemia and Moravia), except those for the upkeep of roads. Even so, the Tyrol, the territories in south-western Germany and the Austrian Netherlands remained special cases. Joseph had wanted to include Hungary and Transylvania too, but the resistance of the Hungarian nobility to paying what was deemed to be their fair share of direct taxation meant that the eastern territories were excluded. They remained in a 'colonial' relationship, as cheap sources of food and raw materials and as captive markets for manufactured products. There was a similar situation and a similarly limited move towards commercial unification in Italy, where internal customs barriers were abolished in Tuscany in 1783 and in the Papal States ten years later.

The Holy Roman Empire and the Habsburg Monarchy were, of course, especially fragmented. Yet conditions were no different in countries, such as France or Spain, which looked like unified states but were in reality conglomerations of separate territories acquired over the centuries. Castile, the Basque Country, Navarre, Aragon and Andalucia were separate states for the purposes of customs revenue, so it was often cheaper to import foreign manufactures by sea than from inside the country. The same applied to France, which in terms of domestic commerce was not a single kingdom at all. Its constituent provinces can be divided into two groups. The first (Normandy, Picardy, Île de France, Champagne, Burgundy, Bourbonnais, Nivernais, Berry, Orléanais, Touraine, Poitou, Aunis, Anjou and Le Maine) was unified in the sense that goods could move freely from one to the other, paying a single duty when leaving or entering the group as a whole. But there was a second, substantial group of provinces (Artois, Flanders, Brittany, Guyenne, Saintonge, Languedoc, Provence, Dauphiné and Lyonnais) obliged to pay dues when trading with each other or with any member of the other group. In addition, three recently acquired provinces (Alsace, Lorraine and Franche-Comté) enjoyed free trade with foreign countries but were separated from the rest of France by customs barriers.

Both Spain and France were also afflicted by a rich variety of tolls – royal, seigneurial and municipal. These were sometimes imposed in return for a real service, such as the upkeep of a road or bridge, but more often than not had degenerated into ways of fleecing travellers. In 1679 Colbert had instructed intendants to pay special attention to reforming abusive tolls (*péages*) but without success. Four years later, the intendant of Limoges reported:

The tolls are multiplying with every day that passes, with the result that goods cannot travel from upper to lower Limousin without paying seventeen to eighteen different tolls on a stretch of road of sixteen leagues. And what is more, the seigneurs charge what they like, for they do not put up a sign advertising the tariff, as the law requires, but take what they like from travellers, who pay up to avoid having their goods confiscated and having to go to court.

Several subsequent attempts were made to root out the worst offenders – 154 tolls were suppressed in Languedoc alone between 1729 and 1782 – but a large number remained in force until the Revolution. The effects of tolls and customs duties on commerce were predictable. In 1696 Pierre Boisguilbert stated that Provence was full of natural produce capable of commanding high prices in the markets of Paris. Alas, he went on, such was the proliferation of man-made obstacles that a journey which need take no more than four or five weeks was stretched artificially to three-and-a-half months. In the same vein, Vauban complained in his *Project for a Royal Tithe, or General Tax* of 1707 that extortion had made transporting produce to market so irksome that cultivators preferred to see their crops rot in the fields.

As if that were not enough to inhibit internal trade, there was also the wide variation in the levels of various forms of excise to contend with. One commodity that every person in France needed, but no one could produce, was salt. Yet the country was divided into six different regions with six different rates of duty (*gabelle*), with the result that the price fluctuated from sixty-two *livres* per *quintal* in the areas of the 'great gabelle' (the twelve central provinces, including the Île de France) to five *livres* per *quintal* in the 'exempt' zone (Artois, Flanders, Hainaut, Béarn and Navarre). It was Adam Smith's view that 'one of the principal causes of the prosperity of Great Britain' was the absence of internal customs barriers and the uniformity of taxation. If only they could be extended to Ireland and the colonies, he added, the prosperity would be greater still. In France, however, 'the different revenue laws which take place in the different provinces, require a multitude of revenue officers to surround, not only the frontiers of the kingdom, but those of almost each particular province, in order to prevent the importation of certain goods, or to subject it to the payment of certain duties, to the no small interruption of the interior commerce of the country'. Together with the other constraints already discussed, this disparity created a great interruption. In the middle of the eighteenth century, it was estimated that the cost of transporting a consignment of wine worth 500 *livres* from Muret (Haute-Garonne) to Paris was 501 *livres*, thanks to haulage costs, tolls, customs dues and the excise.

Where there are two adjacent places with different prices for the same commodity, there will be smuggling; and the greater the discrepancy, the greater the profit margin and the greater the number of smugglers. On his way through France in 1786, Joseph Townsend wrote: 'A nobleman of Berry told me, that on one side of a rivulet which flows by his château, salt is sold at forty *sols* a bushel, and on the other at forty *livres*, that is, at twenty times as much. In consequence of this, no less than two thousand troops of horse and foot were stationed on its banks to check the smugglers.' Smuggling was a major occupation in France at this time. In her classic study, *The Poor of Eighteenth-Century France*, Olwen Hufton states with a confidence born of intimate knowledge of the sources that the number of smugglers certainly ran into hundreds of thousands and perhaps even topped a million. That is not at all surprising when one considers that a child could earn the equivalent of an agricultural labourer's daily wage by carrying a couple of pounds of salt across a *gabelle* frontier. Even dogs could be enlisted to carry the precious substance, thus provoking the authorities to train their own canine agents to intercept them. More dangerously, so manifestly absurd was the law and so many were the people involved, that smuggling bore no stigma. On the contrary, smugglers such as 'Mandrin' and 'Cartouche' were folk-heroes.

THE POST

Travel by water, whether it was sea, river or canal, enjoyed numerous advantages over its terrestrial equivalents. But it suffered from one serious drawback – its slowness. The ocean-going traveller might some-times find a following wind to speed his passage, but more often than not he was condemned to becalmed immobility or laborious tacking. On the inland waterways, the barge could proceed only at the pace dictated by the draught animals, or in other words at walking pace. This was what Arthur Young discovered when he travelled from Venice to Bologna, first by sea and then by canal: 'Of this voyage, all the powers of language would fail me to give the idea I would wish to impress. The time I passed in it I rank among the most disagreeable days I ever experienced, and by a thousand degrees the worst since I left England; yet I had no choice: the roads are so infamously bad, or rather so impracticable, that there are no *vetturini*; even those whose fortune admits posting [travelling by stagecoach] make this passage by water.' Conditions on the cheap but painfully slow barge were so squalid that Young chose to walk most of the 125 miles (200 km). Even on the more hospitable Dutch canals, the funereal pace was too much for impatient Englishmen to bear. Towards the end of the eighteenth century, James Mitchell commented: 'This mode of travelling seems to afford a fair example of Dutch arrangements generally; it is economical of money, but expensive of time ... While a Dutchman travels three miles in an hour, an Englishman travels six or eight, and this is nearly the difference between the spirit and energy of the two nations.'

By this time, Mitchell and his fellow countrymen had a standard of land travel against which to find the Dutch barges sadly wanting. The rapid increase in the speed of road travel in Great Britain, made possible by the turnpikes, has already been noted. In the 1780s the accelerator was pressed further by another innovation – the mail coach. Hitherto, letters had been carried up and down the main postal routes by a mounted messenger known as a 'post boy', defined by one dissatisfied customer as 'an idle boy mounted on a worn-out hack who, so far from being able to defend himself against a robber, was more likely to be in league with him'. The customer in question was the Bath impresario John Palmer, who believed that he could do better. In 1784, his friend William Pitt, prime minister since the previous December, authorized him to run a scheduled mail-coach service from Bristol to London, leaving at four in the afternoon and arriving in the capital early the following morning, carrying both letters and passengers. Such was its success in improving speed and reliability that the service was extended to many more cities during the next two years. In 1786, the travelling time from Edinburgh to London was shortened from three-and-a-half days to sixty hours. It was once thought that it was a combination of the railways and the factory system which introduced a more structured attitude to time. In fact, it was the mail coach which obliged people to think in terms of units as short as minutes. Passengers on the London to Glasgow run, for example, were told that they had exactly thirty-five minutes for dinner, from 4.36 to 5.11 p.m. If they lingered too long over their pudding, they would be left behind when the coach swept away. So the 'railway age' found travellers 'psychologically and horologically prepared', as David Landes has put it.

The contribution of the letter to promoting passenger travel, and vice versa, encapsulates the symbiosis between physical and symbolic communication. It was during the seventeenth and eighteenth centuries that there was a qualitative leap in the movement of private individuals; it was during the seventeenth and eighteenth centuries that there was a qualitative leap in postal services. On the continent the lead was taken by the service run by the Thurn and Taxis family, the lucky but also enterprising beneficiaries of an imperial monopoly first granted at the beginning of the sixteenth century. Although their tenure as Imperial Post-Master was hereditary, it was no sinecure, as they faced bracing competition from several German princes, notably Brandenburg-Prussia and Saxony, with 760 and 140 post offices respectively by the late eighteenth century. By that time, the Thurn and Taxis network was dense enough to mean that no German community was further than a half-day's walk from a postal station, and well-organized enough to move letters 95 miles (150 km) in twenty-four hours and all over Europe. Between 1750 and the outbreak of the French Revolutionary Wars, the family is estimated to have generated 25,500,000 *gulden* (about £2,550,000 in contemporary English currency) in profits. Although finally forced to yield to the pressures of nationalization in 1867, when Bismarck's new North German Confederation took over the last vestiges of their organization, and despite recent indiscretions, it remains one of the richest families in Germany, if not the world.

In France, typically, there was a greater degree of central control. A 'Royal Postal Service' was established as early as 1477, although it was not until 1719 that the University of Paris finally relinquished its ancient right to operate its own postal service. Originally intended simply as a conduit for official business, the opportunities for raising revenue were exploited from 1603, when Henry IV authorized the royal couriers to carry letters for private individuals. By 1671, one of the most celebrated of all correspondents, Madame de Sévigné, could write to her daughter: 'I am full of admiration for the post-boys who are constantly on the move, bringing our letters to and fro; there isn't a day in the week when they cannot bring them; they are always there, at every hour of the day, out in the country. What honourable people! How helpful they are, and what a fine invention the post is!' By 1763 postal services were sufficiently developed to allow a M. Guyot to bring out a *Guide des lettres*, devoted solely to the coming and going of the post. When the Revolution began, there were 1,320 post offices in France, ready to play a major part in the dissemination of stories true and false about what was going on at Paris and Versailles.

Conditions were even more propitious for a postal breakthrough in England, where distances were shorter, population denser, urbanization more developed and the public sphere especially precocious. Characteristically, the Stuarts viewed the post primarily as a source of funds. When the Duke of York ascended the throne as James II in 1685 he was drawing the colossal sum of £43,000 per annum from the profits of the service, a tribute to his elder brother's generosity and the volume of letters being despatched. He was not alone: one of his brother's many mistresses, the Duchess of Cleveland (née Barbara Villiers), drew £4,700 per annum. It is illustrative of the veneration of private property embedded in British political culture that she was able to bequeath this sum to her (and Charles II's) son, the Duke of Grafton, from whom it passed down through the generations until the late nineteenth century, when it was finally commuted for £91,000.

Two developments in particular helped to create a national network of symbolic communication, first in England and then throughout Great Britain and Ireland. The first was a private initiative by William Dockwra of London, who initiated a private postal system just for London, collecting and delivering mail within a 7-mile (11-km) radius at one penny per item. Recruiting hundreds of taverns, coffee-houses and shops as collecting stations, he was able to provide a service more rapid than anything on offer today, as collections and deliveries were made as often as every hour during the daytime. Needless to say, the Duke of York saw this as an infringement of his monopoly and moved quickly to take legal action to close him down. Yet such was the demand – and profitability – revealed by Dockwra's enterprise that the official post office was obliged to offer a substitute. The second was the institution of a 'cross-post' system by Ralph Allen after 1720, to link towns laterally, without having to go up and down the arterial routes to London. By the 1750s, all of England and much of Wales was included. It can be stated with confidence that by the accession of George III in 1760 most major towns were linked with the capital and with each other by an efficient daily mail service.

The north–south gradient, noted with relation to roads, applies with less force to postal services. Despite the difficulties getting about Spain, it had enjoyed a good postal service since the sixteenth century, a legacy of the Habsburg dynasty's need to communicate with its far-flung empire. In Italy too, there was a Habsburg legacy to ensure that mail could be moved about the peninsula with reasonable fluency and security. After 1746 it was also the point of departure for a postal link with the Ottoman Empire, running from Naples to Constantinople via Otranto, Ragusa (modern Dubrovnik) and Salonika. In Russia too there was a long tradition of postal service, based on eastern models. In a country where cheap labour was freely available, nearly 13,000 postal workers could be employed on the route from St Petersburg to Moscow in the 1760s. Writing a generation earlier, the diplomat Friedrich

Christian von Weber found twenty-four posting stages between the two cities and was impressed by their efficiency: 'this great Conveniency, added to the Cheapness of Carriage, renders the Communication between *Petersbourg*, *Moskow* and *Archangel*, extreamly easy'. Elsewhere, however, communication problems both physical, in the shape of enormous distances and minimal roads, and symbolic, in the shape of mass illiteracy, prevented the development of anything but the most rudimentary of services. It took weeks rather than days for a despatch from Moscow to reach even major provincial centres, while communities lying off the main routes lived their lives untouched by news from the world beyond their environs.

Letter-writing was something that could be taught. Manuals and formularies enjoyed enhanced popularity in the late seventeenth century. Aspiring English correspondents could find advice on how best to plead their cause in love or business in, for example, 'W.P.''s *A Flying Post with a Packet of Choice new Letters and Complements: containing a Variety of Examples of witty and delightful Letters, upon all Occasions, both of Love and Business* (1678). One of the most successful of the eighteenth-century guidebooks was written by none other than Samuel Richardson, who published it in 1741, in other words *before* he set about his own great epistolary novels. Usually referred to simply as *Familiar Letters*, the full florid title reveals the extent of his ambition: *Letters Written to and for Particular Friends, on the Most Important Occasions, Directing not only the Requisite Style and Forms to be Observed in Writing Familiar Letters; But How to Act Justly and Prudently, in the Common Concerns of Human Life*. In 172 model letters, Richardson provided all manner of advice, both practical and ethical, as in 'To a young Trader generally in a Hurry in Business, advising *Method* as well as *Diligence*' or 'From a Gentleman, strenuously expostulating with an old, rich Widow, about to marry a very young gay Gentleman'.

This rage for letter-writing owed much to postal improvements. Madame de Sévigné would not have written 1,700 letters to her daughter, nor would Horace Walpole have written 1,600 letters to Madame du Deffand or 800-plus to Sir Horace Mann (whom he did not meet for the forty-four years of their correspondence) if they had not been confident that they would be delivered. Right across Europe (and the Atlantic), the post created a network which ever-increasing numbers of intellectuals could use for the exchange of opinion, information and gossip. The medium also influenced the message, for the relative immediacy now available in long-distance intercourse encouraged a more intimate and subjective style. Indeed, Goethe assigned part of the blame for the effusion of sentimental correspondence to the excellence of the Thurn and Taxis postal service.

2

People

In 1798, at opposite ends of Europe, two major treatises on population were published. The more authoritative of the two was written by Joseph von Sonnenfels, the leading political scientist of the Austrian Enlightenment. In his *Manual of the Domestic Administration of States, with Reference to the Conditions and Concepts of our Age*, he summed up the conventional wisdom, namely that a large and growing population was a Good Thing. Indeed, he went so far as to assert that demographic increase should be made 'the chief principle of political science', for the good reason that it promoted the two chief ends of civil society: material comfort and physical security. The greater the population, Sonnenfels argued, the greater the country's agricultural productivity and the greater the capacity to resist both foreign enemies and domestic dissidents. To clinch it, he pointed out that the more people there were to contribute to the expenses of the state, the less the tax burden on the individual would have to be. This common-sense approach was underpinned by the belief that the population of the world had been declining since classical times. It was a conviction Sonnenfels shared with most of his contemporaries, including Voltaire and Montesquieu. The latter observed gloomily: 'if this decline in population does not cease, in a thousand years the world will be a desert'.

A very different view was expressed in the same year by the young English scholar Thomas Malthus, in *An Essay on the Principle of Population as it Affects the Future Improvement of Society*. At thirty-two, he was almost exactly half Sonnenfels' age, but his vision of the future was at least twice as bleak. His chief concern was to counter the belief in the perfectibility of the human race advanced by progressives such as William Godwin and the Marquis de Condorcet. Malthus proceeded from two premises: 'that food is necessary to the existence of man' and 'that the passion between the sexes is necessary, and will remain nearly in its present state'. These two natural laws were not of equal force, however, for 'the power of population is indefinitely greater than the power in the earth to produce subsistence for man'. A man and a woman could give life to several children, each of whom could do the same. Consequently, demographic growth proceeded in a geometrical progression, whereas agriculture could only expand arithmetically. In other words, the number of people generated by the sequence 1, 2, 4, 8, 16, 32, 64, 128 could not be sustained by resources generated by the sequence 1, 2, 3, 4, 5, 6, 7, 8. The necessary result was that, sooner or later, any expansion of population would be halted naturally when it banged its head against the ceiling imposed by this discrepancy. A combination of misery and 'vice' (by which the Rev. Malthus meant contraception) would soon redress the balance.

In the long run, both men were to be proved wrong, but in 1798 either position seemed credible. During Sonnenfels' lifetime (he had been born in 1732), both the power and prosperity of his country had increased hand in hand with its population. One of the four Emperors he served, Joseph II, stated as a central axiom: 'I consider that the principal object of my policy, and the one to which all political, financial and even military authorities should devote their attention, is population, that is to say the preservation and increase of the number of subjects. It is from the greatest possible number of subjects that all the advantages of the state derive.' Yet all over Europe, periodic subsistence crises lent support to Malthus' gloomy forecast, not least the harvest failure which arguably precipitated the French Revolution. If Malthus had lived a little longer (he died in 1834), he might well have found grim satisfaction in observing the misery of the 'hungry forties', especially the potato famine and ensuing mass emigration which reduced Ireland's population from 8,400,000 to 6,600,000 in just five years. As this ambivalence suggests, in this respect the end of the eighteenth century was on the cusp between old and new. As we shall see, demographically the period 1648–1815 was in many respects more like the fifteenth than the twentieth century, although it also had many modern characteristics.

NUMBERS

It is not difficult to appreciate why, of all the branches of historical scholarship, demography should be among the most contentious. On the one hand, its practitioners have the opportunity to crunch numbers down to several decimal points, thus giving a spurious impression of precision. On the other hand, in any period before the censuses of the nineteenth and twentieth centuries, evidence is so fragmentary that words such as 'estimate', or even 'guess', seem too precise to describe the results. The choice seems to be between bold statements about national totals and the microscopic 'reconstitution' of small communities, on whose microscopic foundations great airy structures are then erected. Especially in regions with poor communications, negligible literacy rates and little or no regular administration, such as Hungary following the Habsburg *reconquista* of the late seventeenth century, virtually nothing can be known about the level of population. However, demographic developments are so fundamental to an understanding of this, or any other, historical period that an attempt must be made to construct some sort of structure, although the straw and even most of the bricks are lacking.

A good place to start is a summary of the best population estimates for a number of European countries between the middle of the seventeenth century and the end of the eighteenth (see Table 2).

Table 2. Population of European countries 1650–1800 (in millions)

	1650	1700	1750	1800
Europe		110	140	190
Austria-Bohemia	4.1	4.6	5.7	7.9
Belgium	2	2	2.2	2.9
Dutch Republic	1.9	1.9	1.9	2.1
England & Wales	5.6	5.4	6.1	9.2
France	21	21.4	25	29
Germany[1]	10	15	17	24.5
Hungary[2]		3		9.25
Ireland	1.8	2.8	3.2	5.3

	1650	1700	1750	1800
Italy	11.3	13.2	15.3	17.8
Poland	3	2.8	3.7	
Portugal	1.5	2	2.3	2.9
Prussia			3.6	6.2
Russia	7	15	19	37
Scandinavia	2.6	2.8	3.6	5
Scotland	1	1	1.3	1.6
Spain	7.1	7.5	9.1	10.5
Switzerland	1	1.2	1.3	1.7

[1] i.e. those parts of the Holy Roman Empire eventually included in the frontiers of the German Empire of 1871

[2] including Transylvania

Source: mainly Jan de Vries, *The Economy of Europe in an Age of Crisis 1600–1750* (Cambridge, 1976)

All of these statistics are approximate but some are more approximate than others. The figure for England and Wales in 1650, for example, can be set down with far greater confidence than that for Russia, which may be completely wrong. To give national figures is also somewhat misleading, as there were wide regional variations within any given country. For example, in Spain the population of provinces on the periphery, notably Catalonia, Valencia and Galicia, increased much more rapidly than in the Castilian centre. In France growth was strongest in Hainaut, Franche-Comté and Berry, moderate in the Parisian basin, Brittany, the Massif Central, the south-west and the Midi, and weakest in Normandy. In Germany, not surprisingly, much higher rates were recorded by the thinly populated east than by the relatively densely populated west – indeed, as we shall see, there was a significant amount of internal migration.

Even after every qualification has been carefully noted, a general picture can be identified. Chronologically, this presents a sequence of stagnation or slow growth (1650–1700), followed by a general if modest increase (1700–50) and then by a more rapid expansion (1750–1800). But its true significance emerges only when it is placed in a much wider time frame. Following the catastrophic population losses caused by the Black Death in the middle of the fourteenth century, recovery began in the late fifteenth and continued throughout the sixteenth. But around 1600, the Four Horsemen of the Apocalypse returned with a vengeance to many parts of Europe, bringing war, plague and famine with devastating demographic consequences. The great plague which struck Castile in 1599–1600, for example, was only the first of many such visitations which reduced the population of the region by a quarter by 1650. Only England and the Dutch Republic managed to avoid the general decline of the first half of the seventeenth century. So the developments of 1650–1800 represent both a recovery and a resumption of growth. However, much more important than what preceded our period was what followed it. Despite the warnings of Malthus, the expansion of the second half of the eighteenth century was not checked by inelastic subsistence. On the contrary, Europe's population went on growing throughout the nineteenth century at an ever-accelerating rate.

Geographically, as Table 2 reveals, there was a shift in the demographic balance of Europe away from the Mediterranean to the northwest. This becomes clearer if the individual countries are grouped by region (Table 3).

Table 3. Population of Europe (in millions)

Zone	1600	1700	1750	1800
I. Mediterranean[a]	23.6	22.7	27.0	32.7
Index	100	96	114	139
II. Central[b]	35.0	36.2	41.3	53.2
Index	100	103	118	152
III. North and West[c]	12.0	16.1	18.3	25.9
Index	100	134	153	216
Total	70.6	75.0	86.6	111.8
Index	100	106	123	158

[a] Spain, Portugal, Italy

[b] France, Switzerland, Germany

[c] England, Scotland, Ireland, Low Countries, Scandinavia.

Source: Jan de Vries, *The Economy of Europe in an Age of Crisis 1600–1750* (Cambridge, 1976)

The eminent Dutch economic historian Jan de Vries, who compiled Table 3, added laconically that he would have added a fourth region – Eastern Europe, embracing Poland and Russia – but there were insufficient data.

The shift in Europe's demographic centre of gravity was momentous. Late medieval and Renaissance Europe had been dominated by the Mediterranean. In manufacturing, trade and banking, its cities had been pre-eminent; in culture, the Italian city-states had created a civilization which bore comparison with classical Greece; in politics, the Spanish branch of the Habsburgs had created an empire on which the sun never set. Yet by the eighteenth century, northerners were coming south as if to a museum, their admiration for its past exceeded only by their contempt for its present. As an English visitor put it in 1778, Rome had once been 'inhabited by a nation of heroes and patriots, but was now in the hands of the most effeminate and most superstitious people in the universe'. As we shall see, the relative demographic decline of the region was both symptom and cause of a wider set of problems.

MARRIAGE AND FERTILITY

One possible explanation for the secular increase in Europe's population was a rise in fertility as a result of women getting married younger. A drop in the average age of marriage by just five or six years could mean a 50-per-cent increase in the number of children born. Indeed, Tony Wrigley has argued that it was just this sort of reduction which accounts for three-quarters of the growth of population in England between 1750 and 1800. It was certainly very easy to get married in England, with an age of consent of fourteen for boys and twelve for girls. Nor was there any need for a church service – an exchange of oaths in the presence of witnesses, or even just an exchange of statements of intent to marry, followed by sexual intercourse, was regarded as sufficient. Yet here, as elsewhere in northern and western Europe, marriage was delayed until long after sexual maturity, the average age lying within a range of 24½ to 26½ years. Although there was certainly a reduction in England during the latter part of the eighteenth century, Wrigley's critics have argued that it may have been offset by women calling an earlier halt to childbearing.

The long delay in contracting marriage – only one English bride in eight was a teenager when she first married – was not offset by any compensating extramarital fertility. By the standards of the twenty-first century, the illegitimacy rates were amazingly low: in most European countries the rate rarely reached 5 per cent and was often below 2 per cent, as it was in England. (In the United Kingdom today the rate is above 30 per cent.) In France it was barely 1 per cent in the countryside and only 4–5 per cent in Paris. However, there was an undoubted move upwards during the course of the eighteenth century. By 1789 the illegitimacy rate had reached 4 per cent in French towns with populations of more than 4,000, 12–17 per cent in full-blown cities and 20 per cent in Paris. In Germany in the same period there was a similar increase from 2.5 to 11.9 per cent. However, the modest increase in fertility these figures represented could have had only a small impact overall, even if all of the children born out of wedlock had survived to adulthood. In the event, as we shall see, they were especially prone to dying in infancy.

In those parts of Europe where a strong degree of social control was exercised by churches, guilds or seigneurs, the decision to delay marriage was often imposed from above. In northern, western and central Europe, however, it was usually a voluntary response to economic circumstances. There appears to have been a strong feeling that marriage should not be contracted until the couple was in a position to set up an independent household. It was also here that the highest numbers of women who never married were to be found. In north-western Europe 10–15 per cent and in some places even 25 per cent of women remained celibate, making this a more important check on population growth than the late age of marriage. In the east and the south, on the other hand, the rate was much lower and there was also less reluctance to accept a subordinate position in an extended household, with a corresponding reduction in the age of marriage. Everywhere dowries posed a problem, especially for fathers blessed with an excess of daughters, such as Mr Bennet of *Pride and Prejudice*. The English social historian, the late Roy Porter, did not believe that Sir William Temple (1628–99) was being unduly cynical when he wrote 'our marriages are made, just like other common bargains and sales, by the mere consideration of interest or gain, without any love or esteem'. Certainly the newspaper announcements Porter cited in support of this generalization have a flavour all the more hard-nosed for their clerical origin:

MARRIAGES

Married, the Lord Bishop of St Asaph to Miss Orrell, with £30,000.

Married, the Rev. Mr Roger Waind, of York, about twenty six years of age, to a Lincolnshire lady, upward of eighty, with whom he is to have £8,000 in money, £300 and a coach-and-four during life only.

Disqualified by celibacy from clerical enterprise of this kind, the Catholic Church made a modest demographic contribution by establishing institutions such as the Italian *monti di maritaggio*, to provide dowries for impecunious girls. The general determination to guard against impoverishment – 'no land, no marriage' – condemned large numbers of males and females to celibacy if not chastity. In Catholic Europe, the most common asylum was the monastery or the nunnery. Unmarried girls obliged to become brides of Christ rather than men were also required to provide a dowry for their nunnery, but the sum was appreciably less. It is not often appreciated just how thriving were the monastic establishments of eighteenth-century Europe. Around the middle of the eighteenth century there were at least 15,000 monasteries for men and 10,000 nunneries for women, with a total complement of *c.*250,000. Voltaire summarized their contribution to society with the dismissive comment: 'they sing, they eat, they digest'. As with most of Voltaire's anti-clerical jibes, this was grossly unfair, as many monks and nuns worked hard in a wide variety of demanding roles. But one thing they did not do was procreate.

They did not procreate, except on very rare occasions, although they may well have engaged in clandestine sexual activity. Indeed, if the increasingly scurrilous anti-clerical literature of the eighteenth century is to be believed, they engaged in little else. Married couples, however, were positively encouraged, if not required, to engage in sexual activity, but still they did not always procreate. Contraception is a branch of demography especially clouded by lack of direct evidence, but it is also one in which there is an unusual degree of consensus. Whether writing about Colyton, Geneva, Besançon or Rouen, there is general agreement that family planning was widely practised, especially among the elites, and on an increasing scale. In Rouen, for example, fertility rates fell consistently from 1642 to 1792, with a brief interlude in the middle of the eighteenth century. Births per family halved from eight in 1670 to four in 1800, as women stopped having babies earlier, or even stopped having them altogether (the proportion of the wholly childless doubled from 5 per cent to 10 per cent during the same period).

As contraception in any shape or form was condemned as vigorously by Protestants as by Catholics, very little evidence has been left of the techniques employed. There were plenty of herbal and/or magical recipes on offer, but it may be doubted whether they were very effective. More reliable, but by no means infallible, was the condom. This was allegedly the invention of a Dr Condom, seeking to limit Charles II's brood of illegitimate children, although the word is more likely to derive from the Latin *condus* for receptacle. Until the discovery of the vulcanization of rubber in the 1830s, the only materials available were cloth (too porous) or animal intestines (too insensitive). Although condoms were certainly in use, by James Boswell for example, they appear to have been used for the avoidance of disease rather than contraception. In the words of an anonymous English poet of 1744:

> Let not the Joy she proffers be Essay'd,
> Without the well-try'd Cundum's friendly Aid.

Indicative of the low esteem in which the condom was held was the attempt to portray it as some other country's invention, the English calling them 'French letters' and the French calling them 'English overcoats'. Less cumbersome but more fallible was a sponge inserted in the vagina, allied with post-coital use of a syringe or bidet for washing out any remaining sperm. Literary evidence suggests that this combination was especially favoured in France, where the ubiquitous bidet remained a source of misunderstanding and mirth for foreign visitors until relatively recently.

The only secure form of contraception was abstinence, or rather abstinence from ejaculation inside the vagina. Demographic historians find it easy to agree that *coitus interruptus* was both the most popular and most effective technique employed. Unfortunately, it raised intractable theological issues. Was it acceptable to engage in copulation solely for the purpose of enjoyment, without the intention of procreation? Was not premature withdrawal of the male member disturbingly close to the sin of Onan ('And Onan knew that the seed should not be his; and it came to pass, when he went in unto his brother's wife, that he spilled it on the ground, lest that he should give seed to his brother. And the thing which he did displeased the LORD: wherefore he slew him also.' Genesis 38:9–10)? How should one interpret, for example, the Anglican Book of Common Prayer (1662), which states that marriage was ordained by God for three reasons: 'for the procreation of children', 'for a remedy against sin, and to avoid fornication; that such persons as have not the gift of continency might marry', and 'for the mutual society, help, and comfort, that the one ought to have of the other, both in prosperity and adversity'? That *coitus interruptus* was widespread, despite these problems, was demonstrated not least by the numerous – and very popular – pamphlets which inveighed against it. The author of *Onania; or the Heinous Sin of Self-Pollution, and all its Frightful Consequences, in both Sexes, consider'd*, which went through twenty editions between 1710 and 1760, was in no doubt about its ethical status: it was absolutely unacceptable. When a reader wrote in to argue that he and his wife could not afford to support any more children and therefore his conscience was clear, he was told bluntly that he was committing 'an abominable sin'. From the opposite end of the theological spectrum, no one summed up better the repertoire of birth control techniques available to an early modern couple than the marquis de Sade, including his own favoured solution. In *Philosophy in the Boudoir* (1795) he has his two arch-rakes explain to the ingénue how to avoid pregnancy:

MADAME DE SAINT-ANGE A girl risks having a child only in proportion to the frequency with which she permits the man to invade her cunt. Let her scrupulously avoid this manner of tasting delight; in its stead, let her offer indiscriminately her hand, her mouth, her breasts, or her arse . . .

DOLMANCÉ . . . To cheat propagation of its rights and to contradict what fools call the laws of Nature, is truly most charming. The thighs, the armpits also sometimes offer him retreats where his seed may be spilled without risk of pregnancy.

MADAME DE SAINT-ANGE Some women insert sponges into the vagina's interior; these, intercepting the sperm, prevent it from springing into the vessel where generation occurs. Others oblige their lovers to make use of a little sack of Venetian skin, in the vernacular called a condom, which the semen fills and where it is prevented from flowing farther. But of all the possibilities, that presented by the arse is without doubt the most delicious.

MORTALITY − FAMINE

Despite the marquis de Sade's wishful thinking, sodomy remained very much a minority taste, not least because it was punished so severely when detected (see below, pp. 80−84). Certainly it does not appear to have had any discernible impact on the fertility figures of old regime Europe. On the other hand, the cumulative effect of birth control techniques certainly depressed rather than elevated Europe's population. The trend towards an earlier age of marriage in some regions certainly pointed in the other direction but not sufficiently to explain the rise. Demographers therefore conclude that explanations based on fertility are inadequate. Instead, they concentrate on a decline in mortality, especially on the diminution, if not disappearance, of the three great killers of the seventeenth century: famine, war and plague.

Perhaps no aspect of everyday life in the twenty-first century separates us more sharply from the early modern period than food prices. Although so taken for granted as to be invisible, the stability and low level of basic foodstuff prices are among the more agreeable characteristics of the modern world. Every now and again, there is a flurry of press interest if, say, adverse meteorological conditions in Brazil sends the price of instant coffee up by more than a few pence but, generally speaking, the cost of a regular shopping expedition is predictable from one year to the next. Moreover, for the great majority, the proportion of a salary spent on food is low and getting lower. This is a necessary consequence of a global division of labour, which in turn derives from quick and cheap transport. But for the early modern household, by far the greatest single item of expenditure was food, and by far the greatest source of anxiety was fear that the harvest would fail. Before steampower opened up the limitless productivity of the North American plains, most food had to be grown locally. As we have seen in Chapter 1, in the age of the quadruped, so difficult was it to transport the staple crop − grain − that any profit disappeared before even a few miles had been covered.

This problem was compounded by a dangerous over-reliance on cereals and thus on the weather. The latter presented two kinds of problems in the period 1648−1815. The first was macroscopic: there is a good deal of evidence that the late seventeenth century formed part of a much longer 'new ice age' which had begun a century or so earlier. Taking the period 1920–60 as a basis for comparison, it can be shown that average mean temperatures were 0.9°C lower during the second half of the seventeenth century and 1.5°C lower during the 1690s. That may not sound very much, but it appears to have had a seriously depressing effect on agricultural productivity. The second meteorological problem was short-term, namely the devastating effect that a wet winter or spring, or even a sudden hailstorm at harvest-time, could have on yields. It is worth remembering that early modern cultivators did not select their seed but simply kept back part of the previous crop; that the varieties they used had not been adapted to make the most of their soil and growing conditions; that even in a good year the yield might be as low as four or five grains to each one retained; that they had no mechanical equipment to harvest, thresh or dry; and that storage facilities were usually anything but watertight.

So, especially in the lands of the north, west and centre, peasant-producers knew that it was not a question of 'if' but 'when' a year of dearth would come. When it did, the signs would already be there by spring, in the form of stunted growth and rotting roots. With rumours of impending crop failure spreading, prices would begin to rise, as the well-off hurried to stock their larders. Those with grain to sell – the noble and ecclesiastical landowners, the grain merchants and the richer tenant-farmers – would then keep back their stocks from market, waiting for prices to reach their cyclical peak. Even in a normal year, late spring and early summer formed a difficult time in the calendar of consumers (and their governments), for it was then that the grain stocks of the previous year were beginning to run out but the new harvest had not yet been gathered in. This window of anxiety was known in France as *la soudure* ('the gap'). If the current harvest then really did prove to be disappointing, prices could start to go through the roof. And that was not the end of it. Most peasants did not cultivate enough land to allow them to be self-sufficient, but needed to enter the market as purchasers to make up the shortfall. To raise the necessary cash, they relied on labouring or some kind of manufacturing activity such as weaving or spinning. However, just when higher grain prices made this supplementary income all the more necessary, demand for manufactured items collapsed, because consumers were now having to spend so much more of their income on food.

By the autumn of a year of harvest failure, a large and growing number of people would find themselves excluded from the market. To survive, they resorted to inferior forms of food, to consuming their seed corn, to begging, to crime, to whatever. The lucky, the young, the healthy and the enterprising might get through the winter, but woe betide them if the following year's harvest also proved to be a failure. In May 1693 a minor official in the French bishopric of Beauvais noted that the price of corn had gone up sharply, causing acute hardship. Eleven months later, he wrote again, this time with a harrowing description of

an infinite number of poor souls, weak from hunger and wretchedness and dying from want and lack of bread in streets and squares, in the towns and countryside because, having no work or occupation, they lack the money to buy bread ... Seeking to prolong their lives a little and somewhat to appease their hunger, these poor folk for the most part, lacking bread, eat such unclean things as cats and flesh of horses flayed and cast on to dung heaps, the blood which flows when cows and oxen are slaughtered and the offal and lights and such which cooks throw into the streets ... Other poor wretches eat roots and herbs which they boil in water, nettles and weeds of that kind ... Yet others will grub up the beans and seed corn which were sown in the spring ... and all this breeds corruption in the bodies of men and divers mortal and infectious maladies, such as malignant fevers ... which assail even wealthy and well-provided persons.

The demographic effects of this sequence are not difficult to imagine, for one need only translate the sickeningly familiar images of present-day famines in the Horn of Africa to a European setting. Most obviously, marriage and birth rates plunged, while mortality – and especially infant mortality – rates soared. It has been estimated that during the terrible *mortalité* of 1692–4, 2,800,000 people, or 15 per cent of the total population of France, perished. The 1690s proved to be particularly destructive all over western, northern, central and eastern Europe. In Finland the famine of 1696–7 carried off at least a quarter and perhaps as much as a third of the population. In Scotland, a poor harvest in 1695 was followed by severe failure in 1696, a modest improvement in 1697 but general failure in 1698. In the worst affected counties, such as Aberdeenshire, the mortality rate reached 20 per cent. As Sir Robert Sibbald observed: 'Everyone may see Death in the Face of the Poor.' Only England and the Dutch Republic escaped the holocaust, perhaps because their agricultural systems were better balanced but more probably because their better water communications allowed both better circulation of surpluses and supplies from outside to be brought in.

There were bad harvests right across Europe in 1660–63, 1675–9, 1693–4 and 1708–9, together with plenty more localized famines in between. But then the situation began to improve. After 1709 there were no more famines in France, although there were plenty of years of acute shortages, not least in 1788–9. There were widespread subsistence crises in 1741–2, in the early 1770s and the late 1780s. Every now and again there would be a local outbreak of horrors of the late-seventeenth-century variety, as there was in Sicily in 1763 when the harvest failed, tens of thousands starved to death and social order broke down. For the reasons discussed earlier, food shortages could not be eliminated from Europe until improvements in communication opened up the grain-growing plains of the New World, but, even so, the eighteenth century marked a distinct improvement on what had gone before. As we shall see in a later chapter, part of the explanation is to be found in improved agricultural methods and part in more effective government action. It is also likely that a gradual improvement in meteorological conditions raised production levels. In any event, one reason for the striking difference between the demographic histories of the seventeenth and eighteenth centuries must lie in the reduction in the number and severity of famines.

MORTALITY – WAR

The first fifty years of the seventeenth century had witnessed some of the most terrible and most sustained blood-letting in human history. At home, faction-fighting turned into civil war; abroad, few parts of Europe were not affected by the epochal struggle between Habsburgs and Bourbons. The result was demographic catastrophe. In 1652, a report to the ecclesiastical authorities on the condition of the region around Paris affected by the '*Frondes*', as the civil war of 1648–53 was known, recorded 'villages and hamlets deserted and bereft of clergy, streets infected by stinking carrion and dead bodies lying exposed, houses without doors or windows, everything reduced to cesspools and stables, and above all the sick and dying, with no bread, meat, medicine, fire, beds, linen or covering, and no priest, doctor, surgeon or anyone to comfort them'. Yet these inhabitants of the Parisian *bassin* were the lucky ones, for at least the conflict which engulfed them was of relatively short duration. To the east, by that time, there was a whole generation which had grown up knowing nothing but the horrors of war. During the Thirty Years War, which began with the defenestration at Prague on 23 May 1618, armies rampaged across central Europe again and again. Only the Alpine regions and one or two favoured parts of the north were spared.

Contemporaries were in no doubt that this conflict was especially brutal, even by the terrifying standards of early modern warfare. Both literature, for example Grimmelshausen's *Simplicissimus*, and the visual arts, for example Jacques Callot's *Les Misères et les Malheurs de la Guerre*, convey harrowing evidence of the looting, rape and murder inflicted by the soldiers. Subsequent scholars have argued long and hard about the quantitative damage inflicted. German nationalist historians of the nineteenth century were only too anxious to believe that foreigners had plunged their country back into a dark age, from which only now – thanks to Prussia – it was at last emerging. That sort of narrative in turn provoked a strong reaction in the later twentieth century, when all kinds of qualifications to the 'doom and gloom' scenario were advanced. However, the consensus still seems to favour the figures first produced by Günther Franz in 1943 which showed that the urban population declined by a quarter and the rural population by a third. Those figures, however, are national averages; depending on the region, they could range from zero losses to well over 50 per cent.

The recovery of Germany's population after the end of the war was clearly in part just that – recovery. Once the armies had gone away, the natural buoyancy could return. Personifying the amazing virility and fecundity of the survivors was Hans Bosshardt, who got married for the fourth time at the age of eighty, his bride being his twenty-year-old goddaughter. He had three children by her, the youngest being born in the same year that its sixty-six-year-old half-brother died. The energetic Hans eventually died aged 100 whereupon his widow kept up the good work by soon remarrying. Unfortunately, it turned out that the war had not gone away for good. It returned with a vengeance in the 1670s, when Louis XIV sought to expand France's frontiers in the east. The Palatinate had barely recovered from the Thirty Years War when it was laid waste by the armies of General Turenne in 1674. The Elector

Palatine, Karl Ludwig, made Louis XIV personally responsible for the destruction of thirty years of *rétablissement*, but that did not prevent the French armies coming again and again in the 1680s. In 1689 the systematic, officially authorized destruction of Heidelberg, Mannheim, Worms, Speyer and many other towns in the region represented a new and ominous departure in the history of warfare. In 1693 the French returned, this time to burn Heidelberg to the ground. Far from being apologetic, Louis XIV had a medal struck bearing the boast '*Heidelberga deleta*'.

It was not only the hapless Germans who suffered repeated demographic setbacks in the second half of the seventeenth century. In the south-east, the new attempt by the Ottoman Turks to take control of the Danube valley, and the ensuing Austrian *reconquista* of Hungary, left huge tracts of territory virtually uninhabited. In the north-east, the long struggle between the Scandinavian countries, Poland and Russia for domination of the Baltic region also decimated the population periodically. In 1658, for example, Polish armies moved into Denmark to drive out the Swedes. What followed was a fine illustration of the old adage that, for civilians, allies were to be feared just as much as enemies. It was reported from southern Jutland: 'The Poles drove us from house and home, treated us brutally, and took away all we had, cattle and corn and everything we possessed, so that many were doomed to die of hunger; and so in the *herred* [district] of Malt there are only two, three or four persons left alive in every parish, and many corpses are eaten up in the houses by dogs.' The parish priest of the town of Malt confirmed this grim news, adding that with but few exceptions all his parishioners were dead and their houses burnt. Mortality rates of up to 90 per cent were reported. The *herred* court was told: 'in God's truth [it is] well known that before this dismal, wretched war and raging pestilence came upon us, the parish and parishioners of Rev. Christian Jensen were in full vigour ... and there were then in the parish of Føvling forty-five farms and seven homesteads, of which no more than six farms and three homesteads now remain ... The other farms are quite deserted.'

So war had not lost its teeth. Yet taking a very long view of the period 1648–1815, or at least 1648–1792, it can be seen that it did gradually lose some of its destructive force. It was not that wars became less frequent: on the contrary, there was a major war between the European powers in every decade of the eighteenth century except perhaps the

1720s. Rather it was the case that armies were now better disciplined and better provisioned. For reasons to be discussed later, one state after another moved to establish control over their armed forces. War was still a terrible affliction for anyone unfortunate enough to get in its way, but conflicts did become shorter in duration and more limited in geographical scope. It was Frederick the Great's declared ambition to isolate warfare from civilians to the extent that they would be unaware that it was underway. Of course, he failed, indeed he himself claimed that the Seven Years War had been as catastrophic from a demographic point of view for Prussia as the Thirty Years War. However, there was no return to the anarchy of the first half of the seventeenth century. It is impossible to imagine, say, one of Wallenstein's officers making the following observation by a Prussian subaltern in the Seven Years War:

We were never short of bread, and it frequently happened that we had a surplus of meat. It is true that coffee, sugar and beer were often not to be had even at high prices, while in Moravia we sometimes ran out of wine. But in Bohemia we had local wine in plenty, especially in the camp at Melnik in 1757. You know how things are in wartime: if you want to be really comfortable, you ought to stay at home.

Similar tributes about life on the other side can also be found, an English volunteer in the Austrian army even maintaining that his colleagues did not desert because they were 'well paid, well dressed and well fed'. So there is a great deal to be said for Sir Michael Howard's canine metaphor to describe eighteenth-century warfare:

It might be suggested that it was not the least achievement of European civilisation to have reduced the wolf packs which had preyed on the defenceless peoples of Europe for so many centuries to the condition of trained and obedient gun dogs – almost, in some cases, performing poodles.

This verdict has been confirmed, albeit more prosaically, by Fritz Redlich, who, in a general account of military depredation between 1500 and 1815, concluded: 'The eighteenth century experienced a fundamental change in outlook and attitude towards looting and booty.' As we shall see later in a different context, there was a return to the bad old days when the hordes of the French Revolution were unleashed on Europe. For the time being, however, another Horseman of the Apocalypse had had his mount muzzled if not gelded.

MORTALITY – PLAGUE

It will be recalled that the hapless people of Malt complained not only about 'this dismal, wretched war' but also about the 'raging pestilence' which had come in its wake. Some victims were murdered by Polish soldiers, a few may have starved to death, but most died from plague. This was the third and greatest source of mortality, although it very often combined with the other two, for bodies enfeebled by hunger were easier prey for pathogens, and it was often armies that spread the epidemics. Günther Franz, in the study of German population losses during the Thirty Years War referred to earlier, argued that violent deaths were much less numerous than had once been supposed – it was plague that had been the main killer.

In the twenty-first century, when epidemic disease is both rare and understood, it is difficult to imagine a time when it was common and not understood at all. With our life expectancy of between seventy-five and eighty years, depending on class, gender and geographical location, and set to continue increasing to one hundred and beyond, death can be disregarded as something that happens to other people. When life expectancy lay between twenty-five and forty, again depending on class, gender and geographical location, death had terrifying immediacy. In England mortality worsened during the third quarter of the seventeenth century, life expectancy falling to its lowest point of around thirty years in the 1680s. It then improved to reach thirty-seven by 1700 and forty-two by the middle of the eighteenth century. Even so, when mourners gathered around an English graveside to hear the clergyman intoning the words of the Book of Common Prayer of 1662 – 'in the midst of life we are in death' – they knew that he was telling the truth. Three years after those chilling words were published, the Great Plague of London killed perhaps between 80,000 and 100,000 in less than a year, out of a total population of fewer than 500,000. Its progress can be followed in a number of contemporary sources, the best being the diary of Samuel Pepys. Even his naturally ebullient disposition was chastened by the rapidly mounting death toll. On 26 July 1665 he recorded: 'The Sickenesse is got into our parish this week; and is hot endeed everywhere, so that I begin to think of setting things in order, which I pray God enable me to put, both as to soul and body.' Two days later he travelled to Dagenham, where he found the people so terrified of contagion from London visitors that he exclaimed, 'But Lord, to see in what fear all the people here do live would make one mad.' Back in the capital on the following day, a headache 'put me into extraordinary fear'. By the middle of August he could write, 'The people die so, that now it seems they are fain to carry the dead to be buried by daylight, the nights not sufficing to do it in.' Particularly alarming was the death of his physician on 26 August. And so on.

Good luck and Pepys's natural high spirits got him through the dark days of the late summer and autumn, after which mortality rates began to fall. Even his anxiety had not prevented him from indulging his two favourite passions – making money and philandering – to such an extent, indeed, that he could record complacently on the last day of the year: 'I have never lived so merrily (besides that I never got so much) as I have done this plague-time.' This turned out to be the last major outbreak of bubonic plague in England, thus bringing to an end a sequence which had begun back in the mid-fourteenth century with the Black Death. The nature of the plague is now well established. The bacillus is transmitted by the bite of a variety of flea (*Xenopsylla cheopis*) which normally lives parasitically on rats. When the bacillus becomes particularly intense and the rats start to die, the fleas need to find alternative hosts from which to draw blood. The most promising candidates are humans living in the vicinity of the rats. The flea bite is followed by an incubation period of usually three to six days, although it can be as short as thirty-six hours and as long as ten days. Then the victim is afflicted by shivering, vomiting, acute headache and pain in the limbs, giddiness, extreme sensitivity to light and a high temperature ($c.40°C$). Inside the body, the bacteria invade the lymph nodes, producing one or more swellings (the eponymous 'buboes') in the neck or the groin and internal bleeding. In between 50 and 75 per cent of cases death follows in approximately two weeks, ultimately as a result of respiratory failure. Even more deadly, although less common, are pneumonic plague and septicaemic plague, which (unlike the bubonic variety) can be easily spread from human to human.

In short, plague depended on a quadrilateral relationship between the bacillus, the flea, the rat and the human. Unfortunately, seventeenth-century Europeans were blissfully ignorant of the nexus and so could do little to break it. Living cheek-by-jowl with the source of infection, they unwittingly encouraged its periodic visitations. The unsanitary conditions of early modern communities has been summed up with particular eloquence by James Riley:

It was a habitat of stagnant waters and steaming marshes and fetid cesspits; of narrow, airless, and filth-ridden streets and passages; of hovels and grand buildings without ventilation; of the dead incompletely isolated from the living. It was, we can now see, a habitat in which the micro-organisms of disease (and the living vectors that transmit those micro-organisms and other pathogenic matter) thrived ... It is inescapable to suppose that fleas, lice, houseflies, mosquitoes, rodents, and other small animals and insects which act as living disease vectors and vector hosts existed in stupendous numbers in these conditions. It was the golden age of these organisms.

Some idea of the havoc inflicted by the plague can be gained from simple statistics: Naples lost about half of its population and Genoa 60 per cent in 1656; Marseilles and Aix-en-Provence lost half in 1721; Reggio di Calabria lost half and Messina 70 per cent in 1743; Moscow lost 50,000 or about 20 per cent in 1771–2; and so on. Behind these stark figures, however, lie deep and dark economic, social, cultural and psychological chasms of grief and suffering. One example must suffice. It was in 1647 that there began what proved to be, in the words of Antonio Dominguez Ortiz, 'the greatest catastrophe to strike Spain in the early modern period', when the first case of plague was reported in Valencia. From there it spread through Aragon and Catalonia to the Balearic Islands and Sardinia, decimating the population as it went. In Barcelona, every possible precaution was taken to prevent infected people entering the city, but in vain. Shortly after New Year's Day 1651 plague was established there. By the time it began to relinquish its grasp in late summer, 45,000 people had died. Observing it all was the tanner Miquel Parets, who left a harrowing record of its effect on his family. In quick succession he lost his wife, his baby daughter and two of his three sons:

God took our little girl the day after her mother's death. She was like an angel, with a doll's face, comely, cheerful, pacific, and quiet, who made everyone who knew her fall in love with her. And afterwards, within fifteen days, God took our older boy, who already worked and was a good sailor and who was to be my support when I grew older, but this was not up to me but to God who chose to take them all. God knows why He does what He does, He knows what is best for us. His will be done. Thus in less than a month there died my wife, our two older sons, and our little daughter. And I remained with four-year-old Gabrielo, who of them all had the most difficult character.

In Barcelona, as elsewhere, the outbreak of plague led to a breakdown of social order, as the healthy struggled to get out of the city while the going was good, the wealthy sought to buy their way out of quarantine restrictions, and the criminals took advantage of the collapse of law and order. For the survivors everywhere, the rewards could be great, as the acceleration of inheritances concentrated property ownership. The greatest beneficiary of all was the Church – indeed it could not lose, for it was the recipient of benefactions inspired both by hope during the outbreak and by gratitude after it. Catholic Europe is still covered with architectural evidence of this confidence in the power of the Almighty to ward off disease, in the shape of chapels, statues and various votive offerings to the 'plague saints' St Rochus (also the patron saint of dogs and dog-lovers) and St Sebastian (also the patron saint of archers). Even if the plague did strike, eventually it would go away, thus confirming God's infinite mercy. Grandest of all these monuments is surely Santa Maria della Salute, the great baroque church built at the entrance of the Grand Canal in Venice to celebrate the end of the great plague of 1631–2. Visually the most exuberant is the Plague Column erected on the Graben in Vienna by the Emperor Leopold I following the plague of 1679.

The most popular explanation for a visitation of the plague was divine wrath; consequently the most popular prophylactic was propitiation. At Marseilles in 1720, Archbishop Belsunce took the lead, dedicating his fellow citizens to the cult of the Sacred Heart and leading penitential processions. In Barcelona, Miquel Parets recorded:

There are no words to describe the prayers and processions carried out in Barcelona, and the crowds of penitents and young girls with crosses who marched through the city saying their devotions. The streets were constantly full of people, many greatly devout and carrying candles and crying out 'Lord God, have mercy!' It would have softened the heart of anyone to see so many people gathered together and so many little girls, all of them barefoot. To see so many processions of clergy and monks and nuns carrying so many crosses and so many rogations that there was not a single church nor monastery which did not carry out processions both inside and outside their buildings.

It was to no avail, and Parets was obliged to add, 'but Our Lord was so angered by our sins that the more processions were carried out the more the plague spread'.

Two other techniques were employed to avert or arrest the plague. Least effective were the various magical and herbal remedies employed, such as the fumigation with juniper ordered by Peter the Great during the wave of plagues which attacked Russia between 1709 and 1713. If juniper were not available, he decreed that horse manure was to be used, 'or something else which smells bad, as smoke is very effective against these diseases'. However, most public authorities did understand enough of the epidemics to appreciate the need for isolating the outbreaks and their victims. Most Italian cities, for example, boasted a public health authority or *sanità*, ready to go into action at the first sign of illness, excluding or quarantining travellers from infected regions, sealing off the houses of the afflicted, establishing pest-houses, disposing of corpses, and so on. Alas, there proved to be too many ways round the regulations: the infected fled, the sick were concealed, soiled garments were not burnt but used again, and plague-controllers were bribed. The need to import provisions meant that no city could be isolated entirely from the outside world, while municipal prohibitions of public gatherings were often overruled by the clergy's penitential processions.

Yet the period 1648–1815 did see, first the retreat, and then the virtual disappearance of the plague from Europe: England was afflicted for the last time in 1665, central Europe in 1710, France in 1720–21, the Ukraine in 1737, southern Europe in 1743 and Russia in 1789–91. Numerous explanations have been advanced. It is possible that the black rat (*Rattus rattus*), which liked to live cheek-by-jowl with humankind, was replaced by the brown rat (*Rattus norvegicus*), which was less sociable. It is also possible that all rats developed a higher degree of immunity to the plague bacillus, so the fleas had less need to abandon them for human hosts. The increasing use of stone for dwellings, as opposed to wood, wattle and daub, probably created a less welcoming environment for rodents of all kinds. Another hypothesis speculates that the bacillus itself naturally transmuted into a less virulent form. The American scholar James Riley has argued that what he calls 'the medicine of avoidance and prevention' made an important contribution to the decline of all infectious diseases, singling out for special mention improved drainage, lavation, ventilation, interment, fumigation and refuse burial, the relocation of refuse-producing industries and waste sites, and cleaner wells. More effective quarantine regulations were also adopted by a number of European states. The most important was the Habsburg Monarchy, which, following the reconquest of Hungary from the Ottoman Turks, issued strict regulations to keep out plague carriers. The long frontier which straggled for 1,200 miles (1,900 km) across the Balkan peninsula, from the Adriatic to the Carpathians, was turned into a great cordon sanitaire. The quarantine period for anyone wishing to cross the frontier from the east was twenty-one days in plague-free times, forty-two days if an outbreak was rumoured and eighty-four days if the rumour was confirmed. Guards were under orders to shoot to kill anyone trying to evade the restrictions. Equally tough action was taken by the French government to confine the 1720 outbreak to Provence.

None of these possibilities can be a sufficient cause for the decline in the incidence and severity of plague. Nor can that decline be a sufficient cause for the increase in Europe's population. In one of those tricks of which malevolent nature is so fond, just as plague was waning, other diseases were waxing. Influenza, typhoid fever, typhus, dysentery, infantile diarrhoea, scarlet fever, measles and diphtheria all played their part in keeping the mortality rate up. The great killer of the eighteenth century was smallpox, an airborne virus which enters the human body through the mouth or nose, then multiplies in the internal organs, causing high fever and a rash which turns into blisters and then pustules. The lucky escape with pock-marked skin, caused when the pustules dry; the less fortunate will be made blind, deaf or lame (or any two of the three); about 15 per cent will die. On occasions, the mortality rate could be much higher: between 1703 and 1707, for example, Iceland lost 18,000 of its original population of 50,000. In Dublin between 1661 and 1745 20 per cent of reported deaths were ascribed to smallpox. James Jurin, secretary of the Royal Society of London, estimated that smallpox had killed a fourteenth of London's population between 1680 and 1743. At Lodève in Languedoc outbreaks in 1726 and 1751 increased the death rate by almost 200 per cent.

Among the high-profile casualties in this period were the Elector Johann Georg IV of Saxony, who was infected when he insisted on kissing his dying mistress goodbye; the Emperor Joseph I, whose untimely death in 1711 at the age of thirty-two gave a decisive twist to the War of the Spanish Succession; Louis XV, who was rumoured to have caught the disease from the pubescent peasant-girl he had raped; and the Elector Maximilian Joseph of Bavaria, whose untimely death in 1777 precipitated the War of the Bavarian Succession. As these examples demonstrate, smallpox was impeccably democratic, decimating the palace as well as the hovel. If less destructive than the plague, it was more ubiquitous. In *Candide*, Voltaire wrote that if two armies of 30,000 each met in battle, two-thirds of the combatants would be pock-marked. The position and severity of the scars were used as a means of identifying criminals and, significantly, it was thought worthy of comment if they were *not* marked. The figure usually given for total European deaths per annum from smallpox in the eighteenth century is 400,000, although this must be a very rough guess indeed. In 1800 in the German principalities of Ansbach-Bayreuth it was recorded that 4,509 people had died from smallpox, or about 1 per cent of the total population. As an ever-present *memento mori*, it also caught the attention of the poets like Lady Mary Wortley Montagu, who contracted the disease in 1715 at the age of twenty-six. She survived the ordeal but at the expense of her beauty, as she recorded the following year:

> How am I changed! alas! how am I grown
> A frightful spectre, to myself unknown!
> Where's my complexion? where the radiant bloom,
> That promised happiness for years to come?
> Then, with what pleasure I this face surveyed!
> To look once more, my visits oft delayed!
> Charmed with the view, a fresher red would rise,
> And a new life shot sparkling from my eyes!
> Ah! faithless glass, my wonted bloom restore!
> Alas! I rave, that bloom is now no more!

MEDICINE

Yet in this case it really was darkest before dawn. It was as a pock-marked spectre that Lady Mary travelled to Constantinople with her husband, the British consul in the city. There she found that Turkish peasant women had found a way of preventing the disease through a form of inoculation. As she explained in a letter to a friend in 1717:

Apropos of distempers, I am going to tell you a thing that will make you wish yourself here. The *smallpox*, so fatal and so general among us, is here entirely harmless by the invention of *engrafting*, which is the term they give it. There is a set of old women who make it their business to perform the operation every autumn in the month of September when the great heat is abated . . . They make parties for the purpose . . . the old woman comes with a nutshell full of the matter of the best sort of smallpox, and asks what veins you please to have open'd. She immediately rips open that you offer to her, with a large needle (which gives you no more pain than a common scratch), and puts into the vein as much matter as can lie upon the head of her needle, and after that, binds up the little wound with a hollow bit of shell, and in this manner opens four or five veins.

These enterprising ladies were exploiting what was common knowledge everywhere – that a mild form of smallpox granted immunity for life. The technique may have been known already in western Europe too, but it was certainly Lady Mary's proselytizing that led to its popularization. Although she could not set a personal example herself, as she already enjoyed immunity, she did the next best thing by having her five-year-old daughter inoculated when she returned to England in 1721. Her example was quickly followed by the Prince of Wales, who had both his daughters inoculated. Other social leaders to set examples included the duc d'Orléans, Frederick the Great of Prussia, the Empress Maria Theresa, the King of Denmark and Catherine the Great of Russia. It proved to be uphill work, not least because inoculation was not without its dangers. There was another major outbreak in London in 1752, when 17 per cent of all deaths were attributed to the disease. This concentrated the minds of potential victims everywhere, with the result that there was a rapid increase in the rate of inoculation during the second half of the century. Members of the Sutton family, who toured rural areas offering the treatment, claimed to have inoculated 400,000 in the thirty years after 1750. The dramatic effect inoculation could have on mortality rates is shown by a number of local studies which demonstrate that by the end of the eighteenth century, inoculation had spread down from monarchs to the common people.

A second breakthrough came at the very end of the century when an English country doctor, Edward Jenner, discovered the much safer and less elaborate technique of vaccination. He had noticed that infection with cowpox, a disease that is relatively benign when contracted by humans, granted immunity against smallpox. In 1796 he inoculated an eight-year-old boy with pus taken from the pustule of a milkmaid infected with cowpox. The boy suffered nothing worse than a mild fever, but when inoculated a short time later with the smallpox virus he proved to be immune and experienced no ill effects whatsoever. This discovery was publicized by Jenner in *An Inquiry into the Causes and Effects of the Variolae Vaccinae*, published in 1798. By 1801 it had gone through two more editions and the technique was well on its way to gaining universal acceptance. It was made compulsory in a number of continental countries: in Sweden, for example, where deaths from smallpox per 100,000 fell from 278 in the late 1770s to 15 in the 1810s. In Bavaria, where the King set a personal example and then made it compulsory in 1807, total deaths from the disease fell from *c.*7,500 per annum to 150 and then to zero by 1810. Napoleon had his entire army vaccinated. When Jenner wrote to him to ask for the liberation of a British prisoner of war, Napoleon is reported to have replied: 'Anything Jenner wants shall be granted. He has been my most faithful servant in the European campaigns.'

Smallpox was not eradicated from the world until 1977, according to the World Health Organization, but it had ceased to be a serious killer in Europe by 1815. Its virtual eradication was a rare example of an unequivocal success story for medicine in this period. It also provides a good example of how folk-remedies (the Turkish peasant women's 'smallpox parties') could combine with scientific observation and experimentation (Jenner's vaccination) to produce real improvements in public health and reduce mortality. Much more typical of early modern attitudes were the other treatments used to combat smallpox. They were based on the Hippocratic-Galenic tradition which still dominated western medicine despite – or perhaps because of – the antiquity of its eponymous founders (Hippocrates had lived 450–370 BC and Galen of

Pergamum AD 129–200). At its heart lay the belief that human health was determined by the interrelationship between four 'humours' in the body. These were blood (hot and wet), black bile (cold and dry), yellow or red bile (hot and dry) and phlegm (cold and wet). According to time of life or time of year, any one of these humours could become predominant, with adverse effects. Too much black bile led to melancholy, too much phlegm led to torpor, too much red bile led to belligerence, and so on. The task of the physician was to restore the desired balance by draining off any excess.

So the preferred treatment of early modern medicine took the form of laxatives, emetics, dehydration and phlebotomy, to encourage purging, vomiting, sweating and bleeding respectively. As Edward Topsell defined the objective in the early seventeenth century: 'the emptiyng or voiding of superfluous humors, annoying the body with their evill quality'. That is why so much literature of the seventeenth and eighteenth centuries refers to the arrival of the barber-surgeon with his bleeding-cups and leeches as soon as illness struck. Indeed, the physician was often referred to as a 'leechman' who charged a 'leech-fee' and worked at a 'leech-house' (hospital). For the smallpox victim, it need hardly be said, none of these treatments did any good whatsoever, on the contrary. Nor did such exotic remedies as the 'red cure', which required the patient to dress in red clothes, sleep in a bed surrounded by red drapes and drink red-coloured fluids. Yet such was the authority of humoralism that its precepts were accepted by most without question. Samuel Pepys had himself bled when he thought he was 'exceedingly full of blood' and believed that it would improve his failing eyesight. Rare indeed was the strong-minded individual such as the Princess Palatine, of whom Madame de Sévigné recorded when she first arrived at Versailles in 1670: 'she has no use for doctors and even less of medicines . . . When her doctor was presented to her, she said that she did not need him, that she had never been purged or bled, and that when she is not feeling well she goes for a walk and cures herself by exercise.'

There was no lack of medical services on offer in the early modern period, indeed there was an embarrassment of riches. For most patients, the first port of call was the household's fund of accumulated wisdom, supported by herbal remedies and magical invocation. If a member of the family was literate, one of the many printed manuals, such as Samuel Tissot's *Avis au peuple sur la santé* (1761) or William Buchan's *Domestic*

Medicine (1769), could be consulted. Resort could also be had to the local wisewoman or wiseman, the village priest, the blacksmith (if bones needed setting) or even the lady of the manor. A community might be lucky enough to have in its midst an individual with special powers, such as the seventh son of a seventh son, or a natural healer identified by being 'born with the caul' (i.e. with a piece of the placenta sticking to his head). There were plenty of travelling salesmen and quack doctors roaming the country, peddling patent medicines in the style of Dr Dulcamara of Donizetti's *L'Elisir d'amore*. And there were also, of course, the official men of medicine – the physicians, the barber-surgeons and the apothecaries. There was no need to confine oneself to just one of these sources of medical advice and probably most sick people sought a second or third opinion.

Any temptation to divide these various resources into the scientific and the superstitious should be resisted. The former often did more harm than good, the latter often did more good than harm. A striking example of the shadowy relationship between the two was provided by the discovery of the cardiotonic properties of the foxglove plant by the Shropshire physician William Withering in 1775. Unable to help one of his patients with a serious heart condition, he was suitably embarrassed when the patient obtained a herbal tea from a gypsy-woman and promptly recovered. Withering systematically tested each of the brew's twenty-odd ingredients until he had isolated foxglove as the benefactor. The *digitalis purpurea* the plant produces increases the intensity of the heart muscle contractions while reducing the heart rate, and can also be used to treat dropsy. After extensive trials on animals and human patients, Withering published in 1785 *An Account of the Foxglove and Some of its Medical Uses etc; With Practical Remarks on Dropsy and Other Diseases*, which advertised its curative properties to the world. It has been used ever since. There were several other 'folk-remedies' which turned out to be based on sound science, such as willow-bark tea, which contained *salicylates*, the active ingredient in aspirin, or 'Jesuit bark', the bark of the cinchona tree which contains quinine. There was plenty to be said for preferring the practical experience of the wisewoman to the book-learning of the quack. Thomas Hobbes observed: 'I would rather have the advice or take physick from an experienced old woman that had been at many sick people's bedsides, than from the learnedst but unexperienced physician.'

Successes such as inoculation, vaccination or digitalis were few and far between. Almost all the staples of modern medicine – germ theory, general anaesthesia, radiology, antibiotics, and so on – were discoveries of the nineteenth and twentieth centuries. For most patients in most places, the situation in 1815 was not so very different from that of 1648. In four ways, however, there can be said to have been progress, in the sense that the chances of patients receiving beneficial treatment improved. First, there was a fitful but definite move away from a humoral view of disease to one centred on the material structure of the body and employing a mechanical metaphor to understand its workings. The chief theoretical influence here was Descartes, whose rationalist philosophy divided soul from body, thus allowing the latter to be studied for its own sake and on its own terms. The chief practical influence was the growing practice of conducting post-mortems, which boosted anatomy and pathology at the expense of humoral theory. A landmark was the publication in 1761 by Giovanni Battista Morgagni of Padua of *De Sedibus et Causis Morborum per Anatomen Indagatis Libri Quinque* (The Seats and Causes of Diseases Investigated by Anatomy in Five Books), which described 640 post-mortems in detail, relating the state of the organs after death to the clinical symptoms displayed during life.

Secondly, in a few places there developed clinical training, which gave aspiring physicians the opportunity to learn their profession at the bedsides of real patients. The most influential figure here was Herman Boerhaave (1668–1738), professor of medicine at the University of Leiden in the Dutch Republic, who applied Cartesian dualism to physiology. He did not invent clinical training, which dates back to sixteenth-century Pavia, but he did popularize it. His clinic came to be a most important institutional influence on the development of eighteenth-century medicine. It was to Leiden that John Monro sent his son Alexander to be trained in anatomy, as part of his plan to give the University of Edinburgh a faculty of medicine, duly established in 1726. It became the most important centre of medical research and training in the British Isles, not least because it was closely linked to the Edinburgh Royal Infirmary, founded three years later. Similar institutions for clinical training were established in Halle, Göttingen, Jena, Erfurt, Strassburg, Vienna, Pavia, Prague and Pest. Perhaps significantly, it was not the university but the hospital that provided the institutional base for medical progress. At the University of Oxford, the primary duty of the Regius

Professor of Medicine was to lecture twice a week during term on the texts of Hippocrates or Galen. Even that modest requirement proved too much for Thomas Hoy, Regius Professor from 1698 to 1718, who preferred to reside in Jamaica and appointed a deputy (who in turn appointed a deputy). Hoy was not untypical: the official history of the University records gloomily: 'The holders of the office between 1690 and 1800, with minor exceptions, performed their duties with so little commitment that they merit no more than passing mention.'

A third form of progress was provided by voluntary movements of various kinds. There is no reason to suppose that human nature became more charitable in the eighteenth century, but the proliferation of private initiatives to relieve suffering was certainly striking. Whether it was the Medical Institute for the Sick-Poor of Hamburg, set up 'to return many upright and honest workers to the state' and 'to reduce distress of suffering humanity', the Society for Maternal Charity to serve 'a class of poor for whom there are neither hospitals nor foundations at Paris, namely the legitimate infants of the poor', or the self-explanatory National Truss Society for the Relief of the Ruptured Poor of London, the amount of medical attention available greatly increased. This phenomenon appears to have been particularly common in Great Britain, although this may simply reflect greater knowledge. Of special importance for medicine was the 'voluntary hospital movement', so-called because the hospitals in question were founded by groups of charitable individuals. The first was the Westminster Infirmary, founded in 1720, followed in London by St George's, the London and the Middlesex. At least thirty more were founded in the provinces, among them Addenbrooke's Hospital in Trumpington Street, Cambridge, founded in 1766 following a bequest from a former bursar of St Catharine's College 'to hire and fit up, purchase or erect a small, physical hospital in the town of Cambridge for poor people'.

Lastly, there was certainly a marked increase in the number of formally educated and certified practitioners. Three broad categories can be identified: at the summit were the physicians, academically trained, officially licensed and enjoying highest status and highest fees. More disparate were the apothecaries and the barber-surgeons, usually organized in guilds and treated as craftsmen. As the name of the latter group suggests, their primary function was to dress hair. They could turn their hand to simple medical tasks such as extracting teeth, lancing boils or setting bones, but usually were prudent enough to work within their limitations. The development noted above of the mechanistic view of the human body and the accompanying development of anatomy led to a corresponding expansion in the barber-surgeons' horizons and the dropping of their tonsorial function. In 1745 the London Company of Surgeons broke away from the Barbers, completing their elevation to professional status with a royal charter in 1800 which made them the Royal College of Surgeons. In France, conventional craft-training for surgeons was ended in 1768. Everywhere there was a gradual convergence of training for physicians and surgeons, with a consequent elevation in status for the latter.

Between 1648 and 1815 there were few decisive medical innovations, but there was probably more change than in the previous millennium, especially in the way in which the working of the human body was regarded. It seems appropriate, therefore, to end this section with the optimistic view of the future voiced in 1794 by William Heberden:

I please myself with thinking that the method of teaching the art of healing is becoming every day more conformable to what reason and nature require, that the errors introduced by superstition and false philosophy are gradually retreating, and that medical knowledge, as well as all other dependent upon observation and experience, is continually increasing in the world. The present race of physicians is possessed of several most important rules of practice, utterly unknown to the ablest in former ages, not excepting Hippocrates himself, or even Aesculapius.

WOMEN, SEX AND GENDER

In 1703 Sarah Egerton published a collection of poems entitled *Poems on Several Occasions*, including 'The Emulation', whose opening lines are:

> Say, tyrant Custom, why must we obey
> The impositions of thy haughty sway?
> From the first dawn of life unto the grave,
> Poor womankind's in every state a slave,
> The nurse, the mistress, parent and the swain,
> For love she must, there's none escape that pain.

> Then comes the last, the fatal slavery:
> The husband with insulting tyranny
> Can have ill manners justified by law,
> For men all join to keep the wife in awe.
> Moses, who first our freedom did rebuke,
> Was married when he writ the Pentateuch.
> They're wise to keep us slaves, for well they know,
> If we were loose, we soon should make them so.

She wrote with the depth of emotion inspired by personal experience. As a penalty for writing a long verse satire, *The Female Advocate*, at the precocious age of fourteen (or so she claimed in her autobiography), she was sent away from London by her middle-class parents to live with relations in rural Buckinghamshire and was then forced into a loveless marriage with a lawyer. Released from this servitude by the death of her husband, she then jumped back into the fire by marrying a widower twenty years older than herself in *c.*1700. Whatever material advantages the Rev. Thomas Egerton brought her – he was rector of Adstock – they were not sufficient to expunge memories of Henry Pierce, a humble clerk with whom she was in love. The unhappy couple's early attempt at divorce was frustrated by legal barriers, so they were forced to struggle on in a notoriously stormy marriage. Another female poet, Mary Delariver Manley, witnessed a 'comical combat', in which both Egertons resorted to violence, he by pulling her hair, she by throwing food. After the death of her second husband in 1720, Sarah enjoyed just three years of comfortable, and one hopes peaceful, widowhood before expiring herself at the age of fifty-three.

In this brief biography can be found some, but by no means all, of the problems encountered by women in early modern Europe: parental tyranny, the arranged marriage, the loveless marriage, and the inability to divorce. At least poor Sarah had the literary skill to leave a record of her resentment. Nor was she a lone voice. In the very same year that she wrote the lines quoted above, Mary Chudleigh published *Poems on Several Occasions*, including 'To the Ladies', whose first lines are:

> Wife and servant are the same,
> But only differ in the name:
> For when that fatal knot is tied,
> Which nothing, nothing can divide,

When she the word *Obey* has said,
And man by law supreme has made,
Then all that's kind is laid aside,
And nothing left but state and pride.

In her case, it was Sir George Chudleigh Bart., Devon squire, who was displaying 'state and pride', although he did also give her six children, only two of whom survived infancy. Although she never criticized her husband directly, it can be inferred with some confidence that he was less than ideal. Two years earlier, in 1701, Lady Mary had written 'The Ladies' Defence' in answer to a sermon advocating the absolute submission of wives to husbands preached by a nonconformist minister called John Sprint. In the preface she stated that what made the greatest contribution to marital unhappiness was 'Parents forcing their Children to Marry, contrary to their Inclinations; Men believe they have a right to dispose of their Children as they please; and they think it below them to consult their Satisfaction'. The poem is a discussion between three men, one of them an Anglican clergyman, and a woman. The chief spokesman for the male camp is the aptly named Sir John Brute, who takes the view that 'Those worst of Plagues, those Furies call'd our Wives', can, and should, be treated roughly:

Yes, as we please, we may our Wives chastise,
'Tis the Prerogative of being Wise:
They are but Fools, and must as such be us'd.

In her reply, the female mouthpiece – Melissa – gives as good as she gets, apostrophizing men as arrogant tyrants, complacent hypocrites, sadistic brutes, self-indulgent sots, idle voluptuaries, 'Empty Fops, or Nauseous Clowns', just to mention a few of her epithets. Sir John is given strong clerical support from the unnamed parson, who patiently explains to Melissa the great gulf separating men from women:

Your shallow Minds can nothing else contain,
You were not made for Labours of the Brain;
Those are the Manly Toils which we sustain.
We, like the Ancient Giants, stand on high,
And seem to bid Defiance to the Sky,
While you poor worthless Insects crawl below,
And less than Mites t'our exalted Reason show.

Because it was Eve's fault that mankind was expelled from Paradise, he asserts, it is only right that her successors should be enslaved. Melissa replies that any intellectual limitations suffered by women are caused by men:

> 'Tis hard we should be by the Men despis'd
> Yet kept from knowing what would make us priz'd:
> Debarred from Knowledge, banish'd from the Schools,
> And with the utmost Industry bred Fools.

Sir John promptly confirms the justice of this complaint by observing that women should not be allowed to read, for 'Books are the Bane of States, the Plagues of Life, / But both conjoyn'd when studied by a Wife'. The fourth member of the party, Sir William Loveall, the sort of bachelor so very keen to establish his heterosexual credentials by boasting of his conquests, tells Melissa that members of the fair sex should content themselves by being just that – fair – and not trouble their pretty little heads with matters they cannot understand. Faced with Brute's misogyny, the parson's theology and Loveall's condescension, Melissa can only look forward to a more equitable existence in the next world.

Just how representative were Sarah Egerton and Mary Chudleigh can never be established, although there were plenty of other straws in the wind. In *Some Reflections upon Marriage* (1706) one of Mary Chudleigh's correspondents, Mary Astell, wrote, 'if all men are born free, how is it that all women are born slaves?' Rather like the 'submerged nations' awaiting discovery by the ethnologist to bring them to the surface, most European women throughout this period were sleeping beauties (to borrow Sir William Loveall's imagery) whose resentment at millennia of oppression was confined to literary expression. That their general grievances were real is easy to establish. In every European country the legal system discriminated against them. In this respect at least, the spread of Roman Law during the early modern period had a regressive effect, for its attitude to women was underpinned by an assumption of their mental and physical weakness – Justinian's Code explicitly referred to their 'fragility, imbecility, irresponsibility and ignorance'. Of course, such empty vessels could not be entrusted with any property they might possess. So whatever a woman brought to a marriage was treated as if it now belonged to her husband; only when he died might she hope to regain control, and even then she might not have first claim on the estate. As for her unmarried daughters, more often than not they found themselves left out in the cold. Even if an estate were not formally 'entailed', a legal device to keep the estate intact from one generation to the next, it was usual if not invariable for the male heirs to be privileged. That was what Henry Dashwood's daughters discovered in Jane Austen's *Sense and Sensibility* (1811) when their father died, leaving everything to his son by an earlier marriage and relying on his heir's good will to 'do something' for his half-sisters. He had not reckoned with his daughter-in-law, who in the space of one chapter succeeds in reducing the sum from £1,000 for each of the girls to nothing:

'He did not know what he was talking of, I dare say; ten to one but he was light-headed at the time. Had he been in his right senses, he could not have thought of such a thing as begging you to give away half your fortune from your own child.'

It might be thought that in this instance Jane Austen did her sex no favours by presenting Fanny Dashwood as the avaricious female bringing out the worst in her well-meaning but weak husband.

The Egertons, Chudleighs and Dashwoods were lucky to be literate, for not the least disadvantage suffered by women was educational. Everywhere in Europe it was men who were more likely to be literate, although there is some fragmentary evidence that rates for women were increasing. In the Electorate of Saxony, for example, the impact of the Reformation with its stress on the need for all believers to be given access to the word of God, meant that by 1580 about half the parishes had licensed German-language schools for boys, but only 10 per cent for girls. By the end of the following century, those figures had increased to 94 and 40 per cent respectively. Elsewhere, the ratio appears to have been less favourable: in France on the eve of the Revolution, for example, about 65 per cent of men but only 35 per cent of women could sign their names. Moreover, where schools for girls existed, there was a growing tendency to concentrate on practical subjects such as sewing and knitting to equip them for their domestic role. In an essay addressed to the two English universities, published in 1655, Margaret Cavendish, Duchess of Newcastle, implored her male superiors not to scorn women's intellectual endeavours, lest 'we should grow irrational as idiots, by the dejectednesse of our spirits'. It was that fatal lack of self-esteem which makes us quit all industry towards profitable knowledge being employed only in looe [*sic*], and pettie imployments, which takes away not onely our abilities towards arts, but higher capacities in speculations, so as women are become like worms, that only live in the dull world of ignorance, winding ourselves sometimes out by the help of some refreshing rain of good education, which seldom is given us, for we are kept like birds in our houses.

As we shall see in a later chapter, for women the intellectual changes of the eighteenth century were double-edged. On the one hand, the development of the salons offered the opportunity for a few favoured individuals to gain real influence and the emergence of the novel gave them a genre ideally suited to the depiction of their world, but the attitude of the Enlightenment proved to be much more equivocal than might have been expected. A better understanding of the physical world and its laws did not necessarily encourage an egalitarian view of the human beings who inhabited it. By the late eighteenth century, women might no longer be burnt as witches, but they continued to be patronized as weaklings. As Merry Wiesner has pointed out, not only did the 'scientific revolution' fail to destroy the traditional belief in the inferiority of women, but by its privileging of such 'masculine' characteristics as reason, order, control and mechanical processes, it may have anchored that supposed inferiority even more firmly in European culture. Nor did the development of new ideas of 'politeness' by progressive intellectuals such as the third Earl of Shaftesbury or David Hume (both of them bachelors) point towards equality. Apologists for the superiority of modern commercial urban society and its civilized discourse might well call for women to be treated with greater courtesy and generosity, but also assumed continuing deference to the dominant males. It was against this kind of patronizing kindness that Mary Wollstonecraft erupted with such eloquence in her *Vindication of the Rights of Woman* of 1792.

The great majority of European women could not have cared less that David Hume or Montesquieu thought they were naturally inferior, for they were the illiterate daughters of illiterate peasants. For them, the absolute priority was scraping together enough money to attract a husband. By the time they were in their early teens, or even earlier, they had left the family unit to seek employment. The main source was domestic service. In France north of the Loire, country girls in service accounted for 13 per cent of the urban population. For every family that came up just a little way in the world, the first luxury was a servant. An exercise of the imagination is required to appreciate the sheer drudgery involved in everyday life before the introduction of public utilities and the harnessing of electricity: fetching water, which in towns often involved long queues; purchasing supplies from the market on a daily basis; clearing and relaying fires and stoves; 'slopping out' chamber-pots; washing, mangling and ironing clothes; taking up and beating carpets; and so on and so forth in an endless round of back-breaking toil. If all went well, then after ten years or so of labour, enough money might have been hoarded to allow a return to the village and marriage. But woe betide the servant who was unwise enough to get pregnant or unlucky enough to fall ill. The division between mere poverty and outright destitution was as thin as it was crucial.

An alternative to domestic service was increasingly found in the rural manufacturing industries that expanded so rapidly in many countries in the course of the eighteenth century, and will be discussed further in the following chapter. To avoid the restrictive practices of the urban guilds, entrepreneurs turned increasingly to 'putting out' the unskilled processes of textile manufacturing – especially spinning – to the homes of the rural population. In some cases, they were all combined in a single building or 'manufactory'. As industrialization developed, so did the large urban manufactures attract ever larger numbers of women from the country-side: silk in Lyon, Nîmes and Tours and across northern Italy, lace in France and the Low Countries, woollens and cottons in the north of England. Spinning was an activity redolent with associations for women at the bottom of the heap: in Amsterdam women arrested for soliciting were sent to the spinning-house (*Spinnhuis*) for corrective labour; in Lyon women thrown out of work by one of the periodic recessions in the silk industry prostituted themselves from the brick kilns where they gathered to keep warm. Everywhere prostitution provided a last resort when destitution threatened. Although the figures must be very approximate, it has been estimated that there were 10,000 prostitutes in mid-eighteenth-century London and double that number in Paris, where one woman in thirteen looked to selling her body for at least part of her income. Needless to say, there was a steep hierarchy, from the courtesan who married a royal duke at the top, down through the brothels of various standards to the street-walker operating in the open air at the bottom. It was one of the last-named that James Boswell met in May

1763: 'At the bottom of the Haymarket I picked up a strong, jolly young damsel, and taking her under the arm I conducted her to Westminster Bridge, and then in armour complete did I engage her upon this noble edifice. The whim of doing it there with the Thames rolling below us amused me very much.'

The opportunities for employment in textile manufacturing also brought unmarried women to the towns, as the term 'spinster' indicates. There were not very many of those in eastern Europe, where the age of marriage was low, but in the north-west somewhere between 10 and 15 per cent never married, indeed in some places as many as a quarter remained spinsters. Significantly, it was in the most urban societies that the unmarried rate was highest, for in the countryside every peasant needed a wife to keep the household going. It was with the authority gained from his rides around rural England that William Cobbett observed that 'a bare glance at the thing shows that a farmer above all men living cannot never carry on his affairs without a wife'. She was needed to look after the livestock, to grow vegetables, to take farm produce to market, to manage the dairy, to organize the pickling and preserving of food to get the family through the winter, and so on. Especially in the poorer regions where the men had to migrate for much of the year to seek work as labourers, she would also have to work in the fields. It was this apparent absence of the men which misled Arthur Young into thinking that they stayed at home with their feet up while their wives toiled.

This mutual dependence did not change during this period, but neither did women's dependent status. However, it has been argued, imaginatively, especially by the American scholar Thomas Laqueur, that there was a radical shift in the way in which women's bodies were viewed. Since the second century AD and the time of Galen, it had been a biological axiom that men and women shared the same sexual organs, the difference being that women's were to be found inside the body. So the vagina is an inverted penis, the labia is the foreskin, the uterus the scrotum and the ovaries the testicles. As a result of improved dissection and observation, it came to be realized that in reality men and women were so different as to constitute two quite separate sexes, leading Laqueur to make the lapidary observation that 'sometime in the eighteenth century sex as we know it was invented'. This most emphatically did not mean that the equality of women was invented at the same time. On the contrary, natural science could now be enlisted as a more authoritative support for old prejudice. For the overwhelming majority of Europeans, of course, it was the Bible which provided the most compelling justification for discrimination. From the rich store to be found in that misogynistic compendium, the following statement by St Paul in his Epistle to the Ephesians is the most unequivocal: 'Therefore as the church is subject unto Christ, so let the wives be to their own husbands in every thing' (5:24).

One thing that did change was the common attitude to female sexual desire. In the past it had been supposed that women were more enthusiastic about sex, as evinced by their ability to experience multiple orgasms. The most popular sexual primer of the late seventeenth century – Nicolas de Venette's *Conjugal Love, or The Pleasures of the Marriage Bed Considered in Several Lectures on Human Generation*, first published in French in 1686 and translated into several other languages – stated firmly: '[women] are much more amorous than men, and, as sparrows do not live long, because they are too hot, and too susceptible of love; so women last less time, because they have a devouring heat that consumes them by degrees'. Although Venette's ingenious mixture of (mis)information and titillation went on being published throughout the eighteenth century, the stereotype gradually came to be reversed. Respectable women were now seen as being passive if not passionless, naturally chaste and virtuous. It was the opposite sex that was portrayed as the lusty sexual predator. If male promiscuity was not excused, it was certainly accepted as the natural order of things, as rueful but not really disapproving adages such as 'boys will be boys' gained currency.

Although there were plenty of lusty women in the eighteenth century, most of them were to be found within the covers of pornographic novels. If prostitution is the oldest profession, pornography must be one of the oldest literary genres, narrowly beaten for first place by religion. However, from the late seventeenth century there was a significant spurt in production, encouraged by the expansion of the public sphere and the allied development of the novel, to be discussed in a later chapter. The appearance in Paris in the 1650s of what were to become two classics – *L'École des filles ou la philosophie des dames* and *L'Académie des dames* – signalled a geographical shift in the leadership of the pornographic books industry from Italy to France, which has lasted to this very day. Copies were soon spreading across Europe, speeded by a demand that was as insatiable as the activity they recounted. On 9 February 1668 Samuel Pepys recorded in his diary: 'Away to the Strand, to my bookseller's and bought that idle, roguish book *L'escholle des Filles* [*sic*]; which I have bought in plain binding (avoiding the buying of it better bound) because I resolve, as soon as I have read it, to burn it, that it may not stand in the list of books, not among them, to disgrace them if it should be found.' Translations followed almost at once. *Vénus dans le cloître ou la Religieuse en chemise* of 1683, for example, could be bought in an English-language edition the same year. For reasons that cannot be explained adequately, there were periodic surges in the publication of pornographic books. The 1740s were vintage years, witnessing the appearance of (among others) the anonymous *Histoire de Dom Bougre, portier des Chartreux* (1741), Diderot's *Les Bijoux indiscrets* (1748), the marquis d'Argens' *Thérèse philosophe* (1748) and John Cleland's *Fanny Hill* (1748–9). In all but the cheapest editions, they benefited from appropriate illustrations. The century achieved a climax with what proved to be the *ne plus ultra* of pornography in the shape of the marquis de Sade's various publications: *Justine* (1791), *Philosophy in the Boudoir* (1795) and *Juliette* (1798). His most aptly titled book – *The 120 Days of Sodom* – was written in 1785 but not published until 1904.

Wherever produced, virtually all the pornography of the seventeenth and eighteenth centuries was written by men for the delectation of men. Women are usually depicted either as jolly, lascivious creatures who thoroughly enjoy male attentions (Moll Flanders, Fanny Hill, Thérèse, Juliette) or as virginal ingénues who prove to be shy but eager when the male seducer hoves into view. In French novels in particular, they are most likely to be initiated by priests or monks. In *Thérèse philosophe*, one of the most successful pornographic works of the entire century and praised by de Sade as 'the only one that has shown the goal, without however quite attaining it', the eponymous heroine secretly watches her friend Eradice conducting her spiritual exercises with a Franciscan friar. These involve first meditation, then the birching of Eradice's bare buttocks and, finally, penetration from behind by what Father Dirrag tells his unsuspecting victim is 'a remnant of St Francis' cord' which he happens to have in his possession. Thérèse recorded the climax of their devotions as follows:

'Is your mind at ease, my little saint?' he asked, as a sort of sigh escaped him. 'As for me, I see the heavens opening, and sufficient grace is carrying me aloft, I . . .'

'Oh, Father!' cried Eradice. 'Such pleasure is penetrating me! Oh, yes, I'm feeling celestial happiness. I sense that my mind is completely detached from matter. Further, Father, further! Root out all that is impure in me. I see . . . the . . . angels. Push forward . . . push now . . . Ah! . . . Ah! . . . Good . . . St Francis! Don't abandon me! I feel the cord . . . the cord . . . the cord . . . I give up . . . I'm dying!'

In other words, no matter how pious a woman might be, the appeal of the male member was irresistible, especially when it was thought to be a sacred relic. Another indication of the male provenance of pornography was the popularity of scenes depicting sexual activity between two women. In the anti-clerical world of French erotic fiction, this almost invariably took place in a convent, Diderot's *La Religieuse* being a fine example of what amounted to a sub-genre.

For male homosexuals, homosexual sub-cultures developed from the late seventeenth century in the major cities of Europe, and probably in the smaller ones too. In London the example was set at court, where a group formed in the 1690s around the Duke of Shrewsbury, the Earl of Portland and – so it was widely but falsely believed – King William III himself and his page Arnold van Keppel (created Earl of Albermarle in 1697). Out on the streets, gay clubs, pubs and open-air cruising grounds proliferated. By 1709 they were sufficiently numerous to catch the eye of the raffish journalist Ned Ward, who in his account of the clubs of London and Westminster reported:

There are a particular Gang of *sodomitical* Wretches in this Town, who call themselves the *Mollies*, and are so far degenerated from all masculine Deportment, or manly Exercises, that they rather fancy themselves Women, imitating all the little Vanities that Custom has reconcil'd to the female Sex, affecting the speak, walk, tattle, courtesy, cry, scold and to mimick all manner of Effeminacy, that ever has fallen within their several Observations; not omitting the indecencies of lewd Women, that they may tempt one another, by such immodest Freedoms, to commit those odious Bestialities, that ought for ever to be without a Name.

In Paris in 1725 the police compiled a '*Grand Mémoire*' containing 113 names of notorious *infâmes*, including the duc de Lorges and the servants who pimped for him, several other servants, the abbé Couatte, the marquis de Villars (son of the maréchal), the duc de Villars-Brancas, the marquis d'Entragues and the duc d'Humières, together with the names of their lovers and the nicknames they gave each other. Maurice Lever, who worked through all the police records, found that all classes were represented, although the world of opera, the theatre and the arts in general were surprisingly under-represented. As he concludes, this was a separate world, a closed society with its own rules, slang, codes, gestures and rivalries. The favoured cruising grounds were particular parts of the Tuileries and Luxembourg gardens, together with nearby inns where private rooms could be hired if inclement weather discouraged alfresco activity. In the Dutch Republic, which gave the world the verb 'to cruise' (from *kruisen*), there appears to have been an embarrassment of riches when it came to places of assignation: public toilets, the Amsterdam town hall, a wooded area near The Hague, numerous pubs such as The Little Dolphin at The Hague or The Serpent at Amsterdam, innumerable parks and churches, the tower of the cathedral at The Hague, and even the very grounds of the building in which the Court of Holland held its sessions.

Woe betide the sodomites (the term favoured by most contemporaries) should they find themselves inside the courthouse, for they were persecuted more vigorously and brutally in the Dutch Republic than anywhere else in Europe. Prosecutions went from being virtually non-existent before 1676 to occurring sporadically, before a veritable craze erupted in 1731 following 'the most extraordinary and accidental discovery of a tangle of ungodliness', possibly motivated by the search for scapegoats in the aftermath of devastating floods. Convinced that there was a nationwide sodomitical network, the Court of Holland determined 'to exterminate this vice to the bottom' (*sic*). In just two years, seventy-five men were put to death and hundreds more escaped garrotting only by fleeing. The most shocking episode occurred near Groning where a local squire, Rudolph de Mepsche, had more than thirty peasants, men and boys, arrested on charges of sodomy. Twenty-two of them were executed. There were further outbreaks of persecution in 1764, 1776, 1797 and almost every year in Amsterdam between 1791 and 1810. Between 1730 and 1811, when the introduction of the Napoleonic Code decriminalized same-sex activity, around 200 men were executed and about as many were condemned to long terms of solitary confinement.

In France executions were relatively few and far between, but they were spectacular enough to catch the public attention. In November 1661, Jacques Chausson, aged forty-three, a former customs official but now unemployed, and his former colleague Jacques Paulmier, alias Fabri, aged thirty-six, were burnt alive at the stake (i.e. without first being strangled) on the Place de Grève in Paris for a homosexual assault on seventeen-year-old Octave des Valons. During the interrogation, they revealed under threat of torture that they had been soliciting young males on behalf of the marquis du Bellay and the baron de Bellefore. The police did not follow up these allegations, but after the execution a song called 'The Complaint of Chausson and Fabri' could be heard on the streets of Paris:

> If we burnt everyone
> Who did what they did,
> Then, alas, in a very short time
> Several nobles of France
> And important prelates
> Would meet their maker.

In 1725 the Paris police chief, Lenoir, estimated that there were 20,000 *infâmes* in the capital. A generation later it was claimed that the police register had inflated to twice that size, and the *Gazette cuirassé* added for good measure that if the names of all those actively engaged in homosexual activity were published, then twice as many volumes as the *Encyclopédie* would be required – and that ran to twenty-eight volumes in the folio edition. Yet of the seven men executed in Paris for the crime of sodomy in the eighteenth century, five had also been convicted of theft and murder, and another was burnt only in effigy. When Jean Diot and Bruno Lenoir were burnt in the Place de Grève in 1750 after having been caught having sex in the middle of the rue Montorgueil (they were drunk), general surprise was expressed at the severity of the sentence. The lawyer Edmond Barbier confided to his diary the opinion that it was designed to serve as a deterrent against a vice which recently had been spreading very rapidly. Yet, if the full rigour of the law was imposed only rarely, homosexuals were subjected to sustained harassment, for the cruising grounds teemed with agents provocateurs seeking to entrap the unwary into making a proposition. In 1749 alone they arrested 234, most of whom ended up serving short but very unpleasant and humiliating terms in jail, not to mention the subsequent social ostracism.

The same sort of fate befell English sodomites unlucky enough to get caught. That danger became much greater from the 1690s when a number of 'reformation societies' were formed to improve public morals. Their first victim was the adventurous Captain Edward Rigby, who was entrapped by nineteen-year-old William Minton, put up to it by Thomas Bray of the Society for the Reformation of Manners. When Rigby made homosexual advances in a private room in the George Tavern in Pall Mall, Minton shouted 'Westminster!', the signal for the entry of a clerk of the court, a constable and two assistants waiting next door. Rigby's sentence was typical – three sessions of two hours each in the pillory, a fine of £1,000 and a year in prison. His subsequent career was the stuff of a picaresque novel. After fleeing to France, converting to Catholicism and becoming a naval officer, he was taken prisoner at sea by the British in 1711 and taken to Port Mahon on Minorca. Escaping from captivity there, he managed to get back to France by stowing away on a Genoese ship.

According to the London newspaper *The Flying Post*, Captain Rigby 'appeared very gay' when he stood in the pillory in Pall Mall on 20 December 1698. If so, he must have been a very tough nut, for it was a truly terrible ordeal. On 27 September 1810 six men were pilloried in the Haymarket after being convicted for sodomy following a raid on a male brothel at the White Swan public house in Vere Street. The route from the Old Bailey to the Haymarket was lined by an enormous crowd many thousands strong, all determined to express their indignation with word and missile: 'it is impossible for language to convey an adequate idea of the universal expressions of execration, which accompanied these monsters on their journey', as one newspaper account put it. So the occupants of the open-topped cart were encrusted with filth by the time they reached the actual pillory, where 'upwards of fifty women were permitted to stand in the ring [in front of the pillory], who assailed them incessantly with mud, dead cats, rotten eggs, potatoes, and buckets filled with blood, offal, and dung, which were brought by a number of butchers' men from St James's Market'. At least they survived. Two other members of the White Swan group were hanged in public the following year, watched by a large crowd including the Duke of Cumberland (son of George III and later King of Hanover), and the earls of Sefton and Yarmouth, all of whom were rumoured to have been clients of the men executed.

Given the numbers involved, executions were very rare and prosecutions of any kind relatively rare. A homosexual seeking public gratification in London could probably escape detection, especially if he were careful, lucky and upper class. A German visitor, Johannes Wilhelm von Archenholz, wrote in 1789: 'it is very uncommon to see a person convicted, and punished for this crime; not on account of the paucity of the numbers charged with perpetrating it, but because they never yield to such a brutal appetite but with the utmost precaution'. Between 1730 and 1830 only seventy cases of sodomy were tried at the Old Bailey. A more common hazard was the male prostitute seeking to improve his earnings by blackmail – Charles Vaughan, also known as 'Fat Phyllis', for example, who went to masquerades and the theatre dressed as a woman. In 1790 he made the mistake of trying to extort money from the Reverend Mr Cuff, who promptly took him to the magistrates.

Perhaps not surprisingly, whenever there was a panic over the alleged prevalence of homosexuality, the blame was assigned to foreigners. This was a national prejudice of long standing: when Parliament petitioned Edward III in the mid-fourteenth century to banish foreign artisans and merchants, one of the accusations levelled at their target was their introduction of 'the too horrible vice that is not to be named'. Attached to Captain Edward Rigby's pillory in 1698 was a ballad entitled 'The Women's Complaint to Venus':

> How happy were good English Faces
> Till Mounsieur [sic] from France
> Taught Pego a Dance
> To the tune of old Sodom's Embraces
> But now we are quite out of Fashion:
> Poor Whores may be Nuns
> Since Men turn their Guns
> And vent on each other their passion.

In the Dutch Republic it was asserted that sodomy had been completely unknown until introduced by the Spanish and French envoys attending the negotiations that led to the Peace of Utrecht in 1713. Henceforth it was known as the 'Catholic vice', part of the great conspiracy by the Antichrist whose headquarters at Rome was also 'catamitorum mater'.

The knowledge that has survived of homosexuality has come down to us mainly through trial records, police reports and satirical pamphlets, so it necessarily appears much more unusual and aberrant than it really was. That was particularly the case of same-sex relations between women, of which only the tiniest tip of the iceberg protrudes above the documentary surface. As we have noted already, the pornography written by men for men liked to pretend that lesbianism was rife in convents, and perhaps it was. Only the occasional flash of evidence from the non-fictional world can be found, in the correspondence of the duchess of Orléans, for example, who in 1685 reported that at the convent school founded by Louis XIV's morganatic wife Madame de Maintenon at Saint Cyr,

some of the young ladies there had fallen in love with one another; they were caught committing all sorts of indecencies. Mme de Maintenon is supposed to have cried her eyes out. She had all the relics put on display to drive out the devils of lechery. Also, she sent for a priest to preach against lewdness, but he talked about such hideous things that none of the modest ladies could bear to listen; they all left the church, but the culprits were overcome by uncontrollable fits of the giggles.

As punishments go, having to listen to a sermon seems to err on the side of severity. More fortunate was Henriette de Castelnau, comtesse de Murat, a notoriously flagrant lesbian, who at about the same time was banished to a remote château under official surveillance. Elsewhere, it was very much a submerged vice, unmentioned and unmentionable, appearing only when the ladies in question decided to flaunt their relationship, as did the wonderfully flamboyant Eleanor Butler ('tall and masculine') and Sarah Ponsonby ('effeminate, fair and beautiful') in England in the 1780s. When an opinion was expressed, the language used was as extreme as that employed to denounce male homosexuality. In a treatise of 1700 Father Ludovicus (Luigi) Maria Sinistrari de Ameno argued that in cases of same-sex relations between women, an enlarged clitoris should be taken as presumption of guilt, and justify both torture and burning at the stake. That ultimate penalty appears to have been rare almost to the point of absence, although a German woman who had lived as a man was executed in Bavaria in 1721 for sodomy with her female lover, with whom she had celebrated a form of marriage.

MIGRATION

As we saw in Chapter 1, physical mobility in early modern Europe was not easy. It was some indication of the intensity of demographic pressure, therefore, that there was so much migration during the course of the period 1648–1815. Most of this was from west to east, from regions which were densely populated, and increasingly experiencing problems of overpopulation, to the thinly populated expanses of Prussia, Russia and what William McNeill called 'Europe's steppe frontier' of Danubian and Pontic (i.e. to the north and north-west of the Black Sea) Europe. Reviewing a range of statistical information, Denis Silagi concluded that the population of the Kingdom of Hungary, including Transylvania and Croatia-Slavonia, more than doubled between the late seventeenth and the late eighteenth centuries. That total conceals some more dramatic regional changes: for example, in the course of the eighteenth century, the county of Bács-Bodrog went from 31,000 to 227,000 and the Bánát from 45,000 to 774,000. Most of those increases were due to immigration, made possible by the epochal defeat of the Turks at Vienna in 1683 and their subsequent retreat into the Balkans. In 1690–91 perhaps as many as 100,000 Serbs moved north to what is today the Vojvodina in northern Serbia, the biggest single migration in Balkan history. More still came from the west, albeit more gradually. From Lorraine, the Palatinate, Hessen and Swabia came peasants seeking land and artisans seeking employment. They were both pushed and pulled. They were pushed by population pressure at home, especially in regions of non-partible inheritance. They were pulled by offers of free or cheap land from landlords eager to populate their vacant estates.

The Habsburg authorities also played an important part in this great resettlement project. To protect their newly won territory, they established a paramilitary zone running right along the frontier of southern Hungary. There they established Croatian, Serbian and Romanian soldier-settlers, organized them into regiments and granted them personal freedom and free land in return for service against the Turks. In the eighteenth century, both Maria Theresa and Joseph II organized recruiting campaigns in the western regions of the Holy Roman Empire. An eyewitness in the Palatinate in 1782 recorded:

There was no town, village or hamlet where printed manifestos were not circulating from hand to hand. The Emperor Joseph's bounty was so highly esteemed that it seemed that the whole region wanted to emigrate. So many family-groups, including those that were well-off, set out on the emigration trail that the roads were crowded and gave the impression that everyone wanted to leave.

From agencies established at Kaiserslautern, Zweibrücken and Worms, Austrian recruiters toured the region advertising the patents of 1781 which promised new settlers in Galicia, recently added to the Monarchy by the partition of Poland, exemption from forced labour dues, forty free yokes of land, freedom of worship for Protestants, exemption from military service for ten years and ample subsidy to cover the costs of the journey. Dangerous and difficult was the journey across Europe and many were those who returned poorer and wiser, but enough stayed to alter permanently the population and ethnic composition of many parts of central-eastern Europe. More intrepid still were the 27,000-odd Germans who responded to similar inducements offered by Catherine the Great of Russia to settle around the Volga. By 1914, they had multiplied to number around 600,000.

Anything the Austrians could do, the Prussians could do better. On 18 October 1685 Louis XIV signed the Edict of Fontainebleau, revoking the Edict of Nantes of 1598 and with it the limited degree of toleration accorded to French Protestants in certain places. This act of Catholic triumphalism led to the emigration of about 250,000 Huguenots. Most went to the two great 'arks of the refugees' – the Dutch Republic and England – but a significant number went east. Just eleven days after Louis XIV's revocation, the Elector Frederick William of Brandenburg issued the Edict of Potsdam inviting the Huguenots to settle in his territories and offering all sorts of material rewards if they did. Around 14,000 responded, a figure which should be multiplied many times if the quality of the contribution to their backward and depopulated new home is to be assessed correctly. There was a further surge of Huguenot immigration in 1689 when Louis XIV's armies devastated the Palatinate and sent the refugees who had taken shelter there fleeing further eastwards. As a disproportionate number of those who took the decision to flee France were young, they enjoyed a correspondingly high birth rate when they reached their destinations. By 1720 every fifth inhabitant of Berlin was a Huguenot or of Huguenot origin.

So common did policies to promote immigration become that a new word was coined to describe the phenomenon: *Peuplierungspolitik*. It became a permanent feature of Brandenburg-Prussia. In 1732 King Frederick William I self-consciously imitated the example of his grandfather when he welcomed to his territories the 20,000-odd Protestants expelled from Salzburg by the Archbishop. He was particularly anxious to repopulate East Prussia, where plague had killed around a third of the population between 1709 and 1710. Frederick William may have been one of the more brutal sovereigns of his – or any – age, but he knew instinctively how to make a gesture. As the first contingent of Salzburgers neared Berlin, he led his court out to meet them, singing hymns and kneeling with them to give thanks to the Almighty for this latest act of Divine Mercy. This proved to be a great public relations coup, advertised to the rest of Europe in word and image and establishing Prussia as the third great 'ark of the refugees'. It was now said that while France was the refuge of kings (James II of England, Stanislas Leszczyński of Poland), Prussia was the refuge of oppressed peoples.

As in so many other respects, there was a strong line of continuity with the reign of his son. In the course of Frederick the Great's long reign from 1740 to 1786, around 280,000–300,000 immigrants entered Prussia, attracted by free land, livestock, equipment and seed, personal freedom, religious toleration and initial exemption from conscription, taxation and labour dues. According to Günther Franz's suspiciously precise figures, they brought with them 6,392 horses, 7,875 cattle, 20,548 sheep and 3,227 pigs and 2,000,000 *talers* in cash. Most were settled on land reclaimed by drainage projects around the Oder, Netze and Warthe rivers, but about a quarter were craftsmen of various kinds and settled in the towns. Well might Frederick claim that he had 'won a province in peacetime'. It was an achievement with important implications. As Christof Dipper has pointed out, as demographic regeneration from a country's own resources was such a long and uncertain process, the states which did best were those able to attract immigrants.

Causes célèbres such as the expulsion of the Huguenots or the Salzburgers were few. Most migrants were pulled by the prospect of material gain rather than pushed by persecution. And most of them moved inside the territorial boundaries of a state. Harold Temperley observed that the Habsburg Monarchy was not so much a single country as a whole continent, a description which could be applied with even greater validity to the Russian Empire. Not surprisingly, it was in these great multinational conglomerates of the east that the highest figures were recorded. Between the first Russian census of 1719 and the third of 1762–3, the population of European Russia increased by 33.8 per cent, but the population of the Siberian provinces by almost exactly twice that rate. The highest figure of all, of course, was scored by the brand-new capital St Petersburg, which went from swamp to metropolis in just two generations. By 1750 its population had reached 75,000 and was still growing fast. There was also a good deal of seasonal migration in Russia. One traveller estimated that in spring the population of Moscow fell by 50,000 as the nobles and their households returned to their estates. Later in the century, especially following the victories of the war of 1768–74, there was a demographic surge southwards to the rich and empty lands secured by the Treaty of Kutchuk-Kainardji. They were particularly attractive to runaway serfs.

Further west, the distances traversed were less impressive but the total numbers were far greater. In northern, western and most of central Europe, there was no serfdom to keep the rural population tied to the lord's estate. In the British Isles, the great magnet was London, the great demographic success story of the western world in the eighteenth century, increasing from c.200,000 in 1600 to c.400,000 in 1700 to 600,000 in 1720 to almost a million by the end of the century. This rate of growth could only be attained by massive migration of around 7,500 per annum in the early eighteenth century, for the imbalance between births and deaths made the capital a 'demographic black hole' (Julian Hoppit). London was a special city for many reasons: unfortified, never captured by a foreign enemy, built by private not public wealth, un-planned, little influenced by court or Church, largely self-governing and, in the words of Sir John Summerson, 'the least authoritarian city in Europe'. Its importance in British life – political, social, economic and cultural – was unmatched by any other country's capital city. The pro-portion of the population of France living in Paris remained steady at around 2.5 per cent, but London's share of England's inhabitants was already 5 per cent in 1600, 7 per cent in 1650 and had grown to 11 per cent a century later. Moreover, ease of communication and a plethora of employment opportunities meant that an even greater proportion spent long or short sojourns there. Tony Wrigley has estimated that one in six of the adult population of England had some experience of London at some stage during their lives. Londoners were well aware of their special status. Typical was Edward Chamberlayne's boast in 1687 that London was 'the largest and the most populous, the fairest and most opulent city at this day in all Europe, perhaps in the whole world, surpassing even Paris and Rome put together'.

In France, as befitted its greater size and more complex geography, there was a wider variation of migration patterns. Broadly speaking, they divided into three kinds: seasonal, involving an absence of several months each year; temporary, involving an absence of some years but ending with a return to the home-base; and permanent. Regionally, there was a marked difference between the relative stability of the north-west and the greater mobility of the centre and south. It was the poorly resourced mountainous regions such as the Massif Central, Alps and Pyrenees that were obliged to send their surplus population down into the cities and plains in search of supplementary income. The seasonal migrant was usually male, young, a family-man, a country-dweller, the owner or tenant of a small plot, unskilled or at best semi-skilled, and poor. The work he sought was most often in agriculture, especially bringing in the harvest, fruit-picking or wood-cutting, although he was often to be found in the building trades. He was both common and ubiquitous. In 1810 it was estimated that there were around 200,000 seasonal migrants moving around France, with another 800,000 people dependent on them for their livelihood.

What this makeshift economy could mean for the wretched inhabitants of villages with insufficient resources was explained by Olwen Hufton in her study of the poor of eighteenth-century France. She reconstructed the annual struggle for survival undertaken by the villagers of Saint-Jean-d'Ollières in the Puy-de-Dôme. Every October, 200 adult males left the village to cut wood. After returning the following summer to work briefly on their own land, they left again to work on the olive harvest in Provence. Meanwhile, another group of the same size, but accompanied by 100 children, had left in November to seek work in Berry, combing hemp. If they failed, they travelled on to Paris to find work where they could or to beg. In any event, shortage of food at home meant that they could not return until the following Easter. After work in the fields, they then set off for Provence to gather mulberry leaves for silkworms, a task which kept them busy until the autumn, when the cycle began again. Three hundred children from the village were also on the road for much of the year, working as chimney sweeps, as were an unspecified number of adults, eking out a living as pedlars and/or beggars. Even the aged were expected to do their bit, sowing the seeds in the field before tottering off to the towns to beg. The only members of the community to spend prolonged periods at home were small children and their mothers.

Tramping the roads of France in search of work must have been as depressing as it was demanding. How much more so was a final form of migration – to the world outside Europe. A long, arduous sea journey took the intrepid emigrant to an uncertain future in a distant land about which very little could be known. Yet large numbers crossed the Atlantic during this period. Between 1630 and 1700 about 378,000 inhabitants of the British Isles went to North America. The pace slackened during the more stable and prosperous century that followed, but, even so, another quarter of a million had left by 1800. It is believed that 40,000 Highlanders emigrated following the failure of the Jacobite rebellion of 1745. They were joined by a large number of Germans, variously esti-mated at somewhere between 100,000 and 200,000. By 1800 it appears that a third of Pennsylvania's population was German by origin. There were repeated waves of emigration from the Iberian peninsula to southern and central America, although the figures are very approxi-mate. The great Prussian scientist and traveller Alexander von Humboldt estimated in 1800 that Spanish America contained a total population of 16,900,000, of whom 3,200,000 were whites but only 150,000 were *peninsulares*, i.e. first generation Spaniards. In fact, according to John Lynch, the real figure was much lower, somewhere between 30,000 and 40,000. Even in Mexico, to which there had been the greatest emi-gration, there were only about 14,000 *peninsulares* in a total population of 6,000,000, of whom 1,000,000 were white. Around a quarter of a million Dutch also emigrated in the course of the seventeenth and eighteenth centuries, mainly to south-east Asia.

Only the French seem to have been reluctant to leave Europe. They had established a footing in North America as early as 1535, but a hundred years later there were only sixty-five French inhabitants of Quebec and one hundred more elsewhere in Canada. Under the energetic direction of Colbert, the pace picked up during the middle decades of the century, with the result that there were 12,000 permanent settlers in North America by the 1680s. Yet the total number of emigrants for the period 1600–1730 amounted to just 27,000. Additional population pressure from the third quarter of the eighteenth century might have led to a rapid increase, but in 1759 the French were defeated at Quebec by General Wolfe and lost Canada to the British. It was a defeat which ensured that English, not French, would become the world language and may also have helped to destabilize politics inside France. The typical emigrant was young, male and, by definition, alienated from conditions in the old country. For example, on 12 May 1785, John Dunlap, who had been responsible for the printing of the Declaration of Independence, wrote to his brother-in-law in Strabane, Co. Tyrone, extolling the advantages of the New World: 'People with a family advanced in life find great difficulties in emigration, but the young men of Ireland who wish to be free and happy should leave it and come here as quick as possible. There is no place in the world where a man meets so rich a reward for good conduct and industry as in America.' So it might be speculated that the British exported their dissidents and so suffered their revolution three thousand miles away from home in the shape of the American War of Independence. The Spanish did the same in the shape of the liberation movements in Latin America in the 1820s. But the French Revolution was a revolution in France.

3

Trade and Manufacturing

TRADE

When Joseph Palmer visited Bordeaux in 1775, he was deeply impressed, recording that it

yields to very few cities in point of beauty; for it appears to have all that opulence which an extensive commerce can confer. It is finely situated on the banks of the *Garonne* ... The quay which is extended on a straight line, for more than two miles, with a range of regular buildings, cannot fail of striking the eye with admiration; which is encreased by the noble appearance of an immense rapid river, and the multitude of ships and vessels which trade here.

Twelve years later the peripatetic agronomist Arthur Young confirmed this favourable verdict. In view of his notorious propensity for making unflattering comparisons between conditions at home in England and what he found in France, his impressions are particularly authoritative: 'Much as I had heard and read of the commerce, wealth and magnificence of this city, they greatly surpassed my expectations. Paris did not answer at all, for it is not to be compared to London; but we must not name Liverpool in competition with Bordeaux.' As he was ferried across the river, he added, 'The view of the Garonne is very fine, appearing to the eye twice as broad as the Thames at London, and the number of large ships lying in it, makes it, I suppose, the *richest* water-view that France has to boast.'

Visual evidence of the accuracy of this description can be found by any present-day visitor, for the city's architecture demonstrates that the eighteenth century was its heyday. For all its splendour, the Place Royale is not the most characteristic site, for it was replicated in other French cities. The same could be said for the new archiepiscopal palace facing the cathedral. It is the great opera-house – the Grand Théâtre – designed by Victor Louis and built between 1772 and 1780 which best exemplifies the Bordeaux boom. What makes it special is not its size, for although it is very large, it is not as big as, say, San Carlo in Naples or La Scala in Milan. Nor is it the fact that it was a free-standing building, for Frederick the Great's opera-house on Unter den Linden in Berlin had anticipated this feature by more than a generation. The Bordeaux opera-house is different because in effect it is three buildings, incorporating not just a theatre but also a concert-hall and a staircase. To identify the staircase as a space of equal importance is less perverse than might appear, for the foyer and staircase were as large as the auditorium. It was there to allow members of Bordeaux high society the opportunity to parade before each other in all their finery – to see and be seen. As Victor Louis grasped, in an opera-house the audience is as important a performer as the singers on stage. In an opera-house built for a king, it is the royal box that is the chief architectural feature, but in a public opera-house built for a great commercial city such as Bordeaux, it is the foyer, staircase and other public rooms. Arthur Young certainly grasped the close connection between commerce and culture in the city:

The theatre, built about ten or twelve years ago, is by far the most magnificent in France. I have seen nothing that approaches it . . . The establishment of actors, actresses, singers, dancers, orchestra, etc. speaks the wealth and luxury of the place. I have been assured that from thirty to fifty *louis* a night have been paid to a favourite actress from Paris . . . Pieces are performed every night, Sundays not excepted, as everywhere in France. The mode of living that takes place here among merchants is highly luxurious. Their houses and establishments are on expensive scales. Great entertainments, and many served on [silver] plate. High play [gambling] is a much worse thing; and the scandalous chronicle speaks of merchants keeping the dancing and singing girls of the theatre at salaries which ought to import no good to their credit.

This conspicuous display derived from commerce. Between 1717 and 1789 Bordeaux's trade increased on average by 4 per cent per annum, multiplying almost twenty times in value, from 13,000,000 *livres* to almost 250,000,000 *livres*; its share of French commerce increased from 11 to 25 per cent and its population doubled from 55,000 to 110,000. Although some of this prosperity derived from increased wine sales to the rest of Europe, the lion's share came from the West Indian colonies

– Guadeloupe, Martinique and, above all, Saint Domingue, the greatest sugar-producing region in the world. The sugar production of the last-named increased from 7,000 tons in 1714 to 80,000 tons in 1789. Moreover, it was not just the merchant-princes who grew rich on the proceeds, for Bordeaux's whole economy was moulded by its leading sector. For example, 700–800 men were employed in the shipyards, 300–400 in the ropeworks, 300 in the sugar refineries, and so on.

As we shall see, the whole European economy expanded during the eighteenth century, but it was international trade that provided the most dramatic success story. The original impetus probably came from outside Europe. In the last quarter of the seventeenth century, there was a marked upturn in the Iberian Pacific, demonstrated by the customs receipts at Manila and Acapulco, which increased by 2,600 per cent in the fifty years before 1720. Simultaneously, a demographic surge in China created a corresponding demand which attracted growing numbers of British and Dutch merchants. The Chinese gold they brought back to Europe, together with the rapidly expanding output of Brazilian mines, helped to alleviate the chronic shortage of coin and, among other things, allowed the stablization of European currencies. With European colonial expansion on the move again after a century of stagnation, in North America, the Caribbean and the Far East, the scene was set for self-sustaining expansion. Between 1740 and 1780 the value of world trade increased by between a quarter and a third; indeed, in Alan Milward's words, 'the mid-eighteenth century was one of the most remarkable periods of trade expansion in modern history'. In France, the volume of foreign trade doubled between the 1710s and the late 1780s, but its value increased five times. French colonial trade increased in value by a staggering ten times during the same period.

The human cost of this great surge is revealed by more chilling statistics, for example that the number of slaves in the French West Indies increased during the course of the eighteenth century from $c.$40,000 to $c.$500,000 in 1789, with the price of each slave quadrupling during the same period, such was the demand for their labour. All the major maritime nations were involved in the trade. The Portuguese and the Dutch imported more than they needed for their own colonies, so sold on their surplus to the voracious Spanish and French producers. The British probably constituted the most dynamic national group; as Paul Langford has written, slavery was 'one of the central institutions of the

British Empire, one of the staple trades of Englishmen'. It was certainly the foundation for the prosperity of Liverpool, from which there were nearly 2,000 slave-trade departures between 1750 and 1780, compared with 869 from London and 624 from Bristol.

If the transatlantic trade provided the most startling statistics, the core of Europe's trade remained within Europe. As Jacob Price has observed, it is remarkable how durable was the traditional 'map of commerce', whose main artery ran from the Baltic via the Low Countries to the Bay of Biscay and the Iberian peninsula, with off-shoots to Norway, the British Isles and the Mediterranean. In the course of the sixteenth century, oceanic connections had been added to reach America and the Far East, but it was the Baltic–Cadiz route that remained the great employer of shipping. In 1660 it was dominated by the Dutch. Despite – or perhaps because of – the eighty-year struggle to break free from Spanish rule (only ending in 1648), the Dutch had put together a trading system of truly amazing size, complexity and prosperity. One simple statistic illustrates their predominance in European commerce: in 1670 their merchant marine totalled 568,000 tons, more than that of France, England, Scotland, the Holy Roman Empire, Spain and Portugal *combined*. The basis of Dutch trade was the huge surplus of grain, chiefly rye, produced by the Baltic countries, especially Poland-Lithuania. It was almost all shipped to the Dutch Republic, 80 per cent of it in Dutch ships. Around 40 per cent was then re-exported to feed the numerous parts of Europe, notably in the south, that were unable to feed their populations from their own resources. This plentiful supply of basic food allowed Dutch farmers to specialize, to concentrate on branches of agriculture best suited to their soil and climate, namely livestock, dairy products, vegetables, barley, hops, tobacco, hemp, flax, cole-seed (for lamp-oil) and various sources of dye (madder, weld and woad). Down their matchless waterways, these cash crops, and the articles manufactured from them, went to markets all over northern and western Europe. More important still, in terms of value, were the 'rich trades', the commodities such as spices, sugar, silk, dyestuffs, fruit, wine and silver that the Dutch gathered in southern Europe and took back to all points north. By the 1660s this branch of commerce was generating seven times as much profit as the bulk freightage from the Baltic. It also provided much of the raw materials that formed the basis of the Republic's flourishing manufacturing sector: fine cloth, silks, cottons, sugar-refining, tobacco-processing, leather-working, carpentry, tapestry-weaving, ceramics, copper-working and diamond-cutting.

Part of the explanation of Dutch superiority was technological. From their first introduction at the very end of the sixteenth century, the famous *fluyts* (known to the English as 'fluteships' or 'flyboats') provided a sharp competitive edge. Thanks to the adoption by the Amsterdam shipyards of standardized designs and labour-saving devices, the *fluyt* maximized carrying capacity and minimized cost. It has been estimated that an English ship of 250 tons cost 60 per cent more to construct than its Dutch rival. As a dedicated carrier of bulk freight with no pretensions to be a warship, the *fluyt* was also much cheaper to run, requiring far fewer sailors – as few as ten for the 200-ton version, as opposed to the thirty for an English ship of comparable tonnage. The result was that Dutch shippers were able to undercut their competitors from other nations by between a third and a half. With that kind of advantage, the Dutch achieved an extraordinary dominance of the carrying trade. By the second half of the seventeenth century, they so dominated the Baltic as to make it appear a colony. The Swedish port of Gothenburg, for example, was built by the Dutch, owned by the Dutch and run by the Dutch – Dutch was even its official language. The Bishop of Avranche wrote in 1694:

It may be said that the Dutch are in some respects masters of the commerce of the Swedish Kingdom since they are masters of the copper trade. The farmers of these mines, being always in need of money, and not finding any in Sweden, pledge this commodity to merchants of Amsterdam who advance them the necessary funds. It is the same with tar and pitch, certain merchants of Amsterdam having bought the greater part of these farms of the King, and made considerable advances besides, so that the result is that these commodities and most others are found as cheap in Amsterdam as in Sweden.

Danish sovereignty was also heavily compromised by coercion on the part of the Dutch to secure most-favoured status for their ships passing through the sound separating the North Sea from the Baltic.

A second major branch of Dutch commerce was supplied by fishing. Not for nothing was their herring industry known as 'the Great Fishery'. Each year, between late June and early December, a specialized fleet of *buizen* (known to the envious English as 'busses') followed the herring-shoals from the Shetlands to the Straits of Dover, catching colossal quantities as they went. The fish were salted, barrelled and sent back to the Maas ports for re-export, the Catholic parts of Europe proving particularly good customers. Out of season, the *buizen* went south to the Bay of Biscay or to Portugal to collect the huge amounts of high-quality salt needed in the curing process. In terms of total value, the Great Fishery vied with English cloth for the title of 'greatest single branch of European commerce'. Less important but also lucrative was the cod-fishing in the North Sea and the whaling in the Arctic. The latter reached its peak in the 1680s, when the Dutch were sending 240 ships a year, returning with up to 60,000 tons of blubber to be turned into lamp-oil and soap.

The Dutch also exploited the resources of the East. In the last year of the sixteenth century, a number of ships returned to Amsterdam from the Spice Islands laden with, among other good things, 600,000 pounds (270,000 kg) of pepper and 250,000 pounds (113,000 kg) of cloves. As this precious cargo yielded a profit of more than 100 per cent, there was a rush to follow. When, three years later, the various companies were amalgamated to form the Dutch East India Company, one of the greatest commercial undertakings in European history was underway. At its peak, in the late seventeenth century, it was the richest corporation in the world, owning 150 trading ships and 40 ships of war, and employing 20,000 sailors, 10,000 soldiers and nearly 50,000 civilians. Dutch pre-eminence in south-east Asia first had to be wrested from the Portuguese. Showing irresistible energy and aggression, they chased the incumbents from one spice island after another. By 1660 the Dutch were in possession of Cochin (on the west coast of India), Malacca (on the west coast of the Malayan peninsula), Indonesia (including Sumatra and Java), Borneo, the Celebes, the Moluccas, western New Guinea, Formosa and Ceylon. All that was left to Portugal in the Orient was Goa in southern India and Macao in China. Later attempts by the British to muscle in on the immensely lucrative spice trade were rebuffed with vigour, not to say brutality, notably at the infamous 'Amboina massacre' of 1623, dramatized by John Dryden fifty years later to drum up support for the Third Anglo-Dutch War.

The total population of the Dutch Republic was only about two million, yet Dutch merchants seemed to be everywhere in the world, leaving their calling cards in the form of place names – Cape Horn, Brooklyn, New Zealand, Van Diemen and Spitsbergen, for example.

From 1625 until 1667 New York was a Dutch colony called New Amsterdam. They established a permanent presence in South America, the Caribbean and South Africa, as well as in eastern waters. Commenting on the ubiquity of the Dutch fleet in 1667, Sir William Batten, Surveyor of the Royal Navy, exclaimed to Samuel Pepys: 'By God! I think the Devil shits Dutchmen!' His fellow countryman Charles Davenant added a little later: 'the trade of the Hollanders is so far extended that it may be said to have no other bounds than those which the Almighty set at the Creation'. Underpinning their global trading complex were the financial institutions of Amsterdam. Founded in 1609, its eponymous bank quickly eclipsed the traditional leaders, Venice and Genoa, as the centre of Europe's money market. It was soon joined by a Loan Bank. Together with the Stock Exchange, which moved to a palatial new building in 1609, the banks gave Dutch merchants a head-start in managing their business affairs. Nowhere else could credit be obtained so easily, quickly and cheaply. Nowhere else could goods be insured with such facility. Symbolic of the methodical approach adopted by the Amsterdam agents was their introduction of printed forms for the registration of insurance policies. So superior were the services they offered that during the Third Anglo-Dutch War of 1672–4, the British fleet was insured at Amsterdam. For all Europe's businessmen, a bill on Amsterdam was the accepted way of financing foreign trade. With this institutional infrastructure in place by the middle of the seventeenth century, the Dutch were in a position to establish quickly what Jonathan Israel has called 'world trade primacy' when peace returned in 1648.

Their primacy was to last a long time. In the middle of the next century, the Dutch still dominated the carrying trade: of 6,495 ships entering the Baltic in 1767, 2,273 (35 per cent) were Dutch. However, figures of this kind conceal a serious decline, both relative and absolute. Many of the Dutch ships now travelling to the Baltic were small vessels from Friesland and the Wadden Islands. The great bulk-carriers of Holland were much diminished. The bulk-carrying fleet of Hoorn, for example, fell from 10,700 lasts in the 1680s to 1,856 in the 1730s and 1,201 in the 1750s. The decisive period for the end of the Dutch Republic's 'Golden Age' appears to have been the second quarter of the eighteenth century, when the 'rich trades' receded and the fishing industry collapsed. The contraction of ship-building was symptomatic of a wider decline, as the number of shipyards on the Zaan, to the north of

Amsterdam, fell from over forty in 1690 to twenty-seven in the 1730s and twenty-three in 1750. Only the re-export of colonial produce continued to expand, but even in this sector there was a decline relative to the massive expansion achieved by the French and the British.

If the Dutch Republic had bucked the European trend in the seventeenth century by increasing its population and its wealth, it now went into reverse, just as general expansion was beginning everywhere else. Between 1600 and 1650 its population had increased from somewhere between 1,400,000 and 1,600,000 to somewhere between 1,850,000 and 1,900,000. But there it stuck. There may have been some slight increase to reach 1,950,000 in 1700 but the eighteenth century was marked by demographic stagnation. The first reliable census in 1795 recorded a total population of 2,078,000. More serious was the distribution of the population. At a time when Europe's urban population was growing, many Dutch towns were experiencing de-urbanization, as Table 4 reveals.

Table 4. Changes in Dutch urban population 1688–1815

	1688	1720	1732	1749	1795	1815
Amsterdam	200,000	220,000	220,000	200,000	200,000	180,000
Leiden	70,000	65,000	60,000	36,000	31,000	28,500
Rotterdam	50,000	45,000	45,000	44,000	57,500	59,000
Haarlem	50,000	45,000	40,000	26,000	21,000	17,500
The Hague	30,000	–	38,000	–	–	38,000
Middelburg	30,000	–	–	25,000	20,146	13,000
Delft	24,000	20,000	20,000	13,910	14,500	12,850
Gouda	–	–	20,000	–	11,700	–
Enkhuizen	14,000	–	10,400	–	6,800	5,200
Zaandam	20,000	–	–	12,500	10,000	8,974

Source: Jonathan Israel, *The Dutch Republic. Its rise, greatness and fall 1477–1806* (Oxford, 1995)

Behind the extraordinary figures for Haarlem and Leiden lay a collapse of the fine-cloth industries which had made them two of the most prosperous communities in Europe. In the latter, annual production fell from 25,000 rolls in 1700 to 8,000 in the late 1730s.

The Dutch Republic had suffered the fate common to many other economies enjoying the initial advantage of being first in the field. So rapid was its expansion, so astounding was its wealth, that it was bound to attract the jealous hostility of other states. This was made all the more likely by the prevailing economic orthodoxy, which held that the amount of silver and gold coinage, or 'specie', in the world was finite and that therefore one country could only prosper at the expense of others. Sir Matthew Decker summed this up in 1744: 'Therefore if the Exports of Britain exceed its Imports, Foreigners must pay the Balance in Treasure and the Nation grow Rich. But if the Imports of Britain exceed its Exports, we must pay Foreigners the Balance in Treasure and the Nation grow Poor.' Moreover, as a state's power was causally related to its possession of specie, the government had a duty to regulate the economy accordingly, by promoting exports and reducing imports. This led the English Parliament, for example, to pass the Navigation Acts of 1651, 1660 and 1696. These required all trade to and from English colonies to be carried in English ships and all colonial produce to be brought to English ports. A similar attitude was adopted by the French. In a report prepared for Louis XIV in 1670, Colbert wrote:

There is only a fixed quantity of money circulating in all of Europe, which is increased from time to time by silver coming from the West Indies. It is demonstrable that if there are only 150 million *livres* in silver circulating [in the kingdom], we cannot succeed in increasing [this amount] by twenty, thirty or fifty million without at the same time taking the equivalent quantity away from neighbouring states.

Like the English, Colbert had his sights set squarely on the Dutch, who, he alleged in the same report, handled nine out of every ten units of commerce passing in and out of French ports. They brought into France very much more than they took out, the balance being paid for by the French in hard cash, 'causing both their own affluence and this realm's poverty, and indisputably enhancing their power while promoting our weakness'. To correct the situation, in 1662 a tax of fifty *sous* per ton had been imposed on every ton of cargo carried in a foreign vessel. The result: 'we have seen the number of French vessels increase yearly, and in seven or eight years the Dutch have been practically excluded from port-to-port commerce, which is [now] carried on by the French. The advantages enjoyed by the state from the increase in the number of sailors and sea-going men, and from the money that has remained in the realm, are too many to enumerate.' Every time a European government imposed a mercantilist policy such as Colbert's, the Dutch were affected adversely. In 1724, for example, the Swedes passed a 'Commodity Act', which barred foreign ships from their ports except when carrying the produce of the ship's own nationality. This hurt both Swedish merchants and Swedish consumers, by driving up freight rates and prices. But it hurt the Dutch even more.

Both the English and the French also took direct action against Dutch commerce by waging war, the former in 1652–4, 1665–7 and 1672–4, the latter in 1672–8, 1689–97 and 1702–13. In all these conflicts, the Dutch showed that they could punch well above their weight. Such feats of arms as the raid on the Medway in 1667 or the three great victories over the combined Anglo-French fleet in 1673 showed that even a demographic imbalance of something in the order of fourteen to one could be overcome. In the long run, however, the God of Battles proved to be on the side of the big battalions. The overexertion necessitated by decades of incessant warfare eventually exhausted the Republic's resources. In particular, the burden of taxation required to service the accumulated debt and maintain the armed forces inflicted structural damage on the Dutch economy. In 1678 the national debt was 38,000,000 guilders; by 1713 it had risen to 128,000,000. As early as 1659 Sir George Downing had marvelled: 'it is strange to see with what readyness the people doe consent to extraordinary taxes, although their ordinary taxes be yett as great as they were duringe the warr with Spaine', adding by way of illustration, 'I have reckoned a man cannot eate a dishe of meate in an ordinary [inn] but that one way or another he shall pay nineteen excises out of it. This is not more strange than true.' At the end of the seventeenth century, Gregory King estimated that although the population of the Dutch Republic was less than half that of England, it was raising more public revenue – thanks to the fact that the average Dutch taxpayer was paying three times as much as his equivalent in England or France.

These high indirect taxes on consumption led to correspondingly elevated wages and diminished competitiveness. Wages for cloth-workers in Leiden were twice as high as those paid to workers across the frontier in the southern Netherlands and three times as high as in the neighbouring Prince-Bishopric of Liège (then an independent principality of the Holy Roman Empire). No wonder that by 1700 traditional customers of the Dutch were finding cheaper suppliers elsewhere. By this time they were also finding it more convenient to transport the goods in their own ships. Sooner or later it was inevitable that other shipbuilders would close the technological gap, construct their own versions of the *fluyts*, develop their own merchant marine and cut out the Dutch middleman. Prussia's direct trade with Bordeaux, for example, doubled between the 1740s and the 1780s. The dynamism the Prussians showed in military matters was also evident in commerce. At Stettin, the number of ships increased from 79 in 1751 to 165 in 1784. And they were getting bigger: the number of ships over 100 *Lasten* increased from two in 1751 to seventy-eight in 1784. In the Baltic there was growing competition from Scandinavian and Hanseatic shipping, with the Swedes developing a rival herring fishery at Gothenburg and the Norwegians supplanting the Dutch as the main suppliers of cod to the region. By the middle of the eighteenth century, the Dutch cod fishery had shrunk to less than 20 per cent of what it had been in the 1690s. By the 1770s the Dutch had only just over 40 per cent of the Baltic grain trade, compared with its virtual monopoly a century or so earlier. They also found their traditional domination of the whaling industry challenged: in 1721, of the 355 vessels engaged in whale fishing around the coasts of Greenland, the lion's share – 251 – were still Dutch, but there were now 55 from Hamburg, 24 from Bremen, 20 from the Biscayan ports of France and Spain and 5 from Bergen.

As the rest of Europe recovered from the Thirty Years War and developed their own commerce, there was decreasing need for the Dutch entrepôt. This did not mean that the great trading complex developed during the Golden Age collapsed in the eighteenth century. Several important sectors continued to expand, at least in absolute terms. Dutch merchants continued to show their old enterprise and energy in developing new branches, as in the lucrative coffee business in the East Indies. At home, however, there was undoubtedly a move away from manufacturing and trade towards finance, especially loans to foreign governments. With so many of the latter eager to pay 5 per cent and more in interest, it made good sense to move accumulated capital into banking. And so the Dutch Republic became what Charles Wilson has called 'a *rentier* economy', if not quite a parasite, then certainly a more passive player in Europe's economy.

Of the countries moving in the opposite direction, the most spectacularly successful in relative terms was Russia. From being a remote and occasional supplier of raw materials in 1660, by 1815 it had emerged as a major commercial power. Peter the Great's victory in the Great Northern War of 1700–21 brought control of the eastern Baltic, including the ports of Narva, Riga and Reval, not to mention his new creation of St Petersburg. The latter was founded only in 1703, yet by 1722 its turnover of freight was twelve times that of Archangel, previously Russia's main port. With the 'window on the west' now secured, Russia's trade with western Europe doubled between 1726 and 1749. Just as important, albeit often overlooked, were the acquisitions made in the south by Catherine the Great. The Treaty of Kutchuk-Kainardji in 1774 brought a foothold on the Black Sea and the right for Russian merchants to navigate on it; the Convention of Ainali Kawak in 1779 added the right to pass through the Straits into the Mediterranean; the annexation of the Crimea in 1783, secured by the war of 1787–91, brought the northern coastline of the Black Sea under Russian control; the war of 1807–12 extended it almost to the Danube delta. The three partitions of Poland of 1772, 1793 and 1795 advanced the frontier of the Russian Empire more than 300 miles (500 km) to the west.

It took a long time for this transformation of the geopolitical situation to be realized in commercial terms. For much of the eighteenth century, Russia continued to be regarded by the west, and especially by its main customer, Great Britain, as a colony, i.e. as a source of raw materials and a market for manufactured commodities. Aware that the Russians lacked any kind of commercial infrastructure, the British drove a hard bargain in their trade treaty of 1734. Although the more onerous provisions were revised in a subsequent treaty of 1766, the basic exploitative outline remained the same. Achieving economic maturity was proving to be a long process: in 1773–7 the average number of Russian-owned ships in all Russian ports was only 227, and only between 12 and 15 of those over 200 tons were genuinely Russian. To put that statistic in perspective, of 1,748 ships visiting Russian ports during the same period, over 600 were British. That Russia had arrived as a maritime power, however, was advertised dramatically on 24–26 June 1770, when a fleet which had sailed from the Baltic via the North Sea inflicted on the Turks at Chesme in the Aegean one of the most crushing defeats in the history of naval warfare. It was intended to pay commercial dividends, for it was followed by the establishment of diplomatic representation in trading centres. In the course of the next decade, sixteen consuls general and thirty consuls were appointed to cover the Baltic, North Sea, Atlantic and Mediterranean. The last two decades of the eighteenth century saw rapid expansion, spurred on by the opportunities presented by the new ports in the south, where Kherson was founded in 1778, Sevastopol in 1783 and Odessa in 1793. In 1794, 406 Russian ships sailed from Russian ports, still outnumbered by the British with 1,011, but clearly now constituting a merchant marine to be reckoned with. It had increased eight times between 1775 and 1787. Foreign trade also showed an impressive surge, as Table 5 demonstrates:

Table 5. Total Russian foreign trade (turnover in 000r.)

Year	Total	Imports	Exports	Balance
1772	31,253	15,563	15,690	127
1782	40,301	19,242	21,059	1,817
1787	48,867	22,753	26,114	3,361
1792	78,218	37,521	40,697	3,176
1794	85,004	39,530	45,474	5,944
1795	90,424	36,652	53,772	11,893
1796	109,519	41,879	67,640	25,761

Source: Isabel de Madariaga, *Russia in the Age of Catherine the Great* (New Haven and London, 1981)

Indicative of this secular transformation of Russian commerce was the shift in its relationship with the British. When the trade treaty of 1766 was about to expire in 1786, the British found to their surprise and dismay that they could not renew it on the old terms. This should not have been surprising. Catherine the Great had given an indication of her intentions in 1780 when she formed the League of Armed Neutrality, a consortium of non-belligerents which, despite its name, was aimed squarely at British maritime supremacy. With a self-confidence born of the knowledge that they now had their own merchant navy and their own mercantile services, the Russians proved obdurate and the treaty lapsed. More alarming still for the British was the commercial agreement the Russians signed with the French in January 1787. This was adding insult to injury, not least because it had important strategic as well as political implications. Both the Royal Navy and the British merchant marine relied very heavily on Russia for their construction materials, not just timber for masts and planks but also timber derivatives such as pitch, tar, resin and turpentine, flax for sail-cloth and hemp for rope and cordage. Now that Russia had opened up direct trade links to the Mediterranean through the Black Sea, the awful possibility loomed that these 'naval stores' would be diverted to Britain's mortal enemy.

The process was in fact already underway. In 1781 a French merchant based at Constantinople by the name of Anthoine had travelled to Kherson, St Petersburg and Warsaw to investigate this possibility. He then journeyed on to Versailles to report to the French authorities. In April 1783, with the war in America drawing to a close, the French foreign minister, Vergennes, urged the minister for the navy, Castries, to accelerate the project, lest the British take counter-measures. Anthoine was duly given the exclusive right to export naval stores to France through Kherson and was granted a credit of 100,000 *livres* on an Amsterdam bank. In 1784 he was joined at Kherson by a master-mastman to assist in the selection of appropriate masts. A contract was duly signed with the Polish magnate Prince Poniatowski for the delivery of 300 masting trees. A further consignment of 263 arrived at Marseilles in 1786. It is difficult to estimate what might have become of this trade. The masts actually delivered were smaller and of poorer quality than the French had hoped, and Anthoine showed more interest in trading on his own account than in promoting the national interest. In the event, the outbreak of war between Turkey and Russia in the summer of 1787 brought the project to an abrupt halt. In 1793 Catherine the Great responded to the execution of Louis XVI by cancelling the agreement.

Although not the main cause, that act of regicide facilitated the entry of Great Britain into the Revolutionary Wars, thus beginning the death-agony of French overseas trade. But even before that terminal crisis, there had been signs of strain. After wresting control of the Levant trade in the early eighteenth century, by the 1780s French merchants found themselves being undercut by cheaper textiles brought by English, German and Austrian competitors. By 1783 their market share had declined to around 40 per cent. That was the year in which the American colonists finally won recognition of their independence and it should also have been the year in which their French mentors and allies entered into their commercial kingdom. It was not to be. The French commercial system proved to be inflexible, over-reliant on the protected colonial trade and especially on its re-exports, which accounted for more than a third of all exports in the 1780s. More specifically still, it was over-reliant on Saint Domingue, which generated three-quarters of trade with the colonies, most of the re-exported goods and absorbed nearly two-thirds of France's foreign investments. The growing exhaustion of over-exploited soil and the rising price of slaves were already enfeebling this golden goose when it was abruptly decapitated by the outbreak of a great slave revolt in August 1791. The French never regained control of the island.

That by itself was enough to reduce the trade of Bordeaux by a third in less than a year, but much worse was to come. After the declaration of war by the National Assembly on Great Britain and the Dutch Republic on 1 February 1793, the Royal Navy ruled the waves to such effect that French overseas trade virtually collapsed. Lorenz Meyer, a Hamburg merchant, reported from Bordeaux in 1801:

The former splendour of Bordeaux is no more . . . The devastation and loss of the colonies have wiped out commerce and have ruined with it the prosperity of the first city of France. This can be seen everywhere. The stock-exchange is still packed with merchants, but most of them go there only out of habit. Business is a rare event. The only branch not to have disappeared is the domestic trade in wine.

In 1789 French re-exports to Hamburg, mainly of sugar and tobacco, had been worth 50,000,000 *livres*. In 1795 – a better year than the previous two – France sent just 291 *tonneaux* of sugar, mainly in neutral vessels, whereas the British sent 25,390 *tonneaux*. In that same year, all French foreign trade had fallen to just 50 per cent of what it had been in 1789. In the first seven years of the Revolution, the proportion of all economic activity in France provided by overseas trade had fallen from 25 per cent to 9 per cent. Even in 1815 it was still only 60 per cent of what it had been in 1789. This decline had a corresponding impact on the manufacturing hinterlands. At Marseilles, for example, the value of industrial production fell by three-quarters between 1789 and 1813.

The great lesson of the eighteenth century was that the key to commerce was shipping and the ability to protect that shipping. It was a lesson that the French were sometimes unwilling and often unable to learn. At times it proved possible for naval and mercantile interests to make their voices heard at Versailles, notably during the long ministry

(1661–83) of Colbert, but more often than not they were shouted down by the military. In the fierce competition for scarce resources, tradition and geography favoured the army. Periodic efforts to construct a navy capable of taking on the Dutch, or – later – the British, invariably faltered. Consequently, all the decisive naval engagements ended in French defeats. This endemic failing was causally linked to the relative weakness of the French merchant navy. It was never more than half the size of that of Great Britain, despite a demographic superiority of three to one, a long coastline and excellent ports on both the Atlantic and the Mediterranean. Sir John Habbakuk described this failure as 'one of the most curious features' of the economic history of the period. In 1767, 203 ships passed through the Sound from the Baltic en route to French ports and 299 travelled back in the opposite direction – but only 10 were French-owned. Consequently, in time of war the French had a pool of only about 50,000 skilled seamen on which to draw when the fleet was mobilized. The British had more than double that figure: the census of 1801 recorded 135,000 sailors in the Royal Navy and 144,000 in the merchant marine.

That is why the Pont d'Iéna and the Gare d'Austerlitz are in Paris but Trafalgar Square is in London. The contrast between the two combatants in the 'Second Hundred Years War', which began with the Glorious Revolution of 1688 and ended at Waterloo, must not be exaggerated. It was not a simple confrontation between an aristocratic French state based on land and a bourgeois British state based on commercial capital. After 1629 French nobles were permitted to engage in ship-owning and overseas commerce, and after 1701 in any form of wholesale trade, without losing their noble status by derogation. Many of them did so. The French historian Guy Chaussinand-Nogaret has written: 'from 1770 onwards . . . the nobility began to be massively involved in great overseas trading companies, which they sometimes founded'. The West Africa Company, founded in 1774 to open up the colony of Cayenne and to supply it with slaves, numbered among its twenty-four shareholders the duc de Duras, the marquis de Saisseval, the comte de Jumilhac, the abbot of Chartreuve, the comte de Fresserville, the marquis de Mesnilglaise, the marquise de Grignon, the comte de Blagny and the marquis de Rochedragon. On the other hand, the British Parliament was still dominated by landowners in 1815. The British peerage admitted no merchant or financier to its ranks during this period. In the view of John Cannon, the aristocrats who ran the country constituted 'one of the most exclusive ruling elites in human history'.

Yet there were important differences. The French seat of government was at Versailles, a wholly artificial creation, built on a greenfield site at the behest of a single individual. The British capital was London, a great port and financial centre. If the importance of its court has sometimes been underestimated, it did not compare with the size, grandeur and prestige of its French counterpart. As we shall see in a later chapter, London was also the centre of a rapidly growing public sphere, in which commercial interests could be articulated and applied. As so often, the 'primacy of foreign policy' had a part to play. The accession of a Dutch king in 1688 created the concept of 'the Maritime Powers', a natural alliance bound together by a common commitment to defending liberty, Protestantism and commerce against the absolutism and Catholicism of France. The checking of Louis XIV's ambitions in the 1690s and the victories of the War of the Spanish Succession appeared to prove that the balance of power in the world had swung the Anglo-Dutch way, especially to the Anglo part. Daniel Defoe claimed in *The Complete English Tradesman* of 1726, 'We are not only a trading country, but the greatest trading country in the world.' He added, perhaps more controversially, 'our climate is the most agreeable climate in the world to live in'. This triumphalist theme was reprised constantly. Edward Young, better known as the author of *Night Thoughts*, crowed in 1730 that the world conspired to make England rich:

> Luxuriant Isle! What Tide that flows,
> Or Stream that glides, or Wind that blows,
> Or genial Sun that shines, or Show'r that pours,
> But flows, glides, breathes, shines, pours for Thee?
> How every Heart dilates to see
> Each Land's each Season blending on thy Shores?
> . . .
> Others may traffick as they please;
> *Britain*, fair Daughter of the Seas,
> Is born for *Trade*; to plough her field, the Wave;
> And reap the growth of every Coast:
> A Speck of Land! but let her boast,
> Gods gave the *World*, when they the *Waters gave*.

> *Britain!* behold the World's wide face;
> Not cover'd half with *solid* space,
> Three parts are *Fluid*; Empire of the Sea!
> And why? for Commerce. *Ocean* streams
> For *that*, thro' all his various *names*:
> And, if for *Commerce*, *Ocean* flows for Thee.

It was a vision shared ten years later, in 1740, by the hermit in Thomson's *Alfred* in his final exhortation to the beleaguered Saxon king:

> I see thy commerce, *Britain*, grasp the world:
> All nations serve thee; every foreign flood,
> Subjected pays its tribute to the *Thames*.

As the British saw it, their four great mutually supportive achievements – power, prosperity, Protestantism and liberty – were all secured by commerce, so the merchant enjoyed a correspondingly high status. In 1722 Richard Steele put the following words into the mouth of Mr Sealand in his play *The Conscious Lovers*: 'I know the Town and the World – and give me leave to say, that we Merchants are a species of Gentry, that have grown into the World this last Century, and are as honourable, and almost as useful, as you landed Folks, that have always thought yourselves so much above us.' John Gay was more forceful in *The Distress'd Wife*: 'Is the name then [of merchant] of Reproach? – Where is the Profession that is so honourable? – What is it that supports every Individual of our Country? – 'Tis Commerce. – On what depends the Glory, the Credit, the Power of the Nation? – On Commerce. – To what does the Crown itself owe its Splendor and Dignity? – To Commerce.' Daniel Defoe agreed: 'trade in England makes Gentlemen, and has peopled this nation with Gentlemen'. To these literary examples can be added the authoritative opinion of a Swiss traveller, César de Saussure, who observed in 1727: 'In England commerce is not looked down upon as being derogatory, as it is in France and Germany. Here men of good family and even of rank may become merchants without losing caste. I have heard of younger sons of peers, whose families have been reduced to poverty through the habits of extravagance and dissipation of an elder son, retrieve the fallen fortunes of their house by becoming merchants.' In the past it had been an axiom of English political theory that a virtuous polity depended on a tradition of civic humanism, sustained by a landed elite whose independence ensured their virtue. Now there emerged a greater willingness to view commercial society, not as a sink of corruption but as a wholly legitimate sphere of private sociability.

Ultimately it is this question of status that distinguishes British from French commerce in the period 1660–1815. In France it was certainly important, but was never more than one course on a rich menu of national attributes. In Great Britain it was paramount. The speed of the country's commercial success was such as to catch the eye of a wide range of observers unconnected with – and unsympathetic to – trade. Horace Walpole, fourth Earl of Orford, told his correspondent Horace Mann: 'You would not know your country again. You left it as a private island living upon its means. You would find it the capital of the world.' That arch-Tory Dr Johnson recognized that 'there was never from the earliest ages a time in which trade so much engaged the attention of mankind, or commercial gain was sought with such general emulation'. It also excited plenty of adverse comment, from John Brown, for example, who in 1758 wrote an eighty-page rant – *An Estimate of the Manners and Principles of the Times* – to show that excessive trade, and the wealth that flowed from it, had brought effeminacy, irreligion and decadence. Behind these subjective impressions lay some impressive statistics, for example that the merchant marine almost trebled from 3,300 vessels (260,000 tons) in 1702 to 9,400 (695,000 tons) in 1776; that imports increased from c.£6,000,000 of goods in 1700 to c.£12,200,000 in 1770; and that exports in the same period more than doubled from £6,470,000 to £14,300,000. If these men had lived until the end of the century, they would have had even greater occasion for celebration or deprecation. As Cain and Hopkins have established, over the whole period 1697–1800 exports from England and Wales grew at a mean rate of 1.5 per cent per annum. However, in the 1780s, when cotton manufactures took off, really impressive acceleration occurred, achieving a rate of 5.1 per cent per annum for the period 1780–1800. Exports' share of national income rose significantly to reach 18 per cent by 1801, having doubled since 1783. If Joseph Palmer, whose admiration of the splendour of Bordeaux was quoted at the beginning of the chapter, had been able to visit London in 1818, he would have found 4 miles (6.5 km) of dockyards, 1,100 ships, 3,000 barges, 3,000 watermen or navigators, 4,000 dockers and – as a depressing final touch

– 12,000 revenue officers. By this time, the city had become a gigantic entrepôt, making England not just the workshop but also the warehouse of the world (Boyd Hilton).

THE RESIDENTIAL CITY

Change caught the eye of contemporaries, and change has caught the eye of historians. The modernizing vigour of commercial centres such as London and Liverpool, Nantes and Bordeaux, Hamburg and Danzig, St Petersburg and Sevastopol, made them seem like the cities of the future. And so they were. Yet for most townspeople, it was not the merchant who provided their livelihood. The characteristic urban economy of the period 1660–1815 was not a port but a court. This was the golden age of the *Residenzstadt*, the 'residential city' whose *raison d'être* was provided by those who resided within its walls: the ruler, his officials, his clergy and his courtiers. Together these privileged groups formed a powerful economic group, spending in the city what they extracted from the countryside in the form of taxes, rents and seigneurial dues. It was the compulsory sacrifices of the peasants that allowed the *Residenzstadt* to flourish. In the post-industrial world, domestic service has been marginalized if not eliminated, but in early modern Europe it was the prime source of urban employment. One example must suffice: in his social survey of Vienna conducted in the late 1780s, Joseph Pezzl identified at least a dozen 'princely' establishments, that is to say households maintained by magnates with the title of Prince (*Fürst*). The richest of them – the Liechtensteins, Esterházys, Schwarzenbergs, Dietrichsteins and Lobkowitzes – each put between 300,000 and 700,000 *gulden* into circulation every year. Below this elite came around seventy Counts (*Grafen*), spending between 50,000 and 80,000 *gulden*, and then fifty or so Barons (*Freiherren*), whose households disbursed between 20,000 and 50,000 *gulden*. It was from the middle group of Counts that Pezzl took a representative establishment to illustrate why the city teemed with servants:

The lady of the house needs for her service one or two chambermaids, a man servant, a washerwoman, two parlourmaids, an extra girl, a porter, a messenger and two general servants.

The man of the house has a secretary, two *valets de chambre*, a lackey, huntsmen, messengers, footmen, two general servants.

For the general service of the house there are a major domo, a waiter, two charwomen, two house-boys and a porter or gatekeeper.

In the kitchen there are a chef, a confectioner, a pastry-cook, a roasts-cook, plus the usual crowd of kitchen-boys, kitchen-porters, washers-up, scullery-maids etc.

The stables are looked after by a master of the horses, a riding-master, two coach-men, two postillions, two outriders, two grooms, four stable lads etc.

This was a culture in which status counted for everything, display determined status, and display could be sustained only by an 'appropriate' establishment. So Pezzl could add: 'the total number of male and female domestic servants in Vienna is estimated to be 20,000 and this estimate is certainly not exaggerated'. At the time he wrote, the total population of the city was about 225,000. Apart from these direct dependants, almost everyone engaged in trade, retailing or manufacturing was part of the *Residenzstadt* nexus. The conspicuous consumption of the privileged orders created an economy in their own image, a web of luxury trades and luxury services which drew to Vienna the labour to serve them. As the author of another contemporary survey, Ignaz de Luca, recorded: 'The great majority of the nobility in the city are courtiers or civil servants. Taken as a whole, the nobility owns great wealth and spends freely, which is a blessing for the working population, especially in a place like Vienna where there is a large number of manufacturers, artisans and other labourers.' David Hume's sour comment in 1768 was that the city was 'compos'd entirely of nobility, and of lackeys, soldiers and priests'.

Even the very first cities to be formed, in the river valley civilizations of the near east, were sustained in part by the residence of a *rentier* class 'living off its rents'. What was special about our period was the dominant role this element exercised in so many parts of Europe. Partly this was due to a new geographical stability on the part of the courts, which by the end of the seventeenth century had ceased to be peripatetic. One weary ambassador to the court of the French King Francis I (1515–47) had complained that 'never during the whole of my embassy was the court in the same place for fifteen consecutive days'. Under Louis XIV (1643–1715), the court came to rest at Versailles and quickly turned a greenfield site into a *Residenzstadt*, the tenth largest city in the country. Vienna did not become the permanent capital of the Habsburg Monarchy until the reign of the Emperor Ferdinand II (1617–37) and could only turn itself from frontier fortress into *Residenzstadt* when the threat from the Turks was finally lifted following their abortive siege of 1683. The subsequent construction of such monumental buildings as the Church of St Charles (*Karlskirche*) or Prince Eugene's summer palace, the 'Belvedere', outside the old fortifications advertised the confidence of the ruling orders that the Turks would never be a threat again. By 1720 no fewer than 200 palaces of various kinds had been built in and around the city, doubling by 1740. Now the city came to be known as the Habsburg Monarchy's 'Capital- and Residential-City' (*Haupt- und Residenzstadt*).

At the centre of these residential cities stood the court, the interface between princely power and aristocratic privilege. It was a place of 'representation', where the authority of the ruler was made visible through display and ceremony; it was a place of recreation, where high society could dine, dance, gamble, attend balls, operas and ballets and generally have a good time; it was a place of negotiation where deals between centre and periphery, capital and province could be brokered. It was a place of conflict, and a place of conflict-resolution. No longer did the great landowning magnates of Europe seek to challenge the monarch by building alternative power-centres on their estates. The English Wars of the Roses (1457–87), the French *Frondes* (1648–53), the Thirty Years War (1618–48), and the Hungarian rising led by Francis II Rákóczy (1703–11) – just to name a few of the more important convulsions – were all followed by a new sociopolitical alliance between ruler and privileged orders. In no case was there a simple victory of absolutism over aristocracy, however much the new court discourse elevated the royal image. To borrow the striking metaphor of John Adamson, at court 'the carapace of authority concealed a diversity of partly complementary, partly competing "foyers of power"'. Between the middle of the sixteenth and the end of the seventeenth century, there developed across Europe what Adamson has called a 'standardisation of expectations' as to what a court should comprise.

As we shall see in a later chapter, the court played a dominant role in the politics and the culture of most European countries during this period. Here it is its economic role that needs further emphasis. In particular, the sheer size of the undertaking needs to be borne in mind. As Olivier Chalines has written about Versailles: 'far from being merely an assemblage of the higher nobility drawn in from the various provinces of the realm, it was a whole society in miniature, with its own priests, soldiers, officials, tradesmen and domestic servants'. There were 10,000 of them by the end of Louis XIV's reign, which made his court the greatest single employer in his kingdom, with the exception of the army, itself also strongly represented at court. Moreover, around the Sun King or his equivalent there revolved many planets, each with its own subordinate moons.

Many of them wore clerical garb. Especially in Catholic countries, the *Residenzstadt* had a strong ecclesiastical flavour. Indeed, demonstrative piety was one of the 'standardized expectations' referred to above. It was at court that both individual prelates and pious institutions could catch the eye of a royal patron. Indeed, in surprisingly many cases, it was the Church that stood at the centre of the residential economy. Most obviously, this was the case in Rome, both the Holy See of St Peter's successor and the capital of his secular patrimony. It was also the preferred place of residence for the great aristocratic families that for so long had dominated the Sacred College of Cardinals, and with it the Pontificate, as the names of the most prominent *palazzi* demonstrate: Altieri, Borghese, Chigi, Colonna, Este, Farnese, Fiano, Pamphili, Ruspoli, Sciarra, and so on. Virtually every Catholic religious order felt obliged to maintain a branch there, with the result that there were 240 monasteries for males and 73 convents for females. Together they owned about a third of the city's real estate and, together with the secular clergy, comprised about 7 per cent of the total population of 140,000 in 1740.

Rome also boasted two other assets that brought visitors flocking from all over Europe to reside within its walls, however briefly. The first was its status as capital of the Catholic Christian world. If less obligatory than the Muslim haj, a pilgrimage to Rome and its innumerable churches and relics had a powerful appeal to the faithful, especially during a jubilee year. In 1650, 700,000 are reported to have made the journey. They were a few years too early for Bernini's great colonnade enclosing St Peter's Square, which could accommodate 100,000 pilgrims at a time. The second asset was the new fashion for old artefacts. For the thousands of wealthy Europeans who set out each year to explore the continent's cultural riches, a visit to the sites of classical antiquity, and especially Rome, was the *sine qua non*. As Dr Samuel Johnson observed: 'Sir, a man who has not been in Italy is always conscious of an inferiority, from his not having seen what it is expected a man should see. The grand object of travelling is to see the shores of the Mediterranean', for 'all our religion, all our arts, almost all that sets us above savages, has come from the shores of the Mediterranean.' Now that it was so much safer and easier to travel, it became de rigueur for young men with pretensions to intellectual attainment to travel to the places they had studied so intensively in the course of their mainly classical education. No one put this better than Joseph Spence, accompanying the Earl of Middlesex in 1732:

This is one of the pleasures of being at Rome, that you are continually seeing the very place and spot of ground where some great thing or other was done, which one has so often admired before in reading their history. *This* is the place where Julius Caesar was stabbed by Brutus; at the foot of *that* statue he fell and gave his last groan; *here* stood Manlius to defend the Capitol against the Gauls; and *there* afterwards was he flung down *that* rock for endeavouring to make himself the tyrant of his country.

If the pious pilgrims still had the numerical advantage, it was the secular tourists, especially the notoriously wealthy and gullible British, who packed the purchasing power. They also flocked to Venice. The beauty of the latter's setting and architecture, its reputation for sexual licence, especially during the Carnival season, and the high quality of its public entertainment, notably opera, combined to attract high-spending visitors from all over Europe.

At the other end of the hedonistic scale was a special sub-category of residential cities in which the military predominated. Unquestioned leader here was Berlin, where every visitor was struck by the ubiquity of men in uniform. When Frederick the Great came to the throne in 1740, the city had a civilian population of 68,961 and a garrison totalling 21,309, including dependants. By the time he died in 1786, the city was surrounded by barracks 'like a necklace', as one observer commented, and those figures had risen to 113,763 and 33,635 respectively. Not far behind came St Petersburg, which in 1789 included 55,600 soldiers and their families among its population of 218,000.

Great cities such as Vienna, Rome, Venice or St Petersburg were the

most conspicuous examples of the importance of the residential economy, but in aggregate terms they were eclipsed by the numerous smaller
versions spread across Europe. The region par excellence of the residential city was the Holy Roman Empire, that loose amalgam of princes,
both secular and ecclesiastical, and Free Imperial Cities subject only to
the nominal authority of the Emperor. Whatever their exact title (and
there was a rich variety), every ruler held sway over a court and capital.
Some were very small – Weimar, for example, home to Goethe, Herder,
Wieland and many other luminaries, had a population of only about
7,000 at the end of the eighteenth century. Only two were really large
cities by the standards of the age – Berlin with 175,000 and Vienna with
225,000. What they all had in common was economic dependence on
the ruler. A good example of a middling *Residenzstadt* was Mainz,
capital of the eponymous Archbishop-Elector, with a population of
about 30,000 in the 1780s. About a quarter of this number were nobles,
clergymen, officials and government employees of one kind or another,
and their dependants. The Elector also exercised considerable indirect
influence on the economy through his expenditure. The court needed
food, drink and entertainment; the Electoral palaces and government
buildings had to be maintained; the various offices of state needed a
thousand different commodities. The economic importance of the court,
nobility and clergy was demonstrated clearly when they departed in the
wake of the wave of French invasions beginning in 1792. The population
fell by a third to just over 20,000, despite Mainz becoming an important
French garrison town and the capital of the Mont Tonnerre *département*.
The missing thousands had followed their sources of livelihood into
exile at the courts of Franconia and Bavaria.

It was not only royal or princely capitals which housed a residential
sector. Every town which attracted *rentiers* to reside within its walls was
to a greater or lesser extent a *Residenzstadt*. This applied to spas such
as Bath or Bad Pyrmont, to provincial centres such as Toulouse or Kiev,
and to ecclesiastical centres such as Valladolid or Angers. No wonder
that Angers was a centre of counter-revolution after 1789. When the
town was captured by the Vendéan insurgents in 1793, a local priest
found a receptive congregation when he preached on the beneficence of
the clergy, claiming they 'received with one hand to give with the other.
They were the beneficent syphon which drew up the water, distributed
it and fertilized the land . . . The clergy were almsgiving itself. Their

property belonged to the people.' In trying to explain why the French Revolution attracted such widespread hostility from the common people, both inside and outside France, historians would do well to look beyond social divisions, or even ideology and culture, to hard-nosed economic interest.

MANUFACTURING

Perceptions of that interest were strongly influenced, if not dictated, by what continued to be the most common form of organization for manufacturers – the craft guild. Its longevity was due not least to the plurality of tasks it performed: quality control, social disciplining, social welfare, status maintenance, religious devotion and collective recreation being just a few. At its heart, of course, stood its monopoly of production of a given commodity in a particular community. In most European towns for most of the eighteenth century, aspiring manufacturers had to join a guild. Typically, the trainee craftsman first had to serve an apprenticeship of three years. As a journeyman, he then left the city to travel from one town to another, collecting en route testimonials from his various employers. This peregrination usually lasted at least two years. On his return to his home town he was not allowed to apply immediately for admission to the ranks of the masters. First he had to work for another two years or so as a simple journeyman. He was then permitted to submit his masterpiece to the guild and, if it were approved, to pay the substantial fees and become a master. This is a very generalized account; the process was often very much longer or, especially if the candidate concerned were a close relation of an existing master, shorter. Needless to say, this long and complicated procedure gave the guilds ample opportunity to keep their numbers down, the regulations governing the presentation of masterpieces being an especially potent weapon.

Like so many other organizations enjoying a monopoly of their chosen activity, the craft guilds had a built-in tendency towards ossification. By the eighteenth century many were showing all the negative conservatism of a vested interest overtaken by events: dogged devotion to old techniques, suspicion of innovation, resentment of competition and xenophobia. They were particularly determined to confine guild membership to 'their kind of people'. The early modern value-system prioritized honour and the guild-masters were just as determined to defend their place in the social hierarchy as was any magnate or prelate. So no applicant for admission to a guild need bother unless male, of legitimate birth and of the right religious denomination. Contamination by contact with a 'dishonourable profession' offered a rich range of reasons for the exclusion, for example, of sons of public executioners, knackermen, tanners, barber-surgeons, shepherds, musicians, actors, pedlars or beggars. More bizarrely, in Germany at least, the offspring of civil servants were ruled out. Significantly, so were factory workers. The pedantry displayed when enforcing these regulations may well have concealed a more personal vindictive agenda. In 1725 in Brandenburg, for example, a cloth-maker was ejected from his guild when it came to light that his wife's grandmother was allegedly descended from a shepherd. A cobbler spotted drinking with the local hangman suffered the same fate.

More serious than these occasional acts of discrimination was the dead weight constantly applied to enterprise and innovation, as the master craftsmen protected their monopoly by reducing competition to a minimum. In France it was the requirement of a masterpiece that was exploited most. The journeyman was often required to produce a fiendishly complicated piece of work, to give presents to the jury members appointed to assess its merits, and then, if successful, to pay an entrance fee to the guild. In Paris, the distillers required 800 *livres* and the apothecaries 1,000 *livres*. Yet the sons and grandsons of existing masters were often exempted from some or even all these requirements. Minutely detailed regulations on size and quality choked innovation and adaptation to changing market conditions. The new code introduced in the Dauphiné in 1782, for example, contained 265 paragraphs. New commodities were seen not as an opportunity but as a threat, as in the case of printed calicoes, banned by a series of ordinances passed between 1686 and 1759. Typical was the attitude expressed by the town council of Strasbourg in 1770 when obstructing an attempt by a cotton manufacturer to get established: 'it would upset all order in trade if the manufacturer were to become merchant at the same time, and infringe the most sensible rules laying down who are allowed to trade in the city'. These and many other abuses were recounted with relish by the enlightened reformer Turgot, when he proposed to Louis XVI in 1776 that the guilds be abolished outright. The excessive demands for useless and expensive masterpieces, he argued, were forcing gifted craftsmen to leave France to work abroad. The guilds' arguments that they ensured quality control he dismissed as spurious: 'liberty of trades has never caused ill effects in those places where it has been established for a long while. The workers in the suburbs and in other fortunate places do not work less well than those living in Paris. All the world knows that the inspection system of the guilds is entirely illusory.' He concluded: 'I regard the destruction of the guilds, Sire, as one of the greatest benefits that you can bestow on your people.' Turgot fell from power, following a court intrigue, before the necessary legislation could be enforced. It was left to the Revolution to complete his work.

Other governments took frequent action against guild abuses. In the Holy Roman Empire the Imperial Trades Edict of 1731 offered both a comprehensive indictment and a programme for reform. Some idea of the pre-modern world in which the guilds operated can be gained from paragraph number one of article thirteen:

That the tanners and the tawers [*Rothgerber* and *Weissgerber*, two tanning trades using different materials and techniques] in some places brawl with one another over the processing of dog skins, and over other useless disagreements among themselves, and those who will not process them call the others dishonourable, and also will have it that apprentices who have worked in places like that should be punished by the others. Similarly if an artisan stones a dog or cat to death, or beats it, or drowns it, or even just touches a carcass, an impropriety is wrung out of that, to the point that the skinners take it upon themselves to pester such hand workers by sticking them with their knives and in other ways, and in such fashion as to oblige them to buy their way out of it with a sum of money.

Significantly, this edict was renewing previous measures dating from 1530, 1548, 1577, etc. and conceded that 'these very salutary provisions have not altogether been lived up to and even other abuses have gradually crept in'. As implementation was conditional on action by the individual principalities of the Empire, very little was actually achieved. The guilds were so deeply entrenched in most places that any attempt to wrench them out by the roots caused social and political disorder. Especially during the difficult years of the mid-seventeenth century, rulers found themselves obliged to do deals with all manner of corporate bodies, including the guilds. Moreover, the latter showed surprising tenacity and even vitality in some trades. Far from being 'decadent', 'moribund' or 'superannuated' – just three of the adjectives often applied to their condition in the eighteenth century – guilds were still being created. Wherever governments valued social harmony and control above productivity, the guilds could find friends. So the troubled times after 1789, and even after 1848, saw the guilds taking on a new lease of life.

As the tanners and tawers knew, there was more than one way of killing a cat, and there was more than one way of dealing with the guilds. Especially popular in continental monarchies was the granting of permission to favoured entrepreneurs to operate outside the guild system, producing certain specified – usually luxury – goods. Setting the pace here was Jean-Baptiste Colbert, who took control of economic policy in France in the 1660s. In 1662 he paid 40,000 *livres* for 'a large house situated on the Faubourg Saint-Marcel les Paris, commonly known as the Gobelins'. He filled it with a number of tapestry workshops under the general direction of the painter Charles Le Brun. Before long there were working there 'over 800 tapestry workers, sculptors, artists, goldsmiths, embroiderers and, in general, workers in all that made for splendour and magnificence'. Their first task was appropriately representational, namely creating a series of huge tapestries to designs of Le Brun illustrating Louis XIV's exploits. To consummate the union between royal economic enterprise and royal display, one of the tapestries depicted 'King Louis XIV visiting the Gobelins Manufactory'. Other similar enterprises followed, the largest for the production of mirrors and soap.

As we shall see in a later chapter, such was the success of the 'Versailles project' that most other European sovereigns felt obliged to follow the French example. Although this emulation was partly a matter of fashion, it was also driven by a mercantilist concern to improve the balance of trade by reducing expensive imports. Right across continental Europe, non-guild manufacturing establishments were founded with government support, encouraged by all kinds of fiscal and financial privileges. In the Electorate of Mainz, for example, they were set up to produce ribbon and braid, cotton, pencils, chocolate, gold and silver chain, hats, silk, surgical instruments, playing cards, sewing needles, Spanish noodles, soap, parchment, cosmetics, taffeta and chintz (and even this is not a complete list). It is next to impossible to assess the overall effect of these and similar enterprises elsewhere. Did they promote the economy by providing capital and enterprise which otherwise would have been absent? Or did they impede development by stifling competition? Certainly many of them were short-lived, bobbing from crisis to crisis, kept afloat only by further injections of capital before sinking when the bottom of the royal purse was reached. Success stories such as Meissen or Nymphenburg porcelain were rare. On the other hand, apologists for royal subsidies have pointed out that the level of subsidy was relatively low. Even Louis XIV advanced only 284,725 *livres* to mirror manufacturing between 1667 and 1683, and about 400,000 *livres* to soap manufacturing between 1665 and 1685. His total subsidy to privileged manufacturing during a twenty-year period was about 16,000,000 *livres*, which sounds a good deal until one recalls that the gross annual domestic product during the same period was around a billion-and-a-half *livres*. It also appears that many of those regions which progressed to full-blown industrialization in the nineteenth century had received privileged treatment during the eighteenth.

Although the products of these luxury industries now line the walls of palaces or fill the display cabinets of museums, at the time their impact on the larger economy was marginal. Much more subversive of guild domination of manufacturing was the expansion of rural industries, especially in the manufacturing of textiles but also of goods such as gloves, ribbons, stockings, shoes and hats, not just on a small scale for local consumption but on a mass basis for export markets. The key figure here was the merchant-capitalist, who co-ordinated the various processes on a 'putting-out' basis. It was he who bought the raw material and had it delivered to the homes of the labourers, first to the spinners, then to the weavers and then to the fullers and dyers who turned it into finished cloth. It was he who paid them on a 'piecework' basis. It was also he who found a cloth factor to take it to market. The advantages of this system were manifold: it exploited cheap rural labour, increasingly available as the population expanded; it minimized the need for fixed capital; it gave peasants the opportunity to supplement the returns from their plots by working after dark or during slack periods of the agricultural year; it allowed the unskilled labour of women, children and the elderly to make a contribution to the household's income; it promoted the division of labour; and it evaded all the rules and regulations of the guilds, especially quality controls and limits on the size of enterprises.

That 'putting-out' to rural labourers suited the needs of the age was demonstrated most eloquently by the large and rapidly rising number of those involved. In Prussian Silesia, production of linen rose from 85,000 to 125,000 pieces between 1755 and 1775 and the number of looms from 19,810 in 1748 to 28,704 in 1790, by which time there were in excess of 50,000 people employed in the industry. Table 6 shows a comparable increase in the number of flax, cotton and wool spinners in Bohemia in the space of just eleven years between 1768 and 1779.

Table 6. Increases in Bohemian textile-spinner numbers during the 1760s and 1770s

Fibre	1768	1776	1779
Flax	79,520	100,454	229,400
Cotton	7,267	6,451	6,410
Wool	22,590	30,996	37,943

Source: James Van Horn Melton, *Absolutism and the Eighteenth-Century Origins of Compulsory Schooling in Prussia and Austria* (Cambridge, 1988)

Melton also estimates that in the province of Lower Austria the number employed in manufacturing rose from 19,733 in 1762 to 94,094 in 1783. Similar figures were recorded from the many other 'industrial landscapes' which developed during the course of the eighteenth century – in Italy: a broad band of Lombardy in the hills north of Milan from Val d'Aosta to Lake Garda, the riviera around Genoa and Tuscany north of the Arno; in the Iberian peninsula: Catalonia, which in 1770 was described by one visitor as 'a little England in the heart of Spain' and by the 1790s boasted the biggest concentration of dyers and weavers outside Lancashire; in France: Brittany, Maine, Picardy and Languedoc; in the southern Netherlands: Flanders and Twente; in the Holy Roman Empire: the lower Rhine, Westphalia, Baden, Württemberg, Silesia and southern Saxony; in the Habsburg Monarchy: Bohemia, Moravia and Lower and Upper Austria; in England: Lancashire, the West Riding of Yorkshire, the Cotswolds and East Anglia. The number of people employed was considerable, as every weaver's loom required around twenty-five ancillary personnel to keep it supplied, including six spinners. A good example of how putting-out could erode the position of the guilds was provided by the expansion of the bleaching industry in Elberfeld and Barmen, two adjacent towns in the Duchy of Berg on the lower Rhine. Originally a guild monopoly, the process moved into the surrounding countryside, making best use of the River Wupper, and expanded from 15 enterprises in 1690 to 100 in 1774 and 150 in 1792. Following the inevitable tussle with the guilds, the government lifted all restrictions on production in 1762.

This summary of the development of rural manufacturing has deliberately avoided use of the contentious concept 'proto-industrialization'. First coined in 1972, it was advanced by its supporters as an explanation for the breakthrough from traditional forms of manufacturing to the industrial revolution, being held responsible for population growth, the commercialization of agriculture, capital accumulation, the generation of surplus labour, proletarianization and the creation of large markets. Subsequent criticism has left little of all this intact. It has been argued in return that the region from which the phenomenon was first derived – Flanders – was exceptional, matched only by England and one or two other small enclaves on the continent. Sheilagh Ogilvie, the most effective critic of proto-industrialization, concludes:

In the rest of eighteenth-century Europe, proto-industry (like agriculture) was regulated by traditional institutions: guilds, merchant organisations, privileged towns, village communities, feudal landlords. The spate of research on proto-industrialisation has shown that industrial development was affected much more strongly by institutional variations than by the presence (or absence) of proto-industry.

From the point of view of the entrepreneur, the least attractive feature of putting-out was the lack of control over the workforce. The labourer worked unsupervised, at his own pace and when he felt like it. When the household's income reached a certain point, there was a tendency to prefer leisure to labour, even if the market – and the merchant – were crying out for more goods. One answer was to concentrate production in a single centre and to move from paying piece-rates to paying wages. That required higher fixed capital in the form of buildings, and consequently greater vulnerability to market fluctuations, but it did allow the workers to be supervised and kept up to their work. These 'manufactories' proved to be an effective way of responding to market opportunities in the eighteenth century. It has been estimated that there were about

1,000 of them in German-speaking Europe in 1800, of which 280 were in the Habsburg Monarchy (140 in Lower Austria and 90 in Bohemia), 220 in Prussia, 170 in Saxony and 150 in the Wittelsbach territories (Jülich-Berg, the Palatinate and Bavaria). Some of the individual units employed large numbers of workers on a central site: to select a few examples from the 1780s, the state-run woollen manufactory at Linz employed 102 dyers and finishers, a calico printing firm at Augsburg employed 350, the royal textile manufactory in Berlin employed *c.*400. Even luxury goods could record large numbers of factory workers, with around 400 at both Meissen and Berlin in 1750. Significantly, the further east one went, the more of these large enterprises were owned and run by great aristocratic magnates, exploiting both the raw materials and the cheap serf labour to be found on their estates. The greatest single entrepreneur in the Habsburg Monarchy was Count Heinrich Franz von Rottenhan, who established two large cotton factories and an ironworks on his Bohemian estates. Although the state was directly responsible for some of the largest concerns – the *Lagerhaus* in Berlin, for example, which made uniforms for the Prussian army – its numerical share was only about 6 per cent. On the other hand, there were numerous private individuals who amassed great fortunes from manufacturing – Schüle the 'calico king' of Augsburg, the Bolongaro brothers of Frankfurt am Main (tobacco), and the von der Leyen dynasty of Krefeld (silk), for example. Nor was the centralized manufactory a phenomenon confined to north-western Europe: in 1779 in Barcelona there were nine woollen factories employing 3,000, and there were many units in Russia with workforces numbered in thousands.

AN 'INDUSTRIAL REVOLUTION'?

Page upon page of evidence relating to the growing size of manufacturing units in Europe at the beginning of the nineteenth century could be paraded, but without adding much, apart from tedium. A more interesting question is whether the quantitative change was accompanied by a corresponding qualitative shift. To put the same question another way: was it just the old system producing more or had a structural change occurred? Until relatively recently, the answer would have been an unequivocal yes to the latter proposition. 'The industrial revolution', beginning in England in the second half of the eighteenth century, was for most of the nineteenth and twentieth centuries as fixed a point of reference as was the French Revolution of 1789. Indeed, they have been often coupled together to mark the start of the modern world, as they were by Eric Hobsbawm in his still-popular *The Age of Revolution*. Hobsbawm also provided a good traditional definition of the economic wing of his 'dual revolution':

What does the phrase 'the Industrial Revolution broke out' mean? It means that some time in the 1780s, and for the first time in human history, the shackles were taken off the productive power of human societies, which henceforth became capable of constant, rapid, and – up to the present – limitless multiplication of men, goods and services . . . The economy became, as it were, airborne.

However, whereas the term 'French Revolution' was in use by contemporaries from the start, 'Industrial Revolution' took much longer to get established. It was first used in the French form '*révolution industrielle*' in the 1820s and it was also a French pundit – the economist Jérôme Adolphe Blanqui – who first pronounced on the world-historical nature of the phenomenon when he wrote in 1831, 'industrial conditions were more profoundly transformed than at any time since the beginnings of social life'. It was yet another Frenchman, the historian Paul Mantoux, who provided the classic historiographical statement of its centrality to the modern world:

The modern factory system originated in England in the last third of the eighteenth century. From the beginning, its effects were so quickly felt and gave rise to such important results, that it has been aptly compared to a revolution, though it may be confidently asserted that few political revolutions ever had such far-reaching consequences.

These cross-Channel observers were perhaps more perspicacious than those directly affected, for in England the phrase did not catch on until much later. In the catalogue of the British Library, there are hundreds of titles published in the twentieth century containing the phrase 'industrial revolution', but only a handful from the nineteenth and none at all from the eighteenth. Although Friedrich Engels made frequent use of the term in *The Condition of the Working Class in England*, first published in 1845, the work was not translated from German into English until 1886. Two years previously, Arnold Toynbee's posthumous *Lectures on the*

Industrial Revolution in England had begun the term's long and busy career as a central organizing concept in British historiography.

Once established, the idea of an industrial revolution which reshaped first England, then continental Europe, and then much of the rest of the world, took a strong hold. Oceans of ink have been spilt debating whether it was a bad thing that reduced the working classes to a 'state of downright bestiality' (Richard Altick) or a good thing that trickled increased wealth down to the meanest mill-operative, but its actual existence was generally accepted. Indeed, the idea of a revolution occurring in the economic history of the world, which then affected every other aspect of human activity (a combination of Prometheus and Proteus, as it were), was given a new lease of life in the middle of the twentieth century. In *The Stages of Economic Growth*, first given as a series of lectures in Cambridge in 1959 and then published as a best-selling book, W. W. Rostow adopted an aeronautical metaphor to summarize what happened when the Industrial Revolution occurred: 'take-off'.

The take-off is the interval when the old blocks and resistances to steady growth are finally overcome. The forces making for economic progress, which yielded limited bursts and enclaves of modern activity, expand and come to dominate the society. Growth becomes its normal condition. Compound interest becomes built, as it were, into its habits and institutional structure.

Few, if any, terms originating in economics have achieved such general currency. Its acceptance was facilitated by the almost simultaneous publication (in 1962) of another hugely influential model of industrialization, namely Alexander Gerschenkron's *Economic Backwardness in Historical Perspective*, although he preferred a more fluid metaphor – 'great spurt'. The belief that such watersheds had occurred in the past and could happen again in the future was very much in the air in the boom years of the 1950s and 1960s, encouraging politicians to coin slogans such as 'the white heat of the technological revolution' (Harold Wilson) or 'the great leap forward' (Chairman Mao). Nor did the checks of the 1970s and 1980s, following the Yom Kippur War of 1973, kill the concept. On the contrary, the rapid developments in information technology in the late 1980s gave birth to the notion of a 'third Industrial Revolution', the first having been based on coal and iron and the second on chemicals and electricals. As such, it remains as vital as ever.

Yet there have always been dissenting voices. Just as political scientists such as de Tocqueville stressed the continuity between the old regime and post-Revolutionary France, so have there always been historians undertaking the same sort of exercise for economic development. While Rostow claimed that the British economy took off between 1783 and 1802, although conceding that it had taken a long time to taxi out from departure-gate to runway, others have suggested that it never got airborne, indeed that it was not an aeroplane at all. They see industrialization not as a revolution but as an evolutionary process, unsuited to mechanical metaphors. Rather it should be likened to an organism growing at moderate speed – something between an oak and a *leylandii* cypress. In particular they have drawn attention to the protean nature of the concept 'Industrial Revolution', lending itself to exploitation by both Marxists and apologists for western-style capitalism (Rostow subtitled his *Stages of Economic Growth* 'a non-communist manifesto'). Michael Fores, for example, has complained that it 'is a sort of turn-coat Vicar of Bray figure of scholarship, infinitely accommodating to the special interests of individual writers'. No one has stated this point of view more trenchantly than the late Rondo Cameron, who in an article provocatively entitled 'The industrial revolution – a misnomer', asserted: 'probably no term from the economic historians' lexicon has been more widely accepted by the public at large than "industrial revolution". That is unfortunate, because the term itself has no scientific standing and conveys a grossly misleading impression of the nature of economic change.'

This controversy has generated a huge amount of scholarly literature. As it involves such fundamental questions as the nature of historical change, indeed the nature of historical explanation per se, it can never be resolved, and certainly not here. However, it is necessary to examine, however briefly, some of the key economic areas involved in the period before 1815. A particularly strong argument in favour of the 'gradualists' can be found in the all-important field of communications. As we have seen in Chapter 1, many improvements were made during our period, none of them revolutionary but together having a cumulative effect sufficient to persuade contemporaries that a really major change had occurred. Looking back in 1784, the sixty-one-year-old German writer Friedrich Carl von Moser identified speed as the great development of his life. He recalled with nostalgia the good old days when the leisurely pace of travel accorded perfectly with the national character of the Germans, slow of thought and slow of motion. It was their neighbours, the French, who thought, acted, marched, shot, hunted, ate, walked and travelled quickly. But all that had changed, he noted, and now the Germans too were rushing hither and thither, as demonstrated by a recent journey he had undertaken on a new highway (*Chaussee*), which had been so fast 'that I ceased to be able to hear or see properly'.

One must wonder how Moser, who died in 1798, would have responded to a railway journey. He might well have joined those who speculated that the human body could not tolerate speeds in excess of 30 miles (48 km) per hour. Although the railway age is usually dated to the opening of the first regular passenger service in 1825, when a train pulled by a steam locomotive began to ply between Stockton and Darlington, even here it did not arrive like a clap of thunder in a blue sky. A clear distinction needs to be drawn between railways and steam locomotives. The great advantage of a railway, defined as parallel tracks along which wheeled vehicles can be drawn, is that it greatly reduces friction, and hence increases proportionally the load that can be pulled by a given motive force. The latter can be human, animal or mechanical. Wooden railways had been in use in German mines since around 1500 and can be found in England about a hundred years later. Their load-bearing capability was greatly increased when iron began to replace wood. Between 1768 and 1771 Richard Reynolds introduced cast-iron rails at the great Coalbrookdale ironworks near Telford in Shropshire, adding an inner flange to the rail to improve stability. Later rails were constructed from malleable iron and the flange was transferred to the wheel. Eventually there were more than 20 miles (32 km) of rails within the Coalbrookdale works.

These early railways were usually purely private enterprises, built, financed and run by mining companies, but there were a few horse-drawn public railways in existence before the end of the eighteenth century, such as the line from Croydon to Wandsworth for freight and from Swansea to Mumbles for passengers. Steam-power was first applied on an experimental basis by Richard Trevithick in the late 1790s. By 1804 he was able to demonstrate a locomotive on the line at the Pen-y-Darran ironworks in Glamorganshire, which pulled ten tons of ore and seventy passengers at 5 miles (8 km) per hour. As is often the way with technology, once the trail had been blazed, others quickly followed, notably John Blenkinsop, whose five-ton locomotive *Salamanca* pulled ninety tons of coal on a level surface at 4 miles (6.5 km) per hour in

1812; William Hedley, another locomotive builder but better known for patenting a smooth wheel and rail system in 1813; and of course George Stephenson, whose locomotive *Blücher* of 1814 was the first successful flanged-wheel adhesion locomotive and could pull thirty tons of coal up a hill at 4 miles (6.5 km) per hour. In short, the 'railway age' was well and truly underway before 1815 and had taken so long to come to fruition that 'revolution' does indeed seem something of a misnomer.

That applies to both aspects of what became known collectively as the 'railway', namely iron rails and steam-power. Indeed, the manufacture of iron had come into common use in Britain as early as the eighth century BC. It was discovered that heating iron-bearing ore to a high temperature with the use of charcoal, fanned by a draught of air, creates a solid lump of metal (a 'bloom'). When re-heated, the metal can be hammered into a shape. This is 'wrought iron'. If additional carbon is added to the ore, the melting temperature is reduced, which allows liquid iron ore to be poured into a mould. This is 'cast iron'. In the course of the fifteenth century, a furnace was developed which used blasts of heated and compressed air to drive up the temperature. This is a 'blast furnace'. The molten iron is run off into moulds consisting of a main channel connected to a number of shorter channels at right angles. As this resembles a sow suckling her pigs, the cast iron which results is known as 'pig iron'. A further innovation known as 'fining' allowed the impurities to be drawn off by oxidation, leaving semi-solid, malleable wrought iron in its place.

Two major innovations were made during our period. By the early eighteenth century, iron production in England was on the decline, not through want of demand but due to a shortage of the timber from which charcoal is made. In 1709, after much experimentation, the Quaker Abraham Darby succeeded in making iron using coke rather than charcoal. Coke is the residue left after mineral coal has been heated to a high temperature out of contact with air. As it is rich in carbon, it can substitute for charcoal both as a heating agent and as a necessary additive to the iron ore. On the other hand, because it is a much firmer, more robust substance, it can bear a much larger weight of iron ore in the furnace, thus allowing much larger furnaces to be built, with corresponding economies of scale. Darby's blast furnaces at Coalbrookdale were each soon producing up to ten tons of pig iron a week. As there were virtually limitless resources of coal, much of it close to the surface, the inhibition placed on iron production by timber shortage was removed.

The second major innovation was a response to the imbalance between improved pig-iron production and slow and inadequate 'fining'. In 1784 Henry Cort patented his 'puddling' process, which used a reverberatory furnace to turn pig iron into malleable iron. A reverberatory furnace uses hot air and gases to heat the metal, without allowing the latter to be polluted by coming into direct contact with the fuel used for heating. Puddling consists of stirring the molten pig iron on the bed of the furnace, thus allowing the circulating air to remove carbon and other impurities from the iron. Together with his development of a more efficient way of creating bar iron, patented the previous year, Cort's invention helped to encourage a rapid increase in iron production, which quadrupled during the next twenty years. Pig-iron output in Great Britain went from 17,350 long tons (a long ton is 2,240 pounds or 1,016 kg) in 1740 to 68,300 in 1788 to 125,079 in 1796 to 258,206 in 1806. Lord Sheffield, a prolific author on economic matters, predicted in 1786: 'it is not asserting too much to say that the result [of Cort's inventions] will be more advantageous to Great Britain than the possession of the thirteen colonies of America, for it will give the complete command of the iron trade to this country, with its vast advantages to navigation'. In 1750 Britain imported twice as much as iron as was manufactured at home, but by 1815 that relationship had been reversed to the extent that exports now outnumbered imports by a factor of five. It should be noted, however, that although iron production increased very rapidly, steel remained very much a minority metal. A technique for making steel in a crucible was discovered in the 1740s but it remained very expensive and confined to cutlery manufacture. Cheap steel did not become available until the middle of the following century.

A similarly gradual story unfolded in the second component of the railways – steam-power. Once again, innovation was driven by need. In this case, it was the need to pump water out of coalmines that had to go deeper as the surface seams were exhausted. In 1702 one mine in Warwickshire was using more than 500 horses to work the pumps. The first mechanical pump was invented by Thomas Savery in 1698. This ingenious device consisted essentially of a large metal container filled with steam. Cool water was then poured on to the metal casing, causing the steam inside to condense, thus creating a vacuum, which in turn drew up water from the mine. This was patented as the 'Miner's Friend', but it was barely practical, since the alternate cooling and heating was hugely wasteful and the tin-soldered joins proved to be positively lethal in their failure to handle the steam pressure consistently. Much more efficient was Thomas Newcomen's 'atmospheric engine' of 1705, which used the partial vacuum created by condensing steam to move a piston inside a cylinder. This machine also had distinct limitations: it was slow and voracious in its appetite for coal. Indeed, its thermal efficiency was only about 1 per cent, or in other words of every hundred units of coal consumed, only one was actually used to pump water. However, the cost of coal was of little concern at the pit-head and Newcomen engines were introduced into almost all the large mines in Great Britain within a few years. By the middle of the eighteenth century there were more than fifty in use in the Newcastle coalfields alone.

The real breakthrough came when James Watt, a Glasgow instrument-maker, found a way of dispensing with the hot-cold routine that had made previous steam-engines so inefficient. While repairing the University of Glasgow's model Newcomen engine, he saw a way of employing all the steam generated: 'the idea came into my mind that, as steam was an elastic body, it would rush into a vacuum, and, if a communication were made between the cylinder and an exhausted vessel, it would rush into it, and might be there condensed without cooling the cylinder'. In 1769 he patented his 'new method for lessening the consumption of steam and fuel in fire engines', formed a partnership with the great Birmingham manufacturer Matthew Boulton and began producing steam-engines for use, not just in coalmines but in all forms of industry. Further developments by Watt, notably the double-action engine invented in the early 1780s, improved efficiency still further. It has been suggested, not without reason, that this was a truly epochal moment, because for the first time in its history, humankind had at its disposal a source of power wholly independent of location. Karl Marx made the point well in *Das Kapital*:

Not till the invention of Watt's second and so-called double-acting steam-engine, was a prime mover found, that begot its own force by the consumption of coal and water, whose power was entirely under man's control, that was mobile and a means of locomotion, that was urban and not, like the waterwheel, rural, that permitted production to be concentrated in towns instead of, like the water-wheels, being scattered up and down the country, that was of universal technical application, and, relatively speaking, little affected in its choice of residence by local circumstances. The greatness of Watt's genius showed itself in the specification of the patent that he took out in April, 1784. In that specification his steam-engine is described, not as an invention for a specific purpose, but as an agent universally applicable in Mechanical Industry.

Marx was writing in the middle of the following century, by which time the full implications of Watt's inventions were there for all to see. At the time, there was less excitement. By 1800 there were only about a thousand steam-engines of various kinds in operation across the length and breadth of the United Kingdom. In terms of horse-power generated, they were still heavily outpointed by traditional energy sources, especially water-power, still very important in the woollen industry. Peter Mathias has estimated that even wind-power may have made a larger contribution than steam-power in 1800 and, moreover, that about 50 per cent of the latter was still being produced by Newcomen-type engines.

If neither metallurgy nor steam-power can sustain the concept of an industrial revolution, the sole remaining candidate is textiles, more specifically cotton. If less ancient than iron, cotton had nevertheless been around for a long time, first reaching Europe from Egypt around AD 900. In the eighteenth century it was mainly imported from Brazil, the Caribbean islands, the Middle East and India. Small amounts were grown around the Mediterranean and on the Portuguese and Spanish islands of the eastern Atlantic. The first cotton from the USA did not arrive until 1784. In understanding the significance of the innovations of the late eighteenth century, it is important to understand why cotton was an attractive but problematic fibre. Its great advantages are that it is flat, hollow, with a natural twist and a long 'staple' (the natural length of the fibre). Consequently, it combines comfort with strength and durability. Its great disadvantage is that it is very labour-intensive. The cotton 'bolls' which grow on the plant have to be harvested, ginned (separating the seed from the fibres), cleaned, roved (drawing out, lengthening and twisting) and carded (combing out, straightening and making the fibres naturally parallel) before it can be spun into yarn and then woven into cloth. The process has been described very well by Henry Hobhouse in his classic study *Seeds of Change*:

It was comparatively easy to grow a good crop of cotton, but picking a hundred pounds of bolls would take two man-days; ginning would take fifty man-days at best; and baling by hand, cleaning and carding another twenty man-days. All this effort resulted in only about eight pounds of spinnable cotton, which would then require twenty-five to forty man-days to spin. An ethnic cotton thread, therefore, cost twelve to fourteen man-days of labour per pound. Even if some of this was cheaper child labour, or adolescent labour, the cost of this boring work was still high and inescapable. Compared to one pound of cotton, one pound of wool at the same date took at most one to two man-days from raw material to thread, linen two to five and silk about six.

As Hobhouse adds laconically, 'No wonder cotton was the luxury cloth in 1784.' Only mechanization could turn it into a cloth for mass consumption. The process came in fits and starts, with a number of inventions designed primarily for other fabrics. John Kay's 'flying shuttle' of 1733, for example, which doubled a weaver's productivity, was intended for woollens. However, it called for a corresponding increase in the spinning of yarn, which encouraged the invention of mechanical spinning devices. Lewis Paul and John Wyatt's roller spinning machine, patented in 1738, James Hargreaves' spinning-jenny, invented in 1764 and patented in 1769, Richard Arkwright's water frame of 1769 and Samuel Crompton's 'mule' of 1779 (so-called because it combined the functions of both the jenny and the frame) combined to bring a massive increase in productivity, economies of scale, improvements in quality and a precipitous fall in the cost of yarn. Such was the degree of change that it caught the eye of poets – of John Dyer, for example, who in 'The Happy Workhouse and the Good Effects of Industry' of 1757 recorded:

> We next are shown
> A circular machine of new design,
> In conic shape: it draws and spins a thread
> Without the tedious toil of needless hands.
> A wheel, invisible beneath the floor,
> To ev'ry member of th' harmonious frame
> Gives necessary motion. One, intent,
> O'erlooks the work: the carded wool, he says,
> Is smoothly lapped around those cylinders,
> Which, gently turning, yield it to yon cirque
> Of upright spindles which, with rapid whirl,
> Spin out in long extent an even twine.

By 1800 the cost of very fine yarn was one quarter of what it had been twenty years earlier. Cotton benefited most from these and other inventions, because its tough composition suited the crude technology of the early machines, because of a long-term shift in fashion towards lighter fabrics, because export markets in warmer climates were opened up and because the wearing of underwear became habitual for all classes. Sidney Pollard has estimated that a labourer spinning by hand needed more than 50,000 hours to work 100 pounds (45 kg) of cotton; Crompton's mule of 1780 needed 2,000 hours; and the power-assisted mule introduced in the mid 1790s needed just 300. In other words, the productivity of labour rose over 150 times in the course of the eighteenth century. The amount of cotton imported into Britain increased from 2,500,000 pounds (1,135,000 kg) in 1750 to 22,000,000 (nearly 10,000,000 kg) in 1787, by which time most of it was being cleaned, carded and spun by machines. As measured by the consumption of raw cotton, production increased ten times between 1760 and 1785 and then more than ten times between 1785 and 1827.

There was a clear appreciation among contemporaries that something momentous had happened. John Aikin wrote in 1795 that 'the rapid and prodigious increase of cotton manufacture is, perhaps, absolutely unparalleled in the annals of trading nations'. Yet numerous qualifications have to be made to what might be looking like a revolutionary scenario. After the promising spurt of productivity represented by the flying shuttle, weaving failed to keep pace with spinning. Edmund Cartwright patented a 'power loom' in 1785 but, despite subsequent improvements, the problem of combining speed with continuity was defeated by repeated breakages of the yarn. By 1815 there were only about 2,400 power looms in operation in the United Kingdom. Mechanical weaving was to be a nineteenth-century phenomenon. It has also been pointed out, by Samuel Lilley for example, that the jennies, frames and mules did not represent a technological breakthrough comparable with, say, the discovery of synthetic dyes or wireless telegraphy. He adds that 'the early stages of the Industrial Revolution – roughly up to 1800 – were based very largely on using medieval techniques and on extending these to their limits'. What Hargreaves, Arkwright and the rest did was to take different parts of the traditional spinning-wheel and put them together in new combinations. It has also been pointed out that in purely quantitative terms, the contribution made by cotton to the national economy was modest. Peter Mathias's figures suggest that in the 1760s it amounted to less than half a per cent and was still less than 1 per cent in the 1780s. In 1770 cotton added £600,000 to the Gross Domestic Product, but wool added £7,000,000 and leather £5,000,000.

Of all the products associated with the British industrial revolution, cotton was also the one that spread furthest, fastest and earliest to the continent. However tedious, the following information gleaned from a number of regional studies gives some idea of the ubiquity of cotton manufacturing by 1815: at Rouen the number of manufactories increased by 1,800 per cent between 1763 and 1785 and by 800 per cent at Bolbec; at Mulhouse in Alsace, the number of printed cotton pieces increased from 30,000 to 120,000 between the 1750s and the 1790s; in 1786 the French imported 11,000,000 pounds (5,000,000 kg) of raw cotton (the British were importing about 18,000,000 pounds (over 8,000,000 kg) at the same time); during the last quarter of the eighteenth century, cotton began to be worked to the north-west of Milan in Gallarate, Busto Arizio and Vercelli; a cotton mill using the mule jenny was established at Monza in 1795; cotton manufacturing in Russia began with the firm of Chamberlain and Cousins in 1755 and spread quickly; between 1782 and 1786 ten cotton factories were set up in Prague; the Catalonian cotton industry was employing 80,000 by 1792; in the Austrian Netherlands, cotton factories were established at Antwerp, Brussels, Mechlin and Tournai; in Alsace in 1806 there were 25,026 people working in various branches of the cotton industry, or nearly half of all industrial workers in the province; in the *département* of the Roër (the northernmost of the four new *départements* created when the west bank of the Rhine was annexed to France) there were 65,000 people – *c.* 10 per cent of the total population – working in 2,500 factories in 1811; in Europe as a whole in 1815 there were 1,500,000 spindles in the cotton industry, of which 1,000,000 were in France, 250,000 in Saxony and 150,000 in Switzerland. This kind of information could be replicated at will, but that will do.

Many of these enterprises were organized on a putting-out basis and many of them were manufactories rather than mechanized factories. Nevertheless, there is plenty of evidence that British technology found its way to the continent. Some entrepreneurs moved there to seek their fortunes, as did none other than John Kay when he failed to maintain his patent rights to his flying shuttle. The French authorities gave him a grant of 3,000 *livres* and paid him an annual salary of 2,500 *livres* to tour Normandy to teach workers how to use his invention, while three of Kay's sons made shuttles in a Paris workshop. It spread through industrial espionage, with machinery being copied and operatives being bribed to divulge secrets. In 1785, for example, a German spy called Baden, arrested in Lancashire, was fined the very substantial sum of £500 for trying to recruit machine operatives. By 1815 local versions of jennies, frames and mules were in operation right across Europe, from Belgium to Russia.

Why were the British first in the field? No one explanation will work, for it is next to impossible to find a single characteristic peculiar to the British economy. Was it perhaps the excellent communications, both natural and man-made? The Dutch Republic was equal if not superior in this regard. Was it the accumulation of commercial and financial expertise, the integrated money market, the advanced commercial agriculture, the flexible social structure, the religious toleration, the relative immunity from war-damage? Here too the Dutch were at least equal and several other European countries boasted at least some of these factors. Was it the availability of raw materials, especially coal and iron ore (which the Dutch lacked)? Yet Belgium and several parts of western and central Germany were equally favoured. And so on. Perhaps a combination of all these advantages was needed to achieve the critical mass.

It is also possible that to look exclusively at the supply side of the economy is to invite certain disappointment. It was on the demand side that the British were so special. As Neil McKendrick has stated firmly in a seminal study, 'There was a consumer revolution in eighteenth-century England. More men and women than ever before in human history enjoyed the experience of acquiring material possessions ... The consumer revolution was the necessary analogue to the industrial revolution, the necessary convulsion on the demand side of the equation to match the convulsion on the supply side.' What in the past had been seen as luxuries now became 'decencies' and what had been decencies now became necessities. The work of McKendrick, Sir John Plumb, Roy Porter and John Brewer has shown how eighteenth-century Britain, and especially eighteenth-century England, was increasingly gripped by a rage for spending which transformed the economy.

As Plumb observed, 'to spend has been the rising chord of Western capitalism' and 'aggressive consumption lies at the heart of successful bourgeois society'. The concept of the classless customer who was always right took hold, as Adam Smith recognized in *The Wealth of Nations* in 1776: 'consumption is the sole end and purpose of all production; and the interests of the producer ought to be attended to, only in so far as it may be necessary for promoting that of the consumer. This maxim is ... perfectly self-evident.' Ultimately, what encouraged the Darbys and the Arkwrights to come up with ways of satisfying the market's appetite was the knowledge that these eager consumers were out there looking for products to purchase. As David Landes has observed, 'what distinguished the British economy ... was an exceptional sensitivity and responsiveness to pecuniary opportunity. This was a people fascinated by wealth and commerce, collectively and individually.' Of course, there were consumers on the continent, notably in the Low Countries and in urban centres, but nowhere were they so numerous and so confident.

The British viewed continental developments with a complacency born of the knowledge that imitation is the sincerest form of flattery. They could afford to be patronizing in 1815, because they knew that the twenty-two years of warfare which had just ended had turned what was already a gap between the British and continental economies into a chasm. The reasons for this development must await consideration in a later chapter; here we can conclude with the question of whether the political revolution in France was accompanied, or perhaps even preceded, by an industrial revolution in Great Britain. A Marxist historian such as Eric Hobsbawm is in no doubt that it was:

If the sudden, qualitative and fundamental transformation, which happened in or about the 1780s, was not a revolution then the word has no commonsense meaning ... The Revolution itself, the 'take-off period', can probably be dated with as much precision as is possible in such matters, to some time within the twenty years from 1780 to 1800: contemporary with, but slightly prior to, the French Revolution. By any reckoning this was probably the most important event in world history, at any rate since the invention of agriculture and cities. And it was initiated by Britain.

There is nothing ideological about such a view, although Hobsbawm likes to think that conservative (i.e. non-Marxist) historians are naturally uneasy with anything to do with revolution. The American economic historian David Landes is equally convinced of the revolutionary nature of what happened in Britain in the late eighteenth century, and almost repeated Hobsbawm's words when he wrote, 'The technological changes that we denote as the "Industrial Revolution" implied a far more drastic break with the past than anything since the invention of the wheel.' On the other hand it is undeniable that scholars who see Great Britain as an 'old regime' see not revolutionary change but continuity. Jonathan Clark has written, with characteristic trenchancy, 'The "Industrial Revolution" is . . . not a thing, still less an event, but a term of historical art adopted long afterwards to celebrate an alleged watershed between premodernity and modernity: where the French Revolution brought to an end the *Ancien Régime* in France, the Industrial Revolution was supposed to have done the same in England.'

The economic historians have provided plenty of statistical evidence to support Clark's view. They have pushed the origins of industrialization further and further back in time, while simultaneously post-dating the effects. As David Cannadine has put it, the industrial revolution has been 'almost written out of modern British history'. In 1989, the bicentenary of the French Revolution, Donald Coleman summed up the current state of play:

If the evidence, largely in the form of contemporary statistics or ingenious modern reconstructions is approximately correct . . . then it would seem that before 1830 economic growth was slow, with neither output nor incomes per head showing much increase; and notable change, economic and technical, was severely limited. Only after the mid-century did the economy show much significant difference and even then it was more a matter of structural change, from agriculture towards industry, than the attainment of higher productivity. In short, continuity has been stressed and the discontinuity implied by the idea of a revolution downgraded or even dismissed.

How are we to resolve this dispute? Paradoxically, a clue to a possible solution is provided by Clark in a piece of evidence which he presents in support of his argument against the notion of an industrial revolution but may perhaps point in more than one direction. It is an extract from a treatise published in 1815 by the manufacturer and social reformer Robert Owen:

Those who were engaged in the trade, manufactures, and commerce of this country thirty or forty years ago, formed but a very insignificant portion of the knowledge, wealth, influence, or population of the Empire.

Prior to that period, Britain was essentially agricultural. But, from that time to the present, the home and foreign trade have increased in a manner so rapid and extraordinary as to have raised commerce to an importance, which it never previously attained in any country possessing so much political power and influence. This change has been owing chiefly to the mechanical inventions which introduced the cotton trade into this country.

The immediate effects of this manufacturing phenomenon were a rapid increase of wealth, industry, population and political influence of the British empire; and by the aid of which it has been enabled to contend for five-and-twenty years against the most formidable military and *immoral* power [France] that the world perhaps ever contained.

Clark believes that this shows Owen looking primarily to Britain's *commercial* prosperity as the key to its survival. It does indeed do that, but it also links the commercial transformation of the country 'chiefly to the mechanical inventions which introduced the cotton trade into this country'. Like most contemporaries, Owen did not make the econometrician's fine distinctions between various forms of wealth creation. What he saw was an expansion of the British economy proceeding so fast and so far as to justify revolutionary status, even if he did not use the phrase 'industrial revolution'. He looked around him and saw paupers going from rags to riches in just a few years. In Lancashire in 1780 it was recorded that within a single decade 'a poor man not worth £5, now keeps his carriage and servants, is become Lord of a Manor, and has purchased an estate of £20,000'. Significantly, Owen also linked this material prosperity to political stability and military success. The 'Second Hundred Years War', which had begun with the Glorious Revolution of 1688, had finally been resolved in Britain's favour on the field of Waterloo in the year that Owen published his pamphlet. As we shall discover in a later chapter, the latest phase of that conflict, between 1793 and 1815, greatly increased Britain's economic lead over her old enemy. To the triumphalist British, this seemed to be a victory not just of one country but of a whole culture, based on liberty, Protestantism and prosperity, the three foundations of their country's greatness. In other words, what contemporaries experienced as a fundamental change in their economy was part of a wider complex of developments, which in just a century had turned an offshore island of marginal economic and political significance into the mistress of the world. Viewed in this way, the changes in commerce and manufacturing do deserve their revolutionary status. The world was transformed by industrialization, it did begin in Great Britain and it did begin in this period.

4

Agriculture and the Rural World

THE PROBLEM OF PRODUCTIVITY

Nothing separates the modern world more from the old regime than the relative importance of agriculture and the countryside. At the beginning of the twenty-first century, just under 400,000 people are engaged in agriculture in England, or 1.7 per cent of the working population. Moreover, the overwhelming majority of those who live in rural areas commute each day to towns and are urban in outlook. Almost none of the food they consume is grown locally, indeed most of it is imported from abroad. In England in 1700 about 80 per cent of the population lived in the countryside, more than two-thirds of them working directly on the land and most of the remainder deriving their income from agriculture indirectly. In addition to supplying almost all the food they ate, English agriculture also produced raw materials for the country's industries (wool, leather, tallow, madder, hops, etc.), provided seasonal employment for many town-dwellers, and generated the capital and credit to sustain the country's manufacturing sector. Moreover, apart from a few metropolises such as London and Bristol, most 'towns' looked more like villages and existed to service the local agricultural economy. If that was true of one of the most commercialized economies in Europe, it applied with correspondingly greater force to the wholly rural regions of the centre and the east. Despite sporadic signs that the economic balance of power was beginning to shift, in 1815, as in 1660, the country was king.

It had been so since the beginning of human history. The predominance of agriculture, in the sense of organized cultivation of the earth, however, was of much more recent origin. It is worth recalling that *Homo sapiens* has existed ten times longer than civilization (and twenty times longer if Neanderthal man is accorded human status). It was only around 10,000 BC that the hand-to-mouth existence of hunting and gathering began to be supplemented by the cultivation of crops and the domestication of animals. The momentous nature of this change can hardly be exaggerated. For the first time, humankind was able to produce and store a surplus, thus making civilization possible. A first but giant step had been taken towards the domination, control and exploitation of the planet.

The early agriculturalists were confronted by a problem which was still acute ten millennia later, namely that although orderly cultivation greatly enhanced production, the soil was soon exhausted. If worthwhile yields were to be achieved, either new land had to be sown or the old plot had to be rested periodically. It was the manner of addressing this fundamental problem that determined patterns of European agriculture between 1660 and 1815. Much depended on the density of population and the availability of land. Where the former was thin and the latter was large, the cultivators could afford to be prodigal. In Finland, the enormous, virtually empty forests allowed swidden farming on a four-year cycle. In the first year, the trees were stripped of their bark and allowed to dry out. In the second year, the desiccated trunks were burnt down and the ash was left to be absorbed into the ground, a process which continued through the third year. Finally, in the fourth year, seed was sown in soil which was now so fertile that yields of between ten and twenty to one could be achieved, or, in other words, for every seed sown, between ten and twenty were produced. Unimpressive by modern standards (yields of eighty to one are achieved for wheat on East Anglian farms) this was an impressive score for the eighteenth century, as we shall see. However, the drawback of this 'slash and burn' approach, which was also employed in Sweden and northern Russia, was that not only did it lead to massive deforestation, but the land was very soon exhausted and had to be abandoned, often for decades. A similar approach was adopted on the steppes of southern Russia, where crops were planted on natural grassland, which was then allowed to revert to steppe when yields fell, as they very soon did.

In more settled and densely populated regions, this kind of agriculture could not be practised. In most parts of Europe a pattern had developed which divided the community's arable land into two alternating parts, one of which was cultivated and one of which was allowed to lie 'fallow'.

Depending on the natural fertility of the soil, the land was left fallow every other year in a 'two-field' system or every third year in a 'three-field' system. In other words, at any one time, half or a third of the arable land was not being cultivated. In France, for example, a three-field system became established in the fertile grain-growing regions north of the Loire, with wheat or rye being grown during the first year, spring cereals such as barley or oats during the second, and fallow for the third. In the less-favoured south, a two-field system had to be employed; indeed, where the soil was thin and the climate harsh, as in the mountains or on the Auvergne plateau, much longer periods of fallow had to be allowed. Throughout the Iberian peninsula, despite periodic attempts to move to a three-field system, soil conditions dictated the dominance of the two-field system, as they also did at the other end of Europe, in Scandinavia.

With at least a third of the land out of cultivation at any one time, productivity was correspondingly low and the proportion of the population required to till the soil was correspondingly high. Progress was impeded in part by sheer ignorance. Until it was known that plants synthesize their proteins from inorganic nitrogen compounds in the soil, the need replace the all-important nitrogen could not be appreciated. Indeed, nitrogen itself was not discovered until c.1770. What eighteenth-century cultivators could observe, however, was that the use of manure increased the fertility of the soil and reduced the need for fallow. That is because animals pass through their system most of the nitrogen present in the food they eat (as well as other fertilizing ingredients, notably phosphorus and potash). However, a great deal of their waste is needed, as a ton (2,240 pounds or 1,016 kg) of animal manure contains only 10 pounds (4.5 kg) of nitrogen. Once these natural ingredients had been synthesized, cheap and plentiful fertilizers became universally available, but that was to be very much a development of the nineteenth century. When Sir Humphry Davy gave a course of lectures to the British Board of Agriculture in 1813, later published as *Elements of Agricultural Chemistry*, his subject was very much in its infancy. As he complained to his audience: 'agricultural chemistry has not yet received a regular and systematic form. It has been pursued by competent experimenters for a short time only; the doctrines have not as yet been collected into any elementary treatise.'

Denied the factories of ICI or BASF to produce nitrates in industrial quantities, early modern cultivators had to rely on their animals, or – if they were more enterprising and less squeamish – on the 'night soil' produced by the human population. But they found themselves trapped by the 'infernal circle of the fallow'. The need for fallow resulted in low productivity. But as the great majority of Europeans relied on cereals for their subsistence, they were obliged to devote a high percentage of their land to arable farming. That necessarily meant that only a low percentage could be devoted to pasture and the maintenance of livestock, which in turn limited the amount of manure available. And that necessitated leaving the land fallow every second or third year, which brings us back to low productivity and square one.

BREAKING THE 'INFERNAL CIRCLE OF THE FALLOW'

This circle could be broken, indeed it had been broken in many places in north-west Europe before 1700. It could be broken, first by planting crops on the fallow land which not only did not exhaust the soil but actually rejuvenated it by putting back precious nitrogen. This was a technique known to the Germans as '*Besömmerung*' ('summering'). Several plant varieties were tried, depending on soil and climate, including peas, vetch (a bean-like fruit of various species of the leguminous plant *vicia*), potatoes, esparsette or sainfoin (*Onobrychis viciifolia*) and buckwheat, but the most effective were various kinds of roots (turnips, swedes, mangelwurzels, etc.) and artificial pasture, especially clover. The last-named were the most effective because they could be stored and used as forage for additional livestock during the winter months. In particular, roots and hay could be used to promote stall-feeding, which in turn facilitated the collection of manure, the maximization of its benefits and the reduction of the need for fallow. In other words, the infernal circle could not only be arrested, it could be put into reverse.

From 'summering' it was a short step to devising rotations of crops which eliminated fallow altogether. In Flanders elaborate sequences had been developed as early as the fourteenth century, although that degree of precocity was exceptional. It was not until the late seventeenth century that significant shifts away from the old open-field system could be registered. In England by 1700 the 'Norfolk' four-course system had spread from its eponymous origin to several other counties. This called for a winter-sown crop, usually wheat, in the first year, turnips in the second, a spring-sown crop, barley for example, in the third, but undersown with clover and rye-grass, which was then grazed and/or cut in the fourth. To maintain nitrogen levels and thus productivity, an optimum balance had to be struck between the production of cereals and the maintenance of livestock in an alternating pattern of 'convertible husbandry'. As in so many other forms of economic progress, it was the Low Countries that were the pioneers, although the English liked to think that they formed the vanguard. Richard Bradley proudly claimed in his *General Treatise of Husbandry and Gardening; Containing a New System of Vegetation: Illustrated with Many Observations and Experiments* of 1726 that, 'The Improvement of Land and the Study of Agriculture, have greatly contributed to render our Nation famous above all other Countries'. Although it was certainly in the north-west corner of Europe that agricultural change had proceeded most generally, contemporary reports show that the elimination of fallow had been achieved in many parts of the Holy Roman Empire too: in Brandenburg, for example, where an enterprising major, Joachim Friedrich von Kleist, introduced new rotations in the second half of the eighteenth century and more than doubled the value of his estate. From Erfurt, whose hinterland had the reputation of being 'the market garden of Germany', Christian Reichardt recorded that he had developed an eighteen-year rotation of cereals and vegetables which eliminated the need for fallow and did not require frequent manuring. Travelling through the Electorate of Mainz in 1765, Thomas Pennant recorded, 'in my road to Hanau passed thro' a flat rich country abounding with Indian Corn [maize], Beets, Kidney Beans, Cabbages and Potatoes'. Even south of the Alps pockets of productivity could be found, in the Po valley, for example, or around Vicenza, where the use of artificial pastures from the mid-eighteenth century soon doubled grain yields, or around Valencia in southern Spain, where Joseph Townsend found sophisticated rotations in operation in 1787.

Agricultural reformers who had witnessed what the rotation of crops could achieve by way of increased productivity could become most indignant when confronted by traditional patterns. Perhaps the most knowledgeable, certainly the most emphatic, was Arthur Young, who travelled extensively in England, France and Italy. He found plenty to admire in French agriculture, although perhaps significantly it was the peripheral regions such as Flanders, Artois and Alsace that caught his approving eye. Again and again he marvelled at the abundance and variety of the country's natural produce. Yet he just as often lamented that what Providence had bestowed with such a generous hand, man spoiled through ignorance, 'for fallows disgrace in some rich districts the finest soils imaginable'. In Picardy, Normandy, the Pays de Beauce or the Pays de Caux, the 'noble soil is full of beggary and weeds'. Warming to his work, he went on:

To detail all the barbarous rotations which ignorance has spread through Bretagne, Maine and Anjou would be tedious. The general feature of their management is to pare and burn the fields exhausted, abandoned, and by time recovered, that a succession of crops may bring it once more into the same situation. A change of the rotation of crops is the only thing wanted to alter the face of these provinces.

In Lorraine and Franche-Comté, the 'miserable routine' of the three-field system was 'a disgrace to the cultivators'. Although he found 'the worst husbandry in Great-Britain' immediately outside Cambridge on the road to St Neots, Young's benchmark had been provided by the agriculture he found in East Anglia and described in considerable detail in his four-volume *The Farmer's Tour through the East of England. Being The Register of a Journey through various Counties of this Kingdom, to enquire into the State of Agriculture* of 1771. Although he did not use the word 'revolution', that in effect was what he was describing. During the previous two generations, he observed, the agriculture of Norfolk in particular had been transformed. This he ascribed to seven reasons:

- enclosures
- the use of marl (a kind of soil consisting principally of clay mixed with carbonate of lime, forming a loose unconsolidated mass, valuable as a fertilizer)
- new rotations
- turnips
- clover and rye-grass
- long leases
- 'By the country being divided chiefly into large farms'

Was Arthur Young right to be so indignant? If eliminating the fallow was such a simple matter, was it just lethargy and ignorance that kept so much land out of cultivation? As we shall see, it was a complicated nexus of cultural, geographical, political, social and economic forces that kept most of Europe's agriculture locked in a cycle of low productivity. Ignorance certainly did play a part. It is no accident that the most innovative regions were also among the most productive. Literate cultivators found it easier to gain access to the rapidly growing body of literature and to give the lie to Voltaire's quip that, 'Many useful publications are written about agriculture and everyone reads them, with the exception of the peasants.' There were certainly plenty of well-meaning agronomists spreading the productivity gospel with missionary zeal. In Italy, an agricultural academy, the Accademia dei Georgofili, was founded in Tuscany in 1753, the first of many such initiatives, often followed by the publication of periodicals and pamphlets. The first Italian chair in agricultural science was founded at Padua in 1765. Travelling through Italy in 1789, Arthur Young was presented by his fellow agronomist Tartini with a copy of his *Giornale d'Agricultura di Firenze*, although the gift was accompanied by the depressing comment that the venture had folded due to lack of interest. However, he did add complacently, 'a professor of agriculture, in Sicily, being sent by his sovereign, and wisely sent, to England for instruction in agriculture, appears to me to be an epoch in the history of the human mind'. The German-speaking world was also prolific: in 1803 an agronomist teaching at the Prussian University of Frankfurt an der Oder compiled an agricultural bibliography with more than 6,000 titles.

OBSTACLES TO AGRICULTURAL GROWTH

However, knowledge of what to do and how to do it was only the first, and by no means the most difficult, step. Let us imagine that a French peasant working in a traditional three-field system found out about the advantages of 'summering' and decided to grow turnips on his share of the fallow field. Just as soon as the first shoot appeared above the surface, he would be confronted by what was arguably the greatest obstacle to agricultural progress, namely the communal structure of cultivation. Every member of the community, both noble and commoner, had the right to graze cattle on the land that was fallow, on the cultivated fields after the harvest had been gathered in and on the meadows after the first hay crop. This right was known as '*vaine pâture*' in France, but its equivalent could be found wherever there were open fields. Together with '*parcours*', the reciprocal right of *vaine pâture* enjoyed by two or more neighbouring communities, it was one part of a community-based approach to economic life which required all decisions to be taken collectively – what to sow, when to sow, where to sow, when to harvest, how to harvest, and so on. No great stretch of the imagination is required to appreciate the inertia built into this system. If a convoy can move only at the pace of its slowest member, communally organized agriculture lay permanently becalmed in a Sargasso Sea of tradition.

Returning to our imaginary enterprising French peasant, his attempt to breathe new life into the motionless sails of his village's agriculture would soon be punished by walking the plank. To prevent his neighbours' cattle consuming his turnips, his obvious course of action was to erect a fence and thus enclose his plot. The most likely response would be direct action to demolish the barrier, but legal action would certainly have been justified. In other words, any cultivator seeking to break with tradition needed not just knowledge, enterprise and courage, he also needed the support of the authorities. There was no excuse for the latter not appreciating the check on productivity imposed by *vaine pâture*, denounced by agronomists as 'barbarous', 'savage' and – that most pejorative of mid-eighteenth-century epithets – 'gothic'. From the rich variety of denunciations, the following, from the leading French agronomist Henri-Louis Duhamel du Monceau, is particularly authoritative:

One would scarcely imagine that customs so barbarous, and so opposite to the progress of agriculture, should be in some sort authorized by prescription, and even encouraged, or at least winked at, by the magistrates: the fact is however certain; and the partisans of this custom [*vaine pâture*] have the confidence to assert, that it is absolutely necessary for the encouragement of the increase of cattle. What a strange error is this! Can we possibly think that the means of increasing the number of our cattle can consist in what deprives us of the opportunity of providing for them a sufficiency of food? Experience has often convinced us that two acres of good lucerne will maintain four oxen, or as many cows, for six months in the year, with a very small addition of ordinary fodder: how many acres of stubble would the same number of cattle require to maintain them? Cows and oxen would be in bad case had they no other food but what the stubbles afford. This custom, far from favouring the increase of cattle, is a real obstacle to it: this is so evident, that I think it quite unnecessary to prove it.

For aspiring reformers like Duhamel du Monceau, the English example seemed to point the way to the future. A magistrate of the Parlement of Metz observed, 'we might perhaps not have realized that this practice was a bad one if the English had not taught us what the land is capable of. Without the shadow cast by the picture of their agriculture on ours, we might still believe like our fathers that rights of *vaine pâture* were a bondage.'

So why was Prometheus not unbound? When the first reliable agricultural census in France was conducted in 1840, it showed that 27 per cent of the soil was still fallow and only 6 per cent devoted to artificial pastures. During the previous hundred years or so, certainly some initiatives had been taken, both at a local and a national level. The most promising was the drive launched by the luxuriously named Henri-Léonard-Jean-Baptiste Bertin, comte de Bourdeilles, who was controller-general of finances between 1759 and 1763. He planned to allow every member of a community to withdraw up to a fifth of his land from the *vaine pâture* on condition that it was then used for the cultivation of artificial pasture and was enclosed with a ditch or hedge. The scheme was sent to the senior provincial officials (intendants) and agricultural societies for comment, a procedure which took a great amount of time and yielded inconclusive results. No national legislation ever was introduced. It was left to individual Parlements, Estates and intendants to do what they could – and although that turned out to be not negligible, neither was it adequate. They were inhibited by a belief that communal rights such as *vaine pâture* represented a legitimate form of property. As Guillaume-François Joly de Fleury, controller-general of finances in the early 1780s, put it: 'The rights of *vaine pâture*, having been established for the greater part by customary arrangements, it does not seem possible to interfere with them since they constitute a sort of property belonging to the community of inhabitants.' Another powerful consideration was the knowledge that the abolition of a communal structure and the introduction of individual initiative would discriminate against those who eked out a living on the margins of rural society. As is so often the case, greater productivity for the whole could be purchased only at the expense of countless vulnerable individuals. As Bertin himself put it, 'it is between the protection that is due to the suffering part of humanity and the greater benefit to agriculture as a whole, that is difficult to decide'. Given the potential for social violence displayed by the suffering part of humanity and the limited police powers at the disposal of the state, no wonder that more often than not it was decided to let sleeping dogs lie. Despite his indignation at abuses such as *vaine pâture*, Duhamel du Monceau did not believe that the kind of legislative coercion employed in England could be applied to France – there it would have to be left to voluntary action.

This reluctance and/or inability of the French state to press ahead with the abolition of communal rights, and thus to permit enterprising cultivators to enclose their land, provide an excellent illustration of the narrow limits within which the absolutist state in practice operated. It was in constitutional, parliamentary Britain that real action that made a real difference was taken. This was because the British Parliament represented the landed interest of the country. A decision taken at Westminster and embodied in an act of Parliament was then enforced by those same landowners, acting in their capacity as Justices of the Peace. Many enclosures in Great Britain took place as a result of agreement among all those affected, indeed Parliament usually declined to act unless four-fifths of property-owners had signalled their consent, but the availability of enforceable legislation certainly accelerated the process. Although the first enclosure act was passed as early as 1604, unfavourable economic conditions confined the total to fewer than fifty between then and the accession of George II in 1727. By this time, however, money was beginning to raise its voice more insistently. In 1722, Robert Vyner was told that enclosure had allowed the rents of land at Withern in Lincolnshire to be raised from 2s 6d (12½ pence) to 13s 4d (67 pence) per acre. That was almost certainly exceptional but even the more common rise of 40 per cent plus was very attractive. As the 'price scissors' between agricultural produce and manufactured commodities began to open more widely during the second half of the eighteenth century, a torrent of acts flowed from Parliament, washing away the traditional agricultural landscape. According to Paul Langford, nearly four thousand enclosure acts were passed between 1750 and 1810, affecting roughly 20 per cent of the total acreage of England and Wales. It allowed rich landowners to become richer still: between 1776 and 1816, Thomas Coke, Earl of Leicester, doubled his rent roll.

In other words, to cut through the dense thicket of traditional communal agriculture, a sharp and heavy legislative instrument was required. An alternative approach was found in Prussia, where the king was the fortunate owner of between a quarter and a third of all farmland. This gave the royal administration a degree of control over the rural economy which Frederick the Great (1740–86) in particular was not slow to exploit. Among many other schemes for maximizing productivity, he issued a general decree in 1769 to encourage enclosures. Elsewhere in northern Europe, rationalization proceeded by example – often emanating from the Low Countries – from the consolidation of strips on the open fields to full enclosure. This process spread along the Baltic littoral during the second half of the eighteenth century, the Swedish Field Consolidation Act of 1749 being an important landmark. In Denmark the main initiative came from above in the shape of a series of agricultural commissions, which after 1757 established regional enclosure laws, superseded in 1768 by the General Land Use Department, which promoted both enclosures and rationalization within the old system. From there it spread south into Schleswig-Holstein, where the initiative appears to have come mainly from free peasants with an eye on the market. In the Austrian Netherlands, the government issued orders encouraging the division of common land and the consolidation of holdings in Hainaut in 1757, Brabant in 1772 and Namur in 1774.

Where the reversal of the 'infernal circle of the fallow' could be achieved, greatly increased production of cereals followed. This was every cultivator's dream, for the grain could be milled into flour, and the flour could be baked into the bread which was the staple of preference for most Europeans. In many parts of Europe, however, neither soil nor climate was suitable for cereal-growing, so the inhabitants had to make do with other forms of food. As Arthur Young observed, 'many of the people in France eat but very little rye and no wheat', concluding: 'to suppose, therefore, that the quantity of land here noted is all under wheat and rye, would be a gross error'. Among the alternative crops he described was a throwback to hunting-gathering days – the chestnut (*Castanea sativa*, not to be confused with the horse-chestnut, *Aesculus hippocastanum*, whose fruit is as attractive as it is inedible). Again and again on his travels through France he commented on the beauty and ubiquity of chestnut trees (known as 'the bread-tree'), especially in the Limousin, La Marche and parts of Languedoc, where 'they eat chestnuts abundantly'. On the road to Limoges in June 1787 he noted, 'chestnuts are spread over all the fields and yield the food of the poor', adding on another occasion that chestnuts were 'the exact transcript of the potato in Ireland'. Its importance for substantial parts of the south was considerable, indeed a historian of Languedoc writing in the 1770s stated that only chestnuts made the Cevennes and the Vivarais habitable at all, because supplies of cereals were so limited that they could not sustain a quarter of the existing population.

NEW CROPS

Less haphazard in their distribution were some crops of more recent origin. Top of the list chronologically was maize, also known as 'Indian corn', brought back from the Americas by Columbus and his successors. As a foodstuff, it has numerous advantages, notably its high yield (up to forty to one), its suitability for reducing fallow or converting a two-field to a three-field system and the length of its roots, which penetrate deeper and take less from the topsoil. By the end of the seventeenth century, maize was well established in northern Italy and south-west France, by the middle of the eighteenth century it was common in Spain and Portugal, and by 1800 it had reached the littoral regions of the Black Sea. By this time it was much more than a fringe curiosity. In France 15 per cent of all grain harvested in the diocese of Toulouse in 1774 was maize, as was 20 per cent in the diocese of Albi in 1786. In Lombardy at about the same time, it has been estimated that 10 per cent of the cultivable area was down to maize. Yet it could not serve as a panacea for Europe's agricultural problems. As the regions just noted indicate, maize flourishes best in a sunny climate. Moreover, it is labour-intensive, is inferior to other cereals in nutritional value, its protein (and especially its gluten) is of poor quality and it is deficient in niacin, making those who rely too heavily on corn prone to pellagra and other niacin-deficiency diseases. Eighteenth-century cultivators would not have known about its nutritional limitations or niacin deficiency, but they could see the other drawbacks without difficulty. According to Maurice Garden, maize made no discernible progress in France in the eighteenth century and there may even have been a retreat after 1750. Even more restricted by its special requirements was rice, confined almost exclusively to northern Italy, where it sustained a prosperous export trade, albeit at the cost of making malaria endemic.

Most important of all, at least in terms of potential, was the potato. First introduced from its native South America to Spain and Italy in 1565, it had reached the Low Countries by 1587, when the papal legate included it in his diet, the German-speaking world a year later, England at some point during the 1580s, and France just before the turn of the century. It did not reach Scandinavia and eastern Europe until the middle of the eighteenth century. Despite this early introduction, the potato took a long time to get established, not surprisingly in view of the unattractive appearance and texture of the early varieties. The compensating advantages, however, were so great that eventually it began to gain acceptance, first in horticulture and then in agriculture. As every gardener knows, the potato is special, for it is easy to plant, requires minimal attention, reaches maturity rapidly, and – most important – produces spectacular yields. In the kitchen it is equally welcome, for it requires very little preparation (it does not have to be threshed or milled like cereals), can be easily cooked in several different ways and is both tasty and filling. According to the Dutch economic historian Slicher van Bath, in the eighteenth century the yield of the potato per acre was 10.5 times higher than wheat and 9.6 times higher than rye, which more than compensated for its lower calorific value. To put that statistic another way, the net calorific value of the potato is 3.6 times that of grain. Writing in The Wealth of Nations (1776), Adam Smith stated firmly: 'The food produced by a field of potatoes is not inferior in quantity to that produced by a field of rice, and much superior to what is produced by a field of wheat. Twelve thousand weight of potatoes from an acre of land is not a greater produce than two thousand weight of wheat.' He also commented that during the previous thirty or forty years the price of potatoes had halved, as their cultivation had moved from the garden to the field. More controversially, he ventured the opinion that the benefit of a diet of potatoes could be witnessed in the impressive physiques of the labourers and prostitutes of London ('the strongest men and the most beautiful women perhaps in the British dominions'), especially when compared with his stunted fellow Scots, subsisting on a diet of oatmeal.

The potato was also less vulnerable to adverse weather than most other staple foodstuffs. As we have seen in Chapter 2, for the early modern European, it was not so much a question of whether a cereal harvest would fail as of when. A community that could fall back on potatoes when this happened was a community that had freed itself from the threat of famine. As the Englishman John Forster claimed in a pamphlet of 1664, the potato was 'a sure and easy remedy' for food shortages. Of course, over-reliance on the potato could also lead to catastrophe if disease struck, as it did in Ireland in the 1840s, but in the eighteenth century the potato was a life-saver. For that reason alone, governments were keen to promote its cultivation. For reasons that are still not clear, their efforts bore least fruit in France, with the exception of isolated regions on the periphery in the Dauphiné and the Pyrenees. Not even the news that potatoes were served to the royal family at Versailles or prints of Queen Marie Antoinette wearing a corsage of potato-flowers were sufficient to overcome a prejudice so deep-seated that *pommes frites* did not appear on French menus until the following century. In Toulouse, for example, Robert Forster found that peasants would not even feed potatoes to their pigs, for fear that their meat would be contaminated. The Burgundians invented the French appellation *pomme de terre* – but they also banned it on the grounds that it caused leprosy. While intendant of Limoges in 1761, the enlightened physiocrat Turgot tried to dispel the popular belief that the purple flower of the potato was a version of deadly nightshade by eating it in public and making peasants sit next to him to observe that he was not poisoned. The French were not, of course, alone in their prejudices. In 1770 famine-afflicted Neapolitans refused to touch a boatload of potatoes sent as a gift; burghers of Kolberg in Prussia told Frederick the Great, 'the things have neither smell nor taste, not even the dogs will eat them, so what are they to us?'; and Russian peasants distrusted the potato because it was not mentioned in the Bible, believed that it caused cholera and rioted when attempts were made to force them to grow it.

Despite popular prejudice, throughout the British Isles, the Low Countries, northern Europe and in many parts of the Holy Roman Empire, the potato had made a major dietary impact by 1815. Unusually, it was the Irish peasants who were in the vanguard of progress. As the potato's most recent historian, Larry Zuckerman, has written: 'No European nation has had a longer, more intimate partnership with the potato than Ireland. The first Europeans to accept it as a field crop in the seventeenth century, the Irish were also the first to embrace it as a staple in the eighteenth.' The French agronomist Duhamel du Monceau, writing in the 1760s, found the English consumption of the potato 'astonishing', but even their enthusiasm paled by comparison with the Irish, 'who are so fond of potatoes, that they spare no pains to have plenty of them'. Their 'lazy bed' cultivation technique allowed a family of six to subsist on the produce of just an acre of land. Travelling through Ireland in 1809–11, Edward Wakefield calculated that each member of such a family consumed on average 5½ pounds (2.5 kg) of potatoes each day. Their British masters had greater reservations but they too succumbed by the end of this period. In 1818 William Cobbett, who regarded the potato as a badge of servitude ('this villainous root ... this root of wretchedness'), raged: 'It is the fashion to extol potatoes and to eat potatoes. Everyone joins in extolling potatoes, and all the world like potatoes, or pretend to like them, which is the same thing in effect.'

On the continent, although the evidence is sporadic it clearly points to a growing willingness to experiment. Potatoes can be found in many parts of Flanders, Brabant and Westphalia before 1700, in Franconia by 1715, in Brandenburg in the 1720s, in the Moselle valley of the Electorate of Trier in the 1730s, and so on. In the Kurmark province of Prussia, the production of potatoes increased from 5,200 *Tonnen* in 1765 to 19,000 in 1779, and to 103,000 in 1801, by which time potatoes were being grown as field crops. The failure of the cereal harvest in the early 1770s had provided a powerful impetus towards diversification. As the great German agricultural scientist Albrecht Thaer (1752–1828) recalled: 'it was not until 1771 and 1772 that the practice of cultivating the potato as a field crop began to acquire supporters, but at that time all the grain crops failed, and the famine which ensued led to the discovery that proper and sufficient nourishment might be derived from those very potatoes which had hitherto been regarded only as a luxury, just as well as from bread.'

SERFDOM AND THE
PEASANT'S BURDENS

An important reason for the reluctance of European peasants to embrace agricultural innovations and increase the productivity of their land was the knowledge that a large proportion of any surplus they generated would go to their various lords. In an age when taxation may seem heavy but is at least simple and transparent, it is difficult to appreciate the sheer number, variety and incoherence of the old regime's demands. At the risk of oversimplification, the beneficiaries can be grouped in three categories: State, seigneur and Church. The first can be left for a later chapter, although it should be noted that in most European countries the 'smash and grab' days of the first half of the seventeenth century had made way for more orderly and more predictable demands. Although rural unrest did not disappear entirely, as we shall see, royal taxation was rarely the main target of the insurgents. That privilege was reserved for the seigneurs. Generalizing about seigneurial dues in any one province, let alone one country, let alone a whole continent, is notoriously difficult, but the nettle has to be grasped if any sort of clarity is to be achieved.

In much of Europe inside the eastern and western peripheries, it can be said that the landowner possessed three kinds of land: the domain he farmed himself, using hired or conscripted labour; the land he rented out, in return for payments in cash or kind, or in return for a share of the crop; and the land that he did not 'own', in the sense that it was his to dispose of as he saw fit, but over which he exercised seigneurial rights and from which he extracted seigneurial dues. The seigneurial rights were in part honorific, designed to emphasize the seigneur's paramount position in the community, such as the right to a special pew in church. They were also in part a combination of the honorific and the economic, such as the exclusive right to maintain a dovecot or the especially unpopular exclusive right to hunt and to preserve game for that purpose. Finally, they were in part nakedly economic, such as the right to extract a fee whenever land in this category changed hands. This last-named due was especially onerous for French peasants, amounting to about one-eighth of the purchase price in most of the country, although it could go as high as a quarter or a third in parts of Lorraine and as much as a half in the Auvergne. In the Holy Roman Empire it was less, being just 2 per cent in Württemberg, for example. Further east, it was rare, except in Prussian Silesia and the German-speaking provinces of the Habsburg Monarchy, where it varied between 3 per cent and 10 per cent. Also nakedly exploitative was the seigneur's monopoly of milling, brewing or distilling, or his right to pre-empt the peasants' produce at less than the market price. Some of the special demands were as quaint as they were onerous. In Hungary, a peasant was obliged to pay special dues at their lord's first communion, on his marriage, and if he needed to be ransomed from Turkish captivity. Quite apart from the financial burden these dues involved, by their very nature they highlighted the subservient and dependent status of the individual peasant and his family. Especially intrusive was the 'Gesindezwangdienst' extracted in Austria and Bavaria, for example, which obliged adolescent children to serve the seigneur as domestic servants for a number of years. More generally it was the case that the seigneur, usually acting through his bailiff, convened village assemblies, presided over them – and told them what to do. It was through the seigneur that the central authorities conducted most of their business, notably recruiting soldiers and collecting taxes.

For the peasants of the Holy Roman Empire east of the River Elbe, Poland, Russia and the Bohemian, Moravian and Hungarian parts of the Habsburg Monarchy, the most onerous seigneurial due was neither honorific nor financial, but physical, in the form of forced agricultural labour. The obligation to work on the royal roads (the corvée) or to perform haulage services for the seigneur was common in the west and centre of Europe, but the nature and extent of the 'robot' (a word used by several languages but deriving from the Slavonic for 'work') in the east were such as to create a difference in kind. This was a contrast between two kinds of domination and two kinds of economy, best summarized by two sets of opposing German composites – Grundherrschaft/ Gutsherrschaft, and Grundwirtschaft/Gutswirtschaft, where 'Grund' means land and 'Gut' means estate, 'Herrschaft' means lordship and 'Wirtschaft' means economy. In western, southern and central Germany, the seigneurial and economic system was based on land, whereas in the east it was based on the manorial estate. In the former, the peasant owed dues in cash or kind to his seigneur by virtue of the land he cultivated; in the latter, the peasant owed dues in cash, kind and labour by virtue of being born on the estate and was to all intents and purposes a serf, for he could not leave, marry or choose his profession without the permission of his lord and was obliged to work on his lord's domain for a certain number of days each year without remuneration. Although the *robot* varied from region to region, it was rarely less than burdensome. In the Neumark province of Brandenburg, for example, three days a week was counted as light, and four, five or even six days as normal.

That there should have been such a fundamental division between eastern and western Europe is not so difficult to explain. The old adage '*Stadtluft macht frei*' (it is urban air that makes one free) operates in both directions. It was in the urbanized west that serfdom disappeared earliest, and it was in the rural east, where one could travel for weeks without encountering anything resembling a town, that it not only survived but periodically enjoyed new leases of life. Its most recent revival had occurred in the aftermath of the devastations of the seventeenth century, when a combination of depopulation and western demand for grain encouraged landowners to anchor their peasants to their estates. Closely allied to this socio-economic explanation was the sociopolitical consideration that the landed nobility was very much more powerful – and the central authorities correspondingly weaker – in the east. Even where rulers felt a duty to intervene to protect their subjects against the depredations of the landlords, their actual capacity for enforcing their good intentions was limited. So Charles VI's pious hope of 1723 that the Hungarian counties would intervene on the side of oppressed serfs stayed on paper, as did Maria Theresa's similar directive a generation later (1751). According to gentry liberal Gergely Berzeviczy: 'The landlord looks on the serf as a tool necessary to cultivate his lands and as a chattel which he inherited from his parents, or purchased, or acquired as a reward. He demands that the serf pays dues and performs *robot* for him and regards him as one with whom he can deal as his self-interest dictates.'

Ruler and lord were competing for the serf's surplus. As fiscal pressure mounted, especially with increasing military expenditure, the ruler would appear to have had a vested interest in protecting the serf against the lord's exactions. The physiocrat Quesnay's maxim, written demonstratively in capital letters, that 'POOR PEASANTS MEAN A POOR KINGDOM' should have been a truism. Yet it was not as simple as that. If peasants were needed to pay taxes and fill the ranks of the army, their lords were also needed, to administer the countryside and to man the officer corps. Only where there were sufficient commoners of sufficient education could the nobles be dispensed with. But that was nowhere. For the time being, a balance had to be struck. The dilemma was explained with characteristic clarity by Frederick the Great in his treatise *On the Forms of Government and the Duties of Sovereigns*. His premise was that the legislator must place himself in the position of the poorest of his subjects and ask himself what abuses he would most want to see corrected. Top of the list in many European countries was serfdom, 'of all conditions the most wretched and the one which most offends humanity'. Yet although it might seem that all that was needed to abolish 'this barbaric custom' was an act of the will, in the real world there were several other countervailing considerations that needed to be taken into account. Among them were the sanctity of contract between landowner and cultivator, the danger of agriculture collapsing through too precipitate action, and the need to indemnify the nobility.

When he wrote those lines in 1777, Frederick could draw on a lifetime of experience, especially on the check he had suffered in Pomerania in 1763. He had sent the following unequivocal instruction to the province's senior civil servant:

Serfdom is to be absolutely and immediately abolished wherever it exists – be it on royal, aristocratic, or municipal lands. Let this decree, issued by His Royal Majesty for the benefit of the entire province, be implemented immediately. All opponents should be persuaded gently of the value of this decree, but coercion may also be employed, in the last resort, if necessary.

What is most odd about this order is Frederick's belief that it could be implemented. As the Seven Years War had just ended, the sacrifices made by the Pomeranian Junkers should have been towards the front of his mind. Not unreasonably, they played this card with some vehemence when protesting against the projected abolition. As one contemporary estimate held that every single noble family in the province boasted at least one serving officer, their objection was cogent. They also argued that the relationship between lord and peasant was not true serfdom (*Leibeigenschaft*) but rested on a 'voluntary and honest' contract, which obliged the landowner to 'feed and maintain the peasant family, including children and servants, even when they become invalids through accident or old age; to supply the peasant with house, stable, arable land, cattle and garden for his use; to pay equitable wages to domestic servants; and to build and maintain central buildings for residential and economic purposes'. Not the least advantage of this welfare state, they argued further, was that it kept the peasants 'in their proper place': severing the ties which bound lord and peasant in mutual obligation would lead to anarchy. Frederick did not press the point.

Justification for his prudence was provided by Joseph II when he did press the point against his various nobilities in the late 1780s. Serfdom, the *Gutsherrschaft* and *Gutswirtschaft* were unacceptable to Joseph for several reasons. First, the system subjected a large proportion of the population to the authority of the landlords, who for all their wealth and pretensions were nothing more than private individuals. That was repugnant to the modern state's claim to sovereignty. Secondly, the notion of hereditary subservience was incompatible with Joseph's belief in the natural equality of man. Thirdly, the control exercised by the landlords allowed them to expropriate an excessive proportion of the serfs' income, thus denying the state its proper share. Fourthly, the abuse of power permitted by the system led to social disorder, as the serfs resorted to the only weapon at their disposal – insurrection. Fifthly, the restrictions imposed on mobility starved the manufacturing and commercial sectors of labour. Finally, those same restrictions also made it more difficult for the state to recruit soldiers.

When Joseph finally acquired complete control of his dominions in 1780, on the death of his mother, the Empress Maria Theresa, he moved quickly to dismantle serfdom. Beginning in 1781, he introduced a series of measures which granted all peasants the right to marry, migrate and choose a trade or profession without their lords' permission. The obligation to provide children for compulsory domestic service was also abolished. This package represented a major step towards emancipation but left untouched the thorny questions of the lords' judicial control and the *robot*. His mind was concentrated by the eruption in 1784 of a peasant rising in Transylvania so widespread that as many as 36,000 insurgents were under arms at its height. In the county of Hunyad alone, 62 villages and 132 noble residences were burnt and 4,000 people, most of them nobles and their families, were killed 'in the most horrific manner'. Investigation of the causes of the outbreak confirmed his long-held belief that the Habsburg Monarchy was sclerotic, with limbs that responded only fitfully to instructions from the brain at the centre. His infuriated reaction provides an eloquent description of what it was to be a reforming monarch in the late eighteenth century:

It has been well known to me that for many years the serfs on the Szalat estates have presented the most pressing complaints about the oppression and brutality of the public officials as well as of the landlords, and I have called repeatedly for the investigation and redress of grievances, but alas up till now it has all been in vain. Commissions of inquiry have indeed been appointed but all they have been able to achieve is that the serfs have been maltreated even worse than before, the officials have been whitewashed and the abuses have never been attacked at their roots. Certainly the situation can be kept under control by force for a while, but when people are oppressed too much and the bow is strung too tightly, sooner or later it is bound to snap.

Even before 'Horja's revolt' erupted, Joseph had initiated a radical reform programme. He worked from a simple first principle: 'The land and the soil which nature has given to man to support him is the sole source from which everything comes and to which everything returns, and whose existence remains constant through all the vagaries of time. For this reason it is incontestably true that land alone should provide for the needs of the state.' Moreover, 'natural justice' demanded that all land should be treated equally, no matter what the status of the owner. Was it not a 'fatuous prejudice', he asked, to suppose that there had once been a time when there had been only lords and no peasants and that the latter, when they materialized, were allowed the land only on certain conditions? The fact of the matter was that primal equality had made way for privilege and inequality as a result of usurpation. It was high time to strip the abuses away, so that the state and all its members could benefit equally. To this end, he announced the creation of an entirely new system, based on the equal taxation of land. Differences in its value, resulting from variations in type, fertility and location, would be dealt with by taking a ten-year average net return (in other words after the costs of cultivation and the seed had been deducted) based on the market value of threshed corn. All other forms of taxation, whether imposed on trade and industry or consumption, were to be abolished.

This was not just a reform of taxation; it also involved a reconstruction of rural relations. In the past, the wretched peasant was kept chained to the estate and forced to contribute so much to his lord in various dues and services that there was precious little left for public service or public funds. So long as the rural economy was based on a personal nexus of subservience and dues were paid in kind rather than cash, the mass of the population would remain beyond the reach of the state's agents, whether in the form of tax-collectors or recruiting sergeants. Joseph therefore ordered that the manifold seigneurial burdens, including the *robot*, should be consolidated into a single cash payment. In this manner, he was convinced, the mighty potential of the Habsburg Monarchy, at present restrained by the bonds of prejudice, could be liberated to serve the state. It was this combination of a reform which was both fiscal and 'urbarial' (i.e. regulating relations between lord and peasant) which made Joseph's programme so radical – and so controversial.

The Transylvanian revolt of 1784 did nothing to change his mind. Never did Joseph show himself more determined and obstinate than in his imposition of his 'Taxation and Urbarial Regulation'. Not even the bitter opposition from most of his senior bureaucrats made him hesitate. On the contrary, the knowledge that they were all landowners complaining through their pockets spurred him on. In 1785 the great land survey, which was a necessary precondition of the new system, was begun and driven on with periodic tirades and visitations. By 1789, knowing that he had not long to live and showing all the impatience of Lessing's modern man who wants the future today, Joseph believed that the time was ripe for implementation. The measure had changed somewhat from earlier drafts: values were now to be based on a six-year average of gross income. The peasant was to keep 70 per cent of his gross produce; of the remaining 30, 12.5 per cent was to go to the state and 17.5 per cent to the lord. This latter sum included all dues and services, including the ecclesiastical tithe and the *robot*. When countering the criticism of a senior official, Count Chotek, who refused to sign the law of 10 February 1789 and insisted on being allowed to resign, Joseph stated that if in the past a peasant had been deprived of more than a third of his income, then he had suffered a grievous wrong which must now be corrected. But it was not to be. As we shall see in a later chapter, by this time the Habsburg Monarchy appeared to be falling apart due to domestic unrest and foreign war, and even the pathologically obstinate Joseph had to appreciate that this radical scheme had to be revoked. More than fifty years were to pass before the peasants were emancipated in the wake of the revolutions of 1848–9.

They had to wait even longer in the Russian Empire, until 1861 indeed, and even then the fruits of 'emancipation' turned to ashes in the mouths of the former serfs. Russia was special, most fundamentally because of its geography. The climate dictates a short growing season of only four months (mid-May to mid-September) in the *taiga* between Novgorod and St Petersburg, five-and-a-half months in the central regions around Moscow and six months on the steppe. To put those figures in perspective, in western Europe the equivalent is eight to nine months. The brevity of the season discouraged individual initiative, and instead placed a premium on co-operation and the pooling of resources. It also kept yields obstinately low, the average being still only between three and four to one in the nineteenth century, or the same as four hundred years earlier. Consequently, in a good year Russian agriculture could support those who cultivated it, but could not generate a surplus sufficient to support a significant urban sector. Behind the glamour of St Petersburg was the reality of an overwhelmingly rural economy, with only around 3 per cent of the population living in towns. Even that figure is misleading because most of the 'urban inhabitants' were landlords and peasants who grew their own food.

The other geographical determinant was space. Even a cursory glance at a map of Europe will demonstrate that Russia was of a different order of magnitude. In 1800, for example, the distance from its western frontier to the Ural mountains (traditionally the frontier of Europe) was greater than from its western frontier to the west coast of Ireland. Just moving information around this great land mass was a difficult undertaking: even after German and Swedish experts had established a postal system in the second half of the seventeenth century, it could take up to a fortnight for a despatch to reach Kiev from Moscow. Communities lying off the main routes – the great majority, in other words – were simply beyond the government's communication range. Yet the need for a strong central authority was paramount, in view of repeated invasions by predators from the west – Poles and Swedes – and south – Mongols and Turks. In response, there developed what Richard Pipes has termed a 'dyarchy', a political system in which the Tsar exercised absolute power at the centre, but farmed out the country to the nobility in return for taxes and services. Running through it like a steel cord was the principle of subjection: the nobles were subjected to the Tsar and the peasants were subjected to their lords. The senior official Mikhail Speransky observed in 1805 that there were only two classes in Russia: 'slaves of the sovereign, and slaves of the landlords. The former are called free only in regard to the latter.' Even as late as the nineteenth century, every noble, whatever his rank, was required to end a letter to the Tsar with the formula 'Your Humble Slave'.

It is difficult to avoid the conclusion that serfdom lasted longest in Russia because it was a response to fundamental conditions of life. In Pipes' words, it 'was not an exceptional condition, but an integral aspect of an all-embracing system binding the entire population to the state. Unlike the slave of the ancient world or the Americas, the Muscovite serf was not an unfree being living in the midst of freemen, a helot among citizens. He was a member of a social system which allowed no one to dispose of his time or belongings.' That did not mean that there was not a great variety of conditions. Not all Russian peasants were serfs and not all serfs were the same. As Simon Dixon has written: 'Though peasants constituted over 90% of the population, this mono-lithic proportion conceals a kaleidoscope of juridical status which fluc-tuated over time.' Much depended on the category of ownership. Peter the Great's census of 1723 showed that 56 per cent of serfs were owned by nobles, 21 per cent by the state, 14 per cent by the Church and 9 per cent by the Tsar. One important distinction to be drawn is between labour services (*barshchina*) and dues payable in cash or kind (*obrok*), although the subcategories were very numerous. Jerome Blum logged forty-four variations of *barshchina*. *Obrok* was favoured where the serfs were engaged in manufacturing and trading of some kind, *barshchina* where access to urban or export markets created a demand for agricultu-ral produce. Where the latter conditions prevailed, in the 'black earth' regions of the south, *barshchina* was in the ascendant, by about three to one, while in the forest heartland the proportion was about fifty-five to forty-five. Dues of all kinds appear to have risen for most of our period, reaching a plateau around the middle of the eighteenth century. There were, of course, large numbers of serfs who worked no land at all but worked full time in the lord's household as indentured domestic servants. Travelling in Russia in the late eighteenth century, the Englishman William Tooke was shocked by the swarms of idle servants who hung about the houses of the nobles: 'it may be affirmed, without exagger-ation, that in the house of a Russian nobleman five or six times as many domestics are kept as in families of equal rank in any other country in Europe, and the retainers for both sexes in some of the great houses in

Petersburg amount to a hundred-and-fifty or two hundred persons'. These house serfs appear to have been especially vulnerable to physical abuse. Simon Dixon cites an episode witnessed by the Jansenist abbé Jacques Jubé on a visit to Russia in the early 1730s when an elderly lackey was forced to grovel on the ground in expiation for a very minor offence before being kicked in the face and stomach.

Everywhere in Europe the pitiable lot of the serf was pitied by a growing number of contemporaries. As a crime against humanity and a crime against productivity, serfdom united in condemnation those whose hearts were soft and those whose hearts were hard. If attempts at reform were often half-hearted or still-born, even before 1789 there was a sense that the institution was moribund. Only in Russia did its vitality appear undiminished. The decisive steps towards the establishment of serfdom as the dominant social institution were taken by Peter the Great, in 1705 with the introduction of conscription and in 1719 with the imposition of the poll-tax (literally 'soul-tax' – *podushnaya podat*). Further deterioration in their position followed, as the lords' power to punish was strengthened. Catherine the Great was no doubt sincere in her often-expressed hostility to serfdom in principle but, in the words of Michael Confino, she presided over 'the golden age of the nobility and the apogee of serfdom'. Only six lords are known to have been punished during her long reign (1762–96) for maltreating their serfs. In 1790 Aleksandr Nikolaevich Radishchev published *A Journey from St Petersburg to Moscow*, fictional in the sense that it did not describe a single journey he had actually undertaken but factual in its account of conditions along the route. Chief among his targets was serfdom, which he condemned because it violated natural right, corrupted both the serf and the serf-owner, and because it was economically unsound:

The bestial custom of enslaving one's fellow men, which originated in the hot regions of Asia, a custom worthy of savages, a custom that signifies a heart of stone and a total lack of soul, has quickly spread far and wide over the face of the earth. And we Slavs, sons of slava [glory], glorious among earth-born generations, both in name and deed, benighted by the darkness of ignorance, have adopted this custom, and, to our shame, to the shame of past centuries, to the shame of this age of reason, we have kept it inviolate even to this day.

Radishchev paid dearly for his indignation. Condemned to death, he spent more than a month on death row before the sentence was commuted to loss of his noble rank and ten years' exile in eastern Siberia. There he remained until Catherine the Great's death six years later. Although he was then allowed to return to European Russia, he never recovered from his ordeal and committed suicide in 1802.

Although visitors knew that serfdom existed in many other parts of Europe, what they found in Russia seemed especially onerous and offensive. Even making allowances for the common tendency for western Europeans to view the east *de haut en bas*, there was plenty to cause offence. Sir Charles Whitworth, the British envoy to the court of Peter the Great, recorded: 'The peasants are perfect slaves, subject to the arbitrary power of their lords, and transferred with goods and chattels: they can call nothing their own.' In fact, it had been technically illegal since 1649 to sell serfs separately from the land to which they were notionally attached, but the practice continued, as the regular repetition of bans throughout the eighteenth century demonstrated. Moscow newspapers continued to advertise serfs for sale 'by the family' or 'individually', and even included them with household utensils as job lots. A serf scullery-maid could be had for fifty roubles, but a 'pretty young girl serf' could fetch ten times that amount, indeed serf harems were fashionable during the late eighteenth century and early nineteenth. So were serf orchestras and serf theatrical troupes. Prince Potemkin paid Field Marshal Razumovsky 40,000 roubles for a serf orchestra. Even quite modest landowners had serfs trained as musicians, putting them to work in the fields or in the house by day. This was a sensible investment, for not only were the serf musicians available to entertain the family in the evening, they also represented a marketable asset and could be sold on if necessary. However eminent, the serf performers were always subject to the whims of their owners, including corporal punishment. Probably untypical but certainly symbolic was the great whip kept hanging in the wings of his private theatre by Count Kamensky, with which he beat performers in the interval if they had not lived up to expectations. Another owner, identified in the source only as 'B', prowled in the wings during the performance, berating those on stage with words and gestures. During a performance of *Dido and Aeneas*, he was so incensed by the inadequacy of the leading lady that he rushed on to the stage and slapped her face, adding a good thrashing in the interval.

It is a measure of the special quality of Russian society that these privately owned serf troupes dominated theatrical and operatic life in the eighteenth century. Princess Yankova recalled: 'In our day, it was considered more refined to go [to the theatre] by the personal invitation of the host, and not to one where anyone could go in exchange for money. And who indeed among our intimate friends did not possess his own private theatre?' In his illuminating study of Russian culture, Orlando Figes records that between the late eighteenth century and the early nineteenth, there were theatres on 173 noble estates and 300 serf orchestras. Russian opera and Russian ballet were born not at court or in the public theatres of St Petersburg and Moscow, but at Kuskovo, the stately home of the Sheremetevs, where in effect an academy was maintained for the instruction of serf musicians and performers. As the family owned estates totalling c.2,000,000 acres together with perhaps as many as a million serfs, and was richer even than the richest English magnate, they could afford to be cultural leaders.

The effect of serfdom on the economy was not so straightforward as might appear at first sight. In the German lands east of the River Elbe and in the Habsburg Monarchy, the anchoring of the serfs to the lord's estate is generally believed to have had a retardative effect, for they were excluded from the capitalist process both as labourers and as consumers. Only when Joseph II, for example, granted them freedom of movement in 1781 could they move off the land to participate in urban manufacturing. In Russia, on the other hand, serfs could actually be obliged to become industrial workers. Beginning with the reign of Peter the Great, entire villages were 'assigned' or 'ascribed' to manufacturing enterprises, often a very long way from their original domicile, especially to iron foundries in the Urals. In the last year of Peter's reign (1725), 54,000 were assigned to metallurgical industries alone. Most of these were state run, although it was not unknown for private entrepreneurs to be given the right to conscript labour. By the middle of the eighteenth century, Russia was the largest iron-producing country in Europe and had replaced Sweden as the main supplier of British markets, so in this odd sense it might be said that serfdom was being used to promote economic progress.

The effect of serfdom on agriculture, however, was unequivocally depressing. No subtle grasp of human psychology is required to appreciate that a forced labourer will approach a task without enthusiasm. The Hungarian Károly Zichy lamented: 'My estate is in a most advantageous situation, in the vicinity of four towns; my villages are on the bank of the Danube River, near the busiest roads; my bailiffs are good; the soil is of the first quality; and yet all my income is spent on administration. I can only retain income derived from the 11,000 sheep on my manorial lands. What can I expect from the weak draft animals, bad ploughs, and wooden carriages of the serfs?' If he had added to the deficiencies of the serfs 'ill-will', he would have been closer to the mark. A growing number of the more intelligent lords, especially in Prussia, began to appreciate that it was in their interests to dispense with the forced labour of the serfs, with all the reciprocal obligations that involved, and to hire and fire free labour as and when it was required. Major Joachim Friedrich von Kleist, whose success in adapting to market conditions we have already noted, employed day-labourers on a seasonal basis, because he found them much easier to exploit than dependent peasants. This was a development accelerated by the increasing share of noble estates (*Rittergüter*) passing into the hands of commoners. Radishchev had seen enough of sulky Russian serfs dragging their feet to know that: 'following this natural instinct [self-interest], everything we do for our own sake, everything we do without compulsion, we do carefully, industriously and well. On the other hand, all that we do not do freely, all that we do not do for our own advantage, we do carelessly, lazily, and all awry.' 'To work as if on the lord's land' was a synonym for 'to go slow'.

But there was more to it than just going slow. Serfdom was also part and parcel of a communal structure of agriculture. As we have seen, even where peasants were legally free, they were the willing victims of communal obligations (*servitudes collectives*). Where they were tied to the soil and/or subjected to their lord, the urge to huddle together for collective security was that much greater. In Russia, serfdom and the village commune or *mir* – a wonderfully protean word which also means 'peace', 'world' and 'universe' – progressed together. Consisting of village elders elected by the male heads of household, the *mir* conducted almost all peasant business, fixing the dates for the agricultural year, deciding what, when and how crops should be grown, distributing plots of land on the open fields, collecting taxes and enforcing basic community discipline. Writing in the 1840s, Baron Hauxthausen commented: 'The power of the Communes, and the obedience shown to them, meet us everywhere.' As he pointed out, there was no proverb in either the Germanic or the Romance languages lauding the virtues of the commune, but there were plenty in Russian, for example:

God alone directs the Mir.

The Mir is great.

The Mir is the surging billow.

The neck and shoulders of the Mir are broad.

Throw everything upon the Mir, it will carry it all.

The tear of the Mir is liquid, but sharp.

The Mir sighs, and the rock is rent asunder.

The Mir sobs, and it re-echoes in the forest.

Trees are felled in the forest, and splinters fly in the Mir.

A thread of the Mir becomes a shirt for the naked.

No one in the world can separate from the Mir.

What belongs to the Mir belongs also to the mother's little son.

What is decided by the Mir must come to pass.

The Mir is answerable for the country's defence.

This was not a structure conducive to change, as a disapproving Friedrich Christian von Weber wrote in 1720: 'their Minds seem so darkened and their Senses so stupefied by Slavery, that though they are taught the most obvious Improvements in Husbandry, yet they do not care to depart from the old way, thinking that no body can understand it better than their Ancestors did'. More sympathetic – and also more perceptive – was the Hungarian liberal Gergely Berzeviczy:

The peasant shows an inborn distrust toward all of his superiors, even toward those who are not responsible for his plight, and believes that he is entitled to extract benefits by craft from those who because of their superior status enjoy so many advantages over him . . . Distrust also exists toward all the administrative and judicial authorities. After all, who make up the authorities? The masters of the serfs and individuals connected with them. All innovations, particularly those initiated by the lords, are hated by the peasants; they oppose them stubbornly because they are aware that the interests of the lord are contrary to their own. Serfs suspect innovations as instruments of the lords' intent to increase their own advantages at the expense of those of the serfs.

Berzeviczy added that the serfs did everything in their power to evade their seigneurial obligations, sending the weakest members of their family, their weakest draught animals and their worst equipment.

TITHES

As if the endless variety of dues in cash, kind and labour exacted by state and lord were not enough, a third group of predators – simpler but more menacing – loomed in the shape of the clergy and their demand for a tithe of the peasant's produce. Like many disagreeable things in life, it enjoyed biblical backing, most authoritatively in Genesis 28:20–22:

And Jacob vowed a vow, saying, If God will be with me, and will keep me in this way that I go, and will give me bread to eat, and raiment to put on, So that I come again to my father's house in peace; then shall the LORD be my God: And this stone, which I have set for a pillar, shall be God's house: and of all that thou shalt give me I will surely give the tenth unto thee.

A more explicit command was to be found in Leviticus 27:30–32:

And all the tithe of the land, whether of the seed of the land, or of the fruit of the tree, is the LORD's: it is holy unto the LORD ... And concerning the tithe of the herd, or of the flock, even of whatsoever passeth under the rod, the tenth shall be holy unto the LORD.

During the intervening millennia, the simplicity of this promise/demand had fragmented into infinite complexity. In theory, all land was subject to the tithe, whether it belonged to highest sovereign, the richest prelate or the humblest serf. When Louis XIV took land at Versailles to form part of his new palace's park, he was obliged to pay compensation to the tithe-lords. Yet nothing was ever that simple under the old regime, least of all in France. A number of religious orders, ever anxious to establish a special status within the Church, had secured exemption, while the nobles of Provence had managed to get their share reduced to well below the rate for commoners. That rate was not, as might be expected from the word's etymology and Jacob's pledge, 10 per cent. Sometimes it was, but very often it was more or less. It could vary from crop to crop, place to place, and even from field to field within a single parish. At Lacépède near Agen on the Garonne, it was a tenth on cereals, a thirteenth on flax and a twentieth on wine. It was very high in parts of the south-west, reaching an eighth in the Condomois, in Lorraine, where a seventh was not unusual, and highest of all in certain benighted parts of Brittany where a fifth and a barely credible quarter were demanded. On the other hand it was negligible in many parts of the south, especially in the Dauphiné and Provence. It should also be noted that where the seigneurial regime was heaviest, the tithe was lightest, and vice versa. Pierre Goubert has estimated that a rough national average would be 7 or 8 per cent.

Just as various was what was tithable. Although it can be said that the cereal harvests were always liable, that was where uniformity stopped. Timber, natural pasture and draught animals were almost always exempt, but not wine, young livestock and artificial pasture. Opportunities for evasion on the part of the producer and sharp practice on the part of the tithe-owner were legion, creating a constant source of social friction – and litigation, especially when new crops such as clover or roots made their appearance. In such a situation the only invariable beneficiaries were the lawyers, when one or other party took the case to court. The most notorious was the 'Five Points' dispute in Flanders, which had been before the court 'for centuries' before the Revolution of 1789 put an end to it. Collecting the tithe was an onerous business, so most owners leased their right to professionals, often grain-dealers, which did nothing to enhance its popularity. Moreover, of all the dues payable by the cultivator, the tithe took precedence, and no harvest could be gathered in until the tithe-lord's share had been paid. With the price of agricultural produce on the rise for much of the eighteenth century, it was almost invariably collected in kind and was not commuted into cash payments.

The peasants might have been more co-operative if their tithes had been kept in the parish and used for the maintenance of the local priest and the upkeep of church buildings. But usually the lion's share went to the princes of the Church, especially to the episcopate and to monasteries, and even to laymen. The great Benedictine abbey of Chaise-Dieu owned tithes in more than three hundred parishes. Only one parish priest in ten was in sole possession of his community's tithe. As a remonstrance from Aulnay-aux-Planches, near Châlons, complained to the Estates General in 1789: 'The tithes represent a considerable burden imposed by religion, which we pay willingly, and would pay more willingly still if we saw them being employed in accordance with the purpose assigned to them by God and man.' The parishioners of Rougeon near Blois were more indignant: 'it makes us wretched to see our parish priests in a state of destitution, misery and poverty, at the same time as we see an endless number of monks, friars, abbés and canons taking away our tithes and denying our priests their due: the patrons of the livings view with indifference our churches without prayer-books, without vestments, in a state of collapse, as filthy as stables'. No one knows how much the Church in France extracted from the laity in the form of tithes: contemporary estimates vary from 70,000,000 *livres* (Lavoisier) to 133,000,000 (de Chasset). The figure offered by Albert Soboul for the closing years of the old regime was 120,000,000.

The tithe was just as common, just as onerous and just as resented in Protestant countries. In England it survived until commuted by Act of Parliament in 1836. Indeed, it positively thrived, as the tithe-owners, a third of whom were lay 'impropriators', proved adept at bringing new crops within their net. From Godalming in Surrey it was reported in 1697 that 'all tithes of corn, grain, clover stfoin [sainfoin] & all upland grass' were paid in kind, as were 'all tithes of set peas and beans . . . tithes of gardens & orchards & fruit trees & shrubs in fields and elsewhere. Also tithes of hops, flax, hemp, woad, saffron, coleseed, plants and all small tithes.' It is some measure of the profitability of the potato that it flourished despite being ruled a tithable crop. The tithe was a heavy burden, as Arthur Young complained in his *Farmer's Letters to the People of England* in 1768:

The tenth of the produce is a very considerable tax; for after a farmer has richly manured a field, drained it at a very large expence, given it a year's fallow, sowed it with wheat, harvested the crop, and paid two years rent on it, to pay a tenth of the product of all his expences and labour is so exceedingly burthensome, that no tax subsisting at present in England nearly equals it.

Courts both lay and ecclesiastical were generally on the side of the tithe-owners: in 1782 it was estimated that of 700 tithe cases recorded in Westminster Hall, 660 had been decided in favour of the clergy. In the previous year an enterprising vicar of Kensington had won the right to tithe the exotic fruits grown in his parish for the wealthy inhabitants of London. After rebuilding his rectory at Epworth, Samuel Wesley's first priority was to build a tithe-barn to hold his corn. However, the cultivators did not make life easy for the tithe-owners. In the words of a traditional harvest song:

We've cheated the parson, we'll cheat him again,
For why should the Vicar have one in ten?

Extracting it may have been unpleasant, but the rewards were considerable. Almost every English village still boasts an 'Old Rectory' built or extended in the eighteenth century, whose splendour pays eloquent tribute to the value of the tithe.

PEASANT RESISTANCE

Right across Europe, landowners and land cultivators battled for advantage in a struggle which became more acute as population pressure increased, and with it the price of agricultural produce. In the seventeenth century, the peasants had been more likely than not to resort to direct action, especially when a war-torn state was desperately trying to raise enough revenue to stay afloat. These 'fiscal wars' often bound other members of the rural community – seigneur, clergy and even neighbouring townspeople – in a joint defensive action against the rapacity of the centre. Even after the *Frondes*, Louis XIV's government was harassed by large-scale rural revolts: in 1662 there were 6,000 peasants under arms in the Boulonnais to resist taxation; the same number in Béarn in 1664 resisting an attempt to impose the *gabelle* (salt-tax) on a previously exempt province; in 1670 5,000 insurgents in the Vivarais in northern Languedoc rebelled against increased taxation; in 1675 a rebel army took control of Bordeaux for four months at the same time as a revolt in Brittany had to be countered by a military campaign by 16,000 regular troops. And so on. By 1700, however, the incidence of rural unrest conducted by large armed bands and directed essentially against royal tax-collectors had greatly diminished.

That did not mean that the French – or indeed the European – countryside matured into the sort of rural idyll depicted in the paintings of Claude Lorraine. Rather, the peasants turned their hostility against a different target, namely the seigneurs, and used judicial rather than direct action to secure redress of their grievances. As the King's control, especially through the intendants, and the authority of his courts improved, so did the latter become more attractive. As Daniel Roche has observed: 'The growth of the state gave the peasantry the ability to protest, as well as new reasons to avail themselves of that ability.' The same phenomenon could be found east of the Elbe, where 'The Junkers' faithless servants' (to borrow the title of a seminal article by William Hagen) also made full use of an enhanced ability to protest. In July 1787 King Frederick William II of Prussia issued a proclamation to be communicated 'especially to the lower orders', in which he observed 'with the highest displeasure that in recent times lawsuits and quarrels between landlords and their subject villagers have greatly multiplied'. However, he did not seek to abolish altogether this 'unbridled passion for litigation', rather to direct it into the proper channels. Indeed, he took the opportunity to issue a warning to lords tempted to abuse their authority:

But if any estate owner abuses his rights and jurisdictional powers to harass his subject villagers wrongly with demands for labour services and fees beyond what they properly owe him; or if he in any way encroaches upon their property or their prerogatives; or if he is guilty of other forbidden exactions or violent mistreatment of his subjects; then not only will such wrongful breach of Our trust in the nobility be punished by the laws of the land, but it will also incur special signs of Our deepest displeasure and disgrace at Our hands.

On the estate of Stavenow, the peasants proved doughty opponents when Major Joachim Friedrich von Kleist attempted – as they saw it – to increase their labour dues unlawfully. Kleist's control of his seigneurial court could give him only temporary advantage, for the peasants hired a lawyer and took their case to the royal court in Berlin. The case was eventually settled in 1797, after more than thirty years of litigation, with the peasants coming out on top. As we have seen, this running battle did not prevent Kleist from promoting agricultural innovation and doubling the value of his estates.

Where royal justice was either absent or mistrusted, the peasants adopted other strategies of resistance. Passive resistance, prevarication, go-slows, feigned incomprehension, dumb insolence – the whole repertoire of non-cooperation was employed by the weak but resentful in the face of authority. Where the terrain was favourable and landlord pressure intolerable, the recalcitrant often turned to crime. In Calabria, the southernmost province of the Kingdom of Naples, for example, banditry with a social edge was endemic. Wracked by disputes between landlords trying to erode communal rights and peasants trying to escape from seigneurial jurisdiction, during the closing decades of the eighteenth century something approaching 'a rural class war' (Giorgio Candeloro) raged. Travelling through Calabria in the late 1770s, Henry Swinburne noted:

The father of a family, when pressed for the payment of taxes, and sinking beneath the load of hunger and distress, *va alla montagna*, that is, retires to the woods, where he meets with fellow-sufferers, turns smuggler, and becomes by degrees an outlaw, a robber and an assassin.

A terrible earthquake in 1783, which killed 40,000 people and destroyed over 200 villages, proved to be the last straw for many long-suffering peasants. A government scheme to draw the teeth of social unrest by expropriating the Church backfired when the land was bought not by local cultivators but by middle-class carpet-baggers. To add injury to insult, the suppression of the monasteries destroyed an important traditional source of charity. By 1787 the bandit gangs had proliferated to the point of ubiquity and were posing a real threat to the regime. In that year D'Agostino of Grotteria, for example, assembled a gang strong enough to rule the Calabrian coast all the way from Catanzaro to Reggio and was suppressed only after a major military exercise. When law and order collapsed completely, following the French invasion of 1798 and the counter-revolutionary crusade of Cardinal Ruffo and the '*Sanfedisti*', the bandits came into their kingdom. Among others to emerge was one of the most celebrated bandits of European history – Michele Pezza, alias 'Fra Diavolo', who became the hero of an opera by Auber (1830), a novel by Alexandre Dumas (1861) and a Laurel and Hardy film (1933). We shall return to him when discussing resistance to the French Revolution in a later chapter.

Bandits like Fra Diavolo were criminals first and social protesters second – usually a very long way second. Their victims were often their own kind. Yet such was the need on the part of the rural poor to find a secular saviour to give them hope of a promised land of plenty and social justice, that some very unpromising material was transfigured into heroic status. The eighteenth century proved to be, in Eric Hobsbawm's words, 'the golden age of bandit-heroes'. It was a period when pressure on rural communities from population growth was intense, when the state's control of the countryside was uncertain, when physical communications were primitive, but when improvements in symbolic communications allowed the propagation of myths by word, image and song. So it was also a period which saw the appearance of Stenka Razin (Russia), Juro Janošik (Slovakian part of Hungary), Louis-Dominique Bourguignon, alias Cartouche (France), Angelo Duca, alias Angiolillo (Naples), Diego Corrientes (Spain), Robert Mandrin (France), Johannes Bückler, alias Schinderhannes (the Rhineland), 'Rob Roy' MacGregor (Scotland), Matthias Weber, alias The Slicer (The Rhineland), Dick Turpin (England), and also a major revival of the cult of Robin Hood. All these men – and untold others – qualify to a greater or lesser extent for the status of 'social bandits', defined by Hobsbawm as 'peasant outlaws whom the lord and state regard as criminals, but who remain within peasant society, and are considered by their people as heroes, as champions, avengers, fighters for justice, perhaps even leaders of liberation, and in any case as men to be admired, helped and supported'.

It is this mythologizing which makes these men interesting. Historians have mercilessly stripped away the thick coats of glamour applied by wishful thinking, to reveal the petty criminals concealed within, but that was not how contemporaries saw them. The marquis d'Argenson lamented Robert Mandrin's ability to cause mayhem in the French countryside in the 1750s: 'Unfortunately, the people are all for these rebels because they make war on the farmers-general, who are reputed to be excessively rich, and bring people goods at lower cost. Hence the officers who must fight in this war do so reluctantly and speak of nothing but their woes.' One of Mandrin's great assets in building a popular reputation was the apparently victimless nature of his crimes, for his main business was smuggling, taking advantage of the chaotic internal customs dues we have already examined (see above, pp. 30–34). Based in the Dauphiné, he organized the smuggling of a wide range of items, including leather, furs, tobacco, gunpowder, lead-shot, various kinds of fabrics and even agricultural produce across a wide area stretching from Auvergne to Provence and Savoy to Burgundy. At his peak he is reputed to have employed around 300 in his gang. He was caught in 1755 and broken on the wheel in public at Valence, to encourage the others, but his reputation as a French version of Robin Hood, stealing from the rich to give to the poor, spread like wildfire through chap-books, woodcuts and ballads. As d'Argenson gloomily observed, 'the whole country is for the smugglers'.

As we shall see later, as the old regime tottered towards its end there was an efflorescence of rural crime with social overtones, but for most of the century the various French police forces were able to contain the problem. It was out on the periphery of Europe, where state control was virtually absent, that really major eruptions of rural resistance could occur. Significantly, the greatest outbreak of the late seventeenth century took place around the rivers Don and Volga, to where fugitive peasants from Poland and Russia had fled. It was led by a Cossack called Stenka Razin, who in 1667 assembled a band consisting mainly of landless immigrants with nothing to lose. For the next three years they preyed on both Russian and Persian settlements before concentrating on the former. By this time, Razin commanded a substantial army of 7,000 which quickly rose to perhaps as many as 20,000, as he captured Astrakhan on the Volga delta, Tsaritsyn (better known later as Stalingrad) and Saratov. When he reached Simbirsk, his army had advanced more than 500 miles (800 km) and was more than halfway to Moscow. However, by this time the government of Tsar Aleksei I had had time to organize a response. In October 1670 an army commanded by Prince Yury Baryatinsky crushed Razin's large but undisciplined horde and sent it fleeing back towards the lands of the Don Cossacks. Razin himself was handed over to the authorities in April 1671 by Cossacks loyal to the regime. He was publicly executed by quartering in Red Square. His revolt did not die with him, however, and it was not until December of the same year that the insurrectionaries' last stronghold – Astrakhan – fell to the regime.

A century later, an even greater peasant insurrection broke out in the same sort of region, for the same sort of reasons and with the same sort of result. It is some indication of the special character of Russian political life that its leader claimed to be Peter III, murdered in 1762 in a palace revolution. Peter had been succeeded by his widow, Catherine II, but her hold on the throne was anything but secure. Not only was it assumed that she had connived at her husband's removal, but their son Paul, born in 1754, had at least as good a claim to the throne as she did. In the event, Catherine ruled until 1796, although not without challenge – twenty-six pretenders appeared during the course of her reign, sixteen of them claiming to be Peter III. By far the most dangerous turned out to be a Don Cossack by the name of Emel'yan Pugachev, who had served in the Russian army in the Seven Years War and against the Turks after

1768. Deserting in 1771, Pugachev then spent two vagrant years living by his wits, until in 1773 he appeared on the Iaik (often transliterated as Yaik) river. There he found the eponymous Cossack Host in a state of feverish unrest following the brutal suppression of a mutiny (also led by a Peter III pretender) the previous year.

It cannot be established – and probably does not matter – just how many of Pugachev's followers really believed his claim to be Peter III. As he was illiterate, and prone to making preposterous claims such as that his trusty sword had been given to him by his 'godfather' Peter the Great (who had died in 1725), it seems unlikely that those closest to him were taken in. What was important was the perceived need to legitimate the revolt by appeal to a traditional authority in countering the evil usurper and her wicked advisers. What made Peter III so attractive as a model was the rumour that he had been deposed to prevent his proclamation of the emancipation of the serfs. He had indeed taken the first steps towards the emancipation of Church peasants, which helps to explain why this group provided some of Pugachev's most enthusiastic supporters. And it is liberty which was the central theme of Pugachev's manifestos: 'the freedom of the rivers from their sources to their mouths, and the land and the growth thereon', freedom of religion, freedom from taxation, freedom from conscription, together with more material inducements such as free land, food (twelve *chetverti* or *c.*70 bushels of grain per annum), arms, and even money (twelve roubles per annum). Although ordinary peasants gave active support to Pugachev, this was really a revolt of those on the margin: fugitives with nothing in their pockets, but a great deal of hatred in their hearts; Cossacks who resented the ever-growing intrusion of the Russian state; Tartar and Bashkir nomads whose way of life was under threat from the same force; Old Believers who viewed Catherine as the Antichrist; 'ascribed' serfs in the factories of the Urals who turned on their masters and then gladly made arms and ammunition for Pugachev's forces; and so on.

When shaken together, these ingredients proved to be truly explosive, not least because the Russian army was still fighting the war against the Ottoman Turks that had begun in 1768. Pugachev's first manifesto was read out on 17 September 1773; he was betrayed to the authorities almost exactly a year later, on 15 September 1774. In the meantime, his followers, numbering tens of thousands, had looted, raped and murdered their way across an area the size of the British Isles. Their final tally was

1,572 serf owners and their dependants, 237 clergy and 1,067 officials put to death – and even these figures are incomplete. For the most part, this was not an organized military campaign but a series of pillaging operations. In August 1774, for example, Pugachev's main army celebrated its capture of Saratov by hanging twenty-four landowners and twenty-one officials, killing an untold number of other inhabitants and looting everything that could be looted. The main host then moved south towards Tsaritsyn, but left behind twenty-nine armed bands to compete for the further devastation of the neighbourhood. It seems that, like Stenka Razin before him, who was operating in very similar territory, Pugachev could not grasp the potential for a full-scale national serf rising and, instead of turning north and west to Moscow, turned back south to Cossack country and 'his people'. It is also possible that the news that peace had been concluded with the Turks in July 1774 convinced him that a wider campaign was no longer viable.

In the badlands around the Volga and the Don, the writ of the imperial authorities ran fitfully, and usually only when it was supported by the regular army. In the *guberniia* of Kazan, which included six provinces and a population of about two-and-a-half million, there were only eighty officials and a negligible military force. So what might have been just a brief riot in a better-policed state was given enough slack to grow into a full-blown rising. Pugachev was the second insurrectionary 'Peter III' to pop up in this unlikely spot in as many years. There was a special flavour to this, the greatest peasant revolt of the eighteenth century in terms of death and destruction. At its heart was a shriek of rage from the dispossessed. As an Old Believer factory serf from the Urals put it: 'Who Pugachev was did not trouble us, nor did we even care to know. We rose in order to come out on top and to take the place of those who had tormented us. We wanted to be masters and to choose our own faith . . . Had we won, we would have had our own tsar and occupied whatever rank and station we desired.' They certainly took their opportunity to exact revenge on their tormentors when it presented itself. It has been estimated that during the closing stage of the revolt, around 1,000 nobles, officials, army officers and clergy – men, women and children – were tortured, raped and murdered. It need hardly be added that the imperial troops responded in kind. Pugachev himself was sentenced to be quartered in public but, to the disappointment of the crowd, was beheaded before dismemberment took place.

PAUPERIZATION AND PROSPERITY

There was one important characteristic shared by the Don-Volga region with other restive parts of Europe – population pressure. David Moon has estimated that between the 1720s and the middle of the following century, the number of male Don Cossacks grew by more than ten times, from 29,000 to 304,000, much of that increase, of course, coming from immigration. As we have seen in Chapter 2, this was a phenomenon common to all of Europe, with common results – the most common being a corresponding increase in the price of food, as demand outstripped supply. In the modern developed world, with bulk-carriers on land and sea and a global agricultural economy, such imbalance can be swiftly corrected by the movement of food from areas of surplus to areas of scarcity. In the age of the quadruped, this option was available only to a very limited extent and was confined to those with access to water communications. The main response had to come from local resources. So everywhere previously waste land was brought into cultivation, in many places there was a shift from pastoral to arable, and in some places productivity was increased by new crops and new techniques. Nowhere did the agricultural system prove to be sufficiently elastic and so everywhere the price of food increased faster than other commodities and services, notably manufactured goods and wages. In the early 1770s there was a surge in prices caused by poor harvests across continental Europe. In Tuscany, for example, the price of grain rose from 12 *lire* a sack before 1763 to 18 in 1771, to 20 in 1783 and 23 in 1790. In Toulouse, according to the figures presented by Robert Forster, the price of grain increased by 67 per cent between 1740–47 and 1780–87.

As the 'price scissors' between the escalating cost of food and the lagging cost of everything else opened up, certain groups were placed in a highly advantageous position, as they could sell for more and buy for less. First and foremost among the beneficiaries were those who owned enough land to grow a surplus. And first and foremost among that elite were of course the great landowners. Their consideration must await a later chapter, but there were also ordinary peasants who found themselves in this happy position. However, one vital qualification needs to be made at the outset – to benefit, the cultivator had to be within reach of a market. There is no point in growing a surplus if it cannot be sold. At Tobolsk in Siberia in 1793, John Parkinson wrote of the local peasants: 'They only seek to have just corn enough for their own service; if they have more, there are no means of disposing it.' On the other hand, the proximity of a market created a strong incentive to produce more. In the Rhineland, for example, the eponymous river encouraged the development of a thriving specialized agriculture, as the traveller J. K. Risbeck reported in 1786:

The earth yields uncommon returns, and the corn of this country is imported [sic] far and wide on the Rhine. There are also large quantities of fruits and greens of all kinds; excellent asparagus and cabbage are the food of the most common people: nor is there a place in Germany where the people are so fond of them, or have a greater supply of provisions of this kind. Great shiploads of their cabbages, as well raw as pickled are carried down the Lower Rhine as far as Holland. The little city of Croneberg, situated on an eminence six miles off the main road, drives a trade with Holland to the amount of eight thousand guilders a-year for apples, cyder, and chestnuts, of which last it has large groves. All the villages of the country lie in orchards of trees and command large fields of corn below.

In the same year at the other end of Europe, Joseph Townsend found similarly prosperous diversity in the market gardens surrounding Barcelona: 'The country around Barcelona is well cultivated, and abounds with vines, figs, olives, oranges. Silk; flax, hemp, algarrobo, fruit, wheat, barley, oats, rye, beans, peas, vetches, Indian corn, millet, with all kinds of lettuce, cabbages, colliflowers [sic], and other vegetables for the service of the kitchen.'

The problems of the peasants in every day and age are so well known through harrowing images, both pictorial and verbal, that it is easy to forget that few communities were so wretched that there were not a few fat cats (coqs de village as they were known in France) who had the luck or the enterprise to make economic conditions work for them. Throughout the German-speaking lands, folk-museums are full of arte-facts – painted chests and cupboards, furniture, clocks, kitchen utensils and clothing – dating from this period and testifying to peasant well-being, not to mention the numerous ornate dwellings that have survived. Anec-dotal evidence of peasants living high off the hog is easy to find for the later eighteenth century. In January 1763, despite the fact that the Seven Years War was still underway, Count Lehndorf recorded in his diary a visit to 'a rich peasant's wedding' at Ottersleben near Magdeburg. As more than three hundred people had been invited, it was just as well that the catering arrangements were generous: forty-two capons, thirty-six *Scheffel* (*c.*440 gallons or 2,000 litres) of wheat-flour for pastries, carp to the value of 150 *talers*, two oxen, fourteen calves, brandy to the value of 150 *talers*, and so on. The bride's trousseau was worth in excess of 3,000 *talers*, her dowry was 14,000 *talers*. Lehndorf added: 'these rich peasants, who still enjoy their ancient privileges, are subjects of the Cathedral. I have a grand time at these rural festivities and I take special pleasure in the fact that these people are content with their lot and enjoy a comfortable standard of living.' Similar accounts of prosperity can be found in southern Bavaria, the Black Forest, on the Hohenlohe plain, in parts of Hessen and Thuringia, Schleswig-Holstein, in the Rhine and Moselle valleys, and on the North Sea coast. One final example must suffice: looking back at the last generation of the eighteenth century, Pastor Harms of the village of Lunden in the Dithmarschen region on the North Sea coast of Germany reflected: 'It was then that a new impetus was given to the life of the inhabitants of the marshland by good harvests and good prices. The houses became grander, the furniture finer, the carriages more splendid, the clothing more sophisticated, the way of life more refined, the mode of expression more affected, the noses higher, the hands more delicate and always full of coins.'

These were the kind of peasants who caught the eye, but they were also of course in a small minority. The great majority did not grow enough to feed themselves and their families and still have a marketable surplus. For them, the price scissors were an instrument of torture. As the price of food climbed and the labour market filled up, real wages fell. In Great Britain between 1760 and 1795 food prices rose by 30 per cent but wages by only 25 per cent. This was enough to be perceived by contemporaries: John Howlett stated firmly in 1786 that 'the price of labour has not advanced in proportion to the advance in the price of provisions'. In France the discrepancy was greater: according to the figures of Ernest Labrousse, the cost of living rose by 62 per cent between 1730 and 1790 but wages by only 26 per cent (although it should be noted that recently his figures have been challenged and a more realistic figure for the decline in real wages of 10 per cent has been advanced). Spain (with the exception of Catalonia) appears to have been worst affected, with cereal prices doubling between 1750 and 1800 but wages increasing only by 20 per cent. All these, and other figures from elsewhere, are open to all kinds of qualifications, but they do point in the same direction – to a worsening standard of living for those obliged to sell their labour in order to enter the market for commodities.

How many peasants owned no land and earned their living as agricultural labourers? No simple answer can be given, as the percentage varied from country to country, province to province, even village to village. In *The Coming of the French Revolution*, Georges Lefebvre stated that landless peasants accounted for 20 per cent of the population in the Limousin, 30–40 per cent in Normandy, 70 per cent in the region around Versailles and 75 per cent in maritime Flanders. In Spain the landless were especially common in the centre and south, the national figure being somewhere between a third and a quarter, but reaching two-thirds in a large swathe of territory extending from Madrid through La Mancha southwards to Granada and Murcia, and 80 per cent in heavily populated Andalusia. Significantly, it was Great Britain, which boasted the most commercialized agricultural system, that showed the highest percentage of rural proletarians. As their number grew faster than the rural economy, their bargaining position was eroded. Writing in *The Case of Labourers in Husbandry* in 1795, David Davies observed: 'The great plenty of working hands always to be had when wanted, having kept down the price of labour below its proper level, the consequence is universally felt in the increased number of dependent poor.' The first reliable figures were not assembled until 1851, when they showed that just over 300,000 people described themselves as 'farmers and graziers', employing 1,500,000 labourers to cultivate their farms covering on average just over 110 acres, a much higher figure than could be found anywhere on the continent.

England probably boasted a higher average per capita income than anywhere else in Europe, but it was also shamed by widespread rural poverty and wracked by periodic unrest. John Stevenson has established that rioting was relatively uncommon in early modern England, picking up only towards the end of the seventeenth century, 'but it was during the eighteenth century that food riots became most pronounced, occurring with increasing frequency as the century wore on and only dying out in the first half of the nineteenth century'. Particularly bad years, marked by harvest failure and/or trade depression, were 1727–9, 1739–40, 1756–7, 1766–8, 1772–3, 1783, 1795–6, 1800–01 and 1810–13. As elsewhere in Europe, this volatility was caused by the volatility of prices in what was still fundamentally an inelastic agricultural system. It has been estimated that the great majority of the British population was still heavily dependent on bread, consuming at least a pound (0.5 kg) a day. Just how much larger bread loomed in a working-man's budget is revealed by this summary of the annual expenditure by a family of eight in Banbury in Oxfordshire:

Table 7. Family average annual expenditure c.1750

	£	s.	d.
Bread (60 pounds/30 kg per week)	27	6	0
Rent	2	12	0
Fuel	2	12	0
Other	2	12	0

Accustomed as we are to a world in which changes in the price of food are so gradual as to be almost imperceptible, it is difficult to grasp the sensitivity of the poor to sudden price surges. Even in a country with such (relatively) excellent communications as Great Britain, the swings could be violent. There were also sharp fluctuations within any given year, depending on the state of the harvest and the stocks of grain. An especially dangerous time for early modern European governments was late spring and early summer, when supplies from the previous harvest were beginning to run out but the new harvest had not yet been gathered in. That was when consumers were hypersensitive to the point of paranoia to rumours that grain was being hoarded against further price rises or was being moved out of the district to make a killing for its owners elsewhere. It was a fear well put by Samuel Jackson Pratt in his poem *Sympathy*:

> Deep groan the waggons with their pondr'ous loads,
> As their dark course they bend along the roads;
> Wheel following wheel, in dread procession slow,
> With half a harvest, to their points they go . . .
> The secret expedition, like the night
> That covers its intents, still shuns the light . . .
> While the poor ploughman, when he leaves his bed,
> Sees the huge barn as empty as his shed.

It was this kind of fear that ignited the French countryside in 1789. In Great Britain there never was a rising on such a widespread and intensive scale, but there was a great deal of popular resistance to anything that smacked of profiteering by middlemen when grain was scarce and prices were high. On this occasion, the Bible was on the side of the poor – 'He that withholdeth Corn, the People shall curse him: but Blessing shall be upon the Head of him that selleth it' (Proverbs 11:26). As Edward Thompson demonstrated in an influential article published in 1971, the English crowd was driven not only by hunger, fear or greed, but by a strong sense of what was legitimate and a determination to maintain a traditional structure of social norms and obligations by imposing a 'moral economy' by direct action. So they did not simply loot the granaries of farmers, millers or grain-dealers, but rather imposed what was deemed to be a fair price. If the 'moral economy' of the English crowd owes much to its creator's patrician determination to see good in every plebeian action, however violent, it did play a well-documented part in many food riots.

THE STATUS OF AGRICULTURE
AND THE PEASANT

Most contemporaries were less inclined to admire the rural poor, whose prevailing image in the late seventeenth century was dismal in the extreme. In 1684 a writer hiding behind the nom de plume 'Veroandro from Wahrburg' denounced them as follows:

It is true that peasants are human beings, but they are somewhat less refined and are coarser than the others. One only has to observe their behaviour and their gestures to see how easy it is to distinguish a peasant from someone with manners . . . Their odious way of speaking and behaving is obvious to everyone . . . When they eat, they don't use cutlery but thrust their hands straight into the bowl . . . It might almost be said that peasants should be treated like dried cod: they are best when they have been properly pummelled and pounded. Moreover, the dear peasants are never easier to control than when they have been given a full load of work to do, for then they are disciplined and regimented. The peasant always wants to be master, if his master allows him to give himself airs and graces. No one knows better how stubborn the peasants are than he who has lived among them for a long time. And one thing is certain, no amount of just saying the right thing will change a peasant, the only thing that he understands is firm language supported by threats of corporal punishment.

According to Gustav Freytag, who reprinted this indictment, the author was a clergyman. One might conjecture that perhaps he had experienced difficulties with his parishioners in collecting his tithes. If not typical, he was certainly not singing solo. A Bavarian jurist of the early eighteenth century defended the non-representation of peasants at the Estates on the grounds that they 'stand somewhere between the unreasoning beast and man'. In 1751 Johann Christoph Gottsched, the most celebrated literary critic of his age, disqualified peasants as subjects for literature because they were too oppressed politically, too exploited economically and too limited culturally. This kind of opinion was not confined to Germany. Travelling in Russia in 1761, the Frenchman Jean Chappe d'Auteroch referred variously to the peasants he encountered as living in a haze of alcoholic stupor and sexual debauchery, as being mischievous, habitually deceitful, dishonest, brutal, cowardly, violent, stupid, and so on.

This dark picture began to brighten during the course of the eighteenth century. To borrow the title of one distinguished study of the subject, by John Gagliardo, the peasant was moving from 'pariah to patriot'. This transition was achieved by a combination of public and private initiatives. As we have seen in the previous chapter, the official approach to economics in the later seventeenth century, personified by Colbert, was dominated by a concern to promote domestic manufacturing and foreign trade. As the limitations of this 'mercantilism' became evident, interest shifted towards agriculture. It came to be realized, in the words of Frederick the Great, that 'agriculture comes first among human activities, and without it there would be no merchants, no courtiers, no kings, no poets and no philosophers. The only true form of wealth is that produced by the soil. The reclamation of uncultivated land is a triumph over barbarism.' By the time Frederick wrote those words to Voltaire in 1775, the view he was expressing had become something of a truism, not least because of the theoretical underpinning provided by the physiocrats. One European ruler after another had made well-publicized gestures to demonstrate that agriculture and peasants were now receiving the attention they deserved. When the Empress Maria Theresa rolled up her sleeves and helped to bring in the wine harvest in the Leitha hills near Eisenstadt, for example, good care was taken to ensure that her subjects found out about it. The same was true of a much more celebrated episode involving her son, Joseph II. En route to meet Frederick the Great in 1769, Joseph stopped his carriage outside the Moravian village of Sclavikowicz, took over the plough of a peasant by the name of Trnka and ploughed a number of furrows. Unusually for Joseph II, this excursion into gesture politics proved to be a triumph, helping to establish his reputation of being 'the peasant's God'. The event was duly commemorated, first by a simple stone monument erected by the locals 'with an inscription in bad German', and then by 'an immense pedestal of marble with bas-relief representing the event and three inscriptions in Czech, German and Latin'. The latter, dismissed by Count Karl von Zinzendorf as 'tasteless and graceless', was commissioned by the local magnate, Prince Liechtenstein. Numerous prints depicting the scene were soon published and within a year the actual plough was on display and being venerated as a relic. This was no isolated royal initiative. Rulers as different as George III ('Farmer George') of England and Catherine the Great of Russia paraded their agricultural enthusiasm.

They were helped by a simultaneous surge of interest from the public sphere. Libraries across Europe are stuffed with eighteenth-century volumes dedicated to agriculture, describing – with varying degrees of indignation – its current deficiencies and explaining – with varying degrees of realism – how it might be improved. Both reflecting and encouraging debate were the numerous periodicals dedicated to the subject, as well as those aimed at enlightening the cultivators. Although many of these were short-lived, interest was keen enough to sustain a large and growing number. The *Annals of Agriculture*, founded by the tireless Arthur Young, was published in forty-six substantial volumes between 1784 and 1806. Serving as a bridge between public and private were the associations formed to promote agriculture. From the cascade of foundations in the eighteenth century, the following selection of foundations made before 1800 will give some idea of the ubiquity of interest: the Royal Dublin Society (1731); the Tuscan Society of Agriculture (1757); the Society of Agriculture, Commerce and Arts of Rennes (1757); the Economic Society of Berne (1759); the Royal Agricultural Society for the Généralité of Tours (1760); the Royal Agricultural Society for the Généralité of Paris (1761); the Thuringian Agricultural Society (1762); the Royal Agricultural Society for the Généralité of Orléans (1762); the Royal Agricultural Society for the Généralité of Rouen (1763); the Carinthian Agricultural Society (1764); the Celle (Hanover) Agricultural Society (1764); the Imperial Free Economic Society for the Encouragement in Russia of Agriculture and House-Building (1765); the Manchester Agricultural Society (1767); the Academy of Agriculture, Commerce and Arts of Verona (1768); the Agricultural Academies of the Republic of Venice (1768); the Academy of the Agrarian Arts of Padua (1768); the Royal Danish Agricultural Society (1769); the Royal Economic Society of Chambéry for Agriculture (1772); the Society for the Advancement of Agriculture in Amsterdam (1775); the Bath and West of England Society for the Encouragement of Agriculture, Arts, Manufactures and Commerce (1777); the Highland Society of Edinburgh (1784); the Agricultural Society of Turin (1785); the Royal Agricultural Society of France (1788); the Cornwall Agricultural Society (1793); the Peterborough Agricultural Society (1797); the Herefordshire Agricultural Society (1797); and the Newark and Nottinghamshire Agricultural Society (1799). Some of these were state creations, such as the Agricultural Society of Turin, founded on the orders of the King of Sardinia, Victor Amadeus III, 'to promote for the public advantage the cultivation of lands mainly in His Majesty's happy dominions in accordance with rules both appropriate and in keeping with their varied nature'. Others were entirely private – the Economic Society of Berne, for example, initiated by means of an advertisement placed in a local newspaper by Johann Rudolf Tschiffeli, seeking like-minded citizens interested in promoting agricultural advance. They organized prize essay competitions, published the results in their *Proceedings*, organized the distribution of seed and the popularization of new techniques, and ran their own model farm to advertise the advantages of progressive agriculture.

Along with this surge of interest in agriculture went a commensurate rise in the status of the cultivator. Agriculture was not the prime concern of the most influential economist of the age, Adam Smith, but he had a high regard for those who tilled the soil, for they 'require much more skill and experience than the greater part of mechanic trades'. Although generally regarded as 'the pattern of stupidity and ignorance', he argued, the common agricultural labourer in fact possessed great reserves of skill and understanding: 'how much the lower ranks of people in the country are really superior to those of the town is well known to every man whom either business or curiosity has led to converse with both'. This kind of opinion was repeated across Europe. The first action of the Russian Free Economic Society, founded in 1765 by a group of enlightened nobles at the instigation of Catherine the Great, was to organize an essay competition on the theme: 'what is most useful for society – that the peasant should own the land or only moveable property, and how far should his rights over the one or the other extend?' The winner was an Aachen academic with the un-German sounding name of Beardé de l'Abbaye. He argued that the peasant was the foundation of national prosperity, that the poorest peasant was worth more to the state than the useless, uncultured and avaricious magnate, that he should be emancipated and allowed to own all forms of property. It says something for the noble landowners who made up the society that they should have awarded the prize to this denunciation of the status quo. However, they voted by sixteen to twelve not to publish it.

Agronomists seeking to raise the status of agriculture and the peasant received powerful support from one of the most original and influential minds of the period. This was Jean-Jacques Rousseau, who in 1749 experienced a Pauline moment of conversion when a sudden flash of insight revealed that despite its superficial attractions, urban civilization had alienated humankind from its natural rural roots. True virtue was to be found in the spontaneous, unspoilt, natural world of the peasant. Rousseau conveyed this insight to a receptive public in theoretical treatises, in his autobiography, in novels and even in an opera – *Le Devin du village* (The Village Soothsayer) of 1752. The plot of the last-named is simple but clear: a shepherd, Colin, is seduced into neglecting his shepherdess, Colette, by the glamour of the lady of the manor. A despairing Colette enlists the help of the eponymous soothsayer. He tells Colin that Colette is cooling towards him, thus exciting Colin's jealousy and effecting a reconciliation. Although *Le Devin du village* was a tremendous success, Rousseau probably reached his largest audience with his epistolary novel *Julie, or the New Héloïse: letters exchanged by two lovers, living in a small town at the foot of the Alps. Collected and published by J. J. Rousseau*, first published in 1761. Voltaire may have said that he would rather kill himself than finish it, but dozens of editions and translations showed that he was the one who was out of step with the reading public of Europe. Indeed, it was 'probably the record best-seller of the whole of the eighteenth century' (John Lough). The peasantry was presented as 'the most useful and indeed the only truly necessary class in society', whose natural state of happiness could only be spoiled 'if the other classes tyrannise it with acts of violence or corrupt it with examples of vice'. Tilling the soil and living from its fruits was the only genuinely natural activity for humankind, and its only true pleasures were to be found in agriculture. So only the peasant could be a truly complete human being.

To explore further this fertilization of high culture by the peasantry would be to stray too far from this chapter's brief. Suffice it to say that all branches of the arts in the second half of the eighteenth century bore witness to the rising status of the rural world and its values. The danger here is that the aesthetic quality of a Gainsborough painting or a Haydn quartet will glamorize what was essentially a bleak scene and, moreover, a scene that was getting bleaker with every year that passed. It is more fitting to end with an observation about the pauperization of the masses of rural England, probably the most prosperous rural economy of the period, made by John Howlett:

There is, indeed, I cannot help thinking, something peculiarly ungenerous in our complaints of the burdensomeness of our poor. Within the last forty years the rent of our houses and land are increased eight or ten millions; the wealth of our farmers and tradesmen is augmented in similar proportion; that of our merchants and leading manufacturers in a degree infinitely greater. And shall we grudge to allow of this abundance two millions a year towards the support of those from the labour of whose hands and the sweat of whose brows we have derived the whole? Shall we grind their faces, and squeeze them to death, and then have the cruel absurdity of ascribing their fate to their increasing vice and profligacy?

PART TWO

Power

5

Rulers and Their Elites

TWO EXECUTIONS AND
TWO ASSASSINATIONS

At ten o'clock on the morning of Friday, 17 January 1793, the result was announced of a vote that had just been concluded in the National Convention after a session lasting more than thirty-six hours. The issue at stake was the sentence to be passed on Louis Capet, formerly known as 'King of the French'. The outcome could not have been closer: of the 721 deputies present and voting, 361 voted for the death penalty without conditions – a majority of just one. It fell to Pierre Victurnien Vergniaud, the greatest of the Girondin orators, to deliver the verdict: 'I declare, in the name of the National Convention, that the punishment it pronounces against Louis Capet is death.' The news was conveyed to the condemned man by the senior member of his defence team, the extravagantly named Chrétien-Guillaume de Lamoignon de Malesherbes. Any remaining hopes Louis might have had of a lesser penalty vanished when his visitor entered the room weeping. Louis sought to console Malesherbes with the assurance, 'I have been trying to think if, in the course of my reign, I did anything that deserved the slightest reproach from my subjects. Alas, M. de Malesherbes, I swear to you with all the sincerity of my heart, as a man who is about to appear before God, I have always wanted the happiness of the people.' It is some measure of his persistent inability to grasp what was going on in France after 1789 that Louis should think that the 'happiness of the people' was the major issue. After first clinging to his lawyer and then pacing up and down the room, he pulled himself together and began to prepare himself for death. The first step was to send his servant, Jean-Baptiste Cléry, to the library of the

Temple, the grim fortress in which he had been incarcerated since the previous August, to fetch a copy of David Hume's *The History of England from the Invasion of Julius Caesar to the Revolution of 1688*, first published in six volumes between 1754 and 1762.

The passage Louis was looking for began as follows: 'Three days were allowed the king between his sentence and his execution. This interval he passed with great tranquillity, chiefly in reading and devotion.' The king in question was, of course, Charles I, or rather 'Charles Stuart' as he was called by the special High Court of Justice established on 1 January 1649 by the Commons of the Rump Parliament. In the event, only 67 of the 135 nominated commissioners turned up to vote on 27 January that 'the said Charles Stuart, as a tyrant, traitor, murderer, and a public enemy, shall be put to death by the severing of his head from his body'. This verdict came after a trial during which Charles had demonstrated appreciably more consistency and panache than his French counterpart was able to muster a century-and-a-half later. His enemies had played into his hands by staging the trial in Westminster Hall, complete with specially erected tiered seating to allow the largest possible audience. It was here on 20 January that he achieved a first rhetorical triumph without actually saying a word, for his immediate response when the charges were read to him was to laugh derisively. In another non-verbal act of defiance, he wore his high-crowned hat throughout his appearances in the Hall, to demonstrate that he did not recognize the court's authority. He also wrong-footed his would-be judges by refusing to enter a plea, thus frustrating their wish for a public hearing of the thirty-three witnesses they had mobilized.

As it began, so the trial proceeded. Even the most committed of Parliamentarians had to concede that their opponent made the presiding judge, John Bradshaw, and the prosecuting counsel, John Cook, look clumsy and foolish. Charles played a strong hand for all it was worth. He had no difficulty in showing that he was being prosecuted by 'a fraction of a Parliament'; that his trial was opposed by the House of Lords, the third part of the constitutional trinity forming the 'King in Parliament'; that the Commons' claim to have the support of the 'people' was fictitious, for not one tenth of the population had been consulted; and that his trial was contrary to both the common law, which held that the king could do no wrong, and to God's law, for was not Holy Scripture unequivocal on the absolute duty of obedience? No matter what side they were on, these were men who knew their Bible inside out, including St Paul's injunction: 'The powers that be are ordained of God. Whosoever therefore resisteth the power, resisteth the ordinance of God: and they that resist shall receive to themselves damnation. For rulers are not a terror to good works, but to the evil' (Romans 13:1–3).

But Charles had a higher objective than proving the incompetence of his judges. Knowing that such a state trial could only produce one verdict (guilty) and one sentence (death), he set about constructing a programme for posterity. Offering no compromise on monarchical authority, he made it more palatable both by invoking divine support and by contrasting the deep historical roots of his own position with the radical novelty of his opponents: 'I have a trust committed to me by God, by old and lawful descent; I will not betray it, to answer to a new unlawful authority.' More importantly, he stressed that it was he who was the true champion of the people of England: 'do you pretend what you will, I stand more for their liberties. For if power without law may make laws, may alter the fundamental laws of the kingdom, I do not know what subject he is in England, that can be sure of his life, or anything he calls his own.' In a particularly memorable utterance combining aristocratic insouciance with populism, he proclaimed: 'For the charge, I value it not a rush; it is the liberty of the people of England that I stand for.'

This dual appeal to religion and liberty he took with him to the place of execution on 30 January 1649. Had he raised his eyes to the ceiling of the Banqueting Hall of Whitehall Palace, as he made his way to the window leading to the scaffold erected against the wall outside, he would have passed under Rubens' great fresco depicting the apotheosis of his father, James I. He was about to achieve his own very different apotheosis. Famously wearing two shirts, lest the crowd might think he shivered from fear rather than cold, he conducted himself with the serene dignity and courage of which enduring myths are made. Well might Andrew Marvell write:

> He nothing common did or mean
> Upon that memorable Scene:
> But with his keener Eye
> The Axe's edge did try:

> Nor call'd the Gods with vulgar spight
> To vindicate his helpless Right,
> But bow'd his comely Head,
> Down as upon a Bed.

His final words could be heard only by those surrounding him, but they were to have a mighty resonance when published. In a brilliant stroke of self-deprecation, he acknowledged the justice of God's retribution – not because he was guilty of the crimes invented by his accusers, but because he had allowed his faithful and guiltless servant Strafford to be judicially murdered by Parliament in 1641. He reaffirmed his commitment to monarchical liberty, presenting himself as 'a martyr of the people': 'Truly I desire their liberty and freedom as much as anybody whomsoever; but I must tell you their liberty and freedom consists in having of government, those laws by which their life and their goods may be most their own. It is not for having a share in government, sir, that is nothing pertaining to them. A subject and a sovereign are clear different things.' So what Cromwell and the army had hoped would be an execution of not just a man but a whole political system turned out to be 'a massive propaganda victory' (David L. Smith) for the royalists. As the axe fell, there rose from the crowd not a shout of triumph but 'such a groan as I never heard before, and I desire I may never hear again', as one observer recorded.

For those who could not attend the execution, there were to be plenty of representations available within a very short time of the event. Prints provided a visual narrative of the events, including the King's last walk to the scaffold, the moment of truth, the executioner holding aloft the severed head, spectators rushing to dip their handkerchiefs in the royal blood, and so on. For the literate, verbal accounts – often also illustrated – flowed from the presses, especially from the enterprising publishers of the Dutch Republic. Both genres were combined in the most successful of all memorial volumes – *Eikon Basilike* [Royal Portrait]: *The Portraiture of His Sacred Majesty in His Solitudes and Sufferings*. Advance copies became available on the very day that the axe fell and hawkers were selling the first print-run of 2,000 within the week. Purporting to be the King's own work, although John Gauden, Bishop of Exeter, had played a major part in turning royal ideas into polished prose, it proved to be the publishing sensation of the century. Despite the high price –

fifteen shillings initially – it had appeared in thirty-five editions by the end of 1649, not to mention eight on the continent. By 1660 it had been translated into Latin (more than once), Dutch, French, German and Danish in twenty foreign-language editions. It might be noted in passing that, when he commissioned his chaplain to translate it into Latin, Charles stated that he wished 'that it should be delivered to the world in a language common to the most part of the world'. For the reader in a hurry, there were extracts and digests; for the poetic reader, there was even a version in verse. The first edition and many of the more expensive editions were adorned with a graphic frontispiece, depicting the King as a martyr, clasping a crown of thorns representing his suffering in this world, but steadfastly directing his gaze upwards to the eternal glory that awaited him in the next. The volume's twenty-eight chapters had three objectives: a justification of the King's actions in the past, a pro-gramme for royalists in the future, and pious edification through prayers and contemplations. Combining all three was Charles's political testa-ment, in the form of an open letter to the Prince of Wales. It will serve as well as any other contemporary document to illustrate the essentially religious nature of political discourse in mid-seventeenth-century Europe. As Charles puts it: 'The true glory of princes consists in advan-cing God's glory, in the maintenance of true religion and the church's good.' It was only after God, the royal soul and the Anglican Church had been attended to that 'the next main hinge on which your prosperity will depend and move' was considered. This was 'civil justice', those settled laws of the kingdom which made the people subjects not slaves and maintained a mutually beneficial relationship between royal pre-rogatives and the people's 'ingenuous liberties, which consists in the enjoyment of the fruits of their industry and the benefit of those laws to which they themselves have consented'.

This artful publication combined firmness with magnanimity, resol-ution with clemency. No wonder that it was showered with encomiums by the royalist pamphleteers who flocked to publicize this 'everlasting stupendous monument of a book, raised higher than the Pyramids of Egypt', whose 'very reading of it aggravateth our loss of so gracious and excellent a prince'. It helped to ensure that royalism remained both a populist and a popular force in English politics. It was the republicanism of Lord Protector Cromwell and his Commonwealth that from this moment was increasingly on the defensive. It also helped to sustain the

English monarchy through the trials and tribulations that awaited it at the inept hands of Charles's two sons. Charles II and James II would have done well to mark, learn and inwardly digest their father's advice: 'Keep you to true principles of piety, virtue and honour, and you shall never want a kingdom.'

By 1793, however, piety, virtue and honour were no longer enough. Louis XVI had demonstrated all three in abundance, yet still lost his kingdom and his head. It is of course impossible to determine exactly when his end became inevitable – perhaps on the night of 20/21 June 1791 when he tried to run away from the Revolution and was caught at Varennes; perhaps on 1 October 1791 when a brand-new National Assembly was convened; perhaps on 20 April 1792 when war was declared; perhaps on 20 November 1792 when compromising documents were discovered in the strong-box that had come to light in the Tuileries. Certain it was that by the time it was decided to put him on trial on 3 December 1792, there could be only one verdict. Louis himself knew this. As he said to his chief defender, Malesherbes, in the course of their first interview: 'I am sure they will make me perish; they have the power and the will to do so. That does not matter. Let us concern ourselves with my trial as if I could win; and I will win, in effect, since the memory that I will leave will be without stain.'

He approached his final ordeal with stolid calm. Not even his gruelling and humiliating appearance at the bar of the National Convention on 11 December to answer to the charges could affect his fabled appetite: on his return to the Temple he consumed six cutlets, a whole chicken and 'some eggs'. Yet he had just made his first mistake. By agreeing to a trial and asking for counsel, he had recognized the competence of the National Convention to try him. So when his defence counsel, de Sèze, pointed out that the constitution of 1791 stated unequivocally that 'the person of the King is inviolable and sacred', the pass had already been sold. Nor was the ingenious appeal to Rousseau's dictum that natural law could not be applied to an individual anything more than a debating point. The deputies of the Convention were indeed acting as both accusers and judges, so that Louis was unique in having 'neither the rights of a citizen nor the prerogatives of a king', but that was just what one had to expect from a system founded on the sovereignty of the people, exercised through a single-chamber legislature – and to which he had given his consent. By the standards of Charles I, Louis XVI had been a model of compromise, not to say compliance. Perhaps it was just because he lacked that haughty Stuart disdain that he cut such a less impressive figure during his own endgame. In a way, it was a tale of two hats: Charles had contemptuously kept his hat on throughout his trial; Louis had feebly donned the Phrygian cap of liberty to placate the crowd that invaded the Tuileries Palace on 17 June 1792.

Reading David Hume's *History of England*, as he awaited the summons to the scaffold, could not have told Louis how to save his life but it did show him how to die. Like Charles, he studiously avoided any sign of fear. On his last evening he enjoyed his usual large meal – on this occasion pan-fried chicken, pastries, boiled beef and turnip purée, washed down by red wine plus a glass of Malaga with dessert – and then slept soundly. On the morning of 21 January 1793 he rose at five, heard Mass at six, conducted by the non-juring Irish priest Henry Essex Edgeworth de Firmont (non-juring in the sense that he refused to take the oath to the Civil Constitution of the Clergy), took communion, and awaited the arrival of the Convention's emissary. As reported by Edgeworth, he remained unshakeably convinced of both his innocence and his redemption, saying: 'My God, how happy I am to have my principles! Where would I be without them? With them even death appears sweet to me! Yes, there exists an incorruptible judge in heaven who will know how to give me the justice that men refuse me here.' Before he could claim his reward, however, Louis faced a prolonged ordeal, as the carriage sent to bring him from the Temple to the place de la Révolution (previously place Louis XV, subsequently place de la Concorde) took an hour-and-a-half to travel through the crowded streets lined by soldiers four ranks deep. Louis kept his eyes on his breviary, probably not even aware of the quixotic attempt to rescue him launched by Baron de Batz and four others. Reaching the raised scaffold at 10 a.m., his hair was cut by the executioner Sanson, as Edgeworth murmured words of spiritual comfort. Louis then attempted to make a speech, first silencing the constant roll of drums by a shout. He had managed only to say 'I die innocent. I pardon my enemies and I hope that my blood will be useful to the French, that it will appease God's anger . . .' when the drummers were hurriedly told to resume. Quickly strapped to the plank, he became the most prominent advertisement of the efficiency of Dr Joseph-Ignace Guillotin's invention, as Father Edgeworth shouted above the sounds of the drums, 'Son of Saint Louis, ascend to Heaven!'

The revolutionaries proved to be much more thorough in their completion of the grisly process than their Parliamentarian predecessors. Whereas the latter had Charles I's head sewn back on his body and buried in St George's Chapel at Windsor, Louis' physical remains were taken straight to the Madeleine cemetery, placed in an open wooden coffin, covered in a double layer of quicklime and interred in a deep grave which was immediately filled. The French revolutionaries were not getting rid of an evil king, rather the institution of monarchy itself. In their eyes, Louis XVI was guilty not so much because he had committed acts of treason as for having reigned at all. In Saint-Just's pithy formulation: 'No man can reign innocently.' From this point of view, the killing of the king was an act of ritual cleansing. They thought they were replacing the myth of magical monarchical authority with the myth of a phoenix-like republic rising from the blood of the dead king (Clifford Geertz). As one revolutionary newspaper put it: 'The blood of Louis Capet, shed by the blade of the law on 21 January 1793, cleanses us of a stigma of 1,300 years.' But it turned out that Louis' twin ideals – Roman Catholicism and monarchism – could not be dissolved by quicklime. However complex the motivation behind their rising may have been, the counter-revolutionaries of the Vendée chose to call themselves the 'Catholic and Royal Army'. If a republican phoenix did soar from the blood that dripped from Louis' severed head, so did its monarchical antithesis.

As we shall see, much can be learnt about the nature of politics in this period from the apparently similar fates of Charles I and Louis XVI, but first it needs to be recorded that monarchs were as much at risk from the assassin's knife as from the executioner's axe. At Versailles on 5 January 1757 Louis XV was fortunate that Robert-François Damiens's knife thrust missed all vital organs when it penetrated three inches between his fourth and fifth ribs. Unwilling to believe that Damiens had acted alone, his interrogators soon resorted to red-hot pincers and other forms of torture to extract the names of his accomplices. He would not – could not – comply, although if he was the nobody he claimed to be, he was 'a nobody not unknown by some pretty important somebodies' (Dale van Kley). The only motivation he would reveal to his torturers was anger at the misery of the people and royal support for bishops and clergy 'who ought not to refuse the sacraments to people who live well'. That last criticism placed him among the supporters of Jansenism, the movement for reform in the Church associated with Bishop Jansen of Ypres (1585–1638), whose stress on the gratuitous nature of divine grace and opposition to the dominant Jesuits had proved especially popular in France. As the Parlement of Paris had always been a hotbed of Jansenism, its members moved quickly to dissociate themselves from Damiens, suggesting indeed that he had been put up to his crimes by the Jesuits. When they tried him, the Parlementaires showed they had nothing to do with him, by decreeing that the form of his execution should replicate the grisly punishment meted out to Ravaillac, the successful assailant of Henry IV in 1610. The details of the sentence provide an excellent if distasteful insight into the judicial attitudes of mid-eighteenth-century France:

The said Robert-François Damiens has been convicted of having committed a very mean, very terrible, and very dreadful parricidal crime against the King. The said Damiens is sentenced to pay for his crime in front of the main gate of the Church of Paris. He will be taken there in a tipcart naked and will hold a burning wax torch weighing two pounds. There, on his knees, he will say and declare that he had committed a very mean, very terrible and very dreadful parricide, and that he had hurt the King ... He will repent and ask God, the King and Justice to forgive him. When this will be done, he will be taken in the same tipcart to the Place de Grève and will be put on a scaffold. Then his breasts, arms, thighs, and legs will be tortured. While holding the knife with which he committed the said Parricide, his right hand will be burnt. On his tortured body parts, melted lead, boiling oil, burning pitch, and melted wax and sulphur will be thrown. Then four horses will pull him apart until he is dismembered. His limbs will be thrown on the stake, and his ashes will be spread. All his belongings, furniture, housings, wherever they are, will be confiscated and given to the King. Before the execution, the said Damiens will be asked to tell the names of his accomplices.

In the event, the actual execution was even more ghastly than this scenario suggests. The four horses proved unable to tear Damiens apart, not even after two reinforcements had been hitched up, so the executioner was obliged to employ an axe to sever what parts of the limbs were still attached. The victim remained conscious throughout, repeatedly shrieking, 'My God, have pity on me! Jesus, help me!', and – according to one observer – was still alive when his torso was thrown on to the pyre. It must be hoped that Damiens found comfort in the Christian charity of the priest in attendance, 'who despite his great age did not spare himself in offering consolation to the patient'. As if that were not enough, the authorities then required Damiens's children and aged parents to 'leave the realm with the injunction never to return on pain of hanging and strangulation without formality or trial'.

Across the Channel, the regicidal tradition also flickered on occasions. George III survived two attempts on his life, the first in 1786 when Margaret Nicholson, who believed she was the rightful sovereign, tried to stab him with a dessert knife as he alighted from his horse at St James's Palace. It was the King who intervened to save her from being lynched by the crowd, calling, 'The poor creature is mad! Do not hurt her! She has not hurt me!' His assailant was committed to a lunatic asylum, where she spent the next forty-two years. A more serious assault was launched at the Drury Lane Theatre in 1800 by James Hadfield, an army veteran who had sustained eight sabre wounds to the head at the battle of Roubaix in 1794. His pistol-shot narrowly missed its target, lodging in a pillar of the royal box. His dementia took the form of religious delusion, specifically the belief that his death at the hands of the state would effect the Second Coming of Christ. We shall never know whether he was right, for the state declined to oblige, incarcerating him instead (for forty-one years in his case). The only effect of these two episodes was to give the English public well-publicized opportunities to express their devotion to their King. At Drury Lane Theatre no less a person than Sheridan quickly improvised an additional verse to 'God Save the King', which was sung to a rapturous audience by Michael Kelly (who had created the role of Don Basilio in Mozart's *The Marriage of Figaro* at Vienna in 1786):

> From every latent foe,
> From the assassin's blow,
> God Save the King!
> O'er him thine arm extend,
> For Britain's sake defend,
> Our father, Prince, and friend,
> God save the King!

If Hadfield's aim had been better, the history of Great Britain would certainly have been different. Such was the case in Sweden, where the aristocratic conspirator Jacob Johan Anckarström shot King Gustavus III at a masked ball at the Stockholm opera house on 16 March 1792.

Although firing at point-blank range, he only just succeeded, his target living on for another fortnight before succumbing to gangrene. This episode is best known for providing the plot for Verdi's opera *Un Ballo in Maschera*, although the librettist, Antonio Somma, took little more than the actual fact of assassination. Far from being driven by the wrath of a cuckold (most improbable in view of Gustavus III's homosexuality), the historical Anckarström was motivated by political hostility. Yet the actual circumstances were dramatic enough for any opera. Gustavus had been warned in advance that an attempt would be made on his life, but insisted on attending the ball, not even bothering to conceal his identity by donning a full mask. On arrival he stood in the royal box for a quarter of an hour watching the dancing, presenting an easy target, before observing to his equerry, Baron Essen: 'They have lost a good opportunity of shooting me. Come let us go down; the masquerade seems bright and gay. Let us see whether they will dare to kill me!' Once that hostage to fortune had duly been claimed, the mortally wounded Gustavus was quick to blame the French revolutionaries he detested so passionately: 'I feel sure the Jacobins must have suggested the idea. Swedes are neither cowardly nor corrupt enough to have conceived such a crime.'

He was quite wrong, at least about Jacobin involvement. There was nothing revolutionary about his murder, it was just another of the aristocratic coups that were such a popular means of conflict resolution in the politics of early modern Europe. For this was not the action of a demented loner in the style of Damiens or Mrs Nicholson, it was a carefully planned attack involving many more than the forty conspirators eventually arrested. So was the even more momentous assassination nine years later in neighbouring Russia. Shortly after midnight on 12 December 1801, a group of Guards officers broke into the Michael Palace in St Petersburg and confronted Tsar Paul I in his bedroom. What then followed was very confused, not least because many of the assailants were drunk. It was their declared intention to force the Tsar to abdicate in favour of his son Alexander, although their leader, when asked what would happen if consent was not forthcoming, had grimly stated that to make an omelette it was first necessary to break eggs. In the event, Paul was dragged from behind the screen where he had tried to hide, and was then abused, beaten and finally strangled, his pathetic requests for a moment to pray being ignored. The news was quickly conveyed to

Alexander, who always claimed that his support for the coup had been conditional on his father not being harmed. Not many believed that, and even fewer accepted the official version of the cause of death as 'an apoplectic stroke'.

As most of the evidence as to what actually happened dates from a long time after the events, the true course of this squalid episode will never be established. What is certain is the heavy involvement of army officers. Of the sixty-eight conspirators identified, two-thirds were from the aristocratic Guards regiments, whose main purpose of course was to guard the life of their Tsar. It was on this occasion that a cynical Russian noble observed, 'Despotism tempered by assassination – that is our Magna Carta.' It was more than a quip, for it had both a long history and a bright future in Russia. Paul's own supposed father, Peter III, had been deposed and then strangled in a coup connived at by his wife Catherine in June 1762. Of Paul's successors, Nicholas I had to overcome an attempted military coup (the 'Decembrist' rising) on his accession in 1825, Alexander II was assassinated in 1881, Alexander III survived several attempts on his life before dying a natural death in 1894, and the last Tsar – Nicholas II – was murdered by Bolsheviks in 1918.

Although most rulers died in their beds, theirs was an uncertain occupation, and nowhere more so than in the country normally associated with 'absolutism'. Of the last nine kings of France, two were assassinated (Henry III in 1589 and Henry IV in 1610), one was executed (Louis XVI in 1793), one died in prison (Louis XVII in 1795), one was exiled (Louis XVIII in 1815) and two fled (Charles IX in 1830, Louis Philippe in 1848). The long period separating these two bursts of regicidal activity was less placid than might appear. Louis XIII fought three wars against his Protestant subjects and had to surmount a major conspiracy led by his brother Gaston, duc d'Orléans. His son, Louis XIV, never forgot the night of 9–10 February 1651, when he was obliged to feign sleep in the Palais-Royal, as a mob of rebellious Parisians forced their way into his room to see for themselves that he was still in the capital and still their hostage. Although they then left, it may safely be assumed that the boy-king – he was twelve years old – had been terrified by the experience. Certainly, his political mentors were sufficiently intimidated to make immediate political concessions to the opposition. On the following day, a royal order was signed releasing from custody three of the leaders of the *Fronde*, as the rebellion was known (*Fronde* means 'sling-shot'), all of them closely related to the King – the prince de Condé, the prince de Conti and the duc de Longueville. And we have already noted that Louis XV survived an attempt on his life in 1757.

The beginning of our period was particularly volatile. It was in the very first year – 1648 – that the *Frondes* began when the sovereign courts united to resist royal policy, supported by more than a thousand barricades thrown up around the royal palace in Paris. Revolts against Spanish rule in Portugal, Catalonia and Naples were already raging, and were now joined by fresh disturbances in Denmark, Poland and Muscovy. In 1649 Charles I was beheaded. In 1650 a coup excluded the infant head of the House of Orange from any political role in the Dutch Republic. Even before this latest great insurrectionary wave began, Jeremiah Whittaker had exultantly told the House of Commons in 1643 that, 'These are days of shaking and this shaking is universal.' Robert Mentet de Salmonet, who enterprisingly published a history of the English Civil War in 1649, preferred a more static image, observing that he was living through an 'Iron Age' which would be 'famous for the great and strange revolutions that have happened in it'.

LOUIS XIV AND
ABSOLUTE MONARCHY

Conflict resolution by means of regime change proved to be rarely successful in the long run. Of the various insurrections listed, only the Portuguese bid for independence can be said to have achieved its objectives. Indeed, for monarchists everywhere, the turbulent 1640s proved to be the darkest decade before the dawn of a new era of authoritarian government, often characterized by historians as 'the age of absolutism'. The lead was taken by France, where Louis XIV was declared to be of age on 7 September 1651, two days after his thirteenth birthday. Just over a year later, on 21 October 1652, he entered Paris in triumph. The return of his chief minister, Cardinal Mazarin, the chief target of the *frondeurs*, the following February was proof positive that the civil war had ended with an unequivocal victory for the royalists.

It was given visual expression by an unknown artist who depicted Louis XIV as 'Jupiter, vanquisher of the *Fronde*', clad as a Roman emperor and surrounded by the trophies of victory, his foot resting on the Gorgon's shield, in his hand the bolts of lightning with which he has quelled her monstrous plots. In the background, Vulcan and his assistants can be seen, busily preparing further thunderbolts, just in case. This process was brought to a triumphant – and triumphalist – conclusion on 7 June 1654 when Louis was crowned in the Cathedral of Reims. On his entry to the city, the Bishop of Soissons greeted him with the assurance that all his subjects prostrated themselves

before you, Sire, the Lord's Anointed, son of the Most High, shepherd of the flock, protector of the Church, the first of all kings on earth, chosen and appointed by Heaven to carry the sceptre of the French, to extend far and wide the honour and renown of the Lily [*fleur de lys*], whose glory outshines by far that of Solomon from pole to pole and sun to sun, making France a universe and the universe one France.

In the course of the coronation ceremony, Louis was anointed with the oil originally brought from Heaven by the Holy Ghost at the behest of Saint Rémy when he baptized Clovis, the Merovingian King of the Franks, as a Christian in *c*.493 (aerial assistance in transporting the oil had been needed on that occasion because the crush of people prevented it being carried into the church by more conventional means). This 'eighth sacrament' raised the King above all other mortals by making him a '*roi thaumaturge*', that is to say, a king on whom the Almighty had conferred miraculous healing powers. Two days later, Louis ceremonially touched more than 2,000 victims of 'scrofula' (a tuberculous infection of the skin of the neck, nowadays easily cured by antibiotics) with the words, 'The King touches you: may the Lord heal you.' As further evidence of the sacral nature of his kingship, he took communion in both kinds, a privilege normally reserved for priests.

The coronation set the seal on the failure of the privileged orders to push France towards a mixed constitution. Out of the struggles of the mid-seventeenth century came, not a constitutional monarchy as in England, but an absolute monarchy that was to last until 1789, at least in its formal arrangements. As the sacramental nature of the coronation dramatized, it rested most fundamentally on the word of God, as revealed in Scripture. The verse from St Paul's Epistle to the Romans quoted earlier in this chapter is a particularly uncompromising statement of the divine origin of secular authority. The Romans themselves could be enlisted in support, as their legal principles included '*quod principi placuit legis habet vigorem*' (what pleases the prince has the force of law), or '*princeps legibus solutus est*' (the prince is not bound by the laws). The former was given a pithy French paraphrase by a sixteenth-century jurist: '*si veut le roi, si veut la loi*' (if the king wishes it, so does the law).

With this subordination of law-making to the royal will, we seem to have arrived at arbitrary tyranny, or 'despotism' as contemporaries called it. Yet advocates of absolute monarchy were careful to maintain that there was a difference in kind between the legitimate exercise of untrammelled authority and the capricious behaviour of a tyrant. The King of France, it was argued, enjoyed a legislative monopoly that could not be challenged by any other human individual or institution, but he was also subject to divine law, whether revealed explicitly in Scripture or implicitly in the form of natural law. For example, the Ten Commandments obliged the King to respect the true religion (Thou shalt have none other gods before me), to respect the lives of his subjects (Thou shalt not kill), to respect their property (Thou shalt not steal, Thou shalt not covet thy neighbour's house, thou shalt not covet thy neighbour's wife, nor his manservant, nor his maidservant, nor his ox, nor his ass, nor any thing that is thy neighbour's), and to respect contracts and the due process of law (Thou shalt not bear false witness against thy neighbour). Bishop Bossuet, Louis XIV's most eloquent mouthpiece on religious matters, maintained that, 'Royal authority is sacred ... God established kings as his ministers and reigns through them over the nation ... The royal throne is not the throne of a man but the throne of God himself', but he denied that this implied that the King could do as he pleased:

It is one thing for a government to be absolute, and another for it to be arbitrary. It is absolute with respect to constraint – there being no power capable of forcing the sovereign, who in this sense is independent of all human authority. But it does not follow from this that the government is arbitrary, for besides the fact that everything is subject to the judgment of God ... there are also [constitutional] laws in empires, so that whatever is done against them is null in a legal sense: and there is always an opportunity for redress.

The laws to which Bossuet was referring were the 'fundamental laws' of the kingdom. Three could be defined quite precisely: the Salic law of succession, which excluded women, bastards and heretics from the throne; the integrity of the royal domain, which no king might alienate; and the maintenance of the Catholic faith. More shadowy were the *'maximes du royaume'*, a totality of laws, customs and principles which did not have full status as fundamental laws but which shared in their limiting nature. There was plenty of scope for uncertainty and disagreement here, especially when the *frondeur* spirit of the Parlements began to revive in the following century. The marquis d'Argenson recorded in his journal in 1753 that the parlementary remonstrances presented to Louis XV were claiming that in a just monarchy the king must obey the fundamental laws, before commenting drily, 'all that remains is for us to know exactly what these fundamental laws are'. Under Louis XIV, however, defeat in the *Frondes* was still too fresh in the minds of the defeated to allow such impertinence. As the intendant of Burgundy observed to Mazarin in 1660, 'noises from the Parlement are no longer in season'.

It was one thing for the King and his apologists to stake a theoretical claim to absolute authority, quite another to translate it into action. What singled Louis XIV out from most other monarchs of the early modern period was his determination to be as good as his word. A crucial step was taken immediately after the death of Mazarin in 1661. Summoning the Council, he told Chancellor Séguier: 'Sir, I have brought you together with my ministers and my secretaries of state, to tell you that until now I was willing to permit the late Cardinal to conduct my affairs. It is time that I govern them myself.' He did just that. Crucially, he proved to have the necessary qualities of intelligence, application and sheer charisma to make a personal monarchy work. He dominated the kingdom's supreme council, the *Conseil d'en haut*, from which he excluded the great and the good, notably the 'princes of the blood', in whose veins the blood of the Bourbons ran thickly enough to encourage independent political ambitions. He was not likely to forget the treason of the prince de Condé, who not only had led the second *Fronde* but had also subsequently lent his formidable military skills to Spanish forces against France. So for his most senior ministers he chose from the 'robe nobles', so-called because of their legal origins. As he told his eldest son the Dauphin, in a memoir drawn up for his instruction,

It was not in my interest to take subjects of more eminent quality. Above all things, I had to establish my own reputation, and let the public know, by the very rank from which I took them, that my intention was not to share my authority with them. I was concerned that they should not harbour for themselves higher hopes than it pleased me to give them: which is difficult for people of high birth.

The three most favoured robe families were those of Colbert (domestic affairs, commerce and the navy), Le Tellier (the army) and Phélypeaux (diplomacy), but whole dynasties of ministers were created. Of these, Jean-Baptiste Colbert (1619–83) stood out for the scope of his activity and the magnitude of his achievements. The greatest of the latter was his reform of the country's ruinous finances, which provided the means for the military victories and territorial expansion of the first half of the reign. Yet Colbert neither aspired to nor was permitted to become a first minister on the lines of Richelieu or Mazarin. When Louis XIV told his grandson, 'Do not let yourself be governed, be the master; never have either favourites or a prime minister', he was summarizing his own practice. Colbert's prudent advice to his own son was, 'Never, as long as you live, send out anything in the King's name without his express approval.'

So Louis imposed his monopoly of decision-making at the centre. Outside the council chamber he was equally imperious. The French institution most closely resembling a Parliament – the Estates General – which had last met in 1614, was simply not convened. The law courts, confusingly known as *Parlements*, together with the other 'sovereign courts', were deprived of their only political weapon in 1673, when they were instructed to register royal decrees first and voice any criticisms afterwards. The same sort of directive was issued to the provincial estates, now required to vote taxes first and present grievances after. In 1671 Mme de Sévigné reported from Brittany: 'The meeting of the Estates will not last long; all that needs to be done is to ask what the King wants; then not a word is spoken, and it's all wrapped up.' By that time the King was well on the way to establishing a monopoly of legitimate force in his kingdom. The dark days of the civil wars, when the great nobles had run their regiments as if they were their own armies, were gone for ever. In 1643 Le Tellier had lamented to Cardinal Mazarin that 'the army has become a republic, with as many cantons or provinces as there are lieutenants-general'. Its most recent historian (John Lynn) has described its state during the *Frondes* as 'a nadir of indiscipline, pillage and mutiny'. Yet by the time Louis began his first war, against Spain in 1667, his army was very much his army and his army alone, with even such former *frondeurs* as Condé and Turenne recognizing their subordination. When the prince de Conti and the prince de La Roche-sur-Yon (both royal cousins) went off to fight for the Emperor Leopold I against the Turks without seeking permission, Louis promptly stripped them of their regiments. This royal army was for use as much inside the country as out of it, as Louis demonstrated when he sent an army to the Auvergne in 1665 to add the necessary muscle to the judges charged with putting an end to the 'murders, abductions, rapes and extortions' perpetrated by the nobility there.

In imposing his will on his kingdom, Louis' most effective instruments were the 'intendants', the provincial officials who constituted 'the king present in the provinces'. Their full title – '*intendants de justice, de police et de finances*' – reveals the wide scope of their authority, '*police*' in this context meaning virtually anything relating to the common good. First sent out by Richelieu after 1635 to speed up funding for the war with Spain, but abolished during the *Frondes*, they returned in the 1650s and 1660s to become permanent fixtures. By the time the last intendant was appointed, in Brittany in 1689, there were thirty-three of them, supported by around seven hundred assistants called 'sub-delegates'. It used to be thought that these 'commissars despatched to execute the king's orders' represented a decisive breakthrough from a state-of-estates, in which authority was diffused through corporate bodies, to a modern state, in which authority is centralized and exercised through bureaucrats. The intendants were indeed appointed solely by the King, could not buy their offices, were not allowed to serve in regions where they had a vested interest, and were moved around at regular intervals to prevent them acquiring any sense of a local identity that might conflict with that of the centre. Their powers were such as to persuade some well-placed observers that they were the real rulers of the kingdom. John Law, the Scottish-born financier who was briefly controller-general of finance (the office once held by Colbert) in 1720, told the marquis d'Argenson: 'Monsieur, I would never have believed what I discovered when I was in control of the finances. You should know that this kingdom of France is ruled by thirty *intendants*. There are neither

1. A section of the new road from Valencia to Barcelona. Although everywhere in Europe travel remained difficult, dangerous and expensive, there was a marked improvement in arterial routes.

2. Goya, *Highwaymen Attacking a Coach*, 1786–7. Better roads brought more travellers – and more opportunities for criminals.

3. Pierre Mignard, *Louis XIV at Maastricht*, 1673. Depicted as a Roman emperor effortlessly controlling his rearing steed, Louis XIV is seen here at the height of his fame.

4. The gardens, palace and town of Versailles in 1668. Built on what was virtually a greenfield site, the studied artificiality of Versailles proclaimed Louis XIV's triumph over nature.

5. The burning of Heidelberg by the French in 1689. The great conflagration was part of a deliberate policy by Louis XIV's armies to lay waste to the western part of the Holy Roman Empire.

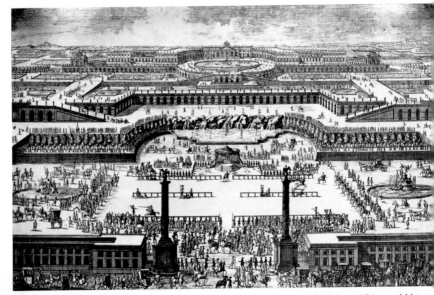

6. Johann Bernhard Fischer von Erlach's design for a new palace at Schönbrunn. This would have been the Austrian answer to Versailles, but shortage of funds prevented its full realization.

7. Louis XIV hunting. Hunting was much more than recreation, playing a vital part in the definition and projection of royal authority.

8. Fox-tossing in the courtyard of the Electoral Palace at Dresden in 1678. The tossing to death of foxes and other animals was immensely popular across central Europe.

9. A hunt at Neckargemünd in 1758 organized for the Elector Karl Theodor of the Palatinate. The deer were assembled in advance in a holding park and then driven down the hill into the water, to be slaughtered by the hunting party firing from the comfort of the pavilion.

10. The Palace of Caserta. Versailles comes to Naples: built for Charles VII, this colossal edifice contained more than 1,200 rooms. As its appearance suggests, in part it served as an office block.

11. Cosmas Damian and Egid Quirin Asam, the high altar of the Benedictine Abbey Church at Weltenburg, 1721. In this epitome of baroque theatricality, St George rides out as the defender of the doctrine of the Immaculate Conception to slay the dragon of heresy.

12. Narciso Tomé, *El Transparente* in Toledo Cathedral. Designed to allow the Blessed Sacrament to be viewed from both sides, this amazing multimedia creation was hailed by Spanish contemporaries as 'the eighth wonder of the world'.

13. Giovanni Paolo Pannini, *The French Ambassador to the Holy See Leaving St Peter's Square, Rome*, 1757. The ambassador in question was the comte de Stainville, better known by his subsequent title of duc de Choiseul. Although he observed the diplomatic forms and abased himself before Benedict XIV, he did not believe in Christianity, let alone papal authority.

14. Bernini, *The Ecstasy of Saint Theresa*, 1647. Saint Theresa dreams of an angel of surpassing beauty who penetrates her heart with a long spear with a glowing tip.

Parlements, nor Estates, nor Governors, I might almost add neither King nor Ministers, but thirty men ... on whom depend the welfare or the misery of the provinces.'

This view of Louis XIV creating a modern, centralized, bureaucratic, absolutist state was to have a long history. Perhaps its most influential advocate was Alexis de Tocqueville, who in *The Old Regime and the Revolution*, first published in 1856, argued that long before 1789 'the government of France was centralized and all-powerful; indeed the range of its activities was prodigious'. Such a view owes much to a special kind of French teleology which sees the state as the great civilizing force in human history – especially when that state (or super-state) is staffed by enlightened French bureaucrats. It has found less support among Anglophone historians, more inclined to be impressed by paradox and idiosyncrasy. They have argued that Louis XIV saw himself less as head of the French state than as head of the house of Bourbon. Although he may well have said on his death-bed, 'I am going, but the State remains', his actions suggest a more dynastic outlook. The immense pains he took to favour his numerous illegitimate children, even to the extent of admitting them to the legitimate line of descent, is certainly persuasive evidence that he put family first. At a more elevated level, his decision to bid for the entire Spanish inheritance on behalf of his grandson, when the last Habsburg King of Spain died in 1700, had little to do with *raison d'état* and rather more to do with the promotion of family fortunes.

Louis' attempt to promote his bastards outraged the French grandees. It was the occasion for one of the duc de Saint-Simon's most intemperate attacks on his kingship: 'contempt for the entire nation ... insult to all the princes of the blood ... high treason in its most rash and most criminal extent ... a crime more black, more vast, more terrible, than that of high treason ...' It was also Saint-Simon who attacked Louis XIV for having established 'the reign of the vile bourgeoisie'. For him it mattered nothing that Colbert became the marquis de Seignelay and married three of his daughters to dukes; that Le Tellier's son and successor in office became the marquis de Louvois and another son rose to be Archbishop of Reims; or that the Phélypeaux family included the comte de Pontchartrain and the comte de Maurepas. All that counted for Saint-Simon was the novelty of their noble status and its origins in the pen-pushing robe nobility. It was the same sort of mentality that allowed the untitled Miss Thorne of Ullathorne in Trollope's *Barchester Towers* to look down from the eminence of her pre-Conquest pedigree on the parvenue Countess de Courcy.

So, did Louis XIV ally with the bourgeoisie – lightly disguised as nobles of the robe – against the grandees? The exclusion of the latter from his councils certainly suggests such a conclusion. Yet the concentration of decision-making in the person of the King did not mean the exclusion of his greatest nobles from patronage, prestige or even power. On the contrary, the expansion of the royal household, court, army and navy expanded their opportunities for enrichment. So did the numerous wars, which allowed the martial code of honour of the 'nobility of the sword' to flourish as never before. As Louis observed to the duc de Vendôme in 1695: 'You know well that the profession of war is that which, of them all, procures more honour to a man who acquits himself well in it, and that it also covers him with as much shame and infamy if he acquits himself badly.' He set an example from the top, leading his regiment personally as late as 1692 and giving 'his orders within musket range'. Together with him at Namur on that occasion were his son, his illegitimate son and his brother. Nearby were several other princes of the blood royal – the prince de Condé, the duc de Bourbon, the duc de Chartres and the prince de Conti, supported by another of the King's bastards, the duc de Maine, and two illegitimate descendants of Henry IV – the duc de Vendôme and his younger brother, the chevalier de Vendôme. The exception that proved the rule of this front-line service by the Bourbons was the duc de Bourgogne, who was only nine years old. Following this example of *noblesse oblige*, a noble of ancient lineage such as Saint-Simon would not have been seen dead pushing a pen as a secretary of state, but was positively anxious to risk death at the head of his regiment (and in Saint-Simon's case was bitterly disappointed when his military career came to nothing). Later in 1692, the abbé de Hocquincourt petitioned Louis to allow him to command the regiment currently leaderless as a result of the death of his brother, the marquis de Hocquincourt. He was clearly not deterred by the knowledge that this latest casualty brought to three the total of Hocquincourt brothers killed while serving at the head of the regiment during the previous eighteen months. Despite – or, more likely, because of – the risks involved, the great nobles came to see that they had much more to gain from working inside and with the establishment than waging war against it. Equally, for his part Louis XIV could see that he and the rest of the Bourbons had more to gain from working in co-operation with the magnates than against them. Among other things, that meant reserving all the smartest regiments for them: by 1691 at least 3,000 nobles were serving in the elite corps, or more than 10 per cent of all nobles serving in the French army.

The nobles were not supplanted from control of the army, nor were they excluded from power in the provinces. The traditional centres of authority – the governors, the Parlements and the Estates (where they existed) – continued in existence and continued to be important. As numerous regional studies have shown, the degree of success enjoyed by an intendant in implementing the royal will stood in direct ratio to the rapport he achieved with the local establishment. If the intendant of Burgundy, for example, fell out with the dominant local dynasty, the Condé, he soon found he had bitten off more than he could chew. Henri François d'Aguesseau, who became chancellor of France in 1717, recorded that his father, who had been intendant of Languedoc, 'realized from the start that the welfare of the province depended principally on a perfect harmony between the principal persons who provided, as it were, the soul and motive force of the state – the Governor, the intendant and the president of the Estates'. The governor in question was the duc de Verneuil, illegitimate son of Henry IV, who was more interested in hunting and 'external display' than in the conduct of business and posed no threat to the intendant's authority. But the president of the Estates was Cardinal de Bonzy, Archbishop of Narbonne, and his standing was such that he had to be very carefully managed.

So was 'absolutism' a myth, as has been argued vigorously by a number of historians? The word itself is certainly an anachronism, not having been coined until the 1830s. However, seventeenth-century contemporaries did have a clear conception of 'absolute authority' and also a clear conception of Louis XIV establishing it. At the centre, the silencing of the Parlements undoubtedly marked a significant intensification of the King's legislative monopoly. That was how Louis XIV saw it, at least. One of the problems confronting him early in his reign he identified as 'the Parlements still in the possession and enjoyment of a usurped authority' and explained why he had to deal with it:

The too great prominence of the Parlements had been a danger to the whole kingdom during my minority. It was necessary to humble them, less for the evil they had already done than for what they might do in the future. Their authority, in so far as people regarded it as being in opposition to mine, produced very mischievous effects, however good their intentions may have been, and thwarted all my greatest and most useful measures.

In the regions there was a keen awareness that Louis XIV's approach to government really was different, and moreover that 'absolute authority' was the best way to describe it. A good example is provided by the abbé Fléchier's account of the activities of one of judges charged with establishing royal authority in the Auvergne:

About this time M. Le Pelletier returned from upper Auvergne, bringing a quantity of evidence against the nobles who live in the highlands. He insistently demanded the continuation of the assizes, fearing lest all the investigations he had made with such peril under such unseasonable conditions might prove fruitless. He had certainly acted with all the authority granted him by an absolute King, and his representation of justice had struck terror to the minds of the people. He sufficed alone to throw the mountain regions into confusion. He had caused law to be recognized where it had never been before, and had brought fear into places which had always been beyond the reach of justice. He exerted the rigour of the law where there had been before nothing but criminal acts: he entered the most strongly fortified castles, he opened the most secret depositories, and sent the most haughty and powerful men in the province under escort to Clermont, where they could give an account of their conduct.

When the turbulent vicomte de La Mothe de Canillac was executed at Clermont on 23 October 1665, he might well have agreed that Louis XIV's authority should be regarded as absolute. So might the citizens of Marseilles five years earlier when they had felt the full force of Louis' authoritarian hand. Following disturbances in the city between rival factions, the King sent an army 6,000-strong to put an end once and for all to the political autonomy enjoyed by the self-styled republic since it first came under French rule in 1486. When the King arrived soon afterwards, he had a symbolic breach made in the medieval walls, demolished the city gates and used the stones to construct the massive new fort of Saint Nicholas, from which the royal garrison was to overawe the turbulent Marseillois. Self-government was replaced by a governor-commandant appointed by the King, and the local nobility were excluded from power. Over the next decade, the city was rebuilt and expanded as part of a self-consciously absolutist project. Nicolas Arnoul, the intendant of the galleys commissioned by Colbert to oversee it, defined his purpose as follows: '[I have] no other intention than the King's grandeur and the good of the city. Marseilles will become another city . . . a great and vast city that will not be able to defend itself against its master, and one that will not be attacked by its [foreign] enemies', so that it would 'start another life . . . [with] principles that are necessary for its service to its master, his grandeur, and the repose of its inhabitants'.

In practice and theory, at the level of both perception and reality, absolute monarchy was an identifiable phenomenon. What it most certainly was not was omnicompetent or totalitarian. The King and his ministers did not try to do very much by present-day standards, and they did not succeed in implementing much of what they did try to do. Given the primitive nature of communications, both physical and symbolic, discussed elsewhere in this book, that is not at all surprising. The great diversity of laws, legal systems, weights and measures, and even languages, defeated even the best standardizing efforts of the French revolutionaries and in some cases survived into the twentieth century. Yet it has to be concluded that Louis XIV did achieve both a legislative and a coercive monopoly in his kingdom. It must also be allowed that he created an absolutist political culture, exemplified by the Versailles project examined below in Chapter 9. One must wonder whether even the most revisionist of revisionist historians could stand in the Hall of Mirrors at Versailles, underneath the painting by Charles Le Brun *Louis XIV Governs by Himself* and still proclaim 'absolutism is a myth'. The wisest words on this topic were written by Peter Burke in his book *The Fabrication of Louis XIV*: 'Ritual, art and architecture may all be seen as the instruments of self-assertion, as the continuation of war and diplomacy by other means.' This is not just 'style', the medium is the message.

ABSOLUTE MONARCHY IN THE HABSBURG MONARCHY

In the Habsburg Monarchy there was a similar drive by successive rulers towards establishing greater control. The problems they confronted, however, were appreciably greater than in France. If the latter was undoubtedly not a unified nation-state but an aggregate of provinces acquired at different times, it could never have been described as 'a mildly centripetal agglutination of bewilderingly heterogeneous elements', which was how Robert Evans memorably summed up the diversity of the Habsburg Monarchy. That diversity is also well conveyed by a simple statement of Joseph II's titles:

Joseph II, Roman Emperor, Apostolic King of Hungary, Bohemia, Dalmatia, Croatia, Slavonia, Galicia, Lodomeria, Archduke of Austria, Duke of Burgundy, of Styria, of Carinthia and of Carniola; Grand Prince of Transylvania, Margrave of Moravia, Duke of Brabant, of Limburg, of Luxemburg, of Geldern, of Württemberg, of Upper and Lower Silesia, of Milan, of Mantua, of Parma, of Piacenza, of Guastalla, of Auschwitz and Zator; Prince of Swabia, Prince-Count of Habsburg, Flanders, the Tyrol, of Hennegau, of Kyburg, of Görz and Gradisca, Margrave of the Holy Roman Empire, of Burgau, of Upper and Lower Lusatia, Count of Namur, Lord of the Windisch March and of Mecheln; Duke of Lorraine and Bar; Grand Duke of Tuscany.

Just in case any titles had been forgotten, the list was usually brought to an end with the formula 'etc. etc.'. The Habsburg possessions included all or part of the present-day countries of Belgium, Luxemburg, the Netherlands, Germany, Austria, the Czech Republic, Slovakia, Poland, the Ukraine, Romania, Hungary, Serbia and Montenegro, Croatia, Slovenia and Italy. As Sir Harold Temperley observed, the Habsburg Monarchy was not so much a country as a continent, all by itself.

France may well have been 'diverse to the point of absurdity' (Fernand Braudel), not least in matters of language, with two distinct forms of French (*langue d'oc* and *langue d'oïl*), four foreign languages (Basque, Breton, Flemish, German) and as many as thirty mutually incomprehensible forms of patois, but even that assortment paled by comparison with the linguistic kaleidoscope that the Habsburgs had to grapple with. Leaving aside the French- and Flemish-speaking inhabitants of the Austrian Netherlands, five main groups of languages can be identified: the German speakers, concentrated in Austria and the Alpine provinces, but also strongly represented in Bohemia, the towns of Hungary, and Transylvania; the Italian speakers, forming a relatively homogeneous bloc in southern Tyrol (but which also included – as it still does – a minority of 'Ladins' speaking a form of Latin similar to the Romansch language of Switzerland), Milan, Parma, Piacenza and Tuscany; the Magyar speakers of Hungary and Transylvania; the Romanian speakers of Transylvania; and, finally, the speakers of Slavonic languages. This last-named group needs to be subdivided further into three: those with a long-standing sense of cultural identity and a written language, such as the Czechs of Bohemia and Moravia or the Poles of Galicia; those with an embryonic sense of separate identity but without yet a clear national consciousness, such as the Croats and Serbs of the Kingdom of Hungary; and those 'submerged nationalities', concealed by illiteracy, whose existence awaited discovery by the ethnologists of the nineteenth century, such as the Ruthenians (or Ukrainians) of Galicia or the Slovaks of northern Hungary. In addition, there were large Yiddish-speaking Jewish minorities in Galicia, Hungary, Bohemia and Moravia. As if that were not enough, Latin was also commonly used for academic and religious discourse and in Hungary for administration and justice too. Even this bewildering categorization fails to do justice to the complexity of the situation, by failing to record adequately just how *mixed* each area was. Especially in Bohemia, Moravia and throughout the vast Kingdom of Hungary and Transylvania, a plethora of different ethnic and linguistic groups lived together with varying degrees of mutual animosity.

By 1648 the Habsburgs had triumphed over two overlapping groups: the Protestants and the nobility of the 'Hereditary Lands', that is to say the mainly German-speaking core territories (Upper and Lower Austria, the Vorarlberg, the Tyrol, Styria, Carinthia and Carniola) and the 'Lands of the Crown of St Wenceslas' (Bohemia, Moravia and Silesia). This was not a foregone conclusion, for by the later sixteenth century the Austrian nobility was predominantly Protestant and the Emperor Maximilian II (1564–76) was sympathetic. The crucial date was 8 November 1620, when a multinational Catholic army comprising Bavarians, Spanish, Walloons, German, French (among them Descartes) and Austrians routed the Bohemian insurgents. Although it took time, eventually both Catholicism and royal authority were imposed, indeed they went hand in hand. In June the following year, twenty-seven Bohemian nobles and burghers were publicly executed in the main square of the Old Town in Prague, the event being visually recorded to serve as an awful warning for the present and posterity. The tongue of Jan Jessenský (Jessenius), rector of the University, was cut out and nailed to the block before he was beheaded. In 1624 Catholicism was declared to be the sole permitted religion; three years later the non-Catholic nobility and burghers of Bohemia were ordered to convert to the true faith or to emigrate. It has been estimated that about 20 per cent of the Bohemian and Moravian nobility (i.e. *c*.85 families) and about 25 per cent of the burghers chose exile. Overall around 150,000 individuals emigrated in the years following the battle of the White Mountain.

Out of the tumultuous decades of the mid-seventeenth century came a triple alliance between the dynasty, the Church and the great aristocratic magnates on which the Habsburg Monarchy was to rest for another century and more. To flourish in this fast-moving world of political and confessional strife, a noble needed to be sure-footed, lucky, Catholic and loyal to the house of Habsburg. The rewards were enormous, as there was a huge amount of land expropriated from the losers available for redistribution. Leaving aside royal and Church estates, about three-quarters of the land in Bohemia changed hands in the course of the 1620s. The major beneficiaries were the magnates. In the mid-sixteenth century, the total acreage of the gentry estates had exceeded that of the magnates, yet a hundred years later the magnates owned 60 per cent of all land and the gentry only 10 per cent. When the victors' lands were expropriated in their turn after the First World War by the newly created Czechoslovak state, the Kinskys lost 170,000 acres, the Liechtensteins 400,000 and the Schönborns and Schwarzenbergs more than half a million each – and those were just their holdings in Bohemia and Moravia. No wonder their loyalty to their Habsburg benefactors was commensurate. While hunting near Prague in 1732, Prince Adam Franz von Schwarzenberg was accidentally shot by the Emperor Charles VI. Although mortally wounded, the luckless prince was able to gasp 'it was ever my duty to give my life for my sovereign' before he expired.

Architectural expression of the new tripartite alliance that dominated the Habsburg Monarchy can be seen in the cityscape of Prague: in the greatly expanded royal castle-cum-palace, the archiepiscopal palace next door, the massive Collegium Clementinum of the Jesuits and the University they directed, the baroque churches and monasteries, the statues of saints on the Charles Bridge, and the numerous aristocratic palaces (Černin, Sternberg, Martiniz, Schwarzenberg, Lobkowitz, Clam-Gallas, Golz-Kinsky, Kaiserstein, Kaunitz, Kollowrat, etc.). After Vienna, Prague was the greatest *Residenzstadt* in central Europe.

In the aftermath of the battle of the White Mountain, Emperor Ferdinand II's chief priority was to advance the interests of the Catholic religion he held responsible for his victory. But this confessional revolution was swiftly followed by a political equivalent, embodied in a new constitution for Bohemia. Although the assembly of the Estates was not abolished, it lost its right to initiate legislation and its claim to elect the king was formally abrogated in favour of the hereditary right the Habsburgs had always claimed was theirs. Decision-making for the province was located firmly in the Bohemian Chancellery in Vienna, where the Habsburg court was now finally fixed. Yet the Estates continued to dominate political life, especially in the crucial area of taxation. Given the absence of a professional bureaucracy and Habsburg preoccupations elsewhere, it could not be otherwise.

The Bohemian, Moravian and Silesian magnates continued to flourish during the second half of the seventeenth century and into the next. The expansion of the Habsburg court, army and diplomatic corps created opportunities for remunerative and prestigious employment. Below the elite, however, rule from Vienna was still resented. In 1720, when the Emperor Charles VI sought the agreement of the Bohemian Estates to the 'Pragmatic Sanction' and thus to the succession of his daughter Maria Theresa, most nobles indicated their hostility by absenting themselves from the vote. A more emphatic demonstration came twenty years later when Charles VI died and the Elector of Bavaria laid claim to the Bohemian crown. At a ceremony at Prague on 19 December 1741, the self-proclaimed king received the homage of more than four hundred members of the Bohemian Estates. Together with the Archbishop of Prague (a Count von Manderscheid), there were representatives from most of the leading aristocratic families of Bohemia present to publicize their desertion of the Habsburgs – Kinsky, Gallas, Königsegg, Kollowrat, Clary, and so on. There was a clear division between officials working on the ground in Bohemia and those operating in Vienna or in the army.

Most of the latter group – 302 of 351 – declared for Maria Theresa; most of the former – 114 of 132 – paid homage to the Bavarian usurper.

Only the sword could decide, and it turned out once again that the Habsburgs had the heavier weapon. By the end of 1742, the Bavarians and their French allies had been chased out, although the wider conflict continued in fits and starts until the Peace of Aachen in 1748. By this time, the fate of Bohemia was subsumed in a more general reform project directed by Count Friedrich Wilhelm von Haugwitz, a Silesian convert to Catholicism. His reforms, which began in 1749, concentrated the state's primal function of arranging security in the hands of the sovereign. To support a large standing army (108,000-strong initially), long-term grants of increased taxation were negotiated with the Estates, or imposed if they could not be negotiated. The tax exemptions hitherto enjoyed by clergy and nobility were abolished. The old-fashioned, baroque-sounding names of the new central and provincial bodies – the *Directorium in publicis et cameralibus*, which combined the Bohemian and Austrian chancelleries, and the Representations and Chambers, respectively – concealed a fundamental change from control by the Estates to control by the sovereign. The creation of a supreme court for the Hereditary Lands (*Oberste Justizstelle*) institutionalized the supremacy of royal justice. All this was accomplished by an act of the will from above: in the striking formulation of Peter Dickson, it amounted to a '*coup d'état*'.

Despite the wobble in loyalty in 1741 – and another one at the end of the 1780s, to be discussed in the next chapter – the history of Bohemia for most of this period demonstrated the relative efficiency of the typically Habsburg alliance with the privileged orders. In the other major kingdom that comprised the Monarchy – Hungary – it was quite a different story. There the opportunity for a similar axis appeared to be even greater, for the concentration of land, wealth and power in the hands of a few magnates was even more pronounced, the greater part of the wealth of the country being owned by just fifty landowning families. But the situation was a great deal more complicated. Although the Habsburgs had nominally ruled the entire Kingdom of Hungary since the last Jagiellon king fell fighting the Turks at the battle of Mohács in 1526, they had been able to make good their claim only to about a third, a crescent of territory stretching from south-west to north-east. Of the rest, another third, comprising the centre, was ruled directly by the Turks, while the eastern third formed the Principality of Transylvania, ruled by a Turkish vassal. Following the great *reconquista* of the 1680s and 1690s, the Peace of Karlowitz of 1699 placed the entire kingdom, including Transylvania, under Habsburg rule *de facto* as well as *de jure*. A second war of 1716–18, ended by the Peace of Passarowitz, added the Bánát of Temesvár, northern Serbia and western Wallachia, although most of these latest gains were lost again in 1739.

As we have seen, Hungary was unusually diverse. At the core, however, both geographically and metaphorically, stood the Magyar gentry, the rock against which every Habsburg attempt at integration foundered. Their fierce sense of separatism stemmed from history, culture, religion, economics and geopolitics. They had sought to dominate the lands of the lower Danube ever since their ancestors first thrust their way over the Carpathians in AD 896. Even during the worst troughs of the ups and downs of the next millennium, they never forgot that once upon a time they had formed an independent kingdom, nor did they lose the ambition to resurrect it. Whether successful or not, the recurring need to repel invaders – German, Mongol, Turkish – periodically sharpened the sense of struggle which seems to be inseparable from acute nationalism. As Count Raimund Montecuccoli informed the Emperor Leopold I in 1662, 'The Hungarians nurse so intense a hatred for the Germans that they even hate those Hungarians who display any sort of inclination towards the Germans.' The integrity of their culture was preserved by their language: as anyone who has even toyed with the idea of learning Magyar will confirm, it is an exceedingly difficult language, not even Indo-European in origin but Uralic, related only to Estonian and Finnish. The Magyar gentry were also kept alienated from Vienna by religion. Of their two great enemies, the Habsburgs were Roman Catholic and the Turks were Muslim – so most Magyars opted for Protestantism, especially in its Calvinist or Zwinglian form. Only in those parts of the country not conquered by the Turks after the battle of Mohács and which therefore felt the full force of the Counter-Reformation was Catholicism dominant. A festering source of grievance was the not unreasonable belief that the Habsburgs treated them like a colony, as a source of cheap food and raw materials to be exploited, and as a dumping-ground for overpriced manufactured goods from other parts of the Monarchy. This resentment was intensified by the loss of Silesian markets in 1740 and the further disruption caused by the first partition of Poland in 1772.

The Bohemians had also been divided from their Habsburg rulers by history, language, culture and material interest. What made the Magyars so much tougher nuts was their capacity for organization. Since time out of mind, the Kingdom of Hungary had been divided into fifty-odd counties (*comitatus*), governed by the gentry who met periodically at county assemblies (*congregationes*). It was here that they gained the political experience, organizational skills, self-confidence and *esprit de corps* which made them so intractable. Whenever the Habsburgs were diverted by trouble elsewhere, the Magyars of Hungary and Transylvania were quick to take advantage. When the Turks marched on Vienna in 1683, they were helped by the Calvinist Prince of Transylvania, Michael I Apafi, and his co-religionist Imre Thököly, appointed by Sultan Muhammad IV as 'King of Upper Hungary' under Ottoman suzerainty. If the Magyar thorn in the Habsburg flesh never proved fatal, it did inflict sharp pain again and again. Thököly's stepson, Francis II Rákóczy, wrote in his memoirs: 'bearing in mind that no fewer than five wars were conducted within a century, one could say they were continuous'. His own rebellion, begun in 1703, was the sixth. It ended in defeat on 30 September 1711 with the Peace of Szatmár, when the Hungarian magnate commanding the Habsburg army – Count János Pálffy – signed an agreement with the Hungarian magnate commanding the rebel army – Count Sándor Károlyi. Rákóczy was dismayed by the settlement and went into exile.

Despite their heavy commitments in the south and the west of Europe, as part of the War of the Spanish Succession, which was still very much underway, the Habsburg forces had been successful yet again. The terms they granted were generous in the circumstances: a full amnesty, restitution of confiscated property, an end to religious persecution, and a pledge to respect the traditional constitution, including the tax exemptions of the nobility. This clemency paid a handsome dividend in the dark days of 1741 when a desperate Maria Theresa went to Pressburg (or Pozsony, as the Hungarians called it) to make a personal appeal to the Estates, carrying in her arms her six-month-old son and heir Joseph. They responded in Latin with the cry '*vitam et sanguinem pro Rege nostro Maria Teresia!*' (our lives and our blood for our queen Maria Theresa). If only slightly more than half of the 100,000 men promised actually materialized, they were enough to turn the tide in her favour. As she later wrote to her younger son, Maximilian Franz: 'Anything can be done with this nation if it is treated well and shown affection . . . You will see this and be astonished at the advantages I have obtained and still obtain from it.'

Maria Theresa wrote those words in 1776, four years before her death. During her forty-year reign, she had demonstrated that a light touch need not be a soft touch. She had succeeded in increasing the central government's share of revenue at the expense of the privileged orders, but without provoking counter-productive alienation. If she had failed to generate the resources necessary to win back Silesia, for whose loss the province of Galicia, won in the first partition of Poland, represented meagre compensation, at least she had kept the Monarchy intact in a particularly perilous period. The magnitude of her achievement was to be thrown into sharp relief by the failures of Joseph II in the 1780s, which will be considered in the next chapter.

BRANDENBURG-PRUSSIA

A 'light touch' is not the sort of image normally associated with the Habsburg Monarchy's great rival – Brandenburg-Prussia – yet in terms of political development they had more in common than might be supposed. If not quite 'a mildly centripetal agglutination of bewilderingly heterogeneous elements', Brandenburg's territory did straggle in bits and pieces more than 600 miles (1,000 km) across northern Europe, from Cleves near the Dutch frontier in the west, to Tilsit (which today is called Sovetsk and is part of the Russian Federation) on the River Memel (Niemen) in the east. If it could not boast such a rich variety of religions, it was sufficiently heterogeneous to pose the same sort of problems for its rulers. If it had a greater potential for a sense of common identity, in 1648 it was still very much an aggregate of separate provinces. In 1650 the Estates of Brandenburg declined to vote money to support the Elector's policy in his neighbouring province of East Pomerania on the grounds that it was 'foreign'. The main point of difference between the Habsburg Monarchy and Brandenburg in 1648 was one of standing. Although the Elector of Brandenburg was a member of the elite group of German princes entitled to elect the Emperor, in terms of resources he was some way behind his secular colleagues (Saxony, the Palatinate and Bavaria).

So rapid was Brandenburg's ascent to a position from which it could challenge the Habsburg Monarchy for the domination of Germany, and then every other power for the domination of Europe, that its historiography was often informed by a sense of inevitability – especially when it was Prussian patriots and/or German nationalists who were writing the history. Yet it seems more likely that the Elector Frederick William 'the Great Elector' (1640–88), who began the process of concentrating and maximizing power, was responding to immediate emergencies rather than following a long-term plan. For any ruler whose territories lay on the great north European plain, which stretches from the North Sea coast to the Ural mountains, the absence of natural frontiers meant that opportunity knocked with the same urgency that danger threatened. Frederick William's predecessor, George William, had tried to stay out of the Thirty Years War. In 1630 he had sent an emissary to his brother-in-law, King Gustavus Adolphus of Sweden, who had just landed in Pomerania, asking him to respect Brandenburg's neutrality. Gustavus Adolphus replied tartly that in an existential struggle between good and evil (Protestant and Catholic), non-commitment was not an option.

He might have added that the choice was between being predator or prey. Frederick William was determined that his Electorate should cease to be the latter. That meant raising an army, which meant raising money, which meant overcoming the opposition of the Estates. In 1643–4 he managed to scrape together a force of 7,800, which allowed him some sort of scope for independent action in the dog-days of the Thirty Years War. His reward came in the final peace settlement. Although bitterly disappointed not to make good his claim to western Pomerania and the all-important mouth of the Oder, he did secure the impoverished eastern part, together with three secularized prince-bishoprics (Kammin, Halberstadt and Minden) and the reversion of the wealthy and strategically important archbishopric of Magdeburg, of which he eventually took possession in 1680. Frederick William now found himself in an upwardly rising spiral: the more troops he had at his disposal, the easier he found it to extract money from the Estates, and the more money he was able to extract, the more troops he was able to recruit. He was assisted by the decision of the Holy Roman Empire in 1654 that princes could raise taxes to maintain essential garrisons and fortifications. He was assisted further by the volatile international situation, which prompted the Emperor to turn a deaf ear to complaints from the various provincial Estates that he was collecting taxes illegally.

Frederick William clearly did not have an 'absolutist' agenda, in the sense that he wished to do away with the Estates altogether. He always preferred the path of negotiation and compromise. On occasion, however, he applied brute force, most notably when dealing with the especially recalcitrant Estates of East Prussia. In 1662 Frederick William announced how he would deal with their most turbulent leader, the Königsberg burgher Hieronymus Roth: '[he] will be interrogated tomorrow, condemned the next and executed on Tuesday or Wednesday'. In the event, Roth was never brought to trial, perhaps because an acquittal was feared, but was simply kept in prison until his death sixteen years later. Even more brutal was the treatment meted out to Count Christian Ludwig von Kalckstein, who was kidnapped in Warsaw, where he had sought refuge, smuggled back to Brandenburg and executed. Two years later, Königsberg's resistance was brought to an end by military action.

By the time he died in 1688, Frederick William had achieved his three principal objectives: he had created his own central administration, his own fiscal system, and his own standing army, and he had also bullied the Estates into accepting all three. He had also brought his scattered bits and pieces of territory intact through the very dangerous times of the mid-seventeenth century. It might be wondered how he succeeded where other aspiring absolute monarchs – the Stuarts, for example – failed. In part it was due to the much weaker economic position of the Brandenburg Estates, due to a combination of the natural poverty of the region and the devastation wreaked by the Thirty Years War. So, in agreements negotiated in 1683 and 1686, it was the Elector who sorted out the Estates' debts, not the other way round. Only gradually did memories fade of the terrible times when Swedish and imperial armies had rampaged across the Electorate, so the argument that a strong army was needed had an enduring cogency.

The noble Junkers might have been more determined in their resistance to the growing burden of taxation – it increased per capita by around four times during the course of Frederick William's reign – if they had carried the main burden themselves. In the event, most direct taxes were paid by the peasants and most indirect taxes, notably the newly introduced excise, by the towns. So long as Frederick William protected the landowners' authority over their serfs, as he did formally in the agreement (*Rezess*) of 1653, they were prepared to give him a free hand in national affairs, however grumpily. Yet it was not quite absolute power for the ruler at the centre in exchange for absolute power for the nobility in the localities, however neat that formula might be. There was never a duality of two adversaries but rather a pattern of constantly shifting coalitions, with co-operation as much in evidence as confrontation. Nor was it clear that the Junkers were the losers, for the enhanced domestic stability, the greater degree of protection against foreign enemies, the territorial expansion and the larger army were all benefits for them as well as the Elector. Indeed, the most recent historian of the Junkers (Edgar Melton) has concluded: 'the triumph of Hohenzollern absolutism went hand in hand with an increase in the power and activity of the nobility at the local and provincial levels'.

It used to be thought that the Hohenzollern rulers of Brandenburg-Prussia could be divided into two types – the exceptionally gifted (Frederick William the Great Elector, Frederick William I, Frederick the Great, William I), and the dim and/or mad (Frederick I, Frederick William II, Frederick William III, Frederick William IV, William II). It was Frederick I's misfortune to be sandwiched between two high-achievers and also to become the target of some of his grandson's most withering comments. More recent biographers have been kinder, drawing attention to two kinds of achievement with important political consequences. The first was to advance mightily Brandenburg's reputation as a state in which culture was valued and promoted (*Kulturstaat*). He did this by founding a new university at Halle, which quickly became one of the most prestigious universities in the Holy Roman Empire, and by creating a number of cultural institutions. Of these, the most important was the Academy of Art founded in 1697, which was to be 'a high school of art or university of art like the academies in Rome and Paris' and the Academy of Sciences in 1700, whose first president was no less a figure than Leibniz.

More important still was his elevation of the Electorate of Brandenburg to be the Kingdom of Prussia. This acquisition of royal status was a necessary response to what Heinz Duchhardt has called 'a wave of regalization' in the Holy Roman Empire. The most spectacular elevation so far had been achieved by Frederick Augustus of Saxony, when in 1697 he was elected King of Poland. It was also becoming increasingly likely that the third major Protestant Elector – of Hanover – would achieve a royal title by becoming King of England when the last Protestant representative of the house of Stuart died. So Frederick's proclamation on 18 January 1701 that he was now Frederick I, King in Prussia, was a necessary response. He had been fortunate that the need for his military and diplomatic support had induced the Emperor Leopold I to recognize this essentially unilateral declaration. To assist credibility, Frederick went out of his way to ensure that the festivities attending his coronation in Königsberg were worthy of the greatest sovereign. Thirty thousand horses were needed to pull the cavalcade of carriages that took the court from Berlin to the coronation. His scarlet coronation robes were studded with diamond buttons costing 3,000 *ducats* each, while the cost of just the crowns created for himself and his queen exceeded the amount raised by a special tax to cover the total cost. Anticipating Napoleon by more than a century, Frederick did the crowning himself – indeed, it was only after the coronation ceremony had been performed in a room in Königsberg Castle that the royal couple proceeded to the cathedral to be anointed by two bishops (one Calvinist, one Lutheran) specially appointed for the occasion.

To call oneself a king and to dress up like one does not, of course, create a kingdom. Leibniz's claim that 'naming a thing completes its essence' is less persuasive than Frederick the Great's sneer that his grandfather had created 'a kind of hermaphrodite, rather more an electorate than a kingdom'. Yet the head of the house of Hohenzollern was now 'King in Prussia' (*in* Prussia rather than *of* Prussia because West Prussia remained under Polish rule) and so had his feet under Europe's top table, even if he was seated below the salt. Although Frederick I's son and successor Frederick William I (1713–40) was content with this modest international position, at home he was turning his inheritance into a springboard for great-power status. This he accomplished by more than doubling the Prussian army to *c.*81,000 men by the end of his reign, financing it entirely from Prussian resources and amassing a great war-chest of 8,700,000 *talers*. He never drew the sword he had forged, but – as his son Frederick put it in *The History of My Own Times* – 'By these means he travelled silently on towards grandeur, without awakening the envy of monarchs'. In the process, he eliminated the last vestige of any political independence on the part of the Estates and created the administrative structure that was to allow Prussia to punch many divisions above its natural weight.

In Hans Rosenberg's judicious, perhaps even charitable, assessment, Frederick William was 'a dangerous, uncouth, and irascible but shrewd psychoneurotic, haunted by delusions of grandeur, but nevertheless the most remarkable administrative reformer ever produced by the Hohen-zollern family'. Intense piety went hand in hand with extreme brutality, as for example on the day when he first had an official found guilty of dereliction of duty garrotted in front of his office, with all senior and junior personnel forced to watch, and then received a group of religious refugees from Salzburg, with his entire court obliged to get down on their knees to give thanks for this deliverance of the Lord's afflicted. When asked, on a visit to East Prussia, to confirm a sentence of imprison-ment passed on Councillor von Schlabuth, Frederick William told the prisoner that he deserved to be hanged. Unwisely, von Schlabuth replied tartly that 'one doesn't hang a Prussian noble'. By way of reply, Frederick William had a gallows erected in the courtyard of von Schlabuth's place of work and had him hanged from it the following day – but not before going to church and weeping as he heard a sermon on the virtue of mercy ('Blessed are the merciful: for they shall obtain mercy' – Matthew 5:7). His views on the nobility as a whole were not flattering: the nobles of Cleves and Mark were 'dumb oxen, but malicious as the devil ... intriguers and false as well, and they drink like beasts – they know nothing else'; those of the Old Mark were 'bad, disobedient people who do nothing in good part, they are always surly and mischievous in their duties to their prince'; while those of Magdeburg were 'like those from the Old Mark, only rather worse'; and so on.

Apart from terrorizing and excoriating his nobility, more construc-tively Frederick William I also reorganized the central organs of government. Essentially, this involved the amalgamation of the body responsible for administering the colossal royal domains (comprising about a third of the cultivable area, according to Otto Hintze, repeating a claim by the Prussian minister von Hertzberg in 1785) with the body responsible for raising taxation, to form the 'General Directory', or 'General-Supreme-Finance-War-and-Domains-Directory', to give it its official title, which began work in 1723. Although to modern eyes it looks distinctly odd, for its four departments combined both regional and topical specialization, relatively it marked a major step towards the integration of the various provinces into a single Prussian state. Although in practice the departmental heads wielded considerable independent power, technically they were the instruments of the royal will. This was communicated to them in the form of marginalia scribbled on their reports and composed in Frederick William's inimitable semi-literate mixture of French, German and Latin. It was on such a document, from Count Karl Truchsess, that Frederick William famously spelt out his political objective: 'I shall achieve my purpose and shall consolidate (*stabilirai*) my sovereignty and anchor my crown like a rock of bronze (*rocher de bronze*)'. This style of government – which was imitated by his successor – was known to contemporaries as 'cabinet government' (*Kabinettsregierung*), but was about as far removed from its English equivalent as it could be, since it meant government-from-the-royal-closet, with no interference by anyone else.

If this form of government has an archaic feel to it, more modern was Frederick William's encouragement of a professionally trained bureaucracy. From 1723 he introduced a system of in-service training for probationers attached to the provincial chambers, complete with examination. Also surprisingly forward-looking was the establishment of chairs of 'cameralism' (applied political science) at the universities of Halle and Frankfurt an der Oder in 1727, with specific instructions that their main task was the training of officials. It was during this period that what was recognizably a bureaucracy emerged: mixed in terms of social origin, meritocratic, non-venal, hierarchical, academically trained and appointed, directed and monitored by the central authorities. Many are the qualifications that need to be made about how this system worked in practice, for nepotism, corruption, obstruction, incompetence – and all the other vices inseparable from public employment in any age – were certainly to be found. The most judicious and also the most authoritative verdict was delivered by the late Betty Behrens in her neglected but important comparative study of France and Prussia in the eighteenth century:

Whatever quarrels, rivalries and injustices may have gone on behind the scenes, it [the Prussian bureaucracy] was a single organisation, with a clear chain of command, whose tentacles stretched over all the Hohenzollern dominions. However conservative and obstructionist some of its members may have been, there developed among many others ... a high degree of professional skill and expertise.

It was a process which reached its consummation with Hegel's designation of the bureaucracy as 'the universal class', freed from the pressures of the market and self-interest, and so able to be aware of society's needs without being corrupted by its divisions.

To Councillor von Schlabuth or Lieutenant von Katte (judicially murdered in 1730 for complicity in the Crown Prince's attempt to escape his father's tyranny), Frederick William's Prussia cannot have seemed like a land fit for nobles. However, as we shall see in the next chapter, when the army is examined, in reality there were many opportunities for the promotion of noble interests on offer. In domestic politics this was shown by the continuing dominance in provincial administration of the noble district councillors (*Landräte*, the singular form being *Landrat*). There were about eighty of them across the Hohenzollern domains, forming the vital interface between central government and local landowners. What little the Prussian state tried to do in the localities was done by the *Landräte*. It was they who supervised the collection of taxes, provided for troops moving through their districts, regulated relations between peasants and landowners, promoted agricultural improvement, prevented or mitigated natural disasters, collected information, and publicized government decrees. In the early days, they were anything but the instruments of royal authority. In 1660 the governor of East Prussia, Prince Boguslaw Radziwiłł, complained that the *Landräte* in his province were 'indifferent to the defence of the country' and were 'true neighbours of the Poles', by which he meant that they were characterized by anarchic disobedience. Even after Frederick William the Great Elector had stamped his authority on them, a Prussian magnate could complain that 'the sovereign must at all times negotiate with these *Landräte* about his rights, even his very bread; so long as this goes on, the Elector will be ruler more *nomine* than *omine*'. That was probably an exaggeration in 1689; it certainly was by the time Frederick William I had finished with them. By then they were partly the king's men and partly the nobility's men, naturally inclined to the latter role but mindful of the need to strike a balance with royal interests. This amphibious quality meant that they were well suited to act as middlemen and to ensure that a proper balance was maintained between the two.

The year 1740 and the accession of Frederick II (he was known as 'the Great' from early on, following his victories in the first war against the Habsburg Monarchy) marked a watershed in Prussian (and European) history, for it was he who struck with the weapon forged by his father. But so far as the political structures of his country were concerned, surprisingly little changed. If anything, he made the system he inherited more incoherent by adding on extra departments to the General Directory as and when he thought they were needed – for commerce and manufacturing in 1740, for Silesia in 1746, and so on. The major change of emphasis he introduced, moreover, was retrogressive, for it was to favour the nobility. He immediately reversed all the measures introduced by his father inimical to noble interests: indeed, one of his first directives to the General Directory put a stop to attempts to reclaim royal domain land appropriated by nobles.

Frederick was loyal to this programme, both in principle and in practice, throughout his reign. In his 'Political Testament' of 1752, which contained his innermost thoughts on government and was not written with an eye to publication, he elevated support for the nobility to the status of a general political maxim: 'a sovereign should regard it as his duty to protect the nobility, who form the finest jewel in his crown and the lustre of his army'. Other social groups might be wealthier, but none surpassed the nobles in valour or loyalty. In practice, this meant an end to the special favour shown to commoners by his father. Even if the aristocratic composition of Frederick's civil service has been exaggerated, he did favour nobles for senior positions, both in the General Directory at the centre and in the 'War and Domains Chambers' in the provinces, and he did restore to the Estates the right to nominate candidates for the crucial position of *Landrat*. Not only did Frederick confirm the public institutions of the Prussian state as instruments of outdoor relief for his nobles, he also did all he could to preserve their private wealth. With the price of grain and the value of land rising sharply, if erratically, it was a time of great opportunity, but also high risks, for the Junkers. For the prodigal, unenterprising or unlucky, danger threatened in the shape of the increasingly numerous, wealthy and acquisitive commoners, who wanted nothing more than a Junker estate – a *Rittergut* – with which to acquire social prestige. Nothing illustrates Frederick's social conservatism better than his letter to Cocceji of 29 December 1750, in which he noted with alarm that estates belonging to old noble families were passing into the hands of nouveaux riches. He ordered that in future no noble estates could be alienated from the class without his express permission. The prohibition was renewed in

1762. (This attempt to turn back the economic tide was a predictable failure: by the end of the century, more than 10 per cent of Junker estates had passed into the hands of commoners.) With the same object in view, Frederick encouraged noble families to entail their landed property, thus making it invulnerable to genetic accident, but with an equal lack of success.

More concrete was the assistance given during the dark days following the Seven Years War, after Junker families had been decimated by the exceptionally high casualty rate suffered by the officer corps and after Junker estates had been devastated by the French, Swedish, Austrian and Russian invaders. Frederick intervened to impose a moratorium on bankruptcy proceedings for two years, to make cash grants for the repair and restocking of farms, and to establish rural credit institutions (*Landschaften*) for the supply of cheap and easy mortgages. It goes without saying that the great majority of army officers were nobles – nine out of ten by the end of Frederick's reign.

Frederick the Great's Prussia was absolute, in the sense that he exercised a monopoly of law-making; it was autocratic, in the sense that *Kabinettsregierung* continued; and it was aristocratic, in the sense that it favoured the nobility. But the whole edifice was underpinned by the need to serve the state to which both monarch and nobles were subordinated. Frederick not only announced that he was 'the first servant of the state', he also demonstrated that he meant it. Life as a military officer or civilian official cannot have been pleasant, as no one knew when or where the King might appear next, to inspect, to interrogate, to harangue, to encourage, to scold, even occasionally to praise and reward. Of course, the Prussian officials had ways and means of warning each other when the King was heading their way; of course, they told him what he wanted to hear; and, of course, he could cover only a small portion of his far-flung and extensive dominions. More important was the image he created of tireless and selfless devotion to duty. It helped to prolong the viability of reform from above many decades beyond its natural life. One of his officials left the following account of Frederick's working day:

He began his work early in the morning with foreign affairs; he had already read the deciphered despatches of his ambassadors and now he dictated to his secretary an answer to every despatch, whether important or not, from first letter to the last, often several pages. Thereupon he dictated to another secretary answers to all the letters on domestic affairs, to reports of the chambers on accounting and finance, and to the reports of the military inspectors on the army. Some of these he had already decreed by marginal notes. While this was being done, another secretary prepared a brief extract of all less important letters and petitions from private persons. This was then placed before the king who decided each item in as few words.

He never took a holiday. As the state expanded, his ability to master each and every detail was stretched beyond even his capacity, with the result that the conduct of business became more haphazard and inefficient. In particular, the secretaries who mediated between him and the bureaucracy acquired a lot of power but no responsibility – a classic recipe for arbitrary government. Yet his example certainly helped to create the ethos of service among the Prussian elites, led by the male members of the royal family, all of whom were obliged to serve in the army. Some idea of how much importance Frederick attached to service can be gained from the following directive to the minister for Silesia, Ernst von Schlabrendorf, in 1763:

Let me make it plain once and for all that I will not sell titles and still less noble estates for money, to the debasement of the nobility. Noble status can only be gained by the sword, by bravery and by other outstanding behaviour and services. I will tolerate as vassals only those who are at all times capable of rendering me useful service in the army, and those who because of exceptionally good conduct and exceptional service I choose to raise into the estate of the nobility.

RUSSIA

When he wrote those words in 1763, Frederick may have been unaware that they had been anticipated a generation earlier by Peter the Great: 'we will allow no rank to anyone until they have rendered service to us and the fatherland'. He would certainly have been aware that Peter had fostered a nobility that even by Prussian standards was distinguished by the emphasis on service. It was not so much that Peter sought to abolish or even dilute the old Muscovite nobility, rather he set about reorientating it towards state service. In the process, he refashioned its education, training, employment and even appearance. Traditional titles – *boiare* (boyars), *okol'nichii, stol'niki* – were allowed to die out. By 1718 there were only six boyars left, the very last one dying in 1750. In their place he instituted a set of titles borrowed from the west – baron, count, prince – and a new hierarchy based on military and civilian service to the state. It was formalized in 1722 when Peter published a 'Table of Ranks', based mainly on Prussian, Danish and Swedish models. There were 14 ranks, 1 being the lowest, embracing 262 different posts – 126 military and naval, 94 administrative and 42 at court. This was not a meritocracy, for existing nobles enjoyed preferential treatment and any commoner reaching the eighth rank acquired hereditary noble status. But if the traditional society of orders was to continue, success within it was to be performance related. Setting an example from the top, Peter demonstratively entered military service as a bombardier. John Perry, who published a first-hand account of Russia in 1716, observed:

By taking upon himself both a Post in his Navy, and in his Army, wherein he acted and took the gradual Steps of Preferment, like another Man, [he wished] to make his Lords see that he expects they shall not think themselves nor their Sons too good to serve their Countrey, and take their steps gradually to Preferment.

Writing a generation later, another foreign observer – Henning Friedrich, Count von Bassewitz – agreed, insisting that Peter had not been in any sense egalitarian: 'What [he] had in mind was not the abasement of the noble estate. On the contrary, all tended towards instilling in the nobility a desire to distinguish themselves from common folk by merit as well as by birth.' On the other hand, status now went with rank not pedigree – a prince in the third class was below a baron in the first. There was no opt-out clause: from 1710 there were regular inspections of young nobles when they reached the age of ten, with those passing a physical and mental aptitude test being despatched to cadet schools until they were ready for full-time service five years later. It might almost be said that Russian nobles no longer enjoyed a private life. In 1716, for example, Peter issued the following order: 'We have received news from Italy that in Venice they wish to accept our people into naval service training: today the French have also responded, saying that they too will accept our trainees. Consequently, select immediately in the Petersburg schools children of well-to-do nobles, bring them to Reval, and place them aboard ships. There should be sixty of them. Send twenty to Venice, twenty to France, and twenty to England.'

This is truly a different world from anything we have encountered so far. There is a mighty paradox here: it was Peter the Great's paramount ambition to bring his state closer to the west, but he succeeded only in driving it further away. Of course, there were all sorts of ways in which the 'westernization' of Russia did proceed. The conquest of the Baltic provinces of the Swedish Empire between 1700 and 1721 provided the famous 'window on the west'. By that time there was no danger of a repetition of the diplomatic gaffe committed by Louis XIV in 1657, when he addressed an official letter to Peter's grandfather, Tsar Mikhail Fedorovich, unaware that he had died twelve years previously. In 1716 Russia impinged on the west as directly as possible, when a Russian army wintered in Mecklenburg. The move of the capital from Moscow to the newly created St Petersburg did much more than wrench the Russian elites 370 miles (600 km) to the west, for it was accompanied by an equally top-down transformation of their culture. Away went the beards, kaftans and pectoral crosses; in came wigs, French fashions and pastimes. The new city was given a German name (hence its Russification as 'Petrograd' on the outbreak of war in 1914) and a Dutch layout. As Geoffrey Hosking has remarked, it was to be not a new Rome but a new Amsterdam. As good an illustration as any of the cultural revolution Peter effected at the apex of society is revealed by a comparison of a portrait of his father, Tsar Aleksei Mikhailovich (1645–76) with a portrait of him by Sir Godfrey Kneller, painted in The Hague in 1697, during one of Peter's visits to the west. The former is made to look more like a bishop than a sovereign, while the latter is every inch a dashing secular warrior-king, the pencil-moustache only serving to emphasize the absence of other facial hair. If this last detail seems trivial, it should be borne in mind that a beard was believed by Orthodox believers to be a sign of a God-fearing man and that without it, admission to the next world might be impeded or even denied.

The secularization revealed by this comparison was expressed in many other ways, most obviously by the seizure of control of the Russian Church from the Patriarch. This found ceremonial expression in a move from religious processions, in which the Tsar participated as a humble servant of God and His Church, to secular triumphs with the Tsar elevated to become the centre of adoration himself. It was an ambulatory equivalent of Versailles. Neatly symbolic of this change was the transfer of the biblical text used on these occasions – 'Blessed is he that cometh in the name of the Lord; Hosanna in the highest' (Matthew 21:9) – from the Patriarch to the Tsar. On 30 September 1696, for example, Peter organized a lavish ceremonial entry to Moscow to celebrate his victory over the Turks at Azov, which involved passing through a triumphal classical arch flanked by gigantic statues of Hercules and Mars and adorned with Caesar's motto 'veni, vidi, vici'. He was also compared with Constantine – not Constantine the Christian convert but Constantine the mighty conqueror. Following the Peace of Nystad, which brought the victorious war against Sweden to an end, the Senate formally gave him the Roman imperial title he had long been using – 'Imperator'.

This might seem a move away from the Byzantine and Greek heritage of Muscovy towards Roman and Renaissance models. Similarly 'western' was Peter's frequent emphasis on the need to serve an abstraction rather than him personally. He variously referred to the 'fatherland', 'Russia', 'the common good', 'general welfare', 'the benefit of the whole nation' and – especially – 'the state'. In the past, the Russian word most closely approximating to 'state', 'état' or 'Staat' – gosudarstvo – designated a specific piece of territory belonging to the Tsar, as in 'gosudarstvo Sibiri' (the state of Siberia), although 'affairs of state' (gosudarstvennye dela) began to be used around the middle of the seventeenth century. Peter sought to take that a great deal further, by separating the idea of an impersonal state from the person of the Tsar. If he never used the phrase 'first servant of the state' to describe his own role, he certainly came close to it, as for example when he struck out the formula 'the interests of His Tsarist Majesty' from a draft decree and substituted 'the interests of the state' as the proper object of soldiers' loyalty. On the eve of the greatest of all his military victories, against the Swedes at Poltava on 27 June 1709, he is reported to have said: 'Do not think of yourselves as armed and drawn up to fight for Peter, but for the state which has been entrusted to Peter.'

So far, so western, but the forces pointing in the opposite direction, back through Muscovy over the Urals and into Asia, were arguably of greater potency. So great was the coercion required to bring about Peter's reform programme that it became counter-productive. A case in point was his new capital, built by tens of thousands of conscripted labourers little better than slaves, many of whom died of disease in the mosquito-infested swamp that was the building site. The Hanoverian F. C. Weber, who worked as a secretary in the British embassy, recorded that no preparations had been made to clothe, feed or accommodate the migrant workers, with the result that 'it is computed that there perished on this occasion very nigh one hundred thousand souls, for in those places made desolate by the war, no provisions could be had even for ready money'. The writer Nikolai Karamzin (1766–1826) was an admirer of Peter's overall achievement and, like Weber, thought St Petersburg was a 'wonder of the world', but even he wrote that the foundations of the city were 'tears and corpses'. Nor did the coercion diminish as the city rose. To people it, a thousand nobles owning more than a hundred serf households were commanded to build residences there, at their own expense but according to plans laid down by the authorities. Thanks to the speed with which they were constructed and the unsuitable nature of the site, the new palaces were crumbling before they were completed. Frederick the Great's friend Count Algarotti jeered: 'Their walls are all cracked quite out of perpendicular and ready to fall. It has been wittily said that ruins make themselves in other places, but that they were built at St Petersburg.' As part of Peter's almost manic attention to detail, the new arrivals were presented with small yachts, in which they were required to present themselves every Sunday afternoon to demonstrate their sailing skills. Attendance at social functions such as balls, soirées and salons was both compulsory and strictly regulated. Well might Dostoevsky call it 'the most rational and premeditated city on earth'.

Peter the Great could get his nobles out of Moscow, but could he get Muscovy out of his nobles? Did he really want to? The example he set himself suggests that his attitude was ambivalent. Even by the standards of the most coarse European sovereign – Frederick William I of Prussia, say – Peter's behaviour was in a different class of crudity. Foreign observers reported with a mixture of horror and ridicule the antics of his court: the aptly named 'cups of sorrow', for example, that is to say the buckets of raw alcohol brought round by guardsmen and from which courtiers were obliged to drink with ladles. Any backsliding was reported by informers and no one was allowed to leave until the Tsar himself arrived around midnight to signal release. Peter's persecution of his son Aleksei also suggests some form of dementia. Constantly bullied and humiliated by his father and told that he should be severed 'like a gangrenous limb', no wonder that Aleksei sought to renounce any claim to the throne and then ran away to seek refuge in the Habsburg

Monarchy. Induced to return in 1718 by promises of good treatment, he was then subjected to what Lindsey Hughes has called 'the first Russian show trial'. During his interrogation in the Peter-Paul fortress of St Petersburg he was repeatedly tortured until mercifully released by death. That rumours at once spread that he had been poisoned, smothered or even strangled by his father give some idea of Peter's terrible – and terrifying – image. By comparison, Frederick William I's brutal treatment of Crown Prince Frederick when he tried to escape paternal tyranny seems like a model of mercy and justice.

When Aleksei foolishly signalled to Peter that he was prepared to return to Russia, he signed his letter: 'your most humble and worthless slave, unworthy of the name of son'. This was more than a form of words. What struck contemporaries repeatedly was the servile nature of relationships in Russian society. It was not invented by Peter, but it was intensified by his terrorist approach to all and sundry and institutionalized by his Table of Ranks. As there was no corporate structure and no sense of corporate identity, interests could only be pursued individually. Together with Peter's rigorous use of coercion and fostering of an ethos of servility and service, this very special quality of the nobility gave Russia a political culture which may have acquired western trappings but fundamentally was growing ever more distant. This phenomenon was recorded by contemporaries so often that it has to be taken seriously, even after every allowance has been made for bias and ignorance. Representative of a rich store of examples was the impression gained by Edward Daniel Clarke, a Fellow of Jesus College, Cambridge, who travelled in Russia at the very end of the eighteenth century, who wrote: 'It is not so generally known as it may be, that the passage of a small rivulet, which separates the two countries of Sweden and Russia, the mere crossing of a bridge, conducts the traveller from all that adorns and dignifies the human mind, to whatsoever, most abject, has been found to degrade it.' Of course, English travellers were particularly fond of this sort of sweeping disparagement, but in among the rhetoric there was a core of truth about what Clarke had to say about the servility which informed Russian society: 'They are all, high and low, rich and poor, alike servile to superiors; haughty and cruel to their dependants.'

Peter's failure to westernize his state was revealed most clearly in his failure to solve what is arguably a monarchy's most fundamental problem: the orderly transfer of power when the current incumbent dies.

'The King is dead, long live the King' is all very well in theory, but who was the new King going to be? In the west, this had been solved by the principle of primogeniture, but in the east there was an elective monarchy in Poland and some uncertainty in Russia, where primogeniture was a matter of custom rather than law. Hence the confusion that arose when Peter's half-brother, Tsar Fyodor, died in 1682. Although Peter was only ten years old and there was another elder half-brother available – Ivan– Peter was proclaimed sole Tsar, partly because Ivan was incapacitated by physical and mental problems but mainly because of the ambitions of his mother's relations. Following a revolt of the 'streltsy' regiments, both Ivan and Peter were made Tsars, but with power being exercised by Sophia, their sister and half-sister respectively, as regent. It was not until Sophia had been elbowed aside in 1689 and the wretched Ivan finally died in 1696 that Peter really took charge.

Decisive in most things, it might have been expected that Peter would have given a firm western direction in this all-important area too. Not only did he not do so, but when he did move, it was in the opposite direction. His only son Aleksei he first disinherited and then judicially murdered. In 1722 he promulgated a new law of succession, making it subject to the current Tsar's will: 'We deem it good to issue this edict in order that it will always be subject to the will of the ruling monarch to appoint whom he wishes to the succession or to remove the one he has appointed in the case of unseemly behaviour, so that his children and descendants should not fall into wicked ways, having this restraint upon them.' Yet when he died three years later he had not made any such appointment. What then followed showed the shape of things to come. Prince Menshikov, Peter's oldest and closest associate, took the widowed Tsarina Catherine to the Guards to win their support for her nomination. All then made their way to the Senate, where the succession issue was in the process of being debated. The senators favoured Peter's grandson, also called Peter, but the Guards officers who entered the chamber put a quick stop to that. With the drums of their soldiers issuing an aural warning outside, Catherine was promptly proclaimed Peter's successor. In a sense, this episode could be advanced as an advertisement for the social mobility of Russia. Allegedly the son of a pie-seller, Menshikov was in fact the son of an NCO, who rose through his friendship with the Tsar to become the richest man in the land and the first to receive the new hereditary title of Prince. For her part, Catherine had been born to a

Lithuanian peasant family and was working as a scullery-maid to a Lutheran pastor in Marienburg when she was carried off by Russian troops in 1702. Passed from one officer to another, including Menshikov, she ended up in the arms of the Tsar, who married her bigamously in 1707.

It was Peter the Great who was responsible for giving the Guards regiments this political role. It was he who decided that they should be permanently posted in St Petersburg, as part bodyguard, part police force; and it was he who gave them elite status, with even junior officers gaining automatic admission to the court. Variously described as 'the kernel of Imperial Russia in the eighteenth century' (Geoffrey Hosking) and 'a kind of repository of the political thought of the ruling gentry class' (Bernard Pares), the Semenovsky, Preobrazhensky and Horse Guards were involved in every succession between 1725 and 1825 bar one (that of Paul I). Given their resemblance to the Praetorian Guard of imperial Rome, it might be said, perhaps, that this represented a form of westernization, but that seems stretching the point rather too far. At least the Russian Guards never actually sold the imperial title, as the Praetorians did, to Didius Julianus in AD 193. Paradoxically, in both cases, it was in the interests of these military emperor-makers to support absolute power. That was revealed in Russia in 1730, following the short reign of Peter II (1727–30). The grandees of the Supreme Privy Council invited Anna, Duchess of Courland, daughter of Peter the Great's half-brother Ivan, to succeed, on condition she shared power with them. But when she arrived in Moscow (which had briefly regained its status as capital under her predecessor), her first action was to visit the Guards regiments, declare herself their Colonel and serve them vodka with her own hands. Neither party wished to see the magnates in power, so two weeks later Anna tore up the conditions to which she had agreed. Baron Christof Hermann von Manstein, a Prussian serving in the Russian army at the time, explained why this alliance between absolutist Tsar and Guards officers was natural:

I much doubt whether this empire, or rather the higher nobility will ever achieve their liberty. The lesser nobility, who are extremely numerous in Russia, will constantly oppose great obstacles to it, being more afraid of the tyranny of a number of the great than of the power of a single sovereign.

He was quite right. Writing from Kazan, one noble commented on the coup that brought Anna to power: 'God forbid that it turn out that, instead of one autocratic sovereign, we have tens of absolute and powerful families, and thus we, the nobility will decline completely.' The alliance was consolidated as the years passed, as the coercive regime of Peter the Great was relaxed. In 1736 the obligation to serve the state was reduced from life to twenty-five years and every noble household was allowed to retain a son to run the estates, if a second did go off to serve, although even those who stayed at home were obliged to learn to read and write in readiness for the civil service if required. However, implementation was delayed by the Turkish War and the flood of requests to leave the service led to a partial repeal. It was not until the brief reign of Peter III (1762) that the nobility was finally emancipated from the service obligation. Although greeted with 'unimaginable joy', as one noble put it, and by a request from the Senate to commission a statue of the Tsar made of solid gold, the small print revealed a number of qualifications, not the least being that officers could not retire in wartime and civilian officials had to secure the permission of the Tsar. It was also firmly stated that those who did not volunteer for service would be excluded from court and denied imperial favour.

It used to be thought that this edict marked a watershed, not just in the history of Tsar–nobility relations, but also in the history of Russia in general. Richard Pipes, for example, was of the opinion that 'it is difficult to exaggerate the importance of the edict of 1762 ... with this single act the monarchy created a large, privileged, westernised leisure class, such as Russia had never known before'. More recent assessments have been rather calmer, seeing the measure as partly a codification of existing practice and partly a recognition that compulsion was no longer needed to make nobles work for the state. If there was indeed a discernible move by some nobles from the army or administration towards the provinces, it did not alter the essentially autocratic nature of Tsarist authority or the essentially servile attitude of the nobility. It certainly did nothing to disturb the pattern of regime change by *coup d'état*. Only four months after issuing the decree, Peter III was deposed. He had been foolish enough to alienate the Guards, by contemptuously referring to them as 'Janissaries', bringing in his uncle, Prince George of Holstein, over the head of the existing commander, introducing Prussian discipline and insisting on leading personally the pointless war against Denmark. The coup that swiftly followed was led by the Tsarina Catherine's current lover Grigori Orlov. After Catherine had been proclaimed

Tsarina in her own right, Peter was murdered, probably by Grigori's brother Aleksei.

Catherine's hold on power was fragile for several years. As she was very well aware, she who rose by one *coup d'état* could well fall by another. Among others waiting in the wings was her son Paul, born in 1754, who could reasonably expect to take over from his mother when he came of age. A co-regency in the manner of Maria Theresa and Joseph II in the Habsburg Monarchy was another option. In 1764 a group of disaffected officers nearly succeeded in freeing Ivan VI, who had been held in captivity since being deposed in 1741 in favour of Elizabeth, the daughter of Peter the Great. He was promptly strangled by his jailer, obeying standing orders, but well might the Prussian ambassador predict, 'it is certain that the reign of the Tsarina Catherine is not to be more than a brief episode in the history of the world'. There was also a rash of pretenders, at least a dozen between 1762 and 1774, variously claiming to be Peter III, Ivan VI, a son of George II of England and the Tsarina Elizabeth, a daughter of Elizabeth, and so on. In the event, Catherine remained very much in sole command until she died in 1796. She achieved this feat by never forgetting where the foundations of her power lay. So Peter III's emancipation of the nobility was not revoked and his scheme for the emancipation of the serfs was not revived. She also tempered her autocracy by giving it a consultative flavour. In December 1766 she issued a manifesto known as the 'Great Instruction' (*Bol'shoi Nakaz*), summoning a commission to Moscow the following summer. When it opened in the Kremlin on 30 July 1767 it was attended by 574 deputies: 38 from government departments, 162 from noble assemblies, 206 from the towns, 58 from assemblies of free peasants, 56 from the non-Christian communities and 54 Cossacks. Conspicuous by their absence were serfs, deemed to be represented by their owners.

The ostensible purpose of the Commission was revealed by its title: 'Commission for the Composition of a Plan of a new Code of Laws'. It also allowed the Tsarina to gain a clearer idea of the aspirations and grievances of her non-serf subjects through the remonstrances they composed for the occasion. Catherine's most authoritative modern biographer, Isabel de Madariaga, takes the view that the information gathered as a result of the exercise proved to be 'invaluable in subsequent legislation'. That may well be so, but it is also likely that the Commission's primary purpose was to consolidate Catherine's hold on the throne: anticipating Tennyson, she knew that 'a doubtful throne is ice on summer seas'. By bringing noble deputies from all over the Empire to Moscow, she reminded the magnates of the traditional alliance between Tsars and the lesser nobility. By confronting the nobility as a class with a large number of deputies from other sections of society, she attached the latter more firmly to her person and demonstrated to the former that they were not the only force in Russian society. By simply calling the Commission and having its members solemnly recognize her on the throne, she legitimized the coup of 1762 and reduced her dependence on those who had brought her to power. When the Commission had fulfilled its task, she discarded it, using the Turkish War as a convenient pretext. Better informed and less naïve than Catherine's sycophantic coterie of French admirers like Voltaire, who compared her favourably with Lycurgus and Solon and dubbed the *Nakaz* 'the most beautiful monument of the century', the foreign diplomats in Russia were under no illusions as to the real purpose of the Commission. The British ambassador reported that: 'By these and other similar measures, glittering enough to dazzle the eyes of the Russians, the power of Her Imperial Majesty increases every day, and is already arrived to such a degree that this prudent princess thinks herself strong enough to humble the guards, who placed her upon the throne.'

The Commission never did discuss constitutional matters, nor was it supposed to. Catherine was quite insistent that the only form of government suitable for the Russian Empire was autocracy. This was made quite explicit in chapter two of the *Nakaz*:

¶ 9. The Sovereign is absolute; for there is no other Authority but that which centres in his single Person, that can act with a Vigour proportionate to the Extent of such a vast Dominion.

¶ 10. The Extent of the Dominion requires an absolute Power to be vested in that Person who rules over it. It is expedient so to be, that the quick Dispatch of Affairs, sent from distant Parts, might make ample Amends for the Delay occasioned by the great Distance of the Places.

¶ 11. Every other Form of Government whatsoever would not only have been prejudicial to Russia, but would even have proved its entire Ruin.

Like every other autocrat in the eighteenth century, however, Catherine knew only too well that commanding was much easier than implementing. During the early part of her reign she favoured a continuation of a bureaucracy staffed by service nobles and directed from the centre. Impressed by the provincial nobility's demands, heard at the Commission, for greater control of their affairs, and appalled by the shortcomings revealed by the Pugachev rebellion (see above, pp. 178–80), in 1775 Catherine instituted a major reform of the administrative system. In place of the existing twenty-five provinces, forty-one smaller units, based on a rational division of population, were established. More important was the devolution of responsibility for a wide range of judicial and administrative functions to nobles elected by their own provincial assemblies. If this seemed to point towards a modest measure of self-government, service was still the watchword, for nobles who had not served or had not reached commissioned rank when they did, were excluded from the elective offices and even from voting in the assemblies. Ten years later 'The Charter of the Rights, Freedoms and Privileges of the Noble Russian *Dvorianstvo*' formalized the nobility's relationship but did not dilute the autocracy. It confirmed Peter III's emancipation of 1762, but it also inserted a crucial qualification: 'at every time necessary to the Russian Autocracy, when the service of the *dvorianstvo* is necessary and needful to the general good, then each noble is bound at the first summons from the Autocratic Authority to spare neither labour nor life itself for the service of the State'.

The state still needed the nobility – and the nobility still needed the state. Peter's failure to persuade his nobles to abandon partible inheritance for entails meant that family fortunes were especially volatile in Russia. One way of keeping a noble head above water was to serve in the army or civil or diplomatic service, not so much because of the salaries – although they could be considerable at the top end – as for the grants of land and serfs that imperial favour could bring. Menshikov's rise from rags to riches was exceptional only in its scale. It is characteristically Russian that the degree of generosity should be measured not in the extent of the land but in the number of serfs that were given. For example, Catherine the Great gave away 400,000 serfs to favourites, senior officials or even as acts of charity – 200 serfs to the widow of a general who had distinguished himself in the suppression of the Pugachev revolt, for example. For the needy and the greedy, this combination of service and reward created a dependent relationship quite unlike anything to be found in the west.

When Catherine died on 5 November 1796, her son Paul succeeded with little fuss. It seems to have been her intention to pass him over and to designate her grandson Alexander as her successor, but she had not yet done so when felled by her fatal stroke. This unusual appearance of normality in Russia's political history was to be of short duration, for Paul lasted less than five years before being murdered in a coup launched by the Guards officers. In political terms, Russia remained very much *sui generis*. Catherine liked to assure anyone who would listen that Russia was not a despotism but a monarchy like any other, but more persuasive was Montesquieu's verdict: 'Muscovy has tried to leave its despotism; it cannot.' Although those words were first published in *The Spirit of the Laws* more than a decade before Catherine seized the throne, they were still applicable in 1796, or indeed in 1815 or any other date in Russian history for that matter. The last word can go to the British diplomat Sir George Macartney, who spent the years 1765–7 in Russia, renegotiating a commercial treaty:

Despotism can never long flourish, except in a barbarous nation, but to despotism Russia owes her greatness and dominion; so that if ever the monarchy becomes more limited, she will lose her power and strength, in proportion as she advances in moral virtues and civil improvement.

SPAIN AND ITALY

From the vantage point of the early twenty-first century, Macartney's prediction might seem to have a good deal to be said for it. Even before Catherine the Great began her great expansion to the west and the south, Russia's 'greatness and dominion' were apparent to all Europe. It was also clear by then that there had been a secular shift in the geographical location of power in Europe. When the period covered by this volume began in 1648, England was disqualified by civil strife; Brandenburg was a third-rate power struggling to recover from the devastation of the Thirty Years War; and, as we have seen, even the name of the Tsar of Russia was unknown to the King of France. By the time Macartney visited Russia in the mid-1760s, England (or rather Great Britain as it should be known after the union with Scotland in 1707) had become the dominant commercial, colonial and naval power; Prussia had confirmed its claim to great-power status by successfully defending its seizure of Silesia against one of the most powerful coalitions ever assembled; and Russia dominated the eastern half of Europe. The two powers lying across the central latitudes of the continent – France and the Habsburg Monarchy – were still undeniably of the first rank, but were beginning to show signs of strain. But in the south there had been a steep decline in the two great empires that had dominated Europe, if not the world, in the sixteenth and seventeenth centuries: the Spanish and the Turkish. In recent years, there has been much revisionist work to qualify the traditional picture of 'the decline of Spain' or 'the decline of the Ottomans'. It is indeed the case that the Spanish Empire in America reached its greatest extent in the course of the eighteenth century. Yet this expansion was more cartographic than real and had involved little more than brushing aside cobwebs.

Among the many reasons for this migration of power from south to north, politics was not the least important and, although it might seem superficial, the personal quality of the ruler proved to be crucial. Spain provides a particularly compelling example of how much can go wrong when a king is not only inadequate but also long-lived. If only Philip IV (1621–65) had brought to politics the same intelligence and enthusiasm that he devoted to the patronage of artists, most notably Velázquez, he might have done more to adapt his empire to an increasingly hostile environment. It was characteristic of his political horizons that, following the fall of the Count-Duke Olivares in 1643, his most influential confidante was a mystic nun, Sor María of the Ágreda convent, with whom he exchanged over 600 letters. In almost every letter he beseeched her to intercede with God on behalf of him, his family and his kingdom (in that order). But he left his most damaging blow to last, siring a successor only four years before his death, although he had experienced no difficulty in producing an illegitimate brood, thought to have numbered eight. His son, who succeeded as Charles II in 1665, was a pitiful creature, handicapped both physically and mentally. In the characteristically bleak verdict of Sir John Elliott, he was 'the last pallid relic of a fading dynasty, left to preside over the inert corpse of a shattered Monarchy, itself no more than the pallid relic of the great imperial past', whose reign was 'a pathetic spectacle of degradation'.

Perhaps a more appropriate word would be 'degeneration'. His father was a Habsburg, of course, and so was his mother, Mariana of Austria, both of whose parents – the Emperor Ferdinand III and the Infanta

Maria Anna – were also Habsburgs. Mariana was originally engaged to Philip IV's son Baltasar Carlos, by his first marriage, but when he died in 1646, she was switched to the father and her prospective father-in-law became her husband. Their first child, Margareta, was married to another Habsburg, her uncle Leopold, the son of Ferdinand III. And so on. In this ever-shrinking gene pool, it is a wonder that the Habsburgs managed to keep afloat as long as they did. In other words, it was no accident that Charles II was a cretin and the last of his line. His flattering but still grotesque portraits provide visual evidence of what a misguided obsession with family interests can bring. (His Austrian cousins seem to have got the message. After marrying and burying two Habsburg relations, Leopold I turned to the Wittelsbachs in the shape of Eleonora Magdalena of Pfalz-Neuburg. Their two sons, Joseph I and Charles VI went still further in the pursuit of an out-cross by both marrying princesses from the Guelph house of Brunswick.)

Throughout his childhood Charles II had to be carried as if he were a babe in arms and even as an adult was usually incapable of walking or speaking. Into the vacuum created by his incapacity moved his mother, advised first by her German Jesuit confessor, Father Nithard, and then by an unsavoury Andalusian adventurer, Fernando de Valenzuela. One particularly alarming manifestation of the implosion of monarchical authority was the intervention in 1677 of Don Juan José of Austria, allegedly one of Philip IV's illegitimate sons, although his paternity was disputed. After assembling an army in Catalonia, he marched on Madrid, issuing en route a *pronunciamento* calling on the Queen Regent to banish Valenzuela and to accept him as her first minister. This was the first such intervention in Spanish history, but it was to have a long future, ending (one hopes) only with General Franco's *pronunciamento* of 17 July 1936. Under this flaccid regime, power fragmented centrifugally in favour of the provincial elites: 'not federalism by conviction but federalism by default' (Elliott).

At the centre, what remained of royal power was in the hand of the councils, dominated by the grandees and run by a tightly knit noble elite educated at the aristocratic *colegios mayores*. On paper, it looked very much like a rationally organized bureaucratic system, indeed one historian of Philip IV's reign has described it as 'the world's first truly bureaucratic state' (R. A. Stradling). Philip himself certainly did his best to justify this accolade, toiling away single-handed at the mountains of documents that accumulated on his desk. He boasted to his conventual confidante:

Sor María, believe me that there is no amount of work which I myself refuse to accept. As anyone will tell you, I am continually seated here, on this chair, with my papers and my pen in hand, seeing and checking upon the pile of *consultas* which come to me from the councils, along with dispatches from abroad. I take my resolutions at once upon the most urgent issues, always trying to adjust my decision to the demands of reason. Other matters which are more weighty and complex, and which demand closer analysis, I refer to different ministers, so that, having heard their opinions, I can arrive at the best policy. But in the end, the decision is taken by no one but me, since this I recognize and understand to be my duty alone.

Following the disgrace of Olivares in 1643, Philip IV had anticipated Louis XIV by announcing that in future he would run the government himself, but he failed to sustain the effort required. Under his son, there was not even the pretence that the King was in charge. As the French fiscal expert Jean Orry observed after Charles II's death, 'It is the councils which rule the state and allocate all the offices, all the favours, and all the revenues of the kingdom.' In theory, Spain was still an absolutist monarchy; in practice, it was run as a joint enterprise by the elites of the centre and the periphery. This has been well put by John Lynch: 'By the end of the seventeenth century, the large and apparently active bureaucracy in Madrid was not an instrument of absolutism or an agent of centralisation but a mediator between the sovereign and his subjects, dealing with nobles, churchmen, tax-farmers, urban oligarchies and other local interests who collaborated with the crown rather than obeyed it.'

Charles II's death in 1700 unleashed a great European war that is usually known as the War of the Spanish Succession, but inside Spain it was a civil war with all the horrors that such a conflict involves. The victory of the Bourbon candidate, Philip V, was also a victory for Castile and a defeat for Catalonia. Indeed, it was a defeat for all the peripheral provinces. The flaccid hand of the last Habsburg was replaced by a much firmer grasp. Symbolic was the destruction of a whole district of Barcelona after its capture and the construction of a great fortress. The new ruler had announced his intentions in the *Nueva Planta* or 'new plan' of 1707, ordering a clean sweep of all those privileges and institutions that had thwarted absolutist rule from Madrid in the past: 'considering that the kingdoms of Aragon and Valencia and all their inhabitants, by reason of the rebellion which they have raised, thus breaking the oath of allegiance they swore to me as their lawful King and Lord, have forfeited all rights, privileges, immunities and liberties which they have enjoyed'. Centralism was the order of the day, as Philip went on to proclaim 'my will to reduce all the kingdoms of Spain to obedience to the same laws, practices, customs and tribunals, each equally subject to the laws of Castile, which are so praiseworthy and acceptable throughout the world'.

In the place of the councils came bureaucratically organized departments on the French model, run by secretaries of state. With this organizational restructuring came a social change too. Under the Habsburgs, according to the Venetian Cornaro in 1683, 'power is entirely in the hands of the grandees. Bound together by family ties and by their own private interests, they care neither for the public weal nor for the interests of the crown. So much has their power increased, and so much has that of the king diminished, that if he wanted to rule in an absolutist and despotic manner, I doubt if he would succeed.' The conclusive military victory of Philip V left the grandees stranded, still rich and still powerful on their *latifundia*, but stripped of the 'aristocratic republicanism' they had previously enjoyed. As the French ambassador Bonnac observed in 1711, 'The opinion that His Catholic Majesty holds in general of the grandees of Spain is that so long as they are not in office they will be incapable of harm, hated as they are by their subjects, and odious to the lower nobility.' Taking the eighteenth century as a whole, nearly a third of the members of the Council of State were newly created nobles, rather more than a third were untitled lawyers or army officers, and only a third were grandees or other nobles of ancient lineage. Not that this represented any sort of 'bourgeois' takeover, rather a 'renovation of the aristocracy by the aristocratisation of the bureaucracy' (I. A. A. Thompson). Also reminiscent of French practice was the introduction after 1711 of a network of centrally appointed and directed officials modelled on the system of intendants.

Any hope that the change of dynasty would bring a return to the palmy days of the sixteenth century, when Spain dominated Europe and created an empire on which the sun never set, was soon frustrated. A century later Spain's position in the states-system was, if anything, weaker and even the colonial empire was beginning to crumble. Of course, that was in large measure due to shifts in power-political and economic structures over which the Spanish had little or no control. Yet they continued to be unlucky in their sovereigns. Part of the problem may have been continuing inbreeding, for the Habsburgs and Bourbons had been intermarrying throughout the previous century: Louis XIV's mother was a Habsburg (the daughter of Philip III) and he himself married his cousin Maria Theresa (the daughter of Philip IV). Whatever the reason, if the first Bourbon King of Spain represented an improvement on his immediate predecessor, it was modest in nature. Philip V was in thrall to two very powerful passions sometimes thought to be at odds with each other: sex and religion. So powerful was his priapism but so awful was his fear of God that he was putty in the hands of his queen. His grandfather, Louis XIV, gave him the following sound advice: 'Kings, exposed to the gaze of the public, are all the more greatly scorned when they suffer their wives to dominate. You have, before your eyes, the example of your predecessor. The queen is your first subject. In that quality and as your wife she ought to obey you . . . Be strong from the beginning.' Yet all his first wife, Marie Louise of Savoy, had to do to reduce him to trembling submission was to banish him from her bed for two nights. His second wife, Elizabeth Farnese, used the same weapon to even greater effect, among other things running Spanish foreign policy in the interests of their two sons (who seemed unlikely to inherit the throne of Spain, as Philip already had two sons by Marie Louise). She eventually succeeded in marrying her children into every significant Catholic family in Europe, from Portugal to Saxony, with the sole exception of Bavaria.

The tension created by Philip's frantic rush from bed to confessional and back again led to periodic breakdowns, which manifested themselves in acute depression, paranoia and fear of dying in mortal sin. When his first major collapse occurred in 1717, the French ambassador reported: 'The king is visibly wasting away through the excessive use he makes of the queen. He is utterly worn out.' As John Lynch laconically adds, the ambassador did not feel it necessary to comment on the condition of the Queen. When experiencing an attack, Philip took to his bed, refusing to rise, dress, wash or even attend to his bodily functions, lying in his own excrement for days or even weeks on end. In 1737, in the midst of yet another attack, relief was found in the unlikely shape of the star opera-singer of the period, the castrato Carlo Broschi, better known as 'Farinelli'. The King was so smitten by the sound of his singing an aria next door to his bedchamber that he asked for an encore, promising any favour in return. Suitably primed by the resourceful Queen, at whose invitation he had come to Madrid in the first place, Farinelli beseeched the King to rise from his bed and return to his royal duties. Farinelli's therapy proved so successful that he became both a close friend of the royal couple and the cultural supremo of the country. But there was a high price to pay. By this time, even when more or less stable, the King had turned night into day, rising at noon, conducting official business during the night, having supper at 5 a.m. and retiring to bed at 8 a.m. After a year of having to adapt, Farinelli lamented: 'Since the day I came I follow the same routine, singing every night for the king and queen who listen to me as on that first day. I pray God to preserve my health in this manner of life; every night I sing eight or nine arias. I never rest.'

Philip V was on the throne for forty-six years. The early prediction of the marquis de Louville – 'he is a king who does not reign and never will reign' – proved to be not far off the mark. For all their superior strength of character, neither of his two queens had the necessary ability – or perhaps even the time, given their bedroom/sickroom duties – to fill the vacuum. That was done by a succession of favourites, the first being the princesse des Ursins, who found plenty of opportunity to indulge that 'masculine longing for fame and power' identified by the duc de Saint-Simon as her driving force. Rudely dismissed by Elizabeth Farnese on her arrival in 1714, she was replaced by Cardinal Giulio Alberoni from Parma and then by a Dutch adventurer, Jan Willem Ripperda. The roller-coaster ride of the latter encapsulates the unstable nature of Spanish government under the first Bourbon: the Queen's patronage raised him to be a duke and a grandee of Spain; its withdrawal turned him into a prisoner and then a fugitive. After adventures worthy of a picaresque novel, which included conversion to Islam (he had already converted from Calvinism to Catholicism) and leading Moorish forces against the Spanish in North Africa, he died in poverty in 1737. Some measure of stability was introduced by José de Patiño, in effect chief minister between 1726 and 1736, who proved to be an effective if conservative administrator.

Philip V's reign was almost a great deal shorter, for in 1724 he quixotically abdicated in favour of his son Luis 'to concentrate my mind on death during the time that remains to me and to pray for my salvation in that other and more permanent kingdom'. Later the same year the new King died of smallpox and Philip reluctantly returned to royal duty. At least this sudden death saved Spain from another grotesque, not so much King Luis, who was an unknown quantity, as his fifteen-year-old queen Louise Elizabeth, yet another Bourbon, believed to have inherited syphilis from her father, the duc d'Orléans, and whose eccentricities included foul language and running around the palace naked. When Philip finally died in 1746, it proved to be a case of *plus ça change, plus c'est la même chose*, for his son Ferdinand proved to be very much a chip off the old block. He too was torn between carnal and spiritual ecstasies, completely in thrall to his Portuguese wife Maria Bárbara, despite her reputed ugliness – 'she was homely in her features, and the original elegance of her shape was lost in corpulence' was the ungallant verdict of William Coxe. Ferdinand was less energetic than his father, being idle and indifferent to the conduct of public business, leaving his queen to fill the gap. The French ambassador's comment on the new reign was 'it is rather Bárbara who succeeds Elizabeth than Ferdinand succeeding Philip'.

In both cases, however, the new reign marked an improvement. Although mentally unstable, Ferdinand was less manic than his father and easier to control. The Queen had no personal dynastic agenda to pursue at the expense of her adopted country, was less selfish and more talented. In particular, she was a gifted musician, both as performer and composer, and a discriminating patron. Domenico Scarlatti was in effect her chamber musician from 1719 until his death in 1757 and she continued her support for Farinelli, without inflicting on him the weird working conditions of the previous reign. She also showed better judgement than Elizabeth Farnese in her choice of ministers, the most notable being Ensenada and Carvajal. If there was much enervating faction-fighting between the two men, significant progress was made in reforming taxation, improving the armed forces, promoting public works with the help of foreign experts and redressing the technological gap with northern Europe. The importance of Maria Bárbara was revealed when she died in August 1758, which sent King Ferdinand's tenuous grip on sanity tumbling over the edge into outright dementia. Inconsolable, he locked himself away in the grim castle of Villaviciosa de Odón near Madrid, wandering aimlessly and endlessly around its rooms, refusing to be washed, dressed or fed. The government of Spain and its empire came to a halt, resuming only when death brought a merciful release to the grieving widower a year later.

The importance of personality in determining the fortunes of an eighteenth-century country was demonstrated by the arrival in Spain of Ferdinand's half-brother Charles, who had ruled Naples since 1735. Compared with the horrors of the previous ninety-four years, this 'giant among Bourbon midgets' (John Lynch) brought a much-needed return to normality. Sound in mind and body, affable, virile without being obsessively priapic (he sired thirteen legitimate children), devout without being a religious maniac, he arrived with a reputation as an enlightened and decisive ruler. As we shall see in a later chapter, when considering 'enlightened absolutism', he was an active reformer, albeit operating within traditional social and political limits. In terms of governmental structures, he began as a pure absolutist, taking all the important decisions himself. Certainly there were no constitutional checks on his authority, as the Cortes of Castile humbly informed him: 'O Sire, the realm is prepared not only to swear an oath of fidelity and do rightful homage, but to perform whatever Your Majesty may propose.' The disturbances of 1766 (see below, p. 324) prompted a change of direction, away from advisers of Neapolitan or Sicilian background, such as Esquilache. Of the two major figures of the second part of his reign, one was a grandee – the conde de Aranda – the other from the lesser nobility – José Moñino, better known as the conde de Floridablanca. The inevitable personal rivalry between the two men reflected a social struggle between the two ends of the Spanish nobility. Although Charles III remained very much in control until his death, government became less personal and more ministerial. Secretaries of state increasingly met in ad hoc committees known as 'juntas' to discuss policy, and may even have begun to develop a sense of collective responsibility.

Charles III died the year before the French Revolution subjected Spain to all sorts of challenges it was ill-equipped to face. The rulers and their elites had adapted erratically, slowly and inadequately. If the grandees had slipped from their seventeenth-century eminence and 'the titled nobility was much more of an aristocracy of merit and public service than it had ever been before' (I. A. A. Thompson), they patently lacked the patriotism that was to become so necessary for success, or even survival, in a revolutionary age. And if the Spanish body politic had roused itself from its moribund condition of 1700, it remained sclerotic, responding only fitfully to impulses despatched from the centre. One potentially ominous sign was the growing influence of the army in public affairs, encouraged by the rapid increase in the number of generals: there were 47 lieutenant-generals in 1788 and 132 four years later. Otherwise the comment of Louis XIV made in 1701 to his new ambassador to Spain, the comte de Marsin, still applied: 'The power of the kings has always been absolute. The people, although impatient for relief, are very submissive; the great, divided among themselves, are unpopular, without adherents, tremble for fear of being removed from Madrid, and are too indolent to be dangerous.'

Among the various states that made up the Italian peninsula, there was a wide variety of relationships between rulers and elites to be found. One characteristic they all had in common, however, was that very little changed in the course of the century – or at least until the French invasions of the 1790s. Perhaps the most extreme example of political stasis was provided by the Papal States. The plural form 'States' is entirely appropriate, for it was a conglomeration of fifteen provinces, including two enclaves in the Kingdom of Naples and two further enclaves in France (Avignon and the Comtat Venaissin). On the surface it looked very much like an elective monarchy, ruled by popes elected and controlled by the Sacred College of Cardinals. In reality, the latter had long since relinquished any formal controlling functions. In the words of the French historian Louis Madelin, Rome was an aristocratic republic that had fallen into ineffectual despotism. There was indeed a discrepancy between papal rhetoric and papal power, neatly expressed by Benedict XIV when he commented, 'The pope commands, the cardinals do not obey, and the people do what they wish.' His army, police force and law courts were all the objects of derision. After an extended visit to Rome in 1728, during the course of which he got to know several cardinals well, including the future Clement XII, Montesquieu wrote, 'The vicar of Christ is very great and the prince is very small.'

There seems little point in even outlining the administrative congregations of the Papal States, presenting as they do 'an almost impenetrable maze to the uninitiated' (Hanns Gross). Clarity at the top was obscured by the existence of three powerful ministers: the Cardinal Secretary of

State, who was both foreign minister and minister of the interior; the Cardinal Camerlengo, whose overlapping responsibilities included finance, agriculture, commerce and public works; and the Treasurer General, who was not subject to the latter but reported directly to the Pope. Also worthy of comment is the extent to which the city relied for its existence on the presence within its walls of the central bodies of Catholic Christendom. Together with their dependants, the staff of the hundred-odd ministries are estimated to have numbered around 80,000, or about half of the total population. Of the remainder, many were lawyers making a living from the inexhaustible flow of petitions for papal dispensations from the faithful across the globe. Although barely credible, it has been estimated that there was one lawyer for every 140 inhabitants.

At least the status of their ruler meant that the people of Rome and the Papal States enjoyed political stability. Elsewhere, the vagaries of international relations created a much more febrile situation. An extreme example was Sicily, ruled by the Spanish Habsburgs until their extinction in 1700, then by the Bourbons in the person of Philip V for the duration of the War of the Spanish Succession, then by Victor Amadeus II of Piedmont for five years, then by Charles VI of Austria for fourteen years, then returning in 1735 to the Spanish Bourbons with Charles VII, who on his elevation to the Spanish throne in 1759 passed it to his third son Ferdinand. For all his shortcomings (and they were many), at least Ferdinand provided continuity, reigning until 1825. In the second half of the seventeenth century, the Sicilian elites had benefited from the 'benevolent devolutionism' (John Lynch) of Charles II. Yet even his feeble grip could clench to some purpose in an emergency, albeit slowly. In the mid-1670s it took four years to suppress the revolt of Messina, not least because after a year of trying, not one regiment of local militia could be raised, and Spanish and German regiments – and even bandits – had to be brought in to supply the necessary coercion. When order was finally restored in 1678, the returning viceroy, Count Santisteban, inflicted such chastisement on the defeated rebels that within a decade the population of Messina had declined by 50 per cent. Revealing the kind of culture underpinning this repression was his decision to have the town hall razed and the site ploughed up and sown with salt ('And Abimelech fought against the city all that day; and he took the city, and slew the people that was therein, and beat down the city, and sowed it with salt', Judges 9:45). The bell that had summoned the people to revolt back in 1674 was melted down and turned into a statue of Charles II, depicted trampling the hydra of rebellion.

Sicily was also special in that it boasted a Parliament, one of only three in eighteenth-century Italy, the others being in the Papal March of Ancona and the Venetian province of Friuli. As representative assemblies go, however, both its ambition and achievements were limited. As its three chambers were dominated by the privileged orders who had most to lose from change, it acted as a brake on what was already a somnolent polity. Victor Amadeus II referred to it contemptuously as 'an ice-cream Parliament', as the deputies spent most of their time consuming refreshments. With a majority of votes controlled by a handful of intermarried clans, the proceedings were a formality. One carriage was usually sufficient to transport all the deputies who bothered to turn up and just two or three sessions were sufficient to complete the business. At least Victor Amadeus II spent a year getting to know his new acquisition. Charles III was just a week on the island before returning to Naples, leaving behind a statue of himself which, for reasons of economy, was made from the melted-down statue of his predecessor.

If Sicily represented the acme of backwardness (and arguably still does), at the other end of the peninsula, Piedmont was already displaying the relative dynamism that was to prompt nineteenth-century nationalist historians to present it as the pre-ordained unifier of Italy, as a 'southern Prussia'. In part this was due to the Duchy's subjection to France during the long reign of Duke Charles Emmanuel II (1637–75). The creation and expansion of a standing army, the concentration of decision-making and the extension of bureaucratic control were all pursued in conscious imitation of the French, if not dictated by them. By the end of the reign there was a network of intendants in place, indeed in this regard the Piedmontese were ahead of their neighbours. Under two long-lived successors, Victor Amadeus II (1675–1730) and Charles Emmanuel III (1730–73), this absolutist policy was continued. It was both symptom and cause of a sustained effort to maximize resources and enhance the Duchy's international position. By the middle of the eighteenth century, the standing army had been expanded to 40,000, an impressive total which was increased further to 70,000 by 1796. Combined with a favourable strategic position, this allowed Victor Amadeus II to become King of Sicily by the Treaty of Utrecht in 1713. Obliged to cede that kingdom to Charles VI, in 1720 he became King of Sardinia by way of compensation.

Only the knowledge that Piedmont-Sardinia was eventually to 'unite' Italy can generate much interest in what was happening a century earlier. It was some measure of the political decadence of this geographical expression that the most progressive and original governmental initiative taken during this period was launched by an Austrian Habsburg. On the death of the Emperor Francis I in 1765, his widow Maria Theresa gave his Grand Duchy of Tuscany to her younger son, Leopold, as a 'secundogeniture'. He proved to be one of the most intelligent, enlightened and effective reformers of the century. Much of what he attempted was familiar, informed by a wish for centralization, rationalization, standardization. What was new was his concern to expand participation in government, by reforming urban councils to involve both landowners and taxpayers. Beginning with Volterra in 1772, this scheme was extended to cover the whole Duchy by 1786. Less successful, indeed ultimately an outright failure, was his attempt to replace the regular army with a militia, but it also indicated a search to move from a top-down authoritarian state to one in which citizens (not subjects) accepted responsibility for their own affairs.

More interesting still were his plans for a constitution for Tuscany. In private correspondence he made it clear again and again just how much he disapproved of his elder brother Joseph's abrasive approach to politics, condemning it as 'despotism'. On his return from an extended stay in Vienna in 1779, he sent a draft constitution to his minister Francesco Maria Gianni, his aim being to find a structure that would allow ruler and people to work together for the common good and would guard against despotism. Indeed, according to Leopold's most authoritative biographer, Adam Wandruszka, this concern to safeguard his Duchy against an arbitrary regime became something of an obsession. Partly this stemmed from his admiration of the traditional constitutions of the Austrian Netherlands and even Hungary, but more modern influences can also be detected. He was very well read in English and French enlightened theory, including Locke, Montesquieu and the physiocrats, and he also took a keen and sympathetic interest in the progress of the American Revolution. He corresponded with Benjamin Franklin and owned a copy of the Pennsylvanian constitution in French translation.

Underlying Leopold's constitutional theory was the belief in a social contract, from which he deduced the equal right of all citizens to happiness, welfare, security, property and liberty, restrained only by the need to respect the liberty of others. From this it followed that the ruler could never be more than the servant of the people, who had the right to monitor legislation and administration. Every state should be underpinned by a fundamental constitution, which would subject the executive to constant monitoring by the citizens' deputies and by the public at large. Such an arrangement would be positively helpful to the ruler because it would guard against corruption and factionalism and would ensure popularity, trust, participation, self-sacrifice – and all the other benefits that spring from a sense of legitimacy. It would help the ruler to do good, but stop him from doing evil. He envisaged both provincial assemblies and a national Parliament, with the franchise extended to all property-owning males over the age of twenty-five. Among other powers, they would enjoy the crucial right to approve taxes and the annual budget. In private handwritten memorandums Leopold gave further compelling evidence of a commitment to constitutionalism:

The present systems of government are no longer viable ... Every government must have a constitution ... Limited monarchy, with executive power in the hands of one individual and legislative power in the hands of the representatives of the nation, is the best of all ... The nation has the right of consent not only to laws relating to taxation but to all other laws as well, without exception.

Whether this project ever stood a chance of success is impossible to estimate. In the event, it was Joseph II who called a halt by informing Leopold that Tuscany was to cease to enjoy its quasi-autonomous status and was to be reintegrated into the Habsburg Monarchy. When he himself succeeded his brother as Emperor in 1790, Leopold had his hands all too full dealing with a crumbling inheritance, not to mention the French Revolution, but, as we shall see in a later chapter, his short reign suggested that his commitment to the Tuscan constitutional project had been sincere.

GREAT BRITAIN

Talleyrand is usually credited with the *mot* that the exiled Bourbons 'learned nothing and forgot nothing'. It could be applied with equal justice to the returning Stuarts in 1660. Like their French successors, they managed to blunder through one reign, only to be sent on their travels again when an even more stupid younger brother squandered the last remnants of goodwill. In a neat juxtaposition of exiles, James II sought refuge in France in 1688, while Charles X fled to England in 1830. There the resemblance ends, for out of the prolonged constitutional crisis in England came a political settlement that has endured with periodic modifications until the present day, whereas France has worked its way through another monarchy, an empire and five republics – so far. The longevity of the settlement of 1688–9 has had much to do with its essentially conservative nature, for it was not so much a compromise as a compendium of what had worked in the past and seemed worth preserving. It has provided powerful support for Michael Oakeshott's celebrated maritime metaphor to explain political success:

In political activity men sail a boundless and bottomless sea; there is neither harbour for shelter nor floor for anchorage, neither starting-place nor appointed destination. The enterprise is to keep afloat on an even keel; the sea is both friend and enemy; and the seamanship consists in using the resources of a traditional manner of behaviour in order to make a friend of every inimical occasion.

The structure of the vessel on which the English political nation embarked in 1688 was described in 'An Act Declaring the Rights and Liberties of the Subject and Settling the Succession of the Crown', better known as the 'Bill of Rights'. It was to this document that William III and Queen Mary had to subscribe before being allowed to ascend the throne that James II was deemed to have abdicated. The Parliament that enacted the measure made clear in the preamble the source of their legitimacy: 'Whereas the Lords Spiritual and Temporal and Commons assembled at Westminster, lawfully, fully and freely representing all the estates of the people of this realm . . .' They were not starting with a blank sheet of paper, on the contrary, they were embarking on a revolution in the old sense – of revolving back to the right order of things before the aspiring tyrant began his 'endeavour to subvert and extirpate the Protestant religion and the laws and liberties of this kingdom'. That also neatly sums up the revolutionaries' objectives: to ensure that never again could there be an attempt to impose Catholicism and absolutism on England. Of these two demons, it was the first that loomed largest and required explicit exorcism, so it was enacted that:

all and every person and persons that is, are or shall be reconciled to or shall hold communion with the see or Church of Rome, or shall profess the popish religion, or shall marry a papist, shall be excluded and be for ever incapable to inherit, possess or enjoy the crown and government of this realm and Ireland and the dominions thereunto belonging or any part of the same, or to have, use or exercise any regal power, authority or jurisdiction within the same.

To prevent any future encroachments on the laws and liberties of the country, the sovereigns were prohibited from suspending laws, interfering with the judiciary or juries, packing or muzzling Parliament, and maintaining a standing army or levying taxes without parliamentary approval. Crucially, in future Parliaments were to be convened regularly and frequently, a requirement reinforced by the Triennial Act of 1694, which stipulated annual meetings and a general election every three years. The subtle and determined William III managed to loosen some of the bounds Parliament drew around him, but his paramount need for war finance kept him under their ultimate control. By its durability this settlement proved that conservative liberty is an oxymoron, not a contradiction in terms. Of the encomia heaped on it during the course of the next century and more, the following from David Hume can stand as representative: 'it gave such an ascendant to popular principles as has put the nature of the English constitution beyond all controversy ... We, in this island, have ever since enjoyed, if not the best system of government, at least the most entire system of liberty, that ever was known amongst mankind.'

If the men who made the Glorious Revolution were unanimous on the Catholic issue, they were more divided about Protestant nonconformity. The outcome was a compromise, the 'Toleration Act' of 1689 being in effect an admission by the Anglican establishment that it could never hope to extirpate Puritanism. On the one hand, England remained a confessional state, with access to all public offices and the universities confined to Anglicans; on the other hand, Protestant nonconformists (Baptists, Congregationalists and Quakers, for example) were not punished if they failed to attend Anglican services and were permitted to establish their own chapels and schools. There followed a very rapid increase in organized dissent: by 1710 3,900 licences for the opening of dissenting meeting-houses had been issued, by which time there were probably around 400,000 nonconformists in England and Wales. In London there were twice as many dissenting meeting-houses as Anglican parish churches. Although still subject to various forms of discrimination, the most onerous being the continuing obligation to pay the church rate and tithe to support a church they never visited, the sting of dissent had been drawn. However distasteful Anglican domination might be, at least it was not Roman Catholic.

The same sort of consideration helped to keep the English elites more or less united. The spoonful of sugar that persuaded most Tories to swallow the rupture of such cherished principles as divine right, hereditary succession and non-resistance was the thought that at least William and Mary were not James II. The latter's brutal trampling on individual and corporate property rights during his brief reign confined what Jacobitism there was to toasts to the 'king over the water'. Although much ingenious effort has been devoted to talking up the Jacobite threat, the obstinate fact remains that outside the Highlands of Scotland support was thin in all ranks of society, even after the unappealing George I succeeded in 1714. His greatest asset was his Protestantism. When the Old Pretender decided that London was not worth a Mass, he also handed to his rivals a priceless advantage. Given the tiny size of the Catholic community in England and the confessional nature of the country's politics, the Stuarts could now only hope to make good their claim to the throne with the assistance of Spain or France. So the associations between Protestantism and patriotism and between Catholicism and treason were correspondingly intensified. A Stuart restoration now meant foreign invasion. When James III's second son, Henry, became a Catholic priest and a Cardinal to boot, the cost of a Stuart restoration became too high for all but a small and diminishing number of Jacobite diehards.

The Glorious Revolution settled the religious problems that had wracked the seventeenth century by tolerating nonconformists and suppressing Catholics in England. The same technique was employed in Ireland, although the situation there was very different because the Catholics constituted around three-quarters of the population (as opposed to *c*.2 per cent in England). But following their decisive defeat at the Boyne in 1690, they were in a hopeless position: 'once again it had been proved that the Stuarts' efforts to reconquer England from Ireland was as fatal for the Irish as for themselves' (Keith Feiling). Catholics were excluded from the Irish Parliament and were subjected to a series of penal laws: for example, in 1695 they were banned from owning weapons or a horse worth more than £5; in 1697 their bishops and regular clergy were banished; also in 1697 it was made next to impossible for Catholics to inherit Protestant land or to pass their own lands intact to a single heir; in 1703 they lost the right to buy land or to acquire it on a long lease but were compelled to divide their own land equally among all heirs. As these last measures suggested, the Protestant Ascendancy was well aware that ownership of land was the key to control. In the course of the 1690s, massive confiscations from Catholic landowners tainted with treason created a new Protestant Anglo-Irish elite. The Catholic share of Irish land fell from 59 per cent in 1640 to 22 per cent in 1688 to 14 per cent in 1703. Just in case there was any doubt as to Ireland's subjection, in 1720 an 'Act for the better securing of the dependency of the Kingdom of Ireland upon the Crown of Great Britain', better known as the 'Declaratory Act', was passed, spelling out the superiority of the English Parliament.

In Scotland it was quite a different story, for the good reason that there it was the Presbyterians who had been William III's most enthusiastic supporters. There was no pretence here that James II had abdicated – he had been deposed, and what the Scottish 'Convention of Estates' had done once, it might well do again. Not only was William obliged to accept this version of events, he had to give the Scottish Parliament a free hand in reconstructing the country's ecclesiastical arrangements. The result was the establishment of the Presbyterian Church of Scotland and the *dis*establishment of the Episcopal Church. More than a decade of upheaval followed, demonstrating yet again that the divisions between Highland and Lowland Scotland were as deep as those between Scotland and England. The domestic dimension of the conflict was dramatized by the massacre of Glencoe when Scots (Campbells) killed Scots (Macdonalds) on the orders of a Scot (John Dalrymple). Both the English and the Scottish political elites – the former rather earlier than the latter – came to see that only a union of the two countries could put an end to more than a century of periodic mutually destructive upheavals. In particular, Scottish reluctance to follow the English lead over the succession issue raised the awful prospect of a Jacobite king north of the border and the war that must inevitably follow. In January 1707 the Act of Union was passed, the very first article showing an impressive grasp of the importance of national semiotics:

That the two kingdoms of Scotland and England shall, upon the 1st day of May next ensuing the date hereof, and for ever after, be united into one kingdom by the name of Great Britain, and that the ensigns armorial of the said United Kingdom be such as Her Majesty shall appoint, and the crosses of St Andrew and St George be conjoined in such manner as Her Majesty shall think fit, and used in all flags, banners, standards and ensigns, both at sea and land.

To sugar a pill which was bound to be deeply unpopular in Scotland, the English negotiators had offered many attractive concessions, especially in economic affairs. In return for their cession of legislative independence, the Scots were given forty-five seats at Westminister (thirty county members and fifteen members for groups of burghs) and sixteen seats in the House of Lords, to be filled by an assembly of Scottish peers from their own members. Within a few years the latter became 'in practice a government list' (Hamish Scott).

Thus was created the 'United Kingdom of Great Britain', a kingdom that was indeed more united than ever it had been in the seventeenth century. The great winners of twenty years of political reconstruction after 1688 turned out to be the great aristocratic magnates. It was they who dominated the Westminster Parliament, so it was they who got their hands first on the pump of patronage. There were surprisingly few of them: just 173 English temporal peers in 1700, a number which held more or less steady as new creations balanced extinctions until Pitt the Younger's flood of creations brought the total to 267 in 1800. Moreover, as John Cannon revealed, the reputation of the British peerage for being open to new men and new money was something of a myth, even towards the end of the century. Of the 113 peers in 1800 whose titles dated from 1780 and after, 25 were promotions, 17 were promotions from the Irish peerage, 7 were promotions from the Scottish peerage, and 2 more were younger sons called up in their fathers' baronies. Only seven of the remainder did not already have some sort of family connection with the peerage and only one was a genuinely self-made man: the banker Robert Smith, the first Lord Carrington.

Smith owed his elevation to his ownership of two pocket boroughs, Midhurst and Wendover, which he sensibly placed at the disposal of William Pitt. That was how many aspiring noblemen caught the prime minister's eye. In Pitt's first tranche of ennoblements were the borough-mongers Thomas Pitt, who became Lord Camelford and controlled Old Sarum and Okehampton; Edward Eliot (St Germans, Grampound, Liskeard and influence in several other Cornish constituencies); and the greatest of them all, Sir James Lowther, who went straight to an earldom (Lonsdale) thanks to his electoral influence in Westmorland, Cumberland and Surrey. It was he who brought Pitt into Parliament in 1780 through his Westmorland pocket borough of Appleby. Uniquely, Lowther gave his protégé carte blanche, requiring only that he should resign the seat 'if ever our Lines of Conduct should become opposite'. Normally he took the view that 'his' members were 'not accountable to any person but myself'. When his own brother took the wrong turning in the division lobby, he was made to resign.

In this way the influence of the peerage on the House of Commons was both considerable and growing. It was a fine irony that just as the House of Lords as an institution was declining in importance, the influence of the peers was going in the opposite direction. There are many statistics to confirm this impression: for example, in 1780 113 seats were controlled by 52 peers, or in other words a quarter of the upper house controlled a fifth of the lower. In addition, account has to be taken of the very numerous relations of peers to be found in the House of Commons. The general election of 1784 returned 107 sons of peers and Irish peers, plus 26 grandsons of peers, 1 great-grandson and 12 nephews, together with 84 baronets (who enjoyed the hereditary title of 'Sir' but did not sit in the House of Lords), 16 sons of baronets and 11 married to the daughters of baronets. Well might John Cannon conclude that 'the cohesiveness of the eighteenth-century House of Commons, from which sprang a sense of common values and a sense of confidence, made it one of the most exclusive ruling elites in human history'.

Peers and their relations were also to be found in large and growing numbers elsewhere on the commanding heights of the British state. As we shall see in the chapter dealing with prelates, by the early eighteenth century the grandees were finding their way back to the upper reaches of the Anglican hierarchy. They had never been away from the armed forces, and now they tightened their grip. Of the 102 colonels of regiments listed in 1769, 43 were peers or sons of peers, 7 were grandsons of peers and 4 were married to daughters of peers. In the Royal Navy it was a two-way process, for many successful admirals were ennobled (Hood, Bridport, St Vincent, Nelson, Collingwood, Keith, Gardner, Gambier and Exmouth) and many younger sons of existing peers joined them. The Earl of St Vincent complained to George III:

A sprinkling of the nobility is very desirable in the Navy, as it gives some sort of consequence to the service; but at present the Navy is so overrun by the younger branches of the nobility, and the sons of Members of Parliament, and they so swallow up all the patronage, and so choke the channel to promotion that the son of an old officer, however meritorious *both* their services may have been, has little or no chance of getting on.

Out in the shires the peers' share of the rising agricultural wealth was steadily – and in some individual cases spectacularly – rising: the share of cultivated land owned by peers rose from around 15–20 per cent in 1688 to around 20–25 per cent in 1790. The twenty-or-so richest peers owned estates in excess of 100,000 acres. Rents were rising from the second quarter of the eighteenth century and positively raced ahead during the 1790s, perhaps doubling by 1815. By that time many of the great landowners were benefiting from the growing demand from industry for the raw materials lying beneath the surface of their rolling estates, especially coal. Physical evidence of the wealth and self-confidence of the great landowners can still be seen in the stately homes dating from this period that dot all parts of the United Kingdom and Ireland, from Carton House (the Duke of Leinster) in County Kildare to Culzean Castle in Ayrshire (the Earl of Cassilis) to Chatsworth in Derbyshire (the Duke of Devonshire), to pick at random three representative examples. It can also be seen in the few great town houses to have survived: Burlington House in Piccadilly (the Earl of Burlington), Marlborough House between Pall Mall and the Mall (the Duke of Marlborough) and Kenwood House in Hampstead (the Earl of Mansfield).

If the great magnates did best, they took the gentry with them into the promised land that opened up after 1688. There were about 15,000 gentry families, renting their land to tenant-farmers and leading increasingly cultured lives on the proceeds. As we shall see in a later chapter, they spent much of their time hunting and horse-racing, although some

– like Mr Bennet in Jane Austen's *Pride and Prejudice* (1813) – preferred the library. In their capacity as Justices of the Peace, they also formed the bedrock on which the country's governance rested, and were described by Maitland as 'so purely English, perhaps the most distinctively English part of all our governmental organisation'. Nominally appointed by the Crown but in reality chosen by the Lord Lieutenant of the County, which almost invariably meant its greatest landowning magnate, they dispensed justice and attended to the few administrative tasks required, such as maintaining roads and bridges, licensing public houses, supervising prisons and workhouses, attending to the police and law enforcement generally, setting the county rate (where there was one), and so on. One JP sitting alone could deal with most petty crimes; two JPs acting together in 'petty sessions' could deal with more serious offences; two or more JPs sitting with a jury at 'the Quarter Sessions' were authorized to try all but the most serious crimes. Unpaid and without any kind of secretarial assistance, the office brought no material reward. In 1693, in a work entitled *The Justice of the Peace: his Calling and Qualifications*, Edmund Bohun, who was himself a JP in Suffolk, warned: 'The Justice of the Peace enters upon an imployment that will occasion him much loss of Time, some Expence, and many Enemies, and after all will afford him little or nothing towards the bearing these inconveniences, but a little unprofitable Honour attended with much Envy.' Many JPs seem to have been mainly if not entirely inactive, others – especially the 'trading JPs' in the capital seeking to make a living out of the office – were notoriously venal. Chapter eleven of Tobias Smollett's *The Life and Adventures of Sir Launcelot Greaves* (1762) is entitled 'Description of a modern magistrate'. The magistrate in question is Mr Gobble, a low-born journeyman hosier who 'had picked up some law terms, by conversing with hackney writers and attorneys' clerks of the lowest order', had married his master's widow and moved to the country, where he acquired a JP's commission from a peer who owed him money. Since then 'he had committed a thousand acts of cruelty and injustice against the poorer sort of people, who were unable to call him to a proper account', thus becoming 'the object of universal detestation'.

Gobble was probably no more typical than the saintly Squire Allworthy of *Tom Jones*. There were enough JPs to allow all sorts to be accommodated: 2,560 in 1680, rising to 8,400 in 1761. The quality may possibly have improved in the course of the eighteenth century, as a growing number of Anglican clergymen were recruited – by 1800 they constituted around a quarter of the total. In any event, the crucial role of the JPs was to serve as the institutional link with the peerage, for the office made the gentry 'partners in oligarchy' (Frank O'Gorman). As it was from their ranks that most MPs were drawn, it was also they who bound together centre and localities. As Trevelyan observed: 'In the eighteenth century the Justices of the Peace might rather have been said to control the central government through the grand national Quarter Sessions of Parliament, than to be under any central control themselves.'

If the magnates and gentry dominated Parliament and the shires, it was the sovereign who dominated the executive. The 1688 settlement left him as a king who ruled as well as reigned. It was he who appointed the ministers and it was he who told them what to do, most obviously in the all-important field of foreign policy. William III used English resources to pursue his war against Louis XIV, and the first two Hanoverians used English resources to promote the interests of their German Electorate, which always took first place in their sense of priorities. By sorting out the religious and financial issues that had hamstrung the Stuarts, it might even be argued that the Glorious Revolution paved the way for a stronger monarchy. Of course, Parliament now had to be called regularly, and Parliament controlled the purse-strings, but Parliament could be managed. In the House of Lords the bishops, the Scottish peers, the soldiers, sailors and courtiers formed a solid base of support on which the king could rely, even in the most troubled times. For example, when George III decided in December 1783 that the time was ripe to bring down the Fox–North administration, all he needed to do was to let it be known that he would regard as his enemy anyone voting for the government's India Bill. In a famous passage Lord Rosebery described what then happened:

The uneasy whisper circulated, and the joints of the lords became as water. The peers, who yearned for lieutenancies or regiments, for stars or strawberry leaves; the prelates who sought a larger sphere of usefulness; the minions of the bed-chamber and the janissaries of the closet; all, temporal or spiritual, whose convictions were unequal to their appetite, rallied to the royal nod.

In moulding the lower house, great was the patronage at the Crown's disposal, not least at election time. In the middle of the eighteenth century it controlled about thirty parliamentary boroughs, mainly through the spending power of the Admiralty. Repeated attempts to reduce royal influence by excluding from the House of Commons those on the royal payroll had only limited success. Even after their number had been reduced by around 20 per cent during the first two decades of George III's reign, there were still around 200 'placemen' in the Commons in 1780 ready to support the King's choice of ministers. Moreover, in normal circumstances most of the independent MPs could be relied on to do the same. In 1782 William Pitt, who had not yet reached his twenty-third birthday, launched an eloquent attack in a speech lasting an hour-and-a-half on 'the corrupt influence of the Crown – an influence which has been pointed at in every period as the fertile source of all our miseries – an influence which has been substituted in the room of wisdom, of activity, of exertion, and of success – an influence which has grown up with our growth and strengthened with our strength, but which unhappily has not diminished with our diminution, nor decayed with our decay'. Less than two years later Pitt was prime minister and making vigorous use of his royal master's patronage to stay in office. The various measures of 'Economical Reform' had certainly reduced the amount, but it was still important.

The recipe for political stability required a minister who enjoyed the confidence of the sovereign who appointed him and the House of Commons that sustained him. One was as necessary as the other. As Fox and North discovered in 1783 (and many other politicians had discovered before them), the royal nod of disapproval was fatal. On the other hand, no king could keep a prime minister in office once he had lost the support of a majority of the House of Commons. Significantly, it was an administration's failure to run the country's foreign policy successfully that was the surest road to ruin. George II got Walpole through the excise crisis by a mixture of dismissals, promotions and even peerage creations, but he could not save him when he first opposed and then mismanaged the war against Spain. Nor could George III at his most obstinate (which is saying something) keep Lord North in office once it was obvious that the American War was lost. Both the long periods of harmony (Sir Robert Walpole 1721–42, Lord North 1770–82 and William Pitt 1783–1801) and the shorter bursts of disruption demonstrated the mutual dependence of Crown, professional politicians and legislature.

All parties could agree that they needed each other, but there was plenty of room for disagreement about how much. Apparently the most unequivocal statement that the balance was out of joint came on 6 April 1780, when the House of Commons voted by 233 votes to 215 to support the resolution proposed by John Dunning 'that the influence of the crown has increased, is increasing and ought to be diminished'. Paradoxically, it would have been better for the cause that Dunning represented if his motion had been lost. As Sir Herbert Butterfield pointed out: 'The inadequacy of corruption could hardly have been more clearly demonstrated than in the carrying of the very resolution that deplored its power.' When, two years later, George III was obliged to dismiss Lord North and then accept no fewer than three ministries he disliked – Rockingham's, Shelburne's and the Fox–North coalition – within the space of eighteen months, Dunning's claim was refuted by events. North himself made the point with his habitual eloquence, when he told the House of Commons:

I was the creature of Parliament in my rise; when I fell I was its victim. I came among you without connection. It was here I was first known; you raised me up, you pulled me down. I have been the creature of your opinion and your power, and the history of my political life is one proof which will stand against and overturn a thousand wild assertions that there is a corrupt influence in the crown which destroys the independence of this House. Does my history show the undue influence of the crown? Or is it not, on the contrary, the strongest proof that can be given of the potent efficacy of the public voice?

Members of both houses of Parliament had to be careful about throwing stones at their allegedly over-mighty monarch, for they were well aware of the crystalline fragility of their own position. By the middle of the eighteenth century it was not at all clear that they were still 'lawfully, fully and freely representing all the estates of the people of this realm', as the Bill of Rights of 1689 had claimed. Especially after the Septennial Act of 1716, elections were few and far between and many constituencies were not contested, encouraging the belief that politics was being reduced to sport for the oligarchy. Although the counties had the reputation of being more open than the boroughs, their seats too were often shared out in advance, to avoid the cost of a contest. In 1768 a Warwickshire freeholder complained that it was more than sixty years since there had been a contest in the county and that 'two or three noblemen, and a few gentlemen have, during that time, thought it sufficient in themselves ... to nominate and chuse representatives for you'. When a contest did take place, no holds were barred and no stratagem thought too base in the quest for victory. Treating to food and drink, outright bribery and intimidation were all commonplace, greatly encouraged by the public ballot. As usual, it was Hogarth who provided the most vivid, if exaggerated, depiction in *An Election Entertainment* of 1755, based on the Oxfordshire election of the previous year. As two Whig candidates provide a riotous banquet for their supporters, the rival Tories parade outside bearing an effigy labelled 'No Jews'. Both parties have adopted 'Liberty' as part of their slogan, the Whigs adding 'and Loyalty', the Tories 'and Property'. Among the rich parade of supporting characters, the gluttonous clergyman is obvious. In the foreground, a document entitled 'An Act against Bribery and Corruption' lies neglected on the ground. On the right a Methodist declines a bribe, much to the disgust of his wife who points to the ragged clothes of their child.

These affairs could prove ruinously expensive. It was said of Sir George Yonge that he had inherited £80,000, that his wife had brought him a dowry of £80,000 and that he had been paid £80,000 by the government, but that six election campaigns at Honiton had devoured the lot. Among the innumerable anomalies that could be found, the practice of bringing back registered 'freemen' of a borough for the vote, even if they had moved to other parts of the kingdom, deserves a mention. When an officer of marines learnt that a number of sailors had been given special leave to return to their home town of Coventry to vote for the government candidate, he did his friend the Duke of Portland a good turn by having them hastily transferred to a ship outward bound to Guinea. However much defenders of the status quo might argue that Parliament did not represent people but property, the discrepancy between a borough such as Old Sarum, which had no inhabitants but returned two MPs, and four great and rapidly growing cities such as Birmingham, Manchester, Leeds and Sheffield, which had no MPs at all, was becoming more obtrusive with every year that passed. In 1780 a group of reformers pointed out that, whereas the total electorate in England and Wales was about 214,000, such were the inequalities of the system that barely 6,000, 'being a majority of the voters of 129 of the boroughs, return 257 representatives, which is a majority of the

English House of Commons, and the efficient representation of above five millions of people'.

Yet reform did not come in this period, having to wait until 1832. Those who advocated it could not find their way round one great obstacle: the only body that could reform Parliament in a constitutional manner was Parliament itself, but the members of both houses of Parliament were the great beneficiaries of the existing system. The closest the reformers ever got to success was in 1782, when Pitt's motion for a committee of enquiry was defeated by 161 votes to 141. When he tried again the following year, he was crushed by 293 to 149. He himself pointed to the reasons: the reformers could not agree among themselves and there was insufficient support in the country as a whole. The *coup de grâce* was delivered by the French Revolution, whose apparent slide into anarchic violence convinced all but a few that the hurricane season was not the best time to be thinking about rebuilding one's house, as the opposition Whig William Windham put it. For many of those who hailed the fall of the Bastille, the September Massacres of 1792 proved to be the last straw. In May 1792 the liberal reformer Sir Samuel Romilly wrote that, despite everything, the French Revolution was 'the most glorious event, and the happiest for mankind that has ever taken place since human affairs have been recorded'; in September he wrote to a French correspondent, 'one might as well think of establishing a republic of tigers in some forest of Africa as of maintaining a free government among such monsters'. For others it was the execution of Louis XVI in January 1793 that was the turning point – for William Cowper, for example, who wrote, 'I will tell you what the French have done. They have made me weep for a King of France, which I never thought to do, and they have made me sick of the very name of liberty, which I never thought to be.' In the context of this chapter's primary concern, the main result of the Revolution was to bind the British elites together more tightly than ever before. When Charles James Fox refused to abandon his support for the new regime in France, the grandees of his party, led by the Duke of Portland, seceded to join Pitt in a government of national unity.

In taking most of the rest of the country with them, it was crucial that they were able to continue to use the language of liberty. They were helped by the judicial system, which intervened to prevent Pitt's worst efforts to appear tyrannical. Few peers – few Englishmen indeed – were more radical than the third Earl Stanhope, hailed by Catherine Macaulay as 'a patriot, a philosopher, and the firm friend of the general rights of man'. Yet for all his unwavering support for the Revolution in France, he could tell a French friend early in 1792: 'we are already free . . . and England is now the richest, the most prosperous and – climate apart – the happiest country in Europe'. At about the same time, Fox wrote to Earl Fitzwilliam identifying the three points that divided them – religious liberty, about which their differences were trivial; the abolition of slavery, on which he was not prepared to compromise; and 'the third point is parliamentary reform, on which the truth is that I am more bound by former declarations and consistency, than by any strong opinion I entertain in its favour. I am far from being sanguine that any new scheme would produce better Parliaments than the present mode of election furnished.' As this suggests, the French Revolution proved to be the most powerful weapon in the British elites' arsenal. There was just enough support at home to encourage solidarity, but not enough to threaten the existing order. To return to the maritime metaphor supplied by Michael Oakeshott at the beginning of this section, the British ship of state sailed through the turbulence created by the French Revolution, if not untroubled then without having to do much more than flog the odd mutineer or trim the odd sail. Most turbulence was caused by the rebellion in Ireland in 1798, leading to the Act of Union of 1801. The creation of the 'United Kingdom of Great Britain and Ireland' settled relations between the two countries at least in the short and medium term. It also provided a further illustration of the metropolitan elite's ability to play off one group of locals against another. Back in 1792 the Lord Lieutenant, the Earl of Westmorland, had observed to Pitt: 'The Protestants frequently declare they will have an Union, rather than yield the franchise to the Catholics. The Catholics will cry out for Union rather than submit to their present state of subjection, it is worth turning in your mind, how the violence of both parties might be turned on this occasion to the advantage of England.'

THE HOLY ROMAN EMPIRE

Following his pact with Mephistopheles, the first port of call for Goethe's Faust was Auerbach's Tavern in Leipzig, where he finds a group of students carousing. One of them, Frosch, sings:

> The Holy Roman Empire, we all love it so;
> But how it holds together, that's what we don't know.

To which his friend, Brander, responds:

> A filthy song! Shame! A political song!
> A tedious song! My lads, thank God in daily prayer
> That running the Empire isn't your affair!
> I reckon it a blessing anyway
> That I'm not Emperor or Chancellor today.

This scene forms part of Goethe's first draft of a poem that was to occupy him off and on for most of his adult life, so dates probably from the early 1770s, perhaps even earlier. Frosch's question has often been posed but rarely answered. Derision has been preferred to analysis, following Voltaire's lead: 'This agglomeration which was called and which still calls itself the Holy Roman Empire was neither holy, nor Roman, nor an empire.' Until the late twentieth century, historians of every stamp perpetuated this bad press. A good example was provided by Geoffrey Barraclough in *The Origins of Modern Germany*, first published in 1946. In his chapter devoted to the last century-and-a-half of the Empire, he denounced its culture as 'servilely imitative of France and Italy', only serving to testify to the 'exhaustion of the German spirit'; its politics as 'petrifaction', for Germany 'existed but it did not live'; and its 'petty absolutisms, whose sole object was self-glorification'. He concluded: 'the historian's only interest in this stultifying ossification lies in the process by which it was brought to an end'.

Yet just a moment's reflection on the Empire's longevity should give pause for thought. No institution lasts for a millennium without having something to be said for it. There was a core of stability lying beyond the obvious absurdities that attracted the derisive attention of nationalist historians such as Treitschke – the geriatric soldiers of the Prince-Bishop of Hildesheim, for example, whose timid motto on their caps read, 'Give peace in our time, O Lord', or the Prince of Hohenlohe who sought to represent his glory by placing outside his remodelled residence at Weikersheim statues of the four great conquerors of the world: Ninus, Cyrus, Alexander and Caesar. The Empire's most durable component was the incorporation of the elites of the German-speaking world in the political process. This was achieved through representation in the *Reichstag*, which after 1663 was no longer occasional and peripatetic but in permanent session at Regensburg. It was divided into three colleges, the first comprising the nine Electors (Mainz, Trier, Cologne, Bohemia, Saxony, the Palatinate, Brandenburg, Bavaria and, after 1692, Hanover). The second and largest college was that of the princes, comprising thirty-four ecclesiastical princes, plus two collective votes shared by about forty monasteries and abbeys, and sixty secular princes, plus four collective votes shared by a hundred-odd Imperial Counts. The third college consisted of the fifty-one 'Free Imperial Cities', the self-governing republics subject only to the authority of the Emperor.

The anomalies were certainly striking. The world had moved on since the institutional structures had been settled in the fourteenth and fifteenth centuries. In terms of the imperial hierarchy, the Archbishop-Elector of Mainz, who ruled over just 350,000 subjects at the end of the eighteenth century and had an army of 2,800, was more important than the Elector of Brandenburg, who as King of Prussia ruled over twenty times as many subjects and had an army a hundred times bigger. Although the Free Imperial Cities included major commercial centres such as Frankfurt am Main and Hamburg, many of them were nothing more than villages. Example could be piled on example without eroding the obstinate fact that the *Reichstag* did allow both the landed and the urban elites from across the Empire to participate in its politics. During the past generation or so, much careful research by German historians such as Karl Otmar Freiherr von Aretin, Karl Härter and Georg Schmidt has shown just how much importance both the Emperor and the princes attached to the conduct of business at the *Reichstag*. So did the major European powers, which took good care to be represented there. Moreover, Regensburg was also the centre of a lively political public sphere, the most important information exchange in central Europe from which pamphlets, printed ordinances and newspapers were disseminated throughout the Empire.

The *Reichstag* was the most important but by no means the only imperial institution. There were also two courts – the *Reichskammergericht* (Imperial Cameral Tribunal) and the *Reichshofrat* (Imperial Aulic Council) – regional groupings of principalities into *Kreise* (Circles), and an imperial army. Judged by the standards of a modern state, all were seriously deficient, indeed it was Klaus Epstein's withering verdict that 'to describe the constitution of the Holy Roman Empire is the same thing as to criticize it'. Shortage of funds meant that instead of the fifty assessors envisaged for the *Reichskammergericht*, there were never more than eighteen actually present and often fewer, with the result that by 1772 a backlog of 61,233 cases had accumulated. Although pursued with his customary vigour, Joseph II's subsequent attempt at reform eventually ran into the sand barrier laid down by vested interests. On the other hand, all the various bits and pieces that went to make up the Empire were bound together by imperial law. Moreover, as several aspiring tyrants found to their cost, it could also be enforced. In Württemberg, for example, the autocratic regent Friedrich Karl was dismissed in 1693 following imperial intervention, bringing 'no small consolation' to the Duchy's Estates. In 1770 the *Reichshofrat* imposed a settlement of a long-running dispute on Duke Karl Eugen which was very much in favour of his opponents. As the episode's historian, James Vann, observed, the Empire thus 'revealed its capacity to discipline a monarch and to preserve the civil liberties of his subjects'. It marked the definitive failure of attempts by successive dukes to wriggle free from constitutional restrictions and led Charles James Fox to observe that there were only two constitutions in Europe – that of Great Britain and that of Württemberg.

As usual, he was wrong. Every constituent part of the Holy Roman Empire had a constitution of some kind, in the sense of a generally recognized framework within which the tasks of government were accomplished and conflicts were resolved. It is commonly supposed that Germans of the old regime were unpolitical creatures, content to live out their unambitious lives under the flaccid hand of their prince. Rather the reverse was true. Thanks to the fragmentation of authority, most Germans were closer to, and more actively involved in, the exercise of power than any other European people, the British included. Whether it was through the Estates still to be found in most principalities, or through the governing councils of the Free Imperial Cities, or through the cathedral chapters of the ecclesiastical states, or through the bureaucracies of the larger states, or through the rural magistracies (*Kreisräte*), they were active – and very often contentious – participants. The political forms involved were never democratic, always restricted, often oligarchic or aristocratic, but they did diffuse authority deep down towards society's roots. In no other European country, it can safely be said, was it possible for a peasant to become a prince in the space of one generation, but that was what could happen in the imperial monasteries of south Germany, where it was common for the sons of peasants to be elected abbot. On the secular side, mention should be made of the 350-odd families of 'Imperial Knights', noble landowners who were not represented in the *Reichstag* but were subject solely to the Emperor. On their estates – about 1,500 in total, covering about 5,000 square miles (13,000 km²) and with a population of about 350,000 – they exercised most functions of government and administration, providing another example of the blurred division between state and civil society to be found throughout the Empire. To borrow Frank O'Gorman's comment on the English gentry, they were 'partners in oligarchy'. As the names of some of the greatest Imperial Knight families – Schönborn, Stadion, Metternich, Greiffenklau, von der Leyen – indicate, many of their members looked to imperial service or to benefices in the ecclesiastical states to supplement the income from their estates.

This fragmentation and diffusion of authority made for profound conservatism, not to say virtual stasis, in the Empire as a whole. Most fundamentally, it was a structure to which such modern concepts as sovereignty, centralization and the maximization of power were alien. In 1756 the young Joseph II was told that, despite its disparate nature,

the German Empire has not disintegrated into a collection of states [*systema civitatum*, which had been Pufendorf's description], but is a single state, whose sole head is the emperor, and whose members are the Estates of the Empire [*Reichsstände* – i.e. all those represented at the *Reichstag*], vassals and subjects in their entirety, whose sovereign rights are exercised partly by the Emperor alone, partly with the consent of the Electors, but in most cases with the fore-knowledge and approval of all the Estates of the Empire together, and where every prince rules with complete freedom and authority albeit according to the laws and customs of the Empire.

That is admittedly not clear, but it cannot be made any clearer. As the constitutional expert Johann Jakob Moser observed in 1766, 'Germany is ruled in German', by a combination of fundamental laws, treaties, privileges and even orally transmitted traditions.

Many were the threats to this museum of corporate privileges. Ever since the Habsburgs had assembled a world empire in the late fifteenth and early sixteenth centuries, the Holy Roman Empire had been dragged periodically into their conflicts. Just as other European countries, most notably England and France, were creating nation-states, the most important German dynasty turned abruptly in the opposite direction. Together with the Protestant Reformation, this brought a prolonged domestic agony which, among other things, destroyed the civic culture of the Free Imperial Cities and elevated the representational culture of the princes. As we shall see in a later chapter, after the Peace of Westphalia in 1648, the way was open for repeated, devastating invasions by Louis XIV and his Swedish satraps. More than ever before, foreign sovereigns acquired imperial territory or imperial princes acquired foreign territory: Sweden-Pomerania, Holstein-Denmark, Saxony-Poland, Zweibrücken-Sweden, Hanover-Great Britain, not to mention the greatest combination of all – Austria-Hungary, for the Habsburgs' did not take full possession of the latter until the end of the seventeenth century.

The most fateful of these extra-imperial connections turned out to be the Duchy of Prussia acquired by the Elector of Brandenburg in fits and starts between 1525, when the last Grand Master of the Teutonic Knights, Albert of Hohenzollern, secularized his state, and 1660, when Frederick William the Great Elector achieved full sovereignty. The latter's son assumed the title of 'Frederick I, King in Prussia' in 1701 and his great-grandson, Frederick II, then proceeded to work out the implications in no uncertain fashion. By seizing Silesia in 1740 and then defending it against all comers over the next twenty-three years, the latter began a German-German struggle for mastery in the Empire. He was greatly assisted by the decline of France. In the past, those German princes seeking assistance against Habsburg hegemony naturally turned to Versailles for assistance. Once the developing colonial rivalry with England meant that French resources had to be spread more thinly, a vacuum began to develop in the Empire. Even if Frederick the Great – to give him the sobriquet awarded by contemporaries after the first of his three Silesian wars – had not moved in to fill it, some other prince would have done so.

Frederick dealt the Holy Roman Empire a terrible blow. His early ingestion of the clear (if thin) draughts of the Enlightenment and his terrible upbringing turned him against his father and everything he stood for, including the 'antiquated, fantastical constitution' of the Empire. He dismissed the *Reichstag* as 'but a kind of phantom ... The envoy which a sovereign sends thither resembles a yard-dog who bays at the moon.' A vignette dating from the Third Silesian War, better known as the Seven Years War, dramatized the abrasive new approach to the Holy Roman Empire adopted by the Prussians. At Regensburg on 14 October 1757, a notary of the *Reichstag* called Aprill delivered to the Brandenburg envoy Baron von Plotho a formal summons, announcing that his master had been put to the ban of the Empire as punishment for his invasion of Saxony the previous year. It was couched in severe, not to say insulting, language. Unimpressed, Baron von Plotho seized the summons, stuffed it down Aprill's shirt and then had his servants throw the luckless notary down the stairs. Needless to say, this episode was then publicized throughout the Empire, growing with the telling. Only three weeks later at the battle of Rossbach, Frederick the Great annihilated an army that was mainly French but included a substantial contingent of imperial troops. If the victory was celebrated chiefly as a German victory over the hereditary enemy, it was also seen as a defeat for the Empire. Ominously, the French commander, the prince de Soubise, complained that his so-called allies had shown little enthusiasm for the conflict and that especially the Protestants among them had been 'entirely Prussian' in their sympathies.

Frederick was strong enough to establish Prussia as a sovereign state, but he was not strong enough to take any other principalities with him. The component parts of the Empire can be divided into five categories: 1. the major secular princes with more than regional significance (Prussia, Bavaria, the Palatinate, Saxony, Hanover, Württemberg, Baden, Hessen-Kassel, Hessen-Darmstadt, and a few others); 2. the lesser secular princes; 3. the ecclesiastical states; 4. the Free Imperial Cities; and 5. the Imperial Knights. Only the first group could aspire to an existence as independent states outside the Empire, but even some of them viewed Prussia with deep hostility, notably Hanover and Saxony, its two main rivals for the domination of northern Germany. Groups two to five all appreciated that they were vulnerable to annexation by the predators in group one and that their only chance of survival lay in the maintenance of the Empire. So in normal circumstances they supported the Habsburg emperor with money, men and their votes at the *Reichstag*.

That should have been enough to sustain the integrity of the Empire against even as ambitious and ruthless a sovereign as Frederick the Great. The situation changed radically however when Joseph II began his restless career. At this point, it may well be necessary to explain the difference between the Habsburg Monarchy and the Holy Roman Empire. The ruler of the Habsburg Monarchy was Joseph II's mother, Maria Theresa, who had succeeded her father, the Emperor Charles VI, on his death in 1740. Her inheritance comprised all those bits and pieces of territory which belonged to the Habsburgs by hereditary right, from the Austrian Netherlands in the west to Transylvania in the east, from Bohemia in the north to Milan in the south. Some of these territories lay within the Holy Roman Empire, but by no means all. The most important of those located outside it was the Kingdom of Hungary, together with the Principality of Transylvania. Maria Theresa could not succeed her father to the elective office of Holy Roman Emperor because she was a woman. After a long interregnum, greatly confused by Frederick's invasion of Silesia, in 1742 for the first time for three centuries the electors chose not a Habsburg but the Wittelsbach Elector of Bavaria, as Charles VII. Following his death just three years later, normal service was resumed – sort of – when Maria Theresa's husband, Francis Stephen of Lorraine, was elected as Francis I. Their son Joseph was elected 'King of the Romans' in 1764, which gave him the automatic right to succeed on the death of his father, which happened the following year. In other words, from 1765 Joseph was Holy Roman Emperor by election but only co-regent with his mother in the Habsburg Monarchy. Only on the death of Maria Theresa in 1780 did he achieve complete control of both Holy Roman Empire and Habsburg Monarchy.

At first he took his imperial duties seriously, but when his attempts to reform the *Reichshofrat* and the *Reichskammergericht* ended in disappointment he threw his hands up in despair and in effect abandoned the Empire. This was hardly a clap of thunder in a clear sky. Throughout the reign of his grandfather Charles VI (1711–40) there had been a struggle for domination between the Imperial Chancellery (*Reichskanzlei*), which dealt with his interests as Holy Roman Emperor, and the Austrian Court Chancellery (*Hofkanzlei*), which dealt with his interests as ruler of the Habsburg Monarchy. The question at stake was:

which interests should Charles VI put first? Should he regard himself first and foremost as Holy Roman Emperor, with an obligation to treat all the members of the Empire in an even-handed way? Or should he give priority to those lands he ruled as hereditary sovereign of the Habsburg Monarchy, whose interests often ran counter to those of the Empire? In a world of increasingly rapid state-formation, it had to be the second option which came to seem more compelling. But Joseph took this development much further. Indeed, by 1778 he was beginning to wonder whether it might not be desirable to sever his links with the Holy Roman Empire altogether, by abdication of the imperial title.

Joseph was not a man of half-measures. Once he had abandoned his attempt to make the Holy Roman Empire work, he turned against it with vehemence, making no secret of his contempt for its institutions and its members. The imperial office was 'a ghost of an honorific power', its business was 'loathsome', the imperial constitution was 'vicious', the princes were spineless ignoramuses, putty in the hands of their pedantic and venal ministers. Of the senior dignitary of the Holy Roman Empire, the Elector-Archbishop of Mainz, he wrote to Count Trauttmansdorff, his envoy at Mainz: 'As I have just come from making my Easter confession on Good Friday and have forgiven all those who trespass against me, I cannot harbour any thoughts of revenge, only contempt for an arrant shit who is bursting with pride.'

In the course of the 1770s, and especially after he escaped from the apron-strings of his mother in 1780, Joseph pursued the interests of his Austrian state in a manner that seemed expressly designed to alienate as many German princes as possible. It would be tedious to follow him through the labyrinth of imperial politics. Two revealing examples must suffice: in 1782 he cancelled all payments made to ministers and other public officials throughout the Holy Roman Empire. Although these 'pensions' were thinly disguised bribes, they had been a vital lubricant oiling the cogs of Habsburg influence at the various German courts. At a stroke, therefore, Joseph had turned the most influential political figures in the Empire from friends into enemies and had cut off a vital source of information – and all for the sake of a modest economy. In the following year he unilaterally abolished all the diocesan rights of the prince-bishoprics that extended into the Habsburg Monarchy, expropriating all their property that lay in the latter into the bargain.

When the Holy Roman Emperor violated imperial law so flagrantly, even those members of the Empire bound to the imperial office by history and self-interest began to feel that the ground was moving beneath their feet. Not for the first time, the Empire's self-regulating mechanism began to operate; help was at hand in the unlikely shape of Frederick the Great. Now that the Austrian gamekeeper had turned poacher, the Prussian poacher could – indeed *had to* – turn gamekeeper. Frederick was able to grasp that plenty could be achieved through the archaic structure of the Empire, but only if the status quo was accepted and impartiality between the religious parties was observed. His reward came in 1785 with the formation of the League of Princes (*Fürstenbund*). This was an association aimed squarely against Joseph's imperial policies, especially the attempt to exchange Bavaria for the Austrian Netherlands. Frederick's ability to enlist two of the most important princes (the Electors of Hanover and Saxony) and many more of the second rank demonstrated the collapse of Austrian influence in the Empire. Perhaps the greatest catch was that 'arrant shit' the Archbishop-Elector of Mainz, the senior prelate of the Church in Germany and the arch-chancellor of the Holy Roman Empire, whose defection was of great symbolic importance – and was recognized as such by contemporaries. Undeterred, Joseph continued in the same vein until his death in 1790. No wonder that his long-suffering foreign minister, Prince Kaunitz, whose imperial policy he had wrecked by his bull-in-a-china-shop approach, remarked, 'that was very good of him', when told that Joseph had died.

In a century that saw 'the state' become the 'master-noun' of political discourse, the Holy Roman Empire was bound to seem out of date, if not anachronistic. It was not a state and never could become a state. Rather it was an organization for the maintenance of law and peace ('*eine Rechts- und Friedensordnung*'). So it should not be judged by the standards of a modern state. It did not seek to centralize authority, maximize resources, build the biggest possible army and conquer other countries' territory. Its failure to do those things brought it into disrepute, not to say contempt, in the power-political world of the nineteenth century, but also ensured a much more understanding assessment after 1945. As for contemporaries, a few shared Joseph II's hostility, some preferred the affectionate mocking of the kind expressed by Goethe's Frosch and quoted at the beginning of this section, and a surprisingly large number appreciated that, for all its faults, the Holy Roman Empire had a lot to be said for it. From the rich store of praise, the following commends itself by the intelligence, objectivity and experience of its author, Christoph Martin Wieland (1733–1813):

From the elected head [i.e. the Emperor] right down to the mayor and corporation of the Free Imperial City of Zell am Hammersbach [a tiny community in the Black Forest], there is not a ruler in Germany whose greater or lesser powers are not limited on every side by laws, tradition and in many other ways, and against whom, should he engage in any sort of illegal activity against property, honour or personal liberty, the imperial constitution does not provide the injured party protection and redress of grievances.

Significantly, Wieland wrote of Germany and the Empire as if they were synonymous. Since the late fifteenth century its full title had indeed been 'the Holy Roman Empire of the German Nation'. Such was the contrast between the polycentralism of the Holy Roman Empire and the central-ism of the German Empire created in 1871 that for too long the ability of the former to accommodate a national identity was overlooked. Friedrich Karl von Moser spoke for many when in 1765 he published a treatise about the German national spirit that derived from the imperial constitution, proclaiming: 'we are one people, with one name, living under a common head and bound together by our constitution, rights, duties and laws for the great common pursuit of liberty'. He went on to lament that a general patriotism of this kind was not as widespread as it was in France, Great Britain or the Dutch Republic, but insisted that the Germans were free and that this liberty could serve to revive national feeling.

Ironically, just as the outbreak of the French Revolutionary Wars in 1792 ushered in the terminal phase in the history of the Empire, its institutions were working better than ever before. During the 1790s both princes and people showed an impressive ability to make the old order work. For all the attention lavished on the tiny handful of Germans who collaborated with the French invaders – the so-called 'German Jacobins' – there was never any danger that the Empire would collapse from within. Much more ominous was the possibility that Austria and Prussia might form an alliance to partition Germany in the same way that they had already partitioned Poland. After nearly going to war in 1790, they did indeed achieve a rapprochement in 1791 and went to war with revolutionary France in 1792. In his *Thoughts on French Affairs* Edmund Burke predicted:

As long as those two princes are at variance, so long the liberties of Germany are safe. But if ever they should so far understand one another, as to be persuaded that they have a more direct and more certainly defined interest in a proportioned mutual aggrandizement, than in a reciprocal reduction, that is, if they come to think that they are more likely to be enriched by a division of spoil, than to be rendered secure by keeping to the old policy of preventing others from being spoiled by either of them, from that moment the liberties of Germany are no more.

Burke was both right and wrong. He was right in the sense that if Austria and Prussia had won the war in 1792, they would have taken 'compensation' in the form of an exchange of the Austrian Netherlands for Bavaria, and more Polish territory respectively. But he was wrong because they did not win and very soon their relations were scarred by vehement mutual recrimination. Prussia left the war in 1795 and signed a separate peace with France. What really finished off the Empire was the decision by the revolutionaries to advance the French frontier to the Rhine and to compensate the secular princes affected with the seculariz-ation of the ecclesiastical states. It all took a very long time, for the good reason that the Austrians proved remarkably resilient. Not until 1806 did the last Holy Roman Emperor, Francis II, abdicate and become the Austrian Emperor Francis I, a title he had created for himself two years earlier. How proud Joseph II would have been. In terms of the categorization identified earlier in this section, in effect what the French revolutionaries and then Napoleon did was to allow group one to gobble up groups two to five. Napoleon was brutally frank about his motives. In 1807 Karl Theodor von Dalberg, who had been the last arch-chancellor of the Empire, went to see Napoleon at Saint-Cloud to recommend the restoration of imperial institutions. He was cut short: 'Monsieur l'Abbé,' Napoleon began contemptuously, 'I am going to let you in on my secret. The little princes in Germany would like to be protected against the big; but the big princes would like to rule as they see fit; but, as all I want from Germany is men and money and it is the big princes who can supply me with them, I shall leave them in peace and the small fry will have to make the best of it.' In this brave new world of power-politics there was no room for such a soft polity as the Holy Roman Empire. Whether it was sensible of Napoleon to destroy it is a different matter.

6

Reform and Revolution

THE STATE

In the middle of the eighteenth century, the abbé de Véri (1724–99) recorded in his journal: 'Today, hardly anyone dare say in Parisian society, *I serve the king* . . . You'd be taken for one of the chief valets at Versailles. *I serve the state* is the expression most commonly used.' Political authority and loyalty had become depersonalized. It was a trend encouraged by some of the monarchs themselves. There is no evidence that Louis XIV said, 'I am the state' (*L'état, c'est moi*), but he did write in his treatise *On the Craft of Kingship* (*Sur le métier du roi*) of 1679: 'The interest of the state must come first.' It must be conceded that he then reintroduced a personal element by adding, 'when one looks to the state, one is really working for oneself. The welfare of the former secures the glory of the latter. The ruler who makes the state content, prestigious and powerful also promotes his own glory.' Succeeding generations were less equivocal. Frederick the Great frequently proclaimed that he was just 'the first servant of the state'. Joseph II, in his first memorandum, written in 1761 shortly after his twentieth birthday, agreed: 'everything exists for the state; this word contains everything, so all who live in it should come together to promote its interests'. Significantly, Catherine the Great of Russia did not say anything of the kind, confining herself to a vague commitment to 'the public good'. The word 'state' does not appear in the 'Great Instruction' (*Nakaz*) she produced in 1766.

The elevation of the state to be the 'master-noun' of eighteenth-century political discourse had been long prepared. In his classic study *The Foundations of Modern Political Thought*, Quentin Skinner showed how the main elements of the modern concept of the state were gradually acquired between the late thirteenth and late sixteenth centuries:

The decisive shift was made from the idea of the ruler 'maintaining his state' – where this simply meant upholding his own position – to the idea that there is a separate legal and constitutional order, that of the State, which the ruler has a duty to maintain. One effect of this transformation was that the power of the State, not that of the ruler, came to be envisaged as the basis of government. And this in turn enabled the State to be conceptualised in distinctively modern terms – as the sole source of law and legitimate force within its own territory, and as the sole appropriate object of its citizens' allegiances.

During those three centuries, three crucial axioms were formed: first, politics came to be regarded as a discrete realm, independent of theology; secondly, the supreme authority in any polity came to be regarded as independent of any international agency such as the papacy or Holy Roman Empire; and thirdly, that authority also claimed a monopoly of legislation and allegiance within its borders.

The confessional strife unleashed by the Reformation and Counter-Reformation, aided and abetted by the closely related struggles between noble factions, advertised the need for a single centre of power in each and every polity. Jean Bodin (1530–96), who lived through the French Wars of Religion, and Thomas Hobbes (1588–1679), who lived through the English Civil War, developed a theory of sovereignty that was to form the bedrock of the modern state. Exercising 'the most high, absolute and perpetual power over the citizens and subjects in a commonwealth' (Bodin), the state was impersonal in two ways, for it enjoyed an existence separate both from the individual who currently happened to rule it and also from those who were ruled. Consequently, it could demand the absolute loyalty of both. This 'conceptual revolution' (Skinner) meant that, although homage was paid to a person, the true object of loyalty was an abstraction. Not every European sovereign was able to detect this sea-change and respond accordingly. Louis XV showed that the old view of the state as an aggregate of estates belonging to the king was still alive and well, when he gave the following dressing-down to the assembled chambers of the Parlement of Paris on 3 March 1766, in a session that became known as the 'séance de la flagellation':

I shall not permit in my kingdom the formation of an association which allows the natural ties of reciprocal duties and obligations to degenerate into a conspiracy of resistance, nor that it introduces to the kingdom a fictitious corporation which can only disrupt harmony. The magistracy does not constitute a corporation, nor an order separate from the three legitimate orders of the kingdom. The magistrates are my officers charged with administering on my behalf my truly royal duty to dispense justice to my subjects . . . Sovereignty resides in my person alone . . . and my courts derive their existence and their authority from me alone. The plenitude of this authority remains with me. They exercise it only in my name and it may never be turned against me. I alone have the right to legislate. This power is indivisible. The officers of my courts do not make the law, they only register, publish and enforce it. Public order emanates exclusively from me, and the rights and the interests of the nation, which it has been dared to separate from the monarch, are necessarily united with mine and repose entirely in my hands.

The constant repetition of the possessive pronoun – '*my* kingdom', '*my* subjects', '*my* courts' – projected a personal, not to say proprietorial, vision of kingship fundamentally at odds with the objective concept of the state.

The theorizing of Bodin, Hobbes and those that followed in their footsteps, undoubtedly did more than reflect – or react against – current practice. If one cannot accept without reservation Hegel's maxim that 'once the world of ideas has been transformed, reality cannot hold out for long', it is an arid view of the political process that ignores the ideological dimension. On the other hand, it is also possible to detect changes in the material world that were moving things along in the same direction. The greatly improved communications discussed in the first chapter provide a good example. When most members of the human race were confined to the community in which they were born and its immediate environs, power relationships were obviously direct and personal. It can be surmised with confidence that today autarkic tribes living in the depths of the Amazonian rainforest do not have much of a concept of the state (although they would be well advised to develop one as soon as Christian missionaries make an appearance). But once the lords started to spend significant periods away from their regions in town or at court, and once their subjects started to move around as migrant workers, or were recruited into a centralized army, political power had to be envisaged in a correspondingly abstract manner. If it was not until the late nineteenth century that peasants were truly turned into Frenchmen, as Eugen Weber has shown, that long-term process had certainly accelerated between 1648 and 1815. In France alone, several million people were uprooted from their provinces by the Revolutionary and Napoleonic Wars, and marched to the four corners of Europe. The same could be said of those other great solvents of the feudal world: urbanization and capitalism.

In the more medium term, military developments made a powerful contribution to the development of the state. As Otto Hintze observed: 'War is the great fly-wheel of the whole political activity of the modern state.' Perhaps due to the nature of their material, military historians are among the most bellicose of their profession, disputing every inch of territory with grim resolution. Yet one thing they seem to be able to agree on is that the cost of warfare grew throughout the early modern period. This was partly a result of the numbers involved. The King of France, Charles VIII, had taken an army only about 20,000-strong to Italy in 1494; by the time of the Treaty of Cateau-Cambrésis in 1559 each side could deploy between 50,000 and 60,000, not to mention naval forces. Those figures kept on rising. When France intervened directly in the Thirty Years War in 1635 it could muster about 125,000. Although the figures are much disputed and very inexact, not least because there was a wide gulf between official figures and the number of soldiers actually under arms, Louis XIV's armies reached nearly 400,000 at their peak in the War of the Spanish Succession. Rather than bombard the reader with an enervating series of statistics relating to every other European country, Table 8 provides an instructive overview.

Table 8. European army numbers 1632–1786

Date	France	Dutch Republic	Sweden	Russia	Austria	England	Prussia
1632		70,000	120,000	35,000			
1640							4,650
1653							1,800
1661	48,900						
1678	280,000						45,000
1679	130,000						
1680				200,000			
1688						53,000	30,000
1690	338,000	73,000	90,000		50,000	80,000	

Table 8. European army numbers 1632–1786 *continued*

Date	France	Dutch Republic	Sweden	Russia	Austria	England	Prussia
1697						90,000	
1710	360,000	100,000		220,000	100,000		39,000
1717	110,000						
1725				215,000			
1738	115,000						
1740	160,000			240,000	108,000		80,000
1756	330,000	39,000		344,000	201,000		143,000
1760							260,000
1778					200,000	100,000	160,000
1786	156,000						194,000

Source: Jeremy Black, *A Military Revolution? Military change and European society 1550–1800* (Basingstoke, 1991), p. 7

The 'Austrian' army is very difficult to disentangle from that of the Holy Roman Empire until the 1740s. When the War of the Spanish Succession began, it was about 100,000-strong; that figure doubled by the beginning of the Seven Years War and rose to over 300,000 by the beginning of the war against the Turks in 1787. It is not quite a tautology to observe that the size of an army and statehood go hand in hand. However, it is significant that the middling German states which failed to emulate Brandenburg-Prussia in achieving full sovereignty also experienced a sharp reduction in military capability. It bears repeating that the chief victim of Prussia's rise to great-power status was Saxony, whose army fell from a peak of around 30,000 during the reign of Augustus the Strong (1694–1733) to just 6,000 in 1792. In the same period Bavaria's army was halved.

To these figures of course must be added the manpower required by the navies of the Maritime Powers. The best statistics are available for the Royal Navy, showing that during the Nine Years War at the end of the seventeenth century the highest total of seamen entered on the ships' books was 48,514; during the War of the Spanish Succession 47,647; during the War of the Austrian Succession 59,596; during the Seven Years War 86,626; during the War of American Independence 105,443;

and during the French Revolutionary-Napoleonic Wars 147,087. Figures for the French navy are much harder to come by. In 1686 the rolls listed 59,494, which was probably the highest figure recorded. The standard history of the French navy during the Revolutionary-Napoleonic Wars, by Martine Acerra and Jean Meyer, takes the view that the total manpower never exceeded 50,000. The Spanish navy's complement was about 25,000 in the late 1730s, when the naval registry was first instituted, rising to 65,000 in the 1790s, although not all of those registered would have been actually available for service. If these figures seem modest when compared with the land forces, it should be borne in mind that the cost of building, equipping and maintaining a fleet was much greater than that of assembling an army. If a sailor packed more firepower than a musketeer, he cost a great deal more to train and was much more difficult to find in the first place. As Acerra and Meyer point out, the Dutch navy never dropped much below the French total, because they had a larger pool of trained seamen on which to draw. Or in other words, the chief constraint on navy size was not financial.

Recruiting, financing and deploying these great hordes naturally led to a corresponding expansion in the powers of the state. We have already seen how the relationship between rulers and elites was influenced by the process. In a later chapter, the financial aspects will be considered. Here the ideological aspects will be examined. The example chosen is Brandenburg-Prussia, because the process there was rapid, relatively complete and found particularly clear expression. Could there be a more eloquent statement of traditional monarchy than Frederick William I's political testament of 1722? Although no attempt has been made to reproduce the weird spelling in the translation that follows, the virtual absence of punctuation has been retained:

My dear successor should be very well aware that all happy rulers have God always in their mind and so do not take mistresses although whores would be a better name for them and live a God-fearing life God will pour on these rulers all the blessings of this world and the next so I implore my dear successor to lead a pure God-fearing life and behaviour and set a good example to his country and army do not drink or guzzle from which an obscene life comes, My dear successor must also not tolerate that in his territories and provinces plays operas ballets masquerades balls are put on but have a horror of such things because they are godless and devilish and greatly add to Satan's temple and empire.

There is a lot more of this kind of thing, but that will suffice to catch the flavour of Frederick William I's political thought. Although his son Frederick certainly never took a mistress, it may be doubted whether his abstinence was a result of either filial or Christian piety. On the contrary, in his own political testament he dismissed Christianity as 'an old metaphysical fiction, stuffed with fables, contradictions and absurdities: it was spawned in the fevered imagination of the Orientals, and then spread to our Europe, where some fanatics espoused it, where some intriguers pretended to be convinced by it and where some imbeciles actually believed it'.

Where Frederick William's thinking was prescriptive, particularist and pious, Frederick's was rational, universal and secular. To legitimate his authority, he postulated a social contract, by which the inhabitants of a state of nature delegated to a sovereign sufficient authority to maintain external security and internal order. By the middle of the eighteenth century, such a concept was hardly original, but its advocacy by a ruler of a backward and hitherto minor state certainly was. Frederick's clearest exposition was given in the course of a discussion of religious toleration in his treatise *On the Forms of Government and the Duties of Sovereigns* of 1777:

One can compel by force some poor wretch to utter a certain form of words, yet he will deny to it his inner consent; thus the persecutor has gained nothing. But if one goes back to the origins of society, it is completely clear that the sovereign has no right to dictate the way in which the citizens will think. Would not one have to be demented to suppose that men said to one of their number: we are raising you above us because we like being slaves, and so we are giving you the power to direct our thoughts as you like? On the contrary, what they said was: we need you to maintain the laws which we wish to obey, to govern us wisely, to defend us; for the rest, we require that you respect our liberty. Once this agreement had been made, it could not be altered.

This is, of course, an authoritarian interpretation of the social contract – the grant of sovereignty is irrevocable and unconditional, the subjects have no right of resistance – but it does impose on the ruler the obligation to serve the interests of the whole. Frederick made that explicit in a passage following that just quoted:

Here we have, in general, the duties which a prince should carry out. So that he never neglects them, he should often recall to mind that he is a man just like the least of his subjects; if he is the first judge, the first general, the first minister of society, it is not so that he can indulge himself, but so that he can fulfil the duties involved. He is only the first servant of the state, obliged to act with honesty, wisdom and with a complete lack of self-interest, as if at every moment he might be called upon to render an account of his stewardship to his fellow citizens.

'The first servant of the state' was a phrase repeated by Frederick time and again: it became the leitmotiv of his political system. In a letter to Voltaire written the year before he came to the throne, he used a striking simile to identify the role of the ruler: he was like a heart in the human body, receiving blood from all members and then pumping it out again to the furthest extremities of the body politic; in return for receiving loyalty and obedience, he sent out security, prosperity and everything else that could further the welfare of the community. It was this sense of responsibility to the whole that rescued Frederick from any charges of despotism. The essence of despotic power was held to be its arbitrary, capricious character, its dependence on the whim of its wielder. That was what led contemporaries to castigate the Russian and Ottoman Empires as 'oriental despotisms'. In Prussia, on the other hand, the absolute power of the king was limited by the obligations imposed by the social contract, especially by the rule of law. Although Frederick did indeed abuse his absolute power on occasions – did act despotically, in other words – he was loyal to his enlightened political thought with sufficient consistency to prompt Prussians to reject with indignation the charge that they lived in a despotism.

They were encouraged in this belief by the reforms Frederick introduced during the course of his long reign. Particularly his expansion of the religious toleration for which Prussia had long been famous, his relaxation of censorship and reform of the civil and criminal law provided evidence that this was indeed 'the age of enlightenment, the century of Frederick', as Kant proclaimed in his essay 'What is Enlightenment?' of 1784. From around the middle of the eighteenth century, similar reforms could be found in other parts of Europe – Spain, Portugal, Tuscany, Russia, Denmark, Sweden, the Habsburg Monarchy and many of the states of the Holy Roman Empire. Whether collectively they justify the description 'enlightened absolutism' has been much contested. For some historians, especially those of a Marxist persuasion, there is a fundamental contradiction between the two components that make up the concept, for the Enlightenment they regard as essentially bourgeois ideology, whereas 'absolutism' was a feudal relic. For others, it was only the absolutism that was real, any enlightened characteristics being dismissed as coincidence or window-dressing.

The view that the Enlightenment was bourgeois can be despatched without further ado. It flies in the face of so much evidence to the contrary, especially that relating to the social origins of both the writers and their audience, that it can be sustained only as an article of faith. The relationship between power and ideology, however, is more problematic, for the tricky question of human motivation is involved. When Catherine the Great plundered Montesquieu and Beccaria to compile her *Nakaz*, did she really intend to make their enlightened precepts the basis of future legislation? Or was she just looking forward to receiving the plaudits of the fawning *philosophes*? Or was it both those things, and, if so, in what proportion: 50/50, 60/40, or what? Although not an entirely pointless exercise, it can best be left to individual judgement. One important consideration that should be borne in mind, although often overlooked by those who deny reality to the concept, is that not even rulers as autocratic as Catherine, Frederick or Joseph were working alone. They all relied on their ministers to a greater or lesser extent, and not only in the implementation of their policies.

Once one expands one's field of vision to embrace this wider constituency of policy-makers, however, the influence of the Enlightenment is next to impossible to deny. The achievement of the Marquês de Pombal (1699–1782) in Portugal as first minister to Joseph I (1750–77) provides an excellent example. He was both a member of the *Academia dos Ilustrados* at home and a Fellow of the Royal Society in London, where he was ambassador from 1739 to 1744. From there he moved to Vienna, where he became a member of the enlightened group led by Baron Gerhard van Swieten, who was not only personal physician to the Empress Maria Theresa but her adviser on a wide range of political and cultural matters as well. Returning to Portugal, Pombal then presided over a radical secularization of perhaps the most clericalist country in all Europe (as we shall see when the great palace-monastery of Mafra is discussed in a later chapter), including the expulsion of the Jesuits in 1759. This intimate relationship between enlightened intellectual and practical politician was especially common in the Holy Roman Empire, where bureaucrats were often university professors and vice versa. Typical was Joseph von Sonnenfels (1733–1817), professor of Political

Science at the University of Vienna, author of many enlightened treatises, notably *The Man without Prejudice* (1773) and *On the Abolition of Torture* (1775), senior civil servant in the Court Chancellery, member of the censorship commission, President of the Academy of the Visual Arts, Freemason and member of the Order of the Illuminati. He was also another good example of the social mobility that talented intellectuals enjoyed, for his grandfather had been a rabbi in rural Brandenburg. These two examples from either end of Europe could be multiplied at will.

Moreover, critics of enlightened absolutism might well be barking up the wrong tree when they concentrate on policies. It was not the post-modern era that discovered that politics is more about style than substance. Whatever reservations have to be made about individual rulers' enlightenment, or lack of it, the obstinate fact remains that most educated people in most countries believed that Kant was right, and that they were indeed living in an age of enlightenment. The following anonymous testimony is taken from a document included in a 'time-capsule', placed in the steeple-ball of St Margaret's Church at Gotha in 1784 and discovered there in 1856:

The days we spent on this earth constituted the happiest period of the eighteenth century. Emperor, kings and princes are philanthropically stepping down from their intimidating heights, disdain pomp and display and become the fathers, friends and companions of their people. Religion sheds its clerical vestments and emerges in pure godliness. Enlightenment marches forward with giant steps; thousands of our brothers and sisters who lived in sacred idleness now contribute to the community. Sectarian hatred and religious persecution diminish; philanthropy and freedom of thought win the upper hand. Arts and sciences flourish, and we are gaining deep insights into the workings of nature. Craftsmen approach artists in their level of skill; useful knowledge spreads through all classes. Here you have a true portrayal of our age. Do not look down on us with arrogance, if you stand higher and see further than we did; rather appreciate from the picture we have given you just how much we elevated and supported your fatherland. Do the same for your posterity and be happy.

The master of what has come to be called 'gesture politics' was Frederick the Great. No sooner did he come to the throne in 1740 than he demonstratively recalled from exile Christian Wolff, hardly a household name today but then regarded as *the* great philosopher of the

Enlightenment. Thus he proclaimed to the intelligentsia of Europe a sea-change in the cultural identity of his state, and, moreover, in a way they could appreciate – a job. Earlier that year Frederick had written to thank Wolff for a copy of his latest work on natural law, praising it to the skies and delivering the following perfect encapsulation of enlightened absolutism: 'philosophers should be the teachers of the world and the teachers of princes. They must think logically and we must act logically. They must teach the world by their powers of judgement, we must teach the world by our example. They must discover, and we must translate their discoveries into practice.'

Joseph II has often been berated for his obstinacy, arrogance and insensitivity by armchair rulers, but one thing he did understand was how to catch a public mood. Shortly after he gained sole control of his dominions on the death of his mother in 1780, he issued a new censorship regulation: 'Criticisms, if they are not slanderous, are not to be prohibited, no matter who their targets might be, whether the humblest or the highest, including the sovereign, especially if the author appends his name as a guarantee of validity, for every lover of truth must rejoice to be told the truth, even if it is conveyed to him via the uncomfortable route of criticism.' It soon turned out that in Joseph's liberty-hall some rooms were still locked – the one marked 'pornography', for example – but so different was his attitude from anything that had gone before in the Habsburg Monarchy (or to be found elsewhere in Europe) that his gesture caused a sensation, not least because of his apparent indifference to personal attacks: 'if the slanders derive from arrogance, the author deserves contempt; if they derive from mental deficiency, he deserves pity; and if simple ill-will is the cause – then we forgive the idiot'.

If this kind of gesture endeared Joseph to the intelligentsia of the Habsburg Monarchy, his ostentatious radicalism had just the opposite impact on the privileged orders. There was nothing inevitable about the systemic clash that brought the Monarchy to the verge of collapse by the late 1780s, especially not the confrontation between Church and state. The reform movement that became known as Josephism did not begin as an attack on the former by the latter. On the contrary, it began as a movement *inside* the Church and *by* the Church to reform itself. Beginning long before Joseph was born, it aimed at the replacement of 'baroque piety' by a form of Catholicism characterized by simplicity instead of display, rigour instead of opulence, austerity instead of indulgence, denial instead of sensuality. As this summary suggests, it was strongly influenced by Jansenism, especially as mediated by the influential Modenese reformer Lodovico Antonio Muratori (1672–1750), whose most important work, *Della regolata devozione dei cristiani* (1723), went through twenty different editions in German translation, eight of them published in Vienna. The reformers' concern to shift power within the Church away from the Pope, Jesuits and regular orders towards the bishops and parish priests was shared by the Empress Maria Theresa. The personal link between the reforms of the bishops and the reforms of the state was provided by Count Christoph Anton von Migazzi, a devotee of Muratori who became Archbishop of Vienna in 1757.

It was only when Joseph became sole ruler in 1780 that this alliance began to crack. He moved quickly to introduce toleration for Protestants and Greek Orthodox; to exclude any form of foreign jurisdiction over the Church in his territories, whether exercised by the Pope or imperial prince-bishops; to dissolve all religious orders that he deemed 'completely and utterly useless' (i.e. the majority); and to re-educate the clergy through new state-run 'general seminaries' in accordance with his fundamental principle that 'the Church must be useful to the state'. He also introduced toleration for the Jews, while stressing that he did not wish to see their numbers increase and emphasizing that his main aim was to make them more useful for the state. Moreover, the language adopted by Joseph was so uncompromising as to suggest that he positively relished putting people's backs up. Although he lived and died a devout Catholic, to his more conservative contemporaries he came to look like a destructive apostate. The desperate journey of Pius VI to Vienna in the spring of 1782 to remonstrate with Joseph both dramatized the possibility of a schism and allowed the plain people of the Monarchy to demonstrate their attachment to traditional forms of worship. They were encouraged by the increasingly noisy opposition of Cardinal Migazzi to Joseph's reforms.

For all his influence on the priests and their parishioners, not even the most turbulent prelate could pose a real threat to the stability of the Monarchy. It was a different matter when Joseph turned his levelling attention to secular privilege. It should be remembered that privilege was not a monopoly of the nobility; on the contrary, it permeated every nook and cranny of society, especially in the towns. Nowhere was that more so than in the Austrian Netherlands, which for the sake of convenience will be referred to as 'Belgium'. Joseph's relations with his subjects there had always been unfortunate. His only visit, in 1781, had been marked by mutual incomprehension; his clumsy attempt to open the Scheldt to international trade, in 1784–5, had ended in failure, convincing Joseph that the Belgians were not worth helping and the Belgians that Joseph was incompetent; his simultaneous bid to use the province as a bargaining-counter in the equally ill-fated Bavarian exchange project completed the process of alienation. However, it was his radical reform programme which took the Belgians from hostility to revolt. The announcement on 1 January 1787 of a fundamental change in the political, administrative and judicial structure led, first to protests and then to a tax strike by the Estates of Brabant, the most important of the Belgian provinces.

Outright revolt was averted on that occasion by concessions made by the governors-general of the province. It was some measure of Joseph's obstinacy and lack of political acumen that he furiously disowned their 'weakness' and then sought to claw back their concessions. Another tax strike in November 1788 by the Estates of Brabant and Hainaut was countered by Joseph's declaration that he regarded their privileges as abolished, their constitutions null and void and their people outlaws. Inflamed by another singularly ill-timed burst of reforms in the spring and early summer of 1789, and encouraged by the revolutionary examples set by adjacent France and Liège, the dissidents took up arms. After a false start in October 1789, they returned in November, quickly expelled the remaining Austrian soldiers and took possession of all the provinces except Luxemburg by the end of the year. On 11 January 1790 the combined Estates proclaimed the independence of the 'United States of Belgium'.

Paradoxically, what appeared to be a weakness of the Habsburg Monarchy – geographical fragmentation – now proved to be an asset, for the secession of Belgium did not imperil the main core of territories. What made the trouble simultaneously brewing in Hungary so much more dangerous was its central location. This latest confrontation in the long-running feud with Vienna was brought on by Joseph's radical assault on the Magyar gentry's social, economic and political power. In 1785–6 the kingdom was divided into ten new districts, without any regard for historical precedent, ethnic distribution or local opinion. The commissars to run them were, of course, appointed by the centre. With equal predictability, the administration of the counties was also nationalized. Their assemblies were forbidden to meet, unless choosing deputies for the national Parliament (which meant never, as the Parliament did not meet). Together with Joseph's refusal to be crowned King of Hungary (thus evading an oath to observe the traditional constitution), his imposition of the German language as the sole *lingua franca* for administration, and his sympathetic treatment of the great peasant revolt of 1784, this clean sweep of traditional institutions threatened to turn the Magyar nobility's world upside down. The last straw was the 'Taxation and Urbarial Regulation', discussed in Chapter 4.

· As the Magyars' ancestors had resorted to armed resistance for much less cause in the past, it was only a matter of time before insurrection was planned. The first conspiracy to be uncovered came in 1786, although the interrogators of the culprit ceased to take him seriously when he revealed under cross-examination that he had intended to publicize his revolt with the help of proclamations distributed by '100,000 trained dogs'. For the time being Joseph was safe. As the Prussian envoy in Vienna, Baron Jacobi, observed in 1787: despite all the angry noises made by the Magyars, the magnates were tamed, the resentment of the Protestant gentry had been blunted by religious toleration, the peasants worshipped Joseph as their emancipator and the massive military presence would nip any revolt in the bud. However, he added with chilling foresight that the situation would be very different if the Prussians could get an army into Hungary to support the insurgents before Joseph or his successor could strike a deal with them. That was exactly the scenario that threatened to develop after the outbreak of war against the Turks in 1787. As early as the autumn of 1788, Joseph knew from intelligence reports that the dissidents were conspiring to turn Hungary into an independent state, to be ruled by the Duke of Saxony-Weimar. He also knew that the Polish nobles in Galicia, the province torn from Poland in the first partition of 1772, were equally anxious to cast off the Habsburg yoke. Even in the normally docile German-speaking provinces at the heart of the Monarchy, rumblings of discontent had become too audible to ignore.

Even by the standards of the Habsburg Monarchy, this domestic crisis was severe. It assumed existential proportions when the threat of military intervention by Prussia became likely. Fresh from his triumphant intervention in the Dutch Republic in the autumn of 1787, the normally indecisive Frederick William II was sorely tempted to take advantage of the wonderfully favourable international situation that had developed. With France bankrupt and subsiding into revolution and the two eastern powers tied down by war in the Baltic and the Balkans, Prussia was presented with a golden opportunity to give the law to Europe. At some point in the late summer of 1789, Frederick William decided on an offensive alliance with the Turks and an invasion of the Habsburg Monarchy from the north in the following spring, to be accompanied by Prussian-sponsored revolts in Hungary and Galicia. Negotiations were also opened with Poland for an offensive alliance. As if that were not enough for the hapless Joseph II to contend with, the Spanish and the Sardinians were getting ready to seize the Habsburg possessions in Italy.

Not for the first or last time in the troubled history of the Habsburg Monarchy, salvation came in the shape of the army. Just as Joseph's numerous enemies thought they could sniff the scent of carrion, there was a sudden surge of vitality. After the disappointments of 1788, the campaign of 1789 went very well for the Austrians. At the very time that the fall of the Bastille signalled the fall of the French absolute monarchy, one Austrian army was advancing into Serbia and another was conquering Moldavia. On 8 October came the climax of the campaign with the taking of Belgrade from the Turks by storm. So much territory was won during this triumphant autumn campaign that both the domestic and the foreign enemies of the Monarchy began to think twice about resorting to arms. Their decision to stay at home was helped by the death of Joseph II on 20 February 1790. He had already revoked many of the most unpopular policies and his successor, his brother Leopold II, hastened to complete the process and to pledge his attachment to the traditional order. Simultaneously, he launched a diplomatic offensive to avert war with Prussia. This he achieved by the Convention of Reichenbach on 27 July 1790. Although this obliged him to hand back to the Turks all the conquered territory, including Belgrade, it allowed him to restore order in Hungary and to reconquer Belgium. On 15 November 1790 Leopold was crowned King of Hungary, swearing 'by the living God, and by His most holy mother the Virgin Mary, and by all the saints, to preserve the churches of God, the lord prelates, the barons, magnates, nobles, free cities and all inhabitants of the realm in their immunities, liberties, rights, laws, privileges and good and approved ancient customs; and to do justice to all'. On 6 September 1791 Leopold was crowned King of Bohemia at Prague. Hungary and Bohemia were to remain part of the Habsburg Empire until 1918.

At the other end of Europe – indeed, at the other end of western civilization – a similar conflict had occurred but with a very different outcome. Although the great victor of the Seven Years War, Great Britain had been left with a National Debt that had almost doubled to £147,000,000 and appeared to be crippling. The unpopularity of the Peace of Paris of 1763 and the post-war economic depression made any increase in domestic taxation more than usually unpalatable. It was natural that the government should look to the American colonies for assistance, for it was they who had benefited most directly from the conquest of French Canada. Moreover, it was well known that their current level of taxation was many times lower: R. R. Palmer estimated that the annual tax burden per head in Britain was twenty-six shillings, as opposed to one shilling in Massachusetts, eight pence in New York (there were twelve pence to the shilling) and five pence in Virginia. Collectively, the thirteen colonies were quite rightly thought to be populous, expanding and rich. In 1700 there were still only 225,000 English-speaking Americans, but fifty years later that number had raced to 2,000,000, with Philadelphia larger than any city in England bar London. More controversially, the Americans were also thought to be feckless and lackadaisical about their own defence, leaving it to the British to deal with the rising of Native Americans led by Pontiac in 1763.

The resulting attempt to make the Americans contribute to the costs of imperial defence, beginning with the Sugar Act of 1764 and the Stamp Act of 1765 led to revolt and secession. For the colonists, the immediate principle at stake was summed up in the simple formula 'no taxation without representation'. As they were not represented in the British Parliament, they did not regard its authority as legitimate: 'A Parliament of Great Britain can have no more right to tax the colonies than a Parliament of Paris' was John Adams' conclusion. Paradoxically they could arrive at this conclusion only by ignoring everything that had happened in England since the 1640s, including the recognition that sovereignty resided in the King in Parliament. In November 1765, Sir Francis Bernard, governor of Massachusetts, told Lord Barrington, secretary of state for war, that: 'In Britain, the American governments are considered as Corporations empowered to make by-laws, existing only during the pleasure of Parliament . . . In America they claim . . . to be perfect States, not otherwise dependent on Great Britain than by having the same King.' Once the issue was one of sovereignty, the irresistible force had struck the immoveable object. That was demonstrated by the Declaratory Act of January 1766, which asserted parliamentary sovereignty in language just as uncompromising as Louis XV's statement of royal sovereignty delivered just two months later and quoted earlier in this chapter:

The said colonies and plantations in *America* have been, are, and of right, ought to be, subordinate unto, and dependent upon the imperial crown and parliament of *Great Britain* . . . the King's majesty by and with the advice and consent of the lords spiritual and temporal, and commons of *Great Britain*, in parliament assembled, had, hath, and of right, ought to have, full power and authority to make laws and statutes of sufficient force and validity to bind the colonies and people of *America*, subjects of the crown of *Great Britain*, in all cases whatsoever.

The last straw for both sides came in late 1773, when the British government sought to help the ailing East India Company by allowing it to sell ten million pounds of tea in the American colonies. The response was the 'Boston Tea Party', when a group of dissidents dressed as Native Americans boarded three ships at Griffin's Wharf in Boston harbour and threw their cargo of tea over the side. In a fine illustration of the superiority of symbol over concept in politics, this essentially trivial episode polarized opinion on both sides. George III was in no doubt: 'the die is now cast, the colonies must now submit or triumph'. In many ways, his attitude towards the Americans resembled that of Joseph II to the Belgians, for he knew that he was right: 'I know I am doing my duty and therefore can never wish to retract', he wrote in July 1775.

By that time the war was underway. Eight years were to pass before the British finally recognized American independence by the Treaty of Paris of 3 September 1783. It was an outcome predicted from the outset by the more far-sighted of British politicians, notably Lord Camden, who in the debates of 1775 argued: 'To conquer a great continent of 1,800 miles, containing three millions of people, all indissolubly united on the great Whig bottom of liberty and justice, seems an undertaking not to be rashly engaged in . . . It is obvious, my lords, that you cannot furnish armies, or treasure, competent to the mighty purpose of subduing America ... but whether France and Spain will be tame, inactive spectators of your efforts and distractions, is well worthy of the considerations of your lordships.' Although public opinion was overwhelmingly anti-American when the war began, Camden was not the only Briton to view with distaste a war against an English-speaking people whose 'great Whig bottom' he shared. The British were used to fighting wars against enemies who were Catholic by religion and absolutist by politics, so the libertarian rhetoric of the Americans was deeply disturbing. On the American side, there was some confusion, or at least disagreement, as to whether they were conservatives fighting to defend old liberties in the plural or revolutionaries fighting for liberty in the abstract. Sensibly, the Continental Congress put the two together in their Declaration of Rights of 1774, appealing to 'the immutable laws of nature, the principles of the English constitution, and the several charters and compacts'.

The Americans had demonstrated that the sovereign state's appetite for power and money could only be stopped by force supported by ideology operating in a favourable international context. They were able to go much further than the Hungarians, for example, in achieving outright independence rather than just the withdrawal of detested reforms, because their force was greater, their ideology was more inclusive and their international context was more favourable. In these respects, the other major problem for the British government – Ireland – was more like Hungary than America. The concentration of British military resources on the colonial struggle after 1775 left Ireland more than usually vulnerable to domestic unrest and foreign invasion. To guard against both, the Anglo-Irish elites, led by magnates such as the Duke of Leinster and the Earl of Charlemont, set about raising companies of volunteers. By the end of 1779 there were around 40,000 under arms, an impressive figure which doubled during the next three years. With the war in America going from bad to worse and with a Franco-Spanish invasion of the English mainland averted in 1779 only by bad weather, the political muscle of the Irish Volunteers grew in proportion. Henry Grattan told an attentive Irish lower house in 1780: 'Never was there a parliament in Ireland so possessed of the confidence of the people; you are the greatest political assembly now sitting in the world; you are at the head of an immense army; nor do we only possess an unconquerable force, but a certain unquenchable public fire, which has touched all ranks of men like a visitation.' British politicians could agree at least with Grattan's boasting about the force at his command. The result was a series of economic and political concessions, which reduced if it did not terminate Ireland's colonial status. Symbolically, the most important was the repealing of 'Poynings' Laws', dating from 1494, which had subjected all decisions taken by the Irish Parliament to English approval. More important materially was the lifting of restrictions on the export of Irish woollens and glassware and on direct trade with other British colonies.

Yet Ireland was to remain under British rule until 1922. The comparison with America and Hungary is instructive. America too was deeply divided, as at least 60,000 and perhaps as many as 100,000 loyalists demonstrated when they preferred emigration to independence. The tumultuous early years of the new republic, leading to the introduction of a new constitution in 1788, also bore witness to deep divisions in both state and civil society. Yet these were but cracks compared with the fissures that prevented a united opposition in Ireland. Between the more than three million Catholics, almost one million Presbyterians and 450,000 Anglicans, there could never be anything more than a temporary marriage of convenience doomed to end speedily in acrimonious divorce. When the Grand National Convention of the Volunteers met in Dublin in November 1783, the deputies debated furiously the issue of Catholic enfranchisement – but decided against it. There was an automatic stop-valve at work here: only with the support of the Catholics could true independence be obtained, but whenever the Catholics began to assert themselves, the Protestants began to have second thoughts. Only when the Catholics had created an ideology and an organization for themselves – and only when the international situation was favourable – could success be achieved. For the time being, even the limited gains of the early 1780s had been won courtesy of the Americans: 'it was on the plains of America that Ireland obtained her freedom', conceded one Irish patriot in 1782. That freedom turned out to be a chimera, for Ireland was united with Great Britain in 1801 to form the United Kingdom.

THE NATION

If the state was one master-noun of eighteenth-century political discourse, the nation was another. Indeed, as a source of inspiration, it was
the more potent. For although the state was an ambitious, omnivorous,
hyperactive agent, the blood it sent pulsing round the body politic was
very much on the thin side. While a dedicated enlightened absolutist
such as Frederick the Great or Joseph II might wish to dedicate his
life to its service, most Europeans found it difficult to work up much
enthusiasm for such an abstract entity. The nation, on the other hand,
proved to be brimful with motivating force, for it triggered both positive
and negative responses in a self-generating dialectical progression. For
every virtue a nationalist ascribed to his own national group, there was a
corresponding vice to be denigrated in the 'other' against which national
identity was defined. Moreover, this was a two-way process, because the
nationalist believed that the other both failed to give credit where it was
due and refused to recognize its own shortcomings. What might be
called 'the dialectic of nationalism' can best be clarified by a simple
diagram:

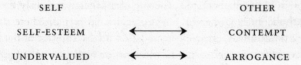

A specific example may help to unravel this secret of the force of nationalism. When the British began to emerge from a prolonged period of
civil strife and to enjoy prosperity at home and to exert influence abroad,
they were also at pains to assert their cultural credentials. The main
beneficiary, as well he might have been, was William Shakespeare, to
whom something of a cult was devoted in the eighteenth century, including the erection of a monument in Westminster Abbey in 1737. As the
German scientist and aphorist Georg Christoph Lichtenberg observed
on a visit to England in 1775: 'Shakespeare is not only famous but sacred;
his moral maxims are heard everywhere.' Justified pride in Shakespeare,
however, was accompanied by denigration of foreign, and especially

French, literature, derided for its pretentiousness, artificiality and super-ficiality. Yet it was well known that the French preened themselves on the absolute superiority of their own culture and dismissed the works of the immortal bard as uncouth and barbaric. Nor was this paranoia, for none other than Voltaire had observed that 'the great merit of this dramatic poet has been the ruin of the English stage', for despite his genius he 'had not so much as a single spark of good taste, or knew one rule of drama' with the result that his 'tragedies' were in reality 'monstrous farces'. What made this verdict all the more galling was that Voltaire knew England well and had gone out of his way to praise many of its institutions in his *Lettres philosophiques*. It might be added here that Voltaire performed the same sort of service for the Germans by satirizing them in *Candide* in the person of the bovine Baron Thunder-ten-Tronck, who 'was one of the most powerful lords in Westphalia, for his castle had not only a gate, but even windows'.

This kind of mutually supportive national prejudice was of long standing by the eighteenth century. In the Middle Ages, satires singled out, for example, the envy of the Jews, the cunning of the Greeks, the arrogance of the Romans, the avarice of the French, the bravery of the Saxons, the bad temper of the English and the lasciviousness of the Scots. As the German scholar Winfried Schulze has cogently argued, the humanists of the fifteenth and sixteenth centuries advanced these simple stereotypes much further by integrating simple prejudices in national historical narratives, especially foundation myths, for 'just about every culture and every religion has its own creation myth, its own equivalent of the Book of Genesis' (Colin Renfrew). In 1526 Heinrich Cornelius Agrippa von Nettesheim (1486–1535), a German who spent most of his life travelling around Europe, wrote in his *De incertitudine et vanitate scientarum*:

All nations have their own special customs and habits that distinguish them from one another and can be recognized by their discourse, manner of speaking, conversation, favourite food and drink, the way they go about things, the way they hate and love or show anger and malice, and in other ways besides. So if you happen to see someone come towards you in a proud and haughty manner, wearing a pugnacious and fierce expression, bellowing like a bull, talking tough, with wild gestures and his clothes in rags, then you can work out at once that he must be a German.

Unusually, Agrippa was much more charitable towards the other European nations whose characteristics he went on to enumerate. Most humanists gave the preference to their own nation: Richard Mulcaster, for example, who in 1582 wrote: 'I love Rome, but London better, I favour Italie, but England more, I honour the Latin, but I worship the English . . . I do not think that anie language, be it whatsoever, is better able to utter all arguments, wither with more pith, or greater planesse, than our English tung is.'

The numerous international forces at work in early modern Europe – dynasticism, classicism and religion, for example – were often powerful enough to deafen national voices. In many 'composite states', regional loyalties and antipathies were much stronger, as the division of Spain between the kingdoms of Aragon and Castile demonstrated. What kept the national option in being and eventually raised it to supremacy was the emergence of national states within the European states-system. In sixteenth-century England, a combination of the Reformation, the development of Parliament and victory over the Spanish Armada promoted a first great surge of nationalism, eloquently expressed in the art and literature of the period. The failure of the Stuarts to understand its force proved to be not the least of the blunders that cost Charles I his head and his son James II his throne. It was only when Crown and Parliament began to work in the same direction again after 1688 that nationalism moved back to the centre of English politics. It was anchored there by the 'Second Hundred Years War' that began in 1688.

Meanwhile in France, a similar if more extreme scenario had unfolded, as the national monarchy of Francis I and Henry II made way for the French 'Wars of Religion' (1562–98). As we have seen in previous chapters, it was only after the renewed civil war of the *Frondes* (1648–53) that Louis XIV was to reassert monarchical authority and to identify the cause of the king with the interests of France. Unlike in England, this was a highly personalized association unmediated by corporate institutions, as the Versailles project proclaimed. That proved to be both its strength and its weakness. On the one hand, it allowed Louis XIV to achieve through the concentration of resources a degree of cultural hegemony for his country unprecedented in European history; on the other, it made the continuation of royal representational culture dependent on the ability of the monarch to make it work.

The hubris shouted from the rooftops of Versailles also invited a visit from Nemesis, the goddess of retribution who reverses excessive good fortune and checks presumption. As we have seen, it is difficult to conceive of anything more triumphalist than the decorative scheme devised for the Salon of War and the Hall of Mirrors. The frescoes are still there, silent but graphic witnesses to Louis XIV's extravagance – and folly. They were foolish for two reasons: first, because when the fortunes of war changed, these artefacts no longer served to glorify but to criticize, by emphasizing the contrast between past victories and present defeats. That was to become a special problem during the dark days of the Seven Years War. How did Louis XV feel, one wonders, as he passed these uncomfortable reminders of the previous reign's glories? By that time, Louis XIV was beginning to look like Shelley's Ozymandias, whose shattered visage peered out from the desert sands with a sneer of cold command: 'Look on my works, ye Mighty, and despair.'

Secondly, the Versailles project was foolish even at the time, at least in its foreign policy aspects, because its triumphalist gloating naturally provoked a reaction of corresponding violence. In particular, the impact on the development of German nationalism was colossal. In the past, several 'others' had served to enhance a sense of identity – the Italians, Spanish, Turks and even the Swedes. But from the 1670s the French moved to pole position. In a flood of pamphlets Louis XIV was denounced as the Antichrist, 'first-born of Satan', deformed by tyranny, aggression, cruelty, vanity, blasphemy, adultery and every other imaginable vice. He was paraded as 'the Christian Turk', right down to his harem of other men's wives, which he seized with the same brutal disregard for the law that he showed in his conduct towards other princes and their territory. The pamphleteers' assault was personal but not personalized. All the royal depravities were projected on to the French, to make a national target. The atrocities committed by the French armies during the Dutch campaigns of the 1670s were broadcast far and wide by word and image. So when Louis turned his attention to the *Reich* in the 1680s, first with the *réunions* (on which see below, pp. 542–3), and then with the devastation of the Rhineland after 1689, German public opinion was ready to believe the worst. And the worst was as bad as it could be: stories of looting, extortion, burning, vandalism, rape, murder and all the other horrors of war were accompanied by savage denunciations of the French national character. That the scorched-earth policy they adopted, resulting in the burning of Heidelberg and the razing of several Rhenish towns, was known to have been ordered from the top only added to the fury. It was reported, for example, that the maréchal de Luxembourg had given a speech in which he called on his soldiers to loot, kill and rape. The French were accused of bombarding defenceless towns, laying waste any territory they thought they could not hold, making land permanently infertile by polluting it with salt, poisoning wells, and so on. Neither babies in the womb nor the dead in their coffins had been spared, so it was claimed. The field of fire was then expanded beyond the military to embrace all French people. In particular, their sexual immorality was attacked: there were no virgins in France above the age of puberty, sodomy was a French invention, syphilis was France's major export, Paris was one great brothel, and so on. These personal vices were reflected in the political system. Originally, the pamphleteers argued, the Franks of France had been as free as their German cousins, but now they had been enslaved and impoverished. The three great bulwarks against royal tyranny – the nobility, the Church and the law courts – had been turned by Louis XIV into meekly obedient instruments of despotic megalomania.

With the help of a veritable thesaurus of antonyms, this vile stereotype was contrasted with the simple, generous, honest, truthful, loyal, modest, chaste, etc., etc. Germans. First among the advantages they enjoyed was their liberty: 'there is no people under the sun that loves liberty more than the German', as a pamphlet of 1684 put it. Indeed, virtually every pamphlet published after 1648 refers to it. It was a liberty secured by the right of the Imperial Estates (*Reichsstände*) to participate in the government of the *Reich*, especially in the election of the Emperor, and by the rule of law. All nations had once enjoyed the same freedoms, it was argued, but only the Germans had known how to preserve theirs, although the Swiss, English and Dutch might be included as well, depending on current circumstances. A fine example of German awareness of national differences was provided by an early eighteenth-century chart entitled 'Short description of the European peoples and their characteristics', arranged in columns headed by a representative figure in national dress, with their national characters defined according to seventeen criteria, including intelligence, knowledge, vices, favourite pursuits, illnesses, attitudes to religion, and pastimes.

German denunciations of the French reached a frenzied peak during the 1690s but continued to influence national discourse throughout the eighteenth century. The main change was from fear of French power to contempt for French decadence. The occupation of Prague between November 1741 and December 1742, for example, was paraded as an example of French cruelty but also of their weakness and incompetence. Together with the defeat at Dettingen the following year by an army commanded in person by Elector George of Hanover (who also happened to be George II, King of England), the retreat from the German theatre of the war suggested that French lions of the past had mutated into bunny rabbits, as one pamphlet put it. The *coup de grâce* was delivered by the battle of Rossbach on 5 November 1757 when a Prussian army commanded by Frederick the Great routed a French army twice its size in half-an-hour. No matter that a significant part of the enemy army was drawn from imperial contingents, contemporary public opinion chose to see it as a victory for the Germans over the French. It was a 'national triumph', as Johann Wilhelm Archenholz put it.

On the other hand, the Seven Years War did mark an important shift in the orientation of German nationalism. The major beneficiary of the surge of Francophobia of the second half of the seventeenth century had been the Habsburg Emperor Leopold I. Presented as gallantly resisting Louis XIV's aggression in the west, while at the same time defeating the Turks in the east, he was able to emerge convincingly as a German hero. The problems began with the death of his son Charles VI in 1740 and the election of the Elector of Bavaria as Charles VII. Although the Habsburgs regained the imperial title by proxy when Maria Theresa's husband, Francis Stephen, secured election in 1745, the imperial office had been demystified and its authority permanently weakened. Worse was to come. The '*renversement des alliances*' engineered by Kaunitz in 1756 may have been a diplomatic triumph, but politically it was a disaster. By allying Austria with the French hereditary enemy, it allowed Frederick the Great to step forward as the saviour of German liberty. The traditional but still vital concept of the German nation represented by the hierarchical *Reich* now increasingly made way for a concept that was more cultural, more Prussian, more Protestant and more north German.

The same combination of Francophobia and liberty was also prominent in England. If a sense of a separate English identity can be found as early as the seventh century, it was the 'Glorious Revolution' of 1688

– 'England's first nationalist revolution', in the opinion of Steven Pincus
– that launched the modern career of English nationalism. The main
driving force was the 'Second Hundred Years War' that began with the
landing of William III in Torbay on 5 November 1688 (thought to be
an especially propitious date, for 5 November was also the day on which
the foiling of Guy Fawkes's 'gunpowder plot' was celebrated). This was
one regime change that did signal a change for the better: Charles II had
been Louis XIV's satrap; William III was his hammer. 'King Billy's War'
was a war that encapsulated all the dichotomies that fuelled the English
version of the dialectic of nationalism identified earlier in this chapter:
Protestant against Catholic, English against Celt, independence against
slavery, liberty against tyranny, prosperity against poverty, even whole-
some food (the roast beef of old England) against filthy foreign muck
(*soupe maigre*, frogs' legs, grass).

Two examples of this potent brew of pride in one's own and contempt
for the other's situation must suffice. The first recommends itself by the
high intelligence of the author – Anthony Ashley Cooper, third Earl of
Shaftesbury; the influence he exerted on contemporaries and posterity,
both at home and abroad; and his Whiggish aversion to anything that
smacked of vulgar prejudice. He saw the War of the Spanish Succession
as an existential struggle by the English to preserve their liberty against
Louis XIV's attempt to impose 'a Universal Monarchy, and a new Abyss
of Ignorance and Superstition'. In his view, the much-vaunted cultural
achievements of the Sun King were vitiated by the absolutist tyranny they
represented. English culture, on the other hand, for all its uncouthness,
was underpinned by a liberty that ultimately must triumph:

We are now in an Age when LIBERTY is once again in its Ascendant. And we
are ourselves the happy Nation, who not only enjoy it at home, but by our
Greatness and Power give Life and Vigour to it abroad; and are the Head and
Chief of the EUROPEAN *League*, founded on this *common Cause*. Nor is it to
be fear'd that we shou'd lose this noble Ardour, or faint under the glorious Toil;
tho, like antient GREECE, we shou'd for successive Ages be contending with a
foreign Power, and endeavouring to reduce the Exorbitancy of a *Grand Monarch*.

Although hardly free from vulgar prejudice, the second illustration is
also of high aesthetic quality, for it comprises two etchings by William
Hogarth collectively entitled *The Invasion*, produced in 1756 at the
beginning of the Seven Years War. In the first, a group of French soldiers

gathers outside an inn on the French coast, waiting to embark for the eponymous attack on England. Hogarth presses all the semiotic buttons: the sign outside the inn bears the legend 'Soupe Meagre a la Sabot Royale', the latter being a wooden shoe, a traditional symbol of poverty; the emaciated soldiers are roasting frogs on a spit over an open fire, carrying a banner labelled 'Vengeance et le Bon Bier et Bon Boeuf de Angleterre'; getting ready to accompany them is a tonsured friar, fingering an axe and gloating over all the tools of his trade – an idolatrous statue, a wheel on which to break heretics, a selection of torture instruments, and a plan for the (re)construction of a monastery at Blackfriars in London; in the background, women plough the fields as their conscripted menfolk are driven on to the invasion fleet at the points of bayonets.

Meanwhile on the other side of the Channel, as the second etching reveals, a group of English patriots assemble outside an inn named 'The Duke of Cumberland' after the younger son of George II, the victor over the Jacobites at Culloden in 1746 and immortalized in music by Handel's 'See the conquering hero come'. The sign also proclaims that here beef is served every day, roast and boiled, a dietary difference emphasized by the brawny physique of the English, contrasting so sharply with the emaciation of their French enemies in the first print. An attractive serving-girl makes the point by admiringly measuring the broad shoulders of an English fusilier. The sexual innuendo is made more explicit by another girl who suggestively fingers a knife positioned in such a way that it appears to protrude from a reclining sailor's groin. Together they are all deriding a caricature of Louis XV, who holds a gallows and from whose mouth comes the message: 'You take a my fine Ships, you be de Pirate, you be de Teef, me send my grand Armies and hang you all, Marblu'. Nor is music neglected: on the table can be seen a song-sheet carrying the chorus of 'Rule, Britannia', while another fusilier is piping the melody of 'God Spare Great George, Our King'. The contrast with the reluctant French conscripts is made by depicting a youth standing on tiptoe to reach the minimum height required for military service, while in the background a platoon of volunteers is being drilled.

If the French or Celtic other helped to intensify English nationalism, the triumphalism of English nationalism helped in turn to inspire counter-nationalisms. In Ireland, the growing prosperity and cultural achievements of the eighteenth century encouraged Protestants to become increasingly restive about what they saw as the condescending exploitation of London. As the generations passed, metropolitan loyalties made way for a sense of Irish identity. It even found dietary expression: a pamphlet of 1762 told the new Lord Lieutenant, Lord Halifax: 'Of this be assured, that now we are thoroughly naturalised we are as warmly attached and bigotted to this little island as the best of yourselves are to old England . . . our bilberries and our potatoes are in our mouths as delicious and high-flavoured as the best grapes and melons in the mouth of an Italian or Frenchman nor should we endure the man who would propose an exchange.' Growing confidence in the future, given concrete (and still extant) form in the shape of urban mansions and country estates, began to grate against the colonial attitude of their masters, who continued to reserve all the plum jobs in Church, administration and army for the English and to charge pensions for English parasites to the Irish establishment. At the end of the eighteenth century, for example, fully a quarter of 'Irish' peers had no connection with the island. As Thomas Bartlett has argued, it was this corrosive conviction that their country was being plundered by English carpet-baggers that fuelled Irish Protestant nationalism. It was intensified by the knowledge that the English looked down their noses at 'Bogg-Land' or 'Teague-Land'. Although the third Earl of Mornington (later Marquess Wellesley and brother of the first Duke of Wellington) had been born in County Meath and knew Ireland well, he could still write to his friend Lord Grenville in July 1790, when travelling through the Low Countries: 'The greatest part of the *pays de Liège* is a dreary, dismal country, something like the best parts of Ireland.'

The lows (the rebellion of 1641) and the highs (the deliverance of 1689–90) of the seventeenth century convinced the Irish Protestants that God had chosen them for special favour. They saw themselves as not one nation of Ireland but as *the* nation, for the Catholics appeared to have been consigned permanently to the rubbish-tip of history. Yet beneath the placid crust of the Protestant Ascendancy, the molten streams of native nationalism still bubbled. As illiteracy in the Irish-speaking population – still at least 50 per cent of the total in 1800 – was the norm and the public sphere was confined to the predominantly Protestant towns, to look to the usual conduits of nationalist feeling such as periodicals and pamphlets is to invite certain disappointment. To detect the continuing ground-swell of submerged hatred of past wrongs and hopes of future vengeance, it is the oral tradition of national-ist ballads and epics that need to be examined, for 'if a man were permitted to make all the ballads, he need not care who should make the laws of a nation', as the Scottish patriot Andrew Fletcher of Saltoun (1653?–1716) put it. That this is not an impossible undertaking has been shown by Vincent Morley, who has demonstrated just how ubiquitous and popular was the long historical poem variously entitled '*Tuireamh na hÉireann*' ('Ireland's Dirge') or '*Aiste Sheáin Uí Chonaill*' ('Seán Ó Conaill's Composition'), first composed in Kerry in the middle of the seventeenth century. This offered all the essential elements of a fully fledged nationalism: a foundation myth (the migration of the Milesians to Ireland from Spain), a mythical hero (Fionn mac Cumhail and his warrior band, the Fianna), special assistance from God (the arrival of St Patrick), cultural achievement (the monasteries), an alibi for failure in the face of foreign invasion ('the betrayer Dermod' was just the first of many), and – above all – a gnawing sense of grievance at foreign oppression (Henry VIII, Elizabeth I, Cromwell, etc.). By the end of this period, the discourse promoted by 'Ireland's Dirge' was beginning to move out of the taverns and fairs of the rural world into the urban public sphere and off the manuscript copies into the printed periodicals. The *Irish Magazine* of 1810, for example, which enjoyed the biggest circulation on the island, fulminated: 'the history of the Universe con-tains nothing more atrocious than the persecutions of the Irish by the English; nothing more repugnant to civilisation; nothing more base or more flagitious; nothing more blasphemous or more profane; bidding a bold defiance to every attribute by which the Creator has distinguished the human species from the ravening beasts of prey.' As Morley con-cludes, the Irish nationalism of the nineteenth century had a long past.

In the short and medium term, the British state could face down Irish nationalism, no matter where it came from. Indeed, the growing assertiveness of the Catholics made it easier to control the Protestants. In 1798 'probably the most concentrated episode of violence in Irish history' (Roy Foster) erupted, resulting in the death of perhaps 30,000 people. Even before the insurgents were routed at Vinegar Hill on 21 June, less than a month after the rebellion began, contemporaries were talking about the conflict as one between Catholics and Protestants. As Lord Castlereagh observed: 'the religious complexities of the Rebellions in the South gradually separated the Protestants from the

Treason, and precisely in the same degree, appeared to embark the Catholics in it'. In short, competing versions of colonial nationalism could make the task of the metropolitan power much easier.

This was also the case in the Habsburg Monarchy, where the multiplicity of ethnic groups offered correspondingly greater opportunities for a policy of divide and rule. When Leopold II came to the throne in February 1790 he needed all the help he could get, for – as we have seen earlier in this chapter – his late brother Joseph II's abrasive reform programme had brought Hungary in particular to the brink of revolt. In persuading the insurgents to pull back from the brink, Leopold made effective use of the nationalist card, reminding the most volatile ethnic group – the Magyar gentry – that they were not alone in the kingdom. On the one hand he offered a carrot in the shape of concessions, on the other he brandished the stick of military coercion. The Magyar-speaking garrison in Budapest was replaced by Croatian units, whose fierce loyalty to the Habsburgs was combined with an equally intense dislike of the Magyars. The Serbs of the Bánát region of southern Hungary were encouraged to hold an 'Illyrian National Congress' at Temesvár between August and September 1790, which then demanded autonomy from the Magyar-run Parliament at Budapest. Simultaneously, government agents circulated petitions among townspeople and peasants protesting against the Magyar concept of an all-noble nation. The Magyar gentry were intimidated further by carefully nurtured rumours that the secret police knew the names of the main conspirators and were preparing to make an example of them. Together with the change in the international situation discussed above, this dexterous campaign had the desired result when the Budapest Parliament agreed that Leopold should be crowned King of Hungary at Pressburg without any new restrictions on his authority. In a ceremonial act of semiotic reconciliation, in November 1790 Leopold and several other Habsburgs travelled to the coronation dressed in Hungarian national costume.

In the other major Habsburg kingdom – Bohemia – a rather different scenario unfolded. There the Czech language had been very much under a cloud since the Catholic victory at the battle of the White Mountain in 1620. With *anything* written in Czech automatically suspected of heresy, the dominant languages for academic and administrative purposes were Latin and German respectively. The initiative for a Czech revival came from above. As part of the campaign to maximize human resources, Czech was made an official language of instruction at the Vienna Military Academy in 1752, the Vienna Polytechnic in 1754 and Vienna University in 1775, the same year that a chair for Czech language and literature was established there. More school textbooks in Czech were published during the reign of Joseph II than during the preceding 150 years. Back in Prague it was the nobles who took the lead in rediscovering their ethnic identity. One of the greatest of the Bohemian magnates, Count František Kinský, wrote a defence of the Czech language in 1773, observing that, 'as a good descendant of Slavs, I have inherited the prejudice that if the mother tongue of a Frenchman is French and of a German, German, then for a Czech the mother tongue must also be Czech'. However, the book itself he wrote in German. He was also co-founder of the Royal Society of Bohemia in 1784, one of a number of voluntary associations established by nobles, including the Patriotic-Economic Society of the Czech Kingdom (1788), the Society of Patriotic Friends of Art (1796), the Academy of Fine Arts (1799) and the Prague Musical Conservatory (1811). These aristocrats had no problem in combining loyalty to the Habsburg Monarchy with a sense of Bohemian patriotism, for they identified with the Bohemian homeland (*česka vlast*) not the Czech nation (*český národ*). This union was exemplified in 1783 by the theatre built in Prague by Count Nostitz, which he called the 'Counts' National Theatre' (*Gräfliches Nationaltheater*) and put 'To the Fatherland and the Muses' (*Patriae et Musis*) over the portico. By the very end of this period, however, there were signs that this balancing act was becoming more difficult as a more assertively Czech non-noble intelligentsia began to form. In 1818 Count Kollowrat, a Bohemian aristocrat of the old school, published a manifesto announcing the creation of a 'Patriotic Museum' (*Vaterländisches Museum*), written in German. Ten days later a Czech translation was published by Josef Jungmann, which described it as a 'National Czech Museum' (*Národní české museum*) and which added that its aim was the preservation of the Czech language and the Czech nation. Many years were to pass before the influx of Czech-speaking peasants into Prague and the other Bohemian cities would create an aggressively Czech national movement, but the signs were there by 1815.

As these examples show, the undeniable power of nationalism did not necessarily point towards instability. It had to be managed, but it could be managed. As the nation developed as an alternative focus of identity, loyalty and commitment, the existing regime had to reposition itself to keep up. What was needed was a grand gesture calculated to appeal to those groups for whom nationalism was proving increasingly attractive, which in this period meant the literate middle classes. The transformation by Joseph II of his court theatre into a 'national theatre' in 1776 ensured him a good press with the German intelligentsia: 'The Germans now have a national theatre, and it is their Emperor who has founded it. What a delightful, what a magnificent thought for everyone capable of feeling that he is a German! Everyone thanks the Emperor with a feeling of the deepest reverence for the great example he has given to the German princes', enthused a periodical devoted to the theatre. His example was indeed followed, most famously by Frederick William II of Prussia, who marked his accession to the throne in 1786 by turning the 'French Comedy House' on the Gendarmenmarkt in Berlin into a 'National Theatre'.

In those countries where there was a constitution associated with national identity, the ruler had to be particularly careful how he trod. It was the attempt to don rough-shod boots that brought Joseph II to grief in Belgium and Hungary. In England, the first two Hanoverians suffered from their very obvious German nationality and ignorance of English conditions – George I, it would appear, did not even understand the ranks of the peerage. They were saved more by what they were not – Catholic Stuarts tied to the apron-strings of the King of France – than by what they did. At least they had the good sense not to tamper with Parliament, the central symbol of English national identity. Any historian who insists that nationalism is a nineteenth-century phenomenon would do well to ponder the following extract from a sermon preached to the House of Commons on 22 December 1641 on the occasion of a special fast prompted by the Irish rebellion:

You that are the representative Body of this Nation . . . You are the Nation representatively . . . you stand in the place of the whole Nation; and if you stand for God's cause, the whole Nation doth it in you. As this is a *Nationall day*, and this Honourable Assembly a *Nationall Assembly*, so this Text is a *Nationall Text*, suitable for the occasion about which we are met, National Repentance will divert Nationall judgments and procure Nationall blessings.

A grateful Commons gave the preacher a massive alms dish bearing his arms and the inscription, 'This is the Gift of the House of Commons to Edmund Calamy, B.D., 1641'. When printed, his sermon, entitled *England's Looking-Glasse*, proved very popular, quickly going through five editions. In this respect nothing changed over the next century-and-a-half. After spending six years in England in the 1770s, Johann Wilhelm von Archenholz concluded that what might seem to some to be the excessive national pride of the English was political in origin: 'The national pride of the English is a natural consequence of a political constitution, by which every citizen is exempted from any other dependence than that imposed by the laws. This pride is carried among them to a great length. Indeed, how is it possible to know and to feel all the merit of such a system of liberty, without attaching an uncommon value to it?' The problems experienced by George III during the early years of his reign stemmed largely from his apparent wish to extend the royal prerogative. After 1783 it was his ability to present himself and his protégé William Pitt the Younger as the defenders of the constitution against the unscrupulous Charles James Fox and his cronies that gave him such a long period of stability.

George's rehabilitation was greatly assisted by the diplomatic triumph in the Dutch Republic in 1787 (see below, Chapter 13) which effaced memories of defeat in the American War. Although this might seem paradoxical, it was then consummated by his brief spell of 'madness' in 1788. When he recovered in February of the following year, he experienced something of an apotheosis, as congratulatory addresses flooded in from all over the country in 'the most brilliant, as well as the most universal exhibition of national loyalty and joy ever witnessed in England', as Nathaniel Wraxall put it. The following extract from the address signed by nearly a thousand of 'the Gentlemen, Clergy, Freeholders, Citizens and Principal Inhabitants of the City of Durham, and its Environs' sums up so well the nature of English nationalism and its sense of identity with King (and God) that it deserves to be quoted at length:

Most Gracious and Potent Monarch,

Great Britain, the Queen of the Isles and Pride of Nations, Arbitress of Europe, perhaps of the World; the Nursery of the Arts, Freedom and Independence; the Terror of her Enemies, and Scourge of Tyrants, is once more raised from a depending, humbled Situation to its present glorious and resplendent Acme of Power, Opulence and Grandeur, by a Descendant of the great and illustrious

Chatham, and his responsible Coadjutors in Administration, under the immediate Direction, benign and spirited Auspices of our most gracious, potent and much-beloved Sovereign, for whose happy Restoration to the inestimable Blessings of Health, Domestic Felicity, and for the Political Salvation and Comfort of these Realms, the humble and grateful Adorations to the Omnipotent be ever due. The Vallies may now again be justly said to laugh and sing, and the Mountains to leap for Joy, praising the One Eternal for His infinite Mercies.

This was not exceptional, as the following statistic demonstrates: no fewer than 756 addresses congratulating the King on his recovery were submitted by various groups and corporations across the length and breadth of the country, or in other words more than double the number generated by the seven most controversial issues of the previous generation (the Jewish Naturalization Act of 1753; the Cider Tax Bill of 1763; the Wilkes affair of 1769; the Catholic Relief Act of 1778; the campaigns for 'Economical Reform' in 1780 and for parliamentary reform in 1783; and the campaign in support of Pitt in 1784) – *put together*.

At just the same time that the good citizens of Durham were composing this tribute, the citizens of France were compiling their lists of grievances (*cahiers de doléance*) in preparation for the meeting of the Estates General at Versailles in May. Although the monarchy itself was not yet an issue, the cleavage between king and nation was already a gulf. In the course of the previous century, an alternative source of legitimacy had developed, alongside but separate from the royal office. This was the nation. The database of the American and French Research on the Treasury of the French Language (ARTFL) shows that between 1700 and 1710 the word '*nation*' was used 45 times in 7 different volumes, that during the next decade it was used 106 times in 12 volumes and that by the 1750s the total had increased to 990 times in 43 volumes and was sustained at that level subsequently. Moreover, the nation had found an institutional base in the Parlements. When Louis XIV sought papal assistance in dealing with the Jansenists, he also created a gap between monarchy and national interest into which the Parlements promptly thrust themselves. By continuing the anti-Jansenist policies, Louis' successors allowed the interlopers to take up permanent residence. By the middle of the eighteenth century, the Parlements were claiming to be the '*tribunal de la nation*', the '*conseil de la nation*', the '*dépôt national*' and '*le temple inviolable des lois nationales*'. In effect, they were advancing the principle of national sovereignty, as for example when the Parlement of Rennes told Louis XV that 'it is the consent of the nation that your Parlement represents and which gives support [*complément*] to the law'. By the end of the reign, during the crisis that followed Chancellor Maupeou's attempt to destroy the political influence of the Parlements, contemporaries were stating bluntly with the comte de Laurangais that, 'It is the nation which is sovereign. It is so by its power, and by the nature of things.' Unfortunately for the Parlements, they were not national enough, revealing their fundamental attachment to the old order by their insistence in 1788 that the Estates General due to meet the next year should be organized in three separate Estates (clergy, nobility, commoners) rather than as one national assembly. As the Parisian lawyer Jacques Godard observed: 'there are now in Paris and in the whole of the Kingdom the names of three parties: that of the royalists, that of the *parlementaires*, and that of the nationals'.

It did not have to be this way. Louis XV's advisers did not have to continue the anti-Jansenist policies. They did not have to return to Versailles from Paris in 1723, keeping the King isolated from the rapidly expanding public sphere of the capital. They did not have to agree to the *renversement des alliances* of 1756, which most French people believed was contrary to the national interest – a belief that was strengthened by the military disasters that followed. Louis XV did not have to behave like a self-indulgent voluptuary, without a care for his public image. Nor did he have to acquire the reputation of being an irresponsible despot by his clumsy attempts to stifle opposition. He did not have to marry his grandson and heir to the Archduchess Marie Antoinette, thus ensuring that the unpopularity of the Austrian alliance would continue to blight the next reign as well. For his part, Louis XVI did not have to lock himself away at Versailles and the other palaces, giving the impression that he was interested only in hunting. When what proved to be the final crisis struck at the end of the 1780s, Louis did not have to relapse into a state of torpor, passively awaiting the end. When the Parisian crowd came to Versailles on 5 October 1789, they found the royal family and the court living in an ossified cultural world from which the spirit had long since departed. It was a museum *avant la lettre*. Of all the monarchy's mistakes, it was this failure to adapt to the growing strength of the nation that was the most fatal. Louis XIV might well have said '*L'état, c'est moi*', but Louis XVI could not say '*La nation, c'est moi*'. That was left to the deputies of the Third Estate of the Estates General, supported by clerical and noble renegades, who declared themselves to be the 'National Assembly' on 17 June 1789.

PEOPLE

The 'people' formed the third part of the troika that pulled the political chariot of the late eighteenth century. In one form or another, it had been part of European political discourse since the very beginning. The task of assessing the concept's importance is made difficult by contours which are blurred to the point of insubstantiality. This is revealed by the problems of translating it satisfactorily. While a dictionary lists '*Nation*' or '*Volk*' as German equivalents for the French word '*peuple*', it only offers '*people*' in English. On the other hand, both '*Volk*' and '*Leute*' can be translated as '*people*' in English but in French '*Leute*' is translated as '*gens, monde, public*' but not as '*peuple*'. Similar uncertainties are to be found in the other European languages. One possible way forward is not to seek what the people were but what they were not, and what they most obviously were not was part of the political establishment. In what follows, the people and their adjective 'popular' will be applied to movements or events that were spontaneous, autonomous and free from direction or control by the regular authorities.

For that reason alone they were regarded with suspicion if not outright hostility by those who recorded their activities. So rudimentary were the police forces, if they existed at all, and so fragile was the social fabric, that fear of violent disorder was shared by almost anyone with anything to lose. So the preferred words to designate ordinary people were not neutral like '*peuple*', '*Volk*' or '*people*' but pejorative like '*foule*', '*Pöbel*' and '*mob*' (defined by Henry Fielding in *Tom Jones* as 'Persons without Virtue, or Sense, in all Stations'). At the top end, the elitism of educated Europeans was well put by Frederick the Great in a famous letter to d'Alembert in 1770. He asked the latter to imagine a state with a population of ten million, from which one would have to exclude at once all peasants, labourers, artisans and soldiers, leaving around 50,000 of both sexes. Once all the women had been excluded, together with all stupid and unimaginative males, one would be left with, at best, around a thousand people capable of intellectual activity – and even among this tiny group there would be marked differences of ability. So, he concluded, there was just no point in trying to educate mankind [*sic*], indeed it would be positively dangerous. All one could safely do was to content oneself with being wise, taking good care to keep the mob under control but abandoning them to their ignorance and stupidity.

Even by the standards of crowned heads, Frederick was unusually snobbish, but his contempt for the unlettered masses was shared by the intelligentsia. As we shall see, Johann Gottfried Herder had great respect for the '*Volk*', but he viewed with disdain 'the rabble of the streets which never sings or creates, but roars and mutilates'. Moses Mendelssohn thought that words like 'Enlightenment' and 'culture' could never form part of the plebeian vocabulary, for 'the mob scarcely understands them'. The French thinkers, or '*philosophes*', were no less elitist. The radical d'Holbach, sometimes described as a 'democrat', made a sharp distinction between property-owning citizens and 'the imbecilic mass of the population which because it is devoid of all enlightenment and good sense can at any moment become the instrument and the accomplice of restless demagogues seeking to disrupt society', and concluded, 'let us never change that inequality that has always been so necessary'.

Even a small sample of the intermittent attempts by 'the blind and noisy multitude' to participate in the political process appears to lend support to this dismissive attitude. Just as our period began, in 1647–8 revolts in Palermo and Naples succeeded in wresting power for a few months from the Spanish viceroys before collapsing in confusion, bloodshed, anarchy and recrimination. In Palermo it was the common people themselves who co-operated with the Inquisitor Trasmiera to carry out a counter-coup, which included the bestially brutal murder of the revolution's 'captain-general' Giovanni d'Alesi and twelve associates. Yet no sooner had they decapitated their movement than they lurched back into violent attacks on the government and the nobility. Divisions within the insurgency, coupled with the traditional hostility between Palermo and Messina, eventually allowed the Spanish government to claw back control, together with all the concessions made along the way. The same sort of self-defeating incoherence was apparent in Naples, where the insurrection was led by the fisherman 'Masaniello' (Tommaso Aniello), first made captain-general by his followers and then beheaded by them. Quickly, albeit posthumously, rehabilitated, his body was exhumed, reunited with his severed head and given a funeral fit for a hero. Like another charismatic leader who soared before plummeting, Cola Rienzi, Masaniello became the subject of a nineteenth-century opera – *La Muette de Portici* with music by Daniel Auber and a libretto by Eugène Scribe. It was an opera moreover that itself sparked off a revolution, for its performance at the Théatre de la Monnaie in Brussels on 25 August 1830 is usually given credit for starting the insurrection that led to the establishment of an independent Belgian state as well as marking the beginning of a new genre – French Grand Opera.

A revolution that ends up being presented as an opera, especially one whose improbable heroine is a deaf-mute, is perhaps difficult to take seriously. Yet, as Helmut Koenigsberger and Peter Burke have shown, there is more than meets the eye to the events in Palermo and Naples. In Palermo the forty-nine new laws – *capitoli* – agreed between d'Alesi's brother and the viceroy indicated that a wide cross-section of the population had been involved. If the abolition of unpopular taxes and the granting of an amnesty were designed to placate the rank-and-file, the proposals to involve the guilds in the administration and to reform legal procedures indicated a longer-term plan for the city's future. In Naples what may have seemed to be mindless violence, not least to Masaniello as he faced his assassins, turns out to have been carefully choreographed rituals of legitimation, which expressed the cohesion of the community at the same time as it created it.

Denied the anthropological insights that have allowed this interpretation of popular revolts, contemporaries were less generous. When the *demos* took charge, law and order inevitably collapsed, or so they concluded. No wonder that 'as it entered the eighteenth century, democracy was still very much a pariah word' (John Dunn). For much of the century there was little or no reason for this attitude to change. As we have seen, the population of most European countries began a sustained increase in the second quarter of the eighteenth century, putting growing pressure on relatively inelastic grain supplies. The result was a wave of bread riots whenever a poor harvest drove prices beyond the average. These usually took the form of '*taxation populaire*', as consumers sought to force bakers to sell bread at a 'fair' price. The rioters were not seeking to loot, rather they had a clear notion of what was right and what was wrong about the way in which grain was stored, milled, baked and marketed. In short, they imposed a 'moral economy' (Edward Thompson).

This instinctive sense of injustice was also lent biblical support: 'He that withholdeth Corn, the People shall curse him: but Blessing shall be upon the Head of him that selleth it' (Proverbs 11:26). They became especially angry when they suspected that grain was being hoarded by unscrupulous producers or merchants waiting for a further rise in prices, or when they saw grain being moved out of their district.

Once the popular genie was out of the bottle, of course, the way was open for it to be sent this way and that by malcontents with more ambitious agendas. A good example was the riots which erupted in Madrid in the spring of 1766, this always being a particularly tense time of the year because the previous harvest was running out but the next had not yet been reaped. In 1765 Charles III's reforming government had relaxed traditional restrictions on the domestic grain trade, in the hope of promoting greater productivity. Unfortunately, it coincided with a poor harvest, so when prices began to climb early the following year, there was a scapegoat conveniently close at hand. The rioting began in Madrid on 23 March, launched by 'a monstrous crowd of the lowest classes . . . a low contemptible people, without permanent residence and altogether abandoned and worthless', as one alarmed observer noted. From there it spread out into the rest of Castile, eventually involving some seventy communities. The forms of protest were traditional: the opening of granaries, the imposition of a just price, the sacking of officials deemed to be corrupt, the election of replacements, and so on, although often purely local issues were also involved. Although these aspects were also apparent in Madrid, other fish were being fried too. Behind the bread riots and the simultaneous agitation against a decree banning the traditional wide-brimmed hat and long cloaks (a public order measure), there appears to have been a conspiracy organized by nobles, clergy and perhaps even the French ambassador too against the Sicilian first minister Esquilache. Although Charles III was frightened enough to flee to Aranjuez, the rioters achieved nothing apart from the departure of Esquilache to Venice, where he served as Spanish ambassador until his death in 1785. Even the hat-and-cloak combination was gradually abandoned, after being cunningly presented by Esquilache's successor, Aranda, as the sort of dress worn by executioners.

The Madrid riots exemplified the problem of popular riots. However elaborate their rituals of legitimation may have been, in practice they proved to be short-term in their objectives and short-winded in their implementation. Sooner or later the authorities regained control. That was also demonstrated by the most extensive and violent riots in pre-revolutionary France, the 'flour war' (*guerre des farines*) of 1775. As in Spain, they were preceded by the coincidence of an attempt to liberalize the grain trade with a poor harvest. By March 1775, the price of a four-pound (1.5-kg) loaf had increased from its normal average of eight or nine *sous* to eleven-and-a-half and then went on rising to thirteen-and-a-half by the end of April. At first concentrated on the region around Paris, the unrest then spread from market to market across northern France, attracting support mainly from the urban poor and those peasants whose plots were not large enough for self-subsistence (the majority). Much violence was directed against the usual targets – the better-off peasants, grain merchants, millers and bakers, in other words anyone suspected of driving up prices by hoarding stocks. Although the Île de France and four adjacent provinces were briefly out of control, the government responded vigorously, not to say brutally, sending in the army with orders to fire on those who failed to disperse. By the end of May 1775 it was all over. Louis XVI gave the following rather complacent account in a letter to the King of Sweden, Gustavus III:

The bad harvest and the wicked intentions of a few people . . . led some scoundrels to come and pillage the markets. The peasants, led on by them and by the false report – sedulously circulated – that the price of bread had been lowered, joined them and they had the insolence to pillage the markets of Versailles and Paris, which forced me to order in troops who restored perfect order without difficulty. After the extreme displeasure I felt at seeing what the people had done, I had the consolation of seeing that as soon as they had been undeceived, they restored what they had taken and were truly sorry for what they had done.

For the time being, Louis XVI could relax, confident in the knowledge that his armed forces were loyal, that the insurrectionaries were easily cowed and – above all – that this subsistence crisis had not coincided with political upheaval. Fourteen years later things were to be very different.

Paris was especially volatile because it was difficult to supply with grain in a bad year, separated from the sea by the long and sinuous Seine. London was quite different, being the greatest seaport in the world and so easily supplied. Moreover, its vast, sprawling suburbs served as a buffer against infection by rural disorder. For those reasons, there were no bread riots there during the eighteenth century, although there were plenty in the provinces: nearly two-thirds of the 275 disturbances between 1735 and 1800 charted by George Rudé. In the capital there were certainly periodic eruptions of popular violence, but they were usually directed against government policy. In 1733, for example, there were noisy demonstrations against the new excise scheme currently making its way through Parliament, including the burning of the prime minister Sir Robert Walpole in effigy. The targets of the London rioters were often national or religious minorities. Attempts to allow the naturalization of Jews in 1751 and again two years later, for example, provoked waves of popular anti-Semitism. The most destructive episode of the entire century was the 'Gordon Riots' of 1780, directed against the Catholic Relief Act. Although they lasted only a week, they caused £100,000 worth of damage and destroyed *ten times* more property than was destroyed in Paris during the entire French Revolution. On the night of 7 June a horrified Horace Walpole counted thirty-six fires raging on both sides of the Thames. When eventually the authorities pulled themselves together, they met violence with violence: 285 rioters were shot dead in the street or died of their wounds, 450 were arrested and 25 were hanged.

The Gordon Riots were led by Lord George Gordon, Old Etonian son of the Duke of Gordon. That an aristocrat should lead a mob of plebeians to inflict a 'time of terrour' (Dr Johnson) producing a 'Metropolis in flames, and a Nation in Ruins' (William Cowper) was viewed with grim satisfaction by those who believed that the future of British politics lay with the middle classes. Their attitude had been articulated most eloquently by William Beckford (1709–70), who as an immensely rich sugar-planter, slave-owner, merchant, financier, alderman of the City of London, Member of Parliament and country gentleman can be said to have personified the interests of his class. In a speech to the House of Commons in November 1761 he defined what he called 'the sense of the people':

I don't mean the mob; neither the top nor the bottom, the scum is perhaps as mean as the dregs, and as to your nobility, about 1200 men of quality, what are they to the body of the nation? . . . When I talk of the sense of the people I mean the middling people of England, the manufacturer, the yeoman, the merchant, the country gentleman, they who bear all the heat of the day . . . They have a right, Sir, to interfere in the condition and conduct of the nation which makes them easy or uneasy who feel most of it, and, Sir, the people of England, taken in this limitation are a good-natured, well-intentioned and very sensible people who know better perhaps than any other nation under the sun whether they are well governed or not.

As his own wealth demonstrated, Beckford was speaking at a time of unprecedented opportunities for middle-class men of talent, enterprise and capital. Yet when the period covered by this volume ended fifty-four years later, the scum were still in command and the dregs were just as difficult as they had ever been. What had gone wrong? One clue was provided by the agitation centred on John Wilkes, which was just getting underway at the time of Beckford's speech. Wilkes (1725–97) was a rakish MP, satirist and journalist, who in 1762 launched a vicious public attack on the Earl of Bute, chief adviser to George III, who had come to the throne just two years earlier. Among other things, Wilkes insinuated that Bute had debauched the Queen Mother to gain influence over the King. Wilkes seemed to bring together all the elements in British politics: he owed his seat in the House of Commons to his connection with the greatest magnate in Buckinghamshire, Earl Temple; he was just as at home in the middle-class public sphere through his journalism; and he also knew how to mobilize and manipulate the common people. This was how he positioned himself in his speech to the Court of Common Pleas in May 1763, when facing a charge of seditious libel:

The LIBERTY of all peers and gentlemen, and, what touches me more sensibly, of all the middling and inferior class of the people, which stands most in need of protection, is in my case this day to be finally decided upon: a question of such importance as to determine at once, whether ENGLISH LIBERTY be a reality or a shadow.

It was on this occasion that the cry 'Wilkes and Liberty!' was first heard on the streets of London. With the help of his various constituencies, Wilkes enjoyed considerable success during his decade in the political limelight – it was Earl Temple who got him released from the Tower of London on a writ of habeas corpus; it was the working-men of London who gave him his extra-parliamentary muscle, shouting slogans like 'Wilkes and the coal-heavers for ever!' as they intimidated his opponents. But it soon became apparent that he was too self-seeking (even by the standards of politicians), too irresponsible and too raffish to attract a genuinely cross-class appeal. His limitations were exposed brilliantly by Hogarth's caricature of 1763, which shows him leering out with undisguised cynicism, his wig curled to resemble the Devil's horns. Behind him can be seen two numbers of his scandal-sheet *North Briton*: number forty-five, in which he attacked the King's speech to Parliament, and number seventeen, in which he attacked Hogarth. This was more than an act of personal revenge on Hogarth's part, for in his diabolic presentation of Wilkes and his cap of liberty he struck a responsive chord with many. For his part, Wilkes soon nestled back inside the establishment, becoming Lord Mayor of London in 1774 and playing a leading role in the suppression of the Gordon Riots in 1780. It was a reconciliation celebrated in a famous caricature of the day entitled *The New Coalition*, in which George III embraces Wilkes, saying: 'Sure! the worthiest of Subjects & most virtuous of men', to which Wilkes replies: 'I now find that you are the best of Princes.' As he himself once said contemptuously of a supporter: 'he was a Wilkite, I never was', confessing that he had been 'a patriot by accident'.

Popular support did help Wilkes to register two lasting achievements: the judicial decision that general warrants were unlawful, and de facto permission to report the proceedings of Parliament in the press. More generally, he demonstrated how a skilful politician could make use of the public sphere. A poor public speaker, Wilkes reached his public through the written word and printed image, in pamphlets, periodicals, newspaper letters, handbills, ballads, verses and political cartoons. Showing a remarkable attention to detail, he sent a card of thanks to anyone who voted for him in his various election campaigns and kept a careful register of all who could be identified as supporters.

Out of the Wilkite agitation of the 1760s came a movement for political reform that was aimed as much at the House of Commons as at the royal prerogative. By 1770 demands were being made for annual elections, a secret ballot, a widening of the franchise to include all householders of substance, the exclusion of place-holders, the increase of county members and the abolition of rotten boroughs. The aspiring reformers had also created an organization, had learnt how to mobilize City interests and opinion and how to make use of popular agitation, and had discovered that there was support to be mustered in the provinces. What they failed to address satisfactorily was the obstinate fact that the only body which could reform Parliament constitutionally was

Parliament itself. Yet all members of Parliament were necessarily ben-eficiaries of the existing order, with a vested interest in its continuation. So what was needed was a group with an ideology or a special interest strong enough to override this fundamental inhibition.

The best candidate was the group of Whigs which came to be known after their nominal leader, the Marquis of Rockingham, for they posi-tively sought to construct an alliance with public opinion: in the words of Edmund Burke, Rockingham's secretary, 'we must strengthen the hands of the minority within doors by the accession of public opinion, strongly declared'. Burke also wrote to a journal about his associates: 'they respect public opinion; and, therefore, whenever they shall be called upon, they are ready to meet their adversaries, as soon as they please, before the tribunal of the public'. This promising way forward to real constitutional change proved to be a cul-de-sac. The exit was soon barred by the realization that the objectives of reformers inside and outside Parliament were fundamentally different. The Rockingham Whigs included in their ranks some of the biggest borough-mongers in England, including their leader and his heir, Earl Fitzwilliam. Any measures aimed at eliminating rotten boroughs and redistributing seats would have cut at the roots of their power and were correspondingly unacceptable. Nor did these aristocrats feel comfortable with any kind of initiative stemming from below. As Rockingham himself put it: 'I must say that the thing which weighs most against adopting the mode of petitioning the King is, where the example was first set.' Edmund Burke's articulation of the same reservation was even more condescend-ing. He told the House of Commons: 'I cannot indeed take it upon me to say that I have the honour to *follow* the sense of the people. The truth is *I met it on my way*, while I was pursuing their interest according to my own ideas', adding in a private letter to Rockingham, 'To bring the people to a feeling, such a feeling, I mean, as tends to amendment or alteration of system, there must be plan and management. All direction of public humour and opinion must originate in a few.' For their part, the radicals outside the political establishment found the 'Economical Reform' favoured by the Rockingham Whigs so pitifully inadequate as to be almost worse than nothing. John Jebb later found the perfect simile: 'moving the People of England to carry so small a Reform would be tempesting the Ocean to drown a fly'. Yet Jebb and his friends could never mobilize enough middle-class opinion even to start to look like an irresistible force. For many it was the Gordon Riots that advertised the dangers of letting the beast out of its cage. One Londoner, J. Brasbridge, recalled: 'From that moment, trusting to the evidence of my own senses, I became a convert to loyalty and social order. I shut my ears against the voice of popular clamour, & have, I trust, ever since maintained the character of a true love of my king, and a well-wisher to my country.' As we shall see later in this chapter, the outbreak of the French Revolution delivered the *coup de grâce* to parliamentary reform and popular politics.

Although the progress of the people towards democracy was fitful even in such a relatively commercialized country as Great Britain, where universal adult suffrage was not achieved until the twentieth century, across Europe there was a discernible increase in the popular element in politics. This can be traced through the politicization of the public sphere. As the number of public spaces proliferated during this period, so did opportunities for the exchange of information, ideas and criticism. An exemplar was the coffee-house. Within fifty years of the founding of the first in Europe – in Venice in 1645 – it had spread across the continent, reaching London in the early 1650s. By 1659 Samuel Pepys could record that he had been to the Turk's Head coffee-house in New Palace Yard, close to Parliament, and had heard 'exceeding good argument against Mr Harrington's assertion that overbalance of propriety [property] was the foundation of government'. For the price of a cup of coffee (although many other beverages were on offer), anyone decently dressed could join in debating the issues of the day. The newly restored Charles II took a dim view of the freedom of expression that prevailed there; according to Clarendon he

complained very much of the License that was assumed in the Coffee-houses, which were the Places where the boldest Calumnies and Scandals were raised, and discoursed amongst a People who knew not each other, and came together only for that Communication, and from thence were propagated over the kingdom; and mentioned some particular Rumours which had been lately dispersed from the Fountains.

An attempt to close these resorts of 'Idle and disaffected persons' at the end of 1675 ended in fiasco when it had to be abandoned in the face of fierce opposition. As Andrew Marvell observed in a poem entitled 'A Dialogue between Two Horses' with more wisdom than command of rhyme:

When they take from the people the freedom of words,
They teach them the sooner to fall to their swords.
Let the City drink coffee and quietly groan;
They that conquer'd the father won't be slaves to the son.

By that time coffee-houses had spread so far so fast across the country as to have become 'a British institution' (Markman Ellis). In 1739 there were 551 in London alone.

Coffee-houses were first opened in Hamburg in 1671, Paris in 1674, Vienna in 1683, Regensburg and Nuremberg in 1686, Frankfurt am Main in 1689, Würzburg in 1697 and Berlin in 1721. The first Viennese coffee-house was opened by a Pole called Koltschitzky, who had served as an Austrian spy during the Turkish siege and was given the concession as a reward by a grateful government. There too discussion of current affairs was the norm. In 1706 a French visitor reported that 'there is an incredible degree of liberty in these places, where not only generals and ministers but even the emperor are torn to shreds'. Things had not changed a generation later, when an observer found 'every kind of discussion of current affairs and loud-mouths sounding forth about the actions and plans of great sovereigns and a thousand-and-one other bits of political business'. Attempts by the city government to control them could not prevent their continuing proliferation: there were forty-eight in Vienna by 1770, sixty-four in 1784 and over eighty by 1790. By that time Johann Pezzl could write that 'as everyone knows, coffee-houses are now one of the most indispensable necessities of every large town'.

The coffee-houses were important centres of recreation, with card-games, chess and billiards being played, often for money. Also very popular in bringing in customers was the supply of newspapers and periodicals. César de Saussure reported from London in 1727: 'What attracts enormously in these coffee-houses are the gazettes and other public papers. All Englishmen are great newsmongers. Workmen habitually begin the day by going to coffee-rooms in order to read the latest news ... Nothing is more entertaining than hearing men of this class discussing politics and topics of interest concerning royalty.' Both the social mix and the propensity for political argument greatly impressed foreign visitors to London. Fleeing France from a *lettre de cachet*, a suitably impressed Abbé Prévost reported in 1729:

I have had pointed out to me in several coffee-houses, a couple of lords, a baronet, a shoemaker, a tailor, a wine-merchant and some others of the same sort, all sitting round the same table and discussing familiarly the news of the court and the town. The government's affairs are as much the concern of the people as of the great. Every man has the right to discuss them freely. Men condemn, approve, revile, rail with bitter invectives both in speech and in writing without the authorities daring to intervene. The King himself is not secure from censure. The coffee-houses and other public places are the seats of English liberty. For two pence you have the right to read all the papers for and against the government and to take a cup of tea or coffee as well.

If the public sphere in England was precociously political, it was not unique. A German writer in 1745 likened the coffee-house to a 'political stock-exchange' where bold spirits and sharp minds from all classes came together to swap information, opinions and judgements. An anonymous account of conditions in Vienna in 1780 revealed that just about everything was discussed in the coffee-houses there, often simultaneously: affairs public and private, high finance, literature, commerce, law suits, academic matters and the fine arts.

The coffee-house was only one kind of social space that reached its first flowering in the eighteenth century. Also important were the various forms of reading clubs discussed below in Chapter 10; voluntary associations such as literary and musical societies; and Masonic lodges. Modern Freemasonry was the creation of the eighteenth century, dating from the founding of the Grand Lodge of England in London in 1717. From there it spread with amazing speed until, by the late eighteenth century, there was no town in Europe of any importance without at least one lodge. In England by the end of the century there were more than 500 lodges, 140 of which were in London, figures which include only those affiliated to the Grand Lodge, so the real total was appreciably higher. In France there were more than 700 lodges by 1789, including about 70 in Paris, with a total membership of at least 50,000, representing perhaps as much as 5 per cent of the urban adult male population.

From this welter of activity in the public sphere, there came a new source of legitimation: public opinion. Its novelty, however, was more a question of scale than kind. The need to attract the approval of the public had been long recognized in England. Writing about the troubled middle decades of the seventeenth century, Kevin Sharpe has observed that, while it had long been a cultural arbiter, now the verdict of the public was sought in politics too and 'such a recognition in turn not only validated the politics of party, it also created a public sphere of news, squib, and coffee-house, a space in which the audience joined in all the action'. In his *Essay Concerning Human Understanding* (1690), John Locke discussed three kinds of law: divine, civil and 'the law of opinion or reputation', that is to say the 'approbation or dislike, praise or blame, which by a secret and tacit consent establishes itself in the several societies, tribes, and clubs of men in the world'.

On the continent, despite an early nod from Pascal, who referred to 'public opinion which, as the proverb goes, is the queen of the world', it took much longer to establish itself. In 1750 Rousseau was still referring to it as immutable collective prejudice, as in: 'neither reason nor virtue nor the laws will subjugate public opinion, so long as one has not discovered the art of changing it'. By 1770 something of a breakthrough had occurred, for in that same year Raynal opined that 'in a nation that thinks and talks, public opinion is the rule of government', and Marsais posed the rhetorical question: 'is not public opinion stronger than fear of the law or even religion?' In 1775 Malesherbes used his maiden address to the *Académie française* to proclaim the coming-of-age of public opinion: 'A tribunal has arisen independent of all powers and that all powers respect, that appreciates all talents, that pronounces on all people of merit. And in an enlightened century, in a century in which each citizen can speak to the entire nation by way of print, those who have a talent for instructing men and a gift for moving them – in a word, men of letters – are, amidst the public dispersed, what the orators of Rome and Athens were in the middle of the public assembled.' Rousseau also changed his tune, writing in 1776: 'among the singularities which mark out the age we live in from all others, is the methodical and sustained spirit which has guided public opinions over the last twenty years'. Now the recognition of a new source of legitimation were coming thick and fast. Two examples must suffice. In 1782 the journalist Louis-Sébastien Mercier claimed: 'During the past thirty years a great and significant revolution has occurred in the way we think. Today public opinion enjoys a power in Europe which is preponderant and irresistible ... It is men of letters who deserve the credit, for in the recent past it is they who have formed public opinion in a number of very important crises. Thanks to their efforts, public opinion has exercised a decisive influence on the course of events. And it also seems that they are creating a national spirit.' By this time, this new source of legitimation had found its way into the commanding heights of government. In 1784 Jacques Necker, who had resigned as finance minister in 1782, published *On the Administration of Finances in France*, in which he proclaimed that 'the spirit of society, and the love of praise and consideration, have constructed in France a tribunal where all men who attract the attention of others are obliged to present themselves. There, public opinion, as from the heights of a throne, distributes prizes and crowns, it makes and unmakes reputations.' He clearly struck a resonant chord with the public, for his treatise proved to be one of the great best-sellers of the century, going through twenty editions during the next five years and selling 80,000 copies.

All this seems unequivocal enough, but there was a serious problem with public opinion, revealed by the two contrasting remarks made by Rousseau quoted in the previous paragraph. He was making a distinction between public opinion that is vulgar prejudice and so should be ignored, and public opinion that is legitimate and should be respected. But who was to decide what was what? One man's prejudice was another man's opinion. To paraphrase George Orwell, who observed that the best books are those that tell us what we know already, legitimate public opinion is what confirms our own opinion. Unfortunately for enlightened intellectuals, more often than not 'the people' proved to be not just unenlightened but positively reactionary, just as likely to riot against attempts to remove discrimination against Jews or Catholics as to demonstrate in favour of 'Wilkes and Liberty!' In the Habsburg Monarchy they were far more likely to turn out to greet the Pope, as more than 100,000 proved in April 1782, than to welcome the enlightened reforms Joseph II was trying to thrust down their throats. Indeed, what prompted Joseph to put the brakes on his liberalization of the public sphere towards the end of his reign was the awful realization that it was not being used to propagate enlightenment, as he had hoped, but rather to incite *conservative* resistance to his reforms. As so often before and since, it was the reactionaries who proved the more adept at exploiting the written word, not least because their arguments struck a much more responsive chord than those of their progressive opponents. The public sphere was a neutral vessel, as receptive to effusions from the right as from the left.

On the other hand, the public sphere was not a space reserved for political dissidents. Its various institutions – the Masonic lodges, for example – were positively eager to parade their loyalty. As the more intelligent European rulers realized, when properly managed it could become a powerful source of support. Frederick the Great proved to be a master of the art of public relations. Despite his conspicuous war-mongering, militarism, snobbery and contempt for German culture, his deft use of gesture politics and active personal involvement in the public sphere earned him such encomia as this from Moses Mendelssohn:

I live in a state in which one of the wisest sovereigns who ever ruled mankind has made the arts and the sciences blossom and a sensible freedom of thought so widespread that their effects have reached down to the humblest inhabitant of his dominions. Under his glorious rule I have found both opportunity and inspiration to reflect on my own destiny and that of my fellow citizens, and to present observations to the best of my ability on the fate of mankind and providence.

In a very different way and in a very different context, George III of England finally learnt how to become a politician during the crisis of the early 1780s. His reward was the seventeen years of political stability provided by William Pitt. At the other end of the scale, not the least important reason for the collapse of the French monarchy was the repeated failure of Louis XV and Louis XVI to modernize their image and re-legitimate their regime. Isolated from the public at Versailles, apparently wallowing in self-indulgent luxury, they allowed the representational culture of Louis XIV to become dysfunctional, a dying weight that eventually dragged them down to perdition. Whichever way the weathervane of public opinion was pointing, whether in a progressive or a conservative direction, regimes wishing to retain their legitimacy had to trim their sails accordingly.

In short, by the late 1780s the people had emerged as a force in European politics, albeit in a multidirectional manner. As the events about to unfold in France were so dramatic, there has been a tendency to overlook the importance of what was happening simultaneously in north America. After the Articles of Confederation of 1781 had proved unsatisfactory, a constitutional convention was convened at Philadelphia in 1787. The new constitution took effect in the summer of 1788. It began by stating unequivocally the principle of national sovereignty: 'We the People of the United States, in Order to form a more perfect

Union, establish Justice, insure domestic Tranquility, provide for the common defense, promote the general Welfare, and secure the Blessings of Liberty to ourselves and our Posterity, do ordain and establish this Constitution for the United States of America.' Article one states that, 'All legislative Powers herein granted shall be vested in a Congress of the United States, which shall consist of a Senate and House of Representatives.' In effect, what the Americans were doing was to adopt a written version of the English constitution, shorn of its objectionable features, most notably the hereditary monarch, and enhanced by certain improvements, most notably a federal structure and an independent supreme court. They had shown already that popular revolt could succeed (albeit with a little help from their friends); now they proceeded to demonstrate that a government that was both pluralist and popular could bring stability, prosperity and power.

Meanwhile, back in Europe 'the people' were being given a prestigious future of a rather different kind, mainly through the agency of Johann Gottfried Herder, who identified the *Volk* as the fundamental unit of human existence. Of all German words difficult to translate into English, *Volk* is one of the most intractable. 'People' seems the most obvious choice, but *Volk* means much more than just an aggregate of individuals (for which the German equivalent is *Leute*). It also denotes a community bound by ethnic and cultural ties, as in 'the German people', together with a populist implication, as in 'the common people'. Especially when used as part of a composite word, it can be translated as 'folk', as in 'folk-dancing' (*Volkstanz*) or 'folk-songs' (*Volkslieder*). Herder's belief in the *Volk* necessarily pushed him towards populism. True value in any nation resided not with the elite's classical culture – dismissed by Herder as a meretricious bird of paradise, being all show and no substance and never touching the ground – but with the common people, especially in the countryside, whose roots were firmly planted in native soil and history. Folk-art, folk-dancing and folk-songs were not to be despised for their roughness but treasured for their authenticity. They were the 'archives of a nationality' or 'the living voice of the nationalities, even of humanity itself' and from them 'one can learn the mode of thought of a nationality and its language of feeling'. That was not the least of Herder's achievements – to relocate cultural value. In Goethe's authoritative verdict: 'Herder taught us to think of poetry as the common property of all mankind, not as the private possession of a few refined, cultured individuals.'

THE FRENCH REVOLUTION –
PEOPLE, NATION, STATE

As we have seen, the last quarter of the eighteenth century witnessed political instability in many parts of Europe. As the century drew to a close, the old regimes of monarchs, prelates and aristocrats appeared to face an irresistible challenge from below. This ubiquity of upheaval has prompted many historians of the period to dub it 'the Age of the Democratic Revolution'. Yet closer examination reveals that the similarities were only skin-deep and rarely went beyond coincidence. The revolts were often conservative rather than democratic (as in the case of Belgium and most of the German disturbances), abortive (as in the case of Hungary or Great Britain), *coups d'état* rather than revolutions (as in the case of Sweden), or easily suppressed (as in the case of Geneva, Poland and Saxony). Only one was progressive, revolutionary and successful by its own efforts – and that was the French.

The unique force of the French Revolution stemmed from the coincidence of two crises in the late 1780s. The first was political, precipitated by bankruptcy. On 20 August 1786, the French finance minister, Calonne, had presented Louis XVI with a bleak assessment: interest payments on the accumulated debt now absorbed more than half the annual revenue, much of the following year's income had been spent, and it was becoming increasingly difficult to raise loans, even at ruinous rates of interest. The attempt which followed to escape the abyss with a radical programme of reform only made the final plunge more certain. Neither consultation nor coercion could persuade the French elites to co-operate. Now that they had the monarch in their grasp, they were determined not to release him until a fundamental change in the way in which the country was governed had been agreed. After two years of squirming, Louis XVI finally ran up the white flag on 8 August 1788, when he announced that the Estates General would meet at Versailles in the following May.

It is just possible – if unlikely – that the old regime might have kept this crisis confined to the world of high politics. What turned an aristocratic *Fronde* into a revolution was the violence generated by the social crisis which now erupted. A run of meteorological disasters in the 1780s reached a terrible climax in 1788 when the harvest failed in many parts of France. As the price of bread soared, demand for manufactured commodities collapsed, so the labouring poor were denied employment just when they needed it most. These two crises were essentially separate but of course they interacted during the winter of 1788/9. They fused in the spring and early summer, the worst time for any regime with an agrarian economy, for it was then that the grain gathered by the old harvest was giving out but new supplies had not yet reached the markets. What made matters worse in 1789 was not just the scale of the price rise but the corrosive belief that a conspiracy was afoot, a *pacte de famine* between government ministers and grain racketeers to starve the French people into submission. All over France, violence erupted as people were mobilized by a potent combination of fear of starvation and hatred of their exploiters.

There had been plenty of bread riots in the past, notably in 1775, but never before had they coincided with a political crisis at the centre. For it was just now that the Estates General at long last met at Versailles. At once they were deadlocked over the issue of whether they should sit and vote as three separate orders, which would allow the clergy (the first estate) and the nobility (the second estate) to dominate the commoners (the third estate) or whether they constituted a single body. Weeks passed in sterile wrangling until the deputies of the third estate cut the Gordian knot with three crucial decisions: on 10 June they announced that they would proceed unilaterally as if they were a single representative body and invited deputies from the other two estates to join them; on 17 June they adopted the title of 'National Assembly', and on 20 June they took the 'Tennis Court Oath' that they would not allow themselves to be dispersed until they had given France a new constitution. Now the issue was well and truly joined. In effect, what the third estate did during these ten great days in June was to proclaim the principle of national sovereignty and to claim for themselves the right to exercise it. This was the true beginning of the French Revolution.

Even Louis XVI could now grasp that the crunch had come. So he reached out for his weapon of last resort – the army – in one last desperate attempt to restore order in Paris and to return the Estates General to obedience. As so often in the past, he contrived to have the worst of both worlds. On the one hand, his decision to call up troops made the Parisian crowds that much more afraid and that much more angry. On the other, it turned out that the 17,000-odd soldiers who reached Paris by the middle of July could not be used. They could not be used because the King became convinced that they would mutiny if ordered to take action against the revolutionary crowds. By deciding he could not use the army, Louis XVI also decided to resign himself to the Revolution. As one of the most clear-sighted observers of the Revolution, Antoine Rivarol, wrote: 'the defection of the army is not one of the causes of the Revolution, it is the Revolution itself'.

Meanwhile, the revolutionaries were creating their own army. They had grasped intuitively that at the heart of any regime is a monopoly of legitimate force. This is the true significance of the storming of the Bastille on 14 July 1789. It was attacked not because it was a symbol of old regime tyranny but because it was thought to contain the ammunition needed by the Revolution's new paramilitary force – the National Guard. By subverting the old regime's army and creating its own, the French revolutionaries had succeeded where scores of insurgents had failed in the past, and were to fail again in the future. In this task they had received crucial assistance from all those inarticulate but violent French men and women who vented their fear and anger on tax collectors, châteaux-owners, grain merchants, and all the other representatives of the old regime. It was the belief that the country was out of control which frightened Louis XVI into accepting that sovereignty had passed from monarchy to nation.

His naturally feeble will had been softened further by the knowledge that what should have been the two stoutest props of the old order – the clergy and the nobility – were riddled with disaffection. It was not the rank and file of the army who first hoisted the flag of mutiny, but aristocratic officers alienated by the progressive collapse of French power and prestige since the glory days of Louis XIV. The last straw had been the failure to prevent the Prussian invasion of the Dutch Republic in the autumn of 1787, thus revealing French impotence in the most humiliating way possible. So the early leaders of the third estate were not bourgeois merchants or manufacturers but aristocratic army officers such as the marquis de Lafayette, the duc de La Rochefoucauld, the comte de Mirabeau, the comte de Lameth, or the vicomte de Noailles. In part, the French Revolution was a military putsch.

The victorious revolutionaries were now able to set about creating a new France from the bottom up. At a very early stage in their deliberations they took an axe to the most fundamental attribute of the old regime – privilege. During a very excited session of the National Assembly, which lasted for most of the night of 4–5 August 1789, one privilege after another was cast aside in the name of liberty. Seigneurial dues and jurisdiction, hunting rights, the sale of offices, tithes and all those special privileges which distinguished one man from another, one group from another, and one part of France from another, all made way for a new order based on uniformity, meritocracy and standardization. In a word, the National Assembly introduced modernization. In fact, what was decided at Versailles was less important than what was actually done by ordinary people at large. In one part of France after another, ordinary townspeople and peasants took the law into their own hands, presenting their legislators with a fait accompli to be rubber-stamped. They were driven not by a concern with rationalization but with a determination to make the shoe that presently pinched so cruelly fit more comfortably.

What the National Assembly was especially well qualified to do was the articulation of the principles which underlay the new France. As it included in its ranks some exceptionally gifted men of letters, it was no wonder that it generated manifestos of corresponding quality. The most eloquent and most important was the 'Declaration of the Rights of Man and the Citizen', promulgated on 26 August. That the legislature of a great power should proclaim that all men enjoyed certain inalienable rights by virtue of their very nature gave the French Revolution a unique universality. By declaring that 'Man' – and not just 'French Man' – had a natural right to liberty, property, security, equality of opportunity, fiscal equality, freedom from oppression and arbitrary arrest, equality before the law, religious toleration and freedom of expression, association and the press, the deputies threw down a challenge to all those regimes which denied their subjects some or all of these. By advertising the concept of citizenship, declaring that sovereignty resided in the nation and reserving to an elected assembly the right to legislate, tax, control the armed forces and supervise ministers, they also established a liberal constitution against which not only patently despotic regimes such as Russia but also more benign but imperfect polities such as Great Britain might be judged.

It was also the National Assembly which had to grapple with the issue which had destroyed the absolute monarchy – the national debt. The Revolution had not solved the country's financial problems, on the contrary it had made revenue collection even more difficult. The obvious way out seemed to be a simple repudiation of obligations, but, quite apart from questions of probity, this escape route was blocked by the simple fact that many of the deputies were themselves creditors of the old regime. The answer was found in the rolling estates of the Catholic Church, covering some 10 per cent of the country's cultivable area. On 2 November 1789, the National Assembly voted by 510 to 346 that all ecclesiastical property was to be placed at the disposal of the nation. In return, the state would assume responsibility for paying the clergy and providing for the poor. Although 'only' 400,000,000 *livres*-worth were ordered to be sold initially, this sale of the century could only end with the total expropriation of what had been France's biggest landowner. In the process, a class of beneficiaries was created with the most deeply committed of stakes in the success of the Revolution.

The fate of the Church under the Revolution exemplified the new order's concern with rational uniformity. In the past, there had been far too many dioceses in the south but not enough in the north. The National Assembly solved that by decreeing that in future there should be one bishop for each of the eighty-three *départements* into which the country was now divided. In similar vein, it also laid down that there should be one parish for every 6,000 souls, a rule which led to a drastic reduction of parishes in many towns. Many clergymen believed that these and the other innovations imposed by the Civil Constitution of the Clergy of 12 July 1790 were long overdue, but few believed that the election of bishops should be entrusted to the laity, a regulation which allowed Jews, atheists and even Protestants to choose the Catholic hierarchy. In the past, the Church had been truly the first estate, both the cultural centre and the great provider of social services in what was officially an exclusively Catholic country. After 1789 it was demoted and marginalized in the name of reason, toleration and secularism – and the great beneficiary was the state.

Sub specie aeternitatis, that was the great irrevocable achievement of the French Revolution – the massive expansion of the competence and power of the state. With all the self-confidence which came from the conviction that nature was on their side, the revolutionaries reached down to touch every aspect of human life. Perhaps their most durable intervention – and arguably their most benign – was to decree that henceforth the basic unit of measurement would be exactly one ten-millionth of the distance from the North Pole to the Equator, to be known as the 'metre'. During the first years of the Revolution, this dirigisme was masked because it was accompanied by a political culture which stressed popular participation. From Rousseau the revolutionaries took the axiom that the power of the people cannot be alienated through representation. As direct democracy is impracticable in a country the size of France, or even in a city the size of Paris, the essential task of the politician is to present himself and his cause in such a way as to personify popular sovereignty. This created a new form of political discourse, as politicians competed to claim legitimacy through all available media – press, pamphlets, theatres, clubs, songs, pageants, processions and symbols of every conceivable kind. The language and ritual of political struggle were not just the external symptoms of some deeper social reality, they themselves were real. Together they established a new political benchmark. After 1789, every regime in France – or indeed in Europe – hoping to rule legitimately had to make some concessions to participatory politics.

On every occasion that the Revolution lurched to the left, there was a further surge of political emigration. Even so, only a tiny fraction of the French population was affected. If counter-revolution was ever to become more than a phantom conspiracy, it needed an issue which would mobilize mass support. This was the role of religion. An early indicator of its undimmed explosive power was provided by the violent reaction to the emancipation of the Protestants, especially in the south-east. However, it was the attempt by the National Assembly to enforce an oath of loyalty to the Civil Constitution on all clergymen wishing to retain their benefices by a decree of 27 November 1790 which launched a decade of civil strife. Especially in the west and in the non-French-speaking regions of the country (such as Breton-speaking Brittany or German-speaking Alsace), most priests refused to take the oath and were supported by their parishioners. Where the revolutionary state tried to enforce its will, violence erupted. The sweeping papal condemnation of the Revolution and all its works in the spring of 1791 added to the revolutionaries' belief that they were threatened by a great international conspiracy.

It was confirmed by the knowledge that Louis XVI deeply disapproved of the Revolution's ecclesiastical settlement, and the suspicion that he disapproved of the Revolution *tout court*. In the final analysis, it could be said that the constitutional monarchy failed in France because the King declined to play the role allotted to him. This was a personal failure, for on the rare occasions that he managed to speak his lines with conviction, he was almost overwhelmed with the great fund of goodwill towards him which persisted until remarkably late in the day. A serious handicap in his fumbling attempts to stay in control was the presence at his side of his formidable queen, 'the only man in the family', as Mirabeau called her. Marie Antoinette was deeply unpopular for her Austrian nationality, undoubted profligacy and fabled bisexual promiscuity. In fact, the revolutionaries had every reason to fear and hate her, for she was indeed busy seeking international military intervention to restore the old regime.

A major milestone on the road leading from absolute monarchy to radical republic was reached on the night of 20/21 June 1791 when Louis XVI and his family tried to escape from France. This advertised for all the world to see that the King was a prisoner in his own country and that his apparent co-operation with the new regime during the past two years had been insincere. This put republicanism squarely on the political agenda for the first time but it did not yet put an end to the monarchy. The soft centre of revolutionary politics was still large enough to prevent the radicals taking control. Republican demonstrations were suppressed, republican clubs were closed, and the new constitution was hurriedly brought to completion. As the new legislature, the 'Legislative Assembly', met for the first time on 1 October 1791, most of its members hoped that the Revolution was over.

It was not, not least because international events now impinged on the situation inside France. Detailed consideration of the origins of the war that began on 20 April 1792 must await a later chapter. Here we need to know that the revolutionaries went to war expecting it to be quick and easy. It was neither. The first foray into Belgium was repulsed by the Austrians with risible ease, as the revolutionary soldiers simply ran away. This did not, however, create a sensible respect for the old regime armies, rather it intensified the belief in an enemy within and a determination to root it out before it could destroy the Revolution. The last straw proved to be the notorious manifesto issued by the allied commander-in-chief, the Duke of Brunswick, from his headquarters at Koblenz on 25 July. Among other things, he promised that if the Tuileries Palace were attacked or if Louis XVI and his family were harmed or insulted in any way, then Paris and its inhabitants would be put to the torch and the sword when he and his army reached the city. Of all the counter-productive declarations in history, this must surely take the biscuit, for it had exactly the opposite effect to that intended. Far from being intimidated, on 10 August the revolutionary crowd stormed the Tuileries, butchered the Swiss Guards defending it, took the royal family prisoner and forced the Legislative Assembly to decree the suspension of the monarchy. France formally became a republic on 22 September 1792.

The Revolution now suffered a prolonged agony. The creation of the republic put radicalism at a premium, as political groups competed to represent the cause of liberty, equality and fraternity in a post-monarchist era. In this competition, the previously dominant group of 'Girondins', led by Jacques-Pierre Brissot, was hopelessly outpointed by forces even further to the left, led on the streets of Paris by radical journalists such as Marat and in the more structured environment of the Jacobin Club by politicians such as Robespierre. So when the King was put on trial in January 1793, the Brissotins dithered while their opponents unequivocally called for the death sentence. The execution of Louis XVI on 21 January 1793 ensured that the Revolution had a long way to go before it reached the limits of extremism.

What made a return to stability impossible was the war. After the early disasters, the revolutionary armies had done well. The allied invasion was checked at Valmy on 20 September 1792 and Belgium and the Rhineland were conquered during the autumn. During the winter of 1792/3, however, the situation deteriorated quickly as tens of thousands of volunteers streamed back from the front and the German powers began to take the war seriously. Moreover, the reckless declaration of war on Great Britain, the Dutch Republic and Spain early in 1793 now meant that France was fighting virtually the whole of Europe, with the significant exception of Russia. To hold the line, the National Convention (which succeeded the Legislative Assembly in September 1792) decreed on 24 February 1793 the conscription of 300,000 men.

The result was civil war. In the Vendée region of the west of France, this latest and most demanding intrusion of the revolutionary state turned long-standing passive resistance and sporadic violence into a general and sustained attempt to destroy the new regime by military force. By the middle of June the 'Catholic and Royal Army' was around 45,000 strong, controlled four *départements*, and was preparing to march on Paris. News from the front was also alarming, as the Austrians won a great victory at Neerwinden on 18 March, reconquered Belgium and prepared to invade. Perhaps the nadir of revolutionary fortunes was reached on 29 August, when counter-revolutionaries surrendered the great port of Toulon and the French Mediterranean fleet to the British. By that time, the patent failure of the Brissotins to win the war they had started with such blithe optimism had led to their fall at the end of May. They were replaced by a much more hard-headed group, prepared to do anything to pacify the country, win the war and save the Revolution. The new centre of power was the 'Committee of Public Safety', in theory only a supervisory committee of the National Convention but in reality the instrument of revolutionary dictatorship for the next twelve months.

The new regime succeeded in checking the invasion and in subduing the Vendée, but at a terrible price in human suffering. With the knowledge and approval of the central authorities, General Turreau sent what became known as 'columns of hell' through the insurgent territory, burning and killing as they went. No one will ever know how many people perished during the 'pacification' of the Vendée. The most authoritative estimate suggests a total of around 400,000 for both sides, which proportionally places the episode in the front rank of the atrocities of modern European history. Back in Paris, the regime was busy eliminating opponents on both right and left. Although its leaders, most notably Robespierre, presented their terrorist laws in the language of reason, humanity and liberty, this was essentially a criminal exercise. Only when the rule of law had been suspended could psychopaths such as the public prosecutor Fouquier-Tinville, or Robespierre's most glamorous and dangerous henchman Saint-Just, emerge to inflict their dark fantasies on their fellow human beings.

The Terror reached a climax in the summer of 1794, by which time it was becoming seriously dysfunctional. As the decisive victory over the Austrians at Fleurus on 26 June showed that the war had been won, a reaction against the blood-letting could not be long delayed. It came on

27 July ('9 Thermidor' in the new revolutionary calendar), when the National Convention seized back the initiative and rushed off Robespierre and his supporters to the guillotine. The Terror was over but its effects were as long-lasting as they were momentous. The experience divided the population so sharply that every subsequent political crisis was influenced profoundly. Right across Europe, the horrors of this terrible year made even mildly progressive reform more difficult and made the political and social establishment both more secure and more conservative. So the Revolution's political legacy was Janus-faced: on the one side benign libertarian ideology, on the other malignant state terrorism. It would be difficult to say which has proved the more influential.

Victory in the west allowed the French to knock the Dutch, the Prussians and the Spanish out of the war in 1795 but left the Austrians and the British still fighting. The conquest of Italy in 1796 by the twenty-seven-year-old General Napoleon Bonaparte brought peace to the continent by the Treaty of Campo Formio in October 1797. This left the French the undisputed masters of western and southern Europe, with Belgium annexed, the Rhineland occupied and the Dutch Republic and northern Italy organized as satellite states. Only the British remained unpacified, but that was enough to make the continental peace nothing more than a truce. Bonaparte's expedition to Egypt in 1798 brought Russia into the war for the first time and gave the British the opportunity to demonstrate the fragility of French power by destroying their Mediterranean fleet at the battle of the Nile (1 August 1798). The result was the War of the Second Coalition, which, in 1799, brought the Revolution to its knees.

That the Revolution would end in military dictatorship had been predicted many years earlier by two observers at either end of the political spectrum – Edmund Burke and Robespierre. Their prophecy was eventually fulfilled because the interminable war naturally led to militarization. The mobilization of the entire population and the cult of the invincible citizen-in-arms promoted the glorification of military values, exemplified by the 'Marseillaise', the most militaristic and bloodthirsty of all the world's national anthems. During the early stages of the war, the government in Paris had kept a tight hold on its generals – indeed, they were far more likely to perish on the guillotine than as a result of enemy action. It was only after Thermidor and the fall of

Robespierre that the civilian grip relaxed and the generals began to be more assertive. Their power to intervene in domestic politics was demonstrated in October 1795, when troops commanded by General Bonaparte dispersed a royalist crowd 'with a whiff of grapeshot', and again in 1797 when the 'Directory' (as the regime was now known) carried out one of its annual *coups d'état* from above with the help of the army. As Bonaparte was incontestably the most successful of the republic's generals, he was also the best qualified to put an end to it. On his return from Egypt in October 1799 he at once got together with Sieyès, the veteran revolutionary politician, to plot a *coup d'état*. They struck on 9 November (18 Brumaire). After two days of confusion, the Directory was overthrown and replaced by a 'Consulate'.

By this time, Bonaparte had discarded the youthful radicalism which once had given him the reputation of being a Jacobin. His experiences in Italy in 1796–7 had left him with a deep distrust of the politics of principle. Indeed, he was opposed to politics of any kind, looking instead for sound government with policy being decided at the centre by a single directing will and then being implemented by professional bureaucrats. This was a view shared by a country which for ten long years had been force-fed with an overdose of ideology. If wounds were still raw and nerves still stretched, only extremists at either end of the political spectrum wished to prolong the struggle between right and left to the bitter end.

At the heart of Bonaparte's success, therefore, was his ability to combine two apparently irreconcilable ideals: liberty and order. He managed this trick by giving the semblance of liberty but the reality of order. Behind the revolutionary rhetoric lay an autocratic will far stronger than anything an old regime monarch could boast. To perform this feat, he relied on plebiscites, ideally suited to his purpose, for they allowed foregone conclusions to be presented as popular choices. Each step on the road to dictatorship – the Consulate of 1799, Bonaparte's appointment as 'Consul for Life' in 1802, and the creation of the empire in 1804 – was given a democratic appearance by plebiscites. The reality was best summed up by the anecdote of the general who told his troops that they were free to vote for or against the new empire, but that the first soldier to register a negative vote would be taken out and shot. In similar vein, an imposing but empty structure of representative institutions was created at the centre. Purged of Bonaparte's critics in 1802, they were little more than docile rubber-stamps franking the First Consul's decisions.

The key figures in the new administration were the 'prefects', one for each of the *départements*, of which there were now ninety-eight thanks to the annexation of Belgium and other conquests. This new administration had many of the characteristics of a modern bureaucracy, being hierarchical, uniform, professional, salaried and trained. It was something less than a meritocracy, however, for the emphasis on personal loyalty to Bonaparte when appointments or promotions were being decided made it look more like a feudal clientage system. Those lucky enough to be chosen were certainly well rewarded, prefects taking home the generous salary of 20,000 francs per annum (about forty times the income of an average artisan). Their social composition demonstrated both Bonaparte's determination to put an end to the Revolution's egalitarianism and his personal preference for men of property, for no fewer than 100 of the 281 prefects who served between 1800 and 1814 came from families which had enjoyed noble status under the old regime.

In spite of, or perhaps even because of, this aristocratic flavour, the new system worked. It can safely be said that France had never been better governed, if quality is assessed in terms of effective obedience to orders issued by the centre. Almost everyone could be pleased by the dramatic improvement in public order which followed Bonaparte's seizure of power. The Vendée was pacified at long last by a judicious mixture of stick and carrot, the sectarian tit-for-tat killings in the Rhône valley were halted and everywhere banditry was suppressed. The prefects and their subordinates passed the acid test – the ability to enforce conscription – with flying colours, at least during the early years of the regime. Together with the repair of existing roads and the construction of new highways, physical communication enjoyed much-needed and long-overdue improvement. The other great failure of the successive revolutionary regimes, public finance, was also rectified. Building on preparatory work by the Directory and enjoying the benefit of a sustained recovery in the economy, Bonaparte established the Bank of France, stabilized the currency, improved revenue collection and brought the national debt under control. It should be noted, however, that although this certainly represented a significant improvement on the chaos of the 1790s, it was not good enough, for France was falling behind her arch-enemy in the struggle for war-sustaining revenue. At the height of the Napoleonic Wars, Great Britain was collecting three times as much money per head of population.

In restoring order to a revolution-torn country and continent, Bonaparte was at his most statesman-like in his search for reconciliation. Proscribing only irreconcilable royalists and Jacobins, he encouraged the rest of the émigrés to return home and rally to the regime. This policy was an undoubted success, as the appearance of aristocratic names among the list of prefects shows. His greatest eirenic triumph, however, was making peace with the Catholic Church by the Concordat of 1802. At a stroke, he took from the counter-revolutionaries their most potent appeal. It was some measure of the catastrophe which had befallen the papacy since 1789 that Pius VII was prepared to accept the terms offered, including recognition of the expropriation of ecclesiastical property and the subordination of Church to state. Although Bonaparte's vaulting ambition eventually led to a new schism, in the short and medium term the Concordat greatly facilitated his hold not only on France but on all Catholic Europe.

His other great positive achievement at home was the promulgation of six legal codes, the Civil Code of 1804 being both the first and the most important. It was renamed the Napoleonic Code in 1806, a not unreasonable personification as it was he who took the chair at most of the sessions of the drafting committee and who gave the final document his own unmistakable stamp. As it was imported into many other parts of Europe, it became the most important single legal document of modern European history. It has often been criticized on the grounds that Bonaparte's personal conservatism was reflected in the provisions dealing with property, women, the family and landed inheritance. No doubt these limitations would fall foul of some cosmic court of human rights, but compared with the chaos of the 400-odd legal codes of old regime France, the Napoleonic Code was a model of rationality and equity and was recognized as such by grateful recipients.

Both to contemporaries and to posterity, the Revolutionary-Napoleonic era seemed a watershed, the divide between the old regime and the modern world. As we have seen, this view seems entirely plausible. So much happened so quickly in so many parts of Europe that it is natural to conclude that a radical change had occurred. Yet when the dust settled after 1815, many important things had changed very little or not at all. French society before 1789 had been dominated by a mixed elite of notables, some of whom were nobles and some of whom were commoners and all of whom were rich landowners. It was the same after 1815. For every aristocrat who had gone to the wall or the guillotine, there were many more who had sailed through unscathed. Catholic prelates had lost their position and civil servants had grown in number and prestige, but it has become something of a cliché to observe that the France of Louis XVIII resembled nothing more than the France of Louis XVI. What was true of France was doubly true of other parts of Europe. Indeed, it would make more sense to argue that the revolutionary experience had consolidated and prolonged the landed aristocracy's hold on social and political power.

Nor had the economy been wrenched forwards into the modern world. Twenty-three years of virtually non-stop warfare had distorted but not modernized the French economy. Its most progressive and profitable sector before the Revolution – overseas trade – had been destroyed by British command of the seas. Although manufacturing had flourished behind the tariff wall built by the continental blockade, most of the beneficiaries were artificial growths which could not survive the cold blast of British competition when peace returned. In 1789 there had been little to choose between British and French industrialization; by 1815 the gulf had become wide and unbridgeable. Indeed, it is difficult to avoid the conclusion that the Revolution put the French economy into shackles from which it proved unable to escape until deep into the twentieth century. In the century after 1815, France fell behind the USA, Germany, Austria-Hungary and Russia in terms of population; in terms of industrial production, France was outstripped by the USA, Germany and the United Kingdom, and in terms of real income per capita by Switzerland, the Netherlands, Belgium, Scandinavia and several parts of the British Empire as well.

What the French Revolution really did change was politics. With amazing speed the revolutionaries created a whole new political culture, quite different in theory and practice from even the most liberal polities of Europe. Underpinned by the principle of national sovereignty, it was an ideology with a short past but a great future, for it wrapped into one explosive package the three great abstractions of modern politics – the state, the nation and the people. The impact was heightened by the accompanying emphasis on mass participation. Through electoral assemblies, demonstrations, marches, lynchings, clubs, pageants and civic ceremonies of every kind, the French people announced its arrival as the main actor in the nation's political life. Moreover, the studied universality of the concepts and language employed ensured that the rest of Europe had to sit up and take notice too.

Much to the disappointment of the revolutionaries and the relief of the old regimes, emulation of the Revolution outside France rarely went beyond declarations of solidarity by progressive intellectuals. The French Revolution was and remained *sui generis*. It was the war which brought it to the outside world, and it did so with shattering impact. So much force was unleashed by the revolutionary state that the old system of checks and balances which had kept Europe more or less intact for a millennium was destroyed. Both Spain and Portugal were so shaken by the depredations of war that, among other things, their great colonial empires fell apart. Although a version of the old regime was restored in Italy in 1815, the clock could not be turned back. The constant reshuffling of frontiers after 1796 and Napoleon's creation of a 'Kingdom of Italy' meant that – *pace* Metternich – the country could no longer be treated as merely 'a geographical expression'. Similarly, the very various experiences of the Belgians ensured that they would not succumb meekly to rule by the Dutch after 1815, breaking away in 1830 to create their own nation-state.

But the most momentous change was the destruction of the Holy Roman Empire, Europe's soft centre. Often threatened in the past by enemies within and without, it had always been saved by a self-balancing mechanism which prevented one power achieving sufficient power to destroy it. Aspiring hegemons such as Charles V, Ferdinand II or Louis XIV had all eventually fallen back exhausted. It was the unprecedented power unleashed by the revolutionary armies, together with the ambition and folly of their political masters, which brought its final demise. This was not the sole responsibility of Napoleon, but he must shoulder most of it. His belief that a drastic reduction in the number of political units in German-speaking Europe would make the region easier to control was right in the short term, but in the long run could not have been more wrong. The humiliation and exploitation he heaped on the conquered Germans stored up a terrible revenge. Only partially exacted in 1813–15, its real day was to come in 1870–71. By that time it was also clear that his assault on German traditions had paved the way for the country to become the richest and most powerful in Europe, if not the world.

PART THREE

Religion and Culture

7

Religion and the Churches

ROME AND THE PAPACY

Of all the innumerable 'view paintings' (*vedute*) produced during the eighteenth century as souvenirs for aristocrats making the Grand Tour to Italy, there can be few as splendid as Giovanni Paolo Pannini's *The French Ambassador to the Holy See Leaving St Peter's Square, Rome* of 1757 (Plate 13). Although the notional subject is well represented by a procession of ten sumptuous carriages in the foreground, the canvas is dominated by the backdrop of St Peter's Basilica, the largest church in Christendom. Its dome by Michelangelo, façade by Maderna and all-embracing colonnade by Bernini combine to form an architectural affirmation of the spiritual supremacy of the Pope: Bishop of Rome, Supreme Pontiff, successor to St Peter. When the comte de Stainville (soon to be promoted as duc de Choiseul) had visited the Pope for his audience, he had alighted from his carriage at the foot of the *Scala Regia*, the grandest of grand staircases, created by Bernini in the 1660s. On the main landing he had encountered Bernini's monumental equestrian statue of Constantine the Great, whose conversion to Christianity had begun the triumphal progress of the True Faith to become the religion of the Roman Empire. Reaching the top of the staircase, Stainville had entered the throne-room of the Vatican Palace, the *Sala Regia*, where he fell to his knees three times, on entering, halfway across the room, and at the foot of the papal throne, where he was permitted to kiss the Pope's slippered foot. When the audience was over, the triple genuflection was repeated, as the ambassador withdrew backwards, never daring to turn his back on Christ's Vicar on Earth.

One can only guess what went through Stainville's mind as he performed this ritual. It seems that he did not believe in Christianity, let alone in the authority of the Pope. His appointment in 1753 had been opposed by the papal Curia, outraged by his loose living and free thinking. Moreover, his audience in 1757 was to take his leave, for, thanks to the patronage of Louis XV's mistress, Madame de Pompadour, he was being transferred to the court of Vienna, a move regarded by everyone outside Rome as a major promotion. When he returned to France as de facto first minister, he dealt the papacy a terrible blow by persuading Louis XV to expel the Jesuits, the most ultramontane of all religious orders. He also paved the way for their total dissolution in 1773. That a pope – in this case Clement XIV – could be bullied into dissolving an order whose members had all sworn him absolute obedience and which had been 'the most important force in Catholic renewal' (Ronnie Hsia) during the previous two centuries, showed how low the papacy had come in the world. Yet it still had much further to tumble before our period ended. If the vignette which best summed up the apogee of papal power was a penitentially clad Henry IV standing barefoot in the snow at Canossa for three days in January 1077, seeking absolution from Pope Gregory VII, its polar opposite was Pius VII being seized at the Quirinal Palace by Napoleon's troops on 6 July 1809 and packed off to captivity.

This discrepancy between external display and effective power was not uncommon in old regime Europe – nor indeed is it uncommon today – but it was especially obtrusive in the case of the papacy. The popes and their more enthusiastic supporters ('ultramontanes') were confined within an absolute discourse which allowed no flexibility. Although the dogma of papal infallibility when pronouncing formally (*ex cathedra*) on doctrines of faith or morals was not established definitively until the Vatican Council of 1870, it had been propagated for many centuries before that. It was just during our period, from the late seventeenth century, that the word 'infallibility' began to be used to describe a teaching authority of the Pope that could not err. The most influential exponent of this view was the Neapolitan founder of the Redemptorist movement, St Alfonso Liguori, whose long life stretched from 1696 to 1787. To paraphrase Hegel, it was only in the twilight of history that the dove of the Holy Ghost began her flight, for the spirit of the age (another Hegelian concept) did not favour the arrogation of infallible authority by an individual human.

The nice distinctions made by ultramontane theologians between the various kinds of authority exercised by the Pope foundered on the common human inability to distinguish between man and office. Just as the claims for the office were being inflated, the quality of the incumbents was diminishing. If the worst excesses of the Renaissance popes were not repeated, there was plenty enough evidence of human frailty to encourage scepticism about infallibility. After the austerity of the Counter-Reformation popes, the long pontificate of Urban VIII (1623–44) signalled a return to lavish display. The arts were no longer patronized only for the purposes of instruction and the propagation of the faith in the manner prescribed by the Council of Trent, they were also there to give pleasure. As Judith Hook has suggested, Urban created 'the greatest and most spectacular baroque court in Europe'. In the process Rome was embellished and his family, the Barberini, enriched. Within a short time of taking office, Urban made two of his nephews and his brother-in-law cardinals. A third nephew was disqualified from this distinction by the need to remain a secular and perpetuate the dynasty, but he benefited in other ways, becoming General of the Church, governor of the Borgo, governor of Castel Sant'Angelo, Prefect of Rome and Prince of Palestrina. No wonder he was one of the richest men in Italy by the time Urban's pontificate ended. Architectural expression of this nepotism (the word itself derives from the favours bestowed on nephews – *nipote* – by popes) was delivered in the shape of the Barberini Palace, one of the largest secular buildings in Europe, including a theatre with a seating-capacity of three thousand. Even the spiritual patronage was employed to glorify the family, as in Bernini's immense *baldacchino* in St Peter's, whose bases are adorned with the Barberini coat-of-arms and whose pillars and canopy swarm with golden bees, the Barberini emblems. Well might a contemporary satirist observe:

> *Queste d'Urban si scriva al monumento*
> *ingrasso l'api e scortico l'armento.*
> (Write this of Urban on the monument
> That he fattens his bees and starves his flock.)

Urban also delivered the ultimate justification for time-serving when he appointed Cardinal Ginetti Vicar of Rome with the comment: 'We have made Ginetti Vicar, and we could really do no less, for in the twenty years he has served us, he has always expressed the same opinions that we have held, and has never contradicted us on any occasion.'

Visitors to Rome, especially those who admire baroque art and architecture, have good reason to be grateful to Urban VIII. His immediate contemporaries were less appreciative. As one sourly observed: 'he wished to be seen as a prince rather than as a pope, a ruler rather than as a pastor'. Unfortunately, he did not command the means to prosecute this secular ambition successfully. Drawn into a ruinously expensive and fruitless war with the Duke of Parma during the last four years of his reign, he left the papacy bankrupt and its subjects rebellious. There were sixteen popes between 1644 and 1815, all of them Italian, all of them high-born and most of them elderly when they took office. The average age at accession of all the popes elected in the eighteenth century was nearly sixty-four, and for the five elected between 1721 and 1758 it was just under seventy. At seventy-eight Clement XII was already a very old man by the standards of the day on his election in 1730, and moreover had failing eyesight. Totally blind after a year and soon bedridden, he simply lacked the physical resources to conduct papal policy during a particularly difficult decade. On the other hand, the relative youth of Clement XI (a stripling of fifty-one on his election in 1700) could not save his twenty-one-year tenure of office from disaster: 'more calamities happened to the papacy during this pontificate than under any Pope since the Reformation' (Owen Chadwick). Victor Amadeus II of Savoy's crushing comment on the luckless Clement was: 'He would always have been esteemed worthy of the papacy if he had never obtained it.'

Human, all too human, good, bad and unlucky popes wrestled with greater or lesser degrees of enthusiasm and success with their intractable problems. They had plenty of able apologists in Rome, and many more elsewhere in Catholic Europe, but their dwindling audience was becoming ever less receptive. Moreover, the most serious damage was no longer inflicted by Protestant heretics fulminating against the Roman Antichrist; it came from Catholic renegades such as Voltaire, whose darts were all the sharper for having been honed on the whetstone of a Jesuit education. His characteristic comment on the failings of the popes in the *Philosophical Dictionary* was: 'It is said that it is evidence of the divine nature of the papacy that it has survived so many crimes; but then the caliphs would have been even more divine had they behaved even more atrociously.' When every allowance has been made for the prejudices of anti-clericals and every credit has been given for good-natured and intelligent popes such as Benedict XIV (1740–58), it has to be allowed that the papacy's serious image-problem was at least partly of its own making. Although the reign of the 'cardinal nephews' was supposed to have ended with Innocent XII's Bull of 1692 decreeing that popes should never grant estates, offices or revenues to relatives, 'the worst nepotist of the age was the last Pope of the [eighteenth] century, Pius VI Braschi' (Chadwick).

It was particularly unfortunate for the popes of our period that their city was attracting a growing number of secular visitors. In the past, Rome had been the great destination of pilgrims; now it was the goal of tourists. The change was not absolute, for the faithful continued to come in large numbers, especially during the jubilee years celebrated every quarter-century. The city's Brotherhood of the Holy Trinity, the charity chiefly responsible for their hospitality, sheltered 280,496 pilgrims in 1675; 299,697 in 1700; and 194,832 in 1750. Although a few – like Tannhäuser and Luther in previous centuries – may have returned home alienated by their Roman excursion, it can be assumed that most were edified by their visits to the holy places and confirmed in their faith. For the wider European public, however, the opinion-formers were the grand tourists from all over Europe, for they usually recorded and often published their impressions. They came equipped with a yardstick against which contemporary conditions were almost certain to be found wanting, namely a classical education. Most famously, the contrast between the classical past and the Christian present inspired one of the greatest historiographical and literary creations of the eighteenth century, as Edward Gibbon recorded in his *Memoirs*: 'It was at Rome, on the 15th of October 1764, as I sat musing amid the ruins of the capitol, while the bare-footed friars were singing vespers in the temple of Jupiter [the Church of Santa Maria in Aracoeli], that the idea of writing the *decline and fall of the city* first started to my mind.'

If no other visitor responded on Gibbon's scale, there were plenty who came 'to admire the past and scorn the present', as Francis Haskell put it. To the fore were Gibbon's fellow countrymen, who combined a fierce pride in their own achievements, founded on the great tripod of Protestantism, liberty and commerce, with an equally intense disdain for a culture based, as they saw it, on the equally interdependent phenomena of Catholicism, despotism and poverty. Horace Walpole wrote home from Rome in 1740: 'I am very glad that I see Rome while it yet exists; before a great number of years are elapsed, I question whether it will be worth seeing. Between the ignorance and poverty of the present Romans, everything is neglected and falling to decay, the villas are entirely out of repair, and the palaces so ill kept that half the pictures are spoiled by damp.' This kind of observation could be repeated ad nauseam. The hatred of the Protestant had made way for a much more insidious and corrosive attitude – the contempt of the educated, whether Protestant, Catholic or indifferent. Writing in his *History of My Own Times*, Frederick the Great gave this account of the papal election of 1740:

The Holy See had lately become vacant by the death of Clement XII of the House of Corsini. The conclave remained sitting twelve months. The Holy Ghost was held in suspense till the factions of the powers of Europe could agree. Tired with these delays, Cardinal Lambertini, addressing the other Cardinals, said, 'I advise you to come to a decision: if you wish for a bigot, choose Aldobrandi; if you prefer a man of learning, elect Coscia; if you like a buffoon, here I am.' The choice of the Holy Ghost fell on this merry Cardinal.

That this fiction was a gross libel on one of the better popes of the period is of less importance than the currency it obtained and the attitude it reveals. Moreover, Frederick's more considered verdict on the papacy's role in the same work is acute, despite its anti-clerical language:

The Renaissance and the Reformation had given superstition a mortal blow. Some saints occasionally were canonized, that the ceremony might not be forgotten; but the pope who would have preached a crusade in the eighteenth century would not have had twenty ragged followers. He was reduced to the humiliating office of exercising his sacerdotal functions, and hastily making the fortunes of his relations and bastards.

This was painfully close to the mark: twenty-nine saints were canonized during the eighteenth century, but they had lived during earlier epochs. There was now a dearth of men and women deemed so holy that they must have gone to Heaven and so would be in a position to intercede for the sinful. As Ronnie Hsia has observed: 'Its political insignificance notwithstanding, the Baroque papacy presided over a heroic Catholicism, peopled with missionaries, martyrs, converts, and living saints. The eighteenth-century papacy, in contrast, drew inward, conscious perhaps of a bygone age of greatness.'

Why should it be thought humiliating to be reduced to carrying out 'sacerdotal functions'? This was not just the jibe of a Deist who thought that all revealed religion was 'the sacred prejudice among the vulgar'. All popes continued to believe that their office was clad in a seamless robe of functions, secular as well as spiritual, political as well as ecclesiastical. In the hierarchy of earthly authority, it was the Pope who came first because it was he who was Christ's vicar, it was he who held the keys of St Peter and it was he who could bind and loose even the greatest of secular rulers from their sins. Every year, on Maundy Thursday (the day before Good Friday), a solemn ceremony took place in the loggia of St Peter's in the presence of the Pope, the College of Cardinals and the entire papal court. First in Latin and then in Italian, the Bull *In Coena Domini* was intoned, listing the numerous offences which attracted an automatic penalty of excommunication (and which therefore consigned the transgressor to Hell for all eternity unless absolution were subsequently obtained). Essentially, it was a warning to laymen in general and the secular authorities in particular to respect the autonomous power of the Church, for among the offences listed were: appeals from ecclesiastical to secular courts; the avocation of spiritual causes from ecclesiastical to lay courts; the subjection of ecclesiastics to lay courts; the molestation of ecclesiastical judges; the usurpation of Church goods, or the sequestration of the same without leave of the proper ecclesiastical authorities; the imposition of tithes and taxes on ecclesiastics without special leave of the Pope; the interference of lay judges in capital or criminal cases of ecclesiastics; and the invasion, occupation or usurpation of any part of the Pontifical States. Of course, these and other claims by the papacy had long been contested by secular rulers but they had not been abandoned. That was discovered by the Duke of Parma in January 1768 when he subjected all communications from Rome to his prior approval. Appealing to the provisions of *In Coena Domini*, Clement XIII responded by annulling the Duke's decree in language worthy of Gregory VII:

[it is] full of outrage and calumny, full of wicked doctrine tending to divide the Church, with the aim of separating the faithful from their head, and with the result that it overthrows the authority of the Church, turns sacred order upside down, lessens the rights of the Holy See and puts them under lay control; and reduces to a state of slavery the Church of God which is free.

But whereas Gregory VII had been able to mobilize the German princes against the Emperor Henry IV, Clement proved to be friendless. His adversary, on the other hand, was positively overwhelmed by support. The Duke of Parma's uncle, Louis XV of France, occupied the papal territories of Avignon and the Venaissin, his Neapolitan cousin seized the papal enclaves of Benevento and Pontecorvo, while his Spanish cousin, Charles III, and his brother-in-law, Joseph II of Austria, lent strident verbal support. The Pope had started a contest he could not win and it is difficult not to agree with Choiseul's withering comment: 'the Pope is a fool and his secretary of state is an ass'. Clement XIII did not climb down, for the good reason that he died on 2 February 1769, but the Duke of Parma's decrees were not revoked and *In Coena Domini* was never proclaimed again. If this did not mark the moment at which the papacy recognized that its temporal power was at an end (that arguably did not come until Mussolini's Concordat with Pius XI in 1929), it was certainly an important staging-post. As we shall see later in this chapter, it also marked the beginning of the death-throes of the Jesuits.

The contemptuous manner in which the Catholic sovereigns treated their spiritual leader in this affair had been anticipated by their disregard of his diplomatic pretensions. When the most important international settlement of early modern times – the Peace of Westphalia, concluded in 1648 – redrew the religious map of central Europe, it did so without reference to the Pope, despite the involvement of all the great Catholic powers. In his Bull *Zelo Domus Dei*, Innocent X lodged a formal protest, taking particular exception to the secularization of bishoprics and monasteries and the drastic reduction in payments to Rome. It made not a scrap of difference; indeed, in the opinion of Gerd Dethlefs, the Bull 'removed the Roman Church from the European order and compromised its authority as the supreme adjudicator among the Catholic powers'. Thereafter every international treaty was negotiated without reference to the Pope. His representatives were excluded from the negotiations which brought the War of the Spanish Succession to an end, while his traditional claim to suzerainty over Naples and Sicily was simply ignored when they were assigned to the Austrian Habsburgs. At a consistory held to review the settlements of 1713–14, Clement XI could only rail impotently against such catastrophes as the Protestant succession in England, the winning of Electoral status by Hanover, the recognition of Prussia's royal title, and so on.

With the advantage of hindsight, we can see that there was both good and bad news for the popes in the long-term development of Church–State relations. As we have seen, right across Europe 'the state' was the 'master-noun of political argument' (Quentin Skinner) and at the heart of the state was the concept of sovereignty. As the essence of sovereignty is its self-sufficiency, by virtue of its definition as 'ultimate authority from which there is no appeal', no state can tolerate the interference of an international authority such as the papacy. The tension had always been there, of course. However, it was in the eighteenth century that the declining power and prestige of the papacy allowed the growing power and ambition of secular states to shift the balance decisively in their favour.

The good news, although it was to be a very long time before the popes developed the necessary organs to hear the glad tidings, was that the modern state's demolition of the various obstacles to its supremacy was also clearing away many of the Church's enemies too. Even the Reformation, arguably the papacy's darkest hour since the Great Eastern Schism, bore with it a chink of light. If the number of Catholics had been greatly reduced, it left those inside the fold much more closely tied to Rome. Something rather similar happened with the secular assault by notionally Catholic states on the papacy – 'it made the centre of Catholicism more supreme as the centre'. For those Catholics who remained Catholic – and there were many more that did than did not – the Pope at Rome could only gain in authority as their own rulers embraced the doctrine of secularism. This was to be especially true of France after 1789 when it became the first completely non-confessional state in European history, but it also applied to enlightened states such as Joseph II's Austria. After charting all the problems and shortcomings of the papacy, it is worth remembering that the Pope is still in Rome, that his flock worldwide is numerically greater than at any time in the past, and that the Catholic share of Christians has increased substantially in recent times. Horace Walpole greeted the election of Clement XIV in 1769 with the gleeful prediction that he would be 'the last Pope'. He was not of course to be the last to underestimate the enduring power of the Pontiff. 'How many divisions has *he* got?' sneered Joseph Stalin when dismissing a protest from Pius XII (1939–58). Although he could not have died soon enough, in a way it is sad that Stalin did not survive to witness papal authority in eastern Europe eclipsing that of the General Secretary of the Communist Party of the USSR (deceased).

PRELATES

Rome was the most papal and the most Catholic city in Europe. It could also claim to be the most clerical, as the forest of church towers and their bells provided constant architectural and sonic emblems of the clergy's domination. Even today, after secularization and expansion have transformed the Roman cityscape, the thousand-odd bells that sound at noon have a powerful resonance, symbolically as well as aurally. But if especially obtrusive in Rome, this semiotic riot was certainly not unique. The physical appearance of virtually every European city, Protestant as well as Catholic, was dominated by churches and other ecclesiastical buildings. Contemporary illustrations even of great commercial centres such as London or Amsterdam bristle with spires reaching for Heaven. Significantly, the only urban centres in which secular buildings set the tone were brand-new creations centred on a court, such as Versailles or Ludwigsburg (in the Duchy of Württemberg).

At least until the devastations of the Second World War, churches destroyed by war, fire or any other natural calamity were quickly rebuilt, usually on a grander scale than before. Sir Christopher Wren was commissioned to design fifty-five churches after the Great Fire of London of 1666. The reconstruction was as good an indication as any of the commonly felt need by governments, clergy and laity to give physical expression to their belief in God and their hope of emulating His resurrection. The same aspiration had motivated the bequests which down the centuries had made the Church the wealthiest corporation in Europe. Moreover, once property had found its way into ecclesiastical hands, it very rarely slipped from their grasp. While a private individual might find it expedient to sell this or that piece of land, an immortal institution held what it had in perpetuity. The result was an accumulation of property which in France amounted to perhaps 10 per cent of the country's cultivable area, including much of the most fertile. Contemporaries chose to believe that the figure was much higher – Barbier, the Paris diarist, for example, put it as high as a third. In Naples, it was thought that the Church owned *two-thirds*, although this was almost certainly an exaggeration. More confidence can be placed in the share of 23 per cent cited for Lombardy or the 20–40 per cent for the Papal States (depending on the actual region). Reasonably secure are the estimates of 56 per cent for Bavaria and 40 per cent for Lower Austria. In Castile the Church owned about a seventh of all arable and pastoral land. In Russia, where ownership of human beings rather than land was a better guide to wealth, the 1678 census showed that the Patriarch, higher clergy, monasteries and cathedrals owned about 20 per cent of all serfs.

With rents and agricultural produce rising in value for much of the eighteenth century, the rich Church was getting richer. Needless to say, its wealth was distributed most unequally. At the top were prelates enjoying princely incomes. Indeed, in the Holy Roman Empire, the elite among them were literally princes too, as they ruled over sovereign secular territories and were represented in the Imperial Parliament (*Reichstag*). At their head were the three Rhenish archbishops – Mainz, Trier and Cologne – who sat in the *Reichstag*'s College of Electors and therefore acquired real political importance when an Emperor died. Two other archbishops (Salzburg and Besançon), twenty-one bishops and around fifty abbots sat in the College of Princes. Not one of them commanded the resources to play an independent political role in Germany, let alone Europe, but their collective importance was considerable. In terms of the confessional identity of the population, the Holy Roman Empire after 1648 divided roughly into two-thirds Protestant to one-third Catholic, but – thanks to these ecclesiastical states – in terms of the confessional identity of the *states*, the Holy Roman Empire divided roughly into one-third Protestant to two-thirds Catholic.

Nothing illustrated better the confessional nature of the old regime than this intermingling, eighteenth-century critics called it 'confusion', between spiritual and temporal. The Archbishop-Elector of Mainz, for example, who was recognized as the Primate of the German Church, exercised metropolitan jurisdiction over the episcopal sees of Worms, Speyer, Constance, Strassburg, Augsburg, Chur, Würzburg, Eichstätt, Paderborn and Hildesheim. As secular ruler, his possessions embraced the city of Mainz, the Rheingau, the area surrounding Bingen, a long strip of territory extending north-east of Mainz into the Taunus, a large bloc of land around the River Main and two distant enclaves in Thuringia. If this archipelago sounds risibly fragmented, it should be borne in mind that its total population was around 350,000 in the late eighteenth century and included some of the richest agricultural land in Germany, notably many of the finest vineyards. The Archbishop-Elector of Trier dominated the Moselle valley, while the Archbishop-Elector of Cologne (usually also Prince-Bishop of Münster) ruled the most extensive territory in Westphalia. Like all the other prince-bishops and prince-abbots, they enjoyed the same sovereign rights as the secular rulers of the Holy Roman Empire.

Judged by the criteria of modern statehood, the amphibious ecclesiastical states, half-clerical and half-secular, were bound to be found wanting. German nationalist historians of the nineteenth century were especially severe on these 'untenable relics' (Treitschke). This was one issue on which the British could agree with the Germans, Coleridge giving poetic expression to the contempt mixed with indignation deriving from the common belief that the German 'princelings' financed their self-indulgent display by selling their soldiers as mercenaries:

> And leagued with these,
> Each petty German princeling, nursed in gore
> Soul-hardened barterers of human blood!

This was to be a prejudice with a long future. Writing about the splendour of the prince-bishops' courts, Geoffrey Barraclough complained that 'the object of these establishments was to create an impression of solidity, permanence and magnificence, which was the very opposite of the truth, with the object of magnifying the distance between prince and subjects and holding the latter in political subjection; the Prince-Bishop of Speyer, in his regal splendour at Bruchsal, did not hesitate to notify his people that "the commanding will of his majesty is none other than the commanding will of God himself"'.

For Protestant Germans and foreigners of any confession, or none, what was most offensive about the prince-bishops was the discrepancy between their pretensions (massive) and the reality of their power (minuscule). Lacking even the rudiments of independent statehood, they erected some of the greatest baroque palaces in Europe – Bamberg, Bonn, Brühl and Bruchsal, just to mention those which begin with the letter 'B', for example. It was one of the great ambitions of the secular princes, Catholic as well as Protestant, to secularize the prince-bishoprics and annex their rolling estates. Their appetites had been sharpened by their partial success in the wake of the Reformation when such great swathes of land as the archbishopric of Magdeburg had passed to Brandenburg and the archbishopric of Bremen to Hanover. The tried and tested principle of 'my enemy's enemy is my friend' was never better tried and tested than by the intimate relationship between Holy Roman Emperor and ecclesiastical princes.

Many of the latter were drawn from the 'Imperial Knights', a quint-essentially old regime group of nobles, whose exact origins are lost in the mists of time surrounding the dissolution of the Carolingian Empire. What distinguished them from all other German nobles was their claim to be 'immediate' (*reichsunmittelbar*), that is to say directly and solely subject to the Emperor. They had not succeeded in gaining full princely status, so were not represented in the Imperial Diet, but in most other respects they were on a par with the princes. They comprised about 350 different families, owning about 1,500 estates covering about 5,000 square miles (13,000 km^2) with a total population of around 350,000. Individually, of course, they counted for nothing, but they were able to punch well above their weight by their control of a large part of the Catholic Church in the Holy Roman Empire. They had been greatly assisted by the conversion to Protestantism of most of the secular princes, leaving only the Habsburgs and most of the Wittelsbachs (plus the Wettins of Saxony after 1697) true to the old faith. So princely competition in the ecclesiastical states failed for want of candidates.

Already present in several cathedral chapters, the Imperial Knights gratefully stepped in to fill the vacuum. They did not succeed in monopolizing all of the prince-bishoprics, for those surrounded by Bavarian territory, such as Regensburg and Freising, were dominated by Bavarian nobles, and those surrounded by Austrian territory, such as Salzburg and Brixen, were dominated by Austrian nobles. Membership of the Cathedral Chapter of Cologne was restricted to Imperial Counts, while in Liège, amazingly, more than half the canons were commoners. Nevertheless, the Imperial Knights took the lion's share of the Imperial Church (*Reichskirche*) and, once they controlled a cathedral chapter and through it the election of the Prince-Bishop, they took great care to keep interlopers at bay by means of stringent membership qualifications. By the beginning of the eighteenth century the Imperial Knights dominated the prince-bishoprics of the Rhineland (except Cologne), Franconia and Swabia. Understandably, the canons almost invariably elected one of their own number, so a series of Imperial Knights ascended the episcopal thrones in Constance, Speyer, Worms, Trier, Würzburg, Bamberg, Eichstätt and Mainz. In other words, the Imperial Knights could usually count on two votes in the Electoral College of the *Reichstag* and several more in the College of Princes. This translated into real influence in Vienna, as every Habsburg emperor – with the notable exception of Joseph II – appreciated the value of their goodwill. Moreover, numerous Imperial Knights entered Austrian service as soldiers, diplomats and bureaucrats: the two most effective Austrian ministers of the Napoleonic period, Stadion and Metternich, were Imperial Knights by origin, from Swabia and the Rhineland respectively. For all of the Knights, the dozens of canonries reserved for them in the cathedral chapters offered comfortable billets for younger sons. For the lucky few who became archbishops or bishops, real power and wealth beckoned. At imperial elections, it was the Elector of Mainz, as Arch-Chancellor and Director of the Electoral College, who summoned the other Electors to Frankfurt for the election, who verified the credentials of the ambassadors, who chaired the discussions about the new 'capitulation' (i.e. conditions) of election, who collected the Electors' votes and who consecrated and anointed the new emperor.

Victory in an episcopal election led to the permanent enrichment of the successful candidate's family, for he had a large amount of patronage at his disposal. Moreover, success could breed success, as prince-bishoprics were often held both in plurality and by several members of the same family. For all the canons of the cathedral chapter, an episcopal election brought substantial perquisites in the form of bribes offered by diplomats canvassing support for the candidate thought to be most sympathetic to their court. The French minister in Mainz observed, 'the Germans are extremely venal, especially most of those who make up the cathedral chapters; they place alongside their principal emoluments the money they receive on the occasion of the various elections', adding wearily, '*point d'argent, point d'Allemagne*' (no money, no Germany). Canons who delayed their decision as to which candidate to support until the last possible moment, holding out for the maximum price for their votes, were said to be 'waiting for the inspiration of the Holy Ghost'. The sums involved could be considerable, reflecting the importance still attached to winning the ecclesiastical states by the great powers. In 1780 the Habsburgs paid out almost one million *gulden* to secure the election of the Archduke Max Franz at Cologne. In 1787 the Prussians spent 180,000 *gulden* in what proved to be a fruitless attempt to get a supporter adopted as heir to the current Archbishop of Mainz.

Across Catholic Europe, the same intermingling of temporal and ecclesiastical authority could be found, albeit in a less spectacular form. The Primate of Poland, the Archbishop of Gniezno, was recognized as the most important person in the kingdom after the King and, as such, served as a regent during the (often protracted) interregnum in this elective monarchy. His equivalent in Hungary, the Archbishop of Esztergom, was made a prince of the Holy Roman Empire in 1715, so was referred to thereafter as the 'Prince Primate'. In France, three prelates became first ministers during the course of the eighteenth century – Dubois, Fleury and Brienne. As an additional prize, all of them were made cardinals. Like every other French bishop of the eighteenth century, they were all of noble birth, they all owed their position to court patronage and they were all appointed to their ecclesiastical benefices by the King. Since the Concordat of 1516, all of the 130-odd bishoprics in France were in the royal gift, the only exception being the archbishopric of Strasbourg, where the cathedral chapter still had the right to elect but never dared to exercise it against the wishes of Versailles.

At Catholic courts the omnipresence of the clergy and the frequency of religious services were equally obtrusive. At Versailles, formal prayers were an important part of the King's ceremonial rising from his bed, known as the *lever*, informal prayers were said after breakfast, Mass was celebrated at noon, evening prayers were conducted after hunting and another formal session of prayers was held when the King ceremonially retired for the night at the *coucher*. To this regular daily round should be added the special services occasioned by the numerous festivals of the Catholic calendar. Around 200 clergy of varying degrees of eminence were present in the palace to assist with these devotions. The most senior was the grand almoner, who attended the *lever* and the *coucher* to lead prayers, and said grace at meals. Proximity to the fount of all important ecclesiastical patronage made Versailles the Eldorado of the more ambitious French clergy. In 1789 the court chaplains, all of noble origin it need hardly be said, between them drew revenues from eighty-three abbeys, without ever having to visit the source of their wealth. They were joined at the palace by the many archbishops and bishops who preferred the pleasures of court and capital to the diocesan grind. Almost half of the episcopate maintained establishments in Paris, prompting the jibe that at least the Gallican Church found it easy to respond quickly to a national crisis by assembling an episcopal quorum without delay. In 1784 Louis XVI felt obliged to issue a circular instructing bishops to obtain permission before absenting themselves from their flocks.

By that time it was too late to save the old regime's hierarchy from its reputation for worldly self-indulgence. It was not entirely merited, for careful research by clerical scholars anxious to rehabilitate the pre-revolutionary Church has shown that many, if not most, of the bishops were well-educated, pious, diligent and effective administrators of their dioceses. The most recent, and arguably the most authoritative, of the historians of the French Church in the eighteenth century, the Reverend John McManners, has concluded that, 'in many ways, this was the golden age of the French Church. An increasing number of bishops, some showing little zeal in their own lives, strove to improve standards among their clergy.' As chaplain of All Souls, an Oxford College richly endowed and untroubled by the presence of students, he is well-placed to sympathize with the *douceurs de la vie* of the French Church and to compose its elegy: 'this was the mellow autumn season adorning the landscape with rich colours before the leaves began to fall and winter came'. But he cannot help but present the Church as a centre for outdoor relief for the nobility. For the younger sons of most aristocratic families, the choice was stark: the army or the Church. As a mother tells her son in one of Marmontel's *Contes moraux*: 'your father's fortune was not so considerable as was imagined; it will scarce suffice to settle your elder brother. For your part, you have simply to decide whether you will follow the career of benefices or of arms, whether you will have your head shaved or broken, whether you will take orders or a lieutenancy of infantry.' Not surprisingly, this attracted men without vocation or even faith, men like Phélypeaux, Bishop of Lodève, of whom Saint-Simon recorded: 'He kept mistresses openly in his palace – kept them there to his dying day; just as openly, he was not ashamed to demonstrate, indeed to say as much in company, that he did not believe in God. And he was allowed to get away with this all his life – but then, he bore the name of Phélypeaux.' And what is one to make of an institution which could find a luxurious niche for Prince Louis de Bourbon Condé, comte de Clermont, son of the prince de Condé and an illegitimate daughter of Louis XIV, who assembled an income of 600,000 *livres* per annum from five abbeys held *in commendam* (i.e. he drew the revenue without any corresponding obligation), maintained a harem of mistresses from the

Opéra, and of whom McManners writes: 'the nearest he came to performing an ecclesiastical function was to build a marble mausoleum for his pet monkey McCarthy'?

Less comical but more dangerous was a prelate like Étienne-Charles Loménie de Brienne, whose composition of a materialist treatise at the Sorbonne in 1751 did not prevent him entering the priesthood and becoming Vicar-General of Rouen the following year at the age of twenty-five. He subsequently became Bishop of Condom in 1760 and Archbishop of Toulouse in 1762. Proposed for the archbishopric of Paris, he was turned down by Louis XVI on the grounds that 'at least the Archbishop of Paris must believe in God'. This check did not prevent him becoming first minister in 1787, Archbishop of Sens (the second richest see in France) in 1788, making his nephew his 'coadjutor' (and thus eventual successor) and acquiring a cardinal's hat. After the outbreak of the Revolution, he showed his gratitude by voting for the Civil Constitution of the Clergy and buying – and then desecrating – the confiscated abbey of St-Pierre-le-Vif. Wrong-footed by the new regime's rush to the left, he died in prison awaiting trial.

Old regime France was not a unified nation-state at all, but a composite, put together over the centuries by the inheritance or conquests of bits and pieces of very different territories. The result was a crazy paving, pleasing in its asymmetry but perplexing in its irrationality. It was characteristic that no fewer than seven archbishops should claim to be Primates of the Church in France. The dioceses were much too big in the north and much too small in the south, where six had only twenty to thirty parishes each, and one (Alais) had only six. The Archbishop of Paris enjoyed an annual income in excess of half a million *livres*, the Bishop of Vence had to get by on just 12,000. The cathedral chapters were often richer than the bishops they elected – that at Chartres, for example, drew around 350,000 *livres* from its estates to support its eighty canons.

Reviewing all of Catholic Europe, it can be said that the concentration of prelates was heaviest in the oldest-settled regions – Spain, Italy and southern France, where, very roughly, there was a bishop for every 150,000 people. In Spain there were fifty-six dioceses for a population of about 9,000,000 in the middle of the eighteenth century. In eastern Europe the bishops were much thinner on the ground. In the 'Lands of the Crown of St Wenceslas' – Bohemia, Moravia and Silesia – there were only six bishops and one archbishop to minister to a population of over 4,000,000. There was a similar shortage in the Kingdom of Hungary, most of which of course was under Turkish domination until the Habsburg *reconquista* of the late seventeenth century. Here in the east, very roughly, there was one bishop for every 500,000 people and such vital episcopal functions as confirmations, ordinations and visitations were correspondingly few and far between. It is difficult to avoid the conclusion that the Catholic Church proved very slow to adapt to changing circumstances and that when it did so, it required a violent *diabolus ex machina* such as the secular state or the French Revolution to shake it from its torpor. In the course of the early modern period, for example, the Habsburg Monarchy became one of the major states in Europe. Yet it had no proper metropolitan or episcopal structure of its own. Much of its territory was subject to prince-bishops of the Holy Roman Empire such as Salzburg, Passau and Regensburg. The see of Vienna covered little more than the city and its suburbs and was raised to archiepiscopal status only in 1717. Similarly, the capital and most important city in Spain, Madrid, had no bishop of its own but was subject to Toledo, while the bishop of the second city, Barcelona, was subject to the metropolitan jurisdiction of the Archbishop of Tarragona. It comes as no surprise to learn that the richest Spanish bishop was ten times richer than the poorest. However, it should be recorded that the Spanish episcopate, mainly drawn from the lesser nobility, was famous for its combination of piety and devotion to duty. The papal nuncio was of the opinion that the Spanish bishops were the most praiseworthy clergy in the Church (together with French parish priests).

The same vices and virtues that characterized the Catholic Church were evident in equal measure in the Anglican Church of Great Britain and Ireland. Having survived trials and tribulations at the hands of the Puritans during the Commonwealth and of the Catholics during the reign of James II, Anglicans were in resurgent mood after 1688. The implementation of the Test and Corporation Acts, first passed during the reign of Charles II, secured their occupation of the commanding heights of the British establishment by confining public office to those prepared to take the sacrament according to the rites of the Church of England. Some Protestant dissenters and Catholics with elastic consciences were prepared to conform just often enough to qualify for office, but until the Acts were repealed in 1828, the Anglicans had a monopoly. There is a good deal to be said for Jonathan Clark's argument that the period after the Hanoverian Succession of 1714 should be described as 'the Anglican Ascendancy' rather than the more usual 'Whig Ascendancy'.

Certainly the upper reaches of British society were more Anglican than ever before. In the middle of the seventeenth century, around 20 per cent of the English peerage were Catholics and another 20 per cent were Puritans. The Restoration of Charles II in 1660 discouraged the latter, while the expulsion of his brother in 1688 checked the zeal of the former. Attainders, apostasies and attrition then reduced the dissidents to the point of near-extinction: by 1800 the House of Lords was over-whelmingly Anglican by profession if not conviction, with just 3 per cent still adhering to the old faith. Nevertheless, at first blush, it looked very much as though the Anglican episcopate was much less aristocratic than its Roman Catholic counterparts on the continent. There were 267 lay peers in 1800 (up from 173 in 1700), but only one was a bishop – Augustus Hervey, fourth Earl of Bristol and Bishop of Derry. He was the exception that proved the rule, as he succeeded to his title only after the death of two brothers. This absence of peers is perhaps surprising, given that Anglican bishops were permitted to marry and sire legitimate heirs. Rather it was the wealth of the great majority of English peers, based on primogeniture and entails, that made it unnecessary for them to seek ecclesiastical preferment.

On the other hand, if the perspective is widened to include younger brothers and sons who were commoners by law but noblemen by culture, the picture changes. Although the great majority of bishops appointed before 1740 were commoners in every sense – 95.3 per cent, to be precise – the trend was reversed during the second half of the century. In 1752 a disgruntled candidate for a see wrote of the vacancy at Durham: 'Reckon upon it, that Durham goes to some noble ecclesiastic. 'Tis a morsel only for them. Our *grandees* have at last found their way back into the church. I only wonder they have been so long about it.' He was right. Durham went to the Honourable Richard Trevor, fourth son of Baron Trevor of Bromham and already Bishop of St David's. Of the seventy-six bishops appointed after 1740, twenty were of noble origin. Moreover, it was these aristocratic clerics who were most likely to secure the plums of Church patronage: half of them eventually reached one of the top six bishoprics (Canterbury, York, Durham, London, Winchester and Ely) as compared with only a quarter of the commoners. All the bishops of the (Anglican) Church of Ireland in 1727 were commoners; by 1800 42 per cent were from aristocratic families.

As we have seen, in the German Church ecclesiastical and secular power could coexist in the same Prince-Bishop. If not quite so intimate, the relationship between the Church of England and the Government of England was certainly close, for the good reason that the two arch-bishops and twenty-four of the bishops sat in the House of Lords. It was a voting bloc that could make all the difference in a close division, as it did when twenty-four episcopal votes helped to save Sir Robert Walpole during the excise crisis of 1733. Not surprisingly, the government of the day took good care that any vacancy on the episcopal bench was filled by a loyal supporter. The rewards were enormous. The annual values of the leading bishoprics were as follows around the middle of the eigh-teenth century: Canterbury £7,000; York £4,500; London £4,000; Durham £6,000; Winchester £5,000; Ely £3,400; Salisbury and Wor-cester £3,000 each. This was at a time when Lord Fellamar in Henry Fielding's *Tom Jones* exclaimed that Sophie Western was 'the best match in England' when he learnt that her father's estate was worth £3,000 a year. Moreover, a bishop had his own patronage to bestow and usually took the view that charity began at home. This is how Bishop Willes of Bath and Wells disposed of the choicer plums in his gift:

19 Aug. 1749 E. Aubrey (son-in-law): Archdeacon of Wells

1 Oct. 1753 L. Seaman (son-in-law): Archdeacon of Taunton

31 Oct. 1755 Henry Willes (son): Chancellor

6 Aug. 1757 Henry Willes (son): Precentor

27 April 1758 L. Seaman (son-in-law): Archdeacon of Wells

15 May 1758 William Willes (son): Chancellor

31 Dec. 1760 William Willes (son): Archdeacon of Taunton

26 May 1764 Charles Willes (son): Chancellor

20 Oct. 1764 William Willes (son): Archdeacon of Wells.

There was the same massive discrepancy between rich and poor prel-ates we have encountered in Catholic countries, with the sees of Bristol and Oxford at the bottom, worth just £450 and £500 respectively. Yet the expenses of all bishops with seats in the House of Lords were very similar, for all were expected to reside in London while Parliament sat. Snugly ensconced in the rich living of St James's, Westminster, William

Wake actually declined his proposed elevation to be Bishop of Oxford with the words:

If I would alter my condition, Oxford is the bishopric of all England I should least desire to fix upon. To say nothing of the revenue, which is but mean, other reasons there are enough to make a man unwilling to come to it, and I have too much approved the bishop's desire and grounds of leaving it to be ever easy in coming myself to it. In short 'tis a post fit only for a Dean of Christ Church or President of Magdalen.

Annual residence in the capital from autumn until the following spring necessarily involved a neglect of episcopal duties, although there is no evidence of any decline in standards after 1714, rather the reverse. Everything depended on the calibre of the incumbent. When Bishop Nicolson was translated to Carlisle in 1702 he found that no one had been confirmed in his diocese since 1684, a situation he manfully tried to correct by confirming 5,449 individuals during his first visitation. The fact remains, however, that the criteria for appointment were political not spiritual. Only clerics with the ear of a politician needed to apply. As Dr Johnson told Boswell on 14 April 1775: 'No man can be made a bishop for his learning and piety, his only chance for promotion is his being connected with someone who has parliamentary interest.'

At the other end of Europe, the claims made by the hierarchy were still greater but the reality was much less. Patriarch Nikon of Moscow and All the Russias (1605–81) proclaimed:

Has thou not learnt . . . that the highest authority of the priesthood is not received from kings or Tsars, but contrariwise, it is by the priesthood that rulers are anointed to the empire? Therefore it is abundantly plain that priesthood is a very much greater thing than royalty . . . In spiritual things which belong to the glory of God, the bishop is higher than the Tsar: for so only can he hold or maintain the spiritual jurisdiction. But in those things which belong in the province of this world the Tsar is higher. And so they will be in no opposition the one against the other. However, the bishop has a certain interest . . . in the secular jurisdiction, for its better direction, and in suitable matters; but the Tsar has none whatever in ecclesiastical and spiritual administration . . . For this cause, manifestly, the Tsar must be less than the bishop, and must owe him obedience.

However, in 1667 he was deposed by a great synod at the behest of Tsar Aleksei, and that was that. The schism with the Old Believers caused by

Nikon's reforms has continued to wrack the Russian Orthodox Church until the present day, but the imposition of the Tsar's authority was accepted without serious resistance. As Pierre Pascal observed, 'after Nikon, Russia no longer had a church: it had a religion of state'. It was left to the even more imperious Peter the Great to reduce the Church to being a department of state. When Patriarch Adrian died in 1700, the office was simply left vacant. The *coup de grâce* was delivered in 1721 when the patriarchal office was formally abolished and its functions transferred to a government-appointed synod. The Orthodox Russian bishops were at a serious disadvantage compared with their Catholic or Anglican colleagues. As canon law required parish priests to marry but bishops to remain celibate, the episcopacy had to be drawn from the monastic clergy. The low and falling status of both kinds of clergy attracted only 'the pious, the insolvent, and the unambitious' (G. Alef) and excluded the participation by the nobility that might have given it the ability to resist state pressure.

MONASTERIES

Few great cathedrals were constructed during our period, the major exceptions being St Paul's in London and Fulda in Hessen, but a large number of monasteries were rebuilt from scratch. Indeed, it might be said that Fulda was the exception that proved the rule, as it was also a Benedictine abbey. The rural landscape of Catholic Germany, Switzerland and Austria is still given a special character by the plethora of baroque monastic buildings, many of them gigantic in extent. Weingarten, Ottobeuren, Zwiefalten, St Gallen, Einsiedeln, Neubirnau, Neresheim, Banz, Osterhofen, Diessen, Weltenburg, St Florian, Wilhering, Melk, Dürnstein, Göttweig, Klosterneuburg – just to mention a few – represent one of the greatest architectural surges of all European history. That it should have occurred when the 'age of reason' was allegedly in full flood is another of those pleasing paradoxes with which the period bristles. In most Catholic countries it was during the second or third quarter of the eighteenth century that monasteries reached their peak. By around the middle of the century there were at least 15,000 monasteries for men and 10,000 for women, housing a total population in excess of a quarter of a million. At either end of Catholic Europe, it was the eighteenth century which saw the final triumph of the Counter-Reformation: in Portugal ninety monasteries were founded between the middle of the seventeenth and the middle of the eighteenth centuries, while in Poland the number of monks and nuns almost doubled during the same period.

Until recently, the history of the monasteries in the late seventeenth and eighteenth centuries attracted little attention from scholars other than architectural historians. A long-rooted aversion to the Catholic exuberance of the baroque, so much at odds with the austerity of the Anglophone Protestant tradition, no doubt played its part. Very recently, however, their importance has been recognized, illustrated and explained by Derek Beales in a trail-blazing work of revision. Among many other things, he demonstrates just how ubiquitous were the 'regular clergy' (i.e. men and women who belonged to a religious order) in old regime Europe. In 1728–9, Montesquieu wrote: 'On the roads of Italy you cannot turn your head without seeing a monk, and in the streets of towns without seeing a priest. All carriages, all boats are full of monks . . . Italy is the paradise of monks. There is no Order that is not lax. The business that all the world's monks have in Rome make the roads crowded.' Italy was, admittedly, the most clerical country in Europe, demographically speaking. A papal inquiry of 1649–50 reported that there were in excess of 6,000 male monasteries and that the major orders alone numbered almost 70,000 members, including lay brothers. It was on the strength of that revelation that in 1652 Innocent X suppressed more than a thousand small houses with fewer than six monks. In the face of Italian enthusiasm for a cloistered life, it was to no avail and the pre-reform total of 6,000 was soon regained. By the middle of the eighteenth century, one in every hundred inhabitants of the Italian peninsula was a monk or a nun. That was just the average. In certain cities, the clerical presence was much more obtrusive, and not only in Rome. In 1781 there were more than 100 male monasteries in the city of Naples housing 4,617 monks, and nearly 100 convents housing 5,871 nuns. As the total population amounted to 376,000, one in every thirty-six inhabitants was a member of the regular clergy. Their share of the *adult* population was, of course, much higher. If the south might be thought especially clerical, it can be recorded as a statistical counterweight that in Florence in the mid-seventeenth century there were more nuns than married women.

THE PURSUIT OF GLORY

No other Catholic country achieved these levels of monastic saturation. Beales has estimated that there were fifteen times more monastic institutions in Italy than in the Holy Roman Empire, although it might be thought that a house such as Ottobeuren counted for more than fifty of the midget *monasteri* and *conventi* that dotted the Italian countryside. Impressive scores were also recorded by Lisbon, which had 50 monasteries – 32 for men and 18 for women; by Paris, which had 58 for men and over 100 for nuns; and by several Spanish towns – Valladolid with a total of 46, Toledo with 39, Madrid with 57 and Seville with 64. If the German towns could not achieve these scores, they too often had a strong monastic flavour – Munich, for example, whose very name means 'little monk', had eighteen male and female houses in 1760 when the population was around 50,000. Everywhere the ubiquity of religious houses and their occupants gave to Catholic towns the same sort of distinctive flavour acquired by Oxford and Cambridge from their Colleges. Like the latter, their extensive buildings occupied large central sites, they owned large amounts of real estate, they gave employment to a significant proportion of the local people, and their clocks and chapel bells tolled the passing of the hours. Also like Oxbridge Colleges, their inmates enjoyed a lifetime of cosseted insulation from the outside world. Indeed, it was not unknown for children to enter a monastic school at the age of five or six and never re-enter the secular world. Three such sisters were released after a number of years to participate in an outing organized by their brother: 'On one of these excursions the girls had the misfortune to encounter a herd of cattle on their way to be slaughtered. In the cloister they had never seen such big animals. Terrified, they begged their guide to take them back as quickly as possible. "That's the world," they said. "Oh, how hideous it is!" They quickly offered themselves to be Carmelites.' In France this period was a golden age for religious women. Founded in 1633 by Vincent de Paul, the Sisters of Charity were running 70 charitable institutions by 1660, more than 200 by 1700 and 420 by the outbreak of the Revolution. That last total included 175 hospitals, prompting Florence Nightingale to observe that if there had been a British equivalent of the Order, her efforts would have been unnecessary. There were many other such orders of women who took simple vows, worked in the community and devoted themselves to practical charity such as educating the poor and looking after the sick. The Breton-based '*Filles de la Sagesse*', for example, founded in 1702, had some 300 sisters in 77 houses by 1789. As Olwen Hufton has observed, the superior rates of literacy above the 'Saint Malo–Geneva' line can be attributed as much to the more active role played by the female orders in the region as to its greater wealth.

During the fourteen hundred years or so that had passed since St Pachomius founded the first monastery at Tabennisi near Denderah in Egypt in 318, a great deal of property of various kinds had passed from secular into monastic hands. The monks had proved to be enterprising cultivators, earning from Guizot (a Protestant) in his history of civilization the sobriquet 'the agriculturists of Europe'. By the eighteenth century, the accumulation of pious bequests, together with the familiar tendency of 'immortal' institutions to keep any land in perpetuity, had made many monasteries rich and some very rich indeed. By the time of the French Revolution, the Benedictine abbey of St Germain-des-Prés had an annual income of a quarter-of-a-million *livres*, and the nearby abbey of St Geneviève almost as much. A popular but necessarily vague guess at the time was that the monasteries owned about a quarter of all real estate in Paris. They probably owned about 5 per cent of the total cultivable area of France, from which they drew around 80,000,000 *livres* in rents and dues, to which must be added around 120,000,000 *livres* from tithes. The contemporary estimate that monasteries owned a half of all land in Naples and Bavaria must have been an exaggeration, although it is well attested that in the latter 28 per cent of all peasants had the larger monasteries as their landlords, so the total must have been higher. In Lower Austria they owned 20 per cent of all land and a half of Church property. The rebuilding of the great abbey of Melk, whose gradual appearance to a traveller coming down the Danube by boat remains one of the most powerful combinations of architecture and landscape anywhere in the world, cost three-quarters of a million *gulden* but was paid for out of income. The grandest of all European monasteries was surely St Sergius-Trinity to the north of Moscow, which owned 106,000 serfs on its over one hundred estates scattered across six provinces. An English traveller, William Coxe, found it 'so large as at a little distance to have the appearance of a small town . . . Beside the convent or habitation for the monks, the walls enclose an imperial palace and nine large churches constructed by different sovereigns.' Simon Dixon has estimated that in 1762, when all monastic land was expropriated, the Russian monasteries owned around two-thirds of Russia's ploughed land, a total which had doubled during the previous two centuries.

With wealth went power. The prestige still enjoyed by the great foundations ensured that their abbots and provosts were well placed to secure further preferment in both the secular and the ecclesiastical world. Of the eighteenth-century popes, Benedict XIII (1724–30) was a Dominican, Clement XIV (1769–74) a Franciscan and Pius VII (elected 1800) a Benedictine. In the Iberian peninsula the relationship between ruling house and the monastic world was especially close, symbolized as it was by Philip II's grim palace-cum-monastery of El Escorial, and was also especially durable. In Spain, Bourbon princes and princesses emulated their Habsburg predecessors by withdrawing to monasteries, while John V of Portugal built his own version of the Escorial at Mafra between 1717 and 1730 with 880 rooms and 330 cells for the monks. Of all the orders, the most successful in gaining that all-important proximity to sovereign power was the Society of Jesus. By the end of the seventeenth century most of the Catholic rulers of Europe had Jesuits as their confessors. Through their control of most universities and many secondary schools, the Jesuits were also well placed to influence the elites in a more indirect fashion. 'Give me a child until he reaches adolescence and he will be mine for life' was a boast popularly attributed to the order, although its validity looks suspect when the educational background of such anti-clericals as Voltaire and Diderot is considered.

In the Holy Roman Empire, the more important abbeys were *reichsunmittelbar*, that is to say represented in the *Reichstag* and ruling over their own secular territories as the monastic equivalents of the prince-bishops examined in a previous section. More remarkably, despite their wealth and power, they had not fallen into the hands of the nobility. Indeed, they offered the fastest route for advancement open to any Catholic commoner, although only a tiny handful could benefit. These were small territories, with just 10,000–20,000 inhabitants, so it is some measure of the fierce cultural competition between them that it prompted the Abbot of Weingarten to build a gigantic church capable of holding a congregation of 12,000, or successive abbots of Ottobeuren to spend more than fifty years completely rebuilding their abbey. Even those abbots who were 'mediated', that is to say subject to a secular authority, could often exert political influence through their membership of the Estates, having benefited at the time of the Reformation from the search by Catholic princes for allies against the predominantly Protestant nobility. Such was the case in Bavaria, where the heads of twenty-five Benedictine, six Cistercian and eight Augustinian houses made up the bench of prelates in the Electorate's Estates. A similar situation prevailed in Austria, where the Abbot of Melk was made President of the First Estate of the Lower Austrian Estates in 1631. In this capacity he became more of a politician and administrator than a spiritual leader, spending much of his time in Vienna, residing at the 'Melkerhof' and leaving his abbatial duties back at Melk to the prior.

Melk had been granted to the Benedictines in 1089 by Margrave Leopold I, so falls into that category of the very old foundations whose members, in the view of McManners, were both the wealthiest and the most idle: 'those who had come earliest to work in the vineyard were the first to retire to the shade'. In truth, the contemporary reputation of all monks was the same, their functions memorably summed up by Voltaire in the lapidary triad: 'they sing, they eat, they digest'. Certainly it would be difficult to reconcile the lifestyle of the monks of Melk or Mafra with the biblical text on which monasticism is based – 'Love not the world, neither the things that are in the world. If any man love the world, the love of the Father is not in him. For all that is in the world [is] the lust of the flesh . . .' (I John 2:15–16). Of course, it might be thought that few, if any, institutions of the Church would survive a rigorous application of scriptural tests. Yet there is more to be said for the old regime monks than the comments by the Reverend McManners and Voltaire might suggest.

In the first place, they appear to have been relatively benevolent landlords. Any peasant offered the choice between a secular and an ecclesiastical lord would have done well to have opted for the latter. Of course, that is to take the short-term view. It must be conceded, *sub specie aeternitatis*, that the grasp of so much property in the 'dead hands' of the monasteries probably stifled enterprise and inhibited agricultural productivity. A Spanish official commissioned by Charles III to look after the interests of the common people expressed the view that 'a town over which a wealthy religious corporation . . . has gained control falls in a few years into the deepest misery. For, more influential than all their townsmen, they buy up today the fields, tomorrow the vineyards, later the houses, and finally all real property, until they have forced once useful subjects down to the miserable level of beggars.' Especially the rural population preferred to see the direct benefits conferred by the monasteries, not least as employers. It has been estimated by Dietmar Stutzer that perhaps as many as one in ten of the Bavarian labour force were employees of the monasteries or their dependants. The monasteries were also sources of charitable relief at times of harvest failure, as in 1768–9 when thousands of Galician peasants flocked to Santiago de Compostela. Many monks served as parish priests, returning to their monasteries only occasionally, as did 600 Premonstratensians in France. In the eighteenth century more than a third of the monks of Melk were engaged full-time in parochial duties (a practice which continues). Those who remained behind certainly liked to make themselves comfortable, introducing stoves to their cells in the late seventeenth century, for example, but they also appear to have been diligent in their observance of canonical duties. They were also assiduous in promoting popular education through their schools and in protecting elite culture through their collections. At Melk music was a special beneficiary: in the course of the 1770s the monks acquired eighty-three symphonies and seventy-three Masses. According to one eminent authority (Richard van Dülmen), the early Enlightenment in Bavaria can be described as 'part of the monastic renaissance beginning c.1700'. If the Enlightenment did not feature prominently on the Spanish intellectual landscape, monks were to the fore in what there was of it, notably the Benedictine Benito Feijoo.

So the monasteries were not moribund in the eighteenth century. As Beales has now shown, it was then that they reached a climax of power and prosperity. However, as he also demonstrates, after the middle of the century, hostile pressures began to grow. It was not that the monks and nuns were less pious or less useful or whatever, rather that the attitude of the secular world had changed. When William Beckford visited the Escorial and was shown their most precious relic – a feather from the wing of the Angel Gabriel – his report neither reflected nor was intended to excite reverence. On the contrary. Plebeian pilgrims from all over Catholic Europe continued to flock to Weingarten to venerate the drop of the Sacred Blood of Christ kept there or to Mariazell to adore the image of the Black Virgin, the *Magna Mater Austriae*, but higher up the social scale, indifference and hostility were growing. Most fatally, sovereigns were beginning to distance themselves from the monastic ideal. The Holy Roman Emperor Charles VI (1711–40) planned to turn the Augustinian monastery of Klosterneuburg outside Vienna into an Austrian version of the Escorial; his daughter, Maria Theresa, cancelled the project and returned to Schönbrunn, the Austrian version of Versailles. Of the pious Portuguese King John V (1706–50), the builder of Mafra, Voltaire wrote: 'when he wanted a festival, he ordered a religious parade. When he wanted a new building, he built a convent. When he wanted a mistress, he took a nun'; his son, Joseph I, abandoned Mafra to its monks.

Joseph I also abandoned the Society of Jesus to his enlightened minister, the Marquês de Pombal. Taking advantage of an attack on the King's life in 1758, Pombal secured royal approval for the expulsion of the Society from Portugal the following year. This proved to be the chink in the dyke, which not even papal support for the Jesuits could close. They were expelled from France in 1764 and from Spain, Naples, Parma and even Malta in 1767. Conspicuously absent from this list was the Habsburg Monarchy, where Maria Theresa and her co-regent Joseph II remained neutral in the campaign which now began to abolish the Society altogether. Joseph may have believed that the regular clergy were 'by their very nature the scourge of all Catholic provinces, and the most implacable leeches of the poor labourer and artisan', but he also recognized the invaluable services performed by the Jesuits in education. Neutrality was not enough to save them. In 1773 Clement XIV abandoned the protracted rear-guard action he had been fighting since his election in 1769 and issued the Bull *Dominus ac Redemptor*, in which he announced: 'We dissolve, suppress, extinguish, and abolish the said Society.' With varying degrees of enthusiasm, the Catholic powers moved to confiscate its assets and expel its members. Ironically, the ex-Jesuits now found refuge in non-Catholic countries such as Prussia and Russia, whose enlightened rulers used them to educate their Catholic minorities. When criticized by d'Alembert for giving refuge to the Jesuits, Frederick the Great rejoindered that he was being tolerant as a matter of principle: 'if you accuse me of being too tolerant, then I am proud of this failing; one could wish that your criticism could be levelled at all princes'.

With the advantage of hindsight, it is not difficult to appreciate why the Jesuits were so hated and so vulnerable. As the complementary principles of state sovereignty and nationalism developed, so did the order's vow of absolute obedience to the papacy become increasingly offensive to the secular powers. As a mainly urban order, whose members frequently moved from place to place, country to country and even continent to continent, it had failed to put down the deep regional roots that made the older monastic orders so resilient. Rich, powerful, privileged and secretive, its apparently over-mighty members naturally attracted hostility from outsiders, including members of other religious orders. All kinds of weird and wonderful stories circulated about the Jesuits, about their penchant for sexual irregularity, about their fabulous wealth, about their regicide conspiracies, about their plans for world domination, and so on. These were believed by people who ought to have been more sceptical, by the marquis d'Argenson, for example, who was convinced that 'nasty Italian monks' were putting together a great army in their possessions in South America, that it was already 60,000 strong and would eventually allow them to take over the world. Their vulnerability stemmed from a long-term shift in the balance between the papacy and the Catholic powers described earlier in this chapter. The pass was sold when the Bourbon powers (Spain, France and Naples, aided and abetted by their close relation Joseph II, who was actually in Rome at the time) combined at the Conclave of 1769 to secure the election of a pope less committed than Clement XIII to Jesuit survival. The successful candidate, the Franciscan friar Lorenzo Ganganelli, may not have given an absolute commitment to dissolve the Society prior to his election but he was known to be less than resolute in its support. And so it proved.

In the view of one Catholic historian (E. E. Y. Hales), the dissolution of the Jesuits was 'the most serious defeat the Church had suffered since Luther's revolt'. Leopold von Ranke, who was nineteen when the Jesuits were restored in 1814, believed that Clement XIV had shown 'serene wisdom' in sacrificing his 'Janissaries', but he of course was a Protestant. Moreover, he also recognized that the dissolution had ushered in a terrible time for the Church: 'since the outworks had been taken, a more vigorous assault of the victorious opinions on the central stronghold would inevitably follow. The commotion increased from day to day, the defection of men's minds took a constantly widening range.' In fact, the attack was already well underway, and significantly it came as much from within as from outside the Church. Emboldened by the expulsion of the Jesuits, in 1765 the Assembly of the Clergy in France petitioned Louis XV to set up a commission to investigate the monasteries. With

Archbishop Loménie de Brienne at the helm, the *Commission des réguliers* reported back with predictably hostile proposals. Eventually about a sixth of all French monastic establishments – 458 houses of 2,966 examined – were suppressed. This was less serious than it looked, as by definition they were small establishments, containing fewer than 3,000 individuals, or about a ninth of the total. What was more serious was the loss of morale inflicted on the other communities and those who might have aspired to join them, leading to a serious crisis of recruitment. A more radical purge was undertaken in the Habsburg Monarchy, where in 1781 Joseph II ordered the United Chancellery to prepare the dissolution of all religious orders that were 'completely and utterly useless' and therefore could not be pleasing to God. These he defined as those that did not run schools or hospitals or help their fellow beings in other practical ways. By the time of Joseph's death, the imposition of this order had changed the Church in the Habsburg Monarchy radically and irreversibly. The 25,000 monks and nuns were reduced in ten years to just 11,000, a weeding out which involved the dissolution of 530 monastic institutions in the central lands (Bohemia, Austria and Hungary) alone. In other words, from constituting 53 per cent of the clergy in 1780, the regulars had sunk to 29 per cent by the end of the decade. The Counter-Reformation in the Danubian lands was over.

POPULAR RELIGION AND 'DECHRISTIANIZATION'

As Derek Beales has written, the popular sobriquet for the eighteenth century – 'the age of reason' – has less justification than 'the age of religion' or 'the Christian century'. It was characterized by dissenting movements within the established Churches which testified to the undiminished and perhaps intensified vitality of lay devotion: Jansenism, Pietism and Methodism in the Catholic, Lutheran and Anglican Churches respectively. In the Catholic world, the period after 1648 saw a great revival in pilgrimages, following the decline caused by the Reformation. Encouraged by the relative security of travelling in an age of numerous but restricted wars, never before had so many faithful been on the road to shrines near and far, old and new. Of the three *peregrinationes maiores* – Jerusalem, Rome and Santiago de Compostela – the two European destinations enjoyed major revivals. In a Holy Year, up to half-a-million pilgrims are said to have sought shelter at the main hospice for pilgrims in the Holy City, Santa Trinità dei Pellegrini, where they were given board and lodging and even a packed lunch for their visits to the seven churches necessary for an indulgence. At Santiago de Compostela in northern Spain, believed to house the body of St James, the crush of pilgrims in 1717 outstripped the supply of confessors. North of the Alps too there was a surge of support. As Henry Russell Hitchcock observed in his study of rococo architecture, pilgrimages in southern Germany became 'unbelievably popular' in the eighteenth century. Among other examples he cites the Benedictine monastery at Ettal in Bavaria, whose cult statue of the Virgin attracted 70,000 visitors a year and worked no fewer than 1,930 miracles between 1600 and 1761. Also popular were pilgrimage places of recent origin, such as Maria Taferl near Melk in Lower Austria, where in 1642 a dying oak tree was miraculously restored to health by the placing of a *pietà* in its branches, a good deed it then reciprocated by performing miracles itself. To accommodate the growing number of pilgrims, construction was begun in 1661 of a magnificent baroque church, designed by Jakob Prandtauer, the architect of nearby Melk. In that year there were 36,000 communicants, a figure which had doubled by 1700 and went on rising to 186,000 in 1751 and 250,000 in 1760, despite the destruction of both the sacred oak and its protective *pietà* by fire in 1755. The greatest pilgrimage place in the Habsburg Monarchy was Mariazell in Styria, where the Black Virgin or *Magna Mater Austriae* attracted between 120,000 and 150,000 pilgrims each year from all over Austria, Bohemia and Hungary, rising to 188,000 in 1727 and 373,000 in 1757. The pilgrimages also had an important influence on the 'sacral landscape' of Catholic Europe. To the parish churches and monasteries they added a plethora of crucifixes, shrines and chapels to mark their itinerary. During the 1680s, for example, forty-four chapels were added to the 'Holy Way' from Prague to Altbuzlau.

First cousins to the pilgrimages, indeed often difficult to separate from them, were religious processions. In the great cities these could be highly elaborate affairs, crossing the boundaries between official and popular initiatives, as prelates, priests and secular authorities were also often involved. In Paris, according to John McManners, their splendour made them important tourist attractions. He cites the annual procession by the parishioners of Saint-Leu-Saint-Gilles to a statue of Notre Dame de la Carolles, reaching a climax with the burning in effigy of the Swiss Guard who, three centuries earlier, had stabbed the statue in a drunken fit of iconoclasm. By 1743 this harmless bonfire party no longer matched the image the Church wished to project, and the ecclesiastical authorities tried to replace it with a High Mass. They were ignored. And so were the Anglican clergy who tried to put a stop to the 'superstitious practices' accompanying the numerous processions that survived the Reformation in Great Britain. On Anglesey, for example, the religious element of the Easter procession was diluted by the secular recreations which followed, such as egg-collecting for the children and football matches and cock-fighting for the adults. Everywhere, beating the bounds of the parish at Rogationtide (Ascension Day) not only thanked God for the fruits of the field but also performed an important practical function. At a time when there was no Ordnance Survey to fix parish boundaries, this formal perambulation gave a 'mental map' of where one belonged, what church one went to, where one's rites of passage were performed, and where one applied for alms. As W. M. Jacob has well put it: 'It established a collective memory for the community and defined those who were inside the community, and who and what should be prayed for.'

Also a blend of sacred and profane were the numerous confraternities and other forms of religious association. If they were not the invention of this period, they certainly flourished during it. Although this was in part due to the encouragement they received from the new Orders, especially the Jesuits, they could not have attained their prominent role in both urban and rural life without a powerful response from the laity. The eighteenth century is often labelled the age of the voluntary association, but it is invariably secular organizations such as reading clubs and Masonic lodges that are advanced as evidence. Yet when it came to membership, it was the confraternities that posted the highest scores. A survey of forty-one parishes in the Electorate of Trier, for example, revealed that all except one had a confraternity and most had two or more. Looking at it from the other direction, Ronnie Hsia has concluded: 'Tridentine Catholicism succeeded in the long term not by suppressing "superstitions" but by grafting orthodoxy onto traditional and popular spirituality.' But it was not always sweetness and light. As enlightened influence permeated the clergy and their secular masters, popular forms of piety came under attack. As we shall see when we examine the issue of toleration as part of the state's modernizing agenda, the motives were various. Together with a distaste for 'superstition' went more materialist concerns such as the maximization of productivity. A good example was provided by the drastic reduction of religious festivals decreed by one government after another. In France, depending on the actual diocese, around a hundred working days per year were lost to festivals, excluding Sundays. Even after the bishops had carried out a purge, there were still thirty-four days of compulsory leisure (*fêtes chômées*) in the diocese of Rouen and more than seventy in Bordeaux and Autun. The same motive lay behind the ban on lengthy pilgrimages. It was at least partly the wish to turn celibate monks and nuns into procreating members of society that lay behind the attacks on the monasteries that gathered momentum during the second half of the eighteenth century.

The devout laity could accept many of these changes. It was when the authorities turned their attention to religious practices that real trouble began. In most cases the decrees ordering the removal of this or that wonder-working statue, or the cessation of this or that pilgrimage, were simply ignored, and that was the end of it. But where this immoveable object met a force that aspired to be irresistible, as it did most spectacularly in the case of Joseph II, violence was sure to follow. One example must suffice. In 1787 the ecclesiastical authorities in the Electorate of Mainz ordered the introduction of a vernacular hymn book. Despite their best efforts to prepare the ground, the rumour soon spread among the laity that it was heretical, the fact that the hymns were written in German and were given numbers – just like the Lutheran books – being regarded as especially suspicious. In fact explicit instructions had been given to the compilers not to include any Protestant hymns. The dissidents remained unconvinced. In most parishes they were content simply to ignore the new hymn book and continue singing in Latin, but where the local priest insisted on carrying out the Vicariate's orders, conflict resulted. Copies which did find their way into the hands of the peasants were promptly torn up and burnt. They may well have been incited by the regular clergy, as the provincial head of the Capuchins was told that if members of his Order continued to preach against singing hymns in German, action would be taken against the Order as a whole. In a number of villages in the Rheingau there were outbreaks of violence and intimidation, and at Rüdesheim something approaching an insurrection broke out. Led by a cooper called Kron, variously described by observers as 'inflated' and 'somewhat unbalanced', the pious citizens took the law into their own hands. On a Sunday in June 1787, Kron and his supporters brushed aside a detail of soldiers outside the church and proceeded to conduct a service themselves in what they believed to be Latin. On the same evening a brawl erupted when one of the Electoral officials was unwise enough to remonstrate with a group of dissidents. The conflict reached a climax a few days later when a group of citizens broke into the local jail and freed one of their imprisoned leaders. At this point the central government in Mainz intervened, and despatched three hundred troops to quell the rising.

The Archbishop had imposed his will, but he was sensible enough to realize that the limits of his authority had been reached. In the following year a new edition of the offending book was published, accompanied by the proviso that 'neither force nor punishments' were to be employed in its introduction. Further concessions allowed a mixture of German and Latin hymns or the two forms to be used on alternate Sundays. In reality, the laity did as they pleased, a state of affairs formally recognized in 1791 when a purely Latin liturgy was allowed once more. By that time, the threat from revolutionary France was making disputes of this kind seem decidedly parochial. The French armies which ravaged the Rhineland repeatedly from 1792 proved to be incomparably less sensitive to popular forms of piety than even the most enlightened reformer of the old regime. Everywhere in Catholic Europe, the revolutionaries' violent anti-clericalism and iconoclasm inflicted the rudest shock to the faith in all of Christian history. The response of the faithful was to intensify their attachment to traditional practices. No matter how hard the occupation authorities tried, they could not put a stop to processions, pilgrimages and all the other public religious demonstrations.

As we shall see when examining counter-revolutionary movements in Europe after 1789, religious enthusiasm could make life very difficult for the French. It was not just faith that was at stake, it was also material existence. For those who believed that God was a presence both permanent and ubiquitous, propitiation of Him was a matter of life and death. The following example from the Rhineland will serve for most rural, and many urban, communities across Europe:

Experience has shown, since time began, that when we do not carry out the usual processions in public in the weeks of the Cross [leading up to Ascension Day], to seek God's blessing and protection for our crops, and now that we are forbidden to do so by the French authorities, that just about every year the harvest fails: sometimes it is the corn which is ruined, sometimes the buckwheat, and the yields are generally poor: if one is sparing in one's worship of God, so will God be sparing in the blessings he bestows on the world. So now we have an almost unbroken run of bad years, one after the other.

It was an unfortunate fact of confessional geography that the regions immediately adjacent to France were among the most clericalist and demonstratively pious on the continent: the Austrian Netherlands (Belgium), the Rhineland, Spain and Italy. Invasion by the first avowedly secular state in European history made them more clericalist and more demonstratively pious. One sign of the intense religious excitement of the period was the rash of miracles which followed. In the Puglian town of Andria, a statue of Christ exhorted the citizens to resist the French invaders, promising a squadron of angels with flaming swords to help them; at Aachen a company of angels intervened to replace a market-cross removed by the French; at Arezzo it was St Donato and the Virgin herself who paid a visit to foment unrest; at the church of St Remigius at Bonn, following a forty-hour prayer, the lights on the altar formed the letters 'V.M.F.' to stand for '*Vivat Max Franz*', the Elector of Cologne, whose capital Bonn was. And so on, and so forth.

This explosion of popular piety would seem to give the lie to the view that the eighteenth century was marked by a process of 'dechristianiz-ation'. On the other hand, many contemporaries can be found lamenting the decline of true religion and the growth of impiety: in Montpellier, Madrid, London, Hamburg, Berlin, Vienna, even Rome. As early as the later seventeenth century, a Parisian parish priest was told by one of his parishioners, a lawyer: 'Sir, I am in no state to confess my sins or receive the sacraments, although you were good enough to clarify my difficulties on the Christian religion which I have professed externally to avoid notice and save appearances. In the bottom of my soul I feel it is all a fairy tale. And I am not alone in this: 20,000 other people in Paris share my views. We know each other, we hold secret meetings, and we strengthen each other in our irreligious resolve.' However fragmentary, this kind of evidence does suggest that important changes were underway. Whether it justifies the use of the word 'dechristianization' is a different matter. It seems reasonable to conclude that in France some people ceased to believe, and that their numbers were probably growing. On the other hand, there is persuasive statistical evidence to show that a very large number of French men and women of all classes remained devout. For example, when a change in the publishing laws in 1778 made it easier for the works of deceased authors to be reprinted, almost two-thirds of the two million volumes which then poured from the presses were religious. Some of the changes, at least, can be explained in terms of a change in the *style* of religious practice rather than its substance. Orthodox Catholics may well have taken the view that Jansenism was like the River Danube – beginning Catholic, becoming Protestant and ending infidel – but the Jansenists themselves believed they were not just devout Christians (which they undoubtedly were) but also true Catholics. Moreover, the boundary between outright rejection and fervent devotion was (and remains) both broad and hazy. Of the occasional conformers jolted out of indifference by the shock of the French Revolution, some became aggressively anti-clerical, while others returned to active defence of the faith. Some historians have detected 'a disintegration of Christian discourse ... the decline of Christian commitment' (Daniel Roche), but others have taken the view that 'it was in the eighteenth century that the piety of the Catholic Reformation won the day ... it was the truly Christian century' (Dominique Julia). If it is impossible to reconcile these generalizations, it can probably be agreed, with John McManners, that 'dechristianization' is too strong a term to summarize developments before 1789 and is best reserved for the blitz launched by the revolutionary regimes.

Outside France, there is little evidence to suggest that Paul Hazard's famous claim that, 'One day, the French people, almost to a man [*sic*], were thinking like Bossuet; the day after, they were thinking like Voltaire', can be exported. As we have seen, in most of Europe, whether Catholic, Protestant or Orthodox, reform came from above, in association with the authorities. In France, Jansenism was persecuted; in the rest of Catholic Europe, it was promoted. Its Protestant equivalent, Pietism, began as a reaction against the established Churches, for its emphasis on the priesthood of all believers and informal devotional groups, on the need for a born-again conversion experience and the priority of the 'inner light', together with its spontaneity and emotion, all conspired to alarm the Lutheran clergy. Yet it was eventually absorbed within the established structure. Consequently, organized religion did not acquire the image of reactionary ossification that afflicted the Church in France.

The Enlightenment's characteristic slogan in France was Voltaire's battle cry '*Écrasez l'infâme!*' but it was not heard elsewhere until the following century. For the mass of the population before the last decade of the eighteenth century, the ecclesiastical authorities came under fire not because they were too conservative but because their enlightened reforms were thought to be ungodly. As we have seen, from Brabant to Tuscany, from Moscow to the Tyrol, trouble only arose when attempts were made to interfere with traditional forms of religious practice. That could cause short-term problems for governments, but in the long term proved to be a great source of strength.

8

Court and Country

HUNTING IN FRANCE

On 14 December 1676 Elizabeth Charlotte ('Liselotte') of the Palatinate, duchesse d'Orléans and sister-in-law of Louis XIV, wrote to her Aunt Sophie, Electress of Hanover, from Saint d'Germain:

I do beg your pardon for not writing for such an eternity. First of all I have been at Versailles, where I was kept busy the whole day long. We hunted all morning, got back at 3 o'clock in the afternoon, changed, went up to gamble until 7 o'clock, then to the play, which never ended before 10.30, then on to supper, and afterwards to the ball until 3 o'clock in the morning, and then we went to bed.

As a summary of court culture, this would be hard to beat for its succinctness. Most European countries during this period were monarchies, all monarchies had courts, and the favoured daytime occupation of courts was hunting. Perhaps influenced by the repugnance expressed by liberal opinion today for hunting, very few historians have felt able to give the activity more than a disdainful mention in passing (a notable exception to this rule is John Adamson, who has noted: 'no court could be without an extensive establishment devoted to the hunt'). Yet its importance to seventeenth- and eighteenth-century elites (and not just the elites, as we shall see) requires that any instinctive distaste should be overridden. Philippe Salvadori, the author of the most scholarly study of French hunting, was not overstating the case when he wrote: '*Vivre en roi, c'est chasser, et chasser régulièrement . . . Ce divertissement est une part du métier de roi: son accomplissement resemble à une liturgie*' (To live as a king is to hunt, and to hunt regularly . . . This recreation is part of the king's job: its realization is like a liturgy). Not for nothing does hunting feature in two of the defining legends surrounding the rise and fall of the French monarchy. On 13 April 1655 the sixteen-year-old Louis XIV was hunting at Vincennes when he learnt that the Parlement of Paris was proposing to discuss edicts it had already registered in his presence. Still dressed in his hunting clothes and boots, and brandishing his riding-whip, he stormed into the chamber and berated the Parlementaires for their impertinence. When the First President of the court, Pompone de Bellièvre (himself a keen hunter), sought to justify their actions by reference to the interest of the state, Louis famously replied: 'L'état, c'est moi!'

If he did not actually use this famous phrase (even Ernest Lavisse referred to it as a 'legend'), the heightened sense of excitement induced by the royal arrival from the chase was authentic. More securely documented is the obverse of this episode, the entry made by Louis' great-great-great-grandson (but only next-but-one successor) in his diary for Tuesday, 14 July 1789: 'nothing'. Even Louis XVI must have been aware that the fall of the Bastille was of *some* importance. What he meant by 'nothing' was that he had not gone hunting that day. To rephrase the Roman Emperor Titus, Louis counted a day without hunting a day lost. The following extract provides a good idea of his priorities: 'July 1789 – Wednesday, 1st, nothing. Deputation from the Estates [General] ... Thursday 9th, nothing. Deputation from the Estates. Friday, 10th, nothing. Reply to the Deputation from the Estates. Saturday 11th, nothing. Resignation of M. Necker ... Tuesday, 14th, nothing ... October, Monday 5th, shooting party at the Châtillon Gate; killed eighty-one items of game. Interrupted by events. Left and returned on horseback.' The 'events' were the 'October Days', when the Queen was nearly lynched by a mob of Parisians and the entire royal family was, in effect, taken prisoner and escorted back to Paris.

The bag of eighty-one was modest by royal standards. Louis kept very careful account in his diary of the game he killed. In December 1775 he recorded the death of 1,564 items, bringing his annual total up to 8,424. The limitations imposed by eighteenth-century musketry did not prevent large scores being achieved quickly. According to the marquis de Dangeau, on 30 June 1706 the ducs de Berry and de Bourgogne (Louis XIV's grandsons) shot more than 1,500 partridges on the plain of Saint-Denis. Another aristocratic chronicler, the duc de Luynes, reported in 1750 that Louis XV shot 318 in three hours at Versailles and another 135 in an hour-and-a-half a few days later. The record seems to have been the 1,700 shot by the King and his entourage on the plain of Saint-Denis on 13 September 1738. Slaughter on this scale required more than a steady hand and a strong stomach. By the end of Louis XIV's long reign, an elaborate, large and very expensive hunting organization had been developed, subdivided into several specialized sections determined by the nature of predator and prey.

Traditionally at the apex was falconry, not least because it was the most ancient and did not involve the use of firearms. In 1750 the Grand Falconry, presided over by the grand falconer, who counted as one of the principal officers of the royal household, numbered eighty-nine birds, to which should be added the forty-odd of the *fauconnerie du cabinet* and the dozen or so of the *fauconnerie de la chambre*. Why the King should need three separate mews of hawks remains a mystery. The most prized birds were the nearly white Greenland falcons, followed by the Icelandic falcon and the Scandinavian gyrfalcon, with the smaller hobbies, merlins (especially favoured by aristocratic ladies) and kestrels (the easiest to train) bringing up the rear. Despite its size and grandeur, the eagle was rarely used, although Salvadori conjectures that the size of the prey – a roebuck and a wild boar – suggests that it must have been an eagle that was employed for Louis XIV's last hawking expedition. By this time hawking had declined to a spring ritual rather than a serious form of hunting. Louis XIV was keen, employing a total hawking personnel of 175 and adding a fourth cast of gyrfalcons to hunt hares in 1682, but even in his heyday he hawked for only between five and thirteen days a year; Louis XV was less enthusiastic and Louis XVI closed down the hawking establishment altogether. Part of the problem may have been the disproportionate effort required, as it required endless training, careful co-ordination of dog, bird, horse and man and often a great deal of time to bring down just one bird (the heron was especially favoured) or small mammal (usually a hare). Charles d'Arcussier claimed in the middle of the seventeenth century that a skilled falconer with one sparrow-hawk could catch seventy quail in a day during their migration, but, even if true, this was clearly an exception.

Also in decline was wolf-hunting, despite the fact that the wolf is the only form of prey that could be described unequivocally as a danger to humankind. Louis XIV's eldest son, the Grand Dauphin, was a very keen wolf-hunter – indeed, he was very keen on any and every form of hunting, even to the extent of hunting stone martens with a pack of basset hounds – but after his death in 1711, the wolf-pack was hunted only by the Master of the Wolf-Hounds and his professional huntsmen. Although the wild boar had its supporters, throughout this period the most popular target of the royal hunt was unquestionably the stag. Its prestige was indicated by the status of the Master of the Stag Hounds (*Grand veneur*) as one of the great officers of the royal household. The stag, which can be defined as a male red deer at least five years old, owed its pre-eminence to more than its size and beauty. Its longevity was fabled: a chronicler of Charles VI (1380–1422) recorded that the King had killed a stag wearing a collar inscribed *Haec Caesar me donavit*, demonstrating that its life had once been spared by a Roman emperor. It was not until the eighteenth century that an average lifespan of thirty to forty years was established. It was also believed that stags liked music and could be tamed by the playing of a flute. Perhaps most important, its elaborate mating rituals and huge antlers were thought to reveal a sexual potency worthy of a King of France.

By the reign of Louis XIV, stag-hunting had long been a ritual in ten parts, helpfully summarized by Gunnar Brusewitz: 1. using a blood-hound or other tracker dog, the chief huntsman locates the stag intended for the hunt, leaving it undisturbed but making careful note of the size of the antlers and any other distinguishing mark; 2. the hunters and their dogs, still on the leash, gather in a forest clearing nearby; 3. the huntsman's horn-call announces that the stag is on the move, the dogs are unleashed and the hunt begins; 4. the hunt moves in pursuit through the forest, the stag's progress is signalled by cry and one of a large repertoire of horn-calls; 5. if the stag should be uncooperative enough to leave the hunting grounds, it is the huntsman's job to use his hounds to bring it back to the main party; 6. as the hunt progresses, the huntsmen need to take care that the pack stays on the line of the original stag; 7. if the hunt is long – and it could take many hours – part of the pack will be rested at strategic points, from which they can be brought back into the chase when required; 8. if 'the hart pants for cooling streams when heated in the chase' (Psalm 42 as paraphrased by Tate and Brady) and takes to the water, the huntsman sounds a special signal to bring the main hunting party to observe what is deemed to be an especially pleasing spectacle; 9. when the exhausted stag stands at bay to face its pursuers, huntsmen creep from behind to cut its tendons, to prevent it harming the dogs as they surround their prey, and the Master of the Hunt goes forward to deliver the *coup de grâce* by slitting the stag's throat with his hunting knife; 10. in the final phase, introduced by Louis XIV, a loud fanfare from the hunting horns proclaims the successful conclusion of the hunt, the pack is allowed to fight for the stag's entrails, the tracker dog is allowed to sink its teeth into the stag's head and the huntsman holds aloft the trophy of antlers.

Given the numbers involved – hunters, horses and dogs often all ran well into three figures – this ritualized slaughter had to be carefully choreographed. It should not be thought that they charged through the forests wherever the stag might lead them. On the contrary, broad tracks, generously proportioned cross roads and specially constructed bridges allowed the hunting party to follow the action in safety and comfort, even in carriages if preferred. Louis XIV cut fifty-four new hunting roads through the forest of Compiègne and his successor added another 400 *lieues* (1,000 miles, or 1,600 km). The elaborate shapes employed for these hunt-ways and the buildings constructed at the intersections combined to create what Martin Knoll has aptly termed 'a scenery of princely presence' – a landscape formed especially for hunting. This symbolic conquest of rude nature was not confined to France. A particularly good example was to be found in Nicolas de Pigage's plan for a game-park attached to the Elector Palatine's residence at Schwetzingen, which combined a circle with eight rides radiating from its centre and a square intersected by six main avenues and several interlocking subsidiaries, the whole linked by a broad avenue to the main palace.

Compiègne was only one of many great hunting grounds. Louis XIV expanded the hunting reserve at Versailles to 30,000 acres and also bought the Rambouillet estate and 57,000 acres to the south-west. In the autumn the whole court moved to Fontainebleau, primarily to hunt in the forests which surrounded the palace. These great tracts were needed if the game were not to be exhausted, for hunting was always a weekly and sometimes even a daily ritual. Towards the end of his reign Louis XIV was hunting between 110 and 140 days a year, Louis XV always hunted three days a week and often more, while Louis XVI hunted on average every other day. Apart from the royal reserves, they could also count on invitations to the hunts of their near-relations, the duc d'Orléans, the prince de Condé and the prince de Conti, at Saint-Cloud, Chantilly and Isle d'Adam respectively. The duchesse d'Orléans,

Louis XIV's sister-in-law, recorded: 'There is hunting every day; on Sunday and Wednesday, it is my son [the duc de Chartres]. The King hunts his own packs on Monday and Thursday; on Wednesday and Saturday the Dauphin goes wolf-hunting, the comte de Toulouse [Louis XIV's illegitimate son] hunts on Monday and Wednesday, his brother the duc de Maine [another illegitimate son] on Tuesday, and M. le duc [d'Orléans] on Friday; it is said that if all the various hunting establishments were mustered together, there would be between 900 horses and 1,000 dogs.' As this suggests, the cadet branches of the Bourbons were almost as active as the King himself: the legendary stables and kennels at Chantilly, rebuilt between 1719 and 1735, could house 240 horses and 250 dogs respectively. This did not change as the century progressed. The prince de Condé's chief huntsman, Jacques Toudouze, kept a careful record from 1748 until 1785 of everything accomplished by the hunt, yielding the scarcely credible but authenticated total of 924,717 items of game killed during those years.

In short, hunting was a major exercise for those at the apex of the French monarchy. In 1750 the duc de Luynes estimated that the two royal stables at Versailles housed 2,100 horses, plus 300 specifically for the hunt; the kennels erected there in 1682 could hold up to 300 dogs and its capacity was doubled by Louis XV in 1737 with another block of kennels custom-built for puppies. Even after Louis XVI's economies, the total cost of hunting was well in excess of a million *livres* per annum. If the amount of game actually killed is a criterion, then the operation was certainly successful. On 27 December 1738 Louis XV recorded that during the course of the current year he had killed 110 stags with one pack of hounds and 98 with the other, a total he was expecting to raise to three figures before the end of the year. But of course even this amount of venison represented a pitiful return on the amount of time and money invested. So, why did three successive Bourbons devote themselves so intensively to the chase and especially to stag-hunting? Part of the appeal may have come from it being seen as a surrogate for warfare: 'the sport of kings, image of war, without its guilt', as the English poet William Somerville put it. His fellow countryman, William Beckford, was more explicit: 'Hunting is a kind of warfare; its uncertainties, its fatigues, its difficulties and its dangers rendering it interesting above all other diversions.' D'Onofri, the panegyricist of King Charles III of Naples, compared his master to Hercules when he hunted, presenting the quarry as an allegory of civilization and arguing that hunting was the sport of rulers because it developed their military skills while 'ameliorating the motions of the sovereign's soul'. He also presented hunting as a special form of magnificence which consequently lent itself to representational display. Indeed, kings did have themselves portrayed conducting a hunt as if they were waging a campaign, as for example in the numerous pictorial depictions of Louis XIV and his stag-hounds in full cry.

Alternatively, they had themselves painted in hunting costume to emphasize the qualities – courage, endurance, skill, mastery over nature, etc. – which characterized the ideal huntsman. An aesthetically brilliant example was Goya's portrait of the undistinguished Charles IV of Spain, who needed all the help he could get. The place of soldiers was taken by the hounds, to which a large part of the pursuit and despatch of the prey had been transferred. As Norbert Elias observed: 'With the delegation by the humans to the hounds of a major part of the pursuit and also of the killing function, and with the submission of the hunting gentlemen to an elaborate self-imposed code of restraints, part of the enjoyment of hunting had become a visual enjoyment; the pleasure derived from doing had been transformed into the pleasure of seeing it done.' A strong bond formed between hunter and hound, as Louis XIV registered when he had his favourites – Diane, Blonde, Bonne, Nonne, Ponne, Folle, Mite, Tane, Zette – painted for display at his private château of Marly.

Hunting the stag in the royal forests was expressly reserved for the King and his immediate family, and woe betide any lesser mortal caught disobeying this prohibition. So it is tempting to see the vigorous promotion of hunting by the Sun King as part of a wider exercise in distancing the monarch from his aristocrats, who in the past had tried to reduce him to being *primus inter pares* and might do so again. The elaborate ceremonial developed on the occasion of the King's getting up (*lever*) and going to bed (*coucher*) are well known. It was played out again in miniature on the occasion of the King's putting on his boots to go hunting (*botter*) and taking them off on his return (*débotter*). There was the same competition among the courtiers to be a participant in this ritual. To accompany the King in his carriage on the way to a hunt or on the way home, or – the ultimate favour – to have supper with the King afterwards, were also hotly competed for. The hunt was also used to promote competition among the courtiers for special favours. Any of them might follow the hunt but only a select few were invited to wear the hunt uniform and thus become formally part of the royal hunting party. To maximize the opportunities for dispensing this distinction, there was a different uniform for different palaces – red with gold embroidery for the Trianon, green for Compiègne, blue for Choisy, and so on.

The integration of hunting in court ritual was cemented when participation in the royal hunt became both a privilege and an obligation for nobles newly presented at court. Chateaubriand discovered this to his cost when, very reluctantly, he succumbed to family pressure and agreed to be presented to Louis XVI at Versailles in February 1787. Following his presentation, he was told by the senior court official, the duc de Coigny, to join the hunting party the next day in the forest of Saint-Germain and so 'set out in the early morning towards my punishment, in the uniform of a *débutant*: a grey coat, red waistcoat and breeches, lace tops, Hessian boots, a hunting-knife in my belt, and a small, gold-laced French hat'. He was provided with a horse from the royal stables but unfortunately 'L'Heureuse' (Happy) did not live up to her name, being 'a fast animal, but hard-mouthed, skittish and full of tricks'. When he eventually managed to clamber on to her back, L'Heureuse bolted and Chateaubriand found himself carried towards the action at uncontrollable speed, first cannoning into a group of courtiers and then committing the cardinal sin of arriving at the kill ahead of the King. Although the latter was good-natured about this faux pas, when they got back to Versailles, Chateaubriand upset his ambitious brother by refusing to wait for the unbooting ceremony – 'the moment of triumph and favour' – and by scurrying back to Paris. 'I took an invincible dislike to the Court', Chateaubriand recorded drily in his memoirs. *Mutatis mutandis*, courtiers seeking to curry favour with the King went out of their way to provide lavish hunting displays. At the Isle d'Adam in 1723 the prince de Conti organized a hunt employing 80 horses and 150 dogs to hunt a single stag, which eventually succumbed after a four-hour chase.

It is obviously impossible to assess what degree of social and political calculation was involved in the Bourbon promotion of hunting. It is possible, as Philippe Salvadori has argued, that the regular ritual slaughter of so many animals enhanced the King's sacral status. It is certainly the case that French treatises – and only French treatises – on hunting drew attention to this aspect. On the other hand, successive kings may have engaged in it simply because they enjoyed it, whether it was because of the beauty of the horses, dogs, hawks, stags or landscape, the appeal of exercise in the fresh air, the good companionship of the hunting party, the pleasures of al fresco refreshment, or whatever. Depicting the pleasures of the hunt and its attendant rituals created a market for painters such as Jean François de Troy, whose depiction of a sumptuous hunt-breakfast captured well *les charmes de la vie cynégétique*. What can be said with confidence is that it was the personal example of Louis XIV, Louis XV and Louis XVI that made French hunting what it was. It was their funds which supported the enormous establishment at Versailles and elsewhere and, perhaps more important, it was their personal example of regular and enthusiastic hunting which served as a model for the rest of the French aristocracy. It was also a sport in which women could participate actively. This was one aspect of French life that found favour with Liselotte of the Palatinate, the rather masculine wife of the rather feminine duc d'Orléans, who had herself painted in hunting costume by Louis Ferdinand Elle in 1673. Not the least attraction of hunting was the opportunities it provided for unchaperoned trysts deep in the forest for couples who strayed off the tracks. Watteau gave this his usual delicately erotic expression in his late masterpiece *Halt during the Chase* of 1720.

FOX-TOSSING AND OTHER ENTERTAINMENTS IN THE HOLY ROMAN EMPIRE

The prestige of the French court, especially after the decline of the Spanish model during the gloomy reign of the cretinous Charles II (1665–1700) and the emergence of the dazzling Versailles project at about the same time, ensured that hunting would assume even greater importance at other European courts than in the past. In the decentralized Holy Roman Empire, there was plenty of regional variation – the Bavarians were especially fond of badger-hunting, for example – but falconry generally enjoyed the highest status. A treatise allegedly written by the Hohenstaufen Emperor Frederick II (1212–50) was still in use in the eighteenth century. The German princes certainly numbered some of the most enthusiastic hawkers of all time, notably the Margrave Karl Friedrich von Brandenburg-Ansbach, whose hunting book recorded that he had hawked 34,429 items of game between 1730 and 1755. Also worthy of mention is Clemens August von Wittelsbach, Elector and Archbishop of Cologne (1700–61), who left iconographic evidence of his passion for hawking in the decorative scheme of the great staircase at Schloss Brühl. He also erected in the grounds of the palace a hunting lodge called 'Falcon's Pleasure' (*Falkenlust*), carefully situated on the flight-path of the herons from their eyries in the palace park to their fishing grounds in the Rhine. Other architectural evidence of the German princes' enthusiasm for hunting of all kinds can still be found in the innumerable *Jagdschlösser* or hunting lodges great and small that dot the forests. Although of only middling status in terms of territorial extent, the Landgraves of Hessen-Darmstadt, for example, built lodges at Kranichstein, Dianaburg, Mönchbruch, Wolfgarten, Wiesental, Bessung, Griesheim, Jägersburg, Bickenbach, Ernsthofen, Neu-Jägersdorf, Jägertal, Zwiefalten and Katzenbach. To call them 'lodges' does justice to neither their size nor their appearance, for several were more like substantial country houses. Jägertal, for example, consisted of fourteen separate buildings, but even so it was a tight squeeze for the hundred-odd courtiers who accompanied Landgrave Ludwig VIII (1739–68) there in autumn to hunt red deer. Kitchen records show that in 1758 the hunting party avoided the monotony of a diet of venison by consuming large amounts of fish: 263 pounds of pike, 727 pounds of carp, 126 pounds of trout, 25 pounds of perch, 54 pounds of eel, 18 barrels of gudgeon and 2,172 crabs. The representational nature of hunting is clearly revealed by the care taken with the appearance of even the smaller lodges – of Dianaburg, for example, an exquisite rococo pavilion in the Kranichstein game-park, used as an observation post and dining room.

The need to keep on the move from one hunting lodge to the next, so that supplies of game were not exhausted, meant that for several months each year the German princely courts led a semi-nomadic existence. As Martin Knoll has pointed out, with specific reference to Bavaria, this peripatetic existence paid political dividends, for it brought the ruler into contact with his rural population and allowed him to take symbolic possession of far-flung territories. As a treatise of 1711 claimed, hunting gave the princes a means of 'displaying their power all over by showing their splendour and magnificence'.

Hunting the stag in the French style, known variously as *parforce* or *chasse à courre*, was disappearing in England, as the stag population had declined so steeply, but it expanded very rapidly in the Holy Roman Empire. It was introduced to the German principalities in the 1680s and quickly became popular, despite the large sums required for huntsmen, horses and hounds and the restriction to hunting one animal at a time. It continued to be popular until the end of the next century, although times of financial stringency could bring temporary or even permanent abandonment. In the aftermath of the Seven Years War, for example, the Elector Karl Theodor of the Palatinate was obliged to abandon both *parforce* hunting and falconry.

The *Oxford English Dictionary* defines hunting as 'the act of chasing wild animals for the purpose of catching or killing them; the chase' or 'pursuit, as of a wild animal; the act of strenuously seeking or endeavouring to find something'. The German equivalent is the word *'Jagd'* but it does not have the same pro-active connotation. *Jagd* was used as a suffix for activities which involved no physical effort on the part of the hunter. The *Kampfjagd* or 'fight-hunting', for example, set one animal against another in a confined space for the benefit of spectators: bears against dogs, stags against wolves, or even lions and tigers against bulls or horses. King Frederick I of Prussia (1688–1713) was so proud of his achievements in this genre that he had a medal struck with his image on one side and the arena used for his *Kampfjagden* on the other. In the same vein was 'fox-tossing' (*Fuchsprellen*), in which a fox was tossed in a net or blanket held by hunt servants or gentlemen and ladies of the court until it expired. This usually took place in the courtyard of the prince's palace, with the assembled courtiers looking on from the palace windows. The Saxons seem to have been particularly fond of this form of entertainment: in the course of 1747 Augustus III, Elector of Saxony and King of Poland, had 414 foxes, 281 hares, 39 badgers and 9 wild cats tossed to death. It could also be found at the imperial court at Vienna, where in 1672 the Swedish envoy found it odd that the Emperor Leopold I should join with the court dwarves and small boys in delivering the *coup de grâce* to the tossed foxes by clubbing them to death.

Only marginally less offensive to modern sensibilities was the form of hunting preferred by most German courts – '*eingestellte Jagd*', which can best be translated as 'park hunting'. It was very simple: a large amount of game was driven by beaters into a specially prepared enclosure where it was shot at close range. Especially popular was an enclosure on a lake or river, so that the game could be shot from boats. This kind of hunting had the advantage of requiring no physical effort on the part of the 'hunter', apart from pulling the trigger, and, above all, of being predictable. A stag hunted *parforce* might possibly escape; a stag driven up to the barrels of the prince and his party's guns was doomed. That predictability allowed hunting to become the centrepiece of representational display when a visiting dignitary had to be impressed. In France, the King was *hors concours*; in the Holy Roman Empire, the plurality of princes made for competition. This was very bad news for the wildlife with which the endless German forests famously teemed. When park hunting began, the dukes of Württemberg were satisfied with a bag of a couple of hundred animals at a time but, once their fellow princes began to ratchet up the standard, a thousand or more were needed if the hunt were to be judged a success.

Predictability also allowed the killing to be accompanied by appropriate pageantry, organized in elaborate architectural structures. One example can suffice: the park hunt organized in 1764 by the Elector Karl Theodor of the Palatinate to mark the visit of the Elector-Archbishop Emmerich Joseph of Mainz. It is particularly well known because the papal nuncio Cardinal Giuseppe Garampi was also invited and left a detailed account of the day's proceedings. The Electoral party first drove in a convoy of carriages from the summer palace at Schwetzingen to the old capital at Heidelberg. There they embarked on the Electoral yacht, which, accompanied by a fleet of 150 boats, took them up the Neckar to the hunting ground. Three hundred peasants had worked for three weeks to beat over a hundred deer into holding pens. The slopes above the river had been deforested and turned into an ornamental garden, surmounted by a huge arch constructed of foliage. On the other bank of the Neckar, a palatial structure had been erected, complete with terraces and the enormous staircase so favoured by the German baroque. From two adjoining pavilions, bands provided appropriate musical accompaniment. Garampi believed that 10,000 spectators had assembled to watch the proceedings. When the Elector gave the signal for the hunt to commence, eighty hunt personnel dressed in green and silvery livery drove the deer in groups of a dozen or so down the hill, into the river and towards the hunting party's guns. As soon as an animal was hit, hunt attendants rowed out to pull it into a barge. The sport lasted an hour, in the course of which 104 stags were killed. As Gunnar Brusewitz drily observed, quoting Corneille's *El Cid*: '*Et le combat cessa faute de combattants*' (The battle ended for want of combatants).

Presumably the Elector's prelatical visitor was impressed, although the actual score was surprisingly modest by contemporary standards. In the previous year, Karl Theodor's near-neighbour, Duke Karl Eugen of Württemberg had celebrated his birthday with two weeks of jollification, including a gala hunt (*Prunkjagd*) at Degerloch in the course of which 5,000 animals of various kinds were driven into an artificial lake and slaughtered. Even that formidable total was exceeded on the occasion of Grand Duke Paul of Russia's visit to Württemberg in 1782, when 6,000 deer and 2,500 boar were killed. Württemberg seems to have been in a class by itself when it came to bloodshed, but respectable scores were at least attempted elsewhere. Duke Joseph Frederick of Saxony-Hildburghausen had assembled 800 deer for a great hunt he organized at Schlosshof near Vienna in 1754 for the delectation of the Emperor Francis I and Maria Theresa. The latter then spoiled the fun by insisting that the animals' lives be spared.

This act of compassion was most unusual, although one or two straws suggested that the wind was beginning to shift away from the killing of animals for sport. Not for the last time, Frederick the Great of Prussia distanced himself from the other princes of the Empire, by sharply criticizing their favourite activity in his *Anti-Machiavell*, published shortly before he came to the throne in 1740. Lamenting that 'most kings and princes spend at least three-quarters of their lives racing through forests, chasing and killing animals', he attacked hunting as non-intellectual:

The hunt is one of those sensual pleasures which excite the body but do nothing for the mind. It is a lethal skill which is used against savage animals. It is a continual dissipation, a tumultuous pleasure which fills the emptiness of the soul, rendering it incapable of any other reflection. It is the ardent desire to pursue some wild beast and the cruel satisfaction of killing it. In short, it is an amusement which builds up the body but leaves the mind fallow.

He conceded that hunting was as old as time, but suggested that all that proved was that 'men have been hunting for a long time, but what is old is not necessarily better'. He also conceded that many great men had loved hunting, but not even the greatest man had been without faults: 'Let us imitate their great qualities and not their petty ones!' In his best Voltairean fashion, he further conceded that the Patriarchs of the Old Testament had been hunters, but pointed out that they had also engaged in all sorts of activities which no longer commanded approval, such as marrying their sisters and practising polygamy. Warming to his work, Frederick denounced the hunting fraternity for its lack of compassion:

Whether or not Adam received the empire over the beasts, I wouldn't know; but I do know that we are more cruel and rapacious than the beasts themselves and that we act like tyrants over this supposed empire. If anything should give us an advantage over animals, it is assuredly our reason; and great hunters ordinarily have nothing else but horses, dogs, and all sorts of animals on their minds. Ordinarily crude, they surrender wholeheartedly to their passion; and it is to be feared that they will become as inhuman toward men as they are toward beasts or, at least, that their cruel indifference to suffering will make them less compassionate to their fellow men. Is this such a noble pleasure? Is this such a rational occupation?

His aversion to hunting was shared by Peter the Great of Russia – perhaps surprisingly, given the gross nature of many of his tastes. Unusually, hunting was not even a noble preserve in Russia.

Frederick could not stop his Junkers going out on their estates with dog and gun, but at least the mass slaughters of the Württemberg or Palatine variety were unknown in Prussia during his long reign. In the other major state – or rather, conglomeration – of the Holy Roman Empire, the Habsburg Monarchy, similar restraint prevailed, albeit in a characteristically more haphazard fashion. Ascending to the throne in the same year as Frederick, Maria Theresa at once ordered a cull of deer and boar in the royal reserves, to bring relief to the peasants and their crops. Her son and successor, Joseph II, went further. In 1786 a new hunting ordinance sought to prevent abuses, to provide compensation for damage caused by hunters or their prey, and authorized peasants to expel game from their woods, meadows and vineyards by any means they saw fit. In effect, that meant the end of the game laws. Two years later, while commanding his army on the Balkan front, Joseph sent back an order for the abolition of his entire hunting establishment. The elderly hunt servants were to be pensioned off, the younger personnel were to be retrained as lackeys or foresters, the dogs were to be given away or sold, and the surplus deer were to be culled, to meet the complaints about the damage they caused to crops. By this time, criticism of hunting was beginning to surface in the public sphere. In 1780 there appeared an anonymous pamphlet entitled *Letter to a Prince from a Stag Hunted by Hounds*:

Today I have had the honour of being hunted by the hounds of Your High-Born Princely Highness; but I most humbly request that in future you may graciously allow me to be spared such an exercise. If only Your High-Born Princely Highness were once subjected to hunting by a pack of hounds, you would not find my request unreasonable. Here I lie, unable to raise my head and with blood flowing from my nostrils. How can Your High-Born Princely Highness have the heart to hunt to death a poor innocent animal who lives from grass and herbs? I would much rather be shot dead and thus have an end put to it.

There is no way of knowing how representative was this *cri de coeur*. The likely author was Matthias Claudius, the son of a Protestant pastor and friend of Herder and Hamann, who scraped a living as a journalist. A more direct if more dangerous way of subverting hunting was to get there first by going poaching. In the great forests that covered so much of the German landscape in the eighteenth century, detection was uncertain enough to encourage risk-taking. Although the usual poacher was the peasant trapping a rabbit for his pot, there were also more ambitious undertakings. The most enterprising was the gang of poachers led by Matthias Klostermeyer, alias 'The Bavarian Hiesel' (Hiesel is slang for Matthias), who poached their way across Bavaria in the late 1760s, fighting regular battles with the authorities as they went. That Hiesel survived for as long as three years, and also inspired a host of legends, suggests that he and his merry men enjoyed the support of the local peasants and might even qualify for the coveted appellation 'social bandits'.

STAG- AND FOX-HUNTING
IN ENGLAND

In England the situation was rather different. Here, too, successive monarchs had hunted with enthusiasm, leaving among other evidence Van Dyck's magnificent portrait of *Charles I at the Hunt*, painted in 1635 and now in the Louvre. The last of the Stuarts, Queen Anne (1702–14), was not deterred by seventeen pregnancies, corpulence or old age from hunting the stag, although obliged late in life to follow the hounds in a light carriage known as a *calèche*. Three years before her death, Jonathan Swift saw her hunting near Windsor: 'driving furiously like Jehu ... [she] is a mighty hunter like Nimrod'. Her successor preferred to do his hunting (and most other things too) in his native Hanover, but hunting by the court continued after 1714. In 1717 the fastidious Alexander Pope wrote to his friend Martha Blount that he had recently met the Prince of Wales and all the maids of honour coming from a hunt near Hampton Court, commenting sourly:

To eat Westphalia ham in a morning ride over hedges and ditches on borrowed hacks, come home in the heat of the day with a fever, and (what is worse a hundred times) with a red mark on the forehead from an uneasy hat! all this may qualify them to make excellent wives for foxhunters and bear abundance of ruddy-complexioned children.

The Prince's father was an enthusiastic hunter in Hanover, where his hunting lodge at Göhrde on the Lüneburg heath was a favoured place for receiving visiting princes, but his interest in the chase in England was fitful. However, when the Prince succeeded as George II in 1727 he immediately took steps to increase his hunting establishment, re-appointing a Master of the Buckhounds (an office which George I had allowed to remain vacant) and setting an energetic personal example. The following description of a hunt on Saturday, 17 August 1728 gives a good impression of what was involved:

Between 10 and 11 o'clock their Majesties, together with His Royal Highness the Duke, and their Royal Highnesses the Princesses, came to the new park by Richmond from Hampton Court, and diverted themselves with hunting a stag, which ran from 11 to 1, when he took the Great Pond, and defended himself for about half an hour, when, being killed and brought out by the help of a boat, the huntsman sounded the French horns. The skin was taken off, and the carcase given to the dogs. His Majesty, the Duke, and the Princesses [sic] Royal hunted on horseback; Her Majesty and the Princess Amelia hunted in a four-wheel chaise, and the Princess Carolina in a two-wheel chaise, and the Princesses Mary and Louisa were in a coach. Several of the nobility attended, and among them Sir Robert Walpole, clothed in green as Ranger. When the diversion was over, their Majesties, the Duke, and the Princesses refreshed themselves on the spot with a cold collation (as did the nobility at some distance of time after), and soon after two in the afternoon returned for Hampton Court.

So far, so conventional – none of this would have been out of place on the continent, although the ladies of the English royal family seem to have been unusually enthusiastic. Yet even during the reigns of the first two Georges, participation was appreciably wider than on the continent. Not only did 'the nobility and gentry' accompany the royal hunting party, but city merchants, professional men and even clergy were also involved. According to the historian of the royal buckhounds, John Hore, especially prominent was Humphrey Parsons, a city alderman and twice Lord Mayor of London. The *après-chasse* was also socially more varied, as George II and his family dined in public at Hampton Court after a hunt, allowing all-comers to witness the event. Shortly before the hunt just recounted, such was the press of spectators in the banqueting-room that the rail collapsed and the crowd fell in on the dinner party, 'at which their Majesties laughed heartily'.

By this time, stag-hunting had become mainly a royal activity, not because it was a Crown prerogative (it was not) but because the agricultural expansion that claimed forests for arable and pastoral farming had destroyed much of the deer's habitat. Also important was the deforestation occasioned by naval expansion, for just one ship of the line needed 4,000 trees for its construction. Only in more remote wildernesses such as Dartmoor and Exmoor could stag-hunting still flourish. This was not a sudden change: the Duke of Beaufort's pack at Badminton continued to concentrate on the stag until the 1770s and another major hunt, the Belvoir, was founded by the Duke of Rutland in 1730 expressly for the same purpose. But in most of the English counties, by the middle of the eighteenth century it was the fox that was becoming the hunters' main prey. It had certain advantages: it was common, it was officially classified as vermin and so could be killed by anyone with impunity (and also with a sense of impunity), and it was characterized by speed, cunning and stamina. On the other hand, unlike the deer or the hare, it could not be eaten, giving rise to one of Oscar Wilde's most celebrated quips: 'The English country gentleman galloping after a fox – the unspeakable in full pursuit of the uneatable' (A Woman of No Importance (1893)). Its inedibility was also the occasion for a telling anecdote recounted by Norbert Elias: 'a Frenchman heard an Englishman exclaim during a hunt "How admirable! the sport which the fox has shown in this charming run of two hours and a quarter", to which the Frenchman replied "Ma foi, he must be worth catching when you take so much trouble. Est-il bon pour un fricandeau?"' In fact, the French did eat fox, judging its meat less unpleasant than that of the wolf: 'dogs as well as men eat it in autumn, especially if the fox has fed and grown fat on grapes'.

As the popularity of fox-hunting increased, so did the ways in which it was hunted change. In the early eighteenth century the fox was usually pursued by hounds that could turn their hand (or rather nose and mouth) to anything that moved, from deer to otter, from hare to badger. They hunted either by sight ('gaze hounds') and relied on speed, or by scent, relying on stamina. Both had their limitations. The former, such as greyhounds, soon ran out of breath and were best suited to smaller game such as hares. The latter were dogged but slow. As the hounds found it difficult to match the fox for speed, the hunting party had to set off very early in the morning, when the nocturnal fox was slowed by a night of feasting. Even so, a hunt could last many hours, until the hounds ground their quarry down, or nightfall brought an end to the pursuit.

The increase in the popularity of fox-hunting prompted enterprising huntsmen to resort to selective breeding to produce hounds specifically designed for hunting the fox. The most influential was Hugo Meynell, who in 1753, at the age of eighteen, rented Quorn Hall in Leicestershire. In the course of the next fifty years he turned his hunt into the most celebrated in England. It was no coincidence that a near-neighbour and near-contemporary was Robert Bakewell, who famously applied selective breeding to sheep with spectacular results. Meynell was greatly assisted by the agricultural developments described in an earlier chapter. By the time he started, enclosures had changed about half of Leicestershire from arable into pastoral land and almost all of it by the time he resigned as Master of the Quorn in 1800. The great expanses of grass carried what was known as 'a screaming scent' for the hounds, allowing fast runs, not as protracted as in the old days but much more exciting. As more of the fields came to be hedged and ditched, jumping – encouraged by the development of a special hunting saddle – brought more thrills and spills. Now that the hounds could keep up with the fox, meets could be postponed until mid-morning, attracting men and women of fashion, previously deterred by pre-dawn reveilles. The development of the turnpike also helped to bring Leicestershire closer to the world of the capital, previously cut off by the county's clay soil which made the old roads 'execrable' (Daniel Defoe). Faster hounds required faster horses and selective breeding duly obliged. Never before (or perhaps since) has there been such a rapid and complementary development of two species. As Raymond Carr, the most distinguished historian of English fox-hunting, has written, 'By 1800 English horses were the best in the world and the English thoroughbred the perfect hunting instrument.'

Together with neighbouring hunts such as the Duke of Rutland's Belvoir, the Earl of Lonsdale's Cottesmore and Earl Spencer's Althorp and Pytchley, the Quorn by the 1780s had made Leicestershire in general, and the town of Melton Mowbray in particular, the centre of English hunting. As these names suggest, peers of the realm were to the fore in the development of hunting. As so often, this process can be charted through the visual arts. In the course of the eighteenth century, a thriving school of English sporting painters emerged in response to a growing demand. Although its exponents enjoyed only a low status in the hierarchy of artists, the same could not be said for their products. The paintings of hunts, hounds and horses were not consigned to the walls of their patrons' stables or gun-rooms. On the contrary, in the 1730s and 1740s, the entrance halls of Longleat, Badminton and Althorp, the stately homes of the Marquess of Bath, the Duke of Beaufort and Earl Spencer respectively, were redecorated with giant paintings of hunting by John Wootton. As Stephen Deuchar has pointed out in his study of sporting art in eighteenth-century England, by reference to contrasting paintings of Longleat by Jan Siberecht in 1678 and of a hunt at Ashdown Park in 1743, whereas in the seventeenth century a hunting scene might be added to the background of a depiction of a great house, by the middle of the next century the positions had been reversed. Like Louis XIV, proud owners had their hounds immortalized in paint. Fittingly, one of the greatest of English fox-hounds, Lord Yarborough's

'Ringwood' (his quality being measured as much by his prowess at stud as on the hunting field), was painted by the greatest of English sporting painters, George Stubbs. Explaining his decision to go to Newmarket, artist Ben Marshall (1767–1835) also revealed his patrons' priorities: 'I have a good reason for going. I discover many a man who will pay me fifty guineas for painting his horse who thinks ten guineas too much to pay for painting his wife.'

If it was the great aristocrats who set the pace in English hunting, it was the gentry and their tenant-farmers who spread it to every corner of the kingdom. For every Earl Berkeley, whose hunting territory stretched in an unbroken swathe from Berkeley Square in London to Berkeley Castle in Gloucestershire, there were dozens of Squire Westerns subscribing to a local pack. Raymond Carr gives the example of the Sinnington Hunt in Yorkshire, whose annual expenses of £32 10s 3d were financed by a ten-shilling subscription paid by local farmers and tradesmen and fines for non-attendance at hunt dinners. It has been estimated that by 1815 in the county of Devon, for example, no fewer than half the resident gentry and most of the tenant-farmers kept hounds of some sort. One Devon squire boasted that he had hunted with seventy-two local packs. By the 1780s there were five packs of fox-hounds and ten packs of harriers hunting within 10 miles (16 km) of Newbury in Berkshire. Fielding's Squire Western may have loudly complained about having to sacrifice a good scenting day to pursue his absconding daughter, but he had not been long on the road before the sound of a hunting horn announced the proximity of a substitute. It was said that in Hampshire one need not sit on any hill for very long before a hunt would announce itself by sight or sound.

The ubiquity of hunting, especially of fox-hunting, in England by the end of the eighteenth century mirrored wider social, economic and intellectual developments: the development of agriculture, the application of science in the form of selective breeding, the move towards uniform regulation, the introduction of standardization by the exchange of fox-hounds among the leading hunts, and so on. It might even be said that hunting formed its own subsection of the public sphere, for – as John Hawkes pointed out – 'The Field is a most agreeable coffee-house, and there is more real society to be met with there than in any other situation of life. It links all classes together, from the Peer to the Peasant. It is the Englishman's peculiar privilege. It is not to be found in any other part of the globe, but in England's true land of liberty – and may it flourish to the end of time!' As this last comment suggests, hunting was also held, not without reason, to promote social integration: 'It came to be looked upon as one of the chief promoters within a country district of unity, stability, harmony, and devotion to traditional, deferential values' (David Itzkowitz). Although only the smart set could afford to hunt with the Quorn or Cottesmore, hunting could never be stigmatized as a pastime of the privileged. This was an argument deployed in defence of hunting, by Christopher Sykes, for example, in 1792: 'When the pleasures of the chase can be made the means of calling the gentlemen of the country together, they become really useful and beneficial to society. They give opportunities of wearing off shyness, dispelling temporary differences, forming new friendships, and cementing old, and draw the gentlemen of the country into one closer bond of society.'

Especially during the early part of the eighteenth century, there was some evidence that hunting also had a political connotation. Steele and Addison's fictional Tory squire Sir Roger de Coverley was satirized, albeit amiably, as a man with a big heart but tiny intellect, who devoted his considerable energies to pursuing various forms of game, especially the fox:

The constant thanks and good wishes of the neighbourhood always attended him, on account of his remarkable enmity towards foxes; having destroyed more of those vermin in one year, than it was thought the whole country could have produced. Indeed the Knight does not scruple to own among his most intimate friends, that in order to establish his reputation this way, he has secretly sent for great numbers of them out of other counties, which he used to turn loose about the country by night, that he might the better signalise himself in their destruction the next day.

Sir Roger was contrasted with Sir Andrew Freeport, an urbane, cultivated, 'polite' Whig merchant, the man of the future. A Whig/Tory, town/country antagonism has indeed been presented by Stephen Deuchar in his study of sporting art, but he takes no account of the hunts owned by great Whig magnates such as the Duke of Richmond, Earl Spencer or Earl Fitzwilliam, let alone the popularity of hunting among the urban population in general and the City merchants in particular. He is also mistaken in believing that 'by the eighteenth century both the king's political power and the nature of his sport had effectively become emasculated'. Against the boorish fictional Squire Western should be set the real Peter Beckford, one of the most celebrated fox-hunters of his day, who was said to 'bag a fox in Greek, find a hare in Latin, inspect his kennels in Italian, and direct the economy of his stables in exquisite French'.

HORSE-RACING, COCK-FIGHTING AND OTHER SPORTS

One reason for this general social impact of hunting was its close links with other sports and other sportsmen. Certainly there were some who viewed any other form of hunting with disdain, the author of *The British Sportsman*, for example, who in 1792 opined: 'Fox hunting is now considered as the only chace [sic] in England worthy of the taste or attention of a high bred sportsman.' William Somerville, who wrote a long poem on the pleasures of hunting, took the view that only the stag and the fox were worthy of the hunter's attention:

> A different hound for every different chase
> Select with judgment; nor the timorous hare
> O'ermatched destroy, but leave that vile offence
> To the mean, murderous coursing crew; intent
> On blood and spoil. O blast their hopes, just Heaven!

But this sort of intolerance was unusual. Most fox-hunters would hunt or course hares, attend cock-fights and – above all – go to race meetings. The period covered by this volume saw the establishment not only of modern hunting in England but also of modern horse-racing. The two sports were always closely connected. Indeed, racing at Newmarket, generally acknowledged as the headquarters of racing in England, if not the world, began by accident when James I went to hunt his hounds and hawks on Newmarket Heath and found it also an ideal location for racing. His successors followed his example, Charles II being particularly enthusiastic, travelling there for racing two or three times a year for two or three weeks at a time. He promoted the sport by personal example, riding in matches and plates, serving as adjudicator in disputes and holding court for his fellow enthusiasts with his habitual profligacy. The diarist John Evelyn, visiting in July 1670, was disappointed by the new residence being built by the King but was impressed by the facilities for the horses, 'of which many are kept here at a vast expense, with all the art and tenderness imaginable'. He returned in October of the following year, finding the 'King and all the English gallants being there at their autumnal sports' and witnessing 'the great match run between Woodcock and Flatfoot, belonging to the King, and to Mr Eliot, of the Bedchamber, many thousands being spectators'. It was the debauchery which accompanied the racing which attracted Evelyn's disapproval. He recorded that it was during this stay that Charles II took the French maid-of-honour Louise de Kéroualle as his mistress and that he 'found the jolly blades racing, dancing, feasting, and revelling, more resembling a luxurious and abandoned rout, than a Christian court'.

The Glorious Revolution of 1688 brought no interruption to royal patronage of racing. William III proved to be just as enthusiastic as his predecessors, although more restrained in his behaviour off the course. When he took the French diplomat the comte de Tallard with him to Newmarket in 1698, he laid on hunting and hawking in the morning, racing in the afternoon and cock-fighting as the *après-courses* entertainment. Queen Anne initiated racing at Ascot, close to Windsor Castle and from the start free of Newmarket's raffish reputation. The close relationship between hunting and racing was revealed by the conditions for many of the races contested there, for example: 'a plate of fifty guineas for horses which had been at the death of three stags hunted by the royal hounds'. This donation of a royal plate as a prize for a major contest came to be the qualification for a racecourse's status as a major enterprise. There were eleven by 1714, raised to sixteen by George II. By that time, racing had spread throughout the length and breadth of England. One observer recorded in 1736: 'It is surprising to think what a height this spirit of horse-racing is now arrived at in this kingdom, where there is scarce a village so mean that not a bit of plate is raised once a year for the purpose.' Nor a ducal palace, he might have added. When the Marquis of Rockingham's administration was formed in July 1765, a pamphleteer derided the 'Persons called from the *Stud* to the *State*, and transformed miraculously out of Jockies into Ministers'. The negotiations had been conducted by the Duke of Cumberland at Newmarket in May and at Ascot in June.

The subsequent history of the sport has been recounted many times, notably by Roger Longrigg. Three developments need at least to be noted here. First, the period saw the rapid development of the English thoroughbred, thanks to selective breeding between native mares and imported stallions. Indeed, for the real purist, racing is not about winning prizes, let alone gambling, but is essentially a means of identifying the best breeding stock. Although barely credible, every one of the countless thoroughbreds to be found today across the world traces its pedigree to one of three stallions imported to England from the Middle East: the Byerly Turk (imported in 1688), the Darley Arabian (1704) and the Godolphin Arabian (1729). Breeding for speed led to younger horses running over shorter courses and ridden by professional jockeys. Secondly, the sport was regularized and standardized, with the emergence of a racing calendar from the late 1720s and the establishment of a recognized authority – the Jockey Club – from the 1750s to adjudicate the disputes that were an inevitable part of any activity involving large sums of money. Thirdly, a pattern of 'classic' races was established to give racing a profile that was both national and public: the St Leger in 1776, the Oaks in 1779 (restricted to fillies), the Derby in 1780, the Two Thousand Guineas in 1809 and the One Thousand Guineas in 1814 (also restricted to fillies). Presumably it was coincidental that the first three of these classics were first run during the American War.

Although often overlooked, or at least underplayed, from the start organized horse-racing was closely linked to another traditional sport: cock-fighting. Wherever horses were raced, cocks were fought, especially when the race meeting extended over several days. At Peterborough in 1789, for example, there was racing over three days, the climax being a sweepstake for hunters of five guineas per entrant, to which Earl Fitzwilliam, the local magnate, had added £50. The advertisement went on:

> There will be an Ordinary [public dinner] at the Angel on Tuesday and Thursday – at which inn there will be a ball on Thursday as usual.
>
> An Ordinary at the Saracen's Head on Wednesday. The Comedians will be at Peterborough in the Race Week.
>
> There will be a regular MAIN of COCKS fought at the Angel Inn during the Races, between the Gentlemen of Leicester and the Gentlemen of Peterboro'.

Racing, dining, dancing, theatricals and cocking – that was what the eighteenth-century sportsman liked. The only surprise is that prizefighting was not thrown in as well. Into such disrepute did cock-fighting fall during the Victorian period, and subsequently, that it is seldom appreciated how important it was during a less sensitive age. So when John Cheny of Arundel published the first calendar of horse-races in 1727, he also included major cock-fights. When the Earl of Derby and his friends decided to organize a sweepstake at Epsom for fillies in 1779, they named it after the former inn in which they lived and fought their cocks during racing: The Oaks. An excellent visual representation of this close relationship between racing and cocking (and hunting) is John Wootton's portrait of Tregonwell Frampton, the Dorset squire who served as racing manager to William III, Queen Anne and George I, with his greyhound, his cock and a portrait of one of his racehorses.

Cock-fighting was a sport of great antiquity, but in its modern form it had been given the lead by royalty. Henry VIII had built a cockpit near Whitehall Palace (later turned into the Privy Council office after a fire in 1697), James I was a regular visitor to the cockpit in St James's Park and Charles II built another in Birdcage Walk. By that time there were cockpits all over England, ranging from elaborate enclosed amphitheatres to simple open-air pits. Nor was this a rural sport, as many inn-signs in market towns still testify – indeed, two of the greatest cocking centres were the rapidly expanding industrial cities of Birmingham and Newcastle upon Tyne. The numerous cockpits in London also testified to the sport's urban appeal, exemplified by the following advertisement from a newspaper in 1700:

At the Royal Cockpit on the south side of St. James's Park, on Tuesday the 11th of this instant February [1700] will begin a very great Cock-match; and will continue all the week; wherein most of the considerablest Cockers of England are concerned. There will be a battle down upon the Pit every day precisely at three o'clock, in order to have done by daylight. Monday the 9th instant March will begin a great match of Cockfighting betwixt the Gentlemen of the City of Westminster and the Gentlemen of the City of London for six guineas a battle, and one hundred guineas the odd battle, and the match continues all the week, in Red-Lion fields. In the following April another match commences, to continue for a week, at four guineas a battle, and forty guineas the odd battle, between the Gentlemen of London, and those of Warwickshire, at the new Cockpit behind Gray's-Inn-Walks.

Like the other sports discussed in this chapter, cock-fighting was socially diverse. It was one of the entertainments laid on for Margrave

Ludwig of Baden when he came on a diplomatic mission from the Emperor Leopold I in 1694. According to Abraham de la Pryme, 'There was bear's baiting, bulls' sport, and cock fighting instituted for his diversion and recreation. But above all he admired cock fighting, saying had he not seen it he never could have thought that there could have been so much vallor and magnanimity in any bird under heaven.' The Earl of Derby, the Gentlemen of the City of London, and the Newcastle miners were all engaged in the same activity, often even in the same place. One historian of popular recreations, Robert Malcolmson, has found that cock-fighting was mentioned 'very frequently' in eighteenth-century sources, the newspapers being full of advertisements for mains. Nor did its popularity decline in the course of the eighteenth century, as is sometimes suggested. A French visitor, Pierre Jean Grosley, commented in 1772 that the English engaged in cock-fighting (and horse-racing) 'to the point of madness', adding that all ranks of society were involved. The first issue of *The Sporting Magazine*, which claimed to be the first periodical devoted to 'the transactions of the turf, the chace [sic], and every other diversion interesting to the man of pleasure, enterprize and spirit', claimed in 1792 that: 'So fashionable is this diversion become, that within a few years past, its regulations have been formed into laws, and, as such, have received the sanction of the COCKPIT ROYAL, as well as the approbation of the best informed, and most skilful fighters in this kingdom.' Perhaps most important was the establishment of cocking and the other sporting pursuits as an acceptable, if not a necessary, form of recreation for the gentry. In George Powell's play *Cornish Comedy* of 1696 a character states: 'What is a gentleman without his recreations? With these we endeavour to pass away that time which would otherwise lie heavily upon our hands. Hawks, hounds, setting-dogs, and cocks, with their appurtenances, are the true marks of a country gentleman.'

The Sporting Magazine also referred to the game cock as 'that prodigy of British valour'. This association with national pride was not uncommon. Almost a century earlier, Robert Howlett in his treatise *The Royal Pastime of Cock-Fighting* had stated firmly that, 'There is not a surer sign of a Nation or Peoples degenerating into effeminacy, and so consequently falling into Poverty and utter Ruin, than when they totally change the Warlike Exercise of Cocking for mimical Plays, silly Dancing, and such like Fopperies', for 'Cocking fits a Man either for Peace, or War, and creates both Courage, and Constancy, with Good-nature, and ingenuity all glued together'. The decline and fall of the Roman Empire, he thought, was a good illustration of the truth of this maxim, as was Gustavus Adolphus of Sweden's comment on entering Germany in 1630 that he had nothing to fear from the imperial forces since they had given up cocking and taken up dancing and drinking. Howlett dedicated his work to 'Sir T. V. Knight', who came from a great cock-fighting family and who had been sent by William III to Ireland, 'where you cut through the Squadrons of the affrighted French, and made the Howling *Teagues* fly to the Boggs for shelter'.

Not only cocks signalled the superiority of the English. In *Thoughts upon Hare and Fox Hunting in a Series of Letters to a Friend*, first published in 1779 but still being reprinted in the twentieth century, Peter Beckford asserted that 'the hounds which this country produces are universally allowed to be the best in the world', a claim warmly seconded by William Somerville:

> Hail, happy Britain! highly-favoured isle,
> And Heaven's peculiar care! . . .
> In thee alone, fair land of liberty!
> Is bred the perfect hound, in scent and speed
> As yet unrivalled, while in other climes
> Their virtue fails, a weak degenerate race.

Two, of course, could play that game, and French stag-hunters derided fox-hunting as suitable only for bad dogs and bad hunters, just the sort of activity one might expect to be favoured by the English. Le Verrier delivered that verdict in 1763, a particularly sensitive year for the French as it marked the conclusion of the disastrous Seven Years War. There was some inconsistency in French attitudes to the English dogs they imported: in the seventeenth century the hounds were criticized for being slow but praised for being docile, whereas in the eighteenth century they were praised for their speed but criticized for their unruliness. There were also complaints that they took a long time to learn the commands of their new masters, which was hardly surprising as, according to Philippe Salvadori, they were addressed in a weird kind of *franglais*. The duc de Luynes, on the other hand, gave honourable mention to the English because at least they rode to hounds, like the French and the Poles. His special distaste was reserved for the Germans, who – as he saw it, at least – just drove game into nets and slaughtered it.

As we have seen, in Germany critics as various as Frederick the Great and Matthias Claudius attacked hunting for its cruelty. In England and France too its advocates did not have matters all their own way. The article on 'La chasse' in Diderot and d'Alembert's Encyclopédie was hostile, defining it as 'embracing all the various ways in which we wage war against animals', although most of the space was devoted to showing how hunting was a natural right but had been usurped by kings and their nobles. In Émile (1762), Rousseau allowed his eponymous pupil to start hunting, but only to keep his mind off sex, adding: 'I do not even profess to justify this ferocious passion' (by which he meant hunting). In England, even the fox-hunting Lord Torrington found the discrepancy between the treatment of animals and humans he encountered on the Duke of Bedford's estate intolerable: 'The dog kennels for these noble animals proudly overtops those miserable mud hovels erected for the sons of Adam; who looking, askance, with eyes of envy at the habitation of these happier hounds, regret their humanity and that they are not born fox hounds.' More usual – and becoming more frequent, it would seem – were attacks on hunting on humanitarian grounds. Alexander Pope acquired first-hand knowledge of hunting when, at the age of twelve, he moved with his family to Bonfield in Windsor Forest. He was particularly revolted by one aspect of the royal hunt, which he condemned as 'barbarous enough to be derived from the Goths, or even the Scythians; I mean that savage compliment our huntsmen pass upon ladies of quality who are present at the death of a stag, when they put the knife in their hands to cut the throat of a helpless, rambling, and weeping creature'. In the words of an anonymous reviewer of Beckford's Thoughts on Hunting: 'in an island so generally cultivated as Great Britain, [hunting] is a very expensive system of tyranny and barbarity in all its circumstances, from the beginning to the end'.

Yet the eighteenth century came and went without hunting having to repel a serious intellectual, let alone a legislative, challenge. Although cock-fighting was finally driven underground (where it is reported to continue to flourish) by Act of Parliament in 1849, hunting and coursing survived into the twenty-first century, albeit very hard-pressed. Until urban interests took command of the House of Commons, the various forms of hunting served as a durable adhesive between king, court and country. It was George III who completed this process of assimilation. Hunting was his favourite outdoor occupation and he was out with his hounds from breakfast to dinner on every day that he spent in the country. By his personal example of unimpeachable morality, not least in sexual matters, he completed the sanitization of the image of both hunting and racing. Not for him the raffish delights of Newmarket, which he never visited, but he was always at Ascot for at least one day of the main meeting in June and gave a plate of £100 for horses that had hunted with his hounds. Nor was it possible to depict him as a mass slaughterer of game on the continental model. After 1783, following the intercession of his second son, the Duke of York, all stags hunted by the royal buckhounds were spared, the dogs being whipped off when their quarry turned to stand at bay. In February 1793 *The Sporting Magazine* was in no doubt that the meet of the royal hunt represented the perfect expression of the King and his elites in perfect harmony. The author of the following lines was, of course, well aware that the King of France had been guillotined the previous month and that the National Assembly had just declared war on Great Britain:

During such enchanting prelude to the ecstatic burst (encircled with carriages and females of the first distinction), we exultingly, nay, rapturously behold the sovereign of our *rich, happy* and *powerful* nation, voluntarily waive the dignity of a court to enjoy the personal gratification, and embrace the grateful services and public attachment of his faithful subjects, with all the affability and politeness of a private gentleman. Here we perceive benignant greatness and majestic grandeur, instinctively bending under the happy sensation of unsullied philanthropy, and all the gentle offices of mutual affection; for during the inexpressible scene of transport, amidst the melody of *horns* and *hounds*, his majesty (divested of every degree of personal parade) pays his most *friendly respects* to, and receives congratulations from every eminent individual and country gentleman in the circle, to each of whom he has long been in the habit of being *most intimately known.*

Constraints of space and information have confined this chapter to just three countries, but hunting was ubiquitous. Even the Pope maintained stables and kennels, complete with a hierarchy of officials. For Philip V, the first Bourbon King of Spain (1700–46), according to his most recent biographer (Henry Kamen), hunting was 'his only serious recreation' (although the duc de Saint-Simon thought that 'the conjugal bed' was a passion of equal intensity). In the last year of Philip's life, another French visitor, the maréchal de Noailles, reported that 'there is not a single hunting rendezvous in the woods at Fontainebleau that he does not recall exactly'. Charles III (1759–88) went shooting twice a day every day except during Holy Week. Not even the imminent death of his son and heir, the Infante Xavier, could interrupt his invariable daily routine: business, hunting, dinner, hunting, business, bed. As one contemporary observed: 'No storm, heat or cold can keep him at home; and when he hears of a wolf, distance is counted for nothing; he would drive over half the kingdom rather than miss an opportunity of firing upon that favourite game.' At the court of Savoy, the master of the horse (*grande scudiere*) was one of a triumvirate of key officials and 'a nodal point of court power' (Robert Oresko), thanks to his daily contacts with the venatorial dukes. Their enthusiasm can be charted through the hunting lodges they built and the hunting paintings they commissioned, in the latter case from the *La curea* (the death of a stag) by Jan Miel (1661) to the *La curea* by Vittorio Amedeo Cignaroli (1773). Architectural reminders of the status accorded hunting by their builders still stretch the length and breadth of Europe – Het Loo (the United Provinces), Aranjuez and La Granja (Spain), Schönbrunn and Laxenburg (Austria), Schleissheim and Amalienburg (Bavaria), Falkenlust (Cologne), Jaegerhof (Düsseldorf), Ludwigsburg (Württemberg), Stupinigi (Savoy), Troja (Bohemia), not to mention Versailles, which began life as a hunting lodge.

9

Palaces and Gardens

REPRESENTATIONAL CULTURE IN A PALATIAL AGE

The period covered by this volume was *the* period for palace-building in all European history. Many palaces had been built in previous centuries but never had there been such a concentrated burst of activity. It is difficult to think of one country in which the ruler's palace was not built, or at least fundamentally reconstructed, between the middle of the seventeenth and the end of the eighteenth century: in Denmark, the Amalienborg Palace in Copenhagen; in Sweden, the Royal Palace in Stockholm and Drottningholm outside the city; in Brandenburg-Prussia, the Royal Palace in Berlin, Charlottenburg on the outskirts, and Sans Souci, the New Palace and the Town Palace at Potsdam; in Russia, the Winter Palace at St Petersburg and the Great Palace at Tsarkoe Selo, and Peterhof, outside it; in Poland, the Royal Palace at Warsaw; in the Habsburg Monarchy, the Leopoldine Tract of the Hofburg and Schönbrunn; in Naples, the Royal Palace in the city and Caserta outside it; in Spain, the Royal Palace at Madrid and the hunting lodges-cum-palaces mentioned in the previous chapter; in Portugal, Mafra; in France, Versailles, Marly and the Trianons; and so on. If the category were expanded to include the second- or third-rank territories of the Holy Roman Empire and Italy, not to mention the great aristocratic magnates of all these countries, the list could be extended almost at will.

Three exceptions must be noted, all of them revealing in their different ways. The most important was Great Britain, for Buckingham Palace in its present form is a nineteenth- and early twentieth-century creation. Much of Whitehall, which had been abandoned by William III, burnt down in 1698 and was revived only as government offices. William did make major alterations to Hampton Court and George III began the process which turned Windsor Castle into the largest occupied castle in Europe, but this was little enough to show for a period in which the country became the greatest world power. The second exception was the papacy, whose continuing pretensions as a major European power were belied not least by architectural stasis, major work at the Vatican being confined to Bernini's *Scala Regia* (1663–6) and in the eighteenth century the conversion of existing buildings to form a museum. The exterior of the second – and de facto main – papal residence, the Quirinal Palace, was essentially complete by 1648. The third exception – the United Provinces of the Netherlands – was, of course, not a monarchy but a confederation sometimes (1672–1795) presided over by a Stadholder from the House of Orange.

Indeed, the 'United Provinces of the Netherlands' were better known to most Europeans as 'the Dutch Republic'. As this suggests, it was in monarchies that most building of palaces took place. That observation seems obvious to the point of banality, on a par with Richard Wollheim's derisive comment, when criticizing reductionist socio-economic interpretations of culture, that nomadic tribes are not responsible for much monumental architecture. It is the British exception which is more helpful, for it suggests that it was not monarchy per se, but a particular kind of monarchy that felt the need to build on a palatial scale. At this point, a historiographical excursus is unavoidable. The most influential work to have been written on European political culture in this period is undoubtedly Jürgen Habermas's *The Structural Transformation of the Public Sphere*, first published in German in 1962. Although his agenda was not that of a historian but rather of a critic of modern culture and politics, he did offer an overview of cultural history which is directly relevant to an understanding of the courts and the spaces within which they operated. In the pre-modern age, those who exercised power – monarch, nobles, prelates – expressed their status in public in a concrete, non-abstract way, through insignia, clothing, gesture or rhetoric. Power was both exercised and represented (in the sense of 'being made present') directly: 'as long as the prince and the estates of the realm still "are" the land, instead of merely functioning as deputies for it, they are able to "re-present"; they represent their power "before" the people, instead of for the people'.

This is representational culture. Confined to those who exercise power, it assumes an entirely passive attitude on the part of the rest of the population, which can communicate with the sovereign only by individual petition. By the baroque age, representation had moved from the cathedrals or streets of the city – the space favoured by medieval sovereigns for their display – to the parks and state apartments of the palace, château and stately home. In a modern house, even the ceremonial rooms (drawing rooms for the rich, front rooms for the poor) are designed to be lived in; in a baroque château, even the living rooms have a ceremonial purpose. Indeed, especially in France, the most intimate – the bedroom – was also the most important. The sumptuous display of what Habermas terms 'the representational public sphere' was not supposed to be recreational or self-indulgent; its purpose was to represent the power of the sovereign before his subjects, beginning at the top with those mighty subjects who aspired to become over-mighty subjects.

The political context is important here. The last part of the sixteenth century and the first half of the next had been scarred as much by domestic strife as by international conflict. The French Religious Wars (1562–98) ended with an uneasy truce frequently interrupted by fresh eruptions of violence – by the assassination of Henry IV in 1610, for example, or by the civil wars (*Frondes*) of 1648–53. It was the insurrection of Bohemian nobles in 1618 against their Habsburg ruler that began the Thirty Years War. And even when that ended, the Habsburg emperors found their Hungarian nobles almost as much a threat as the Turks. Spain was immobilized by the successful revolt of the Portuguese in 1640 and the (ultimately) unsuccessful revolt of the Catalans of the same year. The English Civil War reached a climax in 1649 with the execution of Charles I and the establishment of a Commonwealth. Frederick William the Great Elector (1640–88) spent the first twenty years of his reign struggling to assert his authority over the Junkers of his provincial estates. After the untimely death of Gustavus Adolphus (1632), the Swedish nobility took advantage of the infancy of his daughter and successor Christina, who was just six years old, to raid the royal power and patrimony. Even Russia, usually an exception to any European rule, was wracked by two generations of faction-fighting until Peter the Great asserted his authority in the course of the 1690s. In short, it was a period of sustained and intense challenges to royal authority. For every monarch, the restoration, consolidation and enhancement of that authority was a top priority. The use of representational culture by the organization of courts within a palatial setting offered one apparently potent means of obtaining that goal.

PALACE-MONASTERIES

The secular pageantry of the courts should not obscure the religious certainty which underpinned them. At every court, religious observance was central to its function and architecture. The model was the gigantic San Lorenzo de El Escorial, built by Philip II between 1563 and 1584, which was as much monastery as palace, its central axis dominated by a cathedral. This intimate relationship between court and confession remained a feature of Iberian courts. Even Philip IV's pleasure palace 'Buen Retiro' on the outskirts of Madrid was positioned next to the royal church and convent of San Jerónimo. Its garden was dotted with hermitage chapels, reminding visitors that 'Retiro' implied a spiritual as well as a recreational retreat. Nor did the monastic style of court and kingship die with the seventeenth century. On the contrary, there was a sumptuous last flowering after 1700. At Mafra, north-west of Lisbon, John V (1706–50) fulfilled a vow to build a Portuguese version of the Escorial as soon as he was blessed with a male heir. Although construction did not begin until 1717, three years after the happy event, building was then pushed on with a determination facilitated by the arrival of regular consignments of Brazilian gold. By 1730, tens of thousands of workers, the most popular estimate is 52,000, had got ready for consecration a complex which housed a royal palace, a basilica and a monastery, all on a gargantuan scale. At 761 feet (232 m), the façade is actually longer than that of the Escorial (682 ft/208 m). The monastic section contained accommodation for 330 Franciscan friars. If the royal palace and its 880 rooms is much more prominent at Mafra, the position of the church is as central as it is at the Escorial.

Although located some way inland, its size and prominence made it visible to seafarers making their way to Lisbon. It was also audible, as the great bells of the basilica could be heard 9 miles (15 km) away. Robert Southey also took the trouble to pay a visit overland, sourly writing to his brother Thomas in October 1800: 'You saw Mafra from the sea, a magnificent object, but, like everything in Portugal, it looks better at a distance.' On close inspection, he reported, it had little to commend it apart from its size: 'The church and convent and palace are one vast building, whose front exhibits a strange and truly Portuguese mixture of magnificence and meanness; in fact it has never been faced with stone, a mud plaster is in its place; the windows are not half glazed, red board filling up the work-house-looking casements.' However, he did allow that 'the church is beautiful and the library the finest bookroom I ever saw, and well stored'. William Beckford, on the other hand, was unimpressed at long range – 'The distant convent of Mafra looked like the palace of a giant, and the whole country around it as if the monster had eat it desolate' – but changed his tune when he saw it close up: 'The platform and flight of steps before the principal entrances of the church is grand beyond anything of which I had conceived an idea in Portugal. Looking up to the dome which lifts itself up so proudly above the pediment of the portico, I was struck with pleasure and surprise.' He was greatly impressed by church and palace, especially by the huge amount of well-carved marble employed and the profusion of Persian carpets spread everywhere, adding: 'we traversed several more halls and chapels adorned in the same style, till we were fatigued and bewildered like errant knights in the mazes of an enchanted palace. I began to think there was no end to these spacious apartments.'

Although later poet laureate and a bulwark of the establishment, in 1800 the twenty-six-year-old Southey was still a radical when he wrote, at the conclusion of his visit, 'such is Mafra: a library whose books are never used; a palace, with a mud-wall front; and a royal convent inhabited by monks who loathe their situation'. Yet the epic scale of the palace-convent should serve as a reminder that, for one European ruler at least, representational court culture was essentially religious culture. And so it was for his near-contemporary Emperor Charles VI (1711–40). He showed no interest in Schönbrunn, the Austrian answer to Versailles, giving it to his brother's widow as a dower-house. Although he enlarged the Hofburg in the centre of Vienna by commissioning Fischer von Erlach to build the grandest of all baroque libraries, his main project was the construction of an Austrian answer to the Escorial, by reconstructing and expanding the Augustinian monastery at Klosterneuburg. Before his elder brother's untimely death from smallpox, he had spent a decade in Spain trying to assert his claims to the Spanish throne. Castilian opposition, French armies and British diplomacy ensured that he did not obtain the crown, but he did bring back with him an enthusiasm for Spanish *pietas* which then sought appropriate architectural expression. Alas, he had no Brazilian gold at his disposal, only limitless expenditure demanded by endless wars against the French and the Turks. So only the church and a quarter of the palace-monastery were built, although they still constituted a grandiose pile. Although the imperial court under Charles VI was no different from any other in its pursuit of representational display in and out of doors, its piety was conspicuous. In 1726 the French envoy, the duc de Richelieu, estimated that in the course of the eight days that separated Palm Sunday from Easter Monday he had spent more than a hundred hours in church with the Emperor. He did not regard this as a cause for celebration.

VERSAILLES

In pursuing the palace-monastery, we have rather got ahead of ourselves, chronologically speaking. Shortly after the death of Charles VI in 1740, his successor, Maria Theresa, called a halt to the building at Kloster-neuburg. In Portugal, Joseph I abandoned Mafra to its monks when he succeeded in 1750. By that stage, both palaces were looking like anachronisms: for most European rulers, the palace they all sought to emulate, in overall effect if not in detail, was undoubtedly Versailles. Just how much Versailles differed from the palace-monasteries is clear from its ground plan, which shows the royal bedroom at the centre of the complex. Although the chapel is substantial and lavishly decorated, it is a far cry from the great basilicas of the Escorial, Mafra or Kloster-neuburg in terms of size and location. If hardly an afterthought, it was not completed until 1710, almost thirty years after the palace officially became the primary royal residence. Versailles was unashamedly first and foremost a secular enterprise. Its object was not to celebrate the King of France's subordination to God, but mankind's subordination to the King of France. As the visitor approached Versailles through the great forests which separated it from Paris, a carefully choreographed architectural vista opened up along a central axis culminating in the marble court, at the centre of whose *piano nobile* was situated the holy-of-holies – the King's bedroom. The impact of the palace was intensified by the absence of rivals. In his capital, Louis had three great residences at his disposal – the Louvre, the Tuileries and the Palais Royal – so why build another? It can be conjectured that the plethora of other great buildings in Paris, both secular and ecclesiastical, persuaded Louis to start afresh on what was virtually a greenfield site. Moreover, the visual impact of the Parisian sites was limited by the narrow streets that hemmed them in. Out in the forest, Louis' architects, led by Louis Le Vau and Jules Hardouin-Mansart, had a free hand to create the optimum effects. And so did the gardeners, led by André Le Nôtre, whose transformation of sylvan wilderness into rectilinear order exemplified the royal project for the mastery of nature. As the duc de Saint-Simon observed, 'It was a pleasure to the king to tyrannize nature and to tame it with art and money ... One feels disgusted by the force that is exerted upon nature everywhere.'

Inside the palace, references to the Christian God were confined to the chapel. Elsewhere, the iconographic scheme was dedicated exclusively to the cult of its builder, the Sun King, the earthly embodiment of the pagan god Apollo. In his instructions for the Dauphin, dictated in 1661 after the birth of his heir, Louis explained why the sun had been chosen as his favoured symbol:

by its unique quality,

by the lustre which surrounds it,

by the light which it shines on those other stars which surround it like a court,

by the equal and just distribution of its light which it sheds on all corners of the earth,

by the good which it brings to all places, creating joy and action in every form of life,

by its ceaseless motion while appearing constantly at rest,

by its constant and unchanging course from which it never deviates, it is most assuredly the most vital and the most beautiful image of a great monarch.

The endless speculation and argument about the ultimate purpose of Versailles can never be resolved. Of the possibilities, 'the continuation of war and diplomacy by other means' (Peter Burke) is a strong candidate. A great deal of space and a great deal of money were devoted to the construction of the 'Ambassadors' Staircase', up which a foreign envoy made his way en route to an audience with the King. At the top of the stairs he was confronted by a progression of richly decorated salons, reaching a climax with the *Salon de la Guerre* (the Salon of War). It was then time to turn sharp left into what was then the biggest and grandest parade room in Europe, the Hall of Mirrors, and make the long, slow, ceremonial progress to the presence of the King. By that time, it may be imagined, the ambassador was feeling suitably impressed, not to say overawed. Indeed, it was reported that a Turkish envoy was so overcome that he lost control of his bodily functions and had to be lent a clean pair of breeches before he could complete his journey. If that anecdote is authentic, it is perhaps the ultimate tribute to the success of Versailles and its representational culture.

In the *Salon de la Guerre*, the three foreign enemies of France – the Spanish, the Dutch and the Germans – were joined by a fourth, 'rebellion and discord', as they were sent packing by Bellona, the goddess of war. Together with other pictorial references, such as Louis' assumption of personal government, this identifies a second prime purpose. Versailles both celebrated the end of the civil strife that had wracked France for a century and ensured that it would not recur. It was not only foreign ambassadors who were supposed to be awestruck by the majesty of the King, it was also for domestic consumption. As Louis XIV was well aware, the Bourbon dynasty was barely fifty years old when he came to the throne, and there were many great French families who regarded him as only *primus inter pares*. The representational culture of the kind which reached its climax at Versailles was not an expression of unbounded confidence. On the contrary, the greater the doubts about the stability or legitimacy of a throne, the greater the need for display. There was always a strong undertow of anxiety beneath the smooth surface of courtly confidence. One major impetus behind the construction of the biggest palace in Europe was Louis' determination to put clear water between himself and his magnates. When he appeared at court in a coat encrusted with 14,000,000 *livres*-worth of diamonds, for example, he was demonstrating that no private individual could compete with royal resources. But the courtiers could compete among themselves, constantly outbidding each other in their pursuit of the extravagant fashions set by the King. The colossal expense involved proved to be another instrument of social control, for nobles who spent their revenues on high living at Versailles were nobles with little or nothing left for political intrigue in the provinces. Conspicuous consumption also made most of them dependent on royal largesse. Mme de Maintenon estimated that a single noble at Versailles with a staff of twelve servants would need at least 12,000 *livres* per annum. Only a minority enjoyed that kind of income, the rest could keep afloat only with the financial buoyancy provided by pensions and sinecures. In 1683 1,400,000 *livres* were paid out in royal pensions, a substantial sum representing about 1.2 per cent of total government expenditure, but even so a cost-effective investment in social harmony.

So the court of Louis XIV elevated the King from '*primus inter pares*' to being both '*solus*' (sole) and '*solaris*' (solar). But for a French aristocrat, attendance at court was not just submission to a grim instrument of cultural distancing and social control, it was also an opportunity to participate in the most lavish and exciting entertainment to be found in Europe. No one expressed better the general conviction that the royal court was the only place to be than the marquis de Vardes when he told Louis: 'Sire, when one is away from you, one is not just wretched, one is ridiculous.' From the outset, it was made clear that all that was best in aristocratic forms of recreation would become a royal monopoly. Versailles boasted not just the grandest of palatial settings but also the best hunting, the best theatre, the best opera, the best music, the best balls, the best gambling, the best clothes, the best fireworks, the best gossip, the best sex – the best everything that went to make up an aristocratic lifestyle. Significantly, many of the architects, painters, dramatists and musicians who created the Versailles experience were taken from Nicolas Fouquet, marquis de Belle-Isle, the most pretentious of over-mighty subjects, following his disgrace in 1661. During peacetime the courtiers were entertained three times a week at the '*appartements*', when 'the King, the Queen and the whole royal family descend from their heights to play with members of the assembly', as the official gazette, the *Mercure Galant*, put it in December 1682. 'Play' in this context meant billiards, cards and refreshments, as well as the opportunity for the gossip that was the dominant discourse of a society obsessed with precedence and favour. It also meant dancing. The King himself was, by all accounts, a superlative dancer who could outperform any courtier and hold his own with the professionals. Although he appeared for the last time in a formal ballet in 1669, his continued passion for social dancing ensured that there was no decline in activity. The marquis de Dangeau recorded in his diary that in the six months between 10 September 1684 and 3 March 1685, there were no fewer than seventy royal entertainments involving dancing, including one grand ball, nine masquerades and fifty-eight *appartements*, or in other words, every two or three days.

Life therefore at Versailles was gilded, but was it a gilded cage? Although it was undoubtedly an exercise in political and social control, this familiar image of an emasculated aristocracy pining in luxurious but enervating captivity is misleading. As the exponents of the 'new court history' have pointed out, not even the court of Louis XIV was a monolith but rather a coalition. To use John Adamson's appropriate metaphor: 'The courtier's firmament contained a constellation, not a single blazing sun.' Overemphasis on the concept of 'state-building' has obscured the extent to which the court allowed sovereign and courtiers to renegotiate their relationship in a spirit of co-operation, with the former making as many sacrifices as the latter: 'Far from being the cause of the nobles' ensnarement, as was once supposed, service at court generally appears to have been one of the principal means by which aristocratic authority and influence were maintained' (Adamson). Albeit on Louis XIV's terms, one might add.

One characteristic of Versailles that distinguished it from the other palaces considered so far was the national origin of the various artists involved. Virtually all were French. The exception that proves the rule was the music supremo, Jean-Baptiste Lully. Although the creator of French lyric tragedy, he was a Florentine by birth and was known as Giovanni Battista Lulli until he Gallicized his name and set the seal on his formal naturalization by marrying the daughter of another senior member of the French musical establishment. Thus he managed to meet the maxim of the librettist Pierre Perrin (1620–75) that 'the glory of the King and of France make it unseemly that a nation otherwise invincible should be ruled by foreigners in matters pertaining to the fine arts, poetry and music'. This observation about the national exclusiveness of Versailles is less trite than it might sound, for it was unusual. Of the palaces considered in this chapter, Mafra was the creation of the architect Johann Friedrich Ludwig from Schwäbisch Hall in south-western Germany and an army of Italian sculptors; La Granja was designed by Teodore Ardemans, another German by birth, and its gardens by the Frenchman Étienne Boutelou; the new royal palace at Madrid was the work of Giovanni Battista Sacchetti from Turin; the chief architect of Klosterneuburg was another Italian, Donato Felice Allio; and so on.

With the advantage of hindsight, we can see that it was the visit of Bernini to Paris in 1665 that marked a watershed. Regarded by contemporaries as the successor of Michelangelo, he was invited to take charge of a fundamental reconstruction of the Louvre, the main royal palace in the capital. His reputation was such that the journey from Rome took on the character of a triumphal progress. Louis XIV had ordered that nothing be spared to give an appropriate welcome to the 'King of Art' and sent the head of his household to greet him. The latter, Paul Fréart de Chantelou, kept a daily diary of Bernini's five-month sojourn, so a great deal is known about it and why it ended in failure. Bernini's plans were not adopted and only the east front of the Louvre was completed, to designs by the French architect Claude Perrault. The only lasting memorial of the visit was Bernini's magnificent bust of Louis XIV, 'the most compelling record of absolutism in the visual arts' (Francis Haskell). The project foundered partly because of the personal antipathy displayed by Colbert, in effect chief minister for all domestic matters ('a right c—' was Bernini's terse verdict); partly because of the enormous expense and disruption the plans would have entailed; partly because the King was losing interest in Paris and looking to Versailles; and partly because Bernini's taste was just too Italian. This is revealed by a comparison of his design with what Perrault eventually built. Not for nothing did Perrault produce an edition of Vitruvius' *De Architectura*, the only text on architectural theory and practice to have survived from classical antiquity. Moreover, he intended this not as an antiquarian exercise but as a polemical work, to guide present-day architects. The noble simplicity and calm grandeur of his Louvre colonnade is a world, or at least a mountain range, away from the rhythmic interplay of concave and convex of Bernini's design. As David Watkin has written about Perrault's achievement: 'classical yet modern, rational yet grandiose, French yet universal in its air of authority and detachment, it is the perfect example of the classical baroque style of seventeenth-century France'.

That oxymoronic pairing of apparent opposites could be applied to the rest of Louis XIV's cultural project, exemplified by Versailles. Its authority was underpinned by the creation of a series of royal institutions to codify its practice. The *Académie française* (1634) was later joined by Academies for Painting and Sculpture (1648), Dance (1661), Inscriptions and Letters (1661), Sciences (1666), Poetry and Music (1669) and

Architecture (1671). By that time, there was no branch of high culture not subject to state control. It was also extended to the fledgling press. In 1663, the historian Eudes de Mézeray was granted permission to publish a literary journal on the dual grounds that the arts and the sciences enhanced a state's prestige no less than feats of arms, and that French intellect was in no way inferior to French valour. But although de Mézeray was authorized to report on innovations in every branch of culture, he was strictly forbidden to venture any opinion on matters of morality, religion or politics. The monopoly enforced by the academies ensured that any ambitious and talented artist was obliged to accept state service. Given the scale of Louis XIV's patronage at Versailles and elsewhere, there was also a strong financial incentive to enter the gilded cage. Consequently, almost all the great names of the age – Corneille, Racine, Molière, Lully, Delalande, Couperin, Le Vau, Mansart, de Cotte, Le Nôtre, Le Brun, Mignard, Rigaud, Largillière, Girardon, Coysevox – enjoyed an intimate relationship with the state through pensions or appointments. Their loyalty was total. One example must suffice, namely Racine's fawning declaration that 'all the words of the language, all the syllables seem precious to us, because we look on them as so many instruments which must serve the glory of our August Protector'.

In short, Versailles was only the most spectacular manifestation of a much wider cultural project which aimed at nothing less than the hegemony of French culture in Europe. By the time Louis XIV moved his court officially to Versailles in 1682, there was growing evidence of success. In the same year Ménestrier could claim that the cultural hegemony of Italy was over: 'It is the glory of France to have succeeded in establishing the rules for all the fine arts. During the past twenty years, scholarly dissertations have regulated drama, epic poetry, epigrams, eclogues, painting, music, architecture, heraldry, mottoes, riddles, emblems, history and rhetoric. All branches of knowledge are now conducted in our language.'

Of all these emblems, it was language that was the most important. In 1685 Pierre Bayle observed from his Dutch exile: 'in future it will be the French language which will serve as the means of communication for all the peoples of Europe', adding that every educated person wanted to acquire what had become a mark of good breeding. His forecast was confirmed in 1694 by the official journal, the *Mercure Galante*: 'The range of the French language has crossed the kingdom's frontiers. It is confined neither by the Pyrenees, nor by the Alps nor by the Rhine. French is to be heard all over Europe. The French language is spoken at all the courts: the princes and the grandees speak it, the ambassadors write it and high society makes it fashionable.' When Louis came to the throne in 1643, French was only one of several competing languages: either Spanish or Italian could have made as good if not a better claim to be the *lingua franca* of educated Europe, while Latin still dominated academic discourse. Halfway through his reign it could be claimed by Father Dominique Bouhours SJ that French had become the world language, 'as current among the savages of America as it is among the most civilized nations of Europe'. By the end of the seventeenth century, the marquis de Dangeau could tell the *Académie française* with majestic complacency: 'All our works contribute to the embellishment of our language and help to make it known to foreigners. The wonders achieved by the King have made French as familiar to our neighbours as their own vernacular, indeed the events of these past few years have broadcast it over all the oceans of the globe, making it as essential to the New World as to the Old.' It was a process assisted by the codification of the French language in the great dictionary of the *Académie française*, completed in 1694.

No great acumen is needed to spot that all these tributes to the hegemony of French culture were written by Frenchmen. But there are other, more objective indications that they had a good case. The first international treaty to be drafted in French rather than Latin was the Treaty of Utrecht of 1713; by the 1770s, even treaties not involving France were being drafted in her language, such as the Treaty of Kutchuk-Kainardji between Russia and the Turks in 1774. In 1743 Frederick the Great ordered that the proceedings of the Berlin Academy should be published in French on the grounds that, 'to be useful, academies should communicate their discoveries in the universal language, and that language is French'. In his *Mémoires pour servir à l'histoire de Brandebourg* (Memoirs to Serve as a History of the House of Brandenburg) he added that it was the writers of Louis XIV's reign who had made French the universal language of scholars, politicians, women and courtiers, replacing Latin as the *lingua franca*. It was to be heard in every civilized part of the continent, he added, and was an indispensable passport to polite society. For all these reasons, he defended his decision to write in a language not his own, arguing that it was no more strange for a

German to write in French than it was for a Roman at the time of Cicero to write in Greek.

L'EUROPE FRANÇAISE?

This influence naturally found its way into palace architecture outside France. Virtually all royal, princely and aristocratic patrons included an extended stay at Versailles as part of their Grand Tour (although Frederick the Great was a notable exception). Augustus the Strong of Saxony-Poland even commissioned his court painter, Louis Silvestre, to immortalize in paint the moment when his eldest son was presented to Louis XIV. Those who could not travel to Versailles to experience its wonders at first hand could make their acquaintance through the numerous descriptions and illustrations that were published. In 1663 Louis instructed Israel Silvestre (Louis' father) to engrave 'all his palaces, royal houses, the most beautiful views and aspects of his gardens, public assemblies, Carrousels and outskirts of cities'. This commission initiated a series of magnificent volumes, themselves art-objects of high value, broadcasting French culture across the length and breadth of Europe. As André Félibien, the secretary of the Royal Academy of Architecture, commented: 'it is by means of these prints that all nations can admire the sumptuous edifices which the king has built everywhere, and the rich ornamentation which embellishes them'. Fifty years after the Sun King's death, the architect Pierre Patte wrote in *Monuments Erected in France to the Glory of Louis XV*:

Travel through Russia, Prussia, Denmark, Württemberg, the Palatinate, Bavaria, Spain, Portugal and Italy, and everywhere you will find French architects occupying the most important positions. At St Petersburg, La Mothe is the premier architect, at Berlin Le Geay; at Copenhagen, Jardin; at Munich, Cuvilliés; at Stuttgart, La Guêpière; at Mannheim, Pigage; at Madrid, Marquet; at Parma, Petitot . . . Paris performs for Europe the role of Greece when the arts triumphed there: it provides artists for all the rest of the world.

Patte himself was architect to the dukes of Zweibrücken from 1761 to 1790.

It was authoritative comments such as Patte's that prompted Louis Réau to give his history of European culture, first published in 1938, the title: *L'Europe française*. Those were also the opening words of the book, with an exclamation mark added for emphasis and celebration. His sentiment has been repeated many times since, with a frequency that has increased as actual French cultural influence has declined. Part of the table of contents of a standard general history of Europe, published in 1959 by Roland Mousnier and Ernest Labrousse, reads: '*L'unité de l'Europe: L'Europe française – le français, langue européenne – l'art français, art européen – architecture française – musique française – sculpture française – costume française – cuisine française – L'invasion de l'Europe par la France*'. Yet these celebrations of French hegemony, whether contemporary or subsequent, do not fit very well with visual impressions of the artefacts. Most buildings constructed outside France during this period just do not look French. If a national label does have to be attached to, say, the Winter Palace in St Petersburg, the Amalienborg in Copenhagen, the Royal Palace in Stockholm, the Černin Palace on the Hradčany in Prague, the Esterházy Palace at Eisenstadt, the Liechtenstein Palace, the Belvedere or the Schwarzenberg Palace in Vienna, Bamberg, Würzburg or Pommersfelden in Franconia, Ludwigsburg or Bruchsal in south-western Germany – or whatever – then that label would have to be 'Italian', for the architects of all these buildings were either Italian, had trained in Italy or had studied with Italianate architects. In architecture, and indeed in all the visual arts and music, it would make more sense to write a book entitled *L'Europa italiana*, with or without an exclamation mark.

It is something of a truism that 'Italy' was merely a geographical expression, that particularist antagonisms were rife, that only a small minority of the population could understand the Italian language, and so on. Yet contemporaries clearly did have a clear appreciation of an Italian culture, whether they were Italians themselves or outsiders. Just one example of this kind of sentiment must suffice, but it could be replicated at will. In 1739 the chevalier Charles de Brosses wrote to his brother from Rome that the English were respected 'throughout Italy' because they had lots of money and spent it freely, but the French were universally disliked because of their arrogant prejudice that the only right way of doing things was the French way. He then showed he was no exception by observing sourly that the English visitors spent all their time playing billiards, leaving Rome without knowing even where to find the Colosseum.

This is not to say that French influence was not important. It can be found to a greater or lesser extent in many palaces across the continent: in the Wittelsbach palace of Nymphenburg outside Munich, for example, where the chief architect, Joseph Effner, had been a pupil of Germain Boffrand. A French flavour was even more apparent in the exquisite hunting lodge Amalienburg in the adjoining park, the work of the Walloon François Cuvilliés, who began his career in the Elector's service as court dwarf but was then seconded to Paris to train as an architect. In his photographic survey of 'French architecture in Germany in the eighteenth century', Pierre du Colombier listed eighty buildings in thirty-nine different places and forty-three architects. If that sounds like a resurrection of Louis Réau's *'L'Europe française!'*, it should be added by way of qualification that many of the buildings were either minor (a gate at Heidelberg, a private house at Frankfurt am Main, for example) or represented modest contributions to a structure that was patently not French (the episcopal palaces at Brühl and Würzburg, for example). Moreover, the list of architects includes several of German or Italian origin, apparently on the grounds that they were either lucky enough to work with French architects or were sensible enough to work in the French style. A distinction needs to be drawn between the fashion set by Versailles and the styles in which the attempts at emulation were built. It can also be seen in the subsequent addition of smaller hunting lodges and pleasure-palaces on the lines of Marly or the Trianon, as revealed by the names of the German equivalents – 'Solitude' (Stuttgart), 'Mon Repos' (Ludwigsburg), 'Château de Mon Aise' (Trier), and so on.

It can also be seen in the plethora of secular palaces that covered Europe during this period. It was not so much the architectural style of Versailles that was copied, rather the impetus to create a very large palace on a greenfield site. One example must suffice, but it is a good one. When the younger son of Philip V of Spain became King of Naples in 1735 as Charles VII, he found the royal palace in the capital (previously the residence of the viceroy of Spain) seriously inadequate for his perceived needs. Of course, he set about a major programme of reconstruction, but his main energies were devoted to a brand-new palace 25 miles (40 km) to the north-east at Caserta. His architect, Luigi Vanvitelli, the son of a painter from Utrecht, created for him a structure of colossal size: 800 feet long, 600 feet wide, 120 feet high (245 × 180 × 36 m) and containing around 1,200 rooms. Well might George Hersey comment: 'In its very size and universality it is one of the earliest megapalaces, the forerunner ... of the buildings of the later British Empire, of Fascism and Nazism, and of America's enormous classical temples in Washington.' Although its relative austerity has allowed one architectural historian, Michel Florisoone, to acclaim it as one of the earliest signs of a mid-eighteenth-century turn to neoclassicism, a more common reaction is to find the uniformity of its thirty-six identical bays simply monotonous. As James Lees-Milne tartly observed: 'The serried windows and the detailed ornament are lost in the enormous bulk like a small necklace upon the bosom of an immoderately fat woman.' However, once inside the palace, the visitor's progress from the central arch to the octagonal vestibule and its dramatic staircase has been variously acclaimed as 'superbly successful' (Anthony Blunt) and 'one of the baroque masterpieces of eighteenth century Europe' (Lees-Milne).

Charles was not a Bourbon for nothing and unleashed a panoply of representational display reminiscent of Versailles. When he married Maria Amalia of Saxony (who also knew a thing or two about representation), his historiographer-orator Giambattista Vico compared him to Hercules disembarking at the shrine of Parthenope (the siren-founder of Naples), 'for when he rides on his horse in amiable ferocity, he is seen to be the emperor worthy of his arms; presiding from the royal saddle he hears the desires of his subjects and is seen as the king entering into possession of his kingdom not by virtue of his birth but by virtue of conquest. When, standing in his royal palace, he admits his princes to the adoration of his hand, he is venerated as the simulacrum of God on earth.' In his treatise discussing the design of Caserta, Vanvitelli explained why he had placed four colossi at the southern portal, headed by 'Magnificence': 'they are not the usual symbols used by sculptors, for I have not pretended to represent them abstractly but to particularize them as they reside and are enthroned in His Majesty's great soul'. In the Hall of the Ambassadors, one of several 'Halls of Representation', the fresco on the ceiling depicts *Bourbon Arms Sustained by the Virtues*, including that special Bourbon characteristic: 'Eminence of Rank', floating above a great shield, as with her left arm she prevents an eagle from flying higher, while she herself gazes into infinity.

All this bombast from a kingdom that was large in geographical extent but feeble in terms of international influence makes the size of Caserta seem grossly disproportionate, even if one takes into account the fact that it was also intended to serve as an office-block (like Versailles). Not to mention the cost. The life went out of the project in 1759 when Charles was unexpectedly promoted to the throne of Spain, losing four digits in the process to become Charles III, following the death of his half-brother Ferdinand VI. Vanvitelli lamented: 'The building has a fine effect, but to what purpose? If the Catholic King [of Spain] were here it would be much. Now it is nothing.' By the time it was completed towards the end of the century, the white elephant had become a beached whale.

GARDENS AND POLITICS

As the contemporary illustration of Caserta shows, the palace was surrounded by large and formal gardens. They were also out of date by the time they were finished, a fading reminder of a Bourbon style that had once dominated Europe. Back in 1712, the Elector Maximilian Emmanuel of Bavaria had boasted: 'I can assure you that my gardens, woodlands, lakes and promenades might all be in France' but conspicuously omitted to include 'palaces'. It was indeed out of doors that French influence was felt most unequivocally through the ubiquity of the style of garden architecture perfected by André Le Nôtre at Versailles. This was characterized by formality, regularity and rectilinearity, as can be seen from Plate 14. The gardens closest to the palace were arranged in a series of harmoniously balanced beds and terraces (*parterres*), consisting of water (*parterres d'eau* and *bassins*), grass (*tapis vert*) or elaborate patterns composed of flowers and low boxwood hedges (*compartiments de broderie*). All were arranged around a central axis whose focal point was the centre of the palace and thus the royal bedroom. Further away from the buildings, the gardens became more wooded, but even here the groves (*bosquets*) were carefully ordered in rectilinear groups separated by straight avenues, with the trees trimmed and pruned to form sylvan architecture. Everywhere there were fountains, throwing jets high into the air. Their number and size taxed the ingenuity of Louis XIV's engineers, for natural supplies of water were short at Versailles and had to be supplemented by a series of huge reservoirs linked by an aqueduct to the Seine. Even so, only the fountains nearest the palace could be kept in perpetual motion. Elsewhere they were activated only when the King approached, his impending presence signalled by an elaborate system of whistles and semaphores. Even more numerous were the thousands of statues, carefully arranged to represent the glory of the Sun King. Emblematic was the largest of them, the Apollo Fountain, depicting the Sun God rising from the waves to begin his diurnal journey. As he does so, he looks up the central axis towards the royal apartments. It need hardly be said that the garden statuary was used, among other things, to give three-dimensional expression to Louis' triumphs – Coysevox's 'Vase of War', for example, which depicted the crossing of the Rhine in 1672, or his 'Vase of Peace', which marked the Peace of Nymegen of 1678. In short, in every conceivable sense, the Versailles gardens were artificial, a testimony to the capacity of man to transform a greenfield site from disordered wilderness into disciplined artefact. As Chandra Mukerji has written: 'Versailles was a model of material domination of nature that fairly shouted its excessive claims about the strength of France . . . France was clearly meant to be the new Rome. A few steps into the great formal garden at Versailles provided all that anyone needed to know about the natural authority of the king, the state, and the land of France.'

Nowhere in Europe could the resources and ambition be mustered to replicate Versailles, but its influence was pervasive. Every royal or princely visitor seems to have gone home fired with the ambition to do likewise. If they needed to refresh their memories, they could look at the numerous engravings available, read the guide to the gardens written by the King himself (which went through several editions) or read Antoine-Joseph Dezallier d'Argenville's *La Théorie et la pratique du jardinage*, first published in 1709 and translated into several languages. The results of their sincere flattery could be found in grand schemes such as the gardens at Herrenhausen in Hanover, designed by Martin Charbonnier, a pupil of Le Nôtre; or at Prince Eugène's Belvedere Palace at Vienna, designed by Dominique Girard, another pupil of Le Nôtre; or at La Granja in Spain, where French-born Philip V commissioned several French garden designers and sculptors to make him feel at home. Minia-ture versions of Versailles could also be found on scores of aristocratic country estates right across Europe.

The influence of the Versailles gardens was not only widespread, it was also long-lasting. Gardens *à la française* were still being laid out in the 1770s. By then, however, the formal style it exemplified had long been out of date in most of Europe. Significantly, the challenge had come from England and was as much political as aesthetic. Although this long and complex development has inspired some long and complex studies, only the bare outlines can be indicated here. At the risk of oversimplification, it can be said that the formal gardens of the Versailles variety came to be associated in English minds with French – and Stuart – absolutism. So Charles II's attempt to lure Le Nôtre to England in 1661 was symbolic. As David Watkin has pointed out in his seminal study of landscape gardens, the English climate was conducive to a more natural style reliant on expanses of grass and clusters of trees. Among other things, it facilitated the imitation of the irregular Chinese gardens, the accumulated knowledge of which was now reaching a critical point. Economic developments such as enclosures, which created discrete farming units, and recreational developments such as fox-hunting, which created the need for coverts, also encouraged gardens that melted into the natural landscape. While no wild animal was ever to be found at Versailles, unless imprisoned in the menagerie, in England the invention of a concealed ditch known as a 'ha ha' allowed the illusion that the park and its livestock formed an integral part of house and garden.

The analogy between a freer style of gardening and libertarian forms of government was often pointed out by contemporaries. Addison wrote in number 412 of *The Spectator* in April 1712, in which he considered 'those pleasures of the imagination which arise from the actual view and survey of outward objects':

The mind of man naturally hates everything that looks like a restraint upon it, and is apt to fancy itself under a sort of confinement, when the sight is pent up in a narrow compass ... On the contrary, a spacious horizon is an image of liberty, where the eye has room to range abroad, to expatiate at large on the immensity of its views, and to lose itself amidst the variety of objects that offer themselves to its observation. Such wide and undetermined prospects are as pleasing to the fancy, as the speculations of eternity or infinitude are to the understanding. But if there be a beauty or uncommonness joined with this grandeur, as in a troubled ocean, a heaven adorned with stars and meteors, or a spacious landscape cut out into rivers, woods, rocks, and meadows, the pleasure still grows upon us, as it arises from more than a single principle.

The most eloquent, and possibly the most influential, advocate of this position was Anthony Ashley Cooper, third Earl of Shaftesbury, who in *Characteristicks of Men, Manners, Opinions, Times* included a liking for formal gardens as part of a general denunciation of that 'corruption of taste' which infected the mind of the young by promoting a 'Love of Grandure and Magnificence'. That in turn led to '*Parterres, Equipages, trim Valets in party-colour'd Clothes* . . . In Town, a Palace and sutable [*sic*] Furniture! In the Country the same; with the addition of such Edifices and Gardens as were unknown to our Ancestors, and are unnatural to such a Climate as Great Britain!' For his part, Shaftesbury had experienced a growing passion for views spoiled by 'neither *Art*, nor the *Conceit* or *Caprice* of Man' and for nature which could therefore 'appear with a Magnificence beyond the formal Mockery of princely Gardens'. What was needed, believed Shaftesbury, was a national style for all branches of culture, underpinned by liberty. It was to be a style which sought to follow, rather than assert, mastery over nature. In his three-volume *Ichnographia Rustica* of 1718, the gardener Stephen Switzer contrasted the 'regular designer' and his unnatural obsession with straight lines with the 'natural gardener', who makes 'his Design submit to Nature, and not Nature to his Design'.

Both Addison and Shaftesbury were writing during the closing stages of the War of the Spanish Succession, which saw both the definitive end of French hegemony and the arrival of Great Britain as a front-rank European power. So perhaps it is not surprising that they should have politicized even garden design. *Mutatis mutandis*, the same applied to the construction of several of the great English landscape gardens of the 1730s. As Adrian von Buttlar has shown in his study of the English country house as symbol of a liberal world-view (*Der englische Landsitz 1715–1760: Symbol eines liberalen Weltentwurfs*), a split among the dominant Whigs sent a number of self-proclaimed 'patriot' grandees back to their estates, there to plot the downfall of Walpole and to advertise the superior merits of their own brand of politics. Among the weaponry they employed was garden design. Just how seriously they took their horticultural semiotics is attested by the large sums of money they spent on it. At Stowe, Lord Cobham employed an army of gardeners to create and maintain a garden with a clear political agenda. While the 'Temple of Modern Virtue' was artificially decayed and contained a headless statue (Walpole), the 'Temple of Ancient Virtue' housed Lycurgus, among other Greek heroes, who, in the words of the accompanying inscription, 'planned a system of laws firmly secured against all corruption; and established in the state for many ages perfect liberty and inviolate purity of manners'. In the 'Temple of British Worthies' (completed 1738), the eight worthies of action (King Alfred, the Black Prince, Queen Elizabeth I, King William III, Sir Walter Raleigh, Sir Francis Drake, John Hampden and Sir John Barnard) and the eight worthies of the arts (Alexander Pope, Sir Thomas Gresham, Inigo Jones, John Milton, William Shakespeare, John Locke, Sir Isaac Newton and Sir Francis Bacon) all had in common a dedication to liberty and virtue fundamentally at odds with the despotism and corruption deemed to prevail in contemporary Great Britain.

All over the British Isles, country gentlemen great and small were busy spending their expanding wealth in creating landscape gardens. As Sir John Plumb wrote: 'No one baulked at planting vast woods that could not possibly mature for two centuries. Fifty miles was not an unusual circumference for a park. Sir Robert Walpole used fifty men, women and boys merely to weed his plantations.' Lancelot 'Capability' Brown (1716–83), who worked at Stowe from 1741 to 1751, had at least a hand in the transformation of around 200 estates. Of course, not many of these were on the same sort of scale as Stowe or Stourhead, and only a few had the same kind of ideological agenda, but the collective impact on the countryside was immense and enduring. It was not long before its influence began to spread across the Channel. An increasing number of well-heeled foreign tourists began to travel ever more widely, including in their itineraries stately homes and their gardens. Prince Franz of Anhalt-Dessau and his wife made lengthy and extensive tours of England in 1763, 1767–8 and 1775, paying special attention to country houses and their gardens. On the last occasion they visited Blenheim, Bowood, Chiswick, Kensington, Osterley Park, Painshill, Park Place, Prior Park, Rousham, Sion House, Stourhead, Stowe, Twickenham, Woburn and West Wycome and many less important estates. On their return they set about creating at Wörlitz an English garden worthy of comparison with the greatest of the originals. Among other things, Wörlitz boasts a Palladian Villa, a model volcano, a Gothic House, an 'English Seat', a Grotto and a model of the iron bridge at Coalbrookdale. These buildings and landscape expressed a highly sophisticated cultural and political programme, for whereas Versailles and its German imitators represented the centralized state and its will to power, the gardens at Wörlitz propagated individual cultivation (*Bildung*), virtue, toleration and federalism.

THE HABSBURG ALTERNATIVE

This horticultural trail has taken us a long way in time and space from the Versailles model. As the great palace was being erected from the 1660s, an alternative form of representation was developing across the Rhine in the Holy Roman Empire. One thing the Germans had in common with their French rivals was a clear appreciation of the need to express their aspirations. One of the most prolific writers on public affairs of the period, Johann Christian Lünig, argued that, even though rulers were mortal, their divine commission authorized them to distinguish themselves from the rest of the human race by 'external signs' (*eußerliche Marquen*) and thus increase their prestige and the respect shown to them by their subjects. Most of the latter, he sighed, were not accessible by reason alone, for however many and however excellent were the words employed to demonstrate the religious and rational bases of political obligation, they would pay no attention if the ruler appeared before them in everyday clothes similar to their own. Only when he paraded in magnificent apparel, surrounded by courtiers, foreign ambassadors and life-guards, would the necessary reverence and deference be inspired. So Lünig would certainly have approved of the reaction of Johann Basilius Küchelbecker when he visited Vienna in the 1720s, for he was deeply impressed by the sheer size of the imperial court: 'one's eyes must be delighted when one sees His Imperial Majesty at court surrounded by great princes, counts and nobles, who not only have performed great services but also possess great estates and wealth and so their numerous retinues and costly accoutrements greatly enhance the magnificence of the imperial court'.

This elevation of the Austrian branch of the Habsburgs was of relatively recent origin. It was only under Ferdinand II (1619–37) that the court was finally established at Vienna, and even after that it spent extended periods elsewhere. It was only in 1665, with the death of the last member of the Tyrolean line, that all the German lands of the Habsburgs came to be concentrated in one ruler, Leopold I (1657–1705). The near-certainty that the pitiful Charles II of Spain (1665–1700) would be the last of his line also enhanced the status of the notionally junior Habsburg branch. This consolidation marked the end of a particularly torrid time, when successive emperors had been faced by revolts at home, war in the west against the French and war in the east against the Turks – and often all three simultaneously. That the dynasty emerged triumphant from these trials seemed conclusive evidence to the beneficiaries that God had been walking with them, testing and supporting them in equal measure. The court preacher and Augustinian friar Abraham a Sancta Clara expressed this well when he said that Leopold I had defeated his enemies with his knees, for it was the power of prayer that had triumphed.

The Habsburg style of representation was part of a wider religious project, a special form of baroque piety known as 'Pietas Austriaca'. On his accession in 1657, Leopold immediately signalled his intentions by making a pilgrimage to the Marian shrine at Altötting in Bavaria, where he placed his dominions under the protection of the Virgin. Pilgrimages became a distinctive part of court culture. Seven times during his reign Leopold made his way to Mariazell in Styria, the most important of all Austrian pilgrimage places, the home of the Black Virgin, the Magna Mater Austriae. He was often accompanied on pilgrimage by the entire court: in 1665, for example, to give thanks for the victory over the Turks at St Gotthard the previous year. As the siege of Vienna by the Turks got underway in 1683, Leopold and his wife demonstratively joined a Marian confraternity, and it was with a great shout of 'Mary, help us!' ('Maria hilf!') that the decisive battle to relieve the city began on 12 September. Predictably, the subsequent rout of the Turks intensified the cult of the Virgin and inspired the construction of many churches dedicated to her. At Mariazell, the imperial architect Johann Bernhard Fischer von Erlach was commissioned to add an imposing new high altar. Leopold's devotion to the cult was personal and passionate: in 1665 he signed himself in the pilgrimage book at Mariazell as 'Leopold, the meanest and the least worthy of the Blessed Virgin Mary's serfs', and in 1676 he wrote: 'in time of war I want the Blessed Virgin Mary as my general and in the peace-negotiations I want her as my ambassador'.

This kind of self-abasement would have been signally out of place at Versailles, and the contrast was not lost on contemporaries. Austrian pamphleteers praised Leopold for his modesty, stressing that he built only for the glory of God. They contrasted his modesty and humility with the selfish arrogance of Louis XIV. Thomas da Costa Kaufman believes that the construction of the Leopoldine Tract of the Hofburg in Vienna in the 1660s and 1670s signalled Leopold's 'intentions to revive the grandeur of his house', but it pales by comparison not only with Versailles but also with the projects of some of his own subjects, such as the Černin Palace on the Hradčany in Prague (1668–87) or the Esterházy Palace at Eisenstadt (1663–72). Building on the grand scale was just not Leopold's style. That did not mean that he was reticent, rather that he found other ways to represent his majesty. His favourite was music. Of all European sovereigns, his only rival as a creative musician (so far) has been Frederick the Great. He composed the music for six music-dramas of various kinds, as well as contributing many arias and even whole acts to operas written by his various court composers. One of the latter, Johann Joseph Fux, told him that it was a shame that his imperial office prevented him from becoming a professional musician, to which Leopold replied: 'Yes, I know, but I haven't done too badly, even so.'

His grandfather, Ferdinand II, is usually assigned the blame (or credit, according to taste) for making the Habsburg Monarchy a militantly Catholic, counter-reformatory state, but it was also he who began a long tradition of musical patronage and practice. Among other things, he was responsible for the first performance of opera in the Monarchy, on the occasion of his forty-seventh birthday in 1625. In this he was encouraged by his second wife, Eleonora Gonzaga, from the music-loving court of Mantua, a tradition continued by his son Ferdinand III (1637–57), who also composed, performed and encouraged music – and married another Gonzaga called Eleonora into the bargain. Leopold did not marry a Gonzaga (although one of his three wives was called Eleonora), but he did promote opera, most spectacularly when he married his first wife, the Infanta Margarita Teresa, the daughter of Philip IV of Spain immortalized in several Velázquez portraits, including *Las Meninas*. To celebrate their union, perhaps the most elaborate and extravagant representational display ever staged was performed in Vienna in a specially constructed theatre variously estimated to hold between 1,500 and 5,000 spectators in the space today occupied by the Josephplatz. This was *Il Pomo d'oro* (the golden apple), with music by Antonio Cesti and a libretto by Francesco Sbarra, although Leopold wrote the music for part of Acts two and five. Well might one contemporary exclaim that 'such a work has never been seen in the world before and perhaps the like of it will never be seen again'. Some idea of the scale of the enterprise, enough to make the director of even the best-endowed opera company blanch, can be gained from the cast list, which comprised more than fifty solo roles. To this army of performers, many of them hired from Italy at huge expense, must be added the costs of the special effects, the twenty-three elaborate stage sets, and gorgeous costumes. Needless to say, the performance was carefully captured visually, engraved, reproduced and sent around Europe to advertise to those unlucky enough not to have been present just what unsurpassable magnificence they had missed. It is characteristic of representational culture that this eight-hour work, which had to be divided into two parts given on separate evenings, should have been performed only twice. As can be inferred from the names of the characters, it was a heavily allegorical exercise, designed to celebrate the beauty of the new Empress and the greatness of both her husband and her new home. At its conclusion, flanked on stage by statues of Leopold and his bride and against a backdrop presenting 'The Court of Austrian Glory', Paris awards the eponymous golden apple to the Empress, because she combines the wisdom of Minerva, the beauty of Venus and the greatness of Juno.

Il Pomo d'oro was only the climax of a much longer series of celebrations. When the Infanta had arrived in Vienna, in December 1666, she was greeted by six weeks of festivities, including innumerable balls, banquets and plays, an elaborate equestrian ballet, several operas, and a ballet danced entirely by noble gentlemen of the court (Heinrich Schmelzer's *Twelve Ethiopian Beauties*). Other highlights included a multimedia open-air extravaganza, part ballet and part tournament, called *La contesa dell'aria e dell'acqua* (the contest between air and water), with music by Bertali and Schmelzer, and a German-language 'show' (*Schaustellung*) entitled 'Germany Rejoices' (*Das frohlockende Deutschland*). And Germany did rejoice: the writer Paul Winkler exclaimed after experiencing one of Leopold I's festivities: 'Vienna is the capital of the world, the throne of all the earth'. Later in Leopold's long reign, there was a move towards competing head-on with Louis XIV with monumental structures, perhaps inspired by Austrian victories over the Turks and/or a growing resentment at French pretensions to cultural hegemony. In 1690 Fischer von Erlach built a great triumphal arch to celebrate the return to Vienna of Crown Prince Joseph, following his election as 'King of the Romans' (with automatic right of succession to the imperial title when his father died). The same architect also designed a new palace to be built at Schönbrunn, just outside Vienna. Had it been realized, it would have eclipsed Versailles in every respect, not least aesthetically.

In the event, a much more modest version was constructed, imposing certainly but overshadowed by its French rival in size if not in beauty. Yet the Habsburgs could claim to have won the battle of the palaces, not on account of the buildings they erected themselves but through what can be called 'representation at one remove'. Right across the Habsburg Monarchy, and indeed the Holy Roman Empire, princes and prelates created imperial spaces within their own palaces. A prince Esterházy, an abbot of St Florian or a prince-bishop of Würzburg knew full well that their continued well-being depended on the continued well-being of the house of Habsburg. It is difficult to think of any French aristocratic *hôtel* built in the seventeenth or eighteenth century whose iconography is dominated by the Bourbon dynasty, but across the Rhine it is very easy to find examples of the Habsburgs being apotheosized. At St Florian near Linz, for example, it was the epochal victory over the Turks in 1683 that prompted the massive rebuilding programme that made the institution as much an imperial palace as an Augustinian monastery. In the room designated for imperial audiences, a ceiling fresco portrays the Habsburg Monarchy as the continuation of the four great empires of the past – Babylon, Persia, Greece and Rome. In the Emperor's Hall (*Kaisersaal*) another enormous fresco by Bartolomeo Altomonte celebrates 'The Apotheosis of Charles VI', who in the form of Jupiter stands on a red-white-red-draped podium triumphant above a defeated Turk, while personifications of Austria and Hungary do homage. On a crudely quantitative basis, it is likely that, despite the personality cult of Louis XIV at Versailles, collectively the Habsburgs could boast more iconographic references.

PALACES, COURTS AND POLITICS

Also collective was the great building boom that took place in the wake of the defeat of the Turks and their subsequent expulsion from Hungary. Now that it was safe to build, the aristocrats of the Monarchy set to work with a will: in the half-century after 1683 around 300 palaces were constructed in and around Vienna. They gave visual expression to the alliance of dynasty and magnates which had emerged from the troubled times of the early and middle years of the seventeenth century. As Robert Evans has shown in his classic study *The Making of the Habsburg Monarchy 1550–1700*, the victors of that protracted agony were aristocrats with the political power and material resources to pick up the pieces of a crumbling society. When the dust settled, it was they who stood head and shoulders above the debris. Both relatively and absolutely they had advanced their position in economy, society and the state at the expense of other social groups. But they could not have done it without the support of the Habsburg Emperor. It was he who had the international connections that made possible the defeat of their enemies, whether Turks, Protestants, burghers, lesser nobility or peasantry. Loyalty to the dynasty and the Catholic Church was the price that had to be paid. In the course of just a century it was a deal that could elevate the Esterházys of Hungary, for example, from minor gentry to princes owning an estate the size of Wales.

The Esterházys built an enormous palace at Eisenstadt, a summer palace at Esterháza and, of course, another in Vienna. It was in the capital that they spent the winter, like most of their class, taking advantage of all the recreational possibilities that had developed as the court and its satellites expanded. By 1700 at the latest, Vienna was the undisputed premier playground of the nobility of both the Habsburg Monarchy and the Holy Roman Empire. Even princes and nobles whose main residences were in regional capitals such as Mainz or Darmstadt spent some time in Vienna on a regular basis. For, among many other things, it was the source of imperial patronage: to win a post or promotion at long range was difficult, if not impossible. Proximity to the fount of fortune was all, so in 1711 Prince Schwarzenberg was prepared to pay an enormous sum to become Grand Master of the Horse (*Oberstallmeister*), despite its modest salary, because it guaranteed him regular access to the Emperor, especially when he was on the move. Offices could be supplemented by pensions, loans and outright gifts. In 1773 Maria Theresa gave away 9,000,000 *gulden* from the proceeds of land expropriated from the Jesuits. Such was the cost of maintaining an establishment in Vienna and generally keeping up with the Esterházys that supplementary income was badly needed. So ruler and magnates were bound together politically, economically, culturally and also confessionally (for an absolute requirement for access to the pump of patronage was Catholicism). Even the notoriously fractious Hungarian aristocrats were tamed by the ties that bound them to the Viennese court. As one hostile contemporary observed:

The proud Hungarians, who on their country estates were engaged in planning schemes of liberty, have been allured to court or to town. By the grant of dignities, titles and offers of marriage, and in other ways, every opportunity has been given to them of spending their money in splendour, of contracting debts, and of throwing themselves on the mercy of their sovereign when their estates have been sequestrated . . . Having thus converted the most powerful part of the Hungarian nobility into spendthrifts, debauchees and cowards, the Court has no longer occasion to fear a revolt.

A glamorous court could also be an instrument of foreign policy. This was demonstrated by the Elector of Saxony Frederick Augustus when he secured election as King of Poland in 1697, taking the title of Augustus II. It was one thing to get elected in Poland, quite another to hold on to the prize. In his election campaign, Augustus had been supported by Austria and Russia but had been opposed by a substantial group of Polish nobles supported and financed by France. To make good his claim he now needed to present himself as a king worthy of the name and thus dispel the notion that he was just a middling German prince imposed by foreign powers. In pursuit of regal status, Augustus now created 'the most dazzling court in Europe', which was the authoritative verdict of the peripatetic Baron Pöllnitz in 1729. It boasted the best balls, pageants, opera and hunting to be found anywhere in the Empire outside Vienna. Augustus employed the best portrait-painter (Louis Silvestre) to paint both wife and mistresses, the best jeweller (Johann Melchior Dinglinger), the best porcelain designer (Johann Joachim Kaendler), the best sculptor (Balthasar Permoser), the best architect (Mathhäus Daniel Pöppelmann), the best singer (Faustina) and the best composer (Johann Adolf Hasse). Some idea of Dresden's fabled beauty can be gained from Bernardo Bellotto's justly celebrated *vedute*.

This cultural climbing did pay dividends. The clearest sign that Augustus had thrust his way into the premier league of European sovereigns came in 1719 when his son and heir, Frederick Augustus, was married to the Habsburg Archduchess Maria Josepha, daughter of the late Emperor Joseph I. To celebrate the occasion, Augustus unleashed the full panoply of his court. Two years of preparations, which involved among other things the extension of the 'Zwinger', as the great representational arena next to the Electoral palace was known, and the construction of the largest opera-house north of the Alps, reached a climax with a full month of festivities to greet the bride and bridegroom on their return from Vienna. The ceremonies can be followed with some precision, for Augustus was careful to have each one recorded in word and image and then broadcast to the world by brochure and engraving. Moreover, the marriage paid a recurring dividend for succeeding generations of the dynasty. His son succeeded him as King of Poland and, of his grandchildren, Maria Amalia married Charles III of Spain; Maria Anna married Maximilian III Joseph, Elector of Bavaria; Josepha married the Dauphin of France, and thus was the mother of Louis XVI; Albert married Maria Christina, daughter of the Empress Maria Theresa, and later became Governor of the Austrian Netherlands; Clemens Wenzeslaus became Prince-Bishop of Freising, Regensburg and Augsburg and Archbishop-Elector of Trier; and Kunigunde became Princess-Abbess of Thorn and Essen (where she could seek spiritual consolation for having been jilted by Joseph II). This list alone should be sufficient to remind us that dynastic politics supported by representational court culture could bring concrete material benefits.

Augustus II, whose sobriquet 'the Strong' derived from his fabled strength and even more fabulous sexual potency, was not alone. His near-contemporary Duke Ernst Augustus of Brunswick-Lüneburg (1629–98) undoubtedly strengthened his case for promotion to the Electoral College of the Holy Roman Empire by developing a court of suitable grandeur at Herrenhausen. He eventually became the first Elector of Hanover in 1692. Keeping one step ahead of him in the imperial hierarchy was the Elector of Brandenburg, Frederick III (1688–1713), who, after creating a court fit for a king, became the first 'King in Prussia' in 1701. Of course, the Guelphs and Hohenzollerns gained their promotion mainly as a result of helping Leopold I politically and militarily, but the expansion of the court was an integral part of this process and not just a symptom.

The success of Louis XIV in establishing French political hegemony, albeit only temporarily, and French cultural hegemony, which proved rather more durable, together with the contemporary success of the Habsburgs in consolidating the great-power status of their Monarchy and the achievements of their contemporaries in Saxony, Hanover and Prussia, all suggest that representational court culture was a sound investment. But it could also be dysfunctional. In the Duchy of Württemberg, for example, in the 1670s and 1680s the Regent Friedrich Karl transformed the traditional household from a homely if rather crude 'beer and skittles' operation into a high-gloss and high-cost court. The French provenance of this transformation was not in doubt, as life at court was remodelled according to the precepts of Versailles. The unruly drinking bouts favoured in the past were replaced by opera, ballets and balls. At a '*Divertissement à la française*' staged by the Regent in 1684, for example, the eight-year-old Duke Eberhard Ludwig was obliged to imitate Louis XIV by dancing the role of Cupid. Württembergers attending the Duchy's first salon, introduced by Friedrich Karl's prime minister, the French-educated Baron von Forster-Dambenoy, were expected to speak French and be able to talk about the latest French fashions.

The cultural complex developed in Württemberg during the second half of the seventeenth century cannot have been aimed at the disciplining of the nobles, for the good reason that the Duchy had none to discipline. The nobles of the region had established independence from ducal authority in the sixteenth century by making good their claim to be 'Imperial Knights'. In other words, they acknowledged only the Holy Roman Emperor as their sovereign, were not subject to the Duke of Württemberg and were not represented in the Duchy's Estates. The latter consisted of two houses, one comprising the fourteen Protestant abbots of the secularized monasteries and the other the representatives of sixty towns. Far from being overawed or seduced by the lavish court unfolded by Friedrich Karl and his successors, the Württemberg burghers were horrified and alienated. As the Regent was also seeking to ally with France to create a standing army, an association was made between Francophilia, despotism and profligacy every bit as acute as in Stuart England. In 1681, for example, the Estates campaigned for the dismissal of a French governess and a French dancing master, employed to instruct the young Duke, on the grounds that they were likely to corrupt their charge with 'loose French morals', 'lascivious French ways', 'conversation punctuated with obscene and evil jokes' and 'a style of manners that placed topics of erotic love at the centre of polite discourse'.

As this disapproving but excited obsession with sexuality suggests, a further similarity with contemporary England was the religious flavour of the clash between prince and parliament. The Lutheranism of the

Estates' deputies, which was being given an increasingly Puritanical edge by the burgeoning Pietist movement, was utterly at odds with the secular hedonism of the Regent's court and what his critics called his 'mocking of the very premises of a legitimate, Christian, German-oriented, non-Machiavellian polity'. For his part, Friedrich Karl took the high ground of absolutism, denouncing the Estates for 'shocking expressions touching his *gloire*'. It was he, however, who lost the struggle, being deposed as Regent in 1693 by the Emperor Leopold I. His fate showed that it was the burghers of Stuttgart, Tübingen and the other towns whose co-operation, or at least acquiescence, was most needed, but they were just the people most alienated by the 'loose and lascivious' French culture of the court and correspondingly more determined to resist its political dimension. As so often in early modern Europe, political opposition supported by religious conviction proved especially tenacious. Unlike the aristocratic targets of Louis XIV's representational culture, the Württembergers did not roll over to have their stomachs stroked. They remained upright, usually seeking co-operation rather than confrontation and often obliged to make concessions, but stubbornly resisting attempts to emasculate the ancient liberties and traditional constitution.

A more serious lesson in the dangers of over-indulgence in court culture was provided by the fate of Saxony. While Augustus the Strong was scattering money in all directions, his northern neighbour, the grim Frederick William I of Prussia (1713–40), was hoarding every penny he could lay his hands on. He effectively closed down his father's court, disbanding the orchestra and derisively appointing his court dwarf as President of the Berlin Academy. Augustus is reputed to have told Frederick William: 'When Your Majesty collects a ducat, you just add it to your treasure, while I prefer to spend it, so that it comes back to me threefold.' This may have been sound economics and could also have been supported by the parable of the talents, but it did not help Augustus's son and heir, who succeeded as Augustus III in 1733, when he had to face a challenge from Frederick William's son, who succeeded as Frederick II in 1740.

The latter achieved his sobriquet 'the Great' mainly at the expense of Saxony. When Augustus the Strong died, he left his son a superlative cultural centre but also a mountain of debt. He had increased his army to the respectable total of just under 30,000, but had signally failed to secure Saxony-Poland's great-power status. Frederick William I bequeathed to his son a culture so austere as to be unworthy of the name but an army 81,000-strong, which in terms of quality was the best in Europe, and was supported by a great treasure-chest of 8,000,000 *talers* in hard cash, packed in barrels in the cellars of the royal palace in Berlin. At the beginning of the century, the Saxon and Prussian armies had been almost exactly the same size, indeed, if anything the Saxon army was rather larger; by 1740 the Prussian army was three times larger and much better trained, equipped and financed. The series of wars which began in December 1740 when Frederick invaded Silesia is usually presented as a struggle between Prussia and Austria for the domination of Germany, and rightly so. It was also, however, a struggle between Prussia and Saxony. As the son of an Austrian Archduchess, Augustus III had a much sounder claim to Habsburg territory than did Frederick of Prussia. If he had succeeded in adding Silesia to Saxony and Poland, he would have created an unbroken territorial complex reaching from the heart of Germany to the frontiers of Russia. This was one reason why his Prussian rival was so anxious to strike first.

In the First Silesian War of 1740–42, the Saxons had supported Frederick's raid on the Habsburg Monarchy but deserted him in 1743. So his victory in the Second Silesian War of 1744–5 was a Saxon defeat. That was revealed with brutal clarity when the Third Silesian War (better known in western Europe as the Seven Years War) began. On 29 August 1756 Frederick invaded Saxony, hoping to destroy both his immediate target and the Habsburg Monarchy further to the south before the dreaded Russian juggernaut could be brought into play the following year. In that he failed, but he did succeed in taking control of Saxony and then milking it for all it was worth. The Saxon army he simply incorporated into his own. The Saxon resources he requisitioned and requisitioned until there should have been nothing left. Such was the natural wealth of the country, however, that there was always something to be found by the Prussian foragers. As Frederick himself said, Saxony was like a flour-sack – no matter how hard or often one hit it, a puff of flour would always come out. It can be said with only slight exaggeration that it was the Saxons who financed Prussia's achievement of great-power status, for their involuntary sacrifices financed fully one-third of the Prussian war effort.

10

The Culture of Feeling and the
Culture of Reason

THE CULTURE OF FEELING

Making sense of the cultural richness of the period 1648–1815 would tax even the most synoptic and penetrating of minds. It might be done most satisfactorily by a series of aphorisms, for example Hegel's definition of romanticism as 'absolute inwardness', but that is well beyond my range and would lack illustrative substance. In what follows, I have tried to find a conceptual vessel which steers clear of the Scylla of a list of great names without being sucked down into the Charybdis of overgeneralization. In suggesting that the culture of this period was driven by the dialectical relationship between the culture of feeling (or 'passion', if that seems too anodyne) and the culture of reason, I do not wish to imply that this is the only approach. Any number of craft can put to sea with equal justification, from Hegel's aircraft-carrier to the positivist's fishing-fleet. This particular catamaran just happens to seem to me to be borne along on the twin hulls of speed and stability.

The culture of feeling can be exemplified by Gianlorenzo Bernini's multimedia creation *The Ecstasy of Saint Theresa of Ávila* in the Cornaro Chapel of Santa Maria della Vittoria in Rome, created between 1645 and 1652 (Plate 14). As members of the Cornaro family look on from their box, as if in a theatre, St Theresa experiences the vision she described as follows: 'One day an Angel of surpassing beauty appeared to me in a vision. He held in his hand a long spear whose tip glowed as if it were on fire. This he thrust several times into my heart so that it penetrated to the very depth of my being. The pain was so real that I cried out several times, and yet it was also so unutterably sweet that I could not wish to be spared it. Life can offer no joy which could give me greater satisfaction. And when the Angel withdrew his spear I remained in a state of total love for God.' It would be difficult to think of a better illustration of Sigmund Freud's dictum that 'a dream is a *disguised* fulfilment of a *suppressed* wish'. It should also be sufficient warning to anyone naïve enough to suppose that, just because Christianity preaches against the sins of the flesh, religion and sexuality are opposed to each other. That is why the scoffing comment of the French Parlementaire Charles de Brosses, who visited the chapel in 1739 – 'if that is divine love, then I know it well' – misses the point. Bernini's creation is both spiritual and sensual, devotional and erotic. It is also theatrical, mobile, illusionist, transcendental and organic: the quintessence of the Roman baroque.

By the time Bernini created this extraordinary expression of his own sensual vision of religious experience, the opposing cultural paradigm had been given a potent new articulation by his almost exact contemporary, the French philosopher René Descartes. His portrait by Jan Baptist Weenix (Plate 15) provides as stark a contrast with the sensuous world of Bernini as once could imagine. In *Discourse on Method* of 1637, Descartes provided the conceptual tools which would bring the mystical vision of St Theresa down to earth – mainly in the form of showers of H_2O (one of his first published works was *Meteorology*). The most deflationary was his advocacy of systematic doubt: 'to place our knowledge on foundations which are genuinely secure, we must doubt all of our beliefs, retaining them only if they are absolutely indisputable'. In reassembling the sound parts of the structure that survived, there was only one human faculty that could be trusted – reason. So a fundamental objective of the Cartesian project was 'to lead the mind away from the senses', for they could all too easily deceive the unwary. That did not mean leading the mind away from God. On the contrary, God was allocated the central role in the Cartesian system as the guarantor of human cognition. It was the ability to prove the existence of a perfect God that allowed Descartes to reason his way from the fundamental certainty of his own existence – '*I am, I exist* is certain, so long as it is put forward by me or conceived in my mind', an axiom better known in its Latin formulation '*cogito ergo sum*' (I think, therefore I am). Nevertheless, his philosophy did mark a sharp break with traditional scholasticism. If both Bernini and Descartes worshipped God, the latter's vision was very different from that of St Theresa. The culture he personified was rational, secular, analytical, atomistic, sceptical, activist and optimistic.

If the philosophical future belonged to Descartes, in the mid-seventeenth century the present lay very much with his opponents. He was lucky enough to enjoy a private income, which allowed him to travel around Europe, spending most of his adult life in the relatively tolerant environment of the Dutch Republic, although even here he was harassed by Calvinists. Elsewhere, the firm grasp of the ecclesiastical authorities, aided and abetted by the secular arm, was unrelenting, for every state in Europe was a confessional state. Only during exceptional periods of civil strife, as in England during the Civil War, or in the semi-anarchic borderlands, such as Transylvania, could some sort of de facto pluralism exist. So the dominant culture had a distinct religious character. Moreover, it was also representational, that is to say it sought to 're-present' in the sense of 'making present' the glory of God and the truth of His message. That is perhaps why later ages, more attuned to secular literalism and humanist understatement, have often found the confident resplendence of the baroque uncongenial. This is the sacral equivalent of the representational culture epitomized by Versailles, whose extravagant bombast is now more likely to inspire distaste or derision than the awe that was intended.

Of the innumerable examples from all over Europe that could be presented, the following handful must suffice. Among the most theatrical were the creations of the Asam brothers – Cosmas Damian (1686–1739) and Egid Quirin (1692–1750). Although the former worked mainly as a painter and the latter as a sculptor and architect, in their collaborations they crossed over all visual genres. Their primary objective was to create a total work of art in which the boundaries between this world and the next were dissolved. This they achieved by using all the illusionist techniques they learnt during two years of apprenticeship in Rome: *trompe l'œil* fresco painting, false perspective, chiaroscuro, multimedia transitions, concealed lighting, and presenting church interiors as if they were stage sets, complete with audiences. Among the most successful was the Benedictine Abbey Church at Weltenburg on the Danube, near Regensburg, begun in 1716. Here it is concealed lighting which provides the drama, as St George appears to ride out towards the viewer through a triumphal arch formed by four sinuous 'salamonic' columns, skewering the dragon as he comes, and leaving the Libyan princess cowering away in terror. Behind him, the brilliantly lit fresco displays the Virgin with a serpent coiled submissively around the globe on which she stands, symbolizing the doctrine of the Immaculate Conception, whose defender was St George. As this suggests, the Asams were not thinking ecumenically. On the contrary, they – and all the other Catholic baroque artists – gloried in what made the Catholic Church special. All those aspects of the faith found most offensive by Protestants – the veneration of the Virgin, the Immaculate Conception, the cult of relics and the saints, the Sacred Heart, etc. – were given pictorial and plastic assertion. That could also be seen in the fresco adorning the ceiling of the church at Weltenburg, depicting 'The Church triumphant'. This too is a masterpiece of illusion, in reality an elliptical, double-layered dome with a flat roof, but in appearance a riotously coloured vision of Heaven in which the eye soars up past saints, the Queen of Heaven, God the Father and God the Son to the Holy Spirit fluttering around the topmost drum. Typical of the theatricality of this exercise was the positioning of spectators around the rim of the fresco, including two with the features of the Asam brothers. Indeed, the statue positioned on the left of the triumphal arch from which St George rides out was made to resemble the abbot who had commissioned the project. Through their amazing creations – the Assumption of the Virgin at Rohr is every bit as striking as Weltenburg – the Asams demonstrated that representational art, although created for a third party (in this case God), can also be expressive art. There can be little doubt about the depth of Egid Quirin Asam's piety, at least, for he bought at his own expense four houses in Sendlinger Street in Munich, two of which he turned into an extraordinarily original church dedicated to St John Nepomuk, one he assigned to its priest and one he lived in himself.

The Counter-Reformation's chief arbiter on artistic matters, Johannes Molanus, made the following appeal: 'let the Christian think, when he enters the temple, that he is entering a kind of heaven on earth, where God fills the whole edifice'. At almost exactly the same time as the Asams were doing their best at Weltenburg to obey, the Tomé family were doing likewise at Toledo cathedral. Their creation of the '*Transparente*' there has been variously described by art historians as 'the most sensational' (John Rupert Martin), 'the most outstanding' (Nikolaus Pevsner) and 'the most spectacular' (Barbara Borngässer) achievement of the Spanish baroque. Spanish contemporaries thought it was 'the eighth wonder of the world', although foreign visitors, especially if they were Protestant, thought it epitomized the decadence of Spanish art. Its function was to allow the Blessed Sacrament to be viewed from both sides of the high altar – hence the name 'Transparente'. So the Tomés constructed what is in effect an interior façade, the centre being a tabernacle with a glass aperture through which light would pour and concentrate the eye on the Host inside. At first sight, the creations by the Asams and the Tomés look very different, but they have much in common. Both seek to draw the viewer into a transcendental experience; both make use of trompe l'œil (the best example in Toledo is the stone peeling off the columns to reveal pilasters inside); both make brilliant use of concealed lighting; both use a variety of media to create a total work of art; both were collaborative ventures by families with roots in a popular craft tradition; and both are uncompromisingly, aggressively Catholic. The Transparente in particular was a reaffirmation of the centrality of the sacrament against Jansenism.

In Protestant Europe there is nothing as exuberant as Weltenburg or Toledo, although there are many great churches from the period to demonstrate that the Catholics did not have a monopoly of giving three-dimensional expression to religious devotion. St Paul's Cathedral in London (1675–1708) and the Church of Our Lady (Frauenkirche) in Dresden (1726–43) are two powerful examples. It is in music, however, that the most eloquent expression of the culture of feeling can be found. Indeed, it was exemplified in the work of Johann Sebastian Bach (1685–1750), by common consent the greatest of all composers working in the classical tradition. Everything Bach wrote – and he was amazingly prolific in many different genres – he did for the glory of God, often writing at the beginning of a score 'J.J.' – Jesu Juva (Jesus, help me) and at the end 'Soli Deo Gloria' (to the Glory of God alone). Even into his apparently more austere keyboard music he 'managed to insinuate an attitude of religious contempt for the world' (Richard Taruskin). It was in his church cantatas, however, that he found the genre best suited for the expression of his religious view of the world. In two extraordinary bursts of creativity, at Weimar between 1713 and 1716 and Leipzig from 1723 to 1729, he wrote about 300, of which 200 have survived. To these should be added the three Passions and three oratorios, not to mention his musical last-will-and-testament – the B-minor Mass. If Bach did not write his own texts, he did choose himself the biblical and other sacred verses they comprised, so a 'Bach cantata' is just that (unlike, say, a

'Mozart opera' which is a 'Mozart and Da Ponte opera' or a 'Mozart and Schikaneder' opera).

Any one of the 200 survivors might be chosen as an example of Bach's achievement, for there is not one without superior merit. Here it is number 61 in the Bach catalogue – 'Now come, Saviour of the Heathen' (*Nun kommt, der Heiden Heiland*) that will be discussed, first performed at Weimar in 1714, because it opens the Christian year, being written for the First Sunday in Advent; because it is relatively short (between fifteen and seventeen minutes, depending on the conductor); and because it is of exceptional quality, even by Bach's standards. Like all the others, this cantata was written to form the musical centrepiece of the main Lutheran Sunday act of worship, which began at 7 a.m. and finished around five hours later. It amplified the reading of the Gospel, which had preceded it, and prepared the way for the sermon, which lasted at least an hour and was regarded as the chief part of the service. When it was performed again in Leipzig in 1717, Bach could draw on the choir and soloists of the St Thomas School, of which he was choirmaster, and about twenty musicians. It is scored for a four-part choir, violins and violas, both divided into two, and continuo (bassoon and organ). All soprano parts were taken by boys, a less amazing fact when one considers that their voices often did not break until they were seventeen or even eighteen.

The six sections into which the work is divided – two choral, two recitatives and two arias – take the congregation through four stages of the Christian experience. First, Christ himself is invoked in the opening chorus, as the opening line – 'Now come, Saviour of the Heathen' – is sung successively by sopranos, altos, tenors and basses, before all four unite to proclaim: 'As the Virgin's child recognized'. Then the Church is introduced, as the tenor pleads with Christ to give it 'a blessed New Year' by maintaining sound doctrine and supporting pulpit and altar. Then comes not only the pivot of the whole work but also one of the most electrifying passages in all of Bach's oeuvre, as against a background of pizzicato strings and continuo the bass intones the lines put into Christ's mouth in the Revelation of St John the Divine: 'Behold, I stand at the door, and knock: if any man hear my voice, and open the door, I will come in to him, and will sup with him, and he with me.' Although 'just' recitative and lasting only around a minute, it exemplifies the special power of music to add an extra dimension to even the most eloquent of texts. As if in response, the soprano soloist then tells her heart to let Christ in, for he will make his home in even the humblest dwelling place. The work ends with a four-line, four-part chorale in which music has the last word in every sense: as the choir finishes singing 'Amen! Amen! Come you lovely crown of joy, and do not tarry! For Thee I wait with longing', the violins spiral up to the G above the treble stave and a vision of the life to come after death.

For any aspiring creative artist, it is a sobering thought that Bach not only wrote his cantatas at a rate of one a week, but also supervised the copying of the parts, organized the choir and orchestra, rehearsed them on Saturday afternoon, and directed the performance on Sunday morning – and all that while carrying out his other duties as cantor of St Thomas, including running a second choir. Yet hardly any of his superlative compositions were published during his lifetime and about a third have gone missing altogether. It cannot be known how the congregations of St Thomas and St Nicholas (the cantatas were performed alternately on most Sundays and in both churches on major festivals) responded to this continuous musical feast. A major difference between reception then and today concerns reproduction: the people of Leipzig heard *Nun kommt, der Heiden Heiland* just once, as just one part of a church service. Today it can be heard again and again on any one of the seventeen different recordings currently available (and can be watched as well on an audio-visual recording of a performance directed by Nikolaus Harnoncourt), and divorced from its religious function. It can also be placed in the context of the rest of the 200-odd cantatas, for there are at least half-a-dozen complete recordings available (by German, Dutch, Belgian, English and even Japanese ensembles). On the one hand they reveal great variety, for Bach exploits every conceivable permutation of his vocal, choral, instrumental and orchestral resources. On the other, they all testify to the four foundations of music's universal appeal: melody, harmony, counterpoint and rhythm. Among many other things, Bach laid down a bass line solid enough to appeal to the most basic rock 'n' roller. The cantatas also all testify to Bach's deeply felt religiosity and his successful realization of the ideal articulated by another great Saxon musician, Richard Wagner: 'the emotionalization of the intellect'. Like Wagner, Bach fused text and music to form a total work of art. Even when considering as technical an aspect as the continuo bass line (*Generalbass*) he defined its purpose as 'the glory of God'. This fundamentally religious purpose of Bach's music was well put in relation to the church cantatas by Alfred Einstein:

The art of the Bach cantata is an exposition of the foundations and principles of the Christian faith, and none more searching or more inexorable, deeper or more precise, has ever been. The temporal life and the eternal, works and faith, mortality and death, sin and repentance, suffering and salvation – all the emotions and inspirations of the Christian soul exalted this, the greatest of preachers since Luther, not to theological abstractions but to a passionate presentation by symbolic means of an incomparably vivid musical imagination.

The kind of culture exemplified by Weltenburg, the Toledo *Transparente* and *Nun kommt, der Heiden Heiland* could be illustrated from every different creative genre from every part of Europe, both Catholic and Protestant. From literature good examples would be John Bunyan's *The Pilgrim's Progress* (1678) or Blaise Pascal's *Pensées* (published posthumously in 1670) with its pithy rebuttal of Cartesian rationalism: 'The heart has its reasons which reason knows nothing of.' From painting it would be difficult to exceed the ceiling fresco of San Ignazio in Rome – *The Glory of St Ignatius Loyola and the Missionary Work of the Jesuit Order* (1688–94) – painted by Andrea Pozzo SJ. From the particularly rich range of sculpture, the pulpit created by Hendrik Frans Verbruggen in 1695–9 for the Jesuit church at Louvain, but now in the Church of St Michael and St Gudula at Brussels, so perfectly incorporates baroque religiosity as to justify an extended discussion. It might well be contrasted with the androgynous angels of Ignaz Günther (1725–75) which adorn a number of south German churches.

In music, it would be tempting to compare Bach's cantata with a work by his exact contemporary and fellow Saxon Handel, the most obvious candidate being *Messiah*, not least because the aria 'He was despised and rejected of men' is every bit as dramatic and passionate as 'Behold, I stand at the door, and knock'. But there are plenty of candidates from the Catholic world – one of the numerous oratorios or cantatas by Alessandro Scarlatti (1660–1725) or his son Domenico (1685–1757), for example. Such comparative investigations could be pursued, if not ad infinitum, then at least until many large volumes had been filled. Here it must suffice to have used a few representative examples to establish a point of reference from which development can be measured.

WITCHES AND WITCH-HUNTING

What all these cultural manifestations have in common is a belief in the omnipotence and omnipresence of God. As the baroque artists tried to show, the world below and the world above formed a unity, suffused by the supernatural. The Christian God who directed both was no remote first cause or cosmic clock-maker, but a hands-on deity who liked to make his presence felt. This was a belief that could inspire great art, but could also lead to violent outbreaks of intolerance. None was more terrible for those on the receiving end than the periodic eruptions of witch-hunting. By 1648 the prosecution of witches had largely come to an end in Spain, the Dutch Republic, England, Geneva and France. There was a further wave in Germany during the 1660s and plenty more short but sharp bursts of activity until after the middle of the eighteenth century. In Scotland the last major outbreak was 1661–2. In Poland, Bohemia and Hungary witch-hunting did not reach a peak until after 1700. The last officially sanctioned execution took place in the Swiss canton of Glarus in 1782. During the previous three centuries perhaps as many as 40,000 Europeans had been executed by the authorities, and untold more had perished at the hands of lynch-mobs.

Long after witchcraft had been downgraded from a capital crime to fraud, popular belief in its reality persisted with the occasional deadly consequence. In 1751 a mob at Tring in Hertfordshire, reported to have numbered ten thousand, watched while an elderly couple, John and Ruth Osborne, were 'ducked' in a pond to establish whether or not they had bewitched a neighbour. Although Ruth at once provided proof of her innocence by sinking like a stone, she was subjected to the ordeal three times and drowned. Her husband survived, to help provide the evidence that led to the trial and execution of the mob's ringleader. The last victim of popular belief in witchcraft appears to have been Bridget Cleary of Ballyvadlea, County Tipperary, beaten and burnt to death in 1895 by her husband, other family members and neighbours who believed that she was a fairy changeling magically installed in the place of the real Bridget.

Belief in witchcraft was not confined to the credulous illiterate. Bishop Bossuet (1627–1704), as educated and erudite a man as there was in Europe, could write: 'I hold that witches could form an army equal to that of Xerxes, which was at least 180,000 men', adding: 'I should like them all to be put into one single body so that they could be burned all together in a single flame!' As the author of *The Art of Governing, Drawn from the Words of Holy Scripture*, Bossuet was well placed to appreciate how forthright his God had been on the subject of witchcraft and witches, Exodus 22:18 commanding: 'Thou shalt not suffer a witch to live.' Unlike many modern moral theologians, who first think of an attractive precept and then search for a biblical text to support it, most men and women of all classes believed that what they read in the Bible was literally the Word of God. That was why John Wesley (1703–91) stated that 'giving up witchcraft is, in effect, giving up the Bible'. As his contemporary, the jurist Sir William Blackstone (1723–80) pointed out: 'to deny the possibility, nay, the actual existence of witchcraft and sorcery is at once to contradict the revealed word of God'.

In terms of timing, there seems to have been something of a west–east gradient. Neither Catholic Ireland (despite the later fate of Bridget Cleary) nor Calvinist Holland was much affected in the seventeenth century, nor was Spain after a last outbreak of witch-hunts in Navarre in 1610. In England, where between 300 and 500 had perished since the middle of the sixteenth century, the last witch was executed in 1684, a timetable replicated in France, where the royal government intervened in 1682 to reclassify sorcery as deception, although a priest, Louis Debaraz, was executed at Lyon in 1745. In Sweden there was a last terrible outbreak in 1668–9 at Mohra in Dalecarlia, when several children accused women of taking them to the Witches' Sabbath, leading to around seventy deaths, although the very last execution does not appear to have taken place until 1779.

It was in the south-eastern principalities of the Holy Roman Empire, in Franconia and Bavaria, that witch-crazes kept recurring until deep into the eighteenth century. In the late 1670s, for example, around 140 beggars and indigent children perished in the archbishopric of Salzburg as a result of the '*Zauberer-Jackl*' (Little Sorcerer Jack) trials. Unusually, most of the victims – 70 per cent – were young males, mostly members of vagrant bands of children allegedly led by Little Jack, although he himself was never apprehended. Eighty years later, the new Bavarian Criminal Code of 1751 was still decreeing burning alive at the stake as the penalty for those found guilty of concluding a pact with the Devil, of having sexual intercourse with him or even just worshipping him, and beheading for those who invoked diabolic assistance to do harm to third parties, their property or their animals. Although it is often stated that the last execution in Germany occurred in 1749 at Würzburg, in reality there was a further flurry in Bavaria in the 1750s. Pending further discoveries, the final victim is thought to be Maria Anna Schwägelin, beheaded at the Prince-Abbey of Kempten on 11 April 1775 for confessing to a pact with the Devil. The abbot who signed the death warrant, Honorius Baron Roth von Schreckenstein, added the injunction '*Fiat iustitia!*' (Let justice be done!). In the German-speaking regions of the Habsburg Monarchy and Bohemia, it was the late seventeenth century that saw the worst of the persecutions, but further east, in Hungary and Transylvania, it was not until the very end of the seventeenth century that they began in earnest. In Hungary 209 accused of witchcraft stood trial between 1690 and 1710, of whom 85 were executed; during the next forty years 809 were tried and 213 executed.

In Hungary, as in other parts of Europe, the persecution of witches did not end because belief in witchcraft or magic ceased, but because the government intervened. Travelling through Hungary in 1729, Johann Georg Keysler passed through a village called Nesmel, between Neuendorf and Komárom, where just a few days earlier three women and a man had been burnt at the stake for alleged diabolism, having first confessed to all kinds of absurdities under the most brutal torture. He explained the frequency of persecution there by reference to the Protestantism of the inhabitants. That also explained the horrors at Szeged, where the previous year the local judge, his wife and thirty-four others had been burnt. When Keysler expressed disapproval to the Catholic who was recounting the events, he was told in reply that the judge must have been guilty, because although a tall and corpulent man, he only weighed three-and-a-half ounces. Not unreasonably, Keysler then asked how the judge had been weighed and whether it had been done in public, but soon realized that this was a subject better not pursued. He observed:

It seems it is the opinion of many ignorant persons, that they who will not blindly swallow all such stories, must themselves be concerned in such diabolical practices: others conclude that he who does not believe the stories of witches and apparitions, is not convinced of the existence of God or the devil, Heaven or hell.

In the case of Hungary it was the Empress Maria Theresa who in 1756 ordered that in future all cases should be referred to the central court of appeal for confirmation before sentence could be carried out. The result was a sharp reduction in the number of trials, which came to a complete stop in 1777. By that time, it could be said that the age of witch trials was well and truly over (although they were to resume with a vengeance under a different aegis in the twentieth century). In 1648 witches were being burnt all over Europe; by 1815 anyone attempting to prosecute a 'witch' would find him- or herself in the dock.

THE CULTURE OF REASON

Many have been the explanations offered for this great change, itself symptomatic of an ever more fundamental change. The reasons for both the tenacity of beliefs in witchcraft and their eventual relaxation were revealed by John Wesley in the passage from which the earlier quotation was taken:

It is true, likewise, that the English in general, and indeed most of the men of learning in Europe, have given up all accounts of witches and apparitions, as mere old wives' fables. I am sorry for it; and I willingly take this opportunity of entering my solemn protest against this violent compliment which so many that believe the Bible pay to those who do not believe it. I owe them no such service. I take knowledge these are at the bottom of the outcry which has been raised, and with such insolence spread throughout the nation, in direct opposition not only to the Bible, but to the suffrage of the wisest and best of men in all ages and nations. They well know (whether Christians know it or not), that the giving up witchcraft is, in effect, giving up the Bible; and they know, on the other hand, that if but one account of the intercourse of men with separate spirits be admitted, their whole castle in the air (Deism, Atheism, Materialism) falls to the ground. I know no reason, therefore, why we should suffer even this weapon to be wrested out of our hands. Indeed there are numerous arguments besides, which abundantly confute their vain imaginations. But we need not be hooted out of one; neither reason nor religion require this.

Wesley would not abandon his belief in supernatural forces, because it was based on Scripture, endorsed by scholars down the ages, and confirmed by eye-witness accounts. Indeed, after writing this passage in his journal, he recorded at length the experiences of one of his followers, Elizabeth Hobson of Sunderland, who was repeatedly visited by dead relations. When asked whether he himself had ever seen a ghost, he replied that neither had he ever witnessed a murder, but 'I have not only as strong, but stronger proofs of this [witchcraft], from eye and ear witnesses, than I have of murder, so I cannot rationally doubt of one any more than the other'. Again and again on his travels he encountered unfortunates, especially young women, who were clearly possessed by demons. When told by a doctor that one victim was suffering 'what formerly they would have called being bewitched', Wesley indignantly recorded that the only reason why such a diagnosis was no longer made was 'because the infidels have hooted witchcraft out of the world; and the complaisant Christians, in large numbers, have joined with them in the cry'.

In other words, Wesley believed in witchcraft for what seemed to him to be utterly compelling reasons but was uncomfortably aware that both non-believers and a large number of his fellow Christians did not agree with him. As an intelligent and well-educated man, he supplies a salutary warning to later ages not to scoff at discredited systems of belief. The great majority of Europeans living in the twenty-first century have as little understanding of the science that disproves witchcraft as their predecessors had of the science that proved the opposite. On the other hand, many seventeenth-century scientists now lauded for their contribution to the advancement of knowledge also entertained beliefs that would now be derided as superstition. The greatest scientist of that, or perhaps any, age, Sir Isaac Newton (1642–1727), wrote two million words or more on theology and alchemy, took a keen interest in astrology and believed he could reconstruct the lost chronology of the ancient world from a study of the stars. He also spent a good deal of time trying to unravel the secrets of the Book of Revelation. His near-contemporary Robert Boyle (1627–91) challenged traditional chemistry in *Sceptical Chymist: or Chymico-physical doubts & paradoxes* in 1661 but was also an alchemist and could never abandon his belief in miracles.

Yet it was scientists like these who undermined the foundations of witchcraft and all other forms of magic. Wesley believed that if only one case of diabolic intercourse could be proved, the whole sceptical case would fall to the ground. But equally, once one part of the traditional world-view was shown to be false, despite support down the ages from

15. René Descartes, by Jan Baptiste Weenix, 1647–9. Although almost exactly contemporary with Bernini's sculpture of St Theresa, this austere image could hardly be more different. A central Cartesian concern was to 'lead the mind away from the senses'.

16. Ned Ward, *The Coffeehouse Mob*, frontispiece to Part IV of *Vulgus Britannicus, or the British Hudibras* (London, 1710). Open to anyone who could pay, the coffee-house was a public space in which the issues of the day could be discussed – and fought over.

17. The Court Library, Vienna, designed by Johann Bernhard Fischer von Erlach, 1722.
Magnificent certainly, but designed more to proclaim the glory of the Habsburg Emperor
Charles VI than to encourage the reading of books.

18. Francis Noble's Circulating Library (London, 1746). The growing ability to buy books cheaply or to borrow them for a modest fee from a lending library encouraged a change in the way in which books were read.

19. The blacksmith neglects his work to listen to the tailor reading from the newspaper and expressing his strong views about the contents (1772).

20. The Salon at the Louvre in 1785. The immensely popular biennial exhibitions helped to establish public opinion as the most authoritative judge of art. David's *The Oath of the Horatii* can be seen on the far wall.

21. William Hogarth, *The Invasion*, Plate I (1756). As war begins, the French prepare to impose Catholicism, tyranny and poverty on the British …

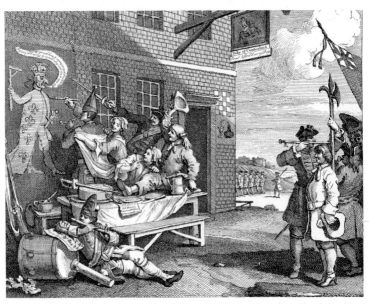

22. Hogarth, *The Invasion*, Plate II (1756) … but on the other side of the Channel, the well-fed, loyal and prosperous British Protestants show their contempt for the French threat.

23. Jean-Baptiste Greuze, *The Village Betrothal*, 1761. Exhibited in the same year that saw the publication of Rousseau's best-selling novel *Julie, or the New Héloïse*, this immensely successful painting demonstrated the popularity of 'sensibility'.

24. Jacques-Louis David, *The Oath of the Horatii*, 1783–4. Commissioned by the royal minister for the arts, it was acclaimed by critics and public alike as the greatest painting of the century. Only after 1789 was it reinterpreted as a revolutionary call to arms. For a visual depiction of its exhibition at the Salon of 1785, see Figure 20.

25. Strassburg Cathedral. It was here that Goethe had the conversion-experience that inspired him to articulate an aesthetic revolution.

26. Georg Friedrich Kersting, *Caspar David Friedrich in his Studio*, 1812. With the outside world shut out, Friedrich paints what he sees inside himself.

27. Franz Stober, *Beethoven's Funeral Procession*, 1827. A comparison between this great public event and Mozart's funeral thirty-six years earlier reveals a radical change in the status of the musician.

28. The impoverished peasant bears the burden of the clergy and nobility.

29. Young, talented and insecure – Bonaparte at Arcole in 1796, by Antoine-Jean Gros.

30. Middle-aged, talented and megalomaniac – Napoleon in his imperial robes, by Jean-Auguste-Dominique Ingres.

both classical and Christian authorities, then the whole edifice began to crumble. Of the many demolition agents, it is the heliocentric view of the universe that has the best credentials. Although expounded as early as the fourth century BC, it was Nicolaus Copernicus' *De Revolutionibus Orbium Celestium* in 1543 that began its slow and fitful progress to acceptance. Along the way, Tycho Brahe (1546–1601) and Johannes Kepler (1571–1630), his immediate successor as Imperial Mathematician to the Emperor Rudolf II, greatly improved astronomical instruments, revolutionized observational techniques, proved that there was no dichotomy between a perfect permanent heaven and a corrupt ever-changing earth, and established the laws of planetary motion. Indeed, Kepler's explanation of the last-named can lay claim to being the first natural law, for it was precise, universal and verifiable.

With just a little casuistry, the Churches might easily have neutered this threat by adapting their cosmology, although such biblical episodes as Joshua stopping the sun in its tracks (Joshua 10:12–13) would always have caused problems. In the event, they painted themselves into a corner by defending the indefensible long after heliocentrism had moved from hypothesis to fact. Although Protestants such as Luther and Melanchthon joined in deriding the heliocentric view as folly perpetrated by attention-seeking neophiliacs, it was the Catholics who proved to be the most inflexible and who suffered accordingly. So famous was Galileo Galilei (1564–1642) that his interrogation, condemnation and abjuration in 1633 became a cause célèbre that branded the Church as a reactionary bulwark against intellectual innovation. The seven cardinals who made up the Inquisition's tribunal stated unequivocally that:

The proposition that the sun is in the centre of the world and immovable from its place is absurd, philosophically false, and formally heretical; because it is expressly contrary to Holy Scriptures.

The proposition that the earth is not the centre of the world, nor immovable, but that it moves, and also with a diurnal action, is also absurd, philosophically false, and, theologically considered, at least erroneous in faith.

The knowledge that the seventy-year-old Galileo had been shown the instruments of torture to encourage his recantation helped to deepen the divide between the religious establishment and natural science.

Beneath the frozen carapace of ecclesiastical authority, however, the relationship between individual Christians and natural science remained mutually supportive. All the great scientists of the seventeenth century were believers, indeed in most cases it was just their belief in the certainty of the next world that drove them to investigate the workings of the one they inhabited. However, what they found there made it difficult to embrace the kind of religion to be found at Weltenburg or to take seriously the notion of diabolic pacts or sexual orgies at the Witches' Sabbath. For in the course of the sixteenth and seventeenth centuries, there was a change in terrestrial physics to match the celestial revolution, as scientists grappled with the two central problems posed by the new cosmology: if the earth was not the centre of the universe, then why did objects fall towards its centre? and, if there were no crystalline spheres to hold them steady, why did the planets orbit in an orderly manner? In finding a solution, the most powerful tool was supplied by mathematics. From Copernicus to Newton, it was the ability of scientists to express their discoveries in the language of mathematics that gave the clarity, the universality and repeatability that provided the necessary authority. Indeed, it could be said that the greatest achievement of the seventeenth century was the discovery that motion could be measured mathematically.

This 'mathematization' of the natural sciences was given magisterial expression by Newton in *Philosophiae Naturalis Principia Mathematica* (Mathematical Principles of Natural Philosophy), first published in 1687. Among many other things, it demonstrated that the same force that caused an apple to fall to the ground also kept the planets orbiting the sun in a regular fashion. By finally destroying the Greek assumption that the celestial and terrestrial worlds are fundamentally different and by demonstrating that both operate according to the same regular, immutable laws of motion, he opened the way for the mechanization of heaven and earth. God might still have a place in a post-Newtonian universe but only as the original creator of a mechanism that then ran according to its own laws. There was certainly no place in it for demons or witches. Most historians of science are anxious to distance themselves from a 'Whig' account of the scientific revolution which sees it as a progression from error to truth. Indeed, many deny that there was anything revolutionary about it at all, preferring an evolutionary process beginning in the Middle Ages. Others like to stress the contributions made by other scientific traditions, notably the organic and the magical.

It has been pointed out how much mathematics owed to Neoplatonism, for example. Yet when every qualification has been given due weight, it is difficult to avoid the conclusion that mechanistic science did triumph in the course of the seventeenth century and that Newton's *Principia* sealed its victory. It was not just a hugely influential scientific treatise, although it certainly was that too – 'No other work known to the history of science has simultaneously permitted so large an increase in both the scope and precision of research' (Thomas Kuhn). It also marked a seismic cultural shift. Moreover, it was a shift that could be perceived by contemporaries. The very heavy demands that the *Principia* made on its readers' intellects ensured that its impact could not be immediate. The panegyric composed after Newton's death by Bernard le Bovier de Fontenelle (1657–1757), the secretary of the French Academy of Sciences, put it well:

at last, when the Book came to be sufficiently known, the approbation, which had been so slowly gain'd, became so universal, that nothing was to be heard from all quarters but one general cry of Admiration. Mankind were amaz'd at the masterly Strokes, which shone throughout the Work, and stood astonish'd at the vast Genius for Invention discover'd in it, which in all the Countries of the learned World hardly ever shews itself in above three or four Persons during the whole extent of a most fruitful Age.

Better known is Alexander Pope's epitaph intended for Newton's tomb-stone in Westminster Abbey:

> Nature and Nature's laws lay hid in night;
> God said, Let Newton be! and all was light.

Assessing the impact of the mechanistic view of the universe on the 'disenchantment of the world' (Max Weber) in general and belief in witchcraft in particular is difficult, not to say impossible. If John Wesley, educated at Charterhouse and Christ Church, Oxford, could still believe in witches half a century after Newton's death, it could not be expected that the illiterate majority would abandon traditional beliefs. Of course, a distinction must be drawn between the end of belief in witchcraft and the end of the prosecution of witches, the latter preceding the former by a century or more. What was needed to bring the trials to a halt was scepticism on the part of those who could stop them or refuse even to start them – magistrates, judges and legislators. If the evidence is patchy, most of it does point towards just this happening during the second half of the seventeenth century. For example, in 1668 Joseph Glanvill (1636–80), very much a believer in demons and witches, admitted ruefully that 'most of the looser gentry and the small pretenders to philosophy and wit are generally deriders of the belief in witchcraft'. Among his opponents was John Webster (1611–82), whose *The Displaying of Supposed Witchcraft* (1677) was dedicated to the Justices of the Peace of the West Riding of Yorkshire. Significantly, the ecclesiastical authorities had tried to prevent its appearance, but it was published with an endorsement from the Vice-President of the Royal Society, Sir Jonas Moore. At the core of Webster's refutation of witchcraft was his argument that the confessions so often paraded by its supporters were inadmissible in principle because 'it is . . . simply impossible for either the Devil or witches to change or alter the course that God hath set in nature'. By 1681 another polemicist, Henry Hallywell, could write that believers in the reality of witches and demons met with derision and contempt. The last witch to be executed in England went to the gallows in 1684. The last known successful indictment occurred in 1712 when a jury found a woman guilty of witchcraft, but the verdict was against the advice of the judge, who then secured a royal pardon for the victim.

The pattern on the continent appears to have been similar: judicial authorities losing confidence in the reliability of witnesses and finally abandoning belief in the crime itself. In Geneva, where surgeons were increasingly reluctant to identify 'the Devil's mark' on the accused, the last witch-burning took place in 1652 and the last trial ten years later. In France, it was the magistrates of the Parlement of Paris who intervened in the 1660s to put a stop to prosecutions in the north of France, and it was the royal government, directed by Colbert, which reclassified witchcraft as fraud in 1682. East of the Rhine, it all took a great deal longer, although treatises casting doubt on witchcraft had been published since the second quarter of the seventeenth century. Here too it was the judicial authorities who eventually took action from above to put a stop to prosecutions initiated by popular action from below.

Fortunately, the evidence needed to sustain a historical hypothesis is less rigorous than the proofs demanded by mathematicians or physicists. If the link between the growth of mechanistic science and the decline in the belief in magic or witchcraft cannot be reduced to a formula or repeated in the laboratory, it can at least be established as a probability. It can be enhanced by two further considerations. First, it should be remembered that science in the seventeenth and eighteenth centuries had not been elevated to realms so abstruse as to be accessible only to professional practitioners. Indeed, the word 'science' did not acquire its modern meaning as being synonymous with the natural sciences until deep into the nineteenth century. Earlier it had meant simply 'knowledge'. Significantly, in the seventeenth or eighteenth century, those who today would be regarded as 'scientists' thought of themselves as exponents of 'natural philosophy' and moved easily between various forms of knowledge that have since become compartmentalized. Virtually all the great scientists of the seventeenth century were philosophers as well as mathematicians, theologians as well as physicists.

Secondly, it was not necessary to understand everything to get the gist of what was being argued. Taking Descartes' advice that 'if you would be a real seeker after truth, it is necessary that at least once in your life you doubt, as far as possible, all things' was not conditional on a close reading of his *Discourse on Method*. Neither did the concept of immutable natural laws depend on mastering the mathematics of Newton's *Principia*. Moreover, there were plenty of popularizers available to make the great discoveries comprehensible to lesser mortals and to point out the implications. James Ferguson's *Astronomy Explained upon Sir Isaac Newton's Principles, and Made Easy to Those who have not studied Mathematics* (1756) went through seven editions. In *New Dialogues of the Dead* (1683–4), *Conversations with a Lady, on the Plurality of Worlds* (1686) and *Of the Usefulness of Mathematical Learning* (1699) Fontenelle provided Descartes-without-tears. As we shall see later in this chapter, both encouraging – and encouraged by – this popularization of science was a rapid expansion of the public sphere.

Before that important dimension can be examined, however, one important historiographical issue needs to be addressed. There was a time when both the radicalism and the speed of the changes discussed so far in this chapter were emphasized. The most memorable formulation was that of the Flemish historian Paul Hazard who, in a book first published in Paris in 1935 with the title *The Crisis of the European Consciousness*, asserted: 'One day, the French people, almost to a man, were thinking like Bossuet; the day after, they were thinking like

Voltaire. No ordinary swing of the pendulum, that. It was a revolution.'
This kind of broad-brush generalization (not to mention sentences without verbs) later fell out of fashion. Continuity became the order of the
day, as Hazard's free-thinking heroes were shown to be much more
conservative than he had supposed, while Bossuet's theocentric world-
view turned out to have a long future. Very recently, however, Jonathan
Israel has presented a similar scenario to that of Hazard in his massive
study *The Radical Enlightenment* (2001). It places the same emphasis
on the revolutionary nature of the change: 'a vast turbulence in every
sphere of knowledge and belief which shook European civilisation to its
foundations'. It identifies the same modernizing forces at work: 'no
other period of European history displays such a profound and decisive
shift towards rationalisation and secularisation at every level'. It shares
Hazard's assumption that there was a single 'European mind': 'there
was just one highly integrated European Enlightenment'. It too is very
much a history of ideas, presenting an 'intellectual revolution', 'battle
of ideas', 'intellectual upheaval'. Where it differs is, first, in the timing:
Hazard's dating of the transformation of the European mind was 1680–
1715; Israel pushes it back to 1650–80. What is usually thought of as
the 'High Enlightenment', he states, was in reality just a process of
'consolidating, popularising and annotating revolutionary concepts
introduced earlier', indeed it amounted to 'often little more than foot-
notes to the earlier shift'. Secondly, he reorientates the focus away from
England and France to the Dutch Republic and, in particular, to Baruch
Spinoza (1632–77). Thirdly, as a result of this privileging of Spinoza,
he makes much more of the atheism, materialism, egalitarianism and
republicanism of the early Enlightenment.

To do justice to a book containing more than eight hundred pages of
small print would require a substantial volume itself. Here it can only
be recorded that, thanks to his phenomenal erudition, Israel has certainly
rescued Spinoza from obscurity, both in his own right and through
the Europe-wide network of those he influenced. He has also brought
the Dutch Republic to centre-stage, both in its own right and as the
great clearing-house of radical ideas in Europe. As with many great
revisions, however, the case is overstated. The members of the 'radical
intellectual underground' were few in number and with limited influence
– gadflies on the margin. They invite the comment made by Edmund
Burke on the British radicals who welcomed the French Revolution:

'half a dozen grasshoppers under a fern make the field ring with their importunate chink, whilst thousands of great cattle, reposed beneath the shadow of the British oak, chew the cud and are silent'. Also open to question is the depth penetrated by the radical ideas. Israel seeks to head off such an objection by remarking that, 'while it is true that the intellectual revolution of the late seventeenth century was primarily a crisis of elites . . . it was precisely these elites which moulded, supervised, and fixed the contours of popular culture. Consequently, an intellectual crisis of elites quickly made an impact on ordinary men's attitudes too and by no means only the minority of literate artisans and small bourgeoisie.' Even if one could accept such an elitist view of popular culture, there remains the problem of just what sort of a proportion of those elites embraced the particular 'intellectual revolution' offered by the radical Enlightenment. Although over a long period of time enough adopted a mechanistic view of the universe to put a stop to the persecution of witches, the overwhelming majority continued to be devout Christians. As we have seen in an earlier chapter, the eighteenth century has as good a claim to be dubbed 'the age of religion' as 'the age of reason'. Not only were the Churches flourishing, but both public and private discourse were dominated by religion. Moreover, most of the debates and controversies that raged did not align believer against non-believer but one kind of believer against another kind of believer.

THE PUBLIC SPHERE

The dissemination of a view of the natural world without the supernatural went hand in hand with the expansion of a new kind of cultural space: the public sphere. Although neither the word nor the concept 'public' was new, hitherto it had been applied either very generally, to denote the whole community – 'pro bono publico', for example – or specifically, to a particular group of people engaged in the same pursuit – 'the theatre-going public', for example. It was only during the period covered by this volume that 'the public', as in 'public opinion', came to acquire its modern meaning as the prime source of cultural and political legitimation. One of the first uses in the English language was by the great scientist Robert Boyle, who in his *Occasional Reflections* of 1665 referred to 'the favourable Reception that the public has hitherto vouchsafed to what has been presented it'. Significantly, Boyle did not go to university and had no academic appointment, but was a younger son of the Earl of Cork and a gentleman-scholar of independent means. Most important, he chose to write in the vernacular, not in Latin. The language of academic discourse was still very much undecided. If Galileo, Boyle and Descartes used their respective vernaculars, Harvey, Huygens and Newton used Latin. Leibniz corresponded with his aristocratic friends in French, his relations in German and his scholarly colleagues in Latin. But the tide was turning fast. In France, even pornography was being published in Latin in 1650, but more than 90 per cent of all titles were in French in 1700, by which time Latin had ceased to be a living language. In the German-speaking world, the percentage of Latin titles fell from 67 per cent in 1650 to 38 per cent in 1700 to 28 per cent by 1740 and to 4 per cent in 1800.

Part and parcel of this rapid and irreversible move to the vernacular was the trickle down of literacy from the academically trained elites to an ever-widening public. Although the evidence is fragmentary, what there is points in the direction of a steady expansion. During the century between the 1680s and the 1780s, literacy rates in France increased from 29 per cent to 47 per cent for men and from 14 per cent to 27 per cent for women. Daniel Roche has concluded that if it is assumed that all those who could sign their names could also read, there were perhaps 10,000,000 potential readers in France. Much higher rates could be found in the north-east, especially in Paris, where something approaching mass literacy had been achieved by 1789. Simon Schama has even written: 'literacy rates in late eighteenth-century France were much higher than in the late twentieth-century United States'. Better figures still have been established for England, Scotland, the Low Countries and Sweden. By the late eighteenth century, 87 per cent of Protestant men and 69 per cent of Protestant women in Amsterdam could sign the marriage register. The figures for Catholics were 79 and 53 per cent respectively. The overall figures for German-speaking Europe must be very approximate guesses, but – for what they are worth – they reveal a rising curve from 10 per cent of the adult population in 1700, to 15 per cent in 1770 and 25 per cent in 1800. Everywhere, men were much more likely to be literate than women, for the good reason that they were much more likely to go to school.

As it was improvements in education that brought the rise in literacy, it can be said to have been at the root of the expansion of the public sphere. The initiative came first and foremost not from the secular authorities but from the Churches. In the Protestant world, the emphasis on the need for all the faithful to have direct access to Scripture made popular education a priority. In the seventeenth and eighteenth centuries this was given renewed impetus by the various reform movements – nonconformity, Pietism and Methodism, for example. Even within the established Anglican Church, it was through private initiatives in founding charity schools at a parish level that literacy was spread. In London alone there were 132 such schools in 1734, educating more than 3,000 boys and nearly 2,000 girls. Although often short-lived, more than 1,700 were established. If such schools were intended to be 'little garrisons against Popery', as Bishop Kennett put it, they were reinforced by more material considerations. As literacy and numeracy were becoming essentials in an increasingly commercialized economy, the market responded with its customary speed to the opportunity. A German visitor recorded in 1782: 'It is here not uncommon to see on doors in one continued succession "Children educated here", "Shoes mended here", "Foreign spirituous liquors sold here", "Funerals furnished here".'

In continental Europe there was the familiar gradient from north-west to east. Although pockets of literacy could be found in Poland, in Russia mass literacy was a twentieth-century phenomenon. As the figures for France, the Rhineland, Belgium and parts of northern Italy show, this was not a Protestant/Catholic divide. Rather it was the need to compete which prompted all confessions to promote education. In Catholic Europe it was most often missionary orders which took the initiative to improve – or even initiate – popular education. In France, the Sisters of the Holy Infant Jesus and the Christian Brothers, both founded at Reims, could claim much of the credit for making north-eastern France one of the most literate parts of Europe. Only later did the state get involved. It was the founder of the Christian Brothers, Jean-Baptiste de La Salle, aided and abetted by the royal mistress (and later morganatic wife) Madame de Maintenon, who persuaded Louis XIV to issue a decree ordering all children between the ages of seven and fourteen to attend a Catholic school.

In the course of the eighteenth century, the state began to encroach increasingly on what had previously been the preserve of the Church:

'[education] is and shall remain for all time a *Politicum*', as an Austrian decree firmly stated in 1770. In support of this claim, Count Pergen, later to become Joseph II's chief of police, complained that the clergy had abused their control of education by creaming off the most talented children to swell their own ranks, leaving only the mediocre for state service. Henceforth, he concluded, 'the state must seize complete and permanent supervision and direction of schools and education'. This was a view shared by Frederick the Great, who in 1743 informed the officials in charge of his new province of Silesia that the purpose of education was to produce young people capable of serving their fatherland by providing them with the knowledge necessary for that elemental task. All over Europe, indeed, the middle decades of the eighteenth century were marked by a burst of reforms with three objectives in common: the assumption of public responsibility for education; the formation of a new secular cadre of teachers; and the modernization of the curriculum to produce what the modernizing state needed: bureaucrats, soldiers, merchants, manufacturers, skilled artisans and a disciplined workforce.

The cumulative effect of the expansion of literacy was to produce a 'reading revolution'. Although slow to come to the boil, by the middle of the eighteenth century, reading was being described as 'an addiction', 'a craze', 'a madness': 'No lover of tobacco or coffee, no wine drinker or lover of games, can be as addicted to their pipe, bottle, games or coffee-table as those many hungry readers are to their reading habit', observed the Erfurt clergyman Johann Rudolf Gottlieb Beyer. Conservatives were appalled, and progressives were delighted, that it was a habit that knew no social boundaries. A German periodical, the *Deutsches Museum*, recorded in 1780: 'Sixty years ago the only people who bought books were academics, but today there is hardly a woman with some claim to education who does not read. Readers are to be found in every class, both in the towns and in the country, even the common soldiers in the large cities take out books from the lending libraries.' Visual evidence of the social spread can also be found, for example in Daniel Chodowiecki's depiction of a peasant reading. Of the rich stock of verbal illustrations available, the following entry in James Lackington's diary from 1791 commends itself. Lackington was a self-made man, who by his own account started with £5 and ended selling a hundred thousand volumes a year by cutting margins to the bone in what he claimed to be 'the cheapest bookshop in the world'. He wrote:

I cannot help observing that the sale of books in general has increased prodigiously within the last twenty years. The poorer sort of farmers, and even the poor country people in general who before that period spent their winter evenings in relating stories of witches, ghosts, hobgoblins etc. now shorten the winter nights by hearing their sons and daughters read tales, romances etc., and on entering their houses you may see *Tom Jones*, *Roderick Random* and other entertaining books, stuck up on their bacon-racks etc. If John goes to town with a load of hay, he is charged to be sure not to forget to bring home *Peregrine Pickle's Adventures*, and when Dolly is sent to market to sell her eggs, she is commissioned to purchase *The History of Joseph Andrews*. In short, all ranks and degrees now READ. But the most rapid increase of the sale of books has been since the termination of the late war [1783].

His impression has been supported by British statistics: during the first decade of the sixteenth century, around 400 books were published; by the 1630s that total had risen to 6,000, by the 1710s to 21,000 and by the 1790s to 56,000. Across the Channel it is impossible to find reliable figures, because of the enormous clandestine trade which escaped the tight official censorship. It is likely, however, that the number of titles doubled between mid-century and 1789, and then increased many times over. In the German-speaking world about 175,000 titles were published during the course of the eighteenth century, two-thirds of them after 1760. If pamphlets, periodicals, newspapers and other ephemera are added, it has been estimated that around half-a-million printed publications reached the German market in the course of the century. The highest *rate* of increase was achieved in Russia, although from the barely credible low base of just 87 titles published between 1725 and 1729, rising to just over 300 in 1796–1800.

This quantitative transformation of the world of books brought with it a qualitative consequence of equal importance. Because there were now so many more books available, both the readers and the way in which they read changed. When few titles were produced in small and expensive editions, the texts were read again and again, mainly for the purposes of devotion, instruction and edification. The typical readers were the priests with their breviaries, the lawyers with their handbooks or the faithful with their bibles. In short, they read intensively. Once there were thousands of titles available, produced in larger and cheaper editions, new kinds of readers joined in, looking for topical information, practical advice and recreation, reading a book once and then discarding it. In short, they read extensively. In the sixteenth century, a library comprising a hundred books qualified the owner as a learned scholar; by the end of the eighteenth century, privately owned libraries numbering thousands of volumes were commonplace.

This of course was a self-sustaining process, as more titles encouraged more readers, who in turn encouraged the production of more titles. The same could be said of the institutions thrown up by the reading revolution. Although increased print runs brought the unit cost of books down, technological constraints – especially in the production of paper – imposed limits to price reductions. One solution was for readers to pool their funds to form a reading circle, passing the purchased volumes around. Most of these associations were informal, but in the larger towns more permanent clubs were founded, with a committee of management and their own premises. In Mainz in the Rhineland, for example, the reading club opened in 1781 aimed 'to provide a suitable opportunity to read at a low cost new publications of all kinds and to enjoy social relationships in which literary and political knowledge will be exchanged'. Its premises near the cathedral comprised two 'quiet rooms' for reading and two clubrooms for discussion and re-freshment. For a modest annual subscription, a member could borrow from the library or consult a large number of newspapers and periodi-cals. By that time there were reading clubs all over the Holy Roman Empire, with about 600 being founded during the second half of the eighteenth century with a total membership of 20,000. More open and commercial were the lending libraries, very much a phenomenon of the eighteenth century. By 1800 it was estimated that there were at least 100 in London and nearly 1,000 more in the provinces. The modest cost of subscription – three shillings a quarter was typical – brought extensive reading within the reach of at least skilled artisans. They also spread on the continent with comparable rapidity: in 1800 there were nine lending libraries in Leipzig, ten in Bremen and eighteen in Frankfurt am Main.

For this new reading public a new literary genre emerged in the shape of the novel. Some form of prose fiction is probably as old as literacy.

By the late seventeenth century it had developed into two forms – 'romances', fantastic stories of chivalric derring-do, and '*novelle*', short stories for popular reading, often issued in collections. The modern novel, as it emerged in the first half of the eighteenth century, combined the substance of the former with the popular realism of the latter. Southern Europe had led the way in romances, culminating in Cervantes' *Don Quixote* of 1605/1615. In the course of the seventeenth century, French authors took over, with Marie-Madeleine de La Fayette's *La Princesse de Clèves* usually presented as the first modern novel in the French language. Although they were not always described as such, almost a thousand French novels were published during the first half of the eighteenth century. This was despite a torrent of criticism of the genre as immoral, exemplified by Abbé Prévost's best-seller *Manon Lescaut* (1731). Despite the author's claim that 'the entire work is a treatise on morality shown entertainingly in practice', the attention of readers and critics alike was drawn by the avarice and promiscuity of the eponymous heroine and the book was banned in France. In 1737 the authorities imposed a blanket ban on all novels, giving tacit permission only on strict conditions – the publication of Prévost's eight-volume novel *Le Philosophe anglais; ou Histoire de Monsieur Cleveland, fils naturel de Cromwell, écrite par lui-mesme, et traduite de l'anglais* (The English Philosopher, or the History of Mr Cleveland, natural son of Cromwell, written by himself and translated from the English) was made conditional on Cleveland being turned into a Catholic. Although the titillating 'French novel', usually published with a false place of publication, was to have a long and lucrative career, in the eighteenth century it was the English novel that became supreme. The extraordinary burst of creativity represented by Daniel Defoe's *Robinson Crusoe* (1719), *Moll Flanders* (1722) and *Roxana* (1724); Jonathan Swift's *Gulliver's Travels* (1726); Samuel Richardson's *Pamela* (1740), *Clarissa* (1748) and *Sir Charles Grandison* (1754); Henry Fielding's *Joseph Andrews* (1742), *Jonathan Wild* (1743) and *Tom Jones* (1749); Tobias Smollett's *Roderick Random* (1748) and *Peregrine Pickle* (1751); and Laurence Sterne's *Tristram Shandy* (1760–67) and *A Sentimental Journey* (1768) made the novel the English literary genre par excellence. The most successful of them internationally was probably *Pamela*, translated into most European languages with the story suitably adapted to local requirements. In France, for example, the eponymous heroine was given noble ancestry to avoid any suggestion that she was marrying above her station.

For every work of genius that appeared, there were a hundred or more of lesser quality, giving rise to familiar complaints from the intellectuals that more meant worse. Representative was the lament from the London periodical *Monthly Review* in 1790:

Novels spring into existence like insects on the banks of the Nile; and, if we may be indulged in another comparison, cover the shelves of our circulating libraries, as locusts crowd the fields of Asia. Their great and growing number is a serious evil; for, in general, they exhibit delusive views of human life; and while they amuse, frequently poison the mind.

Lamentations that popularization meant vulgarization were often given an added edge by misogyny, for it was the novel above all which gave women access to literature both as producers and consumers. In the seventeenth century, the subject-matter of baroque drama, whether secular or religious, classical or courtly, poetry or devotional literature, had been predominantly masculine. The eighteenth-century novel's concern with the 'real' world of the here and now, especially with family relationships, both moved women to the centre of attention and allowed them to write about their own experiences. If woman's role in seventeenth-century literature is best symbolized by Milton's daughter taking dictation from her blind father, in the next century novelists such as Eliza Haywood, Charlotte Lennox, Frances Brooke, Sarah Fielding, the Minifie sisters, Maria Cooper, Jean Marishall, Phoebe Gibbs, Fanny Burney and Maria Edgeworth had established reputations – and sales – the equal of most of their male colleagues. The first woman in Europe to earn a living from her pen was Aphra Behn (?1640–89). Her three-part epistolary novel *Love Letters between a Nobleman and his Sister* (1684–7) went through sixteen editions over the next century. If Fanny Burney received only £20 for her first (and best) novel, *Evelina* (1778), she made £250 from *Cecilia* (1782), £2,000 from *Camilla* (1796) and £2,000 from *The Wanderer* (1814). One of the most durable German novels of the eighteenth century was Sophie La Roche's *Die Geschichte des Fräuleins von Sternheim* (The Story of Miss von Sternheim), while in France, Marie-Madeleine de La Fayette found many successors, among them Françoise de Graffigny, Marie-Jeanne Riccoboni, Marie Leprince de Beaumont and Anne-Louise Elie de Beaumont. In England between 1750 and 1770 more novels were written by female authors than by men during eleven of those twenty years, although the overall average for the century was more like 20 per cent.

If the novel was the queen of the public sphere, there were plenty of other artistic genres that benefited from its development. Its musical equivalent was the symphony, for whose development the eighteenth century was of comparable importance. In 1700 the 'sinfonia' was the term used to describe the overture to an opera; by 1800, the year in which Beethoven's symphony in C, Opus 21 was first performed, its musical pre-eminence was well established. In the meantime more than 16,000 symphonies had been composed. As Richard Taruskin drily observed: 'immense production, of course, implies immense consumption'. It was no coincidence that the century of the symphony was also the century of the public concert. If a public concert can be defined as a musical performance at which there is a clear distinction between performers and audience and to which the anonymous public is admitted on payment of an entrance fee, then the first took place in London in 1672, when John Banister advertised in *The London Gazette* that 'this present Monday will be Musick performed by excellent Masters, beginning precisely at 4 of the clock in the afternoon, and every afternoon for the future, precisely at the same hour'. Although Banister was a serious musician, having been previously director of the royal orchestra, his concerts were small-scale and informal, accompanied by much smoking and drinking.

Of a much higher order were the *Concerts Spirituels* organized in Paris after 1725 to provide music during Lent, when the theatres were closed. Consisting mainly of sacred music, the concerts began, like the operas for which they were substituting, with a 'sinfonia'. As the symphony established itself as an independent form, so it developed away from the simple fast-slow-fast form of the operatic overture to become a self-contained musical drama in four movements. There was a corresponding move away from the baroque concerto sound, with each instrument equally weighted, to a symphonic style – meaning literally 'together sounding'. This development was also closely linked to the development of the sonata form, whose attraction has been summarized very well by Neil Zaslaw as the 'ability to present and develop musical ideas and "arguments" at unprecedented length while imparting a convincing aural unity to the whole'. By the 1760s Giovanni Battista

Sammartini (1700–75) at Milan, Johann Stamitz (1717–57) at Mannheim and Joseph Haydn at Esterháza had given the symphony a secure status in the musical world, from which Haydn himself and then Mozart and Beethoven could take it on to undisputed eminence by the end of this period.

The triumphant progress of the symphony bore witness to a growing standardization of music across Europe as a result of the expanding public sphere. Now that scores could be circulated so much more easily, the composer began to write not just for the orchestra he directed but for all orchestras. This encouraged a standardization of the size and instrumental complement of orchestras. There was now an international market for music: copies of Haydn's *Sinfonies ou Quatuors*, Opus 1 and Opus 2 reached Naples in the south and Königsberg in the north-east, not to mention Pennsylvania in the west. Although these copies were in manuscript, the printing of scores increased rapidly in the eighteenth century. In particular, it was only after 1700 that the long-known technique of printing music by engraving became widespread, thus allowing much more complex scores to be printed more cleanly, cheaply and quickly. London led the field, soon joined by Paris from the 1740s and Vienna from the 1770s. It was also in London in the second half of the seventeenth century that John Playford and his son Henry brought modern business practices to bear on music publishing, going beyond mere printing to assembling a catalogue of scores, and then advertising, promoting and distributing its contents. The growing commercialization of music meant that composers' dependence on individual patrons began to weaken, although the absence of copyright laws slowed the process. Entrepreneurs emerged all over Europe, seeking out talented composers and putting them in contact with consumers, to the benefit of all three parties. The most celebrated example was Johann Peter Salomon's bringing of Haydn to London for two highly lucrative visits in the 1790s.

As the cultural public sphere grew, so did the authority of the public as an arbiter of taste. This can be traced through the history of the public exhibitions of art mounted by the French Academy of Painting and Sculpture that began in 1663. The academicians were aware of a public interest and were prepared to pay at least lip-service to it. In 1699, when announcing the resumption of the exhibitions ('Salons') after a long interval, they stated in the catalogue that they wished 'to renew the former custom of exhibiting their works to the public in order to receive its judgement'. After 1737 the Salons were held at the Louvre every other year, attracting a growing number of visitors: 15,000 in the 1750s and double that number by the 1780s. To mediate between the creative artists and their public, there emerged the critic. Étienne La Font de Saint Yenne (1688–1771), usually regarded as the first of them, wrote in 1747: 'It is only in the mouths of those firm and equitable men who compose the Public, who have no links whatever with the artists ... that we can find the language of truth.' The populist and even democratic implications of the Salon were picked up well before 1789 by the painter and critic Louis de Carmontelle, for example, who wrote of the Salon of 1785, at which the great sensation was Jacques-Louis David's *Oath of the Horatii*:

[The Salon] is a vast theatre where neither rank, favour, nor wealth can reserve a place for bad taste ... Paris comes alive, all classes of citizens come to pack the Salon. The public, natural judge of the fine arts, already renders its verdict on the merits of the pictures which two years of labour have brought forth. Its opinions, at first unsteady and tentative, quickly gain stability. The experience of some, the enlightenment of others, the extreme *sensibilité* of one segment, and above all the good faith of the majority, arrive finally to produce a judgement all the more equitable in that the greatest liberty has presided there.

By the second half of the eighteenth century, the anonymous abstract public had come to be recognized not just as one legitimate source of value in aesthetic matters but as *the* source. From the rich repertoire of illustrations available, the following *cri de coeur* from Friedrich Schiller is distinguished by its intensity. Schiller had been given an excellent free education at the ducal grammar school at Stuttgart but at the cost of his intellectual independence. Forced to study medicine against his will, imprisoned for writing his first sensational play – *The Robbers* – and told to confine himself in future to medical treatises, he protested with his feet and ran away. He issued the following declaration of intellectual independence:

I write as a citizen of the world who serves no prince ... From now on all my ties are dissolved. The public is now everything to me – my preoccupation, my sovereign and my friend. Henceforth I belong to it alone. I wish to place myself before this tribunal and no other. It is the only thing I fear and respect. A feeling of greatness comes over me with the idea that the only fetter I wear is the verdict of the world – and that the only throne I shall appeal to is the human soul.

Those brave words were written in 1784. Three years later Schiller entered the service of the Duke of Saxony-Weimar, accepting a position as Professor of History at the University of Jena. He was ennobled in 1802. As this trajectory implies, the public did not turn out to be the ideal patron. Its shortcomings will be discussed later. For the time being, the importance of the public sphere as a cultural space and of the public as a cultural actor can be acknowledged. The essential characteristics of the public can be defined as follows. It consists of private individuals brought together by the voluntary exchange of ideas to form a whole greater than the sum of its parts. Not only is it independent of the state, it claims a superior status for both quantitative and qualitative reasons: because its numerical strength allows it to claim to be representative of civil society, and because its insistence on free expression and public debate allows it to claim enhanced authority. It is anonymous and unhierarchical, gaining access solely by the capacity to pay for the cultural commodities it consumes. That its discourse is characterized by openness, criticism, spontaneity and reasoned argument is revealed by cognates such as 'publicity', 'publicize' and 'public opinion'.

THE TRIUMPH OF THE CULTURE OF REASON

The years around the middle of the eighteenth century marked the coming-of-age of the public sphere and the apparent triumph of the culture of reason. The publication of Montesquieu's *Spirit of the Laws* in 1748 and the first two volumes of Diderot and d'Alembert's *Encyclopédie* in 1751 had a tremendous impact right across Europe. Representative of the response to the former was Horace Walpole's letter to Horace Mann, the British minister to the court of Tuscany, on 10 January 1750: 'I want to know your opinion of . . . Montesquiou's [*sic*] *Esprit des Lois*, which I think the best book ever written – at least I never learned half so much from all I ever read. There is as much wit as useful knowledge. He is said to have hurt his reputation by it in France, which I can conceive, for it is almost the interest of everybody there that can understand it, to decry it.' Walpole was half right: *The Spirit of the Laws* was acclaimed rhapsodically by enlightened French intellectuals, but denounced with equal enthusiasm by the conservatives. For once, Jesuits and Jansenists could agree on something: that Montesquieu's book was deeply offensive and dangerous – atheist indeed. If they had actually wanted to promote the book's fame, they could not have done better. The ultimate franking of its reputation came when it was placed on the Index of Prohibited Books in 1751, despite Pope Benedict XIV's misgivings. The reception accorded to the *Encyclopédie* was just as contentious and just as international. Of the 25,000 sets, comprising thirty-five volumes, sold before 1789, about half were to subscribers living outside France. Diderot's restatement of Descartes' methodology of systematic doubt in the preface can stand as the mature Enlightenment's manifesto: 'Everything must be examined, everything must be shaken up, without exception and without circumspection.' A generation later in 1781, as the enlightened tide was on the ebb, Kant returned to the same central theme in his preface to the first edition of the *Critique of Pure Reason*: 'Our age is, in especial degree, the age of criticism, and to criticism everything must submit. Religion through its sanctity, and law-giving through its majesty, may seek to exempt themselves from it. But they then awaken just suspicion, and cannot claim the sincere respect which reason accords only to that which has been able to sustain the test of free and open examination.'

Jules Michelet observed that 'the *Encyclopédie* was much more than a book. It was a faction ... all Europe took it up.' 'All Europe', of course, must be refined to mean 'the enlightened European intelligentsia'. This was indeed a self-conscious faction ('party' would be a better word, for the French '*faction*' does not have the same pejorative overtone as its literal English equivalent). The sense that there was an international community of rational progressive educated people, bound together by the same ideals, dated back to the seventeenth century. Its members liked to refer to themselves as 'the republic of letters', which formed part of the title of Pierre Bayle's immensely influential periodical *News from the Republic of Letters*, which began publication in 1684. In his *Age of Louis XIV*, Voltaire wrote about the late seventeenth century: 'A republic of letters was being gradually established in Europe, in spite of different religions. Every science, every art, was mutually assisted in this way, and it was the academies which formed this republic.'

This was of course a wholly informal space. It was the creation of individuals seeking out or responding to the like-minded. Its chief medium was the written word, so it expanded in tandem with the growth of literacy and publications, especially periodicals. Of special importance was the improvement of postal services discussed in an earlier chapter. As John Brewer has remarked, 'correspondence held the Republic of Letters together'. Among other illustrations he cited the boast of the classical scholar Gisbert Cuper that 'I have a hundred or so volumes of letters, with the responses of Scholars, who honour me with their friendship and correspondence'. The importance of letters went beyond mere convenience, for their very nature encapsulated the idea of intellectual intercourse. Most of the periodicals therefore liked to include a 'readers' letters' section, even if many of them were composed or at least rewritten by the editor. For example, the first series of *The Spectator* in 1712 included 250 letters. News and other items were also presented in epistolary form 'from our own correspondent' – in the first four months of 1764 *The Gazetteer* of London received 861 letters, of which 560 were published at length and 262 were noticed under the heading 'Observations of Our Correspondents'. Improvements in physical communications and longer periods of peace encouraged members of the republic to get to know each other personally. Anne Goldgar provides the example of Charles-Étienne Jordan, a Prussian of Huguenot descent, who in 1733 embarked on a six-month *voyage littéraire* which took in Halle, Leipzig, Paris, London, Oxford, Amsterdam and Leiden. If he did not avert his eyes from buildings and paintings, his chief concern was to visit libraries, literary societies, bookshops and fellow intellectuals. Arriving in London, he wrote: 'I saw St Paul's Church: I won't say anything about it, because my Goal is only to speak about Books and Literature.'

From the republic of letters, and the public sphere into which it fed, came a rapidly growing intelligentsia, socially disparate but ideologically cohesive. By the time the *Encyclopédie* was published, they were no longer 'the little flock of philosophes' but a major force in the public discourse of Europe. Like all intellectuals, there was nothing they liked to do more than to argue, but their common axioms allow the identification of a single European Enlightenment. Not the least important was their common use of the metaphor of light. As one of their deadliest enemies, Novalis, observed in *Christianity or Europe* (1799): 'Light became their favourite subject on account of its mathematical obedience and freedom of movement. They were more interested in the refraction of its rays than in the play of its colours, and thus they named it after their great enterprise, enlightenment.' The German word Novalis used was '*Aufklärung*'. If he had been Italian, he would have written '*i lumi*', if Spanish '*ilustración*', if French '*les lumières*', if Russian 'просвещение' (which, confusingly, can also mean 'education'), and so on. Although this was an attractive metaphor, for it could be contrasted with the darkness of ignorance, prejudice and superstition, it also invited charges of superficiality. Voltaire himself said, disarmingly, 'I am like a mountain stream – I run bright, clear and fast, but not very deep.'

The source of the light was reason. Here one has to tread carefully – as indeed the 'philosophes' did themselves. They were well aware of the varieties and limitations of reason and liked nothing more than to deride the great rationalist systems of the seventeenth-century philosophers, including Descartes and Leibniz, the latter being the butt of Voltaire's wit in the shape of Doctor Pangloss in *Candide*. They admired Descartes for his systematic doubt, while rejecting his deductive reasoning in favour of English inductive empiricism: 'Descartes gave sight to blind men; they saw the errors of the ancients and his own' was Voltaire's double-edged compliment. Voltaire also likened rationalist metaphysics to a minuet, in which the dancer displays much skill and grace but ends up in exactly the same place. As Peter Gay has put it: 'the Enlightenment was not an Age of Reason, but a Revolt against Rationalism'. On the other hand, for all its frailty, reason was deemed greatly superior as a means of understanding the world than such alternatives as the Bible, tradition, intuition or faith. Or to put it another way, if an intellectual were to stand Descartes on his head and say, 'my project is to lead the mind away from reason', he would automatically disqualify himself from any claim to be enlightened. This central concern was best expressed by Ernst Cassirer in his difficult but profound *The Philosophy of the Enlightenment*, first published in German in 1932: 'The basic idea under-lying all the tendencies of Enlightenment was the conviction that human understanding is capable, by its own power and without recourse to supernatural assistance, of comprehending the system of the world and that this new way of understanding the world will lead it to a new way of mastering it.'

As Cassirer's final remark indicates, the understanding of nature that reason brought was not for its own sake. It was just the first step towards controlling (or, one might add, exploiting) nature in the interests of humankind. Here the philosophes were following an agenda set out by one of their most venerated ancestors – Francis Bacon (1561–1626), who wrote in *Novum Organum* (1620): 'The true and lawful goal of the sciences is none other than this: that human life be endowed with new discoveries and powers.' A good example was provided by Benjamin Franklin, who flew a kite during a thunderstorm in June 1752 to test his hypothesis about the nature of electricity. The knowledge gained enabled him to invent the lightning conductor: 'I say, if these Things are so, may not the Knowledge of this Power of Points be of Use to Mankind; in preserving Houses, Churches, Ships, etc. from the Stroke of Lightning?' Pre-modern man rang church bells and prayed to God to avert lightning strikes; post-Franklin man installed a lightning conductor.

Understanding and manipulating nature also involved understanding and manipulating human nature. The philosophes were more optimistic about tackling this apparently intractable problem because they rejected the idea of original sin. Nothing separated them more sharply from the traditional Christian world than their epistemology and psychology. Here they were following another English philosopher, John Locke (1632–1704), whose *An Essay Concerning Human Understanding* (1690) laid down the basic axiom:

All ideas come from sensation or reflection. Let us then suppose the mind to be, as we say, white paper, void of all characters, without any ideas: – How comes it to be furnished? Whence comes it by that vast store which the busy and boundless fancy of man has painted on it with an almost endless variety? Whence has it all the materials of reason and knowledge? To this I answer, in one word, from EXPERIENCE. In that all our knowledge is founded; and from that it ultimately derives itself. Our observation employed either, about external sensible objects, or about the internal operations of our minds perceived and reflected on by ourselves, is that which supplies our understandings with all the materials of thinking. These two are the fountains of knowledge, from whence all the ideas we have, or can naturally have, do spring.

This rejection of innate ideas opened up boundless possibilities for social engineering. If man was simply the product of his environment acting on his sensations, then to change the nature of man one only had to change his environment.

From England the philosophes also imported the Newtonian view of the universe and then popularized it across the continent. In Voltaire's influential opinion: 'Newton is the greatest man who has ever lived, the very greatest, the giants of antiquity are beside him children playing with marbles.' It is a safe conjecture that most educated Europeans made their acquaintance with the laws of gravity through Voltaire's *Lettres philosophiques* (1734), published in English with the title *Letters Concerning the English Nation*, rather than the *Principia*. For the enlightened across Europe they helped to consolidate a further axiom: that the natural world was a mechanism, that God was not constantly interfering with His creation and that what appeared to be miracles were delusions or natural phenomena. Hume's celebrated definition of a miracle in his *An Enquiry Concerning Human Understanding* (1748) – 'a transgression of a law of nature by a particular volition of the Deity, or by the interposition of some invisible agent' – was the prelude to what many regarded as the definitive demolition (although it is still disputed by some).

With God banished from the physical universe and relegated to primal clock-maker, the way was free for human beings to concentrate on the here and now. Life was no longer to be regarded as a vale of tears through which the faithful had to pass before gaining admission to Heaven, or being sent down to Hell; it was promoted to be humankind's prime concern. So the Enlightenment can be said to have been secular, although the German word '*diesseitig*' is more eloquent, meaning 'this side of the grave', as opposed to '*jenseitig*' or 'the far side of the grave'. It can also be said to have been anthropocentric, a quality best expressed by Alexander Pope in his *Essay on Man* (1733):

> Say first, of God above, or Man below,
> What can we reason, but from what we know?
> Of Man what see we, but his station here,
> From which to reason, or to which refer?
>
> . . .
>
> Know then thyself, presume not God to scan;
> The proper study of Mankind is Man.

The Man in question was man per se. Reason was a universal attribute, the condition of being human, so differences of nationality or religion were mere externals. So cosmopolitanism was one of the badges worn most proudly by the enlightened – by Diderot, for example, who wrote to his friend David Hume: 'My dear David, you belong to all nations . . . I flatter myself that I am, like you, a citizen of the great city of the world.' They had nothing against love of the fatherland, so long as it was defined rationally as '*ubi bene, ibi patria*', but assigned it a secondary value. In Edward Gibbon's view, 'it is the duty of a patriot to prefer and promote the exclusive interest and glory of his native country; but a philosopher may be permitted to enlarge his views, and to consider Europe as a great republic, whose various inhabitants have attained almost the same level of politeness and cultivation'. Gibbon certainly followed this precept himself, publishing his first book in French. The article on 'nation' in the *Encyclopédie*, written by Jaucourt, put it more neatly: 'I prefer, a *philosophe* said, my family to myself, my fatherland to my family and the human race to my fatherland.' It was an ideal shared by some musicians, for example by Gluck, who aimed for 'a music which can speak equally to all nations and will dissolve the ridiculous national differences'. According to the reviewer of his opera *Alceste* in 1768, he had succeeded too, for such was the power of his musical imagination that he had exploded national constraints, creating a music that was all his own but also in perfect conformity with nature and therefore universal.

Deemed even less important than geographical origin was confessional affiliation. Of all the crimes and follies of mankind that the Enlightenment railed against most often and most passionately, religious intolerance must stand at the top of the list. As we have had occasion to remark already, every state in Europe was a confessional state and everywhere the heavy hand of the ecclesiastical authorities could be felt by the heterodox, despite such appeals as Pierre Bayle's *Letter on the Comet* of 1682 and John Locke's *Letter on Toleration* of 1689. Significantly, both men wrote their treatises while in exile in the Dutch Republic. Across Catholic Europe the fires of the Inquisition still burnt – at Palermo in 1724, for example, when thousands poured in from the surrounding countryside to watch Brother Romualdo and Sister Gertrude being burnt alive at the stake, or at Braganza in 1755, when the Jewish merchant Jeronimo Jose Ramos was incinerated. Even in France long after Louis XIV had died, it was dangerous to be a Protestant. In 1724 a royal decree actually strengthened the laws against heresy: a pastor caught officiating at a Protestant service was to be executed and his congregation to be put away for life, the women in prison, the men in the galleys. So toleration really was a matter of life and death and the philosophes responded with a sense of being secular crusaders.

In short, they deemed religious persecution to be contrary to natural law and to lead to barbaric acts of cruelty. Nor could it be justified on prudential grounds. In the bad old days of religious conflict, it had been argued that a house divided against itself confessionally was doomed to civil strife: only the total victory of true faith could bring harmony and prosperity. The Enlightenment turned this argument upside-down by divorcing politics from religion. Only when sovereigns adopted the famous lines put into the mouth of Henry IV by Voltaire – 'I am neutral between Rome and Geneva' – could the potential of all their subjects be realized. It was no accident, the philosophes argued, that the three most successful states in Europe – the Dutch Republic, England and Prussia – were also the most tolerant.

If the men of the Enlightenment were resolute in their rejection of prejudice deriving from geography or religion, they were more equivocal on gender differences. On the one hand, some of them at least – Diderot, for example – were prepared to recognize that women suffered all manner of discrimination. On the other, they could not bring themselves to grant equality. This was not prejudice, of course: it was presented simply as a case of following 'nature and nature's laws'. As David Hume condescendingly put it in his essay 'Of the Rise and Progress of the Arts and Sciences': 'As nature has given *man* the superiority above *woman*, by endowing him with greater strength both of mind and body, it is his part to alleviate that superiority, as much as possible, by the generosity of his behaviour, and by a studied deference and complaisance for all her inclinations and opinions.' Arguments based on biology were supported by reference to social function.

This exclusion contrasted sharply with the relative liberty enjoyed by women in an institution of central importance to eighteenth-century culture – the aristocratic salon. Its function was well defined by the abbé Morellet when writing that Madame de Geoffrin, the most famous and influential of all the *salonnières*, sought 'to procure the means to serve men of letters and artists, to whom her ambition was to be useful in bringing them together with men of power and position'. Described by Voltaire as 'a lady remarkable for character and genius', her salon flourished from the 1750s to the 1770s. Like many of her colleagues, she was of humble birth, being the daughter of a valet-de-chambre from the Dauphiné, making her way to the pinnacle of Parisian society by virtue of her intelligence and personality. Her late husband's fortune also helped, allowing her, among other things, to advance 200,000 *livres* to help publication of the *Encyclopédie*. Of the Paris *salonnières*, Suzanne Necker was the daughter of a Swiss Protestant pastor and Julie Lespinasse was illegitimate, in Vienna Charlotte von Greiner was the daughter of a soldier, in Berlin Rahel Levin and Henriette Herz were both of Jewish origin. Common to all these salons was an absence of social exclusiveness. Baron Grimm wrote of Madame Geoffrin: 'All ranks are mixed: the noble, the official, the writer, the artist, all are treated the same, so that no rank remains except that of good society.' By the time she died in 1777, the salon had passed its zenith as a cultural interface. Increasingly popular and influential were the all-male institutions of the public sphere mentioned earlier, joined after 1778 in Paris by '*musées*' – debating clubs with a more political, more masculine character. This has led Joan Landes to argue that 'the exclusion of women from the bourgeois public sphere was not incidental but central to its incarnation' and that 'from the standpoint of women and their interests, enlightenment looks surprisingly like counter-enlightenment, and revolution like counter-revolution'.

Ambivalence was also to be found in the philosophes' attitudes to the world outside Europe. By the late seventeenth century, the accumulation of knowledge about other cultures was encouraging the development of relativism. Anything that increased the range of options had implications for traditional authority at home. That was why Voltaire took the view that the discovery of America was 'a species of new creation' and that because it was due entirely to human agency 'all that has seemed grand until then ... vanishes before it'. In particular, the discovery that the great civilizations of the east had existed long before the date usually ascribed to the creation of the world by the Christian God posed fundamental problems for the authority of the Bible. Moreover, the further discovery that those civilizations had enjoyed a high degree of sophistication at a time when the west was barbaric, undermined the previously Eurocentric perspective of world history. Pierre Bayle wrote in his *Historical and Critical Dictionary* (1697):

It would be very curious to see an account of the west written by a Japanese, or a Chinese, who had lived many years in the great cities of Europe. They would pay us in our own coin. The missionaries, who go to the Indies, publish reports, in which they particularize the falsities and frauds they have observed in the worship of these idolatrous nations. But whilst they ridicule them for it, may they not fear that it should be replied to them: 'Why dost thou laugh, changing the name, the story is told of thee' (Horace), or that they should be upbraided as they deserve, who wink at their own faults, and discover with the utmost sagacity the vices of others?

It might be thought that Bayle, and the many philosophes who followed him, were being more than a little disingenuous here, for they turned this methodology on its head, winking at the faults of the alien cultures but discovering with utmost sagacity the vices of Christian Europe. Voltaire wrote in his essay on China in *The Philosophical Dictionary* (1764): 'the religion of the men of letters of China is admirable. No superstitions, no absurd legends, none of those dogmas which insult reason and nature and to which the bonzes give a thousand different meanings, because they don't have any.' Like several of his colleagues, Voltaire also used extra-European civilizations as a stick with which to beat Christian Europe by publishing what purported to be factual accounts written by extra-European visitors. In his case it was the 'Child of Nature', the artless Huron, hero of *L'Ingénu*, who exposed the cruelty and absurdity of religious persecution under Louis XIV. More subtle was Montesquieu's *Persian Letters* (1721), in which a Persian aristocrat travelling through France reported back to a friend at home about his experiences. He was especially offended by the arrogant intolerance of the numerous Churches, all of which claimed to be the sole depository of the truth. He concluded: 'I can assure you that there never was a kingdom where there were so many civil wars, as in that of Christ', and exclaimed: 'Happy is the land inhabited by the children of the Prophet!'

Beyond satire, the increasing knowledge of the great eastern religions through translations of Confucius (1687), Zoroaster (1771) and the Hindu classics (from the 1780s) further helped to relativize Christianity. Disputes between Churches, and disputes within Churches, no longer seemed important enough to justify the inflicting of so much suffering on the heterodox. By this time, attention had moved south from the Far

East to the Pacific, the Enlightenment's 'New World', for it was during the eighteenth century that the voyages of James Cook (1728–79) and Louis-Antoine de Bougainville (1729–1811) began to provide reliable knowledge of the region. It has been estimated that travel literature commanded a larger share of the rapidly expanding reading market than any other genre apart from the novel. In the South Seas the explorers found a native population of noble savages, with the virtues that came from living close to nature but none of the vices of civilization – and none of the conscience-driven guilt of Christians. In particular, their relaxed attitude to sex aroused a mixture of envy and disapproval. More sensitive Europeans quickly came to realize that their civilizing mission must inevitably become brutalizing and exploitative. Captain Cook lamented:

What is still more to our shame as civilised Christians, we debauch their morals already too prone to vice, and we introduce among them wants and perhaps disease which they never before knew and which serve only to disturb that happy tranquillity which they and their forefathers enjoyed. If anyone denies the truth of this assertion, let him tell me what the natives of the whole extent of America have gained by the commerce they have had with Europeans.

The most elaborate and influential expression of this ambivalence was to be found in the abbé Raynal's *Philosophical and Political History of European Institutions and Commerce in the Two [East and West] Indies*, published in 1770. It was his bold opinion that 'there has never been any event which has had more impact on the human race in general and for Europeans in particular as that of the discovery of the new world, and the passage to the Indies around the Cape of Good Hope'. On the one hand, he recognized the moral superiority of cultures untouched by Europe's grasping hand and conceded that no adequate justification of colonization could be found. But he also stated his belief in the '*mission civilisatrice*' that was to become such a trope of French colonial discourse, and the need to exploit the natural resources of the earth.

The interaction between a growing knowledge of the world outside Europe and attitudes to religion inside it can be illustrated particularly well by Daniel Defoe's novel *Robinson Crusoe*, one of the great best-sellers of the century, first published in 1719. Shipwrecked on his desert island, Crusoe at once set about making the best of it: 'as reason is the substance and original of mathematics, so by stating and squaring every thing by reason, and by making the most rational judgment of things, every man may be in time master of every mechanick art'. He soon found himself neglecting worship on Sundays for the good reason that he lost count of the days. When he found barley suddenly starting to grow, he believed a miracle had occurred and turned to God – but rather lost his enthusiasm on discovering that it came from the chicken feed he had thrown out. He became a born-again Christian only following a conversion experience when he believed that God was talking to him personally. But this inner light did not command persecution of others. Although his first instinct on discovering the cannibals was to kill them, more mature reflection prompted him 'to leave them to the justice of God, who is the governour of nations, and knows how by national punishments to make a just retribution for national offences'. It was a resolution that was strengthened by his liberation of Man Friday, who told him about the native religion: 'by this I observed that there is priestcraft even amongst the most blinded ignorant pagans in the world; and the policy of making a secret religion, in order to preserve the veneration of the people to the clergy, is not only to be found in the Roman, but perhaps among all religions in the world, even among the most brutish and barbarous savages'. Crusoe was as good as his word. Man Friday he converted to Protestant Christianity but without coercion, Friday's father was allowed to go on worshipping his pagan Gods, and a Spaniard whom they liberated was allowed to remain a Catholic. Crusoe concluded proudly: 'I allowed liberty of conscience throughout my dominions'.

Advocating toleration went hand in hand with attacking the intolerant, which for the French philosophes meant the Church. For public purposes, Voltaire prudently maintained that the 'infamous' in his famous slogan '*Écrasez l'infâme!*' was 'superstition', not Catholicism, let alone Christianity. No one acquainted with even a small part of Voltaire's vast oeuvre could take him seriously. Almost everything he wrote was steeped in anti-clericalism, even his first great success – *Œdipe* (1718) – in which, for example, Jocasta says: 'Our priests are not what an idle populace imagines,/Their knowledge is merely our credulity.' Voltaire certainly followed the Chinese warrior Sun Tzu's maxim 'know your enemy', for he knew the Bible inside out. A favourite stratagem was to recount with a studiously straight face some of its less edifying passages. One example, from *The Sermon of the Fifty* must suffice:

One of the patriarchs, Lot, the nephew of Abraham, receives in his house two angels disguised as pilgrims; the inhabitants of Sodom entertain impure desires for these angels; Lot, who had two daughters promised in marriage, offers to abandon them to the people instead of the two strangers. These young women must have been strangely familiar with evil ways, since the first thing they do after the destruction of their town by a rain of fire, and after their mother has been changed into a pillar of salt, is to intoxicate their father on two consecutive nights, in order to sleep with him in succession. It is an imitation of the ancient Arabic legend of Cyniras and Myrrha. But in this more decent legend Myrrha is punished for her crime, while the daughters of Lot are rewarded with what is, in Jewish eyes, the greatest and dearest blessing: they become the mothers of a numerous posterity.

As this implies, there was a strain of anti-Semitism in Voltaire, essentially derived from his anti-Christianity. As he wrote in his English notebook: 'when I see Christians cursing Jews, methinks I see children beating their fathers'. The same sly techniques were employed by his fellow philosophes, by d'Holbach in the *Encyclopédie*, for example, who when he ridiculed 'pagan priests' clearly had the Christian variety in his sights. Elsewhere in the *Encyclopédie* the attacks were more direct. Singled out for special treatment were monasteries, celibacy, parasitism, superstition (relics, for example), excessive wealth (one article claimed that half the land in France was in the hands of the clergy), exemption from taxation and control of education. Especially offensive to Christians was the article on 'Cannibals', which recorded that pagans had accused the first Christians of cannibalism, adding disingenuously that this was based on a misunderstanding, before cross-referring to articles on 'Eucharist', 'Communion' and 'Altar'. Frederick the Great wrote to Voltaire, 'you will certainly grant me that neither antiquity nor whatever nation has devised a more repulsive and blasphemous absurdity than that of eating your God. This is the most disgusting dogma of Christian religion, the greatest insult to the Highest Being, the climax of madness and insanity.'

Frederick was the exception that proved the rule – a German who thought like the French philosophes (and wrote like them too). This raises the important question of just how uniform was the Enlightenment. Recently, some scholars have gone back to seeing it as a single intellectual movement with no significant regional variations. Certainly

it can be shown that across Europe there were 'thinkers who saw themselves as members of a wider, European intellectual movement, dedicated to understanding and publicising the cause of human betterment
on this earth' (John Robertson), but, as lowest common denominators
go, that seems to be on the low side. Significantly, the higher one soars
into realms of philosophical abstraction, the flatter the terrain below
comes to seem. Closer to the ground of human experience, the obstinately intractable bumps of national difference become more obtrusive.
The tone and incidence of anti-clericalism is one of many. All over
Europe intellectuals could be found who no longer accepted revealed
religion, but the sort of vehemently anti-clerical discourse we have just
illustrated was chiefly a French phenomenon. This was put very well by
François Furet in his comparison of Voltaire and David Hume:

Of the two, Voltaire was probably not the more irreligious, as he was a deist and
at least regarded religion as indispensable to the social order. But though Hume
discredited rational proofs of God's existence, including that of First Cause, so
dear to Voltaire, there was in his philosophical discourse none of the antireligious
aggressiveness to be found in the sage of Ferney. Hume lived in peace with the
diversity of Protestant churches, whereas the Frenchman made war on the
Catholic Church.

Hume found many kindred spirits when he moved to Paris in 1763 as
secretary to the British embassy. According to Diderot, Hume complained in d'Holbach's drawing room that he had not met a single atheist
in Paris. Looking round at the eighteen other guests, his host retorted
that there were eighteen atheists in that very room.

When Hume travelled through Germany, he was greatly impressed by
much of what he saw – 'Germany is undoubtedly a very fine Country,
full of industrious, honest People, & were it united it would be the
greatest power that ever was in the World' – but he did not find eighteen
atheists in a single drawing room. It is difficult to comprehend how
anyone familiar with the *Aufklärung* can think that it was part of a
single Enlightenment. In such a populous and educated culture, there
were bound to be a few radicals, even the odd Voltairean wit, but
they were peripheral figures. The attitude of German intellectuals to
metaphysics in general and religion in particular was a world apart from
French radicalism. Although very much towards the progressive end of
the spectrum, Moses Mendelssohn (1729–86) wrote to Thomas Abbt

in 1765: 'By their extremism, Voltaire, Helvetius and the encyclopedists have frightened many a good man back to superstition and so have damaged their own cause.' Both the dominant figures of the early Enlightenment, Gottfried Wilhelm Leibniz (1646–1716) and Christian Wolff (1679–1754) were devout Christians, the former claiming to have disproved Spinoza and the latter explicitly distancing himself from both the free-thinking of the British and the atheism of the French. If Kant (1724–1804) found Christianity inadequate, he did not attack it but rather subsumed it in a more elevated moral scheme. When he defined enlightenment as using one's 'own understanding in religious matters, without outside guidance', leading to 'emergence from self-incurred immaturity', he was not looking forward to a world without God. Those words come from his essay 'What is Enlightenment?', published in the *Berlin Journal for Enlightenment* in 1784. Another contributor to the same series argued that, 'Many people think *only* of religion when they hear of *Aufklärung*. No reasonable man will deny . . . that *Aufklärung* is of course of the greatest importance in the field of religion . . . But it must not be confined to this field; indeed one cannot conceive a thorough religious *Aufklärung* without the prior triumph of *Aufklärung* in many other fields of human life. The term extends far beyond the comparatively narrow field of religion.' As no less a figure than Hegel put it, the German version of Enlightenment was 'on the side of theology'.

Kant spent most of his adult life at the University of Königsberg in East Prussia, as student, supernumerary lecturer and finally as professor. As a loyal subject of the King of Prussia, he sought to enlighten the state from within and by consent. Especially to anyone reared on a diet of western liberalism, his political views seem inconsistent, contradictory even. A committed supporter of the French Revolution, even after the Terror, he was against any form of rebellion against legal authority, regarding regicide as the ultimate political crime. He squared this circle by the unconvincing argument that because Louis XVI in effect abdicated when he convened the Estates General, it was he who was the revolutionary by trying to regain his authority. No more likely to command unanimous approval was his view that Frederick the Great and the French Revolution were engaged in essentially the same rational project. In his popular lectures, published in 1798 as *Anthropology from a Pragmatic Point of View*, he stated firmly that progress to a better world had to be achieved 'not by the course of things *from the bottom up*, but *from the top down*' (*nicht durch den Gang der Dinge* von unten hinauf, *sondern den* von oben herab). Karl Marx derided this as 'the German theory of the French Revolution', while Lenin remarked that it only went to show that if the Germans wanted to seize a railway station as part of a revolution, they would first feel obliged to buy platform tickets. At home, Kant hoped for a dual process: self-emancipation by the subject, accompanied by the gradual liberalization of government by free public debate. As a participant in the public sphere, the individual ought to enjoy the right to express his opinions freely; but as servant of the state, his first duty was obedience. It is revealing that Kant should describe the first kind of use of reason as 'public' and the second as 'private', the reverse of what might be expected in the west.

Singling out Kant for special attention is justified, not only because of the intrinsic value of his philosophy but also for the enormous influence he exerted on contemporaries. That he was already an old man by the standards of the age when his great treatises were published in the 1780s did not prevent them having an almost immediate and colossal impact, not just on fellow philosophers or even academics but on the whole of the German educated classes (*Bildungsbürgertum*), Catholic as well as Protestant. A professor of law at the University of Bonn, Bartholomäus Fischenich, reported to Friedrich Schiller in January 1793 that 'even lawyers are trying to work their way through the Kantian labyrinth. I cannot tell you what effect the moral philosophy of this man – to which I myself return time and again – has on most young people.' For those who found his work too demanding in the original, there were plenty of popularizers available to extract the pith and present it in digestible form. Just as an intimate knowledge of *Das Kapital* is not needed for an ardent commitment to the ideals of Marxism, so was a close reading of the *Critique of Pure Reason* unnecessary for adherence to the central propositions of Kant. Not the least of Friedrich Schiller's contributions to German culture was his transfer of Kant's insights to the world of literature. It is difficult to think of any of those involved in the Prussian reform movement (of which more in the final chapter) of whom it is *not* said that they were deeply influenced by Kant. When asked by Eckermann in 1827 as to which recent philosophers he considered the best, Goethe replied: 'Undoubtedly Kant. It is his philosophy which has developed furthest and has imbued our culture most profoundly. He has also affected those who have not actually read his works.'

Kant exemplified the special flavour of the German Enlightenment: serious, profound, academic, philosophical, republican in theory but anything but revolutionary in a practical sense. It might also be thought that he is a fine example of Henry Wickham Steed's sardonic comment that 'the Germans dive deeper but come up muddier' (although the Germans might wish to rewrite that as 'The Germans come up muddier but dive deeper'). Particularly important was the predominance of the universities in the Holy Roman Empire. There were at least forty (twenty-two Protestant and eighteen Catholic), depending on how they are defined, with a total enrolment of about 9,000 – in England Oxford and Cambridge combined were admitting only about 300 students each year in the 1760s. Their centrality to German cultural life was also attested by fourteen new creations between 1648 and 1789, including Innsbruck (1673), Halle (1694), Göttingen (1737), Stuttgart (1781) and Bonn (1786). For all the criticisms levelled by contemporaries at the poor pay and excessive workload of professors (definitely not applicable to their present-day equivalents), the eighteenth century was the 'heyday of the German university' (Notker Hammerstein). Consequently, it was the university that played the role that in other parts of Europe was performed by the learned society or salon. As Herbert Lüthy observed, in Germany it has always been the professors who stand at the top of the intellectual hierarchy, whereas in France it has been the independent writers.

Moreover, German universities were very different from the self-governing communities of scholars to be found in the Anglo-Saxon world. The great majority were founded, financed and directed by the secular authority. Every prince of any standing wanted his own university, as a status symbol, as a means of controlling his young people and as a supplier of suitably trained officials and clergy. Paradoxically, this also made for a generous measure of academic freedom, for what was not permitted at one university might find approval at another. When Christian Wolff was banished from Prussia after a Pietist faction at Halle persuaded Frederick William I that he was an atheist, Wolff simply moved to the University of Marburg in Hessen-Kassel, whose Landgrave was only too pleased to give refuge and employment to such a celebrated academic. Wolff's career also provided a good example of how the plurality of universities encouraged social mobility. Born into a family of Silesian artisans, it was through his education at Jena and Leipzig that he set off on the road to fame and fortune. Recalled to Prussia by Frederick the Great in 1740, he bought a large manor house and landed estate near Leipzig and was made an imperial baron (*Reichsfreiherr*) in 1745.

Outside the German-speaking regions and Scotland, this was an undistinguished period for universities. If twenty-eight new ones were founded – most of them in the Holy Roman Empire – twenty-nine were closed, amalgamated or reduced in status to colleges. In most countries, the survivors became intellectual backwaters, marooned by their clerical conservatism. At Oxford and Cambridge the number of great buildings – the Sheldonian Theatre, the Radcliffe Camera and The Queen's College at Oxford, Trinity College Library, Pembroke College Chapel and the Senate House at Cambridge – stood in inverse ratio to the scholarship being pursued within them. The periodic attempts made to rehabilitate their reputations by historians keen to rescue their *alma mater* only serve to reaffirm their marginal status compared with what had gone before and what was to come. Of the numerous contemporary critics, Edward Gibbon's celebrated denunciation of mid-eighteenth-century Oxford stands out for its vehemence. In his *Autobiography* he wrote: 'to the University of Oxford *I* acknowledge no obligation; and she will as cheerfully renounce me for a son, as I am willing to disclaim her for a mother. I spent fourteen months at Magdalen College; they proved the fourteen months the most idle and unprofitable of my whole life.' Of course, his fabled anti-clericalism, accentuated by a brief conversion to Catholicism, had a good deal to do with this jaundiced impression: 'the schools of Oxford and Cambridge were founded in a dark age of false and barbarous science; and they are still tainted with the vices of their origin. Their primitive discipline was adapted to the education of priests and monks; and the government still remains in the hands of the clergy, an order of men whose manners are remote from the present world, and whose eyes are dazzled by the light of philosophy.' At Magdalen College he found wealth in abundance but very little learning, for the Fellows were 'decent easy men, who supinely enjoyed the gifts of the founder; their days were filled by a series of uniform employments; the chapel and the hall, the coffee-house and the common room, till they retired, weary and well satisfied, to a long slumber. From the toil of reading, or thinking, or writing, they had absolved their conscience; and the first shoots of learning and ingenuity withered on the ground, without yielding any fruits to the owners or the public.' If this seems like a world we have lost, one need only read on to find oneself muttering '*plus ça change*' when one finds Gibbon describing what he heard when he dined on high table, where 'conversation stagnated in a round of college business, Tory politics, personal anecdotes, and private scandal', although admittedly the adjective 'Tory' is no longer appropriate. Cambridge was little better – 'sunk in dullness' was Byron's verdict (as if any university could ever have been exciting enough to satisfy him) – although in Sir Isaac Newton it could boast a scholar of sufficient distinction to carry innumerable mediocrities.

Gibbon possessed the two qualifications necessary for admission to Oxford: the right religion and money. The same combination was required almost everywhere else, although the Dutch universities owed much of their vitality to their tolerant admissions policy. In Spain, it was an elite within an elite that dominated, for here it was members of the great colleges – the *colegios mayores* – of Salamanca, Valladolid and Alcalá that dominated not just the universities but most public offices too. Shortly after his arrival in Spain, Philip V was petitioned by the non-collegial members of the University of Salamanca, who complained that 150 of the previous 200 vacant chairs had been filled by members of the *colegios mayores*. The bishop of the diocese concurred: 'be he noble or plebeian, although the graduate may have spent all his days and nights and exhausted his energy in study . . . if he was unable to gain entry to a *colegio mayor* the most that he could hope for in a civil career would be an alcalde's office or a miserable post of corregidor or a temporary appointment in the administration'. Yet, as at Oxford and Cambridge, awareness of an abuse did not lead to its swift termination. It was not until the expulsion of the Jesuits in 1767 that a determined attempt at the reform of Spanish universities was instituted, including the modernization of the curriculum. Although the *colegios mayores* were suppressed in 1798, this was more for fiscal than educational reasons. The actual reform programme had paused on the death of Charles III in 1788 and then gone into reverse following the outbreak of the French Revolution.

At either end of Europe was to be found the alpha and omega of state dependence. In Russia, where literacy overall may still have been as low as 3 per cent at the end of the eighteenth century, the dependence was 'almost total' (Nicholas Riasanovsky). Moscow had a university from

1755 but there were only forty-eight students in residence ten years later, of whom only one was reading law. This pathetic total had only just crept into three figures when the century ended. Yet just because it was the hand of the state that dispensed what patronage there was, that same hand would reach for the stick if it was bitten. As we have seen in Chapter 4, that was Radishchev's fate when he published a critique of serfdom in 1790. The son of a minor noble, he had been one of twelve Russians sent to the University of Leipzig, but his failure to reciprocate with unconditional obedience was punished by a death sentence commuted to exile in Siberia. There were to be many Radishchevs in the century that followed, including Alexander Ulyanov, who was executed, and his younger brother Vladimir, who was exiled, and lived to take a terrible revenge using his better known sobriquet 'Lenin'.

In England just the reverse situation obtained. So large and rich was the expanding public sphere and so limited was state patronage that intellectuals were driven to the market by both opportunity and necessity. To take a representative sample: Daniel Defoe (1660–1731) led an existence that was both charmed and chequered as merchant and manufacturer; Jonathan Swift (1667–1745) was an Anglican clergyman, eventually becoming Dean of St Patrick's Cathedral, Dublin; Alexander Pope (1688–1744) lived solely from the sales of his publications – 'indebted to no prince or peer alive', as he put it; Samuel Richardson (1689–1761) was a printer and publisher; William Hogarth (1697–1764) started out as an apprentice engraver before setting up in business by himself; Henry Fielding (1707–54), educated at Eton, made a living from writing for the theatre and the periodical press before becoming Justice of the Peace for Middlesex and Westminster, while continuing to write; another Etonian, Thomas Arne (1710–88) earned a good living as house-composer at Drury Lane; Samuel Johnson (1709–84) eked out a living in London as a professional writer before obtaining a government pension at the age of fifty-two; Joshua Reynolds (1723–92), after a brief period of apprenticeship, earned his living as a freelance portrait painter; and so on. Although not every English intellectual was independent, for royal, ecclesiastical and academic patronage did exist and could be important, London's unique combination of size, wealth, literacy and relatively liberal censorship created a special culture whose libertarian character was recognized by contemporaries, Voltaire's *Letters Concerning the English Nation* being only the most celebrated of many encomia. Only the larger towns of the Dutch Republic created anything similar. But it was also a culture that enjoyed an even-tempered relationship with the state. It was just because John Gay, for example, could lampoon Sir Robert Walpole in *The Beggar's Opera* (1728) without fear of being sent to some English equivalent of the Bastille that criticism rarely if ever became systemic. This fundamental difference between two countries geographically so close but culturally so different was identified very well by Norman Hampson:

The essential difference between Montesquieu and Burke can be put in one word: 1688. Both men regarded individual liberty and what we now call civil rights as the main objective of political activity and they agreed that any plans for change must take as their starting point society as it was, with all its accumulated traditions, interests, prejudices and aspirations. What divided them was that Burke was an active political agent within a system whose legitimacy he accepted, and Montesquieu was not.

This same paradoxical correlation between a light touch and amicable relations can also be seen in the difference between cultural organizations. In terms of titles, the two countries appeared to be very similar: for the natural sciences, England had a 'Royal Society of London for the Improvement of Natural Knowledge' (1660), France an 'Academy of Sciences' (1666); for music, England had a 'Royal Academy of Musick' (1719), France a 'Royal Academy of Poetry and Music' (1669); for the visual arts, England had a 'Royal Academy of Arts in London, for the Purpose of Cultivating and Improving the Arts of Painting, Sculpture and Architecture' (1768), France had a 'Royal Academy of Painting and Sculpture' (1648). Yet in each case the initiative for the creation of these institutions was private in England but royal in France. As the dates suggest, the French exercise was part of a general nationalization (or rather 'royalization') of culture in the service of Louis XIV. The English equivalents came about in a haphazard fashion according to the whim of private individuals. In the case of the Royal Society it was the 'invisible college' (Robert Boyle) that started meeting informally in 1646. The grandly named 'Royal Academy of Musick' was set up to provide Italian opera for London high society. George I guaranteed an annual subsidy of £1,000 for five years, granted a royal charter and made his Lord Chamberlain the Academy's governor, but that was the limit of royal participation (and direction). It was a level of support which might reasonably be termed a necessary but not a sufficient cause of the Academy's existence. In a neat demonstration of the mixed nature of London's cultural scene, it was organized as a joint-stock company, with leading members drawn from the peerage (including seven dukes, thirteen earls and three viscounts) and the gentry, and was meant to be run at a profit for its shareholders. Similarly, George III paid the initial expenses of the Royal Academy of Arts, gave it rooms in Somerset House and knighted the first president, Joshua Reynolds, but then left it to its own devices. So successful financially were its annual exhibitions that it had no need of royal subsidy: during the 1780s the 50,000 visitors attracted each year yielded a healthy income of £2,500. In France, on the other hand, so heavy was the hand of the state that even the most pampered beneficiary could see that he was in a cage, however gilded the bars. The Revolution unleashed a furious attack on all the academies – 'the clergy of the sciences, literature and the arts', as a pamphlet of 1790 put it. By 1793 they had all been abolished. So had the universities, perhaps not surprisingly in view of their marginal position in French cultural life. Their most recent historian, Simone Guénée has described them as 'antiquated, ill-adapted to the literary, philosophical, and theological movement which they obstructed, and to the scientific movement of which they were largely ignorant, giving a traditional, out-dated and obsolete education, still organized on medieval lines incompatible with changing institutions and the progress of ideas and techniques'.

Space has permitted the discussion of only a handful of examples. Differences of cultural environment could be found everywhere else in Europe, from the Iberian countries to Hungary, from Sweden to Naples. Sharply divergent patterns of patronage, literacy, religion (and secularism), social composition and institutional organization, just to mention a few of the variables involved, produced cultural artefacts with correspondingly different flavours. As we have seen, among Europe's intellectuals there was a strong sense of being members of the same 'republic of letters' and a great deal of international correspondence and exchange of ideas. But if the cultural landscape did not consist of discrete regions, Europe was not one country, despite the ubiquity of the French language. Even if that realm is defined more tightly to include only enlightened publications, the strong national and regional characters are obtrusive. Only if an idea is abstracted from its context can it be said to have been the same all over Europe. Yet just as a piece of music is much more than notes on the stave and achieves form only when performed in a certain way by certain musicians in a certain place to a certain audience in a certain culture at a certain time, an idea is more than a concept. Liberty is not the same as *liberté* or *Freiheit* – and Enlightenment is not the same as *les lumières* or *Aufklärung*.

In the visual arts and music, the ease with which sound and image could cross frontiers made them seem stronger candidates for truly cosmopolitan status. That was certainly the view of the influential theorist and critic Antoine Quatremère de Quincy (1755–1849), who in 1798 wrote that 'a community of cultivation and knowledge, together with a certain equality of taste, understanding and talent can be observed across all the countries of Europe: indeed it might truly be said that the differences between them are less than those sometimes found between the provinces of the same empire'. Significantly, Quatremère was the product of a culture whose verbal language was French and whose iconographic vocabulary was classical. Although the actual term 'neo-classicism' was not invented until the following century, what it described was very much the preferred style of the culture of reason – 'an emanation of the Enlightenment', as Rémy Saisselin put it. Like most other all-embracing stylistic designations, it has generated a body of literature as extensive as it is contentious. Here only the barest of outlines can be traced with the broadest of brush-strokes.

There is general agreement that behind this particular revival of interest in classical forms lay a reaction against the baroque and especially the rococo. Against what was thought to be the latter's frivolity, hedonism and ornamental excess was opposed an art that was serious, moral, didactic and plain. The essence of the neoclassical ideal was best expressed by Johann Joachim Winckelmann (1717–68) when he praised the Greeks for their 'noble simplicity and calm grandeur' (*edle Einfalt und stille Größe*). That phrase appeared in Winckelmann's first important treatise, *On the Imitation of the Painting and Sculpture of the Greeks* (1755), which also contains the core of his message to contemporary artists: 'there is but one way for the moderns to become great and perhaps unequalled; I mean by imitating the ancients'. By 'imitating' he did not mean 'copying' in the sense of reproducing exactly classical images, statues or buildings; rather, he advocated using their example as a guide. Thanks to their climate, culture and institutions, the Greeks had got closer than any other people, before or since, to the beauty inherent in nature and had then succeeded in expressing that beauty in artefacts and concepts: 'it is not only nature which the votaries of the Greeks find in their works, but still more, something superior to nature: ideal beauties, brain-born images'.

Thanks to his literary gifts, in particular his ability to imbue penetrating analysis with emotional excitement, and to being in the right place at the right time, the impact of Winckelmann's ideas was colossal. Looking back on his youth, Goethe (born 1749) recalled 'the general, unconditional veneration' that Winckelmann excited among his generation: 'all the periodicals were unanimous in promoting his fame, travellers visiting him returned instructed and enraptured, and his opinions were spread throughout the world of scholarship and society at large'. In 1805 Goethe gave the title *Winckelmann and His Century* to a collection of essays on the art history of the eighteenth century. As Winckelmann's works were quickly translated into the major European languages, his influence was as international as his ideas.

If Winckelmann emerged at mid-century as the most influential theorist of neoclassicism, the way had been well prepared. Of his predecessors, the most important was Anthony Ashley Cooper, third Earl of Shaftesbury (1671–1713), whose assault on representational culture proved to be influential throughout the eighteenth century. Baroque artists he regarded as 'corrupters' and Bernini as 'wicked'. Cosmopolitan in theory but Francophobe in practice (like so many progressive English intellectuals), he was outraged when he saw the frescoes by Charles Le Brun in the Hall of Mirrors at Versailles, especially 'his long Peruk'd bare neck'd *Gallo-Grecian* Heroes, these Monstrositys & the *Manière lechée* & florid Colouring with affected Gesture & Theatrical Action of the Womanish Court'. As that comment suggests, Shaftesbury also had a political agenda. In the same way that the art of ancient Rome degenerated with imperialism and Christianity, so was the culture of Louis XIV's France both decadent and tyrannical, threatening all Europe with universal monarchy and 'a new Abyss of Ignorance and Superstition'.

It was revealing that the only French artist of whom Shaftesbury could find anything good to say was Nicolas Poussin (1594–1665), because his style was 'chaste, severe, just & accurate' and because he spent most of his life in self-imposed exile from corrupt, absolutist France. This enthusiasm for Poussin was something of an axiom for all those who rejected the contemporary art scene during the first half of the eighteenth century. They included all those who embraced the cause of reason. Exemplifying everything they detested was the art of François Boucher (1703–70), the darling of the court, as rich as he was productive. From his enormous oeuvre (he claimed to have produced more than 10,000 drawings), *The Triumph of Venus* of 1740 provides a representative example of the languorous eroticism in which he specialized and which so appealed to Louis XV. There is not one straight line in this riot of swirling drapes, flying putti and reclining nudes. Nor is there any ethical component beyond the pleasures of the flesh. Among those who took offence at Boucher's hedonism, none was more forthright than Diderot:

The degradation of taste, of colour, of composition, of character, of expression, of drawing, is a consequence of the degradation of morals. I make so bold as to say that he has never known the truth. I make so bold as to say that ideas of delicacy, decency, innocence, and simplicity have become foreign to him; I make so bold as to say that he has never known the kind of nature that speaks to my soul, to your soul, to the soul of a decently brought up child or sensitive woman. I make so bold as to say he is without taste.

Diderot's attack was, of course, as much political as it was aesthetic. This particular salvo was fired in 1765, the same year in which Boucher became the official 'first painter of the king'. Instead of what he saw as the decadence of the court, Diderot called for an art that was classical in style and ethical in content: 'to show virtue as pleasing, vice as odious, to expose what is ridiculous, that is the aim of every honest man who takes up the pen, the brush or the chisel'. Here he was paraphrasing Shaftesbury, whose work he had translated. The sort of painting that Diderot promoted in the 1750s and 1760s was the work of Jean-Baptiste Greuze (1725–1805). Its nature was revealed by the titles of his hugely successful exhibits at the Salons: *The Father's Curse*, *The Punished Son*, *The Drunkard's Return*, *The Death of the Paralytic*, *Father Reading the Bible to his Children*, and so on. Diderot enthused that any of Greuze's paintings could be turned into a novel – and he meant it as a compliment. Although now out of favour, Greuze's sentimental moralizing enjoyed tremendous success at the time, both with the connoisseurs when the originals were exhibited at the Salons and with the general public when they were distributed as engravings. Most successful of all was *The Village Betrothal* (Plate 23), better known under its French title of *L'Accordée de village*, exhibited in 1761, the same year that saw the publication of

Rousseau's best-selling lachrymose epistolary novel *La nouvelle Héloïse*. As their success demonstrated, there was a strong demand for exercises in what was called 'sensibility'. Although apparently at odds with the simultaneous cult of reason, it was in reality its complement. As Emmet Kennedy put it: 'perhaps the best way to understand the importance given to *sensibilité* is to view it as an emotional force or energy by which people could do the good portrayed by reason'.

In its depiction of ordinary people and in its preaching of the virtues of chastity, thrift, sobriety and decency, the sort of didactic art advocated by Diderot and practised by Greuze certainly marked a sharp break with, say, Boucher. But it was also modest in aim and ambition. What the philosophes wanted was something more heroic, and that could only be supplied by history painting, the genre they – like everyone else – placed at the top of the artistic hierarchy. It was now that the state took a hand. In 1749, Mme de Pompadour, who had become Louis XV's official mistress in 1744, sent her brother Abel-François Poisson (better known by his eventual title of the marquis de Marigny) on an extended tour of Italy to prepare him for the position of minister for the arts (or *Directeur-Général des Bâtiments, Jardins, Arts, Académies et Manufactures du Roi*, to give him his full title). When he returned in 1751 to take up his office, his commissions favoured painters, sculptors and architects working in a classical style. The most important, for a grand new church on the left bank to be named after the patron saint of Paris, St Geneviève, and to embellish further the great eponymous abbey, went to Jacques-Germain Soufflot (1713–80), who had accompanied him on his Italian journey. If it might seem odd to present a church as an exemplar of the culture of reason, a quick visual comparison with, say, Weltenburg should allay doubts. They should also be dispelled by the knowledge that Soufflot believed 'that even a building designed to embody the mysteries of Christian faith could be perfected by the application of human reason' (Barry Bergdoll). He turned the protracted construction process into a continuous experiment with new building methods, including the use of stone reinforced with an iron armature to give the interior a sense of space and light unobtainable by traditional techniques. So it was not inappropriate that the French revolutionaries should have turned his building into a secular Pantheon: 'the temple of religion should become the temple of the *patrie*; the tomb of a great man should become the altar of liberty', as the initiator of the scheme,

Claude-Emmanuel Pastoret, put it. Piling irony on irony, the first hero to be 'pantheonized' was none other than Voltaire, (in)famously denied a Christian burial when he died in 1778. When his remains were moved to his new resting place in 1791, it was estimated that a crowd of around 200,000 watched.

State patronage of neoclassical art intensified under the comte d'Angiviller, who succeeded Marigny in 1774 (after a brief interlude under Terray). His chief concern was to foster patriotism by commissioning biennially eight portraits and four sculptures of great Frenchmen, to be exhibited in what was planned to be a great national museum at the Louvre. Undoubtedly both the greatest and the most successful painting to be commissioned by d'Angiviller was Jacques-Louis David's *The Oath of the Horatii* (Plate 24), conceived in 1781, painted at Rome in 1783–4 and exhibited at the Salon in Paris in 1785, where it was received with rapture and acclaimed as the greatest French painting since Poussin. Because David emerged after 1789 as a fervent supporter of the Revolution, even to the extent of voting for the execution of Louis XVI and becoming a member of the Committee of Public Safety, the picture has often been interpreted as a call to contemporaries to take up arms against the old regime. David himself lent support to such a view by joining Robespierre in 1794 in a ceremonial re-enactment of the oath-taking. Yet this is all retrospective. At the time, David gave no indication that his painting had any topical message. Nor did contemporaries see any: when it was exhibited in Rome for the first time, 'princes and princesses, cardinals and prelates' flocked to see it. If the painting really was intended as a republican call to arms, David had made an odd choice of period, for Rome was still a kingdom in the mid-seventh century BC and was to remain so for another century-and-a-half. Nor is it clear from either the painting or anything David wrote that he followed Horatius in privileging fatherland over family. Both here and in his other great pre-revolutionary success – *The Lictors Returning to Brutus the Bodies of his Sons* (1789) – there is a good case to be made for the moral superiority of the grieving women over the homicidal men. Whatever David's intentions may have been, *The Oath of the Horatii* became a potent icon after the Revolution had broken out, for, as Simon Schama has observed, it had all the ingredients for revolutionary rhetoric – patriotism, fraternity, martyrdom.

If the revolutionary credentials of David's pre-1789 paintings are open to doubt, how much more is that true of the great neoclassical creations of the 1780s in architecture and sculpture! In artistic terms nothing could have been more radical than Claude Nicolas Ledoux's forty *barrières*, whose construction began in 1785. Yet their political complexion was as reactionary as could be, for these were customs posts, established around Paris by the detested farmers-general. It might be added that one of David's greatest portraits was of Antoine Laurent Lavoisier and his wife, painted in 1788. One of the most important scientists of the century, Lavoisier was also a farmer-general and ended up on the guillotine in 1794.

THE RESURGENCE OF THE
CULTURE OF FEELING

If a single incident has to be found to mark the culmination of the culture of reason, a strong candidate is an event at Paris on 30 March 1778. For once, that overworked word 'apotheosis' is entirely appropriate. For it was on that day that Voltaire went to the *Théâtre Français* to attend a performance of his final play, *Irène*. His arrival was greeted with a standing ovation that lasted twenty minutes. When the performance was over, his bust was installed on stage and crowned with a laurel wreath, as the actress playing Irène recited a poem promising Voltaire immortality in the name of the French nation – and then was obliged to give an encore. This was the climax of a triumphal progress across France which had begun the previous month. John Morley observed: 'no great captain returning from a prolonged campaign of difficulty and hazard crowned by the most glorious victory, ever received a more splendid and far-resounding greeting'. When he arrived at the *barrière* at the city limits of Paris, he told the customs officer inspecting his belongings: 'I am the only article of contraband here.' This remark was very much to the point, for he had been kept out of Paris for thirty years by Louis XV, who regarded his irreverent impiety with horror. Louis XVI allowed Voltaire back, but stayed away from the theatre and forbade the Queen to receive him, thus giving an early indication of his fatal propensity for having the worst of both worlds. Voltaire died exactly two months later, aged eighty-four.

By that time the culture of feeling was enjoying a strong resurgence. Of course, it had never gone away. On the contrary, it had flourished as never before, for emotional forms of Christianity such as Pietism and Methodism were flourishing. All the institutions of the public sphere discussed in the previous section were neutral in terms of content. Periodicals were just as well suited to the propagation of the supernatural as the natural: the Jansenist *Nouvelles ecclésiastiques*, for example, which began publication in 1728, proved to be one of the greatest and most enduring success stories of the eighteenth century, despite vigorous persecution. The same applied to books, pamphlets, lending libraries and reading clubs. That was shown in France in 1778–9, when a relaxation of censorship brought a flood of reprints of works by dead authors. Of the more than 2,000,000 copies generated, nearly two-thirds were religious. Voluntary associations lent themselves as much to pious as to rationalist purposes, to 'class meetings' for the study of the Bible as well as to assemblies of Freemasons.

Nevertheless, to most contemporary observers, it seemed that it was the culture of reason that was on the march, especially among the educated elites. In a biography of Voltaire published in 1789, the marquis de Condorcet reviewed the improvements achieved during the lifetime of his hero (born 1694) as a result of his efforts: health had been improved by more rational burial practices and inoculation; 'the clergy of the countries subject to the Roman religion have lost their dangerous power, and will lose their scandalous wealth'; freedom of the press had improved; in Scandinavia, Poland, Prussia and the Habsburg Monarchy religious intolerance had vanished and there were even some signs of improvement in France and parts of Italy; serfdom appeared to be on the way out in most parts of Europe; various beneficial law reforms had been instituted; wars were less frequent; sovereigns and their privileged orders were no longer able to dupe their subjects; and generally 'for the first time reason had started to diffuse over the peoples of Europe a pure and steady light'.

To many European intellectuals, the outbreak of the Revolution in the same year marked the final triumph of reason and the dawning of a new age for all mankind. Georg Forster, a German scholar who had accompanied Captain Cook on his second expedition to the Pacific (1772–5), exclaimed: 'it is glorious to see what philosophy has ripened in the brain and realized in the state'. Yet this proved to be a false dawn, as Condorcet discovered, dying in prison by his own hand in March 1794 rather than face a 'trial' which would have sent him to the guillotine. But the reaction against reason had begun a long time earlier. Of the many candidates, three possible turning points suggest themselves. The first was the epiphany of Jean-Jacques Rousseau on 25 August 1749. In the *Confessions* he recorded:

The summer of that year [1749] was excessively hot. Vincennes is some six miles from Paris. In no condition to pay for cabs, I walked there at two in the afternoon when I was alone, and I went fast so as to arrive early. The trees along the road, always lopped according to the custom of the country, hardly gave any shade; and often I was so prostrated with heat and weariness that I lay down on the ground, unable to go further. One day I took the *Mercure de France* and, glancing through it as I walked, I came upon the question propounded by the Dijon Academy for the next year's prize: Has the progress of the sciences and arts done more to corrupt morals or improve them? The moment I read this I beheld another universe and became another man.

In a letter he wrote to Malesherbes in 1762, Rousseau stressed the suddenness and extremism of his vision: 'all at once I felt my mind dazzled by a thousand lights, a crowd of splendid ideas presented themselves to me with such force and in such confusion, that I was thrown into a state of indescribable bewilderment. I felt my head seized by a dizziness that resembled intoxication.' Seized by palpitations, unable to walk and breathe at the same time, he fell to the ground as if in a trance. When he was able to rise half-an-hour later, he found that the front of his coat was drenched in tears. It was not reason that had shown Rousseau the way to truth, but a sudden conversion experience, comparable to that of Saul on the road to Damascus. The scales dropped from his eyes, as he now realized that the Enlightenment's value-system needed to be stood on its head – it was civilization not ignorance, prejudice or superstition that had led man astray. In his *Discourse on the Arts and Sciences* written in answer to the Dijon Academy's question, he attacked that value-system root-and-branch. To seek to control and exploit nature for the enhancement of man's material well-being was wrong in principle and deadly in practice. All the various branches of the natural sciences were motivated by vice: astronomy by superstition, mathematics by greed, mechanics by ambition, physics by idle curiosity. He regretted the invention of printing, for it had allowed the impious works of

Hobbes and Spinoza to achieve immortality. He ended by predicting that eventually men would become so revolted by modern culture that they would implore God to give them back their 'innocence, ignorance and poverty', 'for that alone can make us happy and precious in Thy sight'.

The second event occurred one night in June 1764 when Horace Walpole, fourth son of Sir Robert, had a nightmare. In a letter to his friend William Cole, he explained what had happened:

I waked one morning . . . from a dream, of which all I could recover was, that I had thought myself in an ancient castle (a very natural dream for a head filled like mine with Gothic story) and that on the uppermost bannister of a great staircase I saw a gigantic hand in armour. In the evening I sat down and began to write, without knowing in the least what I intended to say or relate.

The stream of consciousness continued for two months until his novel – *The Castle of Otranto, A Gothic Story* – was complete. When he published it the following year, Walpole pretended that it had been found 'in the library of an ancient Catholic family in the north of England', having originally been printed in Naples in 1529. In the preface he also speculated that it had been written by a priest of the old school 'to confirm the populace in their ancient errors and superstitions' at a time when they were under threat from the light of reason shed by the Renaissance. Perhaps because it was such an immediate success, Walpole claimed ownership in his preface to the second edition, which came out later the same year, describing the exercise as 'an attempt to blend the two kinds of romance, the ancient and the modern. In the former all was imagination and improbability: in the latter, nature is always intended to be, and sometimes has been, copied with success. Invention has not been wanting, but the great resources of fancy have been dammed up, by a strict adherence to common life.' Walpole certainly gave his own resources of fancy full rein, including such extravagances as a portrait that stepped down out of its frame, a statue that bled, a sword so massive that it needed fifty men to wield it, giant severed body parts, a sundry cast of magicians, goblins, friars and other agents of the supernatural, and so on. Both the original dream and the writing of the novel took place in the ideal environment, for in the course of the previous fifteen years or so, Walpole had turned his house at Strawberry Hill near Twickenham into a Gothic extravaganza, if not the very first example of the 'Gothic revival' then certainly the most influential.

The third possible turning point was Goethe's journey to Strassburg in March 1770, at the age of twenty-one, to study law at the university there. So it was on German-speaking but French-ruled soil that Goethe experienced his cultural conversion. The agent was the cathedral, the first great Gothic building he had seen. Like most educated Europeans, he had been taught to think of medieval architecture as the epitome of barbarism. Representative of German opinion was the definition offered by Johann Georg Sulzer in his very popular encyclopaedia of the arts, first published in 1771: 'The epithet "Gothic" is frequently applied to the fine arts to designate a barbarous taste, although the meaning of the expression is seldom defined exactly. It seems to be used principally to indicate clumsiness and lack of beauty and good proportions, and originated in the clumsy imitations of ancient architecture perpetrated by the Goths who settled in Italy.'

According to his autobiography, published in 1811, Goethe's first reaction to Strassburg Cathedral was to see its spire only as the ideal vantage-point from which to view the surrounding countryside. Gradually, however, it began to arouse an aesthetic response which was as powerful as it was difficult to articulate. In thinking through the problems posed by the discrepancy between his anti-Gothic prejudices and the building's irresistible appeal, Goethe revolutionized his aesthetic code. All the classical canons were refuted by this irregular, asymmetric, idiosyncratic pile, which was not even finished, for one of the two projected spires had never been built, and which resembled an organism that had grown rather than a structure that had been built. What he had been taught to find offensive, he found just the reverse – it was nothing less than 'a new revelation'.

It was a revelation he shared with the world in an essay entitled 'Concerning German Architecture', dedicated to Erwein von Steinbach, Strassburg Cathedral's main architect. Here he used his new enthusiasm for the Gothic to preach a new aesthetic credo. Any idea that beauty could be found by joining schools, adopting principles or following rules was emphatically rejected: they were so many chains enslaving insight and energy. The ghastly good taste, harmony and purity demanded by classical aesthetics did violence to nature's untamed spontaneity. In the essay's key passage Goethe defined his alternative: 'The only true art is characteristic art. If its influence arises from deep, harmonious, independent feeling, from feeling peculiar to itself, oblivious, yes, ignorant of everything foreign, then it is whole and living, whether it be born from crude savagery or cultured sentiment.' The crucial adjective is 'characteristic' (*karakteristische*), by which he meant art which grows naturally and spontaneously from the culture within which it is produced, not something that has been imitated. In the case of Strassburg Cathedral, it was not only characteristic art, it was also art that was characteristically German. It had been produced on German soil 'in authentically German times' (*in echter deutscher Zeit*) and only gained in stature by virtue of being treated with contempt by the Italians or the French. The great tower was all the more wonderful for looking like something that had grown: 'a lofty, wide-spreading tree of God, declaring with a thousand branches, a million twigs, and with leaves as numerous as the sands of the sea, the glory of the Lord, its Master'.

It was also in Strassburg that Goethe met Johann Gottfried Herder (1744–1803), who edited the collection *Of German Identity and Art* (*Von deutscher Art und Kunst*), in which the essay on Strassburg Cathedral appeared. Together they formed the distinguished core of a movement that came to be known as '*Sturm und Drang*', usually translated as 'Storm and Stress', which took its name from the eponymous play by Friedrich Maximilian von Klinger (1752–1831). This was very much an angry-young-man movement against what was perceived as the stultifying rationalism and classicism of the older generation. Instead the *Stürmer und Dränger* stressed the primacy of the 'inner light' they derived directly or indirectly from Pietism. Their heroes were lonely outsiders, still kicking vigorously against the pricks even as they were sent down to perdition by the forces of convention. Subjectivity, originality and passion were their ideals. As Herder's mentor, the Prussian Pietist Johann Georg Hamann put it: 'passion alone gives hands, feet and wings to abstractions and hypotheses; gives spirit, life and voice to images and symbols'.

Within little more than a decade, *Sturm und Drang* had burnt itself out, but not before Goethe had published two highly influential masterpieces: the play *Götz von Berlichingen* in 1773 and the novel *The Sufferings of Young Werther* in 1774. Frederick the Great dismissed the former as 'an abominable imitation of those bad English plays', but it had a colossal impact, because it was a great libertarian manifesto, both in what it said and the way that it said it. Stylistically it was a revolution, not so much abandoning the unities of time, place and action – the defining features of the dominant French model – as turning them on their head. The action sprawls over several months, there are dozens of scene changes, and there are at least two main plots. Also calculated to grate on the classical ear was the language, for Goethe drew on two early sixteenth-century sources, Luther's translation of the Bible and the historical Götz's autobiography, as well as the Upper German dialect spoken in his home town of Frankfurt am Main. The result was a wonderfully expressive idiom but one which was also colloquial, ungrammatical and generally rough-hewn. Substantively, the main message anticipated Kant: any kind of authority that was not self-generated but was imposed from outside was to be rejected. In the most important single line of the play, the anti-hero Adelbert von Weislingen says: 'One thing is for certain: happy and great alone is the man who needs neither to command nor to obey to amount to something!' *Werther* was even more of a sensation, the first international best-seller written by a German. The plot is quickly recounted: Werther, a young man of middle class but respectable station, meets and falls in love with a girl who returns his feelings but has already committed herself to another. Unable to come to terms with his frustrated passion, Werther shoots himself. The challenge it thrust in the face of cultural convention was so fierce that indifference was impossible. On the right, clerical conservatives found its glamorization of suicide repugnant; on the left, enlightened progressives found its disparagement of reason equally offensive. But the book's admirers drowned the criticism with paeans of emotional praise worthy of Werther himself. The journalist Christian Daniel Schubart (1739–91) told his readers: 'Here I sit, my heart melting, my breast pounding, my eyes weeping tears of ecstatic pain, and do I need to tell you, dear reader, that I have been reading *The Sufferings of Young Werther* by my beloved Goethe? Or should I rather say that I have been devouring it?' Within a year there were eleven editions in print, most of them pirated; by 1790 there were thirty. Translated into French and English almost at once, by the end of the century it was available in almost every European language.

From the insights of individuals such as Rousseau, Walpole and Goethe, a new world-view was created. What eventually became known as the 'romantic revolution' opposed emotion to reason, faith to scepticism, intuition to logic, subjectivity to objectivity, historicism to natural law, and poetry to prose. In the view of the romantics, the Enlightenment and its scientific method had analysed and analysed until the world lay around them in a dismantled, atomized and meaningless heap. It was a common accusation that the Enlightenment 'could explain everything, but understand nothing'. Johann Heinrich Merck, a member of the *Sturm und Drang* group, complained of the Enlightenment:

Now we have got the freedom of believing in public nothing but what can be rationally demonstrated. They have deprived religion of all its sensuous elements, that is, of all its relish. They have carved it up into its parts and reduced it to a skeleton without colour and light . . . and now it's put in a jar and nobody wants to taste it.

Reason had looked like a liberator but had turned out to be a particularly demanding tyrant. Hamann asked angrily: 'What is this much lauded reason with its universality, infallibility, certainty, and over-weening claims, but an *ens rationis*, a stuffed dummy, endowed with divine attributes?' In Rousseau's view, the philosophes committed the fault of his lover, Madame de Warens, of whom he wrote in the *Confessions*: 'instead of listening to her heart, which gave her good counsel, she listened to her reason, which gave her bad'. It was in this spirit that Heinrich von Kleist (1777–1811) sneered that Newton would see in a girl's breast only a crooked line, and in her heart nothing more interesting than its cubic capacity, while William Blake (1757–1827) proclaimed that 'Art is the Tree of Life. Science is the Tree of Death'. In the place of the arid abstractions of rationalism, the romantics called for a remystification of the world. Against the natural aesthetic laws of classicism, they opposed the spontaneity and originality of the inner light of genius. As the greatest of the romantic painters, Caspar David Friedrich (1774–1840), put it: 'The painter should not just paint what he sees in front of him, but also what he sees inside himself. But if he should see nothing inside himself, then he should stop painting what he sees in front of him. Otherwise his pictures would become mere screens behind which one expects to find only the sick or even the dead.' This precept was given visual expression by his friend Georg Friedrich Kersting (1785–1847), who depicted Friedrich in a bare studio isolated from the outside world (Plate 26).

To gain access to what really mattered, the romantics believed, reason and its main instrument – the word – were not so much inadequate as misleading, instilling a false sense of precision and clarity. If nature was not an inert mass, governed by the blind, mechanical Newtonian laws, but a vibrant organism pulsating with life, then it could be understood only by allowing the other human faculties to resume their rightful place. It was an indication of their rejection of the Enlightenment's rationalism that they turned its central metaphor – light – on its head. 'The cold light of day' was rejected as superficial, and in its place was enthroned 'the wonder-world night'. Is the owl perched on the artist's shoulder in Goya's *The Sleep of Reason Begets Monsters* a monster to be feared, or is it perhaps the Owl of Minerva, the symbol of wisdom, who 'flies only at dusk' (Hegel)? From Novalis and his *Hymns to the Night* to Richard Wagner and *Tristan und Isolde*, the night was celebrated as 'the mother of all that is true and beautiful'.

THE SACRALIZATION OF ART AND THE STATUS OF THE ARTIST

In the course of the eighteenth and early nineteenth centuries, culture shed its representational or recreational function to become a sacralized activity to be worshipped in its own right. One clue is provided by comparing and contrasting two funerals dating from the late eighteenth and early nineteenth centuries. No one knows exactly when Mozart was buried, not even the day. He died in Vienna at 1 a.m. on 5 December 1791, according to his widow, Constanze. At 3 p.m. on the following day or on the day after that (accounts conflict), the body was taken to St Stephen's Cathedral, where it was blessed in front of the Crucifix Chapel, and was then transported on a hearse through the Stubentor, along the Landstrasse to the new cemetery of St Marx. The actual interment may have taken place on the same day – the 6th or 7th depending on which authority one follows, or more likely on the next, i.e. the 7th or 8th, given the lateness of the hour. If some of the crasser myths surrounding Mozart's obsequies have been exploded, the fact remains that it was a very muted send-off. No one was present at the graveside, apart from the sexton and the priest, and no gravestone was erected to mark the spot.

How different was the treatment of Beethoven thirty-six years later. When he died in Vienna at around 5.45 p.m. on Monday, 26 March 1827, his friends had already selected an appropriate plot in the Währing cemetery. Once life was pronounced extinct, they set about arranging an autopsy, preserving Beethoven's physical likeness for posterity through a drawing and a death-mask by Joseph Danhauser, and safeguarding his possessions. They also kept a vigil alongside the 'polished oak coffin which rested on ball-shaped gilded supports' and which was surrounded by eight candles, as the throngs of those wishing to pay their last respects filed past. Three days later the funeral took place, beginning at three in the afternoon, formal invitations having been issued. As the coffin was carried down into the courtyard of the House of the Black-Robed Spaniard, nine priests from the Schottenstift intoned a blessing and a choir drawn from the Italian Opera sang a chorale by Anselm Weber. So dense had the crowd become that the procession had great difficulty in starting off, as one can see from Franz Stober's celebrated painting, itself a significant phenomenon. When eventually it did get going, a second choir sang the *Miserere* to trombone accompaniment. Along the road, so many people 'from all classes and estates', as a newspaper report put it, had gathered that the procession to the church of the Holy Trinity in the Alsergasse took one-and-a-half hours to cover the 500 yards (450 m). After the funeral service, the cortège, still numbered in thousands, formed up again for the journey to the Währing cemetery. At the gates, the classical actor Heinrich Anschütz delivered an oration written by the Habsburg Empire's most celebrated dramatist, Franz Grillparzer. This became justly celebrated in its own right, and is indeed as commendable for its eloquence as for its brevity. Particularly striking was the complete absence of any reference to God. The deity to whom Grillparzer – and Beethoven – paid their homage was Art: 'The thorns of life had wounded him deeply, and as the castaway clings to the shore, so did he seek refuge in thine arms, O thou glorious sister and peer of the Good and the True, thou balm of wounded hearts, heaven-born Art!' No supernatural being was necessary, only a secular religion of aesthetics mediated by a supreme artist. As Schubert's friend Gabriel Seidl put it in a poem dedicated to Beethoven's memory:

He dominates and reconciles what is strange and incompatible.

He feels through his mind; he thinks through his heart.

He teaches us new jubilation, new laments, new prayer and new jests.

. . .

He lives! For his life is his music; no god will ever uproot that from the
world's breast.

Part of the explanation for the very different obsequial treatments
accorded to Mozart and Beethoven lies in the establishment of art in
general, and music in particular, as an independent, autonomous source
of value and authority in human society. It was in Germany during the
middle decades of the eighteenth century that aesthetics emerged as a
distinct discipline. Lessing's *Laocoön, or The Bounds of Painting and
Poetry* of 1766 synthesized several different strands to form a tie that
was to bind together succeeding generations of German intellectuals.
Not for nothing was Lessing the son of a Protestant pastor, like so many
other of his fellow writers. As Nicholas Boyle has aptly observed in his
biography of Goethe, German aesthetic theory was 'the ex-theology of
an ex-clerisy'.

Neoclassicists such as Lessing, who reacted with such repugnance to
the hedonistic excesses of the rococo, took a great deal from the French
theorists of Louis XIV's academies, but one characteristic they did not
adopt was the subservience of the arts to non-artistic purposes such as
the glorification of the Sun King. This was given magisterial expression
by Johann Georg Sulzer in his *Allgemeine Theorie der schönen Künste*
(General Theory of the Fine Arts) of 1771, where he stated firmly that
the use of the arts for representational purposes such as 'display and
luxury' was 'a complete misunderstanding of their divine power . . .
and their high value'. Even more influential was Winckelmann. To his
achievements already recorded in this chapter must be added his creation
of an aesthetic religion by the marriage of the language of Pietist intro-
spection with sensualist paganism. Winckelmann's account of the Apollo
Belvedere is more than an appreciation of a statue, it is a religious
exercise, because for him the statue does not represent God, it *is* a God
(Leopold Ettlinger).

If the refined formulations of philosophers might have had a limited
appeal (although one should never underestimate the intellectualism of
the German *Bildungsbürgertum*), the same could not be said of the

poets, dramatists and novelists who shifted the literary balance of power on the continent to the east of the Rhine. It was Goethe, who commanded all those genres, and many more besides, who came to be regarded by posterity as the pre-eminent figure, but in his own lifetime and for long thereafter, it was his friend Friedrich Schiller who was the more highly regarded, not least by musicians. Beethoven thought Goethe was too much of the courtier when he met him for the first time in 1812, but he venerated Schiller from an early age, and clearly knew his work intimately, quoting passages from Schiller's plays in his correspondence.

Winckelmann's celebrated call for 'noble simplicity and calm grandeur' permeated Schiller's mature dramas and his aesthetic writings of the 1790s. In his two masterpieces of 1795–6 – *On the Aesthetic Education of Man, in a Series of Letters* and *Naive and Sentimental Poetry* – Schiller addressed the malaise of modern man, analysing him into his rational and sensuous components. The upheavals unleashed by the French Revolution had revealed the impotence of a purely rational 'theoretical culture'. What was needed was the 'practical culture' offered by aesthetic education, which would allow the expansion of the powers of the imagination. Enlightenment by means of concepts could not influence the character of mankind, for most humans are moved to take action by their feelings. So the seeds of rational perception will wither where they fall unless the soil has been prepared by the emotions and imagination: 'The way to the head must be opened through the heart.' And that was the task of aesthetic education, to pave the way for the transition from 'rule by mere forces to rule by laws'. Aesthetic experience was the one area in which the rational and the sensual could interact harmoniously: only in culture was man simultaneously active and free, able to influence the world around him while remaining self-contained. At a time when all Europe was in danger of being overwhelmed by revolutionary change, it was only through culture that humankind could achieve liberty without licence: 'If man is ever to solve the problem of politics in practice, he will have to approach it through the problem of the aesthetic, because it is only through Beauty that man makes his way to freedom' was Schiller's conclusion. Or, in Beethoven's more succinct formulation: 'Only art and scholarship give us intimations and hopes of a higher life.'

It was in the eighteenth century that 'art' acquired its modern meaning. For Dr Johnson, 'art' still meant skill, as in 'the art of boiling sugar', although by this time it was becoming established that 'the fine arts', 'elegant arts' or 'arts of taste' could be distinguished from 'necessary', 'mechanical' or 'useful' arts. It was from the Germans that the English took the belief that literature, the visual arts and music possessed some common quality that raised them above technology. In *On the Plastic Imitation of the Beautiful* of 1787, Karl Philipp Moritz (who also wrote a perceptive account of his travels through England) argued that just because they served no practical purpose, artistic creations enjoyed a self-sufficient, quasi-religious character. That axiom of course carried with it important implications for the way in which artists should be treated. Now promoted to be high-priests, they had the right to enjoy a creative freedom unencumbered by the representational or recreational needs of the patron. In the words of Goethe's friend and portraitist Johann Heinrich Meyer, 'art must feel free and independent; it must rule, as it were, if it is to thrive; if it is ruled and mastered, it is bound to decline and vanish'.

This drive for independence was fuelled in part by a growing restlessness with the often quirky demands of patrons. Did not even the equable Haydn feel exploited as he ground out yet another baryton trio for Prince Nicholas Esterházy? In 1790 he wrote about the previous decade: 'I did not know if I was a *Kapell*-master or a *Kapell*-servant ... It is really sad always to be a slave ... I am a poor creature!' Less than a year later he was whisked off to London by the impresario Salomon, and there he found both fame and fortune. He wrote home to Maria Anna von Genzinger on 8 January 1791:

My arrival caused a great sensation throughout the whole city, and I went the round of all the newspapers for 3 successive days. Everyone wants to know me. I had to dine out 6 times up to now, and if I wanted, I could dine out every day.

Yet Haydn did return to Eisenstadt and remained in the service of the Esterházys until the day he died. He was sharp enough to appreciate that the anonymous public could be just as hard a taskmaster as any prince. The trick was to take the money and the adulation without having to compromise creative freedom. Not easy to do at the best of times, this balancing-act became progressively more difficult as the public rapidly broadened in numbers without deepening in appreciation. A Haydn symphony was one thing, Beethoven's Ninth was quite another. What the public wanted was easy-listening, that is to say plenty of variety, good tunes, regular rhythms, not too long, and all preferably in the key of C-major so that it could be easily played at home on the piano that was increasingly becoming a feature of middle-class parlours. Long and loud were the complaints from musicians that the public did not appreciate them, preferring the jaunty tunes and rumpty-tumpty orchestration of Italian ice-cream opera. Beethoven's own comment on the prevailing fashion for Italian opera, conveyed two years later in a conversation with Hummel, was characteristically pithy: 'It is said *vox populi, vox dei* – I never believed it.'

The way out of this dilemma, to avoid jumping from the frying-pan of aristocratic tyranny into the fire of public philistinism, was to liberate art from both the scum and the dregs of society and to place it on an altar in unsullied safety (just to mix the metaphor once more). So artists of all genres embraced with enthusiasm the sacralization preached by the aestheticians. From the rich range of examples available, the following two recommend themselves by their eloquence and relative brevity. First, Novalis (the Saxon noble Friedrich von Hardenberg):

Whoever feels unhappy in this world, whoever fails to find what he seeks – then let him enter the world of books, art and nature, this eternal domain which is both ancient and modern simultaneously, and let him live there in this secret church of a better world. There he will surely find a lover and a friend, a fatherland and a God.

And secondly, Goethe:

True poetry identifies itself as such by knowing how to liberate us from the earthly burdens that oppress us, by being a secular gospel, by creating inner cheerfulness and outward contentment. Like a hot-air balloon, it raises us into the higher regions and gives us a birds-eye view of the confused labyrinths of the world.

Of all the creative artists, it was the musicians who found this easiest, for their medium speaks directly to the psyche without any mediating word or image. This was put particularly well by Leonard Willoughby: 'The romanticists hoped to reach ultimate reality through music because, through the quasi-identity of its form and content, it seemed to derive from the eternal primordial chaos without having passed first through the ordering faculty of the human mind. It was precisely this Dionysian element in music which the romanticists loved and stressed.' It did not mean that they were obliged to retreat to some remote ivory tower, removed from the grubby tastes of the general public. What it did mean was a self-protective detachment from the worst excesses of the market-place.

This was a process accelerated by the musicians' ability to express with special force the ever-growing importance of the nation in both elite and popular discourse. The late Ernest Gellner was fond of quoting a character in James Hadley Chase's novel *No Orchids for Miss Blandish*: 'Every girl ought to have a husband – preferably her own', and then adding: 'every high culture now wants a state, and preferably its own', which can be augmented to read 'and every nation wants music – preferably its own'. It was this which lay behind the contemporary veneration of Handel in England, who was all the more English for being naturalized. Especially through his oratorios he literally gave a voice to the potent triad that supported English national identity: Protestantism, prosperity and power. When he died in 1759 at the age of seventy-four he was given a grand funeral in Westminster Abbey and a prominent permanent memorial. On the twenty-fifth anniversary of his death, a great Handel Commemoration was organized to celebrate his status as a national icon, attended by the King and Queen, prelates, peers, gentry and 'last, not least in all Matters of Entertainment and Expence, by the Majesty of the People', as a newspaper report put it. The Anglican clergyman William Coxe observed that the Commemoration was 'the most splendid tribute ever paid to posthumous fame' and 'an honour to the profession, the nation and to the Sovereign'. It was no accident that this apotheosis of the musician should have taken place in London, the city with the largest public sphere in Europe. Handel's demonstration of the ability of music to articulate national identity was imitated by the French revolutionaries with the 'Marseillaise' and other songs in a popular idiom, and subsequently by virtually every European country. This elevation of music and musicians marked a sharp change in the traditional hierarchy of artistic genres, for in the past it had been the architects and painters who had been most esteemed by patron and public alike. As the nineteenth century was to show, the inexorable march of music to cultural hegemony had begun.

PART FOUR

War and Peace

11

From the Peace of Westphalia to the Peace of Nystad
1648–1721

FEHRBELLIN

On 22 June 1675, the Elector of Brandenburg, Frederick William, arrived at Magdeburg with an army about 20,000 strong. They had travelled more than 180 miles (300 km) in less than three weeks from Franconia, where they had been billeted since the previous autumn. On arrival, Frederick William paused long enough only to have the gates of the city closed and a strict information blackout imposed. Pushing straight on across the River Elbe, he took his entire cavalry of about 7,000, together with 1,000 musketeers in carts, north towards the River Havel. There his Swedish opponents were stretched out along the east bank, blissfully unaware that they were now not alone. Arriving at Rathenow on the evening of 24 June, Frederick William sent a spy into the town to make contact with the local official, von Briest. According to Frederick the Great's account in *Memoirs to Serve as a History of the House of Brandenburg*, the enterprising councillor immediately organized a banquet for the Swedish officers. While the latter were carousing, Frederick William sent detachments across the Havel to surround the town on all sides. What then happened was graphically described by the Landgrave Frederick of Hessen-Homburg in a letter to his wife written the same day:

Beloved Fatty,
Early this morning we took the fortress of Rathenow by storm, although they put up valiant resistance; just where they were resisting best, the adjutant Canolski sneaked in unnoticed, with three hundred men; Wangelin and his mistress were taken prisoner, and so were their colonel and a major, two captains and several lieutenants, and about a hundred common soldiers; there had been about

600 of them in all, all the rest were slaughtered; we lost the honoured lieutenant-colonel Ückermann, an ensign and between forty and fifty common soldiers; it has been the finest action in the world, to win such an important place in the teeth of the whole enemy army; if God is willing, we shall soon win another action, when we have our infantry with us, we shall smite the enemy again, with God's help.

Goodbye, I cannot write any more

Until death do us part, your faithful husband and servant

Frederick Landgrave of Hessen

in the camp before Rathenow

We shall never know whether 'Fatty' referred to her husband as 'Hessen' during their more intimate moments, in the same way that Madame de Pompadour addressed Louis XV as 'France'. The stratagem of Canolski referred to was to dupe the sentries into opening one of the Rathenow gates by pretending to be a Swedish relieving force.

With the Swedish army now divided, the commander of the southern half, Waldemar, Count von Wrangel, tried to march east round the Brandenburgers to rejoin his brother at Havelberg in the north. Hot in pursuit, Frederick William was told at Nauen by prisoners of war that he had missed the Swedes by only an hour and that their intention was to cross the River Rhin at Fehrbellin. He eventually caught up with his prey at the little village of Hakenberg, a few miles short of the rather larger community that was to lend its name to the battle. With their backs against marshland and the bridge at Fehrbellin already destroyed by an advance guard of Brandenburg cavalry, the Swedes had no option but to turn and fight. As they enjoyed a numerical advantage of two to one, they should have been able at least to organize a defensive action to allow the bridge to be repaired. As it was, Frederick William's decisiveness won the day. General Derfflinger wanted to wait for the infantry and the bulk of the artillery to be brought up, but his superior insisted: 'we are so close to the enemy that he must lose his hair or feathers'. Battle was joined by the precipitate action of the Landgrave Frederick, who had been sent forward with 1,600 cavalry with orders to reconnoitre but not attack. His disobedience would have cost him his life if the ensuing battle had gone badly. In the event, the capture of the only raised ground on the battlefield by the Brandenburg dragoons allowed the artillery to be used to maximum effect. After a series of counter-attacks had been repulsed, the cavalry was unleashed to send the Swedes fleeing in disorder towards Fehrbellin. On the following day, the Swedish defeat degenerated into a rout, as the arrival of the Brandenburg infantry allowed Frederick William to launch a final assault on Fehrbellin. Over the two days of fierce fighting, the Swedes lost around 3,000, many of them butchered by peasants as they fled through the marshlands, their opponents about 500.

As battles go, Fehrbellin was small beer in numerical terms, but the consequences were far-reaching. It was not only posterity, with the benefit of hindsight, that viewed this battle as the beginning of Branden-burg's march to hegemony in Germany, for it was Frederick William's own contemporaries who now began to refer to him as 'Frederick William the Great Elector'. His great-grandson, Frederick the Great, wrote: 'he was praised by his enemies and blessed by his subjects, and his reputation dates from this great day'. In the shorter term, Fehrbellin began a series of military triumphs. What remained of the Swedish army evacuated Brandenburg and retreated into Mecklenburg, its invincible reputation shattered. Among the vultures who flapped down were the Danes, who invaded the Swedish mainland, the Duke of Brunswick, who occupied Bremen, and the Dutch, who sent a fleet to the Baltic. The Elector of Bavaria hurriedly abandoned plans to enter the war on the side of Sweden's French allies. During the next three campaigning seasons, 1676 to 1678, Frederick William kept up the pressure. Although the Swedes proved resilient, they were gradually forced out of their extensive German possessions, losing Stettin at the end of 1677 and Stralsund and the rest of Pomerania the following year. A last-gasp invasion of East Prussia towards the end of 1678 only served to empha-size the Swedish collapse, as the mere approach of Frederick William and his army caused the Swedish army to take flight and then disintegrate, as the Brandenburgers mercilessly pursued and harried it. Only 3,000 of an original invasion-force four times that number eventually struggled back to Riga in February 1679.

Yet the completeness of the military victory could not prevent a resounding diplomatic defeat. The fate of Pomerania was decided not on the battlefields of the east but around the negotiating table at Nymegen, where the great European war that had begun in 1672 with the French invasion of the Dutch Republic was being brought to a conclusion. Here it was Louis XIV who was in control. If he had not achieved total military victory, Louis had conquered more territory, had acquired more prestige and still had more men under arms than any of his numerous enemies. So he was able to pick them off one by one, neutralizing the English in May 1678, and then making peace with the Dutch on 10 August, with the Spanish on 17 September and with the Emperor Leopold I the following February. So when Frederick William returned triumphant from his campaigns, he found himself with only Denmark to support him against a rampant Louis XIV determined that his Swedish allies should regain all that they had lost. For a while it looked as though the irresistible force had struck the immoveable object, as Frederick William refused to disgorge his hard-won conquests. Only after a French army under the maréchal de Créqui had devastated his territories in the west did he very reluctantly agree to a peace that was signed at Saint-Germain on 29 June 1679. All that he had to show for five years of brilliantly successful campaigning was a modest frontier adjustment and the cession by the Swedes of their right to a share in the tolls of the Brandenburg part of Pomerania. All the rest had to be handed back.

THE HEGEMONY OF FRANCE

The Peace of Saint-Germain provides only one of many examples of what can reasonably be called the hegemony of France during the second half of the seventeenth century, 'hegemony' here being used in the dictionary sense of 'leadership, predominance, preponderance; especially the leadership or predominant authority of one state of a confederacy or union over the others'. As we have seen, out of the French monarchy's trials and tribulations of the 1640s and 1650s there developed an apparatus effective enough to make France's overwhelming demographic and material advantage tell. No other country was blessed with human material resources so deep and so varied. The power that resulted was given majestic visual expression in the Salon of War at Versailles, whose decorative scheme was begun in 1678. The room is dominated by an enormous bas-relief by Antoine Coysevox, depicting 'Louis XIV on horseback, trampling on his enemies and crowned by glory', while a smaller bas-relief below shows the muse Clio dutifully recording his exploits for posterity. On the ceiling, the central fresco by Charles Le Brun depicts 'France in arms, sitting on a cloud surrounded by victories', and holding a shield bearing the image of the Sun King. This is surrounded by four further frescoes identifying the vanquished: an impotently menacing Spain, a collapsing Dutch Republic, a grovelling Germany and a subdued spirit of civil strife. As if that were not enough, next door in the Hall of Mirrors, seventeen of the twenty-seven ceiling paintings are devoted to victories in war and diplomacy. Well might Saint-Simon lament in 1695 that this sort of gloating triumphalism had played a significant part in uniting the rest of Europe against the hegemon: 'have they not played a little part in irritating all of Europe and causing it once again to league against the person of the king and his kingdom?'

Louis XIV's power, which had allowed him to reverse the verdict of five years of warfare between Sweden and Brandenburg, rested on several foundations. One was the settlement that brought the Thirty Years War to an end in 1648. The Peace of Westphalia gave France very little in terms of territory – ten towns in Alsace and the fortress of Breisach – but a great deal in terms of security. The formal recognition of Dutch independence by Spain greatly diminished, if it did not entirely dispel, the nightmare dating back to the late fifteenth century of encirclement by Habsburg territory. The agreement with the German princes forced on the Emperor Ferdinand III meant that his father's dreams of turning the Holy Roman Empire into a monarchical state had receded half-way to oblivion. The soft centre of Europe was to remain soft and, now that both France and her Swedish satrap were guarantors of the Westphalian settlement, the way was open for future intervention in German affairs to make sure that it stayed that way. The French diplomat who remarked that the Peace of Westphalia was 'one of the finest jewels in the French crown' would have enjoyed reading Geoffrey Barraclough's later verdict: 'broken, divided, economically weak, and lacking any sense of national unity, Germany became virtually a French protectorate: even in the imperial diet at Regensburg the dominant voice was that of the French ambassador'.

As we shall see later, that contemptuous dismissal of the Holy Roman Empire is at the very least exaggerated. In the short term too, the French voice everywhere in Europe was stifled by the civil disturbances known as the *Frondes*, which began just a few months after the conclusion of the Peace of Westphalia and lasted for the best part of five years. One reason for their prolongation was their cross-fertilization with the continuing war between France and Spain, the only major international conflict not to have been resolved in 1648. Neatly encapsulating this interaction between foreign and domestic strife was the final major battle of the war, outside Dunkirk on 14 June 1658, when the French army was commanded by the vicomte de Turenne, younger son of the duc de Bouillon, and the Spanish army by the prince de Condé, Louis XIV's cousin. Both men had served on both sides during the *Frondes*. Moreover, on the French side there was a substantial force of English soldiers, sent by Lord Protector Cromwell, and on the Spanish side a substantial force of English (and Irish) soldiers, commanded by the Duke of York, brother of the exiled Charles II. The 'battle of the Dunes' ended in a decisive victory for the Anglo-French forces and paved the way for the Peace of the Pyrenees, signed in November the following year. This took France's southern frontier to the eponymous mountain range by the acquisition of Roussillon and Cerdagne, while the northern frontier was extended by the acquisition of Artois and some fortified towns in Flanders. The prospect of far greater gains in the future was also opened up by the marriage of Philip IV's daughter Maria Theresa to Louis XIV. Although she formally gave up all claims to the Spanish throne, her renunciation was conditional on a substantial dowry being paid, a remote contingency in view of endemic Spanish insolvency. Not that anyone supposed that such a pledge would be allowed to interfere with the prosecution of French interests. Back in 1646 when such a match was first mooted, Cardinal Mazarin had stated bluntly, 'once the Infanta marries His Majesty, we can hope for the succession to the Spanish thrones, whatever renunciations she has to make'.

Two years after the marriage, when Mazarin died, Louis took personal control of his country. What is perhaps most surprising about his personal rule is that he took so long to start throwing his weight about. In 1664 the Pensionary of Holland, Johan de Witt, composed a prescient memoir in which he observed that, as France now had 'a twenty-six-year-old king, vigorous of body and spirit, who knows his mind and who acts on his own authority, who possesses a kingdom populated by an extremely bellicose people and with very considerable wealth', war was inevitable, for such a king would have to 'have an extraordinary and almost miraculous moderation, if he stripped himself of the ambition which is so natural to princes . . . to extend his frontiers'. De Witt was the most important official of the most dynamic and prosperous republic in Europe, but his belief that monarchs had an inbuilt expansionist streak was well founded. As John Lynn has argued, war was not a means to an end but an essential attribute of sovereignty, to be pursued by a king for its own sake. For only success in war could bestow the '*gloire*' that formed the core of the royal and aristocratic value-system. As Cardinal de Retz put it: 'that which makes men truly great and raises them above the rest of the world is the love of *la belle gloire*'.

When Mazarin told his protégé that 'it is up to you to become the most glorious king that has ever been', he did not have social welfare or economic prosperity in mind. Louis got his first opportunity to achieve martial glory when Philip IV of Spain died. On behalf of his wife, Louis claimed parts of the Spanish Netherlands (Brabant, the marquisate of Antwerp, Limburg, Malines, Upper Gelders, Namur) and a third of Franche-Comté under the local 'law of devolution', by which the daughters of a first marriage took precedence over the sons of a subsequent union. In fact, the right of devolution was a private not a public law, as the Spanish could easily demonstrate. Undeterred, in 1667 Louis prosecuted this claim by sending an army under Turenne into the Netherlands in May and another under Condé (now back in favour) into Franche-Comté the following February. As if to emphasize the royal virility exemplified by this exercise, he himself set off for war in a carriage containing, among others, his wife and two mistresses. Military success was total, but it provoked a less agreeable diplomatic response in the shape of a hostile triple alliance of the Dutch Republic, Sweden and England. At the Peace of Aachen, signed on 2 May 1668, Franche-Comté had to be handed back, but several towns in the north were gained: Bergues, Furnes, Armentières, Oudenaarde, Courtrai, Douai, Tournai, Binche, Ath, Charleroi and – most importantly – Lille.

This was a triumph sufficient to unleash a torrent of odes, medals, paintings and statues, but the manner in which his progress had been checked clearly stuck in Louis' craw. In particular, he was outraged by the 'ingratitude, bad faith and insupportable vanity' of the Dutch, traditionally France's ally but now taking the view that a flaccid Spain was a more attractive neighbour than a rampant France: *Gallicus amicus sed non vicinus* (France as a friend but not as a neighbour). As the 'royal historiographer' Racine put it, the Dutch Republic had been 'blinded by prosperity, [and so] it failed to recognize the hand that so many times had strengthened and supported it. Leagued with the enemies of France, it preferred to give the law to Europe and prided itself on limiting the conquests of the King.' To add insult to injury, French suggestions that the two countries might partition the Spanish Netherlands went unheeded. There were also commercial considerations at stake, for Colbert believed that whereas the Dutch had 15–16,000 ships and the English had 3–4,000, the French had just 600 and that, as a result, Dutch shipping annually drained 4,000,000 *livres* from France. Dutch retaliation for the protective tariffs imposed in 1667 by banning imports of wines and spirits from France was another bone of contention.

After the slippery Charles II of England had been detached from the Triple Alliance by the secret Treaty of Dover of 1670, the eastern frontier had been secured by the occupation of the Duchy of Lorraine in 1670, and the support of two strategically important German ecclesiastical states (Cologne and Münster) had been purchased, Louis declared war on the Dutch in April 1672. At first, the enormous French army of around 130,000, led by Turenne, Condé and the duc de Luxembourg under the overall command of the King in person, carried all before it, not surprisingly as it enjoyed a numerical advantage of four to one. In twenty-two days they captured forty towns and were within striking distance of Amsterdam, defended by a garrison of just 20,000. Then things went wrong. Indeed, with the advantage of hindsight, it might even be argued that this was the turning point of the reign. For Louis now committed the same cardinal sin that was to preordain the failure of Napoleon: he forgot that war should be nothing more than the continuation of policy by other means and allowed military success to dictate his war aims. With total victory apparently certain, he dictated terms to the Dutch that were 'as brutal and uncompromisingly vindictive as any that European powers have inflicted on each other in the course of their history as nation states' (Simon Schama). They amounted to territorial, financial, economic, religious and military subjection. As a reminder of their subservient status, a Dutch delegation was to attend the King of France each year, bearing a medallion giving visual expression to their repentance, subjection and gratitude for being allowed to retain even a vestige of their independence. Just to rub it in, the cathedral of Utrecht was reconsecrated as a Catholic place of worship and the first Mass for a hundred years was celebrated with suitable triumphalist pomp.

In this crisis the Dutch leadership did not distinguish itself, although victory at sea over a combined French and English fleet on 6 June showed that their enemies were not invincible. On land, the dykes were breached to create a defensive 'water line' running from Muiden before Amsterdam to Gorcum on the River Waal. Yet the mood in the councils remained defeatist and Louis XIV might well have secured a surrender if the common people of the towns had not risen to demand resistance and the appointment of William of Orange to lead it. On 2 and 3 July, William was proclaimed Stadholder of Zealand and Holland respectively. Although the war went badly for some months to come, the corner had been turned. And not just for the Dutch Republic: for the first time, a major European state was in the hands of a ruler with the necessary intelligence, determination and resources to arrest the French juggernaut. This is one of the great might-have-beens of world history. If Jonathan Israel is correct in his view that the 'water line' could have been crossed easily for two weeks after it was flooded, because a dry summer had reduced water levels, a final French advance might well have brought the permanent subjection of the Dutch Republic, its navy, its commerce and its overseas empire.

In the event, William III was now able to exploit an increasingly favourable diplomatic situation, as the inordinate demands made Spain and the German princes wonder whether they might be next on Louis' list if he achieved total victory over the Dutch. Towards the end of 1672 Frederick William of Brandenburg (William III's uncle) and the Emperor Leopold I sent troops to the Rhine to encourage restraint. On 30 August 1673 Spain and the Austrian Habsburg Monarchy joined the Dutch and the exiled Duke of Lorraine to form a new coalition. Louis now had to disperse his war effort to the west and the south. By the end of the year, he had evacuated most of the Dutch Republic and was fighting mainly in the Spanish Netherlands, the Rhineland and Franche-Comté, not to mention the Mediterranean. In all theatres the French had the better of the argument, as was revealed by the three separate peace treaties of August 1678 to February 1679, known collectively as the Peace of Nymegen, the Peace of Saint-Germain of June 1679 and the Peace of Fontainebleau of November 1679. The Dutch did best; their return to the pre-war status quo, plus the withdrawal of the punitive French tariffs, represented a relative triumph. As we have seen, the Swedes were the luckiest, keeping most of their German possessions despite their comprehensive defeat at the hands of Brandenburg. For the same reason, the Brandenburgers were the most dissatisfied. Virtually the *status quo ante bellum* was restored in Germany, the French returning Philippsburg but gaining Freiburg in Breisgau. The Spanish did worst of all, losing Franche-Comté (and thus control of the 'Spanish Road' leading from Italy to the Netherlands), Artois and sixteen fortified towns in Flanders.

If Louis XIV had failed to humble and partition the Dutch Republic, he undoubtedly had succeeded in strengthening French security in the north and the east at the expense of the Spanish. This was not negligible. It should be remembered that Paris was only 90 miles (150 km) away from Spanish Cambrai when Louis began to roll the frontier back. There was always a defensive element in French strategy. To record the qualified success of Nymegen in this way is to imply that Louis had begun the war with a specific war aim. Yet even his friendliest biographers (François Bluche, for example) agree that the most potent motive for war with the Dutch was a simple thirst for *gloire*. Louis was quite candid when referring to his decision to go to war in 1672:

I shall not attempt to justify myself. Ambition and [the pursuit of] glory are always pardonable in a prince, and especially in a young prince so well treated by fortune as I was . . . A king need never be ashamed of seeking fame, for it is a good that must be ceaselessly and avidly desired, and which alone is better able to secure success of our aims than any other thing. Reputation is often more effective than the most powerful armies. All conquerors have gained more by reputation than by the sword.

That last epigram suggests that Louis realized that the manner in which his victories were represented was more important than the victories themselves. That is surely why so much time and money were lavished on the depiction of the Sun King as invincible warrior. Louis' official 'battle painter', Adam Frans van der Meulen, accompanied him on campaign, to make the necessary sketches that would be later worked up into paintings or cartoons for Gobelin tapestries. A particularly good example was his depiction of Louis and his army crossing the Rhine at Tolhuys on 12 June 1672, in reality an unopposed fording exercise but hyperbolically celebrated by Bossuet as 'the wonder of the century and of the life of Louis the Great'. We have already noted the offensively triumphalist iconography of Versailles, much of which derived from episodes during the Dutch War. It was not necessary to travel to the palace in person, for Louis' propagandists ensured that engravings of the frescoes, paintings and all the other martial representations were broadcast far and wide. A good example was the capture of Maastricht in 1673 which was the occasion for one of the most memorable images of the King, the painting by Pierre Mignard known simply as *Louis XIV at Maastricht*, although it also calls out to be subtitled 'hubris'. In all these images, Louis is depicted as young, strong, energetic, handsome, commanding, usually on a rearing charger he effortlessly controls. Among other media pressed into service to proclaim to the world the greatest triumph of the greatest king of the greatest nation were medals, ballets, triumphal arches, verses and plays. With casual disregard for the compromise nature of the settlement that had brought the war to an end, Corneille wrote: 'No sooner have you spoken than peace follows, convincing the whole world of your omnipotence.'

Not surprisingly, this triumphalist effusion provoked a correspondingly bitter reaction from those on the receiving end. In the Dutch Republic, propagandists turned back to the stock of images and metaphors of the eighty-year war against the Spanish to assault this new and even more dangerous enemy. Louis XIV was depicted in the pamphlets as an Old Testament tyrant such as Nebuchadnezzar, the idolatrous King of Babylon who shrieked 'Kill, kill for the hunt is good!' as the sky caught fire and the earth belched smoke. Stories of Spanish atrocities – pillaging, burning, iconoclasm, blasphemy, torture, mutilation, rape (especially of the very young and the very old), murder – were retold with French villains to form a new 'Black Legend'. However exaggerated many of these written accounts and visual illustrations may have been, the reality was ghastly enough to give them credibility and staying-power. In the same way that the demonization of the Spanish had allowed successive generations of Dutch to sustain the long war for independence, memories of the invasion and occupation of 1672–3 kept Francophobia on the boil for the next generation or so.

The same could be said of contemporary events in the Holy Roman Empire. Here, too, the same sort of image of Louis XIV as the scourge of a wrathful God was eagerly propagated, especially after Turenne had deliberately ravaged the Palatinate when retreating in 1674, to send out a warning to the other German princes. That this was not freelance work on the part of individual soldiers but was done systematically on the orders of the commanding general was thought to represent a particularly offensive new addition to the horrors of war. The outraged Elector,

Karl Ludwig, announced that he was making Louis XIV personally responsible for the wanton destruction of so many years of painstaking reconstruction after the horrors of the Thirty Years War. As in the Dutch Republic, France now replaced Spain as German enemy number one, presented as the epitome of tyranny, flourishing only because of the ruthless exploitation of its own people. Louis XIV was presented as the 'Great Turk' who allied with the infidel to subjugate God-fearing Christians in his demonic quest for a universal monarchy. All the atrocity stories broadcast by the Dutch were repeated here, probably for the same good reason. The following lively extract gives a good impression of the rhetoric employed by the pamphleteers:

The diabolic French murderers like Turkish bloodthirsty killers have tormented, tortured, martyred, maltreated, racked, stretched, afflicted, strangled, thumb-screwed, sawed, asphyxiated, roasted, fried, burned, executed, skewered, smashed, shattered, torn apart, disembowelled, broken on the wheel, quartered, wrenched apart, mutilated, hacked, shredded, sliced up, hanged, drowned, punched, shot, stabbed, and gouged the poor, wretched, innocent people of Upper and Lower Germany without discrimination.

The continuing and intensifying cult of Louis XIV as hammer of the Germans during the 1670s could only reinforce this stereotype. For example, after Turenne's victory at Türkheim in Alsace in January 1675 forced a larger imperial army to retreat to the right bank, Louis XIV had a medal struck with the legend '*Sexaginta milia Germanorum ultra Rhenum pulsa*' (60,000 Germans were beaten back over the Rhine). The representational culture unleashed during this period, which was to achieve its climax at Versailles, certainly achieved its object of enhancing Louis' *gloire*, but at the cost of giving German nationalism both a boost and a Francophobe direction. Even the Habsburg Emperor Leopold I could see that here was an asset to be enlisted. In 1673 he called on the German princes to rally 'as loyal patriots' to the defence of the Empire and 'the liberty of the German nation'.

The peace established in 1678–9 was very much a truce; indeed, to adapt Clausewitz, it might be said that for Louis peace was the continu-ation of war by other means. The means in question were 'reunions'. This process was immensely complicated and need not detain us long. Essentially, Louis claimed that if it could be established that any of his new possessions brought with them fiefs, the rulers of the latter were summoned to do homage to the new sovereign. Failure to do so was penalized by 'reunion' to France. In this manner, between 1680 and 1684 a large amount of territory on the northern and eastern frontiers was annexed, including most of Luxemburg, Alsace, Montbéliard and the Duchy of Zweibrücken. The most sensational of these seizures was the occupation in 1681 of Strassburg, where the great cathedral was returned to the Catholic Church. Needless to say, Louis' triumphal entry into his new possession was well publicized through the various media. The most elaborate engraving of the event was headed 'The king in his council arbiter of peace and war'. Indeed, it was some indication of the dominant position he enjoyed in Europe in the aftermath of the peace treaties of 1678–9 that Louis was able to achieve all this without provoking a major war. There was a scuffle with the Spanish at Luxemburg in 1681–2, but the Austrians were too preoccupied with the Turkish invasion that led to the siege of Vienna in 1683. In August 1684 Leopold I accepted a truce of thirty years at Regensburg, by which Louis XIV was to keep Strassburg and territory 'reunited' up to and including 1681.

THE DECLINE AND FALL OF
FRENCH HEGEMONY

The year 1683 represented the high-water mark of French hegemony in Europe. 'Not a dog barks in Europe unless our king says he may', was the hubristic boast of one French diplomat. There is good – if not conclusive – evidence that Louis was hoping (and expecting) to see the Turks defeat the Austrians, capture Vienna and annex the Habsburg Monarchy. That would allow him to step forward as the champion of Christendom and, more specifically, as the only possible defender of the Holy Roman Empire. He encouraged the Turks to begin their invasion, discouraged the Poles from intervening and declined a request from the Pope to rally to the Christian cause, on the grounds that crusades were no longer appropriate and that he would not risk French commercial interests in the Levant. By means of agreements with the Electors of Saxony, Bavaria, Brandenburg and Cologne, he had already paved the way for the election of himself or a member of his family as the next Holy Roman Emperor.

It was not to be. John Sobieski of Poland did bring an army south, the Turks were defeated, it was Leopold I who emerged as the champion of Christendom and the Holy Roman Empire, and it was Leopold's son Joseph who was elected 'King of the Romans', thus guaranteeing him the imperial succession. At least part of Louis' response was, first, to bully the Huguenots into converting to the True Faith and then, in 1685, to revoke the Edict of Nantes, which had permitted freedom of worship for Protestants. Despite an official ban on emigration, around 250,000 refugees then gave the lie to Louis' claim that his forcible conversion campaign had succeeded. Protestant Europe was outraged. It was not just universal monarchy that Louis now seemed to be seeking but a religious dictatorship too. What he had done to the Protestants in his own country, he might very well do to their co-religionists outside it. At the very least, it can be said that it made the task of the hawks easier in constructing an anti-French coalition. In Brandenburg, Frederick William the Great Elector abandoned his long-standing alliance with Louis. More crucially, in the Dutch Republic, William III now found it much easier to persuade the towns of Holland of the need to pursue a forward policy. The English envoy noted in October 1685, 'they beginne to exclaime very loudly here against the usage which the French Protestants have in France and a day of humiliation and fasting is to be appointed throughout these provinces by reason of that persecution'. That cry of execration could only gain in strength as around 60,000 French refugees poured into the Dutch Republic. In August 1687 the Dutch in effect abrogated the commercial clauses of the Peace of Nymegen and resumed a trade war with France. By the early summer of 1688, the French envoy was reporting that the Dutch were convinced that Louis was seeking 'to destroy their religion and especially their commerce'. On 10 June 1688 the birth of a healthy son to James II of England not only dashed the hopes of his daughter Mary and her husband William III of succeeding, it raised the awful spectre of a permanently Catholic England in alliance with an aggressively Catholic France. So when shortly afterwards 'the immortal seven' English grandees invited William over to liberate them from the Jacobite yoke, he was able to win the support of the States of Holland, without which he could have done nothing. The French threat that a Dutch landing in England would be regarded as a declaration of war was ignored.

This marked the beginning of the 'Second Hundred Years War', which was to end only on the battlefield of Waterloo 127 years later. The first phase was dominated by James's attempt to regain the throne he had abandoned so precipitately in November 1688. The decisive battle was fought in Ireland on the River Boyne north of Dublin on 12 July 1690, when William III's multinational force defeated James II's French and Irish troops. Among the casualties was Frederick Schomberg, once a marshal in the army of Louis XIV, until his refusal to abandon his Protestant faith sent him into exile and the service of William III, who made him a duke in the peerage of England. Meanwhile Louis XIV had embarked on what he hoped would be a limited war on the Rhine but which turned out to be a world war lasting nine years (and variously known as the Nine Years War, the Ten Years War, the War of the League of Augsburg or the War of the Grand Alliance).

By the late 1680s Louis had become increasingly alarmed by the continuing run of success enjoyed by the Habsburg Emperor Leopold I in the east. On 2 September 1686 Buda fell to an Austrian assault, bringing to an end 145 years of Turkish rule; on 12 August the following year, a Turkish counter-attack was crushed by an Austrian army commanded by Prince Charles of Lorraine at Mohács on the Danube, at a cost of 30,000 Turkish dead – a victory all the more sweet because it had been at the same place in 1526 that a Turkish victory had established their domination of Hungary; also in 1687 Transylvania recognized Austrian sovereignty; in 1688 the Hungarian Parliament recognized Leopold's son Joseph as his heir to the Hungarian throne; and on 6 September Belgrade fell to an imperial army commanded by the Elector of Bavaria. With Austrian influence now extended deep into the Balkans and the Turks cowed for the foreseeable future, Louis might reasonably fear that Leopold would turn west and exact retribution for the reunions. Such a step had been prepared diplomatically in 1686 by a league formed at Augsburg by Austria, Spain, Sweden and several German princes.

Louis now committed what John Lynn has called 'the great miscalculation'. He believed that, with William III preoccupied by events in England and almost certain to come to grief there, a short sharp campaign of intimidation on the Rhine would be sufficient to persuade the Emperor and the German princes to turn the truce agreed at Regensburg in 1684 into a permanent settlement. In the event, he had the worst of both worlds. His own move to the east allowed William III a free hand in the west, where far from coming to grief he had succeeded in deposing

James II by the end of the year, while his intended *Blitzkrieg* turned into a prolonged war of attrition. To follow all its twists and turns would consume easily the rest of this chapter. However, one sinister aspect of the war does need to be identified, because of its far-reaching consequences. The manifesto of 24 September 1688 announcing the French war aims stressed their moderation. All Louis was seeking, it was stated, was formal recognition of the reunions, compensation for abandoning French claims to the Palatinate (where a cadet branch of the Wittelsbachs had just succeeded) and to make a protest against the election of Joseph Clement of Bavaria as Elector of Cologne.

As far as it went, that was a not entirely disingenuous summary. French policy and strategy can indeed be described as defensive from now on. The means adopted were quite a different matter. The same brutal scorched-earth tactics adopted during the Dutch War were now employed again, but magnified to the power of ten. The two men responsible for advising Louis on military policy – the marquis de Chamlay and the marquis de Louvois – persuaded him to authorize the physical destruction of western Germany on such a scale that a buffer-zone of devastation would be created. As a bonus, it was believed, the other princes would be so intimidated as to offer no further resistance to French demands. At the very start of the campaign, Louvois instructed General Montclair to pillage Württemberg systematically, while Chamlay proposed to go further. In a letter to his colleague of 27 October 1688 he wrote: 'I would dare to propose to you something that perhaps will not be to your taste, that is the day after we take Mannheim [in the Palatinate], I would put the city to the sword and plough it under.' Mannheim was indeed levelled to the ground 'like a field' (Chamlay) the following March. When the inhabitants declined to help by destroying their own homes, peasants were conscripted to do the job for them. This was a policy dictated from the top, as Louvois revealed when he wrote to Montclair on 18 December 1688: 'His Majesty recommends you to ruin completely all the places that you leave along the upper and lower Neckar so that the enemy, finding no forage or food whatever, will not try to approach there.' The King gave his express approval to Louvois' list of communities earmarked for eradication, exempting only certain religious buildings.

This ghastly process is usually referred to as 'the devastation of the Palatinate', but in fact it embraced a much more extensive swathe of

German territory on both the left and the right banks of the Rhine. About twenty substantial towns were destroyed, including Bingen, Oppenheim, Worms and Speyer, and untold numbers of villages. Predictably, resistance and retaliation on the part of the wretched inhabitants unleashed a second, less organized but even more terrible wave of atrocities. Heidelberg had been targeted for destruction in March 1689, but the enterprising townspeople had made preparations to extinguish the flames, with the result that only about 10 per cent of the buildings were destroyed. It was to no avail, for the French came back in 1693 and this time made no mistake. They then advertised their achievement by striking a medal bearing the motto '*Heidelberga deleta*' (Heidelberg obliterated), thus paraphrasing the demand with which Cato famously ended all his speeches in the Roman senate: '*Ceterum censeo Carthaginem esse delendam*' (Furthermore it is my opinion that Carthage must be destroyed). Needless to say, those on the receiving end reciprocated with a flood of pamphlets and visual images recording French barbarism and calling for retribution. It was from this episode that German demonization of France as the 'hereditary enemy' (*Erbfeind*) dated and was utilized by Leopold I, for example in his submission to the *Reichstag* in 1689 which led the Holy Roman Empire to declare war: 'Germans, arm yourselves against France ... all Germans, Catholic and non-Catholic alike, have the most pressing reason to resist the French, as the common enemies of all Germans, with united hearts, means and weapons.' This was no longer a war against Louis XIV and his armies but a war of German against French. The diabolic image of the French was to have a long future. That the events of 1689 lingered powerfully in the German collective memory was shown by the centenary, which occurred just before the fall of the Bastille, and was commemorated by a flood of pamphlets. Travelling through the Rhineland in the mid-1770s, John Moore wrote of the devastation of the Palatinate: 'the particulars of that dismal scene have been transmitted from father to son, and are still spoke of with horror by the peasantry of this country, among whom the French nation is held in detestation to this day'.

In the war against soldiers, the French achieved the same success they enjoyed against civilians, at least on land, in the four main theatres of the Spanish Netherlands, the Rhineland, northern Italy and Catalonia. The war became a dreary succession of indecisive battles, sieges, manoeuvres and counter-manoeuvres, from whose narrative only the most dedicated military historian can derive much pleasure. It was now that the great dual necklace of fortresses around northern and eastern France constructed by Vauban proved its mettle. Suffice it to say that by 1693 it was clear that neither side would be able to land a knock-out blow and that some sort of compromise would have to be arranged by means of diplomacy. In one respect only was it decisive, but that was important enough. The battle of the Boyne really did put an end to James II's attempt to impose a Catholic and absolutist regime on England and it really did lead to the imposition of a Protestant ascendancy on Ireland and the expropriation of its Catholic landowners. Across the water in London, the English were developing the political, administrative and, above all, financial institutions that would enable them to offset their demographic weakness in dealing with the French threat, founding a National Debt in 1693 and the Bank of England in 1694. It was during these years that the foundations of the English 'military-fiscal state' were laid. With Louis XIV committed to a Jacobite restoration, Anglo-French hostility became as much an axiom of the European states-system as did Franco-Dutch and Franco-Habsburg.

In negotiating a peace, Louis was greatly assisted by the mutual jealousies and resentments that naturally flourished in the enemy 'grand coalition' after so many years of indecisive warfare. The first to crack was the Duke of Savoy, extracted from the war by the generous terms of the separate Peace of Turin of 29 August 1696. That prompted the Austrians and Spanish to conclude a truce in Italy to protect their now dangerously exposed position there, thus allowing the French to move 30,000 troops to what became the main front in the Low Countries. This additional pressure increased William III's determination to bring the war to an end. He had no qualms about abandoning his Austrian allies, for Leopold I had devoted most of his attention and resources to the war in the east against the Turks. All combatants, it need hardly be said, were by now so exhausted financially and economically that they were under pressure from their long-suffering subjects to settle. Once Louis XIV had decided to swallow the bitter pill of recognizing William III as King of England, the necessary treaties were signed at Ryswick in September and October 1697. France retained Alsace and Strassburg but was obliged to give up the rest of the 'reunited' territory and the Rhenish fortresses, to restore Lorraine to its duke and to evacuate the territory conquered in Spain. Although not obvious at the time, recognition of French sovereignty over Saint Domingue in the Caribbean opened the way for the development of the most profitable sugar-island in the region.

Did this represent a French victory? The marquis de Dangeau was in no doubt: 'The king gave peace to Europe on conditions which he wished to impose. He was the master, and all his enemies acknowledged this and could not forbear from praising and admiring his moderation.' Certainly Alsace and Strassburg were now more firmly part of France, but whether that was enough to justify nine years of ruinously expensive warfare is a different matter. Derek McKay's summary of the French response suggests that Dangeau was whistling in the dark: 'The peace was very unpopular in France, where it was difficult to understand why territory had been returned when France had not suffered military defeat.' Leopold I was disgruntled too, for he had failed to return France to the frontiers of 1648, but he could draw consolation from his continuing success in the east. On 11 September 1697, or nine days before the first of the Ryswick treaties was signed, an Austrian army of about 50,000, commanded by Prince Eugène of Savoy, defeated a Turkish army twice that number and commanded by Sultan Mustafa II in person, at Zenta in central Hungary. So crushing was the victory – one of the most complete in the history of European warfare – that it effectively ended the centuries-old struggle between Habsburg and Turk for the domination of Hungary. By the Treaty of Karlowitz of January 1699, the Turks ceded Transylvania and all of Hungary except for the Bánát of Temesvár. Symbolic of its definitive nature was the fact that this was the first time that the Turks had agreed to make a peace rather than a truce with a non-Muslim power. For the next two centuries, Hungary was to prove a thorn in Austrian flesh, but its sheer size – much greater than the present-day state of that name – ensured that the Austrian Habsburgs had finally emerged from the shadow of the senior Spanish branch to become a truly major European power in their own right.

The Nine Years War undoubtedly marked a shift by Louis XIV to a more defensive strategy. The sudden death of the arch-hawk Louvois in 1691 may have contributed to this, as may Louis' advancing age – he was now in his fifties and entering old age by contemporary standards. During the early stages of the war he still campaigned personally, as his war artists dutifully recorded, most sumptuously in Jean-Baptiste

Martin's painting of Louis directing the siege of Namur in 1692. But that proved to be his swansong, for in the following year he formally announced that he would no longer command his armies in person. Yet if his youthful thirst for *gloire* was now sated, his concern to promote the interests of the house of Bourbon burnt no less intensely. This was revealed by his actions over the long-festering but now critical question of the Spanish inheritance. Although Charles II had surprised everyone by living so long, by the late 1690s it was becoming clear that he could not last much longer. The much-simplified family tree opposite reveals the conflicting claims of French Bourbons and Austrian Habsburgs. As neither side could tolerate the entire Spanish inheritance passing to the other, and both sides were anxious to avoid yet another major war after the exertions of the Nine Years War, the obvious solution was to agree to a partition. In 1698 the first such treaty found what looked like a viable compromise by allocating the lion's share – Spain itself, the Spanish Netherlands and the colonial empire to one of Philip III's numerous great-great-grandsons, Joseph Ferdinand of Bavaria. France would get Naples, Sicily and some fortresses in Tuscany, while the Austrian Habsburgs would get the Duchy of Milan. Unfortunately, the Bavarian prince died the following year. Attempts to find another compromise foundered as the two main claimants in turn dug their heels in. First, the Austrians refused to consider an agreement reached by France and the Maritime Powers that would have given Leopold I's second son, the Archduke Charles, the whole Spanish inheritance apart from the Italian possessions, insisting that they must have everything. Under this scheme, France hoped to obtain Lorraine and Savoy in exchange for Milan and Naples. When Charles II died on 1 November 1700, it was the turn of Louis XIV to reject a compromise. Anxious above all else to preserve the territorial integrity of his empire, the late king had left a will bequeathing everything to Philip, duc d'Anjou, great-grandson of Philip IV and the younger of Louis XIV's two grandsons. It did not take Louis long to make up his mind whether to stick to the partition agreement already reached with William III or *va banque*. He was encouraged to opt for the latter by the knowledge that if it was declined for Philip, the Spanish envoy bearing the invitation had orders to go straight on to Vienna to offer it to the Austrian candidate, the Archduke Charles. News of the death of the Spanish king reached the French court on 9 November; a week later, Louis presented the duc d'Anjou to his court with the words:

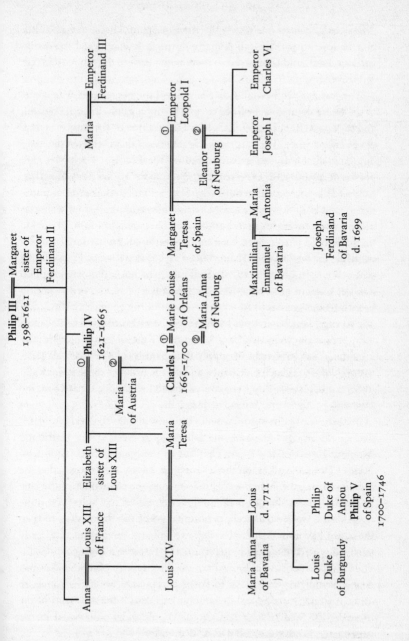

'Messsieurs, before you stands the King of Spain. His birth has called him to this crown; the whole nation wished it and asked me for it without delay, and I granted it to them with pleasure. It is the command of Heaven.'

War was not yet inevitable. In the wake of the Nine Years War, none of the weary combatants wished to sally forth yet again. In both England and the Dutch Republic, William III was restrained by constitutions that gave peace a voice. The Austrians had plenty on their hands in the east, digesting the enormous gains secured by the Peace of Karlowitz and nervously awaiting the expected reaction from the Hungarians. Whether Louis XIV's subsequent actions should be regarded as a series of blunders depends on how one assesses his overall objective. If it were simply his intention to see his grandson peacefully installed as King of Spain, then he could hardly have been more ham-fisted. He declared that in principle the new King of Spain could also become King of France if the senior Bourbon line were to fail; Spain received not just a new king but a whole team of French experts too, thus advertising its satellite status; French troops were sent to take possession of the Spanish Netherlands and to expel Dutch garrisons from the ten 'barrier fortresses' established with Spanish agreement in 1698; the new King of Spain granted the fabulously lucrative right to supply the Spanish colonies with slaves – the *asiento* – to French merchants; and on the death of ex-King James II in September 1701, Louis recognized his son as the legitimate King of England, Scotland and Ireland as James III.

By then war really was inevitable. It followed with the declaration of war on France by England, the Dutch Republic and the Habsburg Monarchy on 15 May 1702. The War of the Spanish Succession had begun. The campaigns of the 1660s and 1670s had shown that in military terms, the French were predominant; the campaigns of the late 1680s and 1690s showed that in military terms the two sides were now more or less evenly balanced; the campaigns of the 1700s showed that the allies had now achieved a decisive military advantage. This was partly due to the superior quality of the respective high commands. Following the retirement or death of the three French generals acknowledged by military historians to be of exceptional ability – Condé in 1674, Turenne in 1675 and Luxembourg in 1695 – the next generation proved to be sadly lacking in enterprise, although Villars did prove capable of effective direction, as he demonstrated in 1711–13.

On the other side, Prince Eugène for the Austrians and the Duke of Marlborough for the English demonstrated repeatedly a degree of energy, enterprise and aggression that their opponents could not match. Ironically, Eugène had first sought to enter the service of Louis XIV. It was only when he was rebuffed, in 1683, that he went to Vienna, arriving just in time to grab the opportunity offered by the Turkish siege to catch the imperial eye. Rewarded for his distinguished service with the command of a regiment of dragoons, he was a field marshal before he reached the age of thirty. His meteoric career well illustrates the cosmopolitan nature of the Habsburg army; nothing indeed could sum it up better than his trilingual signature: 'Eugenio von Savoie'. His three great building projects – the winter palace in the old city of Vienna, the summer palace 'Belvedere' just outside it and his hunting lodge Schlosshof – provide three-dimensional evidence of the riches that could be accumulated by the gifted and the lucky. It was said that Eugène had arrived in Vienna with just twenty-five *gulden* in his pocket but that when he died in 1736 he left an estate worth twenty-five million.

Not the least of Prince Eugène's merits was his ability to establish a good relationship with allied commanders, most notably the Duke of Marlborough, who deserves similar credit for his diplomatic skills. Their most important joint achievement was the victory at Blenheim on 13 August 1704, when they routed a Franco-Bavarian army, taking 14,000 prisoners, including the French commander, the comte de Tallard, and inflicting 20,000 casualties. As the first major land victory (part-) won by an English army since Agincourt nearly three centuries earlier, its importance has been consistently overrated by English historians. Yet, if it did not open to England 'the gateways of the modern world', as Marlborough's descendant Winston Churchill claimed, it did have a major impact on the course of the War of the Spanish Succession. With Hungary and Transylvania in revolt, there was every danger that the French, supported by their Bavarian allies, would be able to march on Vienna and knock the Habsburg Monarchy out of the war. Blenheim put a stop to that potentially decisive initiative, turned Bavaria into an Austrian dependency for the duration of the war and forced the French to adopt a defensive strategy.

The allied victories kept coming. On 23 May 1706 Marlborough, commanding 62,000 allied troops, defeated a slightly smaller French army under the duc de Villeroi at Ramillies, south-east of Brussels in the

Spanish Netherlands, and then spent the rest of the campaigning season seizing one city after another. On the Italian front, on 7 September Prince Eugène, with an Austro-Piedmontese army, defeated the duc d'Orléans at Turin, with the result that the French signed a convention the following March by which they withdrew from northern Italy altogether. After inconclusive campaigning in 1707, Marlborough and Eugène together inflicted another heavy defeat on the French at Oudenarde on 11 July 1708 which led to the conquest of most of the Spanish Netherlands. The last great set-piece victory was at Malplaquet near Mons on 11 September 1709, but it was bought at so great a cost that it hardly deserves to be called a victory. As the French commander, the duc de Villars, reported to his King: 'if God gives us the grace to lose another similar battle, your Majesty can count on his enemies being destroyed.'

After this Pyrrhic victory, the war became a stalemate. French forces had been ejected from northern Italy and the Spanish Netherlands, but the allies had neither the military means nor the political will to deliver a knock-out punch to metropolitan France. In Spain, the war had become a messy civil conflict between Castile, supporting Philip V, and Catalonia, Aragon and Valencia supporting the Archduke Charles, with neither side able to achieve a decisive advantage. All parties were beginning to scrape the bottom of the financial and demographic barrel, not least due to poor harvests and, in 1708–9, one of the coldest winters in recorded history. Peace negotiations were long overdue, but so much was at stake for so many that they took a long time to get going and even longer to reach a conclusion. An important step in the right direction was taken in England in the course of 1710, when Queen Anne freed herself from the 'duumvirs', the Earl of Godolphin and Marlborough (and his wife Sarah), and called an election which brought a Tory landslide. Both the dominant figures in the new administration, Robert Harley (Earl of Oxford from 1711) and Henry St John (Viscount Bolingbroke from 1712) were keen to bring the war to an end. Their enthusiasm was strengthened by the sudden death of the Emperor Joseph I in April 1711, leaving his younger brother, the Archduke Charles, as his sole heir. This created the prospect of a Habsburg hegemony in Europe no more appealing to the English than the Bourbon version against which they had been fighting for so long.

Once the English paymasters had decided to settle, their allies had no option but to follow suit, although the Austrians in particular did so very slowly and reluctantly. Indeed, they declined to sign the Peace of Utrecht when England, France, the Dutch Republic, Savoy, Philip V of Spain, Portugal and Prussia did so on 11–12 April 1713. Only after Villars had captured Landau and Freiburg in Breisgau later that year were they finally convinced that they could gain nothing further and might lose a lot if they continued the war alone. So peace was concluded between France and the Habsburg Monarchy on 7 March 1714 at Rastatt. In effect, the Utrecht–Rastatt agreements amounted to a new partition treaty. Louis XIV secured his primary war aim by gaining international recognition of his grandson Philip V as King of Spain. But there was no question of Philip or his descendants ever succeeding to the French throne. This was less academic than it might seem, for between April 1711 and March the following year, a rash of fatalities in the house of Bourbon had carried off Louis XIV's son, grandson and eldest great-grandson, leaving just one legitimate heir, born in 1710. The Treaty of Utrecht stated categorically that, if this senior line were to fail, succession would pass to the descendants of Louis XIV's brother, the duc d'Orléans. Moreover, Philip V did not succeed to the entire Spanish inheritance, only to Spain itself and its overseas possessions, and was obliged to recognize the English conquest of Gibraltar and Minorca. Louis might console himself, however, with the thought that he had retained Alsace and Strassburg and had only had to give up a few towns in Flanders, a result which compared very favourably with the catastrophe that had threatened in 1709.

For all their mutterings about English perfidy, the Habsburgs had done very well, becoming a major force in western Europe by the acquisition of the Spanish Netherlands, and the dominant force in Italy by the acquisition of the Duchy of Milan, the enclaves in Tuscany known as the 'Stato dei Presidii', and the Kingdom of Naples. Sicily and a royal title went to the Duke of Savoy. Of the two Maritime Powers, the Dutch certainly achieved a greater degree of security by the restoration of the 'barrier fortresses' in what should now be called the Austrian Netherlands. The Austrians were also obliged to confirm their adhesion to the clauses of the Peace of Westphalia relating to their new possessions, including the continued closure of the River Scheldt. This modest return for a decade of exertion was made no more palatable by the knowledge that the British (as the English should be called following the Treaty of Union with Scotland of 1707) had negotiated the peace with France without reference to their Dutch allies. Another bone of contention was their failure to win British support for their claim to Gelderland, most of which passed to Prussia. That the latter now had its feet firmly under the top table of European powers was confirmed by French recognition of its status as a kingdom and its inheritance of the principality of Neuchâtel in Switzerland.

Such was the 'rage of party' in Great Britain that the Peace of Utrecht was bound to be divisive. This was not helped by the accession of George I in August 1714, for he was known to regard the treaty as a betrayal of the Protestant cause, indeed the French were even afraid that he might abrogate it altogether. Responding to his first speech from the throne, the new Whig-dominated Parliament lamented 'the reproach brought on the nation by the unsuitable conclusion of a war, which ... was attended with such unparalleled successes'. Oxford went to the Tower and Bolingbroke went into exile. Yet not too much hindsight should have been required to see that Utrecht marked a major step on England/Great Britain's march to world-power status. Louis XIV was now obliged, not just to recognize the Protestant succession but to expel James II's son, the 'Old Pretender', from France. While France was still the dominant power in Canada, recognition of Britain's possession of the Hudson Bay territory and the return of Nova Scotia and Newfound-land had obvious political implications as well as immediate economic benefits. The same might be said of the cession of St Kitt's in the Caribbean. The acquisition of Gibraltar and Minorca made Britain the dominant power in the western Mediterranean. The transfer of the *asiento* from French to British merchants was lucrative in its own right and also symbolized the defeat of the threat that Spain would become a French satellite. On the European continent, the best possible result was achieved: Louis XIV's bid for hegemony had been finally defeated; the Low Countries were now buffered against French pressure; and a balance of power had been achieved. More generally, the peace treaties established the British objective of a continental 'balance of power' as the goal of the European states-system.

THE NORTHERN WARS

Although the dust had settled on the War of the Spanish Succession by the time Louis XIV died in 1715, the 'Great Northern War' continued to rage in the east. It was known as 'great' to distinguish it from an earlier conflict of the 1650s and 1660s involving the same combatants. At stake in both wars was the domination of the Baltic and the domination of Poland. In 1660 at the Peace of Oliva Sweden confirmed its control of a Baltic empire stretching unbroken from Danish-ruled Norway all the way round the northern, eastern and southern coasts of the Baltic as far as Riga, not to mention the better part of Pomerania obtained in 1648. Poland also survived the '*Potop*' or deluge of invasions that washed over it during the 1650s and 1660s, albeit at the cost of ceding the eastern Ukraine plus Kiev to Russia (still more commonly referred to as 'Muscovy') in 1667. Five years later, the Turks annexed that part of the western Ukraine known as Podolia. King John Sobieski's successful expedition to Vienna in 1683 to assist the defeat of the Turks was a brief flash of achievement in an otherwise gloomy period of civil strife at home and defeat abroad.

Benefiting from the Austrian defeat of the Turks in the 1690s, which among other things brought the return of Podolia in 1699, the Poles went back on to the offensive, led by their ambitious new ruler, Augustus II, Elector of Saxony, elected king in 1697. In 1700 a coalition of Poland, Denmark and Russia attacked Sweden with the intention of partitioning its Baltic empire. The Polish share was to be Livonia and its great port Riga. Not for the first, or last, time, what had been expected to be a short and easy war turned out to be long and laborious. The seventeen-year-old King of Sweden, Charles XII, turned out to be exceptionally energetic and enterprising, although much of his success was attributable to the military and financial resources stockpiled during the previous reign. With the help of an Anglo-Dutch fleet, he first knocked the Danes out of the war in just a couple of months, and then had his army shipped to the other end of the Baltic, where, although only 8,000-strong, it inflicted a crushing defeat on a Russian army three times that size at Narva on 20 November. That left Augustus II, but he proved to be a harder nut to crack, partly because he had the resources of Saxony behind him and partly because of the notoriously intractable nature of

Polish politics. It was not until 1704 that Augustus could be deposed and replaced by a Polish magnate, Stanislas Leszczyński. Two years later Charles XII took the war to Saxony, forcing on Augustus the Peace of Altranstädt, by which he accepted the loss of the Polish crown.

Unlike the war in the west, where armies traversed the same terrain in the Rhineland and Flanders again and again, the Great Northern War sprawled across thousands of miles, from Norway to the Ukraine. But the pace of events was correspondingly slow. It was not until late 1707 that the next phase began, with Charles XII's invasion of Russia with the declared intention of dethroning Tsar Peter and dividing his empire into 'petty princedoms'. For the next eighteen months, no less, the Swedish army marched slowly through Lithuania, winning the occasional engagement but finding it impossible to bring their elusive enemy to battle on the great empty plains, made all the emptier by Peter's scorched-earth tactics. In the autumn of 1708 they turned south into the Ukraine, attracted by the promise of support from the Cossack commander Ivan Mazepa and the belief that supplies would be more plentiful. After enduring the terrible winter of 1708–9, Charles XII finally got the battle he had been looking for, at Poltava on 27 June 1709. By this time his army had dwindled to somewhere between 22,000 and 28,000 and he was facing a Russian army perhaps double that. Moreover, it was a much better trained and equipped force than it had been at Narva, not least in its artillery, which 'laid our men low, as grass before a scythe', in the words of a Swedish eyewitness. The Swedish lost nearly 7,000 in dead and wounded, 2,760 were taken prisoner on the battlefield and the rest surrendered three days later. Charles XII escaped into Turkish territory, where he spent the next five years in exile.

Poltava was a truly world-historical event, much more momentous than Blenheim, for example. Peter the Great's (and his sobriquet was now merited) own comment was: 'now, with God's help, the final stone has been laid in the foundation of St Petersburg'. Leibniz summed up the response of the rest of Europe when he described the battle as a 'great revolution', adding: 'It is being said that the Tsar will be formidable to the rest of Europe, that he will be a sort of Turk of the North.' But Poltava did not bring peace. In 1711, indeed, Peter only narrowly escaped disaster at the hands of the Turks on the River Prut in Moldavia. As this location suggests, the 'Great Northern War' is something of a misnomer. This prolongation of a war the Swedes had irretrievably lost was due in part to Charles XII's refusal to face facts, more evidence, if it were needed, of the importance of the individual in determining the fate of millions. He returned to the north in 1714, but not even an amazing equestrian feat – he rode 900 miles (1,500 km) in a fortnight – could arrest the further contraction of Sweden's Baltic empire. His obduracy was strengthened by the interference of other powers once the War of the Spanish Succession had come to an end. Both George I of England, in his capacity as Elector of Hanover, and the Dutch went fishing in the troubled waters of the Baltic.

The negotiation of a peace was assisted by the shooting of Charles XII at the siege of Fredrikshald in Norway in the autumn of 1718, possibly by one of his own soldiers, but was complicated by the fierce mutual rivalry of Sweden's enemies, especially Hanover and Russia. The first treaty in what amounted to the partition of the Swedish Empire was signed in November 1719 between Sweden and Hanover, ceding the substantial principalities of Bremen and Verden to Hanover. Early the following year, peace was signed between Sweden and Prussia, giving the latter most of Pomerania, including Stettin and control of the River Oder. In July 1720 Denmark also made peace, gaining full sovereignty over the Duchy of Schleswig, previously shared with the Duke of Holstein-Gottorp. Peace with Russia proved more problematic, for the Swedes hoped for French and British-Hanoverian assistance to force Peter the Great to moderate his demands. Only when it became clear that they were on their own did the Swedes agree to settle. By the Treaty of Nystad in August 1721 Russia gained the provinces of Livonia, Estonia, Ingria and a large part of Karelia. This was not so much the 'window on the west' that Peter had long sought as a whole panorama, and confirmed that Sweden had been replaced by Russia as the dominant power in north-eastern Europe.

The collapse of Sweden and the reduction of Poland to a satellite of Russia posed a serious problem for France, which in the past had relied on a 'leap-frog' strategy of encouraging countries in the north and east to bring pressure to bear on the Habsburgs in between. It was a problem that had been exacerbated by further defeats suffered by the Turks at the hands of Prince Eugène in the war of 1716–18, which cost them the Bánát of Temesvár and Belgrade. With all three traditional French allies in a greater or lesser state of decay, adaptation was clearly called for. One way forward had been proposed by Peter the Great when he visited

Paris in 1717. He told the comte de Tessé, the government minister deputed to look after him during his stay: 'France has lost its allies in Germany; Sweden, almost destroyed, cannot be of any help to it; the power of the Emperor has grown infinitely; and I, the Tsar, come to offer myself to France to replace Sweden for her . . . I wish to guarantee your treaties; I offer you my alliance, with that of Poland . . . I see that in the future the formidable power of Austria must alarm you; put me in the place of Sweden.' Denied the advantage of hindsight, which would have allowed them to see that the seismic shift in the distribution of power in eastern Europe was going to be permanent, the French did not respond. As we shall see, this failure to adapt was to be damaging.

One aspect of the wars that came to an end between 1713 and 1721 that does not always attract the attention it deserves is the importance of simultaneous domestic conflicts. Most obviously, perhaps, the 'Second Hundred Years War' was also, at least in its early stages, a civil war in Ireland between Catholics and Protestants, and on the mainland an only slightly less virulent struggle between Jacobites and Hanoverians. Neither the battle of the Boyne nor the defeat of the Jacobite rising of 1715 put an end to this dimension, for the French were constantly looking to invade England through a Celtic backdoor, whether Irish or Scottish. At the other end of Europe, for most of the War of the Spanish Succession the Habsburgs were also fighting Hungarian and Transylvanian insurgents in a full-scale war that did not end until 1711. In the Holy Roman Empire, the Bavarians were forced to evacuate the Tyrol in 1703 after a pro-Habsburg rising, while in the following year the Habsburgs abandoned the attempt to annex Bavaria in the face of a popular rising in support of the Elector. Nor was France exempt: in March 1704, Louis XIV felt obliged to transfer his best general, the duc de Villars, from the German front to the Cévennes to put an end to the 'Camisard war' waged by Protestants there since 1702. It may be conjectured that Marlborough and Prince Eugène would have found the campaign that resulted in Blenheim much more demanding if Villars had been directing the French armies. In the north, Charles XII was constantly at risk from the sort of aristocratic coup that put an end to absolutism on his death and ushered in the 'age of freedom'. Peter the Great's campaigns against the Swedes were constantly hampered by Cossack revolts – by the Don Cossacks in 1707 or by the Ukrainian Cossacks in 1708, for example. And so on. The interdependence of foreign power and domestic stability may seem a truism but is often overlooked. It did not diminish in importance in the century that followed, as we shall see in the next two chapters.

12

From the Peace of Nystad to the French Revolutionary Wars

1721–87

DYNASTIC PROBLEMS AND THE DEVELOPMENT OF THE PENTARCHY

The treaties of the second decade of the eighteenth century might have ushered in a peace as durable as that which followed the Congress of Vienna at the very end of this period. Alas, Utrecht–Rastatt–Nystad turned out to be more like 1919 in their fragility. Even before the Great Northern War had been brought to a close, the western powers were at it again. However, this was rather different from the earlier war, for Great Britain and France were now on the same side. Just how this remarkable volte-face – in its way just as radical a diplomatic revolution as that of 1756 – came about tells us a lot about the continuing importance of dynastic, as opposed to national, considerations in determining foreign policy. Of course, Louis XIV, for example, had always been concerned to press the interest of the Bourbon family; indeed, this has been something of a leitmotiv of recent historiography. Yet he was always careful to identify family and national interests, in the same way that he identified his person with the state. Even if he never actually said 'I am the state', he did say much that amounted to the same thing. And he did write in *On the Craft of Kingship* in 1679:

Kings are often obliged to act contrary to their inclination in a way that wounds their own natural good instincts. They should like to give pleasure, and they often have to punish and ruin people to whom they are naturally well disposed. The interests of the state must come first . . . When one has the State in view, one is working for oneself. The good of the one makes the glory of the other. When the State is happy, eminent and powerful, he who is cause thereof is covered with glory, and as a consequence has a right to enjoy all that is most agreeable in life in a greater degree than his subjects, in proportion to his position and theirs.

If he conceded on his deathbed that he had liked war too much, and if even his most adulatory biographers allow that his early wars were motivated primarily by a search for personal *gloire*, his strengthening of the frontiers did benefit the whole nation.

Purely dynastic, on the other hand, was the policy adopted by Spain, which proved to be the rogue elephant of international politics. Or rather one should write: the policy adopted by the Queen of Spain, for the driving force was supplied by Elizabeth Farnese of Parma, whom Philip V had married as his second wife in 1714. Dominating her husband to a degree that very few consorts have achieved, she used the resources of her new country to carve out a patrimony for the two sons she bore – Don Carlos in 1716 and Don Philip in 1720. Neither seemed likely to succeed to the Spanish throne, as Philip V already had two surviving sons by his first marriage, so she turned her attention to Italy. In this she was aided and abetted by Giulio Alberoni, a turbulent priest originally from Piacenza who had first gone to Spain as secretary to the duc de Vendôme, had then become the envoy of the Duke of Parma and had been responsible for the selection of Elizabeth as Philip V's new wife. An adventurer by temperament, he also appears to have harboured a strong antipathy towards the Austrians, the new masters of the Italian peninsula, and so was an enthusiastic accomplice.

In 1717 the ambitious duo despatched a mighty armada (the largest Spain had assembled since Lepanto in 1571) comprising 300 ships bearing 33,000 troops and 100 pieces of artillery to conquer Sardinia from the Austrians. As the latter were preoccupied with their latest war against the Turks, this proved to be a soft target. So too did Sicily, to which the victorious Spaniards moved the following year. This violent revision of the peace settlement then attracted the hostility of the other great powers, notably France and Great Britain. Both wished to see the status quo preserved, mainly for dynastic reasons. The Regent of France, the duc d'Orléans, naturally still entertained hopes of becoming king if the infant Louis XV were to die and so, equally naturally, was at daggers drawn with Philip V, the only other possible claimant. It was in pursuit of a possible Orleanist succession that he sought a rapprochement with Britain against Spain. George I was turned into a responsive listener to his overtures by the thought that an alliance would both neutralize the threat from the Stuart pretender and secure Hanover. The latter looked especially vulnerable in 1716 when Peter the Great went into winter quarters with a large army in the Duchy of Mecklenburg, next door to Hanover. So it was that the 'natural and necessary enemies' (as the British envoy to the French court, Lord Stair, put it in 1717) sank their differences and combined to put a stop to Elizabeth Farnese's Mediterranean adventures. On 11 August 1718 a British fleet commanded by Admiral Byng destroyed the Spanish fleet off Cape Passaro, the southernmost point of Sicily, capturing seven ships of the line in open waters and then destroying the remaining seven that sought refuge inshore.

Two years of horror followed, both for the marooned Spanish army and their involuntary hosts, until the inevitable surrender was signed. Meanwhile, in 1719 a British expeditionary force landed in Galicia, taking Vigo and Pontevedra, and a French army invaded the Basque country, taking San Sebastian. Alberoni was dismissed and expelled. As John Lynch has written, 'rarely has a war been so resoundingly lost, or a fall from favourite to scapegoat been so precipitate'. France and Britain now imposed a settlement to tidy up and stabilize the Utrecht–Rastatt treaties: Philip V was to renounce any claims to Italy or the southern Netherlands, but the succession to the duchies of Parma and Tuscany was assigned to his son by Elizabeth Farnese, Don Carlos; Charles VI finally abandoned his claim to the Spanish throne but received Sicily; Victor Amadeus II of Savoy had to give up the latter but received Sardinia in exchange and kept his royal title.

The complete package took a very long time to be implemented. Even the most gifted narrator would find it difficult to construct an account of the 1720s both coherent and interesting, or indeed either of those things. Only intense concentration and repeated reference to the chronology can reveal which abortive congress was which, which short-lived league brought which powers together, who was allied to whom, who was double-crossing whom, or whatever. Suffice it to say that this was a period when Great Britain enjoyed a preponderant influence on the European states-system that was as rare as it was brief. Among other things, the British succeeded in forcing the Spanish to recognize the commercial concessions granted at Utrecht and the Austrians to abandon their project for a commercial empire based at Ostend. One lucky beneficiary of all this hustling and bustling was Elizabeth Farnese, for whom sixteen years of scheming finally paid off when Don Carlos entered Parma in March 1732 as its new duke. The Spanish troops sent to assist him were transported across the Mediterranean in British ships, as was the garrison sent to Tuscany to protect his claim against the day when the current childless Grand Duke died.

By 1730 the French had recovered sufficiently from the exertions of the War of the Spanish Succession to contemplate resuming what they believed to be their rightful position at the apex of the European states-system. Not only had Louis XV survived childhood and adolescence, he was now a hale and hearty adult, who had sired a male heir in 1729 and gave every sign of producing many more. In 1726 he had sacked the incompetent duc de Bourbon and announced – in conscious imitation of his predecessor – that he would henceforth be his own first minister, although adding almost in the same breath that Cardinal Fleury would be present at all meetings with his ministers. Fleury was indeed the new director of French policy, bringing to foreign affairs an impressive combination of subtlety and resolution. He disliked the high-handed manner in which Sir Robert Walpole had imposed a *pax britannica* on the Mediterranean in 1731 and he was also alarmed by the Austro-Russian axis: 'Russia in respect of the equilibrium of the North has mounted too high a degree of power, and its union with the House of Austria is extremely dangerous.' So he began to distance France from the entente with Britain and to resume the leap-frog relationships with Denmark, Sweden, Poland and the Ottoman Empire.

Opportunity for the French to flex their muscles came from the succession problems that were afflicting several of their rivals. In Great Britain, the Stuarts were still a threat. Peter the Great's failure to establish primogeniture destabilized the Russian state every time a Tsar or Tsarina died; indeed, his decree that the incumbent should designate the successor positively invited instability. Most importantly, Charles VI had proved unable to produce a male heir, thus calling into question the succession to the Habsburg Monarchy. To guard against its partition, in 1713 Charles issued a 'Pragmatic Sanction' proclaiming that, in the event of his dying without a male heir, all his possessions in their entirety would pass to his elder daughter, the Archduchess Maria Theresa. This was bound to be problematic, not least because it involved passing over the daughters of his predecessor, his elder brother Joseph I. Charles now set about gaining international recognition for the Pragmatic Sanction and not without success, for Spain in 1725, Bavaria, Cologne and Russia in 1726, Great Britain and the Dutch Republic in 1731, and Denmark and the Holy Roman Empire in 1732 all gave their consent. It was not given freely, of course, but had to be bought by concessions of one kind or another. Whether it was worth all the diplomatic effort involved is doubtful. It is hard to disagree with Prince Eugène's opinion that a large army and a well-stocked treasury would have been more help than these paper promises.

In the event, the next major European war was precipitated not by the Austrian but by the Polish succession. When Augustus II of Saxony-Poland died on 1 February 1733, Austria and Russia supported the election of his son as Augustus III, while France resurrected the candidature of Stanislas Leszczyński, who had been briefly King of Poland from 1704 until 1709 as the puppet of Charles XII. In the meantime, Stanislas had secured French support by the marriage of his daughter Maria to Louis XV in 1725. However, his son-in-law gave him only token support in Poland, choosing instead to campaign on the Rhine and in northern Italy. Here the French were uniformly successful and by 1735 were ready to dictate terms to the hapless Charles VI. Their diplomatic position had been greatly strengthened by an alliance with Spain, the 'First Family Compact' of 7 November 1733. The war was finally brought to an end by the Treaty of Vienna in May 1738, three years after the actual fighting had stopped. Its terms showed once again how important were dynastic considerations in determining the map of Europe. Augustus III was confirmed as King of Poland, with Stanislas Leszczyński receiving as compensation the Duchy of Lorraine, which on his death was to pass to France. The current Duke of Lorraine, Francis Stephen, who had married Charles VI's heiress Maria Theresa in 1736, was to receive Tuscany, whose last Grand Duke had died in 1737. The Habsburgs were also to take the Duchy of Parma from Don Carlos, who was to receive Naples and Sicily, where he was to become 'King of the Two Sicilies'. Although for the time being his brother Don Philip was not provided for, Elizabeth Farnese's dream of setting up her boys as independent rulers had taken another giant step forwards.

So the *pax britannica* had been short-lived. It was the French who directed the peace-making of 1735–8 and it was they who seemed in control, for they had established a solid axis with their Spanish relations and extended Bourbon control over southern Italy. Their victory over Charles VI seemed all the more complete when financial exhaustion and military failure forced him to accept French mediation to bring to an end the war he had been fighting against the Turks since 1737. By the Peace of Belgrade of September 1739, the Turks regained most of the territory they had lost in 1718, including Belgrade, although the Austrians kept the Bánát of Temesvár. In the east, however, the situation was less encouraging, for the new King of Poland, Augustus III, was under no illusions that he owed his crown to Russian and Austrian support and was also married to a Habsburg. French leap-frog diplomacy was still intact, but was going to be more problematic in the future.

Another long-term problem that loomed ever larger was colonial competition with the British. The latter had gained enough at Utrecht to whet their appetite for more. They now controlled the entire Atlantic seaboard of North America, with the exception of Spanish Florida, and also claimed a vast swathe of territory to the south of Hudson Bay. In between were the French, whose first expedition to the St Lawrence river had been made as early as 1534 and who now controlled the river valley to the Great Lakes and beyond. More recently, the French had also laid claim to territory far to the south, at the mouth of the Mississippi, naming their new possession 'Louisiana' after their king and founding New Orleans in 1718. Their obvious strategy was to link up these new acquisitions with their older colonies in the north via the Mississippi and Ohio river valleys. It was in the latter that increasingly they collided with settlers from the British seaboard colonies moving west across the Appalachians in search of new land. By the 1730s it was clear that armed struggle was inevitable.

So was a war between Britain and Spain. Spanish hostility to Britain was determined by the loss of Gibraltar and Minorca at the Peace of Utrecht in 1713 and by the obligation to allow the British to supply Spanish colonies in America with African slaves. In the course of the 1730s war became increasingly likely, as growing numbers of enterprising and unscrupulous British merchants flouted Spanish commercial restrictions. A more specific bone of contention was the formal settlement of Georgia, which intensified disputes about the northern limits of Spanish Florida. The war which eventually broke out between Britain and Spain in 1739 is known to the British as 'The War of Jenkins' Ear'. The owner of the ear was Captain Robert Jenkins of the British merchant marine, who displayed it, pickled in a jar, to a committee of the House of Commons in 1738. He claimed that it had been amputated by a sword swipe from a Spanish coastguard, who had boarded and looted his ship off Havana. No matter that the alleged incident had occurred seven years earlier, together with other horror stories it was enough to galvanize British public opinion by triggering all those powerful anti-Spanish, anti-Catholic associations, from the Inquisition to the Armada. Hispanophobia had been given a recent impetus by the assistance given by Spain to an abortive Jacobite invasion in 1719. The war-party inside and outside Parliament made the most of popular indignation, pressuring a reluctant Walpole to declare war.

At first it looked as though the hawks' optimism was well founded, for in November 1739 Admiral Vernon, commanding a fleet of just six ships, took Porto Bello on the Atlantic coast of Panama by storm. But the Royal Navy flattered to deceive. It simply did not have the resources or the bases to operate with success in the Caribbean, the Mediterranean and home waters. One dramatic exception to a depressing tale of abortive expeditions was the success in July 1742 of Captain William Martin in bringing Charles VII of Naples 'to a just sense of his errors' in assisting the Spanish campaign in northern Italy. Dropping anchor with his squadron within easy firing range of defenceless Naples, Martin gave Charles half-an-hour to withdraw from the war, which he did. As Nicholas Rodger observes, 'No more economical demonstration of naval power has ever been given.' Other British successes were few and far between, but they did include the capture of the great French fortress of Louisbourg in Canada and two small-scale victories over the French off Cape Finisterre in May and June 1747.

'The War of Jenkins' Ear' had been underway for little more than a year when it was subsumed in a much greater conflict with a much more portentous title – the War of the Austrian Succession. At one level, this represented a resumption of the centuries-old conflict between Bourbon and Habsburg for the domination of continental Europe, but it was accelerated by the fortuitous death of three monarchs in 1740. The first to go was Frederick William I of Prussia on 31 May. This brought to the throne his mercurial son as Frederick II, as complex as he was intelligent and with quite a different approach to the assertion of his kingdom's interests. Although brutal to the point of madness, Frederick William I's foreign policy was unassertive, timid even. He was restrained by three kinds of loyalty – to the Hohenzollern dynasty, to the Holy Roman Empire and its Emperor, and to his terrible Calvinist God. His son, on the other hand, never cared anything for his family, demanding that the interests of the Hohenzollern dynasty be subordinated to the interests of the Prussian state; he had only contempt for the Holy Roman Empire, despising its 'antiquated, fantastical constitution'; and he dismissed Christianity as 'an old metaphysical fiction, stuffed with fables, contradictions and absurdities: it was spawned in the fevered imagination of the Orientals, and then spread to our Europe, where some fanatics espoused it, where some intriguers pretended to be convinced by it and where some imbeciles actually believed it'.

Frederick William I had nursed many grievances against the Emperor Charles VI, who had ignored his interests in Poland in 1732, snubbed him over Mecklenburg in 1733 and disregarded his claims to the duchies of Jülich and Berg in 1738, but apart from a brief period of alienation in the mid 1720s he had remained loyal. He concentrated his demonic energies preparing for rather than waging war, leaving his son an army 81,000-strong, which in terms of quality was the best in Europe, supported by a great treasure-chest. Although he had every reason to hate his father, Frederick II hailed his achievement, writing in *The History of My Own Times*:

The fame to which the late king aspired, a fame more just than that of conquerors, was to render his country happy; to discipline his army; and to administer his finances with the wisest order, and economy. War he avoided, that he might not be disturbed in the pursuit of plans so excellent. By these means he travelled silently on towards grandeur, without awakening the envy of monarchs.

It was these tools that his son was now to put to such devastating use. There is no reason to doubt his own candid admission that, first and foremost, he wanted to make a name for himself and Prussia, to wipe the sneer off the face of George II of England, for example, who had derided Frederick William I as 'the corporal', 'king of the high-roads' and 'arch-dustman of the Holy Roman Empire'. Despite the formal elevation to royal status in 1701, Prussia was still 'a kind of hermaphrodite, rather more an electorate than a kingdom', as Frederick put it. To make its masculine identity unequivocal, he first canvassed the possibility of acquiring Jülich and Berg, but got nowhere. It was then that the grim reaper came to his assistance, carrying off the Tsarina

Anna of Russia on 23 October 1740 and Charles VI three days later. On hearing the news, Frederick resolved 'immediately' to 'reclaim' Silesia. Writing of himself in the third person, he went on: 'this project accomplished all his political views; it afforded the means of acquiring reputation, of augmenting the power of the state, and of terminating what related to the litigious succession of the Duchy of Berg'. Unmentioned but probably also important was the thought that if he did not claim Silesia, someone else would. He was especially anxious to keep it out of the hands of the Saxons, for the province would form a territorial link between the Electorate and Poland. The almost simultaneous death of the Tsarina was crucial, for on past form Russia would be disqualified from giving the Austrians any assistance by a struggle over the succession. Indeed, Frederick claimed that 'the death of Anna . . . finally determined [me] in favour of this enterprise'. He was proved to be right, for Anna was succeeded by the infant Ivan VI, who was deposed a year later in favour of Elizabeth, daughter of Peter the Great by his first marriage.

On 16 December 1740 the Prussian invasion of Silesia began. Frederick received important assistance from religion – 'that sacred prejudice among the vulgar' – for about two-thirds of the Silesians were Protestants anxious to escape the vigorous persecution inflicted on them by the late emperor. The capital, Breslau, surrendered without resistance early in January 1741. There were only just over 7,000 Austrian troops in the whole province, so it was not long before the Prussians completed their occupation. It was not until 10 April 1741 at Mollwitz that an Austrian army under General von Neipperg mounted a military challenge. This was certainly not Frederick's finest hour. With the superior Austrian cavalry apparently winning the day, he was persuaded by his second-in-command, Count Schwerin, to leave the battlefield. In his absence, Schwerin rallied the apparently defeated Prussians and won the day with the infantry. As Frederick recorded ruefully: 'it is difficult to say who committed the most faults, the King or Marshal Neipperg', giving all the credit to his army: 'the battle was one of the most memorable of the present century; because two small armies then decided the fate of Silesia, and because the troops of the King there acquired that fame of which they can never be deprived, either by time or envy'.

Mollwitz was no more decisive militarily than any other battle of the period, but it did have an extremely important political consequence.

By showing that Prussia could defend its new conquest, it encouraged the war-party in France, led by the marquis de Belle-Isle, to conclude an alliance with Frederick and join the war. Louis XV and his chief minister Fleury thought Frederick was 'a fool' and 'a cheat' respectively, but that low opinion did not stop them following the rush to settle accounts with the Habsburgs once and for all. If the war had gone according to plan and they had been in a position to dictate terms to the new ruler of the Habsburg Monarchy, the twenty-three-year-old Maria Theresa, they would have enforced a radical reconstruction of central Europe. The cunning French plan was to create four roughly equal states, by giving Lower (northern) Silesia to Prussia; Bohemia, Upper (western) Austria, the Tyrol, Breisgau and the imperial title to Bavaria; part of Lower Austria, Moravia and Upper Silesia to Saxony, and leaving the Habsburgs with just their remaining Austrian territories and Hungary. France, of course, would hold the balance between these four, and would take the Austrian Netherlands into the bargain. The Habsburg lands in Italy would be divided between Sardinia and Spain.

Unfortunately, they could neither achieve the necessary degree of military supremacy, nor could they control the mercurial Frederick. As the latter wrote, he had no intention of creating a yoke for his own neck, so instead of behaving like a loyal ally of France, he rather sought to maintain a balance between France and Austria. Intercepted despatches had revealed that the French would desert him at once if the Austrians agreed to cede Luxemburg and Brabant. So in October 1741 Frederick signed a secret truce with the Austrians at Klein-Schnellendorf, by which he ceased hostilities and the Austrians evacuated Silesia. Maria Theresa badly needed this respite, for the Saxons and the Bavarians had moved smartly to assist the French military effort. By early 1742, the Elector of Bavaria, Charles Albert, had been crowned King of Bohemia and Archduke of Austria and had also been elected Holy Roman Emperor. In the north, French diplomacy had encouraged the Swedes to attack Russia, thus ensuring that Maria Theresa could expect no help from that quarter. With a French puppet on the imperial throne – the first non-Habsburg for three centuries – and a Franco-Bavarian army occupying Prague, French influence in Europe had reached a point far in excess of anything achieved by Louis XIV.

This success was short-lived. Although Frederick briefly re-entered the fray late in 1741, he left it altogether in June 1742 after victory at

Chotusitz in May allowed him to negotiate the Treaty of Breslau, which fulfilled his essential aim – the cession of most of Silesia. Almost all of Frederick William I's treasure-chest had been spent, but, as Frederick recorded, 'provinces that do not cost more than seven or eight millions are cheaply purchased'. Meanwhile Maria Theresa had succeeded in raising sufficient troops, mainly from Hungary, to expose the French and Bavarian armies as paper tigers – 'sybarite courtiers' was Frederick's derisive comment on the quality of the French. By the end of 1742, the Austrians had regained control of Bohemia and had occupied Bavaria. The diplomatic situation was also improving, for in Britain the fall of Sir Robert Walpole in February 1742 led to the appointment of Lord Carteret as secretary of state and a much more forward policy on the continent. British subsidies financed the formation of a 'Pragmatic Army' of British, Hanoverians, Hessians and Dutch, which in June 1743, led by George II, scored a major victory over the French at Dettingen near Frankfurt am Main. This was to be the last time that a British sovereign commanded his troops in battle personally.

This revival of Austrian fortunes was not to the liking of Frederick of Prussia at all. By the beginning of 1744 he was becoming increasingly anxious that Britain and Austria might force a peace settlement on France that would cost him Silesia. He claimed to have in his possession a copy of a letter from George II to Maria Theresa stating: 'Madam, that which is good to receive is good to return.' Also alarming was the defection of Saxony to the enemy camp in December 1743, which revived the nightmare of a Saxony-Silesia-Poland bloc. On the other hand, Frederick had not rested on his laurels, using the period of peace to bring his army up to 140,000, to improve the cavalry and to form a war-chest of 6,000,000 *talers*, or enough – so he (wrongly) thought – for two campaigns. Only too well aware that his thinly resourced state must be at a disadvantage in any prolonged war of attrition, his strategy was to deliver sharp shocks to gain limited objectives in short wars. On this occasion, the war began brilliantly with the invasion of Bohemia and the capture of Prague on 16 September 1744 but nearly ended in disaster, as he greatly underestimated the dangers of a winter campaign in hostile territory. With his army melting away through desertions, he was forced to retreat back into Silesia, there to await the inevitable Austrian retribution.

The decisive battle came on 4 June 1745 at Hohenfriedberg when

Frederick's army of about 55,000 routed roughly the same number of Austrians and Saxons in four-and-a-half hours of savage fighting, capturing 7,000 and killing 4,000 for the loss of just over 1,000 Prussians. It was enough to save Silesia and to secure peace with Great Britain but not yet enough to bring the Austrians to the negotiating table. Only after further Prussian victories at Soor on 30 September, at Katholisch-Hennersdorf on 22 November and at Kesselsdorf on 15 December, which led to the capture of Dresden, could Maria Theresa be persuaded that, for the time being at least, Silesia would have to be abandoned. On Christmas Day 1745 the Peace of Dresden was signed, by which Frederick gained Silesia from Austria and a million *talers* from Saxony. In return, he recognized the election of Maria Theresa's husband Francis as Holy Roman Emperor, which had occurred without Prussian participation the previous May. Frederick returned to Berlin to a hero's welcome; it was from this time that he acquired the sobriquet 'the Great'. He himself knew that he owed his triumph more to the army created by his father than to his own leadership, although an unusually favourable international situation helped, not to mention a good slice of luck. 'From now on I shan't hurt a fly, except to defend myself', he wrote. It was to prove easier said than done.

Meanwhile, on the western front the Austrians were also finding the war heavy going. Although George II's victory at Dettingen in 1743 had expelled them from Germany, the French found campaigning in the Austrian Netherlands much more congenial. Beginning in 1744 their armies, commanded by the maréchal de Saxe, an illegitimate son of Augustus the Strong of Saxony, won one victory after another, most spectacularly at Fontenoy near Tournai on 11 May 1745 in the presence of their king. When the battle was over, Louis XV and the Dauphin made a triumphal procession from one regiment to another to be fêted. It was undoubtedly the high point of the reign. Shortly afterwards, the outbreak of the second great Jacobite rising sent most of the British contingents rushing back across the Channel. In the course of the next two campaigns Saxe's army completed the conquest of the Austrian Netherlands and set about invading the Dutch Republic.

All this success should have allowed Louis XV to impose the sort of settlement his predecessor had achieved in 1678–9. Unfortunately, in other theatres, the war did not go so well. In Italy the Austrians and their Sardinian allies had achieved total control by the end of 1746, while in Great Britain the Jacobite rising came to an abrupt end at Culloden on 16 April 1746. Overseas, the capture of Madras by the French East India Company was counterbalanced by the loss of Cape Breton Island and Louisbourg. Growing British maritime supremacy brought a blockade of French trade and fears that the French sugar-islands in the Caribbean would be conquered. With neither side able to land a knockout blow and all combatants suffering from varying degrees of financial exhaustion, a settlement was painfully worked out and eventually signed at Aachen (Aix-la-Chapelle) on 18 October 1748. Almost a decade of fighting across the globe did not yield a commensurate amount of territorial change. Outside Europe, Britain and France exchanged their Canadian and Indian conquests. On the continent, the French restored to the Dutch and the Habsburgs all their conquests in the Low Countries. Their only territorial gain was by proxy, Louis XV's son-in-law Don Philip of Spain acquiring the Italian duchies of Parma, Piacenza and Guastalla. So at long last, after thirty years of scheming, Elizabeth Farnese had succeeded in setting up her two sons by Philip V as independent sovereigns. Not surprisingly, a settlement that left France empty-handed, despite all Saxe's great victories, was deeply unpopular, '*bête comme la paix*' (as stupid as the peace) passing into everyday speech as an expressive simile.

Some consolation might be drawn from the humbling of the Habsburgs, indeed one French envoy at the Aachen peace conference proclaimed that 'France has achieved her great aim, the humiliation of the House of Austria'. Certainly Maria Theresa was very bitter about her treatment at the hands of her notional allies, the British – as bitter as her father had been back in 1714. A longer-term perspective would have yielded some consolation to soothe her wounded pride. At least she had survived the dark days of 1740–1 when the very existence of the Monarchy was in doubt. If she had had to give up Silesia to Prussia, Parma, Piacenza and Guastalla to Don Philip, and a small portion of the Duchy of Milan to Sardinia, the great bulk of her bulky empire had been preserved, despite the adverse military verdict. With her husband given international recognition as Holy Roman Emperor, there was every reason to hope that the house of Habsburg-Lorraine would be as long-lived as its predecessor.

On the other hand, it would be difficult to exaggerate the importance of the loss of Silesia to Prussia, for it was populous (about 1,000,000 inhabitants), economically advanced (a flourishing textile industry and excellent water communications) and fiscally productive (yielding about 25 per cent of the total tax revenue of the Austrian and Bohemian lands). To lose all that was bad enough, but the damage did not stop there. As Silesia had formed an integral part of the economies of the neighbouring provinces of Bohemia and Moravia, they too suffered serious and lasting damage. Moreover, the fact that this great asset had passed to Prussia doubled the depth of the wound: if all the various resources of Silesia were added together and expressed by the algebraic symbol 'x', then the power relationship between the Habsburg Monarchy and Prussia changed as a result of its transfer not by 'x' but by two times 'x', for what had been taken away from the one was added to the other. The same applied to its strategic position. In the hands of the Habsburgs, Silesia was a tongue of territory stretching into northern Germany; its loss not only reduced Habsburg influence there, it also put Prussian armies within 100 miles (160 km) of Prague and 130 miles (210 km) of Vienna. The great victor of the War of the Austrian Succession was undoubtedly Frederick the Great. He had established his supremacy over his great rivals for the domination of northern Germany – Hanover and Saxony – and was now challenging Austria for the mastery of the whole German-speaking world. As Spain and the Dutch Republic had clearly forfeited their great-power status, Prussia joined France, Great Britain, Austria and Russia to form a pentarchy of states capable of acting independently in international affairs.

THE DECLINE AND FALL OF
FRANCE: THE SEVEN YEARS WAR

In the aftermath of the Aachen treaties, both groups of allies were heartily fed up with each other. Maria Theresa deeply resented the peace that had been dictated to her by the British, who clearly welcomed the rise of Prussia as a bulwark to any renewal of a Habsburg bid for hegemony in the Holy Roman Empire. For their part, the British complained with equal venom about an Austrian greed for subsidies that was matched only by their failure to meet their commitments. On the other side, not only were the French alienated from Frederick by what they saw as his recurring acts of treachery but Louis XV also harboured a personal dislike for this agnostic upstart with a taste for making obscene jokes about the royal mistresses. For his part, Frederick was well aware that the French would have been just as negligent of his interests if it had suited them. In short, the way was clear for a fundamental reorganization of the alliance system. It probably would have happened anyway, but in the event the catalyst proved to be the reappraisal of Habsburg policy undertaken by Count Wenzel Anton von Kaunitz. He was well placed to carry out this task, for he had served in senior diplomatic positions in both Italy and the Netherlands during the 1740s and had been the Austrian representative at the Aachen peace negotiations. Direct experience had taught him that neither Italy nor the Austrian Netherlands could be defended successfully against a determined French attack and that in every other respect too their value was greatly inferior to that of the central provinces. Habsburg policy, therefore, had to be reorientated from periphery to centre and its primary objective had to become the recovery of Silesia. That was easier said than done: the pitiless exposure of the Monarchy's military weakness during the previous two decades made this an impossible task without powerful allies. But where were they to be found? The traditional alliance with the Maritime Powers had proved a broken reed, the Dutch being neutral and the British being perfidious. There was the additional consideration that Silesia was landlocked. Even if the Maritime Powers were to put their best feet forward, there was little they could do to help Austria regain the lost province. A continental target required continental allies. Russia was already an ally, indeed it had been Charles VI's anxiety to preserve that alliance that had prompted him to participate in the disastrous war against the Turks of 1737–9. There was nothing less certain than the quality and quantity of Russian assistance, however, as Maria Theresa had discovered to her cost in 1740. Immobilized by palace revolution and diverted by Swedish invasion, Russia had played no part in the Silesian wars of 1740–5. So it was essential that the Monarchy should obtain at least the benevolent neutrality (and preferably the active assistance) of the greatest continental power – France.

This was the analysis presented by Kaunitz to Maria Theresa and her senior ministers in the spring of 1749. Not surprisingly, so radical a proposal aroused scepticism, if not hostility. Nevertheless, Kaunitz was sent to France as ambassador in 1750 and allowed to make his case. What eventually turned the French into a receptive audience was the likelihood and then the certainty that war with the British would resume for the domination of North America. There the French were adopting a forward policy. In 1752 a new governor, the marquis de Duquesne, was sent to Canada, with instructions to reassert possession of the Ohio valley and thus the geographical link with Louisiana. In 1754 he built a fort at the confluence of the Allegheny and Monongahela rivers, which together form the Ohio river, and named it after himself. By that point it was only a matter of time before the undeclared war with Great Britain was made official. With Anglo-French interests also clashing with ever-increasing vehemence in the Caribbean, Africa, India and on the high seas, French policy-makers now faced a choice: should they continue to concentrate on maintaining the domination of continental Europe against the Habsburgs ('to play in Europe that superior role which suits its seniority, its dignity and its grandeur', as the abbé de Bernis complacently put it), should they switch the emphasis to challenging the British for domination of the world outside Europe, or should they try to do both? If the French chose the second of those options, it made good sense to seek a rapprochement with Austria which would neutralize Germany and the Austrian Netherlands and allow them to devote most of their resources to a naval war.

In Austria the crucial decision was taken at two meetings of the Council of State held on 19 and 21 August 1755, attended by Francis I, Maria Theresa, their senior counsellors and, of course, Kaunitz, who had become foreign minister in 1753. It was agreed to pursue an alliance with France, Russia, Sweden and Saxony that would reduce Prussia to its frontiers of pre-1618. In return for benevolent passivity, France would be rewarded by the cession of Luxemburg to Don Philip, who would of course be a French puppet. Austria would also help the French to secure the election of their candidate, the prince de Conti, as King of Poland when there was a vacancy. On 3 September 1755 the Austrian envoy Prince Starhemberg had a first meeting with the abbé de Bernis of the French foreign office at Bellevue, the château of Madame de Pompadour, Louis XV's mistress-in-chief. The French were hesitant, not surprisingly perhaps, as they were being asked to abandon nearly three centuries of hostility.

Their reservations were eventually overcome by a chapter of accidents.

The British too were anxious to neutralize continental Europe, to avoid Hanover being seized by Prussia, still of course France's ally, and then being used to offset any British colonial conquests. Unable to get any sort of undertaking from Austria, they turned instead to Russia, concluding a convention in September 1755. This had the effect of frightening Frederick the Great, who was only too pleased to sign the Convention of Westminster on 16 January 1756, guaranteeing the neutrality of Germany. As the name suggests, this was in no sense a treaty of alliance, just an ad hoc agreement with a specific purpose. However, it proved to be the last straw for the French, who now decided to drop Frederick once and for all. He had blithely supposed that France and Austria must always be enemies, forgetting – as Friedrich Meinecke pointed out – that even oil and water can mix briefly when shaken. But this left the French isolated in Europe with war looming, so at long last they accepted the Austrian offer of an alliance. Even then, the first Treaty of Versailles, signed on 1 May 1756, which effected the 'diplomatic revolution', was purely defensive: only if Austria were attacked by a third party would the French be obliged to respond.

It was now that the consequences of a British miscalculation became apparent. They had seriously underestimated the strength of anti-Prussian feeling in Russia, where both main factions shared a fierce determination to cut Frederick the Great – 'a second Charles XII' – down to size. So the Russian response to news of the Convention of Westminster was a proposal to Austria to launch a joint attack on Prussia later that year. On 22 May the Austrians informed their Russian allies that they would not be able to mobilize in time for a campaign in 1756 and so the assault on Prussia would have to wait until the following year. But the Russian mobilization had already begun and news of it reached Berlin on 17 June. Frederick the Great had not been unduly concerned by the news of the Treaty of Versailles, for that was a defensive alliance, but this latest news was really alarming: if the Russians were arming despite Frederick's agreement with Britain, then the Austrians must be at the back of it. The awful possibility of a two-front war loomed. He also knew that Saxony-Poland was part of the conspiracy and was making a major military effort to maximize its share of the spoils when Prussia was partitioned. As if that were not enough, it was very likely at least that Sweden, now firmly under the control of the French, would also join the predators. As he wrote to his sister, the

Margravine of Bayreuth: 'I am in the position of a traveller who sees himself surrounded by a bunch of rogues, who are planning to murder him and divide up the spoils among themselves.'

It had taken Frederick some time to wake up to the deadly peril he faced, but by June 1756 he was getting reliable information from a mole in the Saxon foreign office. It was from that source that he learnt of the postponement of the Austro-Russian offensive. Knowing that it would be coming the following year, he decided to launch a pre-emptive strike at Austria through Saxony, hoping to knock the Habsburgs out of the war before the Russian steamroller could be launched. On 29 August 1756 his army marched into Saxony. His intended *Blitzkrieg* was to last seven years. At first all went well. By October, the Saxon army had been forced to surrender, the King-Elector was sent off to exile in Poland along with his officers, while the 20,000-odd rank-and-file were simply incorporated into the Prussian army (from which most of them deserted as soon as possible, it need hardly be added). But although he won a hard-fought victory over the Austrians commanded by Field Marshal von Browne at Lobositz on 1 October, Frederick was not able to force them out of the war. As his strategy had failed, he appeared to have the worst of all worlds, for his attack on the Habsburg Monarchy had activated the Treaty of Versailles, obliging the French to enter the war. On the other hand, it could be said in his defence that at least he had knocked Saxony out of the war and had put a stop to any invasion of his territory down the River Elbe. In any event, by the spring of 1757 he was confronted by perhaps the most formidable coalition ever assembled in Europe: France, Austria, Russia, Spain, Sweden and most of the German princes, against which he could only count on Great Britain, Hanover, Brunswick and Hessen-Kassel. It could be said, however, that Louis XV would very likely have joined the war anyway, lured by the prospect of the Austrian Netherlands becoming a French satellite and outraged by Frederick's unprovoked assault on his close Saxon relation – for the Dauphin was married to a daughter of Frederick Augustus III. Moreover, the unfortunate Saxons now found themselves making by far the biggest single contribution to the Prussian war effort, albeit involuntarily, for they supplied about 40 per cent of the total cost of the war in levies and requisitions.

Extracting the pith from the Seven Years War is not easy, for it was both complex and fast-moving. With the advantage of hindsight, we can see that the first full year of conflict was decisive, for it was then that the great coalition had its best chance of destroying Prussia. By the autumn of 1757, indeed, it looked very much as though success was within their grasp. In the spring Frederick had launched a sudden invasion of the Habsburg Monarchy from the north, through Bohemia, hoping to eliminate at least one of his numerous enemies before the remainder could close. Catching the Austrian army off guard had been no more difficult than usual, but inflicting a mortal wound on this soft but infuriatingly slippery target had proved beyond him. Although he had managed to win a hard-fought victory outside Prague on 6 May, the city itself had held out and the ensuing siege had taken more time than he could afford. Turning east to confront a relieving force under Marshal Daun, Frederick had been defeated decisively at Kolin on 18 June and forced to retreat back north into Saxony.

Now the bad news came thick and fast. On 26 July Frederick's Hanoverian and other German allies, commanded by the Duke of Cumberland, were defeated at Hastenbeck, on the Weser near Hamelin, by the French, who then advanced eastward towards the Elbe. On 8 September they imposed the Convention of Kloster Zeven on Cumberland, which in effect neutralized his army and opened up Frederick's flank in the west. It also released the duc de Richelieu's forces to march south to join the main French army advancing from the south-west under the command of the prince de Soubise. Meanwhile in the east, a huge Russian army had invaded East Prussia, inflicting a bloody defeat on the Prussians at Grossjägersdorf on the Pregel river on 30 August. As if that were not enough, the Austrians now sent a raiding party against Berlin, briefly occupying the city on 16 October.

Frederick's only chance was to prevent the French and the Austrians uniting their armies, so he hurried west to meet the former. On 5 November he found them at Mücheln, some 15 miles (25 km) west of Leipzig. They were 30,200 strong, an imposing total swelled further by 10,900 imperial troops under the command of Prince Joseph Friedrich of Saxony-Hildburghausen. Although outnumbered almost two to one, Frederick was anxious for battle and took up position facing west between the villages of Bedra and Rossbach, about 2.5 miles (4 km) from the French camp. What followed was one of the most decisive victories against the odds in military history. Unnerved by a bombardment from the Prussian artillery cleverly positioned above them, the advancing

French and imperial infantry were demoralized further by having to watch their cavalry being routed. So when the dreaded Prussian infantry advanced into view in battle-order, there was little resistance. So quick, easy and complete was the Prussian victory that most of the French infantry never even got the chance to fire their weapons. Prussian casualties amounted to 23 officers and 518 soldiers, of whom just 3 and 162 respectively were killed. Their opponents' losses comprised 700 dead, 2,000 wounded and more than 5,000 prisoners of war, including 5 generals and 300 officers. The results were far-reaching. The suitably impressed British now repudiated the Convention of Kloster Zeven and kept their purse-strings untied for subsidies to their Prussian ally. For their part, the French withdrew into winter quarters to lick their wounds, never again to play a major part in the continental campaign. From then on, their effort was confined to north-western Germany, where the wounds inflicted at Rossbach were regularly reopened by defeats at the hands of the combined forces of Hanover and Brunswick, now under the command of Frederick's brother-in-law, Prince Ferdinand of Brunswick.

At Rossbach Frederick managed to pull one foot out of the mire, but the other was still firmly stuck. Indeed, it sank deeper when the Austrians moved into Silesia in force and took its capital, Breslau (Wrocław) on 24 November. Outnumbering the Prussians by at least two to one, they allowed themselves to be drawn out of the city to offer combat at Leuthen, to the east of the River Oder. Here, on 5 December 1757, Frederick won perhaps his greatest victory, all the more meritorious for being gained at the expense of a much better trained and motivated army than the undisciplined rabble he had blown away at Rossbach. It was after this battle that the grateful survivors sang the Lutheran hymn 'Now Thank We All Our God'. With the Austrians now forced to evacuate Silesia, including Breslau, the first year of full campaigning in what was to become the 'Seven Years War' ended very much in Prussia's favour.

For contemporaries, of the two battles it was Rossbach which made the greatest impact. Austrian defeats, after all, had scant rarity value in the history of warfare. The rout of a major French army was something else again, especially in view of the numerical superiority it had enjoyed and the upstart nature of its opponent. A story was soon making the rounds that, on the eve of the battle, French officers had observed loftily that they were doing 'great honour' to the 'margrave of Brandenburg' by condescending to fight him. So Voltaire was not alone in thinking that Rossbach represented a greater humiliation for his country than Crécy, Poitiers or Agincourt. When news of the battle reached France, it had a predictably chilling effect on a public that had never shown any enthusiasm for the war. Earlier in 1757, a government ordinance had sought to intimidate newspapers denouncing royal foreign policy by threatening the death penalty for anyone convicted of writing seditious publications. Rossbach completed the alienation. In April 1758 Bernis, now foreign minister, lamented: 'Our nation is now more hostile than ever to the war. The King of Prussia is loved here to the point of madness, because those who organize their affairs effectively are always admired. The court of Vienna is detested, because it is regarded as a bloodsucker battening on France and there is very little enthusiasm for seeing it – or indeed France – gaining territory.'

Although France was now neutralized and the German princes were losing interest, Frederick still faced a two-front war against Russia and Austria. The next four years were spent in a desperate struggle to keep them apart. In the spring of 1758, bolstered by a new subsidy treaty with the British, he tried to conquer Moravia, with a view to threatening Vienna and forcing Maria Theresa to make a separate peace. No sooner had that failed than he had to rush to the eastern front, where the Russians had conquered East Prussia and were now moving into Brandenburg proper. At Zorndorf on 25 August 1758, Frederick fought them to a standstill in one of the bloodiest encounters of the war. Then it was time to move south to face the Austrians again, but this time he suffered a heavy defeat at the hands of Marshal Daun at Hochkirch on 13–14 October. Increasingly on the defensive, as his opponents began to make their crushing numerical superiority count, in 1759 Frederick was unable to prevent the Russian and Austrian armies combining. At Kunersdorf on 12 August 1759 they won their greatest victory of the war. More than half the Prussian army was killed, wounded or taken prisoner. Frederick contemplated suicide, acutely aware that his tactical miscalculations had lost the battle. He wrote to his minister Count von Finckenstein: 'I have no more resources and, to tell the truth, I think all is lost. I shall not survive the ruin of my country. Adieu for ever.'

What then followed illustrates very well the importance of that unity of command that Napoleon was to put to such effective use. Frederick pulled himself together and, combining as he did both political and military authority, was able to stumble to safety. He was helped by the disunity of command that impeded his opponents from co-operating effectively. Count Saltykov and the Russians, who had also suffered terrible casualties, first paused to lick their wounds and then withdrew east from the Oder to the Vistula. Their Austrian allies also hesitated, worried that an army to the south, commanded by Frederick's brother, the enterprising Prince Henry, would cut their lines of communication. So they too moved back towards Saxony. Meanwhile better news had arrived from the western theatre, where on 1 August Prince Ferdinand of Brunswick, commanding an international force of British, Hanoverians, Hessians and Prussians, had defeated a Franco-Saxon army under the marquis de Contades, which led to the reconquest of Hanover, Hessen-Kassel and most of Westphalia.

Kunersdorf proved to be the best and possibly the last chance of a decisive outcome to the war. In 1760 Frederick again managed to keep his enemies at bay, defeating Daun and his Austrians at Torgau on 3 November, although the Russians did occupy Berlin briefly in October. In 1761, it was the same pattern of marches and counter-marches, with the allies never quite managing to make their numerical superiority tell. But the circle was narrowing: at the end of the campaigning season, the Austrians wintered in Silesia and the Russians in Pomerania. Very welcome relief for Frederick came on 5 January 1762, when the Tsarina Elizabeth finally succumbed to the series of strokes she had been suffering. As was well known, her successor, Peter III, greatly disapproved of Russian participation in the war and promptly put a stop to it. On 23 February he renounced all conquests and advised his allies to make peace. A formal peace with Prussia followed on 5 May. As an added if modest bonus, Sweden also made peace. On the debit side, British subsidies now ceased. Significantly, now that Frederick could concentrate exclusively on the Austrians, he began to gain the upper hand, reconquering Silesia by the end of the year. Financially exhausted and close to collapse, even Maria Theresa – 'an ambitious and vindictive enemy, who was the more dangerous because she was a woman, headlong in her opinions and implacable', as Frederick put it with his characteristic misogyny – had to accept that Silesia could not be regained. On 15 February 1763 the Peace of Hubertusburg was signed between Austria and Prussia on the basis of the *status quo ante bellum.*

Prussia's success in holding on to Silesia, and with it great-power status, was no fluke. It is sometimes suggested that it was the death of the Tsarina which saved Frederick. Indeed, he himself lent support to this myth by writing in his *History of the Seven Years War* that Prussia was on 'the brink of ruin' at the end of 1761: 'yet one woman only dies, and the nation revives; nay is sustained by that power which had been the most eager to seek her destruction ... What dependence may be placed on human affairs, if the veriest trifles can influence, can change the fate of empires? Such are the sports of fortune, who, laughing at the vain prudence of mortals, of some excites the hopes, and of others, pulls down the high-raised expectations.' But a myth it was. Contrary to popular belief, when Frederick wrote of the 'miracle of the house of Brandenburg', he was referring not to the death of Elizabeth but to the failure of the Austrians and the Russians to follow up their victory at Kunersdorf. By 1760 at the latest, all the combatants in the continental war were suffering from exhaustion. By the close of the following campaign they resembled boxers who had fought themselves to a standstill, still able to stand upright but unable to land a punch that was anything more than a gentle pat. Frederick believed that it was overconfidence which had prompted the Austrians to reduce their armed forces by 20,000 at the end of 1760: in fact it was impending bankruptcy. During the closing stages of the war, it was the Prussian administration that was raising men, money and supplies and it was the Prussian army that was winning battles.

The simultaneous war between France and Great Britain began badly for the latter, not least because of one of those recurring bouts of political instability that persuaded continental Europeans that a parliamentary constitution prevented the maximization of a country's power. In the administration led by the Duke of Newcastle ('a child driving a go-cart on the edge of a precipice', according to the Elder Pitt), the doves led by the Earl of Hardwicke struggled with the hawks led by the Duke of Cumberland. It was not until the summer of 1757 that George II grumpily allowed Pitt to take control of the war. In the meantime, the French under the marquis de Montcalm had captured a string of forts in Ontario, while in the Mediterranean Admiral John Byng's squadron had lost a sea battle against de la Galissonière and with it the island of Minorca. The luckless Byng was court-martialled and executed – 'to encourage the others', as Voltaire put it in *Candide*. Although very unlucky to lose his life, Byng's execution really did remind his fellow officers that the one cardinal sin in the Royal Navy was not to attack the enemy: 'Byng's death revived and reinforced a culture of aggressive determination which set British officers apart from their foreign contemporaries, and which in time gave them a steadily mounting psychological ascendancy' (Nicholas Rodger).

With Pitt's energy and control of Parliament allowing a massive expansion of the army to 150,000 and the navy to 400 vessels, the tide began to turn rapidly in 1758. In July Louisbourg, handed back to the French in 1748, was captured again, this time for good. In May 1759 the immensely rich sugar-island of Guadeloupe was taken. A less immediately lucrative but strategically far more important prize was the capture of Quebec on 12–13 September by an amphibious force led by General James Wolfe, mortally wounded during the engagement, as was his opponent Montcalm. Although there was more fighting to come – Montreal did not fall until 1760 – this marked the end of French Canada. Also in 1759, 'the year of victories', on 20 November Admiral Hawke, with twenty-three ships of the line, chased the comte de Conflans' fleet of twenty-one into Quiberon Bay, capturing one, sinking six and scattering the survivors up and down the coast. This marked the end of a French bid for naval domination in home waters, in preparation for an invasion. As one French captain lamented, 'the battle of the 20th has annihilated the navy and finished its plans'. With half of its budget diverted to the land war in Germany, there could be no recovery. In January 1762 Admiral Rodney captured the other great sugar-island, Martinique, commenting sourly, 'we are highly obliged to the inhabitants for their pusillanimous defence'. In the same month that Martinique fell, Spain belatedly entered the war in the 'Third Family Compact', but this only served to provide the British with more targets for their combined operations. Havana fell in August 1762 and Manila in the Philippines in October.

In India the war was fought by proxy between the French and British East India Companies. Here the French had a deserved reputation for being the more dynamic and enterprising. They had captured the great trading centre of Madras on the south-eastern coast in 1746, handing it back only at the peace of 1748 in exchange for Louisbourg. British policy received fresh impetus in the 1750s when Robert Clive, who had been in India in the service of the East India Company since 1743, pushed himself into the front ranks, combining political manipulation of the viceroys of the Mughal emperor with military action to browbeat them into submission. It was this combination which allowed him to take control of Bengal and its capital Calcutta, together with the adjoining state of Bihar, in 1757. Direct military confrontation between the two European powers began when the newly arrived comte de Lally sought to reconquer Madras in 1758. The decisive battle here was at Wandiwash near Pondicherry in January 1760, when de Lally was defeated by a British force led by Sir Eyre Coote. Pondicherry itself fell a year later after an eight-month siege, Lally's capitulation marking an end to French hopes of dominating the subcontinent. Given his lack of naval support, the unfortunate commander's task was next to impossible, but that did not prevent his execution for dereliction of duty when he returned to France. Unfortunately, his fate was too late to give courage to the French commanders in the Seven Years War.

At first sight, the degree of military supremacy achieved by the British was not reflected in the peace settlement eventually signed at Paris on 10 February 1763. This was due in part to the upheaval in domestic politics occasioned by the accession of the twenty-two-year-old George III in 1760 and his reliance on the Earl of Bute. If Pitt had still been in office, much harsher terms would at least have been demanded. But Pitt had resigned in October 1761 over the refusal of his king and colleagues to agree to a pre-emptive declaration of war on Spain. The French retrieved their West Indian islands, some of their Indian enclaves (Chandarnagar in Bengal, Yanam, Pondicherry and Karaikal on the Coromandel coast, and Mahe on the Malabar coast) and their fishing rights in Newfoundland and on the St Lawrence. On the other hand, their presence in North America vanished, their Canadian possessions going to Britain and Louisiana to Spain as an inducement to make peace. The implications of this loss were not apparent at the time. In Voltaire's *Candide*, immediately before the passage referred to earlier, the eponymous hero discusses Anglo-French relations with the philosopher Martin:

'You are acquainted with England,' said Candide; 'are they as great fools in that country as in France?'

'Yes, but in a different manner,' answered Martin. 'You know that these two nations are at war about a few acres of barren land in the neighbourhood of Canada, and that they have expended much greater sums in the contest than all

Canada is worth. To say exactly whether there are a greater number fit to be inhabitants of a madhouse in the one country than the other, exceeds the limits of my imperfect capacity; I know in general that the people we are going to visit are of a very dark and gloomy disposition.'

Voltaire can hardly be criticized for failing to spot that Wolfe's victory at Quebec and the subsequent expulsion of the French from North America was a world-historical moment. Indeed, if he had lived long enough to witness the granting of American independence in 1783, he might well have gone further and concluded that the British victory in the region had brought them only a poisoned chalice. Only gradually did it become apparent that it also marked the beginning of a process that made English the world language in place of French. In view of their defeats at the hands of the British, the Spanish did well to win Louisiana, not to be confused with the present-day state of that name, for it embraced the entire drainage basin of the Mississippi, from the Rockies to the Appalachians, and so complemented nicely the existing 'Vice-Royalty of New Spain', which included, in theory if not in actual settlement, everything to the west of Louisiana, from the Gulf of Mexico to the North Pacific coast. Spain returned Minorca to the British but regained Havana and Manila.

It was France that had been damaged most by the war. By seeking to wage war simultaneously at sea, in the colonies and on the continent, France was defeated in all three theatres. Unwilling to recognize that their country was suffering from a decline that was both absolute and relative, most French people looked for a scapegoat and found it in the diplomatic revolution of 1756. If it had performed its main task and had allowed the French to defeat the British, it might have proved acceptable to French public opinion – although even then many would have preferred a continental to a 'blue water' strategy. But, as we have seen, in fact it was followed by disaster. From the rich stock of contemporary accounts, the following brief extracts will give some impression of the depth and bitterness of feeling it aroused: 'The treaties of 1756 and 1757 with Austria were regarded by all the powers as the disgrace of Louis XV ... These treaties transformed France from being a great and victorious power into being the auxiliary of Austria' (Soulavie); 'The Seven Years War was a war undertaken without reason, conducted without skill and ended without success ... The wound which the defeats inflicted on national pride was sharp and deep ... The French monarchy ceased to be a first-rank power ... The sense of shame evoked by this royal lethargy, this political decadence, this monarchical degradation, both wounded and aroused French national pride. From one end of the kingdom to the other, to oppose the Court became a point of honour' (Ségur); 'The treaty of 1756 demonstrated the first law of international relations – that there can never be a sincere and solid alliance between natural enemies. This treaty was monstrous in principle and disastrous for France in practice' (Peyssonnel).

THE FIRST PARTITION OF POLAND AND THE EASTERN QUESTION

The Peace of Paris of 1763 did not put an end to France's suffering. In the following year, the collapse of her once-dominant influence in eastern Europe was revealed by the election of Stanislas Poniatowski as King of Poland. By imposing her own candidate – and superannuated lover to boot – the new Tsarina, Catherine II, demonstrated that Poland was now a Russian satellite. When the last vacancy had occurred, in 1733, France had gone to war to try to impose her candidate. She had failed in that object, but at least had gained Lorraine from the resulting imbroglio. In 1764 she stood helplessly by. Worse was to come, when in 1768 a great upheaval in the affairs of eastern Europe began. The outbreak of war between the Ottoman Empire and Russia in that year posed the great 'Eastern Question'. The scale of Russian victories, which included the astonishing feat of sending a fleet from the Baltic to the Mediterranean to destroy the Turkish fleet at Chesme in June 1770 (a battle to compare with Lepanto or Trafalgar), raised the possibility of a Russian conquest of the entire Balkan peninsula and the expulsion of the Turks from Europe.

That was a threat the Habsburg Monarchy was obliged to counter, especially because Russia had been allied to Prussia since 1764. With every Turkish defeat, military intervention to prevent a total Russian victory became more likely. To no one was this more unwelcome than Frederick the Great, who had no real interests at stake in the Balkans and was still preoccupied with the reconstruction of Prussia after the devastation of the Seven Years War. It was to avoid being dragged into the war that he came up with what Hamish Scott has called his 'diplomatic masterpiece': the partition of Poland. Joseph II later rightly claimed that it had all been the work of Frederick, who had set about his task 'with as much shrewdness as malice'. The proposal was that the three great powers of eastern Europe should settle their differences at the expense of Poland. In return for moderating her demands against the Turks, Catherine the Great of Russia was awarded a huge slice (35,500 square miles/92,000 km^2) of eastern Poland. Frederick took little more than a third of that, but for him it was very much a question of 'never mind the width – feel the quality'. By linking East Prussia to the central core of the Hohenzollern territories and by gaining control of the lower reaches of the River Vistula, this acquisition brought to Prussia colossal strategic, economic and fiscal advantages.

For the Austrians, the advantages were much less obvious. The province of Galicia which they obtained was four times as populous (2,650,000 inhabitants) as the Prussian share and almost as extensive (32,000 square miles/83,000 km^2) as the Russian, but its value was certainly far less than that of either. Strategically, Galicia was a liability, lying to the north of the Carpathian mountains, which formed the natural frontier of the Monarchy in the north-east. Economically and socially, it was primitive, destined to become a burden rather than an asset. When he visited Galicia for the last time, in 1787, Joseph II lamented that not all the vast sums lavished on the province had made it a going concern. Politically, it posed a constant irredentist threat, as the Polish nobles there never ceased to look for an opportunity to achieve reunion with Poland. As the events of 1789–90 were to show, this could prove to be a serious problem. In any case, it is difficult to appreciate what benefit accrued to the Habsburgs from the expropriation of a Catholic country which was traditionally pro-Austrian, mainly to the benefit of Protestant Prussia and Orthodox Russia. It had been a Polish king – John Sobieski – who had led the army which relieved the siege of Vienna in 1683. Yet Maria Theresa and Joseph II, who were joint rulers of the Habsburg Monarchy after the death of Francis I in 1765, really had little choice once Frederick had won Russian approval. As Joseph II complained, the only way to stop the partition was to go to war – a war that Austria could not afford and was unlikely to win. Frederick's comment on Maria Theresa's reluctant acceptance of what she called 'this cruel necessity' was characteristically pithy: 'she wept – but she took'.

The partition of Poland did not end the war. On the contrary, the Russians continued to push the Turks back across the Danube and beyond, so that when peace was concluded by the Treaty of Kutchuk-Kainardji on 10 July 1774, they made important gains around the northern coastline of the Black Sea: to the east control of the entrance to the Sea of Azov, to the west control of the Bug and Dniester estuaries, and in between 'independence' for the Khanate of the Crimea from the Turks. Freedom of navigation and the right to send merchant ships into the Mediterranean meant that the Black Sea was no longer a Turkish lake. No one supposed for a moment that this represented the limit of Catherine's ambitions in the region. Turkish vulnerability was further exposed when in 1775 Joseph II exploited their helpless state to annex the Bukovina on the grounds that it had been a dependency of Podolia, which the Habsburg Monarchy had acquired in the partition of 1772. The massive readjustment of the frontiers of eastern Europe that took place between 1772 and 1775 dramatized a long-gestating eastward shift in the location of power. It was the first major war in the region to be concluded without any kind of western mediation. The latter was eagerly offered, but just as enthusiastically rejected. Well might the British and French rage against the criminal rapacity of 'the barbarians, the Goths and Vandals of Germany and Russia' (David Hume) or 'the most impudent association of robbers that ever existed' (Horace Walpole), but there was nothing to be done. At least Walpole could console himself with the thought that it was France that had suffered the greatest loss of prestige, crowing about 'the affronts offered to France, where this partition treaty was not even notified. How that formidable monarchy is fallen, debased.'

In fact, France had a lot further to fall before it reached rock bottom. As its star waned in central and eastern Europe, so did that of Russia rise. The next episode to illustrate this seismic shift was the Bavarian succession crisis, occasioned by the death of the Elector Maximilian III without an heir. There was no shortage of other Wittelsbach lines, but the incorrigibly acquisitive Joseph II took the opportunity to negotiate a settlement with the next in line – Karl Theodor of the Palatinate – which ceded a substantial part of Bavaria to the Habsburg Monarchy in return for uncontested succession to the remainder. Frederick the Great's prompt response was to invade the Habsburg Monarchy through Bohemia. The war which followed – the grandly named War of the

Bavarian Succession – is always described in dismissive or derisive terms, and understandably so. As the last major encounter between two great powers before the French Revolution, it was appropriately the apotheosis (or perhaps caricature) of old regime warfare. There were no battles, only sedate manoeuvring at a safe distance, while diplomats hurried to find a peaceful solution. The result of their labours was the Treaty of Teschen of 13 May 1779, which was undeniably a defeat for Joseph. All Bavaria had to be abandoned, apart from a modest strip of territory on the River Inn. It also represented the climax of Russian influence in Europe. For the first – but not the last – time, Russia had a decisive say in German affairs. Not only had the Russian threat to enter the war on the Prussian side played a major part in forcing Joseph to abandon his forward position, it was Russian mediation which shaped the peace settlement. The reward of Catherine the Great was to become a guarantor of the status quo in the Holy Roman Empire and thus to achieve parity with France. For the next decade, Russia took the place of France as the dominant foreign power in the Holy Roman Empire.

Meanwhile Catherine was also extending her influence over the notionally independent Khanate of the Crimea. She was helped by the fact that Joseph II had learnt the wrong lesson from the events of the 1770s. What (relative) success in the first partition of Poland and (relative) failure in the Bavarian imbroglio seemed to show was that it was Russia which held the ring. When the Russians co-operated, the Habsburg Monarchy had acquired the huge province of Galicia; when the Russians opposed, the Habsburg Monarchy had been obliged to hand back Bavaria. As Joseph told his man in St Petersburg: 'Russia with us, and we with Russia, can achieve anything we like, but without each other we find it very difficult to achieve anything important and worthwhile.' Those words were written less than a month after his mother's death in November 1780. While Maria Theresa was alive, there was no prospect of an Austro-Russian alliance, although Joseph had been allowed to visit Catherine earlier in the year. Now that the apron-strings had been severed, Joseph could initiate a closer relationship. Catherine felt the same way, for it was Austrian opposition that had prevented her exploiting fully Russian military superiority at Kutchuk-Kainardji. By 1780 she had been persuaded by Potemkin, her ambitious ex-lover, favourite adviser and probably husband too, that the best way forward was in alliance with the Austrians. With both partners so eager, consummation was not long delayed: by an exchange of letters in May 1781 the alliance was sealed.

Its first fruit was Catherine's famous 'Greek plan'. This envisaged nothing less than a partition of the European provinces of the Ottoman Empire. Russia's own share would be relatively modest – more land to the north-west of the Black Sea and 'one or two islands' in the Aegean. However, Catherine also proposed the creation of two new states, both of which would be Russian puppets: a new 'Kingdom of Dacia', comprising Moldavia, Wallachia and Bessarabia, to be ruled by a Christian prince (Potemkin was not mentioned by name but he was the most likely candidate); and a new Byzantine kingdom with its capital at Constantinople, to be ruled by the younger of Catherine's two grandsons, who had been equipped at birth with the auspicious name of Constantine (the elder was christened 'Alexander'). This kind of armchair map-making was not taken seriously in Vienna, but they had to sit up and take notice when, shortly afterwards, Catherine struck again, not with a project this time but with action. In April 1783 she announced the annexation of the Crimea, an acquisition of colossal strategic and economic importance for Russia.

No other power was more outraged by this latest act of international piracy than was France. For two-and-a-half centuries the French had regarded the Ottoman Turks as their natural allies in eastern Europe and were horrified by the Russian seizure, which seemed to herald the end of Turkey as a European power. When launching a diplomatic offensive to induce the Russians to withdraw, they demanded – and had every right to expect – the assistance of their Austrian ally, and so were suitably angry when they discovered that not only was Joseph doing everything he could to support Catherine but that he had been secretly allied to her for the past two years. No wonder that the unfortunate Austrian ambassador at Versailles, Count Mercy, was subjected to several 'lively exchanges' with the French foreign minister, Vergennes.

The French initiative was toothless, for the good reason that they had just concluded a ruinously expensive war with the British over America. The architect of this policy was the comte de Vergennes, who became foreign minister on the accession of Louis XVI in 1774. He was a career diplomat with wide and deep experience of foreign courts, especially Stockholm and Constantinople. The central conviction of his policy was that the power of the two countries on the periphery of Europe – Great

Britain and Russia – had increased, was increasing and ought to be diminished. As a member of Louis XV's clandestine parallel diplomatic service, the 'secret du roi', since 1755, he was concerned to defend France's traditional allies – Sweden, Poland and the Turks – against the new breed of predators, led by Russia. In the immediate aftermath of the first partition of Poland, there was nothing he could do in the east, but the growing conflict between the British and the American colonists was an opportunity not to be missed.

When that became a shooting war in 1775, Vergennes began to edge towards participation. Money and weapons were sent to the colonists and the navy was got ready for war. The trigger proved to be the surrender of General Burgoyne to the Americans at Saratoga in October 1777, which made it clear that there would be no quick and easy victory for the colonial power, as had seemed likely the previous year. Years later, after the outbreak of revolution in France, Louis XVI expressed regret that he had authorized the American intervention, complaining that his advisers had taken advantage of his youth, but all the evidence suggests that his approval was given willingly at every stage. Without the assistance of the French, not to mention the Spanish, who joined the war in April 1779, and the Dutch, against whom the British launched a pre-emptive declaration of war in December 1780, the Americans could not have won their independence in the manner and at the speed they did. The decisive battle took place in the autumn of 1781 at Yorktown in Virginia, where a British army of 8,000 under Lord Cornwallis found itself trapped on a peninsula between a Franco-American army commanded by George Washington and the marquis de Lafayette and a French fleet of twenty-four ships of the line commanded by the comte de Grasse. When news of the inevitable surrender reached London, the reaction of the prime minister, Lord North, was, 'Oh God, it is all over.' Although George III was determined to fight on, on 27 February 1782 a motion in the House of Commons calling for an end to war passed by 234 votes to 215.

Yet it proved to be darkest before dawn, for if 1781 had been the worst year for the British, 1782 was the best. On land, they held on to New York and Charleston and went on the offensive in Connecticut. At sea, the combined forces of Rodney and Hood won a crushing victory over the French at the Saintes on 12 April, winning back control of the Caribbean and the Atlantic. A triumphant Rodney told the Earl of

Sandwich, the secretary of state, that the French fleet had been given 'such a blow as they will not recover', concluding: 'you may now despise all your enemies'. In the autumn of the same year, the final attempt by the combined Franco-Spanish force to capture Gibraltar failed comprehensively. In India, de Bussy's major expedition to achieve French control of the subcontinent, as part of a grand scheme for national economic regeneration, was delayed by British naval action and did not get going until after the peace preliminaries had been signed. Fortified by these successes, early in 1783 the British delegation were able to negotiate a peace better than anything that could have been imagined even a year earlier. The independence of the United States of America was recognized, of course, but Canada, Newfoundland and Nova Scotia remained British. The French secured Tobago, a share in the Newfoundland fishing and a few trading stations in Senegal and India. The Spanish did rather better, regaining Minorca and Florida. In India the *status quo ante bellum* was restored.

The most common reaction in Europe to the news of this Treaty of Versailles, however, was the exclamation: '*Finis Britanniae!*' Crippled by debt, immobilized by political instability, with not a single ally to offset the abundance of declared enemies and hostile neutrals, it is not surprising that most contemporaries believed that the loss of America would prove to be only the first stage of a total dissolution of the British Empire. Joseph II, for example, offered the following analysis of Britain's international standing in the spring of 1783: 'England's position beggars description; it shows just how much this nation has degenerated. If France had gained from the late war nothing beyond her demonstration to the rest of Europe of the desperate and pitiable condition of her rival she would have still achieved a great deal.' Nor was he untypical in his belief that Great Britain had suffered more than France in a financial sense, that her material base was more brittle, that her power, prestige and prosperity had all been shattered and that the all-pervading corruption of her public life would impede if not prevent her recovery.

In France, a more jaundiced – and more realistic – view was taken. Yet again, it seemed, the French had expended their blood and their gold for the sake of third parties, in this case the Americans and the Spanish. Vergennes complained: 'Neither the expulsion of the English commissioner resident at Dunkirk nor a little less restriction in fishing off Newfoundland, nor the recovery of the little islands of Dominique and Grenada were great enough reasons for us to go to war and yet these are the only objectives which the King would propose after a successful war.' Moreover, if the British had failed to win the war, they certainly won the peace. As Jonathan Dull concluded, 'ironically, the European state that ultimately benefited most from the war was Britain'. Every passing year confirmed the accuracy of the prediction of Shelburne, one of the British opponents of the war, that loss of political control over America would be followed by a compensating expansion of commerce between the two nations. British trade with the rest of the world, especially with the East, quickly regained, and then exceeded, pre-war levels. Industrial output grew in proportion, benefiting especially from the resumption of uninterrupted supplies of raw cotton. In Europe, the impotence of France revealed by Catherine the Great's unilateral seizure of the Crimea was compounded by a similar inability to control events in the Holy Roman Empire when Joseph II renewed his Bavarian project in 1784. It was not France but Prussia which intervened to form a league of German princes to defend imperial integrity (or so Frederick the Great claimed).

'THE SINEWS OF WAR ARE INFINITE MONEY' – WAR AND PUBLIC FINANCE

In August 1786, little more than three years after the end of the war, the minister in charge of French finance (the 'controller-general'), Charles Alexandre de Calonne, was obliged to inform Louis XVI that his monarchy was facing bankruptcy. The terminal agony of the old regime was beginning. In the same year, the British prime minister, William Pitt 'the Younger', introduced his 'Sinking Fund' for the progressive reduction of the National Debt and was counting on an annual surplus of £1,000,000 to finance it. In the view of his most penetrating and succinct biographer, Lord Rosebery, it was this achievement of Pitt 'which his contemporaries regarded as his highest claim to renown'. These contrasting fortunes exemplify an underlying national difference. The 'Second Hundred Years War' was not won at Quebec or Trafalgar or Waterloo, or even on the playing fields of Eton, but in the Treasury in London.

To understand why British public finance was so resilient and that of their hereditary enemy so fragile, we need to go back to the different ways in which the two countries emerged from their simultaneous political crises in the middle decades of the seventeenth century. As we have seen, the *Frondes* of 1648–53 ended with a victory for the monarch, now 'absolute' at least in the sense that he exercised undisputed control over public finance. In England a more prolonged struggle produced a very different result, the 'Glorious Revolution' of 1688 confirming that here public finance would be subject to regular parliamentary control. Indeed, this was seen as the central achievement of the constitutional conflicts: 'The Security of our Liberties are [*sic*] not in the Laws but by the Purse being in the Hands of the People' (Carteret). That might seem to make the raising of revenue more difficult, but in reality it proved to be the decisive step towards the maximization of the country's resources. Just because the political nation controlled public expenditure, and just because so many of its members benefited from it, Parliament was that much more willing to give its consent to new or enhanced taxation. Moreover, in its direct form, it was taxation that was both national and local: national in the sense that it was applied equally to all parts of the kingdom, local in the sense that it was assessed and collected by representatives of those who paid it – the landowners.

Direct taxation – the land tax and taxes on other forms of personal wealth or indicators of status – was not, however, the most important form of revenue, for it yielded only about 42 per cent of the total during the Nine Years War, 38 per cent during the War of the Spanish Succession, and went on falling to 18 per cent in the 1780s. Even the introduction of income tax in 1799 did not raise the share to more than a third. The main burden was carried by customs and excise. After 1660 responsibility for their collection was shifted from private tax-farmers to public officials, bureaucratically controlled. The advantages of indirect taxation were twofold. First, although it bore heaviest on the poor, because it was a tax on consumption, the fact that it was paid at the port of entry or in the manufactory and was incorporated in the price meant that it was relatively 'invisible'. Secondly, it allowed the state to benefit from the expansion of commerce, through customs dues, and from the consumer revolution of the eighteenth century, as excisable commodities such as tea, sugar and tobacco passed down the social scale to become the necessities of the masses. The apparatus grew in proportion. Between the beginning of the Nine Years War and the end of the War of the Spanish Succession, the number of customs officials rose by a third and that of excisemen by almost half. By the end of the War of American Independence there were 14,000 revenue officers of all kinds, or in other words there were more tax-collectors than Anglican clergymen. This expansion was accompanied by professionalization. As John Brewer has written: 'Dependent upon a complex system of measurement and book-keeping, organised as a rigorous hierarchy based on experience and ability, and subject to strict discipline from its central office, the English Excise more closely approximated to Max Weber's idea of bureaucracy than any other government agency in eighteenth-century Europe.'

In short, the fiscal system that evolved in England in the course of the seventeenth century was universal, bureaucratic, professional and public. Consequently, it enjoyed the vital ingredient of trust. As Martin Daunton has written, 'Taxpayers have little incentive to pay their taxes in the absence of a high degree of "trust" that other taxpayers and the government are fulfilling their obligations.' The parliamentary dimension also ensured that any war that was fought was a national war. William III may have taken England into his long-standing struggle with Louis XIV but only national interest could keep her there. Sir John Wildman told the House of Commons in 1689: 'We talk not here for the King, but for the Kingdom. I have heard a doctrine preached here, "Take Care we be not principals in the war against France", but against King James we are principals in that war to defend us from popery and slavery.' By supporting the Jacobite pretenders and persecuting Protestants, the ham-fisted Louis XIV ensured that the full weight of the English state would be deployed against him.

Relatively modest in 1689, it quickly became formidable. In the 1680s total annual expenditure was less than £2,000,000; during the 1690s it more than doubled; in the War of the Spanish Succession it reached almost £8,000,000. By that time public spending accounted for 7 per cent of the Gross National Product, having doubled since 1688, and it went on increasing steadily to 16 per cent in 1783 and 27 per cent in 1801. Revenue also increased, from £4,300,000 in 1700 to £31,600,000 in 1800, but could not keep up. The only way in which the 'military-fiscal state' could be kept afloat was through borrowing. During the Nine Years War the government raised £16,000,000 in loans; during the

Revolutionary-Napoleonic Wars it raised £440,000,000. State indebtedness grew from £14,200,000 in 1700 to £456,000,000 in 1800. How was this possible? Much of the answer is revealed by what the debt was called, for this was a 'public' or 'national' debt. In 1712 Robert Walpole wrote a pamphlet, part of whose long title ran 'The debts of the nation stated and consider'd in four papers: viz: I. A letter to a friend concerning the publick debts'. The money was lent not to the monarch but to the nation, with the nation's entire landed wealth, represented in Parliament, as the collateral. The relationship was institutionalized in 1694, when an Act of Parliament created the Bank of England, with the immediate task of lending the government £1,200,000. As the annual interest of 8 per cent enjoyed a parliamentary guarantee, the money was raised in less than two weeks from 1,268 investors, including the King himself. By the middle of the next century, the number of investors had risen to 60,000 and reached half a million by 1815, including many from continental Europe. As Adam Smith observed in *The Wealth of Nations*: 'The stability of the Bank of England is equal to that of the British government. All that it has advanced to the public must be lost before its creditors can sustain any loss ... It acts, not only as an ordinary bank, but as a great engine of state.' This was a far cry from the bad old days when lending to a king was more an act of faith than a rational investment. It was an arrangement that allowed successive British governments to raise all the money they needed at acceptable rates of interest. As confidence in the system grew, so did the rates of interest decline – from 6–8 per cent during the War of the Spanish Succession to half that during the Seven Years War. The dazzling success of the latter could only encourage further investment, for success bred success. As the Reverend Benjamin Newton put it in a sermon in 1758: 'The event of war is now generally decided by Profusion of Treasure; the richest Nation is victorious and the Glorious Wreath of Triumph is become the Price of Gold.'

This combination of taxes and loans allowed the British state to double, double and double again its war effort. When the Second Hundred Years War began, the Royal Navy had 173 ships of all types; when it ended it had almost 1,000. The average annual size of the British army during the Nine Years War was just over 75,000; by 1809 it exceeded 300,000. Although manpower figures are notoriously unreliable – especially when they appear to be most precise – one good estimate is that in 1809 there were more than three-quarters of a million men serving in the various branches of the armed forces. The participation ratio of men of military age went from 1 in 16 in the 1740s to 1 in 8 in the American War to 1 in 5 or 6 in the Napoleonic Wars.

One significant advantage enjoyed by the English as they set about creating their military-fiscal state in the second half of the seventeenth century was that they were relative newcomers. Despite occasional excitements such as the defeat of the Spanish Armada, they had mainly kept out of continental wars and had engaged in only limited colonial expansion. All their rivals, however, had been hard at it for a century or more, most intensely during the Thirty Years War. As a result, all kinds of concessions had been extracted by particular interest groups that were to prove very resistant to change. Of no country was this more true than France, whose existential struggle with the Spanish Habsburgs had begun in 1494 with Charles VIII's invasion of Italy and was still underway when this period began. Living from hand to mouth, lurching from one short-term expedient to another, no French king had been able to create an orderly public fiscal system.

Characteristic was the importance of 'venality' or the sale of offices, described by its most authoritative historian (William Doyle) as 'a French addiction'. First marketed in 1522, venal offices were to enjoy a long future because of their popularity with both parties. For the invariably hard-pressed monarch they offered cash in hand; for the purchaser they brought income, privileges (such as exemption from billeting and certain forms of taxation) and, above all, status, in some cases even nobility. And in return for an annual fee (the *Paulette*) they were hereditary. A survey carried out by Colbert in 1664 revealed that there were 45,780 venal judicial and financial offices with a market value of 420,000,000 *livres*, yielding 2,000,000 for the *Paulette* but costing 8,000,000 in payments to the holders as fees (*gages*). Colbert's attempt to reduce venality, the last made under the old regime, was frustrated by Louis XIV's need for money for his war against the Dutch. By 1789, Doyle has estimated, there were 70,000 venal offices, or in other words about 1 per cent of the male population held venal office, so perhaps as many as a third of a million people depended on them. Louis XV's last controller-general, Terray, cheerfully conceded that venality was unjust but the King had to find his money somewhere.

That such a colossal amount of capital should be tied up in

non-productive investment undoubtedly had a serious long-term effect on the French economy, but that is not our concern here. What it meant in financial terms was that reform was rendered next-to-impossible. In the neat formulation of J. F. Bosher, the French kings could not change the system because it was not theirs to change. He also identified a related fundamental failing – the collection of taxes in old regime France was not a public responsibility. It was a commercial exercise, undertaken by private entrepreneurs who contracted with the Crown to collect certain taxes in certain parts of the country in return for an advance payment. The result was private affluence but public squalor. In the course of the Nine Years War, the contracts concluded between the King and the financiers yielded 329,000,000 *livres* for the former but a profit of 107,000,000 *livres* for the latter. No wonder that the price of a position as 'Farmer General' in Louis XVI's reign was 1,500,000 *livres*, for the post gained admission to a company of the forty richest men in the kingdom, the collectors of indirect taxes. There was a yawning gulf between what their minions collected and what finally found its way into the royal purse. In fact, that should read 'royal purses', for there was no central treasury commanding an oversight over revenue and expenditure. Most of the taxes collected went straight to royal payers of one kind or another. There was no hierarchy of officials and no bureaucratic controls. As a result, not even the first step towards financial rationality – a budget – could be taken. Significantly, in 1784 the *Encyclopédie méthodique* defined 'budget' as an English parliamentary term. So whereas the *Compte rendu au roi* (account rendered to the king) presented by the controller-general Necker in 1781 claimed that there was a substantial surplus, his successor Calonne claimed that there was in fact a large deficit – and neither of them could be proved right or wrong. Nor was there a state bank. As J. H. Shennan put it, Louis XIV had preferred to melt down his plate and silver furniture rather than copy the banking practices of his enemies. The ignominious failure of John Law's national bank scheme in 1720, defeated by the financiers who stood to lose most from a nationalization of the country's finances, meant there would be no further attempt under the old regime.

It used to be asserted that the financial problems of the French monarchy stemmed from privilege, from the fiscal exemptions enjoyed by the first and second estates. It was certainly the case that the Church only made a modest voluntary contribution (*don gratuit*) and that nobles were exempt from the main form of direct taxation, the *taille*. However, it has been argued by John McManners that the Church was in fact paying 'a fair share' by the 1780s, and by Betty Behrens that French nobles actually paid more in direct taxation than did their British equivalents, thanks to the imposition of a universal tax of 5 per cent (hence the name *vingtième*) on landed income in 1749, which was doubled in 1756 and trebled in 1782. However well-founded objectively, these counter-arguments seem rather beside the point, for what mattered most was how the situation was perceived by the great mass of taxpayers. As the flood of pamphlets and prints in the late 1780s revealed, there was a widespread belief that the two privileged estates were carried on the backs of commoners.

Consequently, the trust referred to earlier could never inform the French fiscal system. This was all the more serious because of its heavy reliance on direct taxation, which supplied between 48 and 61 per cent of revenue, depending on the period. Unlike in England where the land tax was relatively invisible because it was paid by landowners, who then passed it on to their tenants in the form of increased rents, in France the *taille* was collected directly from the cultivators. As Peter Mathias and Patrick O'Brien have observed in a comparative study of the two countries' fiscal arrangements: 'Had England been a nation of peasant proprietors paying *taille*, collected by tax officials, the direct presence of the tax-gatherer would have created an identifiable object of hostility for most families in rural society, creating and focussing political hostility.' Even the main form of indirect taxation in France – the salt-tax (*gabelle*) – involved a highly visible direct confrontation between individual household and tax-collector.

Trust was also eroded by the widespread variations in types and rates of taxation. As we have seen, just for the *gabelle* France was divided into six different regions with six different rates of duty. Quite apart from fostering a sense of injustice, this incoherence made domestic smuggling a major industry, involving hundreds of thousands of people – perhaps even as many as a million, according to Olwen Hufton. Exemplifying the absurdity was the enterprising use of dogs by smugglers to carry salt across the frontier from Brittany into Maine. The same discrepancies could be found in direct taxation too: in the *élection* of Sens, for example, the ratio of tax to income varied from as little as 5 per cent to as much as 53 per cent with no account taken of the value of the land or its actual productivity. Less quantifiable was the belief that public revenue was being squandered on the private delights of the court. Although in fact accounting for only 6–7 per cent of total expenditure, the well-publicized extravagance of, first, Louis XV and his harem of mistresses, and then of Queen Marie Antoinette, did nothing to encourage ordinary taxpayers. Even as bankruptcy threatened in the 1780s, Calonne was engaging in some high-profile expenditure, including the purchase of the palaces of Rambouillet for 18,000,000 *livres* from the duc de Penthièvre and Saint-Cloud for the Queen, together with a shower of pensions to the latter's friends at court. On 19 July 1787 Louis XVI's ministers tried to give him an elementary and belated lesson on the relationship between public relations and fiscal success:

Duc de Nivernais: 'We cannot hide from Your Majesty that the public mood is bad.' 'But why so?' said the King. No one replied. [Then the marquis de Castries] spoke up: 'Because the public views with some surprise, Sire, that whilst Your Majesty prepares to place new burdens of taxation on the people, he makes no personal sacrifice; that whereas he has made a bad choice [Calonne] which has led to the ruin of his finances, he seems disposed to make his subjects pay the price; that his building continues on all sides etc.

In François Furet's shrewd judgement: 'Had he attacked court wastefulness, Louis XVI would not have saved his finances, but he might perhaps have salvaged even more – the monarchy itself.'

By this time it was too late. Even the limited success achieved in the American War had been won at too high a price, for it had cost as much as the three previous wars put together. The cost of the navy alone had quadrupled between 1778 and 1783. By the time Calonne went to see Louis XVI on 20 August 1786, the situation was desperate. The monarchy was now locked in an interest-deficit spiral – the cost of servicing the debt had grown to the point at which it could only be financed by raising more loans, which increased the deficit, which increased the need for more loans, and so on. The annual deficit was thought to be currently in excess of 100,000,000 *livres* on what was thought to be a total revenue of about 475,000,000 *livres* – although no one could be sure about any of these figures – and debt repayments were consuming about half of income. The third *vingtième*, which had been imposed with so much difficulty in 1782, was due to expire in 1787. Over a billion *livres* had been borrowed since 1776 and loans could now be filled only slowly and at escalating rates of interest. It was now that the earlier failure to make the King's finances public and national proved to be so damaging, for it was a credit strike that forced a reluctant Louis XVI to convene the Estates General.

HOW TO WIN ON LAND UNDER THE OLD REGIME

In military terms, the three great success stories of the period 1648–1815 were France 1648–97 and 1792–1809, Russia and Prussia. The Habsburg Monarchy had its moments, especially against the Turks before 1718, but suffered too many defeats to merit inclusion in the first division. This pattern would suggest that force of numbers was the key to success.

Table 9. Armed forces numbers during the eighteenth century

Country	Early eighteenth century	Mid-eighteenth century	Late eighteenth century
Sweden	110,000 (1709)	53,000	45,000
Russia	220,000 (1715)	284,000 (1756)	300,000 (1796)
Habsburg	100,000 (1705)	157,000 (1756)	312,000 (1786)
Monarchy	140,000 (1710)	202,000 (1760)	
Prussia	40,000 (1713)	260,000 (1760)	194,000 (1786)
Savoy-Piedmont	25,000 (1710)	30,000 (1738)	?
France	400,000 (1703)	280,000 (1760)	180,000 (1789)
	300,000 (1710)		800,000 (1794)
Spain	40,000 (1703)	56,000 (1759)	140,000 (1800)
Great Britain	93,000 (1702–13)	62,000 (1739–48)	108,000 (1775–83)
& Ireland	139,000 (1710)	93,000 (1756–63)	800,000 (1803)

Source: Walter Demel, *Europäische Geschichte des 18. Jahrhunderts* (Stuttgart, 2000)

Apparent confirmation is provided by Table 10, which demonstrates the intensification of warfare during this period.

Table 10. The intensification of warfare 1648–1815

	I	II	III	IV
Thirty Years War	19,000	1.5	1	.24
Wars of Louis XIV	40,000	1.75	7	
Spanish Succession				.77
Wars of Frederick II	47,000	3.33	12	
Austrian Succession				.82
Seven Years War				1.40
Wars of French Revolution	45,000	–	12	
First Coalition				3.0
Second Coalition				4.4
Wars of Napoleon	84,000	3.5	37	
Third Coalition				7.0
War of 1809				11.0
War of 1812				5.2

Explanation of columns:

I. Average size of an army in battle, computed where possible from thirty battles in each war

II. Number of cannon per 1,000 combatants

III. Number of battles in which the opposing armies together numbered over 100,000

IV. Average number of battles per month

Source: R. R. Palmer, 'Frederick the Great, Guibert, Bülow: from dynastic to national war', in Peter Paret (ed.), *Makers of Modern Strategy from Machiavelli to the Nuclear Age* (Oxford, 1986)

Yet even a moment's consideration reveals the inadequacies of a quantitative approach. The colossal armies raised by Louis XIV at the beginning of the War of the Spanish Succession could not prevent Blenheim, Ramillies, Oudenarde and Malplaquet. Nor could the colossal numerical advantage enjoyed by the coalition of France, the Habsburg Monarchy, Russia, most of the Holy Roman Empire and Sweden in the Seven Years War be translated into military victory over Great Britain and Prussia. The population of Great Britain and Ireland was less than half that of France alone in 1756, that of Prussia less than one-eighth.

Demographically, Prussia was a third-rate state when Frederick came to the throne in 1740, yet by the Treaty of Hubertusburg in 1763 it had its feet firmly thrust under the top table of European powers. Expressed most generally, the key to its success lay in the ability to maximize resources. By seizing Silesia in 1740 and then defending it successfully against all comers, Frederick demonstrated that the God of battles was not always on the side of the big battalions. With understandable complacency he observed in the preface to *The History of My Own Times*: 'I have seen small states able to maintain themselves against the greatest monarchies, when these states possessed industry and great order in their affairs. I find that large empires, fertile in abuses, are full of confusion, and only are sustained by their vast resources, and the intrinsic weight of the body.' As a summary of the relationship between Prussia and the Habsburg Monarchy, that is hard to beat.

Frederick's three predecessors had created a system which rested most fundamentally on close co-operation between ruler and landed nobility. By an agreement concluded in 1653 (the '*Rezess*'), the latter were given freehold tenure to their land (previously held as revocable fiefs), the sole right to own estates, and control over their peasants. But in return they guaranteed the taxation necessary for a standing army. There was still a long way to go. The Brandenburg army remained relatively small (about 30,000 in 1688), dependent on foreign subsidy and unable to translate military performance into territorial gain. As we have seen in the previous chapter, most of the land won in the successful war against Sweden between 1675 and 1679, for example, which had taken the Brandenburgers to the gates of Riga, had to be handed back at the Peace of Saint-Germain at the behest of Louis XIV. A deeply resentful Great Elector had a memorial struck, inscribed with a menacing motto from Virgil: '*exorietur aliquis nostris ex ossibus ultor*' (may an avenger one day arise from our bones). The instrument of his vindictive appeal was to be his great-grandson.

However, it was his grandson, Frederick William I, who forged the instrument. Part of his achievement was social. By a deft combination of stick and carrot, he made the Junkers synonymous with the Prussian officer corps. If young nobles were backward in coming forward to volunteer their services, military search parties were sent to fetch them to the cadet schools. Their training was brutal, their early years in the service penurious, but once they rose to the rank of captain and the command of a company, their financial future was assured. By the time Frederick II came to the throne, the Junkers were well and truly assimilated. Part of Frederick William's achievement was cultural. Through personal example he raised the status of the military profession to paramountcy. Never seen out of uniform (of the Potsdam Life Guards) after 1725, he led from the front – and made his children follow suit. Part of his achievement was military. Although a timid player on the international stage, it was he who supervised the transformation of the Prussian army into the most effective in Europe, as his son duly acknowledged:

The late king, by his infinite assiduity, introduced a wonderful order and discipline among his troops, and a precision before unknown in Europe in their motions and manœuvres. The Prussian battalion became a walking battery; the quickness of the charging of which tripled the fire, and made a Prussian equivalent to three adversaries ... So many new inventions transformed the army into a moving fortress, the access to which was formidable and murderous.

Moreover, quality was matched by depth. In 1740 Frederick William left an army with a peacetime strength of 81,000, raised from a population of just 2,240,000. This was made possible by the 'canton system' introduced in 1732–3, by which each regiment was allocated a district for recruiting. This marked an important step towards the nationalization of recruiting, for all able-bodied males were obliged to register on the cantonal rolls. If the quota could not be met by volunteers, then conscripts were taken. This limited form of conscription was not a Prussian invention – Sweden had been the first country to organize a permanent army based on the principle of military obligation – but it was the Prussians who pushed it furthest. Ludwig Dehio estimated that if the Habsburg Monarchy had made the same effort in 1740, it would have had an army 600,000 strong instead of the 108,000 actually available.

Frederick William also completed the process of social militarization which turned Prussia into 'not a country that has an army but an army which has a country, in which, as it were, it is just billeted', as his son's adjutant von Berenhorst famously put it. This primacy of military policy influenced government policy in every sector. The main beneficiaries, of course, were the nobles, who provided the officers. They were given control over their serfs, control of local government, a monopoly of landed estates (so that a Junker could sell his land only to another member of his class), cheap mortgages and subsidies to repair war damage. They also benefited from the preferential treatment given to rural interests when fiscal and commercial policy was determined. The peasantry benefited too, for a regular supply of cannon fodder depended on a tolerable level of existence. In Otto Büsch's lapidary formulation: 'Protection of peasants was protection of soldiers.'

It was a militarism which suffused all sections of society. The Junkers and Frederick went through fire together in the three Silesian wars between 1740 and 1763, in which some 1,550 officers perished. If the von Kleist clan was exceptional in losing twenty-three members, including the distinguished poet Ewald, who died of wounds sustained at Kunersdorf, there were several other families whose losses reached double figures. As the wars had ended with Prussia achieving great-power status against all the odds, the survivors were now tied to their warlord like blood-brothers: as one of his veterans put it, it was a relationship similar to that between a Scottish chieftain and his clan. Frederick set the example of selfless devotion to duty from the top, sharing the privations of his soldiers and requiring the same from the members of the royal family, all of whom were obliged to serve. As Count Lehndorff boasted: 'what distinguishes our army from all others is that our princes are soldiers themselves, and put up with the same hardships as the private soldiers'. It was a pride shared by civilians, as a French visitor found: 'The common people in Prussia, even the lowest classes, are permeated with a militarist spirit, they speak with respect of their army, recite the names of their generals, recount their victories and the times they have covered themselves in glory.' It was an impression confirmed by Prussians themselves, such as Ludwig Tieck, who recorded in his memoirs:

The King appeared at military parades and reviews as the great war-lord, who had defied successfully a coalition of all the rest of Europe, and at the head of his troops, who had won so many battles. When there were military exercises or manœuvres outside one of Berlin's city-gates, perhaps the Hallesche or the Prenzlauer, then the citizens of Berlin streamed out in their hordes to watch. My father [a master-carpenter] also used to take his children out to these popular festivals. Among the pressing crowds of people, the rush of artillery-trains and the marching soldiers, we were prepared to put up with the dust and the heat for hours on end, just to catch sight of our old Fritz surrounded by his dazzling retinue of celebrated generals.

In short, in the course of the eighteenth century, Prussia became a militarized state supported by a militarized society. There was nothing inevitable about this. In 1610 the Berlin militia had refused to obey their ruler's order to conduct a training exercise on the unheroic if sensible grounds that firing their muskets with real gunpowder would frighten their pregnant wives. It was the Thirty Years War which taught the hard lesson that on the north German plain, with its lack of natural frontiers, it was a case of 'eat or be eaten'. It was the series of remarkable Hohenzollern rulers who made sure that it was the Prussians rather than the Poles, Danes, Swedes, Saxons, Bavarians or Austrians who called for the menu. Indeed, even as the eighteenth century began, it was by no means certain that it would be the new kingdom of Prussia rather than some other German principality which would pose the main challenge to the Habsburgs in the Holy Roman Empire, as the following table of troop strengths and their subsequent development, compiled by Peter Wilson, eloquently shows.

Table 11. Militarization of the German principalities during the 1700s

Year	Austria	Prussia	Saxony	Hanover	Palatinate	Bavaria
1702	110,000	26,000	27,000	18,900	18,000	27,000
1726	113,000	60,000	15,000	14,400	8,540	4,950
1740	108,000	81,000	27,800	22,700	8,390	9,000
1744	161,000	132,000	37,400	26,100	10,730	19,500
1750	150,000	137,000	22,320	21,940	12,500	6,290
1762	150,000	120,000	12,100	37,000	12,000	9,000
1765	170,000	150,000	26,620	14,000	11,590	8,000
1777	220,000	158,000	21,840	21,000	11,850	8,000
1790	281,850	200,000	22,900	17,000	15,750*	

* The Elector of Bavaria inherited the Palatinate at the end of December 1777

But militarization was not enough. Prussia could not achieve great-power status until two adjacent rivals had been eliminated: Sweden and Poland. As we know what was to come, it is easy to forget what power the Swedes had wielded in the seventeenth century, when their empire covered much of the Baltic littoral and their armies ranged deep into southern Germany. It is even easier to underestimate the potential of

Poland, given its disappearance from the map of Europe as a result of the three partitions of 1772, 1793 and 1795. Yet the combination of the Electorate of Saxony with the Commonwealth of Poland-Lithuania in 1697 as a result of the election of Frederick Augustus of the former as king of the latter seemed to offer the perfect match of quality with quantity: Saxony was perhaps the most advanced state in central Europe, while the Polish lands stretched from the Baltic almost to the Black Sea. In both cases it was Russia which did Prussia's work for her. By reducing Sweden to a third-rate power and taking control of Poland in the Great Northern War (1700–21), Peter the Great inadvertently also created the conditions for the rise of Prussia.

As we saw earlier in this chapter, the international situation was unusually favourable for Frederick in the autumn of 1740, but nothing could have been achieved without his intervention. No war has just 'happened' simply because the circumstances have been favourable. An act of the will is always required. Frederick's decision to use the weapon his father had forged and to exploit the wonderfully favourable international situation was, if not *the* primal deed, then certainly a world-historical moment, after which nothing would be the same again. In his treatise *General Principles of Warfare*, written in 1746 and based on his experiences during the first two Silesian wars, Frederick impressed on his commanders the need for 'short and lively' wars. As he enjoyed the priceless advantage of unity of command, being both commander-in-chief and head of state, he was able to seek a decisive engagement with a speed denied to his enemies. He also brought to combat a 'do-or-die' nihilism which gave Prussian warfare a desperate aggression which more than compensated for any numerical deficiency. On 20 September 1806, just three weeks before Napoleon's crushing victories at Jena and Auerstadt, Captain Carl von Clausewitz wrote to his fiancée that when Frederick marched off after Rossbach to confront the Austrians at Leuthen in December 1757, 'he was just like a desperate gambler, determined to lose everything or to win everything back, and (if only our statesmen would take note of this fact!) it is in this passionate courage which is nothing more than the instinct of a mighty character that the highest form of military wisdom resides'. In fact, Frederick's aggression diminished as the war progressed and the numerical superiority of his numerous enemies began to tell. Rushing from one front to the next in a desperate effort to keep them at bay, he sought to fight a war of position, of manoeuvre and small gains. As he himself put it: 'to win a battle means to compel your opponent to yield you his position' and so 'to gain many small successes means gradually to heap up a treasure'. During the campaigns of 1761 and 1762, and again during the War of the Bavarian Succession of 1778, he fought no major battle. As we shall see in the next chapter, the French revolutionaries and Napoleon took a great deal from Frederick the Great's military practice and consequently conquered most of Europe; but they fatally failed to imitate his subordination of military means to political ends.

13

The Wars of the French Revolution and Napoleon
1787–1815

THE BEGINNING OF THE FRENCH REVOLUTIONARY WARS

The wars of the French Revolution are usually dated from 20 April 1792, for that was when the National Assembly in Paris declared war on the 'King of Hungary' (which was how the new ruler of the Habsburg Monarchy, Francis, was known until crowned as Holy Roman Emperor in July). In reality, the wars had been underway since 17 August 1787, for it was then that the Turks had imprisoned the Russian ambassador, Count Bulgakov, in the Seven Towers of the Topkapi Palace in Constantinople, which was their ceremonial way of declaring war. As Paul Schroeder has sagely observed, it was a war that began, 'as many wars do, from the decision of a threatened defensive power to halt its decline and regain security by violence'. In the same way that the assassination of the Archduke Franz Ferdinand at Sarajevo on 28 June 1914 unleashed a chain reaction that eventually engulfed the world, this action by the Turks was to have momentous consequences.

First, it activated the defensive alliance between Catherine the Great and Joseph II concluded in 1781, which required each party to come to the assistance of the other if attacked by a third party. Although Joseph recognized his obligation at once – the *casus foederis* in diplomatic parlance – he did so with a heavy heart. As he lamented to his brother Leopold, 'these damned Turks' had forced him to wage war in regions where plague and famine were endemic and all for the prospect of very little gain. With the Austrians tied down in the Balkans for the foreseeable future, the way was clear for the new King of Prussia, Frederick William II, to make a name for himself. The opportunity was already waiting, in the shape of the political crisis in the Dutch Republic. This was essentially a re-run of the factional strife that had wracked the country periodically ever since its foundation, between the maritime provinces led by the merchant oligarchs (the 'Regents') and the landed interests led by the current head of the house of Orange, who exercised ill-defined executive authority as 'Stadholder'. For the past decade or so it had been the former who had got the upper hand, progressively stripping the Stadholder William V of his powers. In the course of the 1780s a sharper edge entered the contest by the emergence of a group of 'patriots' looking for more radical and even democratic reforms, including the total abolition of the Stadholderate. At the same time the domestic struggle had taken on an international dimension by the Dutch treaty of alliance with France concluded in 1785 and the accession to the Prussian throne in 1786 of Frederick William II, whose sister was married to William V.

Nothing less than the future of world domination appeared to be at stake in this imbroglio. Now that the French had control of Dutch naval bases at the Cape of Good Hope and in Ceylon to add to their existing possessions in the Indian Ocean of the Île de Bourbon (Réunion) and the Île de France (Mauritius), they were very well placed to do to the British in India what they had just done in America, for their rivals had no naval base between St Helena and India. Certainly the British viewed French domination of the Dutch Republic with great alarm, and some at least of the French ministers viewed it gleefully as an opportunity not to be missed. The death in February 1787 of the French foreign minister, Vergennes, also removed a brake on the hawks, led by the navy minister, the marquis de Castries. The Dutch patriots were now encouraged to take complete control of the regime.

The incident that sparked off the denouement was the arrest on 28 June 1787 of the Princess of Orange by a detachment of Freikorps, the paramilitary wing of the patriots, as she was trying to make her way to The Hague to rally support there for her husband's cause. Although she was soon released, the Prussians were encouraged by the British to take advantage of the episode to solve the Dutch problem by force. After much hesitation, they agreed, by now secure in the knowledge that the Austrians would be diverted by the war in the Balkans. Stubborn to the point of folly, the patriots had refused the satisfaction demanded, confident that their French sponsors would honour earlier promises of military assistance. As it was, with the new chief minister Loménie de Brienne vetoing any intervention on financial grounds, the French could only stand by in fuming impotence as their Dutch allies were imprisoned or forced to flee. Once the Stadholder had been restored to his previous dominant position, the Dutch Republic was duly steered into a new alliance with Prussia and Great Britain (March and June 1788). For the British, the sense of relief was intense. The Dutch navy was back where it belonged (at the disposal of the Admiralty), the threat of French control of the Channel had dissolved and, above all, sea routes to India were safer than they had ever been. George III spoke for everyone when he told Pitt: 'Perhaps no part of the change in Holland is so material to this country as the gaining of that Republic as an ally in India.'

As the British crowed, the French wailed and gnashed their teeth. To be proved impotent over Poland, the Crimea or even the League of German Princes was one thing, but to be unable to act in one's own backyard to defend a vital national interest was quite another. When Louis XVI supported Brienne and financial prudence against the hawks, de Castries resigned, as did the secretary of state of war, the comte de Ségur. The latter's son was almost certainly correct when he wrote in his memoirs:

Our situation was critical: this was the time when our court should have taken bold action; a vigorous and decisive initiative would probably have thrown our enemies into confusion, reassured the Dutch, checked the Prussians, made the Turks see reason, and so would have diverted abroad that turbulence of opinion which was convulsing France and which urgently required occupation outside the country if it were not to provoke an explosion at home.

Speculation on what might have happened, if only this or that had been done, can sometimes be helpful, especially when the exercise is conducted by contemporaries. The military men among the latter were agreed that a golden opportunity had been lost. Lameth, for example, recorded the 'general opinion' that stopping the Prussians would have been easy, especially as the Dutch opposition party had offered an immediate grant of 12,000,000 *livres*. The political benefits of intervention, he argued, would have far outweighed any cost, for whereas a successful campaign would have restored the loyalty of the army, the actual betrayal of France's allies by the supine ministry had completed its demoralization. Ségur was not the only contemporary to realize that a watershed had been reached: 'France has collapsed', recorded Joseph II, 'and I doubt whether it will rise again.' It is no exaggeration to say that the Dutch fiasco represented the terminal humiliation of the old regime.

As the French monarchy began to lurch towards the abyss, problems were also intensifying for Joseph II. The Turkish declaration of war on Russia had come too late to allow any serious campaigning in the Balkans that year. It was not until 1788 that the war began in earnest. It did not go well for the allies. Despite increasingly desperate pleas from Joseph, the Russian commander-in-chief, Prince Potemkin, stayed resolutely on the defensive. Nor was there any chance that the Russian fleet might appear in the Mediterranean to inflict another Chesme, for the British declined the necessary assistance to transfer it from the Baltic, and a rumour began to spread that the mercurial Gustavus III of Sweden would take advantage of Russian commitments in the south to launch an invasion through Finland (which indeed he did, in July). During the course of a long hot summer, the Austrian army began to fall prey to their oldest enemies – shortage of food and disease. Its inability to seize the initiative was dramatized in August, when a Turkish force broke into the Bánát of Temesvár, inflicting terrible devastation.

The situation was to get a great deal worse before it got better. Joseph's radical reform programme had alienated a wide swathe of opinion across a wide swathe of his territories. In the Austrian Netherlands in 1787 a revolt had been headed off only by concessions by the governors-general – concessions that Joseph promptly denounced and sought to claw back. Encouraged by the outbreak of revolution in France, a full-blown rebellion erupted in the autumn of 1789. With most of the government forces away fighting on the eastern front, the insurgents found it easy to take control of the province. On 11 January 1790 the combined Estates proclaimed the independence of the 'United States of Belgium'. By this time, Joseph II was on his deathbed, finally succumbing to tuberculosis on 20 February. When his brother and successor Leopold arrived in Vienna the following month, he found his inheritance apparently in a state of dissolution. Belgium was gone and it looked very much as if Hungary was about to go the same way.

These troubled waters naturally attracted the attention of Frederick William II, flushed with the success of his Dutch conquest. Now that the British were deeply in his debt, the French paralysed by revolution and the Russians preoccupied by a two-front war, the moment seemed to have come to settle accounts with the Habsburg Monarchy once and for all. In August 1789 Frederick William decided to launch an invasion in the spring of the following year to accelerate a dissolution that seemed to be already underway and to pick up the pieces. Among other things, he proposed to create an independent Belgium and an independent Hungary, the latter to be ruled by a Prussian client, the Duke of Saxony-Weimar. Alliances were negotiated with Poland and the Turks and an army of 160,000 was massed in Silesia. As if that were not enough, the Spanish got ready to claim their share of the spoils in Italy.

Yet when the dust settled, in the summer of 1790, nothing had happened. The Prussian hand had never been as strong as it looked. Indeed, the Austrian position began to improve even before the end of 1788, when their Russian allies at last began to get moving. The Swedish invasion of July 1788 had soon come to a halt, when the Finnish officers mutinied and the Danes threatened to open up a second front. Indeed, only the diplomatic intervention of Prussia and Great Britain saved Gustavus III from total disaster. The armistice they mediated in September relieved, if it did not end, pressure on Catherine the Great in the north. Better news still came at the end of 1788 when at long last the Russians captured the great Turkish fortress of Ochakov, which controlled the estuary of the Dnieper and was the key to the Black Sea coast between the Bug and the Dniester. As a result, the campaign of 1789 went very much better for both allies, ending with a series of Austrian victories in Transylvania and Moldavia and climaxing with their capture of Belgrade on 8 October.

It was these victories, won by Joseph's armies, that allowed Leopold to negotiate a settlement with Prussia. In the spring of 1790 war still seemed the most likely outcome of the crisis, but at one minute to midnight, on 27 July 1790, it was resolved by the Convention of Reichenbach, mediated by the British. In return for Prussia's agreement to demobilize and halt the campaign of subversion in Belgium and Hungary, Leopold undertook to conclude his war with the Turks on the basis of the *status quo ante bellum*. Although this involved giving up all the conquered territory, including the great prize of Belgrade, and thus recognizing continued Turkish hegemony in the Balkans, the agreement rescued the

Habsburg Monarchy from what had seemed certain disintegration. An immediate dividend was paid when an Austrian army reconquered Belgium in November 1790.

While continental Europe had been wracked by revolutions, wars or rumours of war, the British had observed events with majestic complacency. In July 1789 Bishop Porteous recorded in his diary the following entry: 'This day Mr Pitt dined with me at Fulham. He had just recd. News of the French Revolution & spoke of it as an event highly favourable to us & indicates a long peace with France. It was a very pleasant day.' Although Pitt did not know it, an episode had already occurred that was to confirm his optimism, at least in the short term. In May 1789 three British merchantmen had been arrested by Spanish warships in Nootka Sound, on the west coast of Vancouver Island. So remote was the location that it took almost a year for news to filter back to Europe. The occasion may have been trivial, but the issues it raised were of great importance to both sides. Essentially, it was a collision between the relentless surge of British commercial expansion and the traditional Spanish claim to a monopoly of trade and settlement on the Pacific coast. Both sides armed and both sides blew hot in the negotiations which dragged on acrimoniously throughout the spring and summer of 1790. If Spain had been given the support she requested and had every right to expect from her French ally, war could not have been avoided. In the event, none was forthcoming and the Spanish had to concede virtually every British demand.

FRANCE JOINS THE WAR

With this revelation that French foreign policy was still in a state of immobility, it is high time to examine the effect of the Revolution. One preliminary point that needs to be made is that nothing could have been further from the thoughts of the other European powers than a concerted effort to come to the rescue of Louis XVI. When his younger brother, the comte d'Artois, asked for assistance from Joseph II (who was, after all, Marie Antoinette's brother), he received the tart reply: 'It is in my interest to be perfectly neutral in all this business, no matter what happens to the King and Queen, and I shall certainly not interfere.' The general reaction in the chanceries of Europe was well summed up by the

Prussian foreign minister Count Hertzberg: 'The French Revolution presents a peculiar spectacle to the rest of Europe, who can regard it, if not with indifference, then at least with tranquillity.' Catherine the Great of Russia engaged in some inflammatory rhetoric against the revolutionary 'barbarians', but she was much more interested in Poland than France.

Inside France, the National Assembly was preoccupied with domestic reconstruction. Only when the Spanish request for assistance over Nootka Sound forced them, did they look outside the country. The debates of May 1790 revealed that their main concern was to take control of foreign policy away from the King, that there was a strong strain of Anglophobia among the deputies, and that they were determined to make a clean break with old regime diplomacy. 'In future, let us recognize as allies only those peoples who are just', proclaimed Jean François Reubell, 'we no longer wish to have anything to do with dynastic pacts or ministerial wars, conducted without the nation's consent but at the cost of the nation's blood and the nation's gold.' So out of this debate came the Revolution's first great programmatic statement on foreign relations. On 22 May 1790 the National Assembly decreed that 'The French nation renounces the undertaking of any war with a view to making conquests and [declares that] it will never use its forces against the liberty of any other people.'

This 'declaration of peace to the world' appeared to be quite unequivocal. Yet within two years a virtual unanimity of the same Assembly declared war. At first sight this looks like an inevitable clash of ideologies, and indeed there were issues of principle at stake. Two stand out. The first concerned the German princes whose jurisdiction and seigneurial dues in Alsace had been abolished by the decrees of 4–5 August 1789. Not unreasonably, they protested that the National Assembly could not abolish unilaterally what was theirs by treaty. In this clash between the principle of national sovereignty and contractual obligations incurred by the old regime, there could be only one winner. When presenting the report of the committee on feudalism, Merlin de Douai was careful to stress that French claims were also based on history and law, but the essence of his case rested on the indivisibility and inviolability of the nation. What he called the 'social contract' concluded by all French citizens in 1789 took precedence over any political contracts concluded by rulers without the consent of their people: 'in short, it is not the treaties of princes which govern the rights of nations'. With those words, Merlin tore up by their roots the foundations of the European states-system.

At least Alsace had been ceded to France by treaty. It was a different matter in the two enclaves in the south of the country ruled by the Pope – Avignon and the Comtat Venaissin. Supporters of the Revolution there had clamoured from the start for 'reunification' with France. Although there could be no doubt that sooner or later the National Assembly would oblige, the deputies took their time, uncomfortably aware of the furore any recognition of the principle of self-determination would unleash. For that reason, the eventual decree was careful to combine traditional and revolutionary arguments: 'The National Assembly declares that from this moment the territories of Avignon and the Comtat Venaissin form an integral part of the French state, by virtue of the rights of France to their possession and in accordance with the wish to be incorporated in France expressed freely and solemnly by the majority of the communities and citizens.' Again, the careful choice of words could not disguise the explosive implications of the principle advanced as a central axiom of the Revolution's foreign policy.

Both of those issues could have been solved by financial compensation. Not one major power was interested in going to war for the small fry of the Holy Roman Empire or the Pope. Indeed, both Prussia and Austria would have liked to emulate the revolutionaries in annexing irritating enclaves. What was pushing France and the German powers towards war was not issues but their sharply differing assessment of their mutual power relationship. The revolutionaries looked at old Europe and thought they saw a moribund political system in its death agony, with all the states at each other's throats: Prussia against Austria, Austria against the Turks, the Turks against Russia, Russia against Sweden, Sweden against Denmark, Spain against Britain, Britain against Russia. They knew only too well that the Dutch patriots had revolted against their Stadholder and that the Belgian patriots had revolted against their Emperor, for Paris was full of Dutch and Belgian refugees, all looking forward to the day when they went home as part of a French army of liberation. They also knew that the Poles wished to throw off the Russian yoke, that the Hungarians wanted to throw off the Austrian yoke, that the Irish wanted to throw off the British yoke, and so on. For their part, the old regime powers drew quite a different lesson from the events after

1787. What they saw was a French state immobilized by bankruptcy and civil unrest – 'the ablest architects of ruin that had hitherto existed in the world', as Edmund Burke put it. As for the 'patriots' elsewhere in Europe, they had shown themselves to be paper tigers. The Spanish had fought for eighty years to conquer the Dutch Republic – in vain; Louis XIV at the height of his power had tried to conquer the Dutch Republic – in vain; yet in 1787 a small Prussian army had done it in just a few weeks. If anything, the Austrian victory over the Belgian insurgents three years later had been even easier. So why should the French revolutionaries be any different?

In the course of 1791 it became ever more likely that this argument would be settled by military means. In the east, the war against the Turks was drawing to a close. A joint initiative in March by the British and the Prussians to restrain Catherine's appetite for Turkish territory by forcing her to give up Ochakov ended in humiliating failure. Then a further surge of Russian victories brought a preliminary peace at Galatz on 11 August, by which the Turks ceded all the territory between the Bug and the Dniester, including Ochakov. A week earlier the Austrians had also finally concluded their own peace with the Turks at Sistova after one of the most protracted and tedious negotiations in the history of European diplomacy. So both of the eastern powers were now free to turn their attention westwards. For Russia it was high time, for the Polish problem now loomed large. Not for the last time, the Poles had taken advantage of Russian preoccupations in the Balkans to reassert their independence. In May 1789 Russian troops had been ejected and a sustained attempt to modernize Poland's political institutions had recently reached a climax on 3 May 1791 when a new constitution was voted. This strengthened central authority by securing hereditary succession to the house of Saxony when the current King Stanislas Augustus died, by abolishing the 'liberum veto' (the individual deputy's right to blackball legislation) and by abolishing the right of confederation, which in effect had made insurrection legal. In future, it was hoped, a constitutional but strong monarch would be able to mobilize the country's enormous but untapped potential against foreign predators. Now that Catherine had her hands free, retribution loomed.

For their part, the Austrians too were looking west, to France. Leopold's sister, Queen Marie Antoinette, had issued her first appeal for international assistance against the Revolution as far back as 12 June

1790. It went unheeded. In March of the following year Leopold was still advising his sister not to attempt to escape from France but to play for time, and was still stressing that he could do nothing to help without the agreement and co-operation of all the other European powers. What changed his mind was the sharply deteriorating situation inside France and the news that the flight of the royal family was imminent. Even then he warned that he could take no action until they had reached safety and Louis XVI had issued a formal appeal for help. That he was not quite such a cold fish as this chilly prudence suggests was shown by his reaction to the (false) news that the great escape had succeeded. In an excited, not to say passionate, letter, he praised his sister as the saviour of the King, of the state, of France – of all monarchies indeed – and concluded: 'Everything that I have is yours: money, troops, in fact everything!'

In reality, of course, he could do nothing until he was sure of at least the benevolent neutrality of Prussia. By the summer of 1791 the Prussians were in a receptive mood. For all their dominant position on the continent since 1787, they still had nothing concrete to show for it. Not without reason, they blamed their faithless British allies, who had bullied them into accepting a compromise at Reichenbach and then had left them in the lurch over Ochakov. So now they began to think in terms of a military expedition to suppress the French Revolution, for the failure of the 'flight to Varennes' on 20/21 June 1791 had provided clear proof of what everyone had long suspected: that Louis XVI was opposed to the Revolution and was a prisoner in his own country.

Events now moved quickly. On 6 July 1791, Leopold issued the 'Padua Circular', calling on the crowned heads of Europe to combine to restore liberty to the French royal family. On 25 July, a convention was signed between Prussia and Austria which settled outstanding disputes, pledged co-operation over France and paved the way for a formal alliance. On 27 August, Leopold and Frederick William II met in Saxony, at Pillnitz, issuing a joint declaration that the present plight of Louis XVI and his family was a matter of common interest to all the crowned heads of Europe. They called for a concerted effort by their colleagues 'to restore to the King of France complete liberty and to consolidate the bases of monarchical government in accordance with the rights of sovereigns and the welfare of the French nation'. Once this international concert had been formed, they promised, prompt action would be taken in pursuit of its objective. In the meantime they would issue 'appropriate orders' to their armed forces.

This counter-revolutionary initiative led to a triple misunderstanding which was to result in war. First, the émigrés were greatly encouraged by the Declaration of Pillnitz, redoubled their military preparations and even formed a government-in-exile in preparation for the return to France they believed to be imminent. Secondly, the Austrians and Prussians concluded that the apparent move back towards the political centre in France, which had followed the flight to Varennes, was due to their campaign of intimidation. What they had done once, they concluded, they could do again – should the need ever arise. For the time being, they seemed to have got just what they wanted – a weak but stable constitutional monarchy. Thirdly, the revolutionaries took the Padua Circular, the Declaration of Pillnitz and the antics of the émigrés to represent an international conspiracy against the Revolution which would end in invasion. In fact, nothing could have been further from the truth. The Declaration of Pillnitz had been deliberately nullified by a crucial phrase – *'alors et dans ce cas'* ('then and in that case'). If all the European sovereigns agreed to co-operate, 'then and in that case' Austria and Prussia would agree to take action. With Russia preoccupied with Turkish and Polish affairs, with Spain and Sardinia known to be passive and, above all, with Great Britain anxious to see the disorders in France continue ad infinitum, there was not the remotest prospect of that condition being fulfilled. As Leopold complacently wrote to Kaunitz immediately after the declaration had been issued: *'Alors et dans ce cas* is with me the law and the prophets. If England fails us, the case is non-existent.'

The endgame in the move to war began with the meeting of the new legislature in Paris on 1 October 1791. So much confusion is occasioned by the terminology of the revolutionary assemblies that a word of explanation is necessary. The Estates General proclaimed itself to be the 'National Assembly' on 17 June 1789. As its primary task was to draw up a new constitution, its full title was the National Constituent Assembly (*Assemblée nationale constituante*), so it is sometimes referred to as the 'National Assembly' and sometimes as the 'Constituent Assembly'. When at long last it completed its task in September 1791, one of its last actions was to pass a self-denying ordinance excluding its members from seeking election to its replacement. This was to be called the

'National Legislative Assembly' (*Assemblée nationale législative*), so it is sometimes referred to as the 'National Assembly' and sometimes as the 'Legislative Assembly'. Its brand-new membership included many fewer clergymen, many fewer ex-nobles (noble titles had been abolished in June 1790), was much younger and was also much more radical.

In this new body the initiative was soon seized by a group of radical deputies led by Jacques-Pierre Brissot and known variously as the 'Brissotins' or 'Girondins', the latter title alluding to the fact that many of them came from the *département* of the Gironde in the south-west. Their strategy rested on one key insight: that the approval Louis XVI had given to the new constitution was bogus and that he and his queen were conspiring with the German powers to destroy the Revolution. To expose this treason, they began a campaign for war against Austria. They calculated, quite correctly, that war would radicalize the Revolution, destroy the monarchy, establish a republic and – last but not least – bring themselves to power. Nothing looked less likely in the autumn of 1791, for only 38 of the 745 deputies could be classified as Brissotins. But helped by their superlative oratory – the great speeches of Vergniaud, Isnard, Guadet and Brissot belong in any anthology of political eloquence – by the following spring they had assembled almost a unanimity – only seven intrepid deputies voted against the war on 20 April 1792.

The Brissotins had managed this feat by appealing to both the interests and the prejudices of the deputies. Some of the arguments employed were eminently practical – that war would restore the creditworthiness of the revolutionary paper money, the *assignats*, for example. The same could be said of the prediction that it would put an end to civil strife and restore the revolutionary dream of social and political harmony. Others were more emotional, not to say atavistic, especially the repeated exploitation of the hatred of Austria. Vergniaud's denunciation of the Treaty of Versailles of 1756 – 'We can see that the abrogation of this treaty is a revolution as necessary in foreign affairs, both for Europe and for France, as the destruction of the Bastille has been for our internal regeneration' – brought both the deputies and the public galleries to their feet, cheering and shouting their support. France, it was claimed by speaker after speaker, had been humiliated and exploited by their treacherous 'ally'; now it was time for '*la grande nation*' to stand up again and resume its rightful place as the greatest power in the world. Perhaps most persuasive was the argument that a war would be quick and easy. As the Dutch and the Belgians had shown, the oppressed peoples of Europe were sighing for liberation and would rise in revolt against their feudal tyrants the moment a French army crossed their frontier. The Austrian mercenaries would desert in droves, the revolutionary freedom fighters would be irresistible.

If the military signals were propitious, the international situation was equally promising. The great European concert, it was predicted, would prove impotent, immobilized by internal decay and irreconcilable differences. Of the powers which mattered, Great Britain would be kept neutral by public opinion, ministerial instability, the enormous National Debt and problems in India; Russia was preoccupied by Poland; Spain was bankrupt in every conceivable sense of the word. Most important of all, it was more likely that Prussia would fight on the side of France than against her. This confidence in Prussia was one of the most striking – and misguided – of the war-party's assumptions. It was based in part, of course, on the Austrophobe rejection of the old regime's diplomatic system. To return to a Prussian alliance would be to return to the golden age of French greatness before the fall from grace in 1756. It was also based on a surprising but patently sincere admiration of Frederick the Great. The 'immortal glory' of this 'philosopher king' and his stable, just and prosperous state were praised repeatedly. Nor was it only his pacific enlightened virtues which appealed. He was also held up to the Assembly as the model on which the Revolution should base its foreign policy, for when he had been confronted by an Austrian-led concert, he had known just what to do: strike first. In short, far from having to fight the rest of Europe, France would only have the feeble Habsburg Monarchy to contend with.

Hatred, pride and confidence were just three of the emotions excited so effectively by the hawks. As the debates of the autumn and winter of 1791 wore on, they began to fuse to form a critical mass. What was needed now was a detonator. It was found in anger and was supplied by the Austrians. In Vienna, Emperor Leopold and his advisers had watched events in the Legislative Assembly in late 1791 with a growing sense of disappointment and alarm. The stability promised by the royal acceptance of the new constitution was not materializing. On the contrary, the leaders of the new legislature seemed determined to provoke conflict at home and abroad. As the entreaties from Marie Antoinette for intervention became more insistent and more reproachful, the decision was taken to repeat the exercise in intimidation first employed with such apparent success in the previous summer. On 21 December 1791 the chancellor of state, Prince Kaunitz, sent a note to the French ambassador in Vienna couched in deliberately threatening language. If a French army did cross the German frontier to take action against princes harbouring the émigrés, he stated, then Austrian forces in Belgium would intervene at once. Moreover, retribution would also swiftly follow 'from the other sovereigns who have united in a concert for the maintenance of public order and for the security and honour of monarchs'.

Nothing could have served better the cause of the Brissotin war-party in the Legislative Assembly. Just when the wind seemed to have been taken out of their sails by Louis XVI's approval of action against the émigrés, their enemies had come to their rescue. If there was one thing calculated to rouse every deputy, no matter what his position on the left–right spectrum, it was the threat to intervene in French politics, for this conflicted with the essential foundation of the French Revolution: national sovereignty. It also gave credibility to the Brissotin argument that, as the Austrians intended to make war on the Revolution anyway, there was nothing to be lost and everything to be gained from a preemptive strike. Not only did Leopold and Kaunitz fail to appreciate the counter-productive effect of their clumsy initiative, they believed that it had had the desired result. They were deluded partly because they were denied reliable intelligence of events in Paris (their ambassador, Count Mercy, having fled to Brussels long ago) and partly because they received from the French foreign minister, Delessart, a feeble and temporizing reply. Apparently unaware that real power was now in the hands of the legislature, they sent an even more provocative note on 17 February 1792. Only the need to force Louis XVI to dismiss his current executive delayed the now certain declaration of war for a couple of months.

No sooner had the war begun than the miscalculations of the Brissotins began to be revealed. The rest of Europe did not rise in revolt; the Austrian soldiers did not mutiny; the revolutionary armies did not prove to be irresistible; Prussia did not join the French – on the contrary it entered the war at once on the Austrian side. However, Brissot did get one thing right, albeit inspite of his confident predictions. It was the invasion of France by the German powers and their imminent arrival in

Paris that brought the fall of the monarchy and the creation of a republic, on 22 September 1792.

REVOLUTIONARY FRANCE
CONQUERS WESTERN EUROPE

To follow the twists and turns of the war is rendered impossible by its complexity. The French military historian Arthur Chuquet needed eleven substantial volumes just to cover the first fifteen months. Two essential points need to be made, however. One is the fluctuating nature of military success during the 1790s. Neither side was able to gain a decisive advantage until General Bonaparte invaded Italy in 1796 – and even that success proved short-lived. The other relates to the close interaction between success or failure on the battlefield and events on the home front. After a first invasion of Belgium at the end of April ended in disaster, the war went quiet for three months, as the cumbersome Austro-Prussian war machine was cranked into first gear. When it finally did start to move forward, early in August, at first it carried all before it, as French fortresses fell like ninepins. The feeble resistance offered by the garrisons convinced the Parisian radicals that they were being betrayed by the enemy within. The result was the 'September Massacres', when between 1,100 and 1,400 prisoners were butchered. The great majority were social offenders such as prostitutes or common criminals, innocent of the remotest connection with politics, although one or two aristocrats perished as well. Prominent among the latter group was the princesse de Lamballe, whose severed head was paraded to the Temple, where the imprisoned Marie Antoinette was invited to kiss the dead lips of the woman alleged by the gutter press to have been her lesbian lover.

The advance of the Prussians through Champagne stuttered to a halt at Valmy on 20 September when they ran into, not the demoralized rabble they had been expecting, but a large army of well-disciplined and well-armed soldiers, commanded by men who clearly knew what they were doing. As battles go, it was unspectacular: after a prolonged exchange of artillery fire and one abortive advance, the Duke of Brunswick, the Prussian commander-in-chief, ordered a halt. Under cover of darkness, it was the French who left the field of battle, but not even the most sanguine Prussian felt anything other than defeated. That night, the greatest poet of the age, Goethe, who was accompanying the invasion with his employer, the Duke of Saxony-Weimar, told his companions: 'From here and today there begins a new epoch in the history of the world, and you can say that you were there.'

By now the French were pressing forwards on all fronts. On the day after Valmy, General Montesquiou invaded, and then occupied almost without resistance, the Duchy of Savoy. General Custine and the Army of the Vosges moved into Germany, taking Speyer on 30 September, Worms on 4 October, Mainz on 21 October and Frankfurt am Main two days later. The most important battle of the campaign, however, came on 6 November at Jemappes in Belgium, where General Dumouriez won a hard-fought but decisive victory over the heavily outnumbered Austrians commanded by the Duke of Saxony-Teschen. Within a week Brussels had fallen, within a month most of Belgium had followed suit. Together with the effortless conquests in the Rhineland and Savoy, this quick and apparently total victory generated a mood of triumphalism in Paris. But it also presented problems, the most obvious being: what was France to do with the territory the armies had won? If a truism, it bears repeating that the Revolution had gone to war without any actual war aims. So it was now high time to invent some. There were plenty of suggestions, it need hardly be said, the most popular – because the most simple – being the doctrine of 'natural frontiers'. After Jemappes, Brissot himself wrote to Dumouriez: 'I can tell you that there is one idea which is spreading here, namely that the French Republic should have no other frontier than the Rhine.' At the end of January 1793, the doctrine was given its classic expression by Danton in the National Convention: 'The frontiers of France have been mapped by nature, and we shall reach them at the four corners of the horizon, on the banks of the Rhine, by the side of the ocean and at the Alps. It is there that we shall reach the limits of our Republic.'

One glance at the map should have been enough to demonstrate that there were problems with the plan to establish natural frontiers other than the linguistic, ethnic and historical diversity of the people affected. Quite simply, the Rhine flows into the sea not in Belgium but in the Dutch Republic, much of which would therefore have to be included in the new 'natural' France. That in turn would guarantee the hostility of the British, who believed that 'Holland might justly be considered as necessary a part of this country as Kent', as Burke put it to the House of Commons in March 1791. So the French advance through Belgium to the Dutch frontier in the autumn of 1793 turned British neutral observation into active intervention. The National Convention (as the new revolutionary legislature installed in September 1792 was called) had few qualms about adding to a growing list of the republic's enemies because they believed that Britain would be incapacitated by domestic insurrection, especially in Ireland and Scotland. A French secret agent reported from London: 'England offers precisely the same prospect as France did in 1789.' So when the motion was put on 1 February 1793 that war be declared on both Britain and the Dutch Republic, there was not one dissenting voice. The same sort of blithe overconfidence allowed them to add Spain to the list on 7 March.

By that time, the fortunes of war were beginning to spin round once again. An important symbolic moment had come on 2 December 1792 when the Prussians had recaptured Frankfurt am Main. Not only did it show that the German powers were beginning to take the war seriously, it also demonstrated that French confidence in the revolutionary potential of the rest of Europe was entirely misplaced, for the local population had risen in support of the Prussians and had opened the gates to them. Moreover, the great armies that had won Valmy and Jemappes were beginning to melt away. With the Revolution's frontiers secured by the victories of the autumn and with winter approaching, the volunteers began to drift home. They were fully entitled to do so after 1 December 1792, having enlisted only for one campaign. Estimates of the total strength of the armies at this – or any other – stage of the war can only be approximate, but it seems likely that from around 450,000 in the autumn of 1792, numbers fell to 350,000 by the beginning of 1793, of whom only about 220,000 were in any sense 'effectives'. To fill the gaps in personnel that began to yawn, on 24 February 1793 the National Convention introduced conscription. Although the total to be raised was only 300,000, nowhere could the quotas be filled. Across France the average response was about 50 per cent; in the south it dropped to a quarter, while in the west it precipitated civil war in the Vendée.

Thus by the spring of 1793, the Revolution looked as if it were imploding. In the south the Spanish invaded Roussillon; in the east the Prussians went back on the offensive, driving the French out of the Rhineland; in the north the Austrians gained a great victory at

Neerwinden on 18 March, reconquered Belgium and advanced on to French soil; in the north-west a British expeditionary force commanded by the Duke of York besieged Dunkirk; inside France, the 'federalist' insurrectionaries seized control of a large part of the country, including the great port of Toulon, which surrendered to the Royal Navy at the end of August. It was as a response to this critical situation at home and abroad that on 23 August the National Convention finally completed the long transition to revolutionary war begun four years earlier. At long last they heeded the call for every citizen to be a soldier and vice versa and decreed:

From this moment until that in which our enemies shall have been driven from the territory of the Republic, all Frenchmen are permanently requisitioned for service in the armies.

The young men shall fight; the married men shall forge weapons and transport supplies; the women will make tents and clothes and will serve in the hospitals; the children will make up old linen into lint; the old men will have themselves carried into the public squares to rouse the courage of fighting men, to preach the unity of the Republic and hatred of Kings.

The public buildings shall be turned into barracks, the public squares into munitions factories, the earthen floors shall be treated with lye to extract saltpetre [for the manufacture of gunpowder].

All firearms of suitable calibre shall be turned over to the troops: the interior shall be policed with shotguns and with cold steel.

All saddle horses shall be seized for the cavalry; all draft horses not employed in cultivation will draw the artillery and supply-wagons.

This decree is usually referred to as instituting the 'levée en masse', but it was much more than that. It was also the first declaration of total war. From now on, until total victory was achieved, every man, woman, child, animal and inanimate object was conscripted for the war effort.

The result was the conscription of what was probably the largest army ever seen in Europe. No one knows – least of all the revolutionaries themselves – just how many men were under arms by 1794. If the popular figure of a million is a myth, the best guess of around 800,000 is still a tremendous total. Probably of equal importance was the raw aggression that was brought to the conduct of the war by the new regime that replaced (and guillotined) the Brissotins, who had been unable to make a success of the war they had started. Deputies of the National Convention were sent to the front as omnipotent commissars, to terrorize the generals out of defeatism and on to the offensive. Arriving at the eastern front on 24 October 1793, Saint-Just at once advertised his intentions by having the luckless veteran General Isambert shot in front of his troops for showing insufficient resolution in the face of the enemy. As Lafayette had deserted to the Austrians in 1792 and Dumouriez in 1793, it was not surprising that the revolutionaries were suspicious of the generals they had inherited from the old regime. A great cull followed.

Uncomfortably aware of the fate of their predecessors, the new men were just what was needed to turn the tide after the disasters of the spring and summer of 1793. And turn it they did. A first success was gained at Hondschoote in August, when the Duke of York was forced to abandon his siege of Dunkirk and start what was to prove a very long retreat. After mixed fortunes on the eastern front in the autumn, the twenty-five-year-old General Hoche had forced the Austrians back across the Rhine by the end of the year. When campaigning began in the following spring, it was Belgium that was the main battleground. Following defeats at Tourcoing on 18 May and at Fleurus on 26 June, the Austrians were forced to retreat back into Germany. By early 1795, the French had conquered not only Belgium but the Dutch Republic and the left bank of the Rhine apart from the fortresses of Luxemburg and Mainz. The west had been won.

Its conquest had been greatly assisted by simultaneous developments in the east. The major beneficiary here was Catherine the Great of Russia, who was delighted to see Prussia and Austria embroiled in an unsuccessful war in the west, leaving her in control – 'der lachende Dritte', or 'the happy third party', as the Germans say. As soon as she learnt of the French declaration of war, she ordered her armies into Poland 'to restore the traditional constitution'. It is worth repeating that Russia, Prussia and Austria were primarily eastern European powers and more concerned with Poland than France. But their interests were not identical. Prussia viewed the Polish constitution of 3 May 1791 with horror, for, in making the crown hereditary in the house of Wettin, it recreated the nightmare of a Saxon-Polish state. With fear went greed – a desire for more Polish territory, especially the key towns of Danzig and Thorn, plus their surrounding territories.

It is possible that the Prussians were thinking in terms of a second partition even before the Russian invasion; certainly they were putting out feelers immediately after it. That their greedy tentacles would grasp something solid was then made certain by a terrible blunder on the part of the Austrians. Believing that the war against France would be quick and easy, they began to rearrange the map of Europe in advance, in best balance-of-power style. They themselves, they suggested, would seek compensation for the costs of their punitive expedition against the French Revolution by exchanging their Belgian territories for Bavaria, while the Prussians should recoup their outlay by taking a slice of Poland. In the severe but judicious verdict of Paul Schroeder, this was 'an egregious error' – not only had the Austrians walked into a trap, they had helped to lay it and dig it deeper: 'in other words, Austria gave hard cash to a notorious swindler in exchange for his conditional promissory note'. The cash was banked on 23 January 1793 when Prussia and Russia signed a partition treaty, which gave the latter the whole of the eastern half of the country, including the Ukraine, with a population of more than 3,000,000. The Prussian share was three times smaller in terms of population and four times smaller in terms of area, but its value was relatively greater, for it embraced not only the long-coveted prizes of Danzig and Thorn but also all of Great Poland, up to within a few miles of Warsaw and Kraków.

In the west during 1793 the Prussians scored a number of military successes, recapturing Mainz on 23 July and defeating the French at Pirmasens in September and at Kaiserslautern in November, but their strategy was now essentially passive. The Polish rising against the partitioning powers launched by Tadeusz Kościuszko in March 1794 ensured that the Prussian focus would be kept firmly on the east. Indeed, it is no exaggeration to say that the Poles saved the French Revolution from military defeat: by ensuring that both Austria and Prussia, but especially Prussia, went to war with one eye looking behind them and one hand tied behind their backs; by creating dissension between the two German allies; and by keeping Russia out of the war altogether. The Poles also inadvertently pushed the Prussians towards a separate peace with revolutionary France. Excluded from the partition of 1793, the Austrians were determined to have a good share in the next, signing a treaty with Russia on 3 January 1795 which earmarked a huge slice of territory that advanced their frontier almost to Warsaw. Fearing they would be left out in the cold, the Prussians hurried to conclude peace negotiations with France, which had first been mooted immediately after Valmy and had been pursued in earnest since October 1794. The result was the Peace of Basle of 6 April 1795, by which Prussia abandoned her alliance with Austria, withdrew from the war and agreed that France should occupy the left bank of the Rhine until a final peace was concluded with the Holy Roman Empire. In return, France guaranteed compensation on the right bank for losses on the left, and allowed the Prussians to gather together the states of northern Germany in a neutrality zone, thus greatly enhancing their political influence. Thus strengthened, they were able to join the third – and final – partition of Poland by a treaty with Russia signed on 24 October the same year.

The Prussian desertion of the first coalition encouraged two other powers to do likewise. On 16 May 1795 the Dutch concluded the Treaty of The Hague, purchasing peace at a terrible price: an indemnity of 100,000,000 guilders, a huge loan at a low rate of interest, a commitment to maintain a French army of 25,000 until a general peace was concluded and the cession of Maastricht, Venlo and Dutch Flanders. Returning to Paris in triumph, the French negotiator Sieyès rushed to the session of the Committee of Public Safety and flung a fistful of guilders on the table with the words, 'I have brought you a hundred million of these!' The Spanish took longer to come to terms. The campaign at both ends of the Pyrenees had gone very much the French way in 1794, as both Guipuzcoa and Navarre in the north-west were overrun and Figueras in the north-east was captured. Even so, the Spanish armies were still intact and the French had not penetrated beyond the periphery. So when peace was signed at Basle on 22 July 1795, the Spanish secured the best terms achieved by any enemy of revolutionary France in the 1790s: a return to the *status quo ante bellum* with the exception of the Spanish share of Saint Domingue, a prize of dubious value.

The two great victors of this first phase of the war were the peripheral powers. Without being a combatant against France, although very definitely being a combatant against the Poles, Catherine the Great had won an enormous swathe of territory that propelled the Russian frontier some 300 miles (480 km) to the west. The acquisitions made further gains in the south at the expense of the Turks very much easier. At the other end of Europe, the Revolution had conquered the west. Belgium was formally annexed on 1 October 1795, the Dutch Republic had been turned into a docile satellite state as 'the Batavian Republic' and the entire left bank of the Rhine was in French hands, only the fortress of Mainz still holding out. On two occasions – in the summer of 1792 and almost exactly one year later – the Revolution had appeared to be on the brink of total collapse; by 1795 it had achieved greater conquests than even Louis XIV in his prime.

That left the British and the Austrians to deal with. It was in the Atlantic that the war against Great Britain would be won or lost. On 1 January 1793, a confident Kersaint had promised the National Convention that their navy could launch an invasion across the Channel without further ado: 'by this expedition we shall bring the war to a close: on the ruins of the Tower of London we shall sign with the English people a treaty to settle the destinies of the nations and to establish the liberty of the world'. This prediction proved to be no more accurate than his Brissotin colleagues' earlier boast about the invincibility of the land forces. When Admiral Morard de Galles sailed out from Brest in March 1793 with three ships of the line and five frigates, the sortie ended in disaster. After multiple collisions and dismastings, the squadron had to return ignominiously to port. Morard's report revealed that some of his officers had failed to carry out orders through ignorance of what was required of them, while many of the terrified 'seamen' had refused to go aloft. Captain Duval of Le Tourville was killed by a loose block when trying to secure a sail himself. Nor was the first actual encounter with the Royal Navy encouraging. When Sir Edward Pellew and his frigate the Nymphe met the French frigate Cléopatre in the Channel off Prawle Point, it was the latter which was forced to strike her colours after a brisk forty-five-minute exchange of broadsides. A similar encounter between the frigates Crescent and Réunion outside Cherbourg in October ended in the same way.

Yet it was to take a long time for the Royal Navy to establish its superiority. Although not obvious at the time, its greatest success came as a result of domestic strife in France, for the surrender of Toulon in August 1793 allowed the destruction of its great stock of timber – 'possibly the single most crippling blow suffered by the French navy since Quiberon Bay [in 1759]', in the opinion of Nicholas Rodger. On 1 June 1794 Admiral Lord Howe caught the Brest fleet about 400 miles (650 km) out into the Atlantic and captured or wrecked a dozen French ships of the line without loss. For all the wild celebrations the 'Glorious

First of June' unleashed in Great Britain, however, this was a muddled affair with as many opportunities missed as taken. It also failed in its main objective, which was to seize a massive French convoy. In the Caribbean, the British found it relatively easy to seize the French islands – Tobago, Saint Domingue, Martinique, Guadeloupe and Saint Lucia – but much more difficult to hold these in the face of disease and revolts. The only unequivocal successes were gained at the expense of France's new Dutch allies. As soon as the subjugation of the latter looked certain, the British moved to secure the Cape of Good Hope – 'a feather in the hands of Holland but a sword in the hands of France', as the expedition's Commodore John Blankett put it. They also sent an expedition from Madras to capture the Dutch port of Trincomalee on the eastern coast of Ceylon, another crucial acquisition, for it was the only secure port in the region during the monsoon. With their communications with Europe now secure, the British could embark on the consolidation and expansion of their possessions on the mainland of India.

REVOLUTIONARY FRANCE
CONQUERS SOUTHERN EUROPE

Even if the British had got into their naval stride more quickly, they could never have defeated the French Revolution by themselves. That could only be done by a land power, and that meant Austria. Even when deserted by their continental allies, the Austrians continued to demonstrate their marvellous, but usually unsung, resilience. Late in 1795, after months of inactivity, the French had launched a two-pronged attack across the Rhine. The Army of the Sambre-et-Meuse under Jourdan crossed in the north at Düsseldorf and then swung south towards Mainz. The Army of the Rhin-et-Moselle under Pichegru crossed in the south, capturing Mannheim on 20 September. A vigorous Austrian counter-offensive soon had both armies reeling back to the left bank, the year ending with a formal armistice signed on 15 December. For the following campaign, a three-pronged assault on Austria was planned, with the intention of bringing the war to an end. The main thrust was to be through Germany. The Sambre-et-Meuse under Jourdan was to invade from the north and the Rhin-et-Moselle under Moreau from the south, before uniting for a final assault on Austria culminating in the capture of Vienna. Meanwhile, a revitalized Army of Italy was to be sent through Piedmont and Lombardy, up the Alpine passes and into the Tyrol, to complete an irresistible trident.

At first all went well north of the Alps. During July the Sambre-et-Meuse advanced rapidly south-eastwards through Franconia, reaching Amberg by the middle of August, at which point it was less than 50 miles (80 km) from the Bohemian frontier. Meanwhile the Rhin-et-Moselle had also advanced, through Swabia into Bavaria. But the Austrian commander, the Archduke Charles, succeeded in preventing the two armies combining, while at the same time concentrating his own forces. On 24 August he inflicted a decisive defeat on Jourdan at Amberg, forcing him to begin the long retreat to the Rhine. As soon as he learnt of this reversal, Moreau ordered his own army to withdraw. By October both were back where they started from.

Their bacon was saved by Bonaparte and the Army of Italy, who had started earlier and had moved much faster. He enjoyed the inestimable advantage of moving into territory hitherto unravaged by war, whereas his northern colleagues were trying to subsist on the dregs of a cup that had been drained once too often. The story of the conquest of Italy has been told many times in great detail. If only the bare bones can be presented here, at least a simple narrative reveals just how quickly events could move. Bonaparte arrived at Nice on 27 March 1796; in the course of the next month he defeated the Piedmontese army and imposed a truce on them at Cherasco on 28 April; on 10 May he scored his first virtuoso victory over the Austrians at the bridge of Lodi; on 15 May he entered Milan; by the end of May, all Austrian Italy had been conquered except for the fortress of Mantua. In other words, Bonaparte had completed his part of the great plan before either of the northern armies had even started. He spent the rest of the year imposing extortionate settlements on one hapless ruler after another, extracting huge sums of money and cartloads of works of art. Most important were the settlements imposed on the papacy and the Kingdom of Naples on 5 and 24 June respectively. Together with the occupation on 27 June of the port of Livorno, the centre of British commercial activity in the region, they established French hegemony in Italy. Periodically, his presence was needed in the north, to defeat four separate attempts by the Austrians to descend from the Alps and relieve Mantua. After the last such had ended with a comprehensive defeat at Rivoli in January 1797, Mantua finally surrendered.

With his southern flank now secure, Bonaparte could turn north for the long-delayed thrust into the Habsburg Monarchy. Sending Joubert to cover any Austrian intrusion from the Tyrol, he headed north-east, across the Brenta and the Piave into Friuli. By 16 March he had reached the Tagliamento and was poised to enter the Habsburg province of Carinthia. By this time, his enemy's will was crumbling. Francis II was still determined to continue the war, but the new commander on the southern front was not. This was none other than the Emperor's brother, the Archduke Charles, the victor of 1796, but now convinced that nothing could stop Bonaparte marching to Vienna. On 29 March Bonaparte reached Klagenfurt, by 7 April he had marched through Carinthia and had reached Judenburg in Styria. Indeed, his advance units reached the Semmering pass, from which, according to one improbable report, they could see the spires of Vienna 75 miles (120 km) away to the north. With the Sambre-et-Meuse and the Rhin-et-Moselle armies about to cross the Rhine yet again, the Austrians agreed to an armistice.

The war was then brought to an end in two stages. First, Bonaparte negotiated a preliminary peace at Leoben on 18 April 1797. He then set about imposing puppet regimes on northern Italy. By the time the definitive treaty was signed at Campo Formio on 17 October, the terms had changed in France's favour. This was essentially a partition treaty: France received Belgium, most of the left bank of the Rhine, Lombardy, the Ionian Islands and Venetian Albania; Austria received Venice, including its territories on the mainland and along the Adriatic coast, and the promise of the archbishopric of Salzburg when peace was concluded between France and the Holy Roman Empire. The Austrians also agreed to recognize formally the Cisalpine Republic and to cede to it Mantua. The Duke of Modena was to be compensated for the loss of his duchy with the Austrian possessions in the Breisgau in southern Germany.

As an exercise in cynical, old-regime-style, balance-of-power politics, this could not be bettered. Indeed, it was even more outrageous than the partitions of Poland, for in Venice there was not even the excuse of a new constitution, or 'Jacobin' agitation, or a rising in the style of Kościuszko to justify its elimination. If proof were needed that 'revolutionary' France was just another great power, this was it. For their part, the Austrians were certainly acting under duress, but their abandonment of the Holy Roman Empire was an act of self-mutilation if not suicide. For the secret articles of Campo Formio stipulated that the Emperor would use his good offices to secure the left bank of the Rhine for France and also that the dispossessed secular princes would be compensated with ecclesiastical land. The Austrian acquisition of Salzburg was the first stage in this process. In the event, nine years were to pass before Francis II abdicated as Holy Roman Emperor and became Francis I, Emperor of Austria, but with Campo Formio the death-knell of the 1,000-year-old Holy Roman Empire had tolled.

Nine years were needed because the Peace of Campo Formio turned out to be only a truce. The regime in Paris, known as 'the Directory' since 1795, had been rejuvenated by the *coup d'état* of Fructidor (4 September 1797) which had brought a sharp shift back to the left. The French hold on the Italian peninsula was then consolidated in February 1798 by the occupation of the Papal States, the proclamation of the Roman Republic and the deportation of Pius VI to France. Even more important from a military point of view was the corralling of Switzerland by means of the now familiar device of lending the military muscle necessary to allow local collaborators to seize power and set up a satellite republic. The last block was to be eased into place in December 1798, when the King of Sardinia, Charles Emmanuel IV, was forced to abdicate and Piedmont was occupied. For the Directory and its most successful general, Bonaparte, peace was clearly the continuation of warfare by other means.

With western and southern Europe under their control and central Europe about to be remodelled at the Congress of Rastatt, convened to negotiate peace between France and the Holy Roman Empire, the French turned their attention eastwards, to Egypt. Both the foreign minister, Talleyrand, and Bonaparte were enthusiastic about an expedition to conquer it. Egypt would compensate for the loss of the Caribbean islands, pre-empt any attempt by the Austrians to create a Mediterranean empire based on Venice, protect vital French commercial interests in the Levant, provide both a source of raw materials and a market for French manufactured goods, and serve as a base from which to conquer British India. So on 19 May 1798 a huge armada of 280 vessels all told, escorted by 55 warships, including 13 ships of the line and 6 frigates, left Toulon and headed east.

Nemesis swiftly followed. Indeed, there is a good case to be made for

1 August 1798 being the turning point in the history of Revolutionary-Napoleonic France. It was on that day that Rear Admiral Sir Horatio Nelson and a squadron of fifteen ships of the line found Bonaparte's battlefleet at anchor in Aboukir Bay near Alexandria and destroyed it. Of the thirteen French ships only two escaped capture or destruction – and they were hunted down and sunk later. When the smoke cleared, Nelson commented: 'Victory is certainly not a name strong enough for such a scene.' It restored British control of the Mediterranean, it bottled up Bonaparte in Egypt and it may also have marked the end of a French naval challenge to the British hegemon. That was the view of Martine Acerra and Jean Meyer, the authors of the most recent scholarly history of the French navy during the revolutionary period: 'After Aboukir, in reality everything was decided, including the fate of the Empire, Trafalgar being just the inevitable consequence of Aboukir ... Aboukir changed everything, as the navy lethargically resigned itself to its fate and left it to the army to ensure the survival of the Revolution ... Aboukir marked the end of France as a naval power.' Bonaparte himself now accepted British naval supremacy. As he reported to the Directory on hearing of the destruction of his fleet, 'On this occasion, as so often in the past, the fates seem to have decided to prove to us that, if they have granted us hegemony on land, they have made our rivals the rulers of the waves.'

WHY THE FRENCH WON ON LAND AND THE BRITISH AT SEA

As we saw in the previous chapter, it was Frederick the Great of Prussia who proved to be the most efficient maximizer of a country's resources. His reward was promotion to the Premiership of the European states-system, missing out a couple of divisions en route. It was as well that he died in 1786, for the Revolutionary Wars that began the following year brutally exposed the inadequacy of his system. The armies of the French Revolution and the Napoleonic Empire outbid every aspect of Frederickian warfare. The differences were identified helpfully by Hans Delbrück in tabular fashion:

Frederick the Great	Napoleon
Army forms a single unit	Army divided into corps and divisions
Commanders of various units have no other function than to pass on orders or to set an example of personal bravery to the troops	Middle-ranking officers are given independent tasks and scope for using their own initiative
Commander marches and attacks according to a preconceived plan	Commander begins battle on all fronts and decides from one moment to the next how to proceed
No or very few reserves	Very strong reserves
Strongest blow first	Strongest blow last
Chance plays a large part	Chance plays a part but is not allowed to disturb superiority in numbers, and leadership is assigned a decisive weight

Napoleon inherited the tools for victory from the old regime. Revolutionary warfare was not revolutionary. Everything commonly regarded as its essence had been invented earlier: 'The French Revolution *coincided* with a revolution in war that had been under way through the last decades of the monarchy. Soon the two meshed' (Peter Paret). This fusion was made easier by the fact that in old-regime Europe it had been French theorists and practitioners who had formed the vanguard of military change. Partly this was due to the traumatic shock inflicted by defeat at Rossbach. As the Prussians were to do almost exactly fifty years later after Jena and Auerstedt, some far-sighted French military reformers made the best of misfortune to prepare for revenge. They did so in two vital areas. In Jean-Baptiste Vaquette, comte de Gribeauval (1715–89), they found an artilleryman of genius. Seconded to the Austrian army in 1757, he had experienced at first hand just how effectively the Prussians could use field artillery. Recalled by Choiseul (foreign minister after 1758 and secretary of state for war as well after 1761), Gribeauval set about implementing and improving the lessons he had learnt in Germany, most notably standardization, interchangeability of parts, improved accuracy and greater mobility.

At about the same time, Choiseul encouraged his commander in Germany, the maréchal de Broglie, to experiment with more flexible troop formations to allow greater speed and mobility. Broglie broke up his army into more manageable columns or divisions, not exceeding sixteen battalions each, reinforced with their own artillery, covered by their own cavalry and preceded by their own light troops. When one of these rapidly moving columns made contact with the enemy, it was expected to hold on until the others could arrive on either flank and intervene as appropriate. This decentralization gave divisional commanders greater opportunity for initiative and allowed quicker redeployment from column into line of battle.

The Austrians and Prussians went to war with revolutionary France in 1792 confident of a quick and easy victory: 'a promenade to Paris', as one émigré put it. In the event, twenty-two years were to pass before the allies could hold their victory parade down the Champs-Élysées. What had gone wrong? In his treatise *On War against the New Franks*, published in 1795, a bewildered Archduke Charles asked: 'How was it possible that a well equipped, balanced, disciplined army had been defeated by an enemy with raw troops, lacking cavalry, and with inexperienced generals?' His answer at least identified part of the problem: the Austrians had failed, he believed, because they had conducted a defensive war, because they had been too concerned with protecting their lines of communication, and because their use of an extended but thin defensive cordon system had allowed the French to concentrate superior forces at the critical point.

This belief that it was not so much that the French had got it right, rather that the allies had got it wrong, was widespread. It was reassuring but dangerous, because it was an explanation which encouraged a continuing underestimation of revolutionary power and a consequent conviction that tinkering with the old system would be enough to bring eventual victory. The observer who got closest to the truth was rewarded for his insight by repeatedly being passed over for promotion. This was the Hanoverian artillery officer Gerhard Scharnhorst, who also in 1795 published in an obscure military periodical an essay entitled 'A Discussion of the General Reasons for the Success of the French in the Revolutionary Wars'. He singled out for special mention the revolutionaries' intrinsically superior strategic position, which allowed them to operate on interior lines; their superior numbers; their use of light troops; their unified political and military command; their adoption of a coherent, aggressive strategy in the service of national not dynastic interests;

their greater speed and energy; their ruthless acceptance of unlimited casualties; and their nihilistic do-or-die, all-or-nothing approach – 'the struggle was indeed too unequal: one side had everything to lose, the other little'. Paradoxically, it was the allies who had done most to mobilize French resources: 'The terrible position the French found themselves in, surrounded by several armies which sought (or so they believed) to enslave them and condemn to eternal misery, inspired the soldier with courage, induced the citizen to make voluntary sacrifices, gathered supplies for the army and attracted the civilian population to the colours.' Scharnhorst also appreciated how important a part traditional French pride in their allegedly superior civilization fired their indignant rejection of foreign interference: 'The French nation has always deemed itself to be the only people which is enlightened, intelligent, free and happy, despising all other nations as uncultured, bestial and wretched.' More radical was his recognition that a free society could generate more strength because it could call on the enthusiasm of the individual citizen-soldier. So, Scharnhorst concluded, the French victories had been no fluke or a temporary aberration: 'the reasons for the defeat of the allied powers must be deeply enmeshed in their internal conditions and in those of the French nation'.

This is an attractive and popular notion, especially when applied to the pre-nuclear period, but it cannot be accepted as an explanation for the military success of the French Revolution without some qualification. It was certainly the case that many soldiers did see themselves as citizens in uniform, fighting for the Republic and liberty with a fervour born of ideological conviction. Representative of the rhetoric this inspired were the words of twenty-five-year-old Joachim Murat as he set off for war in 1792: 'Do not weep, my father, if you learn of my death. Without a doubt, the most glorious sacrifice I could make of my life would be to die with my comrades in the defence of the Republic'; or the comment of an anonymous soldier making light of the loss of an arm: 'It doesn't matter. I still have one left for the service of the Republic and the extermination of its enemies.'

The belief that it was revolutionary *élan* which brought victory seems problematic when one considers the inconsistent pattern of success. The essential characteristics of the citizen-soldier – his commitment to the Revolution, identification with the nation and willing obedience – were constants and therefore should have had constant results. Yet in fact the campaigns of 1792, 1793 and 1794 (and those which followed) were anything but constant, being rather a bewildering zigzag of success and failure and close-run things. The revolutionaries won at Valmy in September 1792 but lost at Neerwinden the following March, won at Jemappes in November 1792 but lost at Mainz the following July, won at Fleurus in June 1794 but lost at Kaiserslautern (three times in 1793–4). It would be absurd to suppose that when the citizen-soldiers were defeated they were somehow having an off-day and were not feeling very revolutionary. This may seem facetious, but it does show that arguments based on motivation are both impossible to prove and tautological. On the other hand, examination of the battles fought during the 1790s shows that the Austrians and Prussians too were capable of feats of heroism, both individual and collective, which cannot be explained simply in terms of iron discipline making the soldiers fear their officers more than the enemy. Two awful possibilities loom: either that ideological commitment had little to do with fighting effectiveness or that the values of the old regime were just as powerful motivators as the ideals of the Revolution.

This difficult question will never be resolved to everyone's satisfaction, if only because it involves motivation. A more concrete, and to my mind more convincing, explanation for the French victory in the west can be found in the numbers of soldiers mobilized by the two sides. The table of major battles during this period, together with the troop strengths of the two sides involved, printed as an appendix to Gunther Rothenberg's *The Art of Warfare in the Age of Napoleon*, reveals that whenever the allies were able to assemble even roughly the same number of troops as the French, they won. It seems difficult to avoid the conclusion of Gilbert Bodinier: 'All the victories achieved by the republican armies were due to their numbers ... On every occasion that their numerical superiority was slight ... or when they were numerically inferior to the enemy, the French were defeated.'

Yet undoubtedly there was also a qualitative element involved. Nothing distinguished the revolutionary army from its predecessor – and all the other armed forces of Europe, for that matter – more than its meritocracy. The declaration of the National Assembly on 28 February 1790 that henceforth 'every citizen has the right to be admitted to every rank' began a rapid transformation of the officer corps. Away went the courtiers and the parvenus who had bought their commissions for social prestige. Away went the die-hard supporters of the old regime. Into the positions they vacated came those whose careers had been blighted in the past by the need to be noble – the 'officers of fortune', commoners who had won their commissions by exceptional service but remained anchored to the lowest ranks; those confined by lowly birth or lack of funds to such unfashionable branches as the artillery and the engineers; and, above all, the non-commissioned officers. So the armies which conquered western Europe for the Revolution were commanded by men who had acquired their military training under the old regime but had enjoyed rapid promotion after 1789. The great majority (87.3 per cent) of the generals of 1793–4 came from a professional military background, indeed the majority (67 per cent) had completed thirteen years of service or more by 1789. Brigade and battalion commanders enjoyed similar degrees of experience, 86.9 per cent and 73.1 per cent respectively having been professional soldiers at the outbreak of the Revolution. Yet this was also a young army, with more than a third of its colonels under thirty-five years of age and nearly two-thirds under forty-five.

Doing well was not just a question of showing gratitude to the Revolution. It was a matter of life and death. Following the defections of General Lafayette in 1792 and General Dumouriez in 1793, the regime in Paris was hypersensitive to anything which smacked of treason, including failure. No general had been cashiered before 10 August 1792, but 20 had gone by the end of the year, 275 in 1793 and 77 in 1794. Mere dismissal was often not thought to be enough. No fewer than seventeen generals were guillotined in 1793 and sixty-seven more in the following year, making the execution of Admiral Byng by the British in 1757 seem positively slack by comparison. Nothing illustrated better the violence of the French Revolution than the fact that its generals were more likely to die at the hands of their own government than as a result of enemy action. Not that the latter was a negligible risk, for the regime was insistent that its generals should lead from the front, with the result that eighty were killed in action during the 1790s. When one also takes into account the generals lynched by their own men (such as Dillon in 1792), one must concede that the revolutionary generals earned every last morsel of the fame and fortune lavished on them.

Young, talented and insecure, the commanders of 1793–4 broke the mould of European warfare. The generals of Louis XIV and Louis XV had pottered around for years in the Low Countries without ever achieving a decisive result. In 1793-4 the names of the fortresses and even of the battlefields were the same, but the attitude was quite different, with the result that the war left 'the cockpit of Europe' for more than twenty years, returning only for a brief flurry in 1815. Of all the statistics with which the period bristles, perhaps the most revealing is that which tells us that there were 713 battles between 1792 and 1815, but only 2,659 during the previous *three hundred* years. This was partly due to the remorseless insistence by the Committee of Public Safety that the armies must attack, attack, attack, until the enemy was totally defeated: 'shock like lightning and strike like a thunderbolt' was the pithy instruction of 21 August. The ruthlessness bred by this absolute attitude led the National Convention to decree on 26 May 1794 that no British or Hanoverian prisoners should be taken alive. Fortunately, only one French sea-captain ever obeyed this murderous command and, although he was promoted, his example was not followed.

The naval supremacy established by the British in the course of the eighteenth century, and at an ever-accelerating pace after 1793, was to last until the twentieth century. Yet nothing had seemed less likely in 1783, or even 1793, when there were twelve European states with a good claim to be naval powers: four major powers (Great Britain, France, Spain and Russia), five notable powers (Sweden, Denmark, Naples, the United Provinces and Turkey) and three small but not negligible powers (Portugal, the Knights of St John of Malta and Venice). By 1815 there was one superpower (Great Britain) and – a very long way behind – one secondary power (France). All the others had been eliminated. This shift was all the more remarkable in that France had used her land power to capture the navies of four of these (the United Provinces, Spain, the Knights of St John and Venice). Well might a disconsolate General Bonaparte lament in the wake of the defeat at Aboukir Bay that fate seemed to have decided that Britannia should rule the waves.

Two kinds of shortages fatally handicapped the French naval effort. The first was human. When the Revolutionary Wars began, the population was probably about 28,000,000, whereas the total for England, Scotland, Wales and Ireland was less than half that. As we have seen, by means of strenuous overexertion, the revolutionaries were able to mobilize the largest land army ever seen in Europe, yet they could never repeat this feat for the benefit of the navy. There was a deep structural reason for this, deriving ultimately from the relatively small part played by deep-sea fishing and seaborne commerce in the French economy. This confined the pool of skilled seamen on which a navy might draw in time of war to about 50,000. That was why defeats such as the Glorious First of June (1794) or the Nile (1798) were so serious, for just two such bloody encounters could cost the French navy 10 per cent of its effectives in dead and prisoners of war. By 1802 there were 70,000 French sailors held captive in British prisons or hulks and 80,000 by 1814. A comparison of French and British losses in the period is revealing.

Table 12. French and British naval casualties during the Revolutionary-Napoleonic Wars

| Battle | British Losses | | | French Losses | | | | |
	Killed	Wounded	Total	Killed	Wounded	Total	Prisoners	Grand total
1st of June	287	811	1,098	1,500	2,000	3,500	3,500	7,000
St Vincent	73	227	300	430	570	1,000	3,157	4,157
Camperdown	203	622	825	540	620	1,160	3,775	4,935
The Nile	218	677	895	1,400	600	2,000	3,225	5,225
Copenhagen	253	688	941	790	910	1,700	2,000	3,700
Totals	1,034	3,025	4,059	4,660	4,700	9,360	15,657	25,017

Source: Michael Lewis, A Social History of the Navy 1793–1815 (London, 1960), p. 362

Moreover, with long-range fishing and trade virtually closed down by British command of the high seas, these terrible losses could not be made good. It was a problem exacerbated by a lack of interest and understanding on the part of the Revolution's legislators, very few of whom had ever *seen* the sea: two-thirds of the deputies of the revolutionary assemblies came from rural communities with fewer than 5,000 inhabitants. This indifference contrasted sharply with attitudes in England, where nothing less than a myth of naval power dated back at least to the wars of Elizabeth I, which had provided a stock of Protestant sea-dog heroes to complement Foxe's Martyrs. Seen as inseparable from national liberty and commercial prosperity, 'it made English sea power the ideal expression of the nation in arms' (Nicholas Rodger).

The other fatal shortage suffered by the French was of materials. The navy ministers of the old regime, notably the marquis de Castries, had not only built an impressive number of warships, they had also stockpiled the huge amounts of timber, cordage and other naval stores necessary to keep a fleet seaworthy. They had done so, however, only with increasing difficulty and only by incurring enormous debts – by 1789 the navy ministry was 400,000,000 *livres* in debt. The final bankruptcy of the old regime and the collapse of discipline in the naval bases (in large measure due to long and lengthening arrears of pay) led to a serious deterioration in the condition of the stockpiled reserves. When war broke out with Great Britain, it became increasingly difficult to replenish them with supplies from the Baltic and the Black Sea. The brief loss of Toulon was particularly serious in this regard, for the British succeeded in burning almost all the great stocks of naval stores in the arsenal before they evacuated. By 1795 the French shipbuilders had exhausted their stocks of wood suitable for ships of the line and had to switch to building frigates. In 1793 the fleet had consisted of eighty-eight ships of the line and seventy-three frigates; by 1799 there were just forty-nine and fifty-four respectively.

British problems over both men and materials were much less acute. With a maritime base both wider and deeper than its enemy's, the Admiralty experienced less difficulty in supplying the navy with skilled seamen. It was helped greatly by the apparently inexhaustible financial resources which allowed attractive bounties to be offered to recruits. Contrary to popular belief, the notorious and dreaded press-gangs were not the only means of filling the ranks. Unlike in France, the Royal Navy had first call on the budget: 'To its immense good fortune the Navy had enjoyed almost a golden age of public and parliamentary support in the decade preceding 1793' (Paul Webb). That continued: Parliament voted the necessary funds for 24,000 seamen in 1793 – and for 120,000 in 1797. The census of 1801 recorded 135,000 sailors in the navy and 144,000 in the merchant marine. Moreover, the British took good care to keep their sailors healthy: 'the great thing in all military service is health', as Nelson observed. A French visitor to a British frigate after the American War was suitably impressed: 'it is kept in such scrupulous cleanliness that we were astonished, I saw nothing like it on a frigate in Toulon. They blame the uncleanliness of the French, and say it causes more casualties than the English. They wash the entire ship every day.'

Under the energetic administration of Sir Charles Middleton (comptroller of the navy from 1778 to 1790), the naval dockyards were characterized by greater efficiency in management, economy in the use of resources and professionalism on the part of the officials – at a time when their French equivalents were being ravaged by pilfering and neglect. Command of the routes to and from the Baltic ensured an uninterrupted supply of naval stores, so the gulf between the size of the British and French navies could only grow.

The qualitative gap also widened. While the Royal Navy enjoyed the priceless advantage of being able to train its crews at sea, the French were confined to exercises inside their blockaded ports. After months at anchor, it was no wonder that skills proved rusty when eventually they had to be applied on the high seas, as was demonstrated by the chaos which often attended the sailing of a fleet from Brest. Of the 12,000 men in Admiral Martin's squadron, which fled from the British off the Île de Hyères in July 1795, two-thirds had *never even been to sea before*. There is also some doubt as to whether the much-vaunted superiority of the French vessels was really as great as some pessimistic British experts believed. As Acerra and Meyer have pointed out, much of the criticism of British boatbuilders reflected the traditional contempt felt for civilian landlubbers by aristocratic naval officers and must be taken with a large pinch of salt. The French ships were certainly sleeker and faster, but there was a price to be paid: they were also less durable, more fragile and could carry fewer guns relative to overall tonnage. Some of them were also simply too big. The three-decker 120-gun *Commerce de Marseille*, captured at Toulon, greatly impressed Admiralty experts, but it proved to be of little use at sea and was converted into a prison ship in 1796. When conditions were right, a brand-new French ship could go very fast indeed, but at the cost of high building and maintenance costs and a short working life. These were defects greatly exacerbated by the generations of low investment in dockyards.

The widest and most serious gap between the two navies was in the field of gunnery. Iron discipline and constant training at sea helped the British gunners to deliver broadsides which were more co-ordinated, more accurate and – above all – delivered at a much quicker rate, probably twice as fast. Their firepower was enhanced further by superior gunpowder. The British conquest of Bengal had given them access to the best supplies of saltpetre in the world and it is likely that the muzzle velocity of their guns was correspondingly higher. As they closed with the enemy, they could put it to good use in the new 'carronade', a fearsome cannon developed by the Carron ironworks in Scotland, which had reduced 'windage' (the gap between bore and ball) by about 50 per cent and made up in weight of metal delivered what it lacked in range. (French guns, on the other hand, were so poorly maintained that the British could not use those they captured.) The cumulative effect of these and other, smaller innovations, such as standardized blocks, flexible ramrods and more sophisticated signalling, was to create a navy which could be confident of winning every time it encountered the enemy.

Confidence bred aggression. That relentless drive forwards which was so characteristic of the revolutionary armies in their heyday was conspicuously absent from the revolutionary navy, but just as conspicuously present in the Royal Navy. It was best summed up by Nelson's instruction before Trafalgar: 'In case signals can neither be seen nor perfectly understood, no captain can do very wrong if he places his ship alongside that of the enemy.' At Trafalgar, the battle was over in just five hours, by which time Nelson's fleet had taken seventeen prizes and burnt another. As the French and Spanish fought with tenacious courage, so complete a defeat despite the many advantages they enjoyed can only be explained by 'the crushing superiority of British gunnery tactics' (Nicholas Rodger). By this time, British commanders were crazy for battle because they knew they were going to win, even when outnumbered. As Sir John Jervis stood on the quarterdeck of the *Victory* on 14 February 1797 as the much more numerous Spanish fleet approached off Cape St Vincent, his captain, Sir Robert Calder, called out the numbers of the enemy:

'There are eight sail of the line, Sir John.'
'Very well, Sir.'
'There are twenty sail of the line, Sir John.'
'Very well, Sir.'
'There are twenty-five sail of the line, Sir John.'
'Very well, Sir.'
'There are twenty-seven sail of the line, Sir John.'
'Enough, Sir, no more of that: the die is cast, and if there are fifty sail I will go through them.'

It was on this occasion that one of Jervis's subordinates, Commodore Horatio Nelson of the *Captain*, led in person one of the boarding parties that captured the *San Nicolas* and then moved on to board the *San Josef* as well. Not every British commander shared this taste for the offensive. For every Jervis there was a Bridport and for every Nelson there was a Hotham. Several years had to pass before all the dead wood was sent ashore, but gradually the British naval officer corps was culled to become a body distinguished by professionalism, skill and aggression. Its collective quality allowed commanders such as Jervis, Duncan and Nelson to cut the enemy line, knowing that the individual captains would know what to do and would not shrink from doing it. No such *esprit de corps* could be found on the side of their opponents. There were many instances of skill and determination, even heroism, shown by both commanders and crew on the French side but they remained isolated. The general picture was that painted by Admiral Ganteaume: when ordered to sea from Toulon in 1801, he protested that his fleet was in no fit state to do so, for his sailors had received no pay for fifteen months, they were badly fed, their clothes were ragged and their morale was hopeless. Predictably, he failed in his mission to rescue the French army marooned in Egypt since Nelson's victory at the Nile in 1798.

THE WAR OF THE
SECOND COALITION

In the short term, the most serious consequence of Bonaparte's ill-fated Egyptian adventure was the formation of a new coalition. The Tsar of Russia, Paul I, had observed the events of 1796–7 with a mixture of anger and anxiety about what he saw as the 'insatiability' of revolutionary France. Ever since their conquest of the northern coast of the Black Sea, the Russians had been hypersensitive about any threat to their rapidly expanding commercial interests in the eastern Mediterranean. Especially since the annexation of the Crimea in 1783, old ports had been expanded and new ones created, and the value of exports passing through them had more than doubled between 1786 and 1797. Moreover, the Russians were equally anxious about their tenuous hold on the lands they had gained in the second and third partitions of Poland.

Unlike Bonaparte or Talleyrand (or many western historians), they knew just how closely interlinked were Polish and Turkish problems. So when intelligence reports warned of a great fleet of military transports fitting out at Toulon, many Russian ministers nervously concluded that it was directed at them. Some thought it was heading for Albania, from where the troops it carried would march to Bessarabia to link up with Polish rebels; some thought it was heading for Salonika, with the same object in mind; others thought it might sail direct to the Crimea. These economic and political considerations were strengthened by the Tsar's personal involvement in the Knights of St John, the military-cum-religious order which ruled the island of Malta. Bonaparte's seizure of the island in June 1798 en route for Egypt only confirmed Paul's belief in the diabolic nature of the enterprise.

The result was the formation of a grand new coalition, comprising Great Britain, Austria, Russia, Turkey, Portugal and Naples. It was in the course of 1799 that the full folly of Bonaparte's eastern expedition became apparent. He had misjudged the Russians and underestimated the British. It was a supreme irony that he would prove to be the major beneficiary of his own errors, for the failures of the early part of 1798 set up the *coup d'état* of Brumaire which brought him to power. With their most successful general, many of their most talented subordinate commanders and the elite of the French army bottled up by the Royal Navy more than a thousand miles (1,600 km) away, the Directory proved incapable of dealing with the enemy coalition they had done so much to form. The ultimate indictment of their foreign policy was the spectacle of Russians and Turks co-operating during the winter of 1798/9, surely one of the most improbable alliances in the history of the European states-system.

The 'War of the Second Coalition' got off to a false start when the King of Naples jumped the gun in November 1798 and invaded the Roman Republic. Despite initial success, by the end of the year he had taken refuge on Nelson's flagship and his kingdom had been turned into yet another French satellite state as the 'Neapolitan Republic'. When the war proper got going in the spring of 1799, the French suffered one reverse after another in each of the three theatres. In Germany an advance across the Rhine was checked and repulsed by two victories in March scored by the Archduke Charles. In Switzerland too the Austrians occupied Zurich in June and took control of the main Alpine routes. In

Italy it was the elderly but energetic Russian General Count Suvorov who swept the French from the peninsula, with the exception of an enclave around Genoa. In just two months he had conquered Italy more quickly and completely than had Bonaparte in 1796. As in the summer of 1792 and 1793, the last hour of the Revolution seemed to have come.

That the French revolutionaries had found it so difficult to maintain a firm grip on their conquests was due in large measure to the great gulf which had opened up between their rhetoric and their practice. They went to war with the slogan 'war to the châteaux, peace to the cottages', promising to liberate the oppressed peoples of Europe. They were unable to honour this commitment because they could not afford to do so. As the regime was bankrupt and any funds available had to be devoted to the urgent task of feeding the volatile citizens of Paris, the revolutionary armies were obliged to live off the land they liberated. So for the hapless Belgians, Germans, Spanish, Dutch and Italians in their path, they brought not liberation but exploitation in the form of cash levies and the requisition of everything that could be consumed or moved. As the armies were both exceptionally large and exceptionally undisciplined, they also inflicted looting, murder and rape on an unprecedented scale. Although attempts by the locals to resort to armed resistance were ruthlessly crushed, persistent passive resistance ensured that the French could maintain their conquests only by force.

It was a dismal experience for the revolutionaries. They had expected to be welcomed with open arms by a grateful humanity, so when they were rejected, they hardened their hearts and put France first. The rest of Europe, they concluded, had shown that they were still steeped in ignorance and prejudice, unworthy of liberation. Robespierre was not alone in thinking that the French people had outstripped the rest of the human race by two millennia and now constituted what amounted to a different species. This kind of arrogance, which also expressed itself in a rigorously Francophone policy towards the occupied territories, naturally provoked a strong reaction. If nationalism was not an invention of the French Revolution, it was certainly given a powerful impetus by revolutionary cultural and political imperialism.

Widespread anti-French revolts in 1799, the most spectacular of which was the reconquest of the Kingdom of Naples by Cardinal Ruffo's *armata cristiana* (Christian Arm), helped the allies to push the revolutionaries back to their own frontiers. But just when victory seemed to be within their grasp, the coalition began to fall apart. There had always been a fundamental difference of objective between the Russians and the Austrians, the former looking for a restoration of the old regime in Italy, the latter looking for territorial acquisitions at the expense of the Piedmontese and the Pope. To make matters worse, the British pay-masters of both parties were using their financial muscle to insist on dictating strategy from London. Their obsessive mistrust of the Austrians was another self-inflicted handicap. As a result, when yet another coup in Paris injected fresh life into the French war effort, the allies could not make an adequate response. Although the Austrians won another crushing victory in Italy at Novi in August, it was at Zurich that the campaign was decided when General Masséna defeated the Russians under Korsakov. Tsar Paul ordered his armies home. At the same time a joint Anglo-Russian invasion of Holland ended in disaster.

These successes did not come in time to save the regime in Paris. By 1799 the Directory had lost its last shreds of legitimacy by its repeated interventions to overrule the verdict of the electorate. The key figure was now the abbé Sieyès, the veteran operator who had deftly negotiated the whirlpools of revolutionary politics with a pragmatism best summed up by his celebrated response to the enquiry about what he had done during the Terror: 'I survived.' It was he who engineered the *coup d'état* that brought General Bonaparte to power in November 1799. That the General was only one of three Consuls fooled no one – the man on horseback was patently the man in charge.

The military situation confronting him after Brumaire appeared evenly balanced. On the credit side, the counter-revolutionary risings inside France had fizzled out, the Anglo-Russian expeditionary force had gone home with its tail between its legs, and Switzerland had been secured by Masséna's victory at Zurich. On the other hand, an attempt by Lecourbe and the Army of the Rhine to invade Germany had ended in defeat by General von Szataray's Austrians at Sinzheim at the end of November, while in Italy the last fort in French hands apart from Genoa – Coni – fell on 14 December 1799. It was now that Bonaparte took full advantage of the unity of command that his coup had made possible, formulating a plan of campaign, assembling the necessary resources and directing its implementation. The key proved to be his formation of a large reserve army at Dijon, under the command of Berthier, which he could then deploy to capitalize on the central position of Switzerland.

The critical battle was fought at Marengo on 14 June 1800, when Bonaparte won what was arguably the most important battle of his career. If he had lost – and he very nearly did – while militarily he might have lived to fight another day, politically he would have been dead in the water. Even in the few weeks that had passed since he left Paris on 6 May, there had been intensive plotting at home, with ambitious and jealous Jacobin generals such as Bernadotte and Moreau to the fore. Only a decisive victory could have secured the new regime; a decisive defeat might well have destroyed it and plunged France back into the maelstrom of revolutionary politics. In the event, Marengo both screwed down the lid of the French Revolution's coffin and decided the fate of the War of the Second Coalition. Formal peace was still a long way off and many thousands of men would still have to die to secure it, but not much hindsight is needed to appreciate that it was only a matter of time. As Paul Schroeder has written: 'Once again, the only surprise is that Austria stayed in the war another 6 months after Marengo, passing up another chance for a relatively easy escape.' Granting his shattered opponent a badly needed armistice, Bonaparte hurried back to Paris to bang heads together and consolidate his power.

The war did not come to an end until Moreau had defeated the Austrians at Hohenlinden on 3 December 1800. The Peace of Lunéville, concluded on 9 February 1801, confirmed and extended the gains France had made at Campo Formio. It also began the destruction of the Holy Roman Empire, as Bonaparte presided over a great simplification of the map of Germany. Almost exactly two years later, on 23 February 1803, the Imperial Diet approved a settlement which wiped from the map scores, hundreds, of territories. The great beneficiaries were the larger secular princes, notably Prussia, Bavaria, Württemberg and Baden; the losers were the ecclesiastical states, the Free Imperial Cities and the Imperial Knights. It was Bonaparte's intention that the survivors would be large enough to be useful to France as providers of men, money and materials, but not large enough to pose a threat to French security. In the short and medium term, this worked very well, but the more far-sighted could see that the soft centre of Europe had just got appreciably harder – and might well get harder still.

After Lunéville, only Britain remained at war. Her failure to prevent French hegemony on the continent was dramatized when the Spanish invaded Portugal in April 1801 at Bonaparte's behest and forced it into the French orbit. On the other hand, Britannia continued to rule the waves, as Nelson's spectacular victory at Copenhagen in the same month demonstrated. So this particular phase of the Second Hundred Years War had ended in a draw, although in terms of territorial gain the French had come off by far the best. When peace was finally concluded, after many months of wearisome negotiations, all the British had to show for nine years of naval victories was Spanish Trinidad and Dutch Ceylon. Everything else had to be handed back, even the Cape of Good Hope. Lord Grenville, who had been foreign secretary from 1791 until his resignation in February 1801, expressed a very popular sentiment when he told the House of Lords that 'this disgraceful and ruinous treaty . . . [is] the most disgraceful and ruinous measure that could have been adopted'.

THE NAPOLEONIC WARS

General Napoleon Bonaparte did not become the Emperor Napoleon I until 1804, but there is a real sense in which the Revolutionary Wars came to an end in 1802. This has been argued with special cogency by Paul Schroeder. As he shows, the wars that began in 1787 with the Turkish declaration of war on Russia represented a breakdown in the eighteenth-century balance-of-power system. Beginning as a conflict about the future of central and eastern Europe, they expanded after 1792 to include the question of the role of a revived France in the European states-system. When they came to an end, they confirmed British domination of the world overseas, French domination of western and southern Europe and Russian domination of the east. As both Prussia and Austria accepted the settlement, it could have had a long life, but only if the three dominant powers accepted their assigned sphere of influence and their separation either by geographical barriers such as the English Channel or by intermediary zones, the most important of which was the rump of the Holy Roman Empire, including Prussia and Austria.

These conditions could not be realized. As he had shown after the Treaty of Campo Formio, Bonaparte believed that peace was the continuation of warfare by other means. Not only did he refuse the negotiation of a free-trade commercial treaty with the British, he excluded their manufactured goods from every country under his control. The extortion of Louisiana and the attempted extortion of Florida from the Spanish, the re-establishment of slavery and the despatch of an expedition to the Caribbean island of Saint Domingue proclaimed his intention to rebuild a French colonial empire. Contrary to the terms of the 1802 Peace of Amiens with Great Britain, he did not evacuate French troops from the Batavian Republic, annexed Piedmont and Elba to France and occupied Parma. In February 1803 he intervened in Switzerland to impose a new constitution and a new alliance, and to take control of the Alpine passes. The Cisalpine Republic was retitled the 'Italian Republic', with Bonaparte as its president and his stepson, Eugène de Beauharnais, as his viceroy. The reconstruction of the Holy Roman Empire under his aegis ensured that his influence would be predominant there too. In January 1803 a French general who had recently visited Egypt was quoted in the government newspaper as saying that 6,000 men would suffice for a reconquest. Against this background of continuous provocation, it is perhaps not surprising that the British refused to evacuate Malta, as required under the terms of Amiens, and declared war on 18 May 1803.

With the rest of the continent still at peace, albeit uneasily so, the next two years were dominated by Bonaparte's attempt to organize an invasion force at Boulogne. 'Let us be masters of the Straits but for six hours, and we shall be masters of the world', he declared. A colossal amount of time, effort and money was expended, with the result that, by the spring of 1805, 2,240 barges had been assembled, ready to transport an army of 165,000 men and 23,000 horses. Admirers of Bonaparte – or rather Napoleon as he should be known following his self-coronation as 'Emperor of the French' on 2 December 1804 – would do well to examine closely this preposterous enterprise. As Nicholas Rodger has demonstrated, 'his idea of the time and conditions necessary for the operation was completely divorced from reality'. Simply to embark this great armada would have required a week of good weather, and two days more of perfectly calm conditions would be needed to cross the Channel. And even that scenario assumes that the Royal Navy would be completely inactive. Well might the navy minister, Decrès, despair over Napoleon's 'bizarre, shifting and contradictory projects'.

They did, however, have one side-benefit: they allowed the *La Grande Armée*, as Napoleon called his invasion force, to be trained up to peak efficiency. This was just as well, for during the course of 1804 a third coalition was in the process of formation. Napoleon's reconstruction of Germany, the kidnapping and judicial murder of the Bourbon duc d'Enghien in March 1804 and the assumption of the imperial title all helped to propel the Austrians and Russians into a secret agreement at the end of the year. Napoleon's creation of the Kingdom of Italy in May 1805, with himself as king it need hardly be added, and annexation of Genoa to France the following month, completed the process. From August 1805 most of the continent was at war again, only Prussia remaining at peace. It was now that Napoleon enjoyed his finest hour. If the Boulogne episode had shown him at his most bone-headed, his conduct of the campaign in Germany showed just why so many contemporaries believed him to be a military genius. That he surely was, although it must also be allowed that his opponents provided the dull background against which his star could shine all the more brightly. Assuming that Italy would be the main theatre, the Austrians assigned only 60,000 troops to Germany. Their commander, General Karl Mack, believed that Napoleon could muster only 70,000 and would take eighty days to reach the Danube. In the event, the Grand Army was 190,000-strong and marched 300 miles (480 km) in *thirteen* days, achieving complete surprise and forcing Mack to capitulate at Ulm on 20 October. For once, the official army bulletin was not exaggerating when it recorded: '30,000 men, among them 2,000 cavalry, together with sixty guns and forty standards have fallen into our hands . . . Since the beginning of the war, the total number of prisoners taken can be assessed at 60,000 . . . Never have victories been so complete and less costly.'

Much more costly, but much more complete in terms of results, was the victory Napoleon scored six weeks later over a combined Austro-Russian army at Austerlitz in Moravia. Every account of this, the greatest of his victories, agrees that Napoleon showed again and again on the battlefield that '*coup d'œil*' so prized by Clausewitz – 'a sense of unity and a power of judgement raised to a marvellous pitch of vision'. The grim post-battle statistics reveal the extent of his victory: on the allied side 15,000 dead or wounded and 12,000 taken prisoner; on the French side, 8,000 dead or wounded and 573 taken prisoner. Napoleon wrote home to the Empress Josephine: 'I have beaten the Austro-Russian army commanded by the two Emperors. I am a little weary. I have camped in the open for eight days and as many freezing nights. Tomorrow I shall be able to rest in the castle of Prince Kaunitz, and I should be able to snatch two or three hours sleep there. The Russian army is not only beaten but destroyed. I embrace you.' The Russians withdrew eastwards, to fight another day. The Austrians hastened to make peace, signed at Pressburg on 26 December. They gave up Venice, Venetia, Istria and Dalmatia to the Kingdom of Italy; Trentino, the Tyrol and Vorarlberg to Bavaria; and the Breisgau to Baden and Württemberg.

By the end of 1805 Napoleon was on top of Europe, but he was not on top of the world. On the day after his triumph at Ulm, disaster struck at Trafalgar. In just five hours of fighting, Nelson's fleet of twenty-seven captured or destroyed more than half the Franco-Spanish fleet of thirty-three, suffering no losses in the process. In a devastating demonstration of the superiority of their gunnery, the British inflicted ten times as many casualties on their enemy. The consequences proved to be of immense importance. Although Napoleon spent enormous sums in an attempt to reconstruct the battlefleet he had 'thrown away' (Rodger), British maritime supremacy was now absolute. They were safe from invasion and could continue to expand their already immense colonial and commercial empire. The wealth thus generated enabled them to keep on subsidizing their continental allies. As we shall see later, their invulnerability led Napoleon to pursue a blockading policy which eventually brought the fatal campaign against Russia in 1812. Most could now see that the British could not lose the war, but few realized that they must win.

Back on the continent, Napoleon's focus swivelled to the north. Prussia had been neutral since 1795, but in the autumn of 1805 had moved closer to the third coalition. Austerlitz put a stop to that. Napoleon now applied both the carrot and the stick, allowing a Prussian occupation of Hanover but also extracting commitments to provide troops for the next campaign against Russia and to close Prussian ports to British shipping. Prussia's half-hearted co-operation with Austria during the first Revolutionary War and their inactivity during the previous decade have won the Prussians a bad press from historians enjoying the benefit of hindsight. Yet more territory was added to Prussia during the reign of Frederick William II (1786–97), usually depicted as a gross voluptuary who squandered his inheritance, than during the reign of Frederick the Great. It is also worth remembering that, however inglorious, over the years neutrality had paid handsome political, economic and cultural dividends. Indeed, the years 1795–1806 were something of a golden age. Some sympathy might also be felt for the Prussians' dilemma, situated as they were between the French frying-pan and the Russian fire.

Nevertheless, there was undoubtedly much confusion and indecision to be found in Berlin, where there were two foreign ministers – Haugwitz and Hardenberg – pursuing different policies. By the summer of 1806, those advocating a showdown with the insatiable Napoleon were gaining the upper hand. The formation of the 'Confederation of the Rhine' in July revealed Napoleon's intention to turn the German states into satellites. The last straw proved to be the news that he was planning to buy peace with the British at Prussia's expense by handing back Hanover. Early in October Frederick William III in effect declared war by issuing an ultimatum he knew would be rejected. The war was over in a week: at the twin battles of Jena and Auerstedt the Prussian armies were routed. So sudden and total was the collapse that the decision to fight alone has seemed incomprehensible to most non-Prussian historians. Typical was Felix Markham's dismissive comment, 'having ruined the Third Coalition in 1805 by her selfish neutrality, Prussia proceeded in 1806 to commit suicide by taking on Napoleon single-handed'. That was not how it seemed at the time: the Prussians believed that their very large army could achieve sufficient military success to force Napoleon to treat them as equals not as satraps. However misplaced their optimism may have been, they did not go to war expecting to lose. No less a figure than General Blücher proclaimed that 'the French will find their grave on this side of the Rhine and those that make it back home will take with them news of disaster, just like after Rossbach!'

Perhaps even more depressing than the battles themselves was the way in which the Prussian state imploded. Not always noted is the fact that the French had not even reached the frontier, for Jena and Auerstedt are in Saxony. Yet one Prussian fortress after another surrendered with little or no resistance. The commander of Küstrin hurried across the River Oder to greet the advancing enemy, so anxious was he to capitulate. This might have been *finis Borussiae*, if Frederick William III had agreed to the armistice Napoleon now offered. The crucial council took place on 21 November 1806, with the reform party led by Baron vom Stein successfully arguing for continued resistance. In the view of Ranke this was one of the great turning points in the history of the Prussian monarchy. It meant that Prussia's fate was now yoked to that of Russia (which had entered the conflict in 1805) and it also led Napoleon into making a fateful error. By advancing further east he allowed himself to be drawn into the labyrinth of eastern European politics. Although it took some time for the consequences to work themselves out, he was never to escape.

In the short term Napoleon advanced into Poland, acquiring a mistress in the attractive shape of Countess Marie Walewski and encouraging her fellow countrymen to shake off the Russian yoke. From there he moved north into East Prussia, where on 8 February 1807 at Eylan he fought one of the bloodiest battles of his career, gaining a technical victory but losing perhaps as many as 25,000 men in the process. '*Quel massacre! Et sans résultat*', exclaimed Marshal Ney as he rode over the battlefield afterwards. The battle also marked an important step towards the rehabilitation of the Prussian army, for a corps under General Lestocq had performed effectively. Eylau proved to be only a brief setback on Napoleon's triumphant progress towards the total domination of the continent, however, for on 14 June in the same year he defeated the Russians decisively at Friedland, south-east of Königsberg, and forced them to make peace at Tilsit on the River Niemen on 9 July. As Napoleon was anxious to get back west to complete the reorganization of Italy and Germany, the settlement was surprisingly favourable to Russia. All that had to be ceded were the Ionian Islands, indeed a good slice of Prussian Poland was gained. In effect, the two powers agreed to an alliance which divided Europe into two, with France dominating the west, centre and south-west and Russia the east and south-east, with the prospect of further expansion in the Balkans at the expense of the Turks and in central and southern Asia at the expense of the British. Tsar Alexander I positively welcomed the requirement to join the continental blockade and to make war on Britain. The real victim was Prussia, which lost more than a third of its territory and half of its population, had its army reduced to 42,000, and was required to pay an enormous financial indemnity and to maintain a large French army of occupation. To make matters worse, the old nightmare of Saxony-Poland was revived, for the King of Saxony (as the Elector was now called) was to be hereditary ruler of the new Grand Duchy of Warsaw, comprising what had been Prussia's share of the second and third partitions.

THE NAPOLEONIC EMPIRE
UNRAVELS

When these two hectic years of warfare were over, the map of Europe had been redrawn and recoloured. In the process a great new dynasty had been created. The Netherlands had been changed into a kingdom, ruled by Napoleon's brother Louis. The Bourbons had been ejected from the Kingdom of Naples, in favour of another Bonaparte brother, Joseph. Among the beneficiaries of the destruction of the Holy Roman Empire (finally laid to rest in 1806) was yet another Bonaparte brother, Jerome, who became the ruler of the newly created Kingdom of Westphalia. Another new creation, the Grand Duchy of Berg, was given to Joachim Murat, married to Napoleon's sister Caroline. Napoleon reserved northern Italy for himself, creating the 'Kingdom of Italy' there and installing his stepson, Eugène de Beauharnais, as his viceroy. The Duchy of Guastalla he gave to his favourite sister, Pauline, and her husband Prince Camillo Borghese, although they sold it to Parma for 6,000,000 francs. Another sister, Elisa, and her husband, Prince Bacciochi, were given Tuscany in 1808. In the same year Napoleon promoted his brother Joseph to be King of Spain, transferring Murat to the vacancy thus created at Naples.

This parody of old regime dynastic politics brought disaster. The imposition of Joseph Bonaparte on Spain led to risings across the country, fuelled by a variety of resentments, as much internecine as directed against the new regime. After a French army around 20,000-strong capitulated at Bailén in July 1808, the following month a British expeditionary force under the command of Sir Arthur Wellesley landed in Portugal. Thus began the 'Spanish ulcer', which over the next five years was to prove a serious drain on Napoleon's resources. Time and again – most notably when Napoleon went to Spain himself to take command – it looked as though the insurgency might be overcome, and just as often it revived. Wellesley (or Wellington as he should be known following his elevation to the peerage in 1809) retreated from Spain back to Portugal twice in 1809, held on by the skin of his teeth in the lines of Torres Vedras outside Lisbon in 1810–11, retreated from Spain again after another invasion in the autumn of 1812, but in 1813 did finally begin an inexorable advance that took him over the French frontier in October of that year. What ultimately gave him the decisive advantage was naval support. As he himself wrote, 'if anyone wishes to know the history of this war, I will tell him it is our maritime superiority gives me the power of maintaining my army while the enemy are unable to do so'.

During this roller-coaster road to victory, Wellington was given powerful if often incoherent assistance from the guerrilla movements that ravaged the peninsula. A French officer complained that the guerrillas 'attempted to destroy us in detail, falling upon small detachments, massacring sick and isolated men, destroying convoys and kidnapping messengers'. If they ran into a superior force, they melted away into the countryside, hiding their weapons and pretending to be peasants. On average they killed about a hundred French soldiers a day, not enough to achieve victory by themselves but a very useful auxiliary. If social tension and simple criminality played obtrusive parts in mobilizing them, so did religion. The old Spanish sense of being in the front-line of Christendom against the Moors in the Mediterranean, the heretics in the north and the pagans in the New World was still strong. The association of the French Revolution with a new and peculiarly dangerous threat to the True Faith – atheism – gave both the war of 1793–5 and the more intense conflict of 1808–14 a traditional crusading flavour. The transfer of old fervour to a fresh target was neatly symbolized by a ceremony in Cadiz on 25 July 1808, the feast day of St James. The procession to a specially venerated statue of the saint was conducted as usual, with one important difference – the Moorish captives depicted lying prostrate at his feet had been reclothed in the uniforms of French soldiers. This association between national identity and religion was as widespread as the fighting itself. Just a few days earlier, on 16 July, a Spanish force had cut the French line of retreat at the ford of the Menjibar, in the manoeuvres which were to lead to the French disaster at Bailén three days later. The commander reminded his men that it was the anniversary of the battle of Las Navas, the day on which, six centuries before, Alfonso of Castile had defeated the Moors, saving Christianity and founding national independence. The junta of Seville proclaimed:

We are going to fight in defence of the Fatherland and of Religion and our actions must show that we are true Spaniards and Christians. This junta therefore urges the armies, the towns and persons of all classes to improve their habits, to be modest and to endeavour to appease the righteous wrath of God through ... virtue and by means of ceaseless prayer.

A similar combination of national and religious fervour caused problems for Napoleon in many other parts of Europe, not least in Russia. Indeed, it provided the one chink of light to radiate from an otherwise gloomy episode in 1809 when the Austrians tried yet another fall with their old enemy. Rightly concluding that no permanent peace with Napoleon was possible but wrongly assuming that he had been immobilized by the Spanish imbroglio, they declared war in April 1809. After victory at Aspern near Vienna in May they once again paraded their fabled ability to snatch defeat from the jaws of victory by losing at Wagram on 6 July. Yet if their hopes of a German rising in their support had been frustrated by the speed with which Napoleon moved against them, events in the Tyrol revealed the military potential of anti-French insurrections. Annexed to Bavaria by the Peace of Pressburg in 1805, the Tyroleans rose in revolt for 'God, Emperor and Fatherland', as their peasant leader Andreas Hofer proclaimed. After every victory the insurgents conducted services, processions and pilgrimages to give thanks for divine assistance and to supplicate for further marks of favour in their struggle with their anti-clerical tyrant. At the battle of Bergisel on 13 August 1809, when 15,000 Tyrolean peasants defeated 20,000 French and Bavarian regulars, it was a Capuchin – Father Joachim Haspinger – who commanded the left wing. Once the main Austrian army had been defeated, of course, it was only a matter of time before the Tyroleans were brought to heel. Finally defeated in November 1809, Hofer was taken to Mantua and executed.

The Austrians had learnt their lesson. After yet another humiliating peace had been signed at Schönbrunn on 14 October 1809, by which they lost two-thirds of their Polish territory to the Grand Duchy of Warsaw and the other third to Russia, their remaining Adriatic possessions to the Kingdom of Italy, a slice of Bohemia to Saxony and Salzburg to Bavaria, they abandoned resistance and tried conciliation. This was a change of tack with momentous long-term consequences. In Prussia the defeats at Jena and Auerstedt had brought the reformers to power, so that when success eventually came, it was reform that was franked. In Austria the defeat at Wagram led to the dismissal of the reformers and the appointment of Metternich as chancellor, so when success eventually did come, it was his way of thinking that was franked – and he remained in office until the revolutions of 1848. In the short term, Metternich adopted a traditional Habsburg precept – 'Bella gerant alii, tu felix Austria nube!' (Let other countries wage war, may you fortunate Austria marry!) – and arranged a match between Napoleon and the Emperor Francis I's eldest daughter Marie Louise. The knot was tied between the happy couple (and they were a surprisingly happy couple) on 11 March 1810.

Once again, the Habsburg sense of timing was seriously awry, for by now the Napoleonic Empire was beginning to unravel. With Britain invulnerable to direct attack after Trafalgar, Napoleon proposed 'to conquer the sea by the land', as he told his brother Louis. The prohibition of any kind of trade with Britain imposed by the Berlin Decrees of November 1806 was designed to destroy her economy. This was less visionary than it looked. For a year or so after the Peace of Tilsit, Napoleon really was able to impose an effective boycott, prompting the British prime minister Lord Grenville to exclaim, 'I am more alarmed than I can say.' Then the opening up of the Iberian peninsula allowed British exports to flow once more. All the while Napoleon himself was undermining his own policy by authorizing the issue of special licences to allow the import of vital goods and simply to raise revenue. A deep depression in the whole European economy, beginning in 1810, then brought a new crisis for the hard-pressed British and it is a good question as to what might have happened if Napoleon had been able to sustain the pressure.

He could not, because, of all the European powers, it was the British who coped best with the blockade. Their insular position, continuing trade with the rest of the world (which took about two-thirds of British exports) and superior credit institutions allowed them to sit out the economic storm with relative equanimity. As Paul Schroeder put it: 'with all his power, Napoleon not only could not bring the British down, he could not even gain their full attention'. But there was one power whose increasingly hostile attention Napoleon certainly did grasp, and that was Russia. Of all the treaties that Napoleon concluded, it was Tilsit that most clearly revealed his insatiability. No sooner was the ink dry than he was seeking to expand his power into the Russian zone of interest. He gave the Turks covert assistance in their war with Russia, underway since 1806, and also sought to extend his influence over

Persia. Closer to home, he expanded his empire by annexing to France the Kingdom of the Netherlands, Hanover, the Grand Duchy of Berg, Hamburg, Bremen and Lübeck and also occupied the Duchy of Oldenburg. That last action was a particularly provocative breach of the Treaty of Tilsit, for the current duke was Tsar Alexander I's brother-in-law. The choice by the Swedes of Marshal Bernadotte as heir and regent to their childless king in 1811 was interpreted by the Russians as a further French incursion into the Baltic, although in fact Napoleon deeply – and correctly – mistrusted the new Crown Prince.

More fundamental was the running sore that was the Grand Duchy of Warsaw, whose status as a French satellite was underlined when it was allocated the lion's share of Austrian Poland by the Treaty of Schönbrunn in 1809. Perhaps more fundamental still was the economic issue: Russia simply could not survive without British markets and British shipping. Between 1802 and 1806 Russia had sent to Britain 91 per cent of its flax exports, 77 per cent of tallow, 73 per cent of hemp, 42 per cent of linen and even 71 per cent of iron. During those years more than half of all ships docking at St Petersburg were British. When they stopped coming, goods piled up on the quayside and prices collapsed. The main victims were the Russian magnates, whose estates relied on exporting cash crops. Alexander I was of course uncomfortably aware that it was from just this class that the assassins of both his father and his grandfather had come. By the end of 1810 the blockade had been abandoned. Within a year, the number of ships arriving at Kronstadt had doubled.

From the summer of 1811 Napoleon was actively planning the war that was certain to come. Within the course of the next twelve months he assembled a gigantic army in East Prussia, well over 600,000-strong, of whom about 300,000 were French, 190,000 German, 90,000 Polish and 30,000 Italian. Another 50,000 second-line forces and reinforcements followed later. This grandest of grand armies was accompanied by 200,000 animals and 25,000 vehicles when it crossed the River Niemen on 22 June 1812. The most elaborate plans had been laid to feed this horde, but they went awry almost at once. It was not 'General Winter' that defeated Napoleon, as he later maintained, it was sheer distance. When he formally opened the campaign at Erfurt, he was closer to Galway on the west coast of Ireland than he was to Moscow. With every mile his army marched and with every day that passed, the more certain became his eventual defeat (as Charles XII could have told him, or as he himself could have told Hitler). His only hope was to bring the Russians to battle quickly and to defeat them so decisively that they sued for peace. They declined to oblige, not least because they soon discovered that they were heavily outnumbered – they had only just over 200,000 serving in their front-line armies when the war began.

Just how calculated was the Russian refusal to fight the sort of war Napoleon wanted, choosing instead to retreat and retreat, remains an open question. Its effectiveness is undoubted. By the time the Russians did make a stand, at Borodino on 7 September, the Grand Army had already dwindled alarmingly. The Bavarian corps, for example, had lost half its strength through illness before it even made contact with the enemy. Borodino cost Napoleon 30,000 killed and wounded. It was undeniably a victory, for the Russians lost even more and the Grand Army was able to resume its advance to Moscow, which it took a week later, but the Russian general Kutuzov had been able to withdraw the bulk of his army in good order and could look forward to being reinforced continuously – unlike his enemy. Just a month later the Russians enjoyed a numerical superiority. So the retreat from Moscow which began on 20 October was soon degenerating into disaster. Captain Roeder noted in his diary: 'It did not take long for hunger to attack the French army, the regiments began to dissolve and collapse, horses perished in their thousands . . . All the common people in the provinces of Moscow and Kaluga were under arms to avenge the atrocities they had suffered.' That last remark points to an important force accelerating the disintegration of the Grand Army, namely the unofficial action of tens of thousands of partisans, both organized and freelance. The scale of the disaster was stupendous. Of the 655,000 troops that had crossed the Vistula only 93,000 remained. Some 370,000 had died as a result of enemy action or disease, or had simply frozen to death; around 200,000, including 48 generals and 3,000 other officers, had been taken prisoner. From the point of view of Napoleon's long-term military prospects, just as serious as this human carnage was the loss of virtually his entire stock of horses, as many as 200,000.

It says a great deal for the accumulated stock of credibility that Napoleon had built up during the palmy days that it took more than year before his empire finally fell. Whatever one thinks of his prolongation of Europe's agony, it is difficult not to be impressed by the resilience he and his army displayed as the shadows lengthened. The first of his unwilling allies to jump ship was Prussia, neutralized by the unilateral action of General von Yorck in signing the Convention of Tauroggen with Russia on 30 December 1812, and confirmed officially by the Treaty of Kalisch on 28 February 1813. The Austrians were more hesitant, for Metternich had no desire to see French hegemony replaced by a Russian version. It was only when it became clear that Wellington had achieved total victory in Spain, followed by the revelation of Napoleon's total intransigence in an interview with Metternich at Dresden in June, that Austria moved from cautious neutrality to belligerence. By the Treaty of Teplitz of 9 September 1813, the three great continental powers pledged to provide armies of 150,000 each and not to make peace until Napoleon had been defeated.

This was the first time since the Revolutionary Wars had begun that Russia, Austria and Prussia had acted in concert. The effects were soon felt. In the course of a terrible four-day battle at Leipzig between 16 and 19 October, Napoleon's hold on Germany was shattered. At two crucial moments during the battle, the troops of his German puppet princes turned against him: on the very first day, the refusal of General Normann and the Württemberg cavalry to charge saved the Prussian infantry from being routed by Marshal Marmont; on the third day the defection of the Saxon units proved to be 'the decisive event' (Jean Tulard). According to Major Odeleben, who was situated close to Napoleon, it was this that visibly demoralized him. On the following day, he ordered the retreat. What was already a disaster was made worse by the premature destruction of a bridge across the Elster which trapped the rearguard. In all, the French lost 38,000 during the battle and at least another 30,000 as prisoners. A huge amount of ordnance fell into allied hands, including 325 pieces of artillery. Napoleon went straight back to Paris, leaving the remnants of his army to trudge back through the debris of his empire. By the end of 1813 the Prussian army under Blücher had crossed the Rhine into France.

In the course of his interview with Napoleon at Dresden on 26 June 1813, Metternich told him that a favourable peace could be secured with the allies today, but perhaps not tomorrow. Napoleon's reply was uncompromising: he would not dishonour himself; he would rather die than give up an inch of territory; the old regime sovereigns could lose as many battles as they liked and still keep their thrones, whereas he, as a 'parvenu soldier', could not afford even one defeat; his rule would not last a day longer if his force failed and he was no longer feared. Metternich then gave him a piece of his mind (by his own account), telling him that everything Napoleon had said demonstrated that Europe could never secure a durable settlement with him; that his peace treaties had only been truces; that both defeats and victories impelled him to war; that the final struggle between him and Europe was about to begin – and that it was not Europe that was going to lose. Napoleon was in fact quite wrong about the impossibility of accepting peace. On that occasion and repeatedly afterwards, even after the defeat at Leipzig, he could have obtained a settlement which kept him as ruler of a France with natural frontiers, for Metternich's desire to maintain a balance between France and Russia never did weaken. Napoleon would have none of it. Although he demonstrated great skill during the campaigns of early 1814, he was inexorably forced back by the overwhelming numerical superiority of the allies. Deserted by his marshals, Napoleon abdicated on 6 April and went into exile on the island of Elba.

WHY THE FRENCH LOST (EVENTUALLY)

As in 1914, both sides went to war in 1792 expecting to be home before Christmas. 'In the face of our brave patriots, the allied armies will fade away like the shades of night in the face of the rays of the sun', predicted Gaston to a cheering National Assembly, while on the other side a senior Prussian official, Bischoffwerder, told a group of officers: 'Do not buy too many horses, gentlemen, the comedy will not last long. The army of lawyers will soon be crushed and we shall be back home by the autumn.' In the event, neither side could achieve a decisive victory, with the result that peaces proved to be only truces. In view of the roll-call of great French victories – Valmy, Jemappes, Fleurus, Marengo, Hohenlinden, Ulm, Austerlitz, Jena, Auerstedt, Friedland, Wagram, just to mention the more spectacular – that might seem very odd. Yet the obvious question is not often posed: if each of these was so overwhelming a victory, why did there have to be so many of them? The answer lies, of course, in the simple fact that the decisive quality of any battle is more a subjective than an objective concept. The decision-makers of the old regime just refused to believe that all was lost, even after the most catastrophic of defeats. They had good reason for their obstinacy, which only a close reading of the military history of the period will reveal. The Austrians, in particular, kept coming back for more, rather like those infuriating lead-weighted toys which always right themselves after being knocked over, with the same fatuous grin painted on their faces. Napoleon observed contemptuously that the Habsburgs were always one idea and one army behind the rest of Europe, but – as Albert Sorel remarked – they always had an army and they always had an idea. It was Napoleon who ran out of both.

Even in its Napoleonic version, revolutionary France was never able to convince old regime Europe that it had come to stay. Its successes, however dazzling, were thought to be ephemeral – just one more push, its enemies thought, and down it would come. In the event, many more pushes were needed, but in the end they were right. Although the operation took twenty-three years longer than had been hoped or expected, the allies did eventually achieve their war aims. This is not always appreciated, because the counter-revolutionary nature of the war of 1792 is so often exaggerated. The Prussians and Austrians did not go to war in 1792 to restore the old regime, they went to war to induce the revolutionaries to maintain a constitutional settlement which would keep France monarchical but weak (a kind of western version of Poland) and also, of course, to gain territory. That was exactly what they got in 1815.

By that time both sides were poorer but wiser. They had had to learn the error of their ways in a school where discipline was brutal and there were no vacations. Napoleon never learnt, so his empire fell as fast as it had risen. Before he had time to finish the Arc de Triomphe, it was the allies who were holding a victory parade on the Champs-Élysées. He himself liked to think that he had been the victim of bad luck (the early onset of the Russian winter in 1812, for example) and treachery (the desertion of his marshals in 1814), but with the advantage of hindsight we can see that his problems were more structural in nature. Perhaps the most intractable was demographic imbalance. Although the population of France had increased by about 30 per cent in the course of the eighteenth century, this was a rate of growth eclipsed by the other countries of Europe. This relative decline was due less to any deficiency in virility or fecundity than to the simple fact that, by contemporary standards, France had been a densely populated country when the century began, so the population was soon banging its head against the demographic ceiling imposed by inelastic food supplies. By the time the Revolutionary-Napoleonic Wars began, the demographic dominance which had made Louis XIV so formidable was a thing of the past.

To conquer Europe from a base that was too narrow and shallow involved overexertion. The French were obliged to exert so much pressure on both their own population and that of occupied Europe that the law of diminishing returns soon began to operate. In the short term, the problem was dealt with by the establishment of the satellite state, an inspired invention which was to have a future as long as it was dishonourable. Wherever the French went in Europe, they found dissidents prepared to collaborate with the invaders to obtain support in dealing with their political enemies. If peace had ever been restored long enough to allow these new regimes to strike roots, this might have proved a permanent solution. In the event, the need to extract ever-increasing amounts of men, materials and money to feed the French war machine made them reliant on force for their survival. As soon as the prop of the French army was removed, they collapsed in a heap. The same process of alienation occurred in Napoleon's satellite kingdoms. Even those German princes who were given royal titles and vast amounts of land began to wonder whether the game was worth the candle as the price escalated and their subjects became increasingly restive. The number of troops required by Napoleon from his German satraps rose from 63,000 in 1806 to 119,000 in 1809, finally reaching 190,000 with the invasion of Russia in 1812.

For the plain people of Europe, Napoleon's rule had promised much, delivered little and ended in disillusionment. When sending to his brother Jerome a constitution for the Kingdom of Westphalia, Napoleon stated: 'What people will wish to return to the arbitrary rule of Prussia when it has once tasted the benefits of a wise and liberal administration? The peoples of Germany, France, Italy and Spain demand civil equality and liberal ideas.' Some benefits they undoubtedly did receive, in the shape of civil equality, careers open to talent, legal reform and the metric system. But against that had to be set an increased and constantly growing burden of taxation, conscription and a government much more tyrannical than anything they had experienced under the old regime.

The longer the Napoleonic regime lasted, the more unpopular it became.

By 1813 the empire was crumbling from within, as confidence and support were eroded further by failure in Spain after 1808, growing resistance to conscription, and a severe economic crisis which had begun in 1810. What was worse, Napoleon's enemies were beginning to put their own house in order. They had been prevented from mobilizing their full weight by three main failings: their preoccupation with eastern Europe, their mutual antipathies and their reluctance to fight fire with fire. It was Napoleon's personal achievement to bring the western and eastern theatres of the war together, first in 1798 and then terminally after 1806. He also dealt with the second handicap under which his enemies laboured – their mutual distrust. By treating them all so brutally during his glory years of 1805–7, he drummed into their thick skulls the message that they must sink their differences and unite against him. The lesson took some time to penetrate, for in 1809 the Austrians once again had to take the field alone, but eventually it was learnt.

It was also Napoleon who forced the old regime powers to adopt revolutionary methods to combat revolutionary force. It was not so much that they could not grasp what to do, rather that they could not face the terrible side-effects. Certainly the French revolutionaries had constructed a state of colossal power but they appeared to have done so at the cost of killing their king and queen, expropriating their Church, abolishing their nobility, instituting a reign of terror, plunging the country into civil war, unleashing galloping inflation, and so on and so forth. By 1808, however, Napoleon was busy rearranging the thrones of Europe. If he could depose the Bourbons in Spain and Naples, why not the Hohenzollerns and Habsburgs? Indeed, it was well known that he had toyed with just such an idea in 1807 and 1809 respectively. As it now seemed to be all or nothing, even radical reforms had to be risked in the search for survival. By 1812–13 it was the allies who were arming their peasants and mobilizing mass armies.

More fundamentally still, Napoleon was bound to fail because his appetite for *gloire* was insatiable. Like the French Revolution from whose culture he sprang, he never had any war aims beyond victory. This was grasped at an early stage with special insight by the Prussian officer Carl von Clausewitz, the greatest military theorist of the age (or of any age for that matter). His celebrated dictum – 'war is nothing but the continuation of policy by other means' – is often misunderstood as an advocacy of militarism, whereas in reality it is a normative statement and better formulated as: 'war *should* be nothing but the continuation of policy by other means'. Napoleon, on the other hand, always made war first and determined his policy according to the degree and nature of his success. So even after the Prussian defeats at Jena and Auerstedt, and his own experiences as a French prisoner of war, Clausewitz remained convinced that Napoleon would eventually be defeated and that his destruction would be certain if he invaded Russia.

THE CONGRESS OF VIENNA

After Napoleon's departure to Elba, more than eighteen months were to pass before the Revolutionary-Napoleonic Wars were finally brought to an end by the Second Treaty of Paris of 20 November 1815. Such a major reconstruction of Europe would necessarily have taken a long time, but further delay was occasioned by Napoleon's return from Elba on 1 March 1815 for a last, desperate attempt to regain his empire. This episode has received excessive attention because of the dramatic way it ended at Waterloo on 18 June after the 'Hundred Days', but it was really nothing more than a coda marked '*diminuendo*'. Although the actual battle may have been 'a damn close-run thing', as the Duke of Wellington put it, the numerical superiority of the allies was such that the outcome of the campaign was certain before it ever began.

Twenty-three years of fighting had probably killed around 5,000,000 Europeans, or proportionally at least as many as the First World War. The two great victors were the peripheral powers. Great Britain had achieved all its war aims: French hegemony on the continent had been destroyed; the Low Countries were reorganized as a single 'Kingdom of the Netherlands' under the house of Orange; the sea-routes to India were secured by the acquisition of Ceylon, Mauritius and the Cape of Good Hope; and continuing British influence in the Mediterranean was secured by the retention of Malta. In terms of territory, Russia had done even better, acquiring Finland from Sweden in 1809, Bessarabia from the Turks in 1812 and most of Poland in the Vienna settlement. Although not so obvious at the time, the Prussians had also done very well. Quantitatively they were a long way down the list, but qualitatively they were at the top, for their acquisitions included at least four regions with great economic potential: northern Saxony, the Aachen-Cologne-Krefeld triangle, the Saarland and the Ruhr. The peace-makers gave them most of the left bank of the Rhine and Westphalia to create a buffer against French expansion, but in doing so they also made Prussia much more of a German power than it had been in the past.

It took a long time for the implications of these Prussian gains to be worked out. In the short and medium term, it appeared that the Austrians had done best. If they had to abandon their Belgian territories (lost since 1794) and the bits and pieces in the south-west, they regained everything they had lost between 1797 and 1809, including Salzburg, the Tyrol and Galicia. As the Emperor of Austria was to be president of the new 'German Confederation' of thirty-nine states, he was much better placed to dominate central Europe than the Holy Roman Emperor had ever been. Austria was also now indisputably the hegemonial power in Italy, ruling Lombardy, Venetia and the Dalmatian coast directly and Tuscany, Modena, Parma, Piacenza and Guastalla as 'secundogenitures' of the Habsburg family. Yet not much foresight was needed to see the problems that were to become so acute a generation or so later. As Austria was now much more of an Italian power than it had ever been in the past, the hostility of France was inevitable. Savoy-Piedmont-Sardinia, restored and strengthened by the addition of Genoa, was intended to be a buffer against France but potentially was a French ally, as indeed events were to prove in 1859. As Austria was now much more of a Balkan power than it had been in the past, the hostility of Russia was inevitable. That was also to become clear in 1859 when Tsar Alexander II gave Napoleon III of France the all-clear to expel the Austrians from Italy, thus preparing the way for Prussia to expel them from Germany.

All too immediate were the losses inflicted on the two Iberian powers, albeit indirectly. Both retained or regained their territorial integrity, but both emerged from the wars so drained of resources as to be unable to sustain their great overseas empires. With the advantage of hindsight, we can see that Spain had been the chief loser at Trafalgar. The seizure of Caracas in 1810 by a group of patriots including Simon Bolivar ('The Liberator') marked the beginning of a rapid collapse of metropolitan authority. By 1830 almost all of South America had achieved independence. Moreover, the acute polarization of opinion inside Spain after 1793 bedevilled the country's politics throughout the nineteenth century. In particular, the impoverishment of the Church and consequent reduction of its social role encouraged the development of the radical anti-clericalism that was to play such a disruptive role deep into the twentieth century. Spain had benefited from its French connection during the eighteenth century but the Revolution brought only disaster.

The fate of France is less easy to assess. On the face of it, she was treated with extraordinary generosity by the allies, being allowed to go back to the frontiers of 1790 (or in other words to retain the papal enclaves of Avignon and the Comtat Venaissin), and even to regain most of the Caribbean islands. Yet during the twenty-three years of the war, French power had been dealt a series of terrible blows, most of them self-inflicted. The 1,400,000 Frenchmen lost as a result of the wars (some estimates go much higher) left the country with a low male/female ratio (down from 0.992 in 1790 to 0.857 in 1815) and a falling share of Europe's population. The Revolution's agrarian settlement, confirmed and reinforced by Napoleon, both accentuated this demographic weakness and put the whole French economy in lead boots. The collapse of French maritime power allowed the British to establish an unassailable colonial, commercial and industrial advantage. It was Britain not France that became 'the workshop of the world'. As the French economic historian François Crouzet concluded: 'France was not disastrously behind [in the 1780s], and the Industrial Revolution might have taken off there with only a few years' delay in relation to England. But the "national catastrophe" which the French Revolution and the twenty years war meant to the French economy would intensify the discrepancy and make it irremediable.' In short, France no longer had the financial, economic and demographic resources that had made Louis XIV's hegemony possible. But the world had become a much more dangerous place as a result of the destruction of the Holy Roman Empire.

For a generation or so, this structural vulnerability was masked by a long period of peace. There was to be no major war in Europe until the outbreak of the Crimean War in 1854. As Paul Schroeder has argued persuasively, the selfish brutality of Napoleon eventually persuaded the other great powers that they had to change their attitude fundamentally:

He finally convinced the statesmen of Europe, hard persons to teach, that what was at risk was not merely certain goods in international politics (peace, security, territorial integrity) but the very life principle of European politics which made these goods and others possible, the independence of European states, the exist-

THE WARS OF THE FRENCH REVOLUTION AND NAPOLEON

ence of a European states system. He made them see that the kind of politics they had hitherto practised themselves had made his rise to power and his colonial rule possible; that to preserve the international system on which they depended from being wholly destroyed and replaced by colonial rule, they would have not only to defeat or curb him but also to abandon their own old politics, and discover or invent something else.

Most important was the conversion of the two powers of the periphery, Russia and Great Britain, increasingly invulnerable by dint of size and insularity respectively and so the natural hegemons of post-Napoleonic Europe and the only true world-powers. The three master-builders of the Vienna settlement – Castlereagh for Britain, Alexander I for Russia and Metternich for Austria – came to see that 'the chief cause of a generation of war and disaster had not simply been revolution or Napoleonic imperialism, but the arbitrary, lawless use of power in general, and that this had to be stopped'. So they did three crucial things: they established a reciprocal guarantee of territories, security and status, supported by recognized norms of behaviour; they fenced off Europe from colonial, commercial and maritime conflicts; and they created a network of 'intermediary bodies'. The last-named were not just buffer-states, but served also as links between one great power and another. Thus the Kingdom of the united Netherlands not only blocked any further French attempt to control the Low Countries but also formed a bridge between the German powers and Great Britain. *Mutatis mutandis*, the same sort of role was played by Scandinavia, Switzerland, Italy, Turkey and the German Confederation. The last-named was the most important, for although it did not bring unity – 'an impossible and undesirable goal' in Schroeder's view – it did create concord without unity, making Germany secure at home and safe for Europe. In other words, Europe after 1815 was rather like a catamaran, with the two outriggers (Great Britain and Russia) holding a vulnerable centre above the waves. There is a great deal to be said for this argument, although it might be added that the longevity of the Vienna settlement also stemmed from the decisive nature of the war that preceded it. After Napoleon had been defeated and Paris had been conquered not once, but twice, even the most nationalist Frenchman had to appreciate that the war had been lost.

One final paradox of great importance needs to be stressed. The war

which the French revolutionaries unleashed in April 1792 was intenc
to be the most universal war there had ever been, a war for the liberat
of all humanity. Their jaunty confidence was soon frustrated by w
Hegel called 'the cunning of reason'. By the spring of 1793 the war h
ceased to be universal and had become national: as Danton told
National Convention on 13 April, 'above all things we need to look
the preservation of our own body politic and to lay the foundations
French greatness'. The next stage in this ideological contraction tc
much longer because it had so much further to go: by 1808 the war v
being fought for the benefit of one family, the Bonapartes. Yet e
that was not the limit of the contraction, for by 1810 Napoleon v
concluding that his siblings were not sufficiently obedient and v
clawing back what little independence they enjoyed. His brother Lo
for example, was obliged to abdicate as King of the Netherlands.
war had become a war for one man.

Meanwhile, the Revolution's enemies had been moving in the oppo
direction. Their aims in 1792 had been as limited and precise as
means they sought to employ. They did not even suppose they w
embarking on a full-blown war in the spring of 1792; rather they thou
they were organizing an armed demonstration which would send
revolutionary rabble skulking back into submission. In fits and sta
prodded and pushed by the revolutionary challenge outside and th
more far-sighted advisers at home, the 'cunning of reason' took th
from the particular to the universal. As Napoleonic France slip
into military dictatorship, it was the old regime states that introdu
programmes of modernization, mobilized citizen militias, declared tc
war and used the rhetoric of liberation. Alas, after 1815 only the Bri
were able to sustain the relationship, as the continental powers mo
back towards reaction, but that is a story for the next volume in
series.

Conclusion

The most beneficial legacy this period bequeathed to the nineteenth century was the awful warning of what could happen when state power was divorced from traditional restraints and placed at the disposal of one man. So rapacious and brutal was the treatment meted out by Napoleon to the powers he vanquished that even the dimmest of them had to recognize that a new basis for international relations had to be found. It was not enough to defeat Napoleon militarily, for he was only the most malignant symptom of a disease that stretched back deep into the previous century. The competition and conflict engendered by a preoccupation with the balance of power had to make way for a system based on concert and political equilibrium. The result was that during the ninety-nine years that separated Waterloo from the outbreak of the First World War the only major wars were the short, sharp conflicts leading to Italian and German unification. Relative to population, *seven times* fewer men died in battle in the nineteenth century than in the eighteenth.

On the domestic front, the signs were much less clear and much less easy to read. The horrors of the French Revolution were still too fresh in most people's minds to allow a dispassionate assessment of its positive contributions. It was not only the French Bourbons who had forgotten nothing and learnt nothing. If they were unique in having to go on their travels again (in 1830), all the European monarchies had to learn the hard way that after 1789 no regime could be regarded as legitimate if it did not find some way of assimilating the principle of popular sovereignty. Even the British old regime began to look shaky before refreshing its mandate with the Great Reform Act of 1832. The Russians never did learn. Even more difficult to read was the relationship between liberal constitutionalism and nationalism. Although highly intelligent,

Metternich showed a fatal lack of judgement when he treated them as if they were independent. It was to be left to Bismarck to demonstrate that the one could be exploited to emasculate the other.

The future of this and other phenomena can safely be left to the next volume in the series. Reviewing what had happened since 1648, two opposing kinds of narrative might be constructed. The first could be labelled 'progressive' and 'optimistic' and might be presented as follows in 1648 the belief that the earth was the centre of the universe was almost universal; by 1815 it had been discredited even in the most conservative circles (Pope Benedict XIV lifted the ban on heliocentric works in 1757). In 1648 prayers were said and church bells were rung to ward off electrical storms; by 1815 lightning conductors were being installed. In 1648 heretics and witches were being burnt across Europe by 1815 it was their accusers who found themselves in the dock. The dominant leitmotiv was expansion, for this was a period when population, literacy, towns, ease of communication, voluntary association economic activity, overseas empires – just to mention a few of the tastier items from a much longer menu of possibilities – all grew. It was also period when humankind made the decisive breakthrough from the feudal world of the society of orders, the domination of landed wealth and authoritarian government to classes, capitalism and democracy, for witnessed both the American and French Revolutions and the beginning of the industrial revolution.

But there is also more than enough material to support quite a different kind of exercise, which might be labelled 'conservative' and 'pessimistic' This would draw attention to the superficial nature of much of the apparent change and the illusory quality of much of the apparent achievement. At the end of the period, the land-owning elites were still firmly in charge of even the most advanced countries, the overwhelming majority of Europeans were still illiterate peasants, superstition was still rife and a major religious revival was underway. The French Revolution turned out to be all sound and fury, if anything making France more conservative than it had been under the old regime. France after 18 was run by the same sort of mixed elite of noble and commoner *notables* as had ruled before 1789. As for the 'agricultural revolution', 'commercial revolution' and 'industrial revolution', they were not revolutions all, just labels attached retrospectively to an evolutionary process. The changes that had occurred had been for the worse: states were more intrusive, more demanding and more despotic; armies were bigger and more destructive; for the poor, work in the 'dark satanic mills' and life in the mushrooming shanty towns was even nastier and more brutish than in the past. The emancipation offered by the Enlightenment had turned out to be a chimera, being merely the exchange of one kind of tyranny for another and opening the gates that led to the totalitarianism and genocide of the twentieth century. Women, ethnic minorities and those considered to be sexual deviants were still the victims of discrimination and persecution. The fine houses and fancy clothes of the few were financed by the involuntary sacrifices of the many, not least by serfs and slaves. Moreover, the period had ended in the twenty-three years of a world war that in terms of loss of life and suffering put every previous European conflict in the shade.

As this book has tried to show, neither of these narratives is valid in isolation. There is no obligation to accept one or the other in its entirety: a selection can be mixed and matched according to individual taste. While no attempt has been made to disguise the author's own preferences, it is hoped that sufficient illustration, evidence and stimulation has been provided to induce the reader to make a critical choice and, above all, to engage actively with the period and its problems. Here it is appropriate to return to the lines from Goethe's *Faust* with which the Introduction concluded. Faust's alienation led him to make a wager with Mephistopheles that he could never achieve satisfaction sufficient to make him say: 'beautiful moment, do not pass away'. If that were to happen, he agreed, then Mephistopheles could take him. In old age, after many adventures, Faust does at last find contentment in organizing a land reclamation project. But he is redeemed because of his active engagement in the world and his constant striving to understand nature, human nature and his own nature. And that provides a suitably constructive note on which to end.

Suggested Reading

This list is not intended to be in any way comprehensive. I have just included those books and articles I found particularly interesting. Each of the national histories listed below contains a substantial bibliography.

National histories

Jonathan Israel, *The Dutch Republic. Its rise, greatness and fall 1477–1806* (Oxford, 1995)
Simon Schama, *The Embarrassment of Riches. An interpretation of Dutch culture in the golden age* (London, 1987)
Simon Schama, *Patriots and Liberators. Revolution in the Netherlands 1780–1813* (London, 1977)

Wilfrid Prest, *Albion Ascendant. English history 1660–1815* (Oxford, 1998)
The New Oxford History of England
   Julian Hoppit, *A Land of Liberty? England 1689–1727* (Oxford, 2000)
   Paul Langford, *A Polite and Commercial People. England 1727–1783* (Oxford, 1989)
   Boyd Hilton, *A Mad, Bad and Dangerous People? England 1783–1846* (Oxford, 2006)

William Doyle (ed.), *Old Regime France* (Oxford, 2001)
Colin Jones, *The Great Nation. France from Louis XV to Napoleon* (London, 2002)
Emmanuel Le Roy Ladurie, *The Ancien Régime. A history of France 1610–1774* (Oxford, 1996)
Daniel Roche, *France in the Enlightenment* (Cambridge, Mass., 1998)

Hajo Holborn, *A History of Modern Germany*, vol. II 1648–1840 (London, 1965)
Georg Schmidt, *Geschichte des Alten Reiches. Staat und Nation in der Frühen Neuzeit 1495–1806* (Munich, 1999)
James J. Sheehan, *German History 1770–1866* (Oxford, 1989)
Brendan Simms, *The Struggle for Mastery in Germany 1779–1850* (Basingstoke, 1998)
Peter Wilson, *From Reich to Revolution: German History 1558–1806* (Basingstoke, 2004)
Peter Wilson, *The Holy Roman Empire 1495–1806* (Basingstoke, 1999)

R. J. W. Evans, *The Making of the Habsburg Monarchy 1550–1700. An interpretation* (Oxford, 1970)
Charles Ingrao, *The Habsburg Monarchy 1618–1815*, 2nd edn (Cambridge, 2000)
Laszlo Kontler, *A History of Hungary: Millennium in Central Europe* (London, 2002)
Paul Lendvai, *The Hungarians. A thousand years of victory in defeat* (Princeton, 2003)
Derek Sayer, *The Coasts of Bohemia. A Czech history* (Princeton, 1998)

Roy Foster, *Modern Ireland 1600–1972* (London, 1988)

Gregory Hanlon, *Early Modern Italy 1550–1800. Three seasons in European history* (London, 2000)
John A. Merino (ed.), *Early Modern Italy 1550–1796* (Oxford, 2002)
Denis Mack Smith, *A History of Sicily*, 2 vols. (London, 1968)

Norman Davies, *God's Playground. A history of Poland*, rev. edn, 2 vols. (Oxford, 2005)
Jerzy Lukowski and Hubert Zawadzki, *A Concise History of Poland* (Cambridge, 2001)

C. B. A. Behrens, *Society, Government and the Enlightenment: The experiences of eighteenth-century France and Prussia* (London, 1985)
Christopher Clark, *Iron Kingdom. The rise and downfall of Prussia, 1600–1947* (London, 2006)
Philip G. Dwyer (ed.), *The Rise of Prussia 1700–1830* (London, 2000)

Simon Dixon, *The Modernisation of Russia 1676–1825* (Cambridge, 1999)
Paul Dukes, *The Making of Russian Absolutism 1613–1801*, 2nd edn (London, 1990)
Geoffrey Hosking, *Russia. People and empire 1552–1917* (Cambridge, Mass., 1997)
Richard Pipes, *Russia Under the Old Regime* (Harmondsworth, 1977)

H. A. Barton, *Scandinavia in the Revolutionary Era 1760–1815* (Minneapolis, 1986)
Thomas Munck, *Seventeenth-Century Europe 1598–1700* (Basingstoke, 1990) (for Scandinavia)
Franklin D. Scott, *Sweden. The nation's history* (Minneapolis, 1977)

Raymond Carr (ed.), *Spain. A history* (Oxford, 2000)
J. H. Elliott, *Imperial Spain 1469–1716* (London, 1963)
John Lynch, *Bourbon Spain 1700–1808* (Oxford, 1989)

Introduction

Johann Wolfgang von Goethe, *Faust*, Parts One and Two, translated by David Luke (Oxford, 1987, 1994)

Life and death

Philippe Ariès, *Western Attitudes toward Death: From the Middle Ages to the present* (London, 1976)
C. B. A. Behrens, *The Ancien Régime* (London, 1967)
C. B. A. Behrens, 'Government and society', in E. Rich and C. Wilson (eds.), *The Cambridge Economic History of Europe*, vol. V (Cambridge, 1977)
Paula Bennett and Vernon A. Rosario II (eds.), *Solitary Pleasures. The historical, literary and artistic discourses on autoeroticism* (New York and London, 1995)
Jerome Blum, *The End of the Old Order in Rural Europe* (Princeton, 1978)
Clarissa Campbell Orr (ed.), *Queenship in Europe, 1660–1815. The role of the consort* (Cambridge, 2004)
Carlo M. Cipolla (ed.), *The Fontana Economic History of Europe*, vol. III *The Industrial Revolution 1700–1914* (Brighton, 1976)
Ralph Davis, *The Rise of the Atlantic Economies* (London, 1973)
Christof Dipper, *Deutsche Geschichte 1648–1789* (Frankfurt am Main, 1991)
Christof Dipper, 'Orders and classes: eighteenth-century society under pressure', in T. C. W. Blanning (ed.), *The Short Oxford History of Europe: The eighteenth century* (Oxford, 2000)
William Doyle, *The Ancien Régime*, 2nd edn (Basingstoke, 2001)
Martin Duberman, Martha Vicinus and George Chauncey (eds.), *Hidden from History: Reclaiming the gay and lesbian past* (London, 1991)

Robert S. Duplessis, *Transitions to Capitalism in Early Modern Europe* (Cambridge, 1997)

Richard J. Evans, *Rituals of Retribution: Capital punishment in Germany, 1600–1987* (London, 1996)

Richard J. Evans and W. R. Lee (eds.), *The German Peasantry* (London, 1986)

Michael Flinn, *The European Demographic System 1500–1820* (Brighton, 1981)

Roderick Floud and Donald McCloskey (eds.), *The Economic History of Britain since 1700*, vol. I *1700–1860*, 2nd edn (Cambridge, 1994)

Netta Murray Goldsmith, *The Worst of Crimes. Homosexuality and the law in eighteenth-century London* (Aldershot, 1998)

Emma Griffin, *England's Revelry: A history of popular sports and pastimes, 1660–1830* (Oxford, 2005)

Janet M. Hartley, *A Social History of the Russian Empire 1650–1825* (London, 1999)

A. D. Harvey, *Sex in Georgian England. Attitudes and prejudices from the 1720s to the 1820s* (London, 1994)

Karen Harvey, *Reading Sex in the Eighteenth Century. Bodies and gender in English erotic culture* (Cambridge, 2004)

Peter Hersche, *Italien im Barockzeitalter 1600–1750. Eine Sozial- und Kulturgeschichte* (Vienna, Cologne and Weimar, 1999)

Henry Hobhouse, *Seeds of Change. Six plants that transformed mankind* (London, 2002)

R. A. Houston, *The Population History of Britain and Ireland 1500–1750* (Cambridge, 1992)

Olwen Hufton, *The Poor of 18th-century France* (Oxford, 1974)

Olwen Hufton, *The Prospect Before Her. A history of women in western Europe*, vol. I *1500–1800* (London, 1995)

Isabel V. Hull, *Sexuality, State and Civil Society in Germany 1700–1815* (Ithaca and London 1996)

Lynn Hunt (ed.), *The Invention of Pornography. Obscenity and the origins of modernity 1500–1800* (New York, 1993)

P. M. Jones, *The Peasantry in the French Revolution* (Cambridge, 1988)

H. Kamen, 'The economic and social consequences of the Thirty Years War', *Past and Present*, 39 (1968)

Sarah Knott and Barbara Taylor (eds.), *Women, Gender and Enlightenment* (Basingstoke 2005)

David Landes, *The Unbound Prometheus. Technological change and industrial development in western Europe from 1750 to the present*, 2nd edn (Cambridge, 2003)

Thomas Laqueur, *Making Sex. Body and gender from the Greeks to Freud* (Cambridge, Mass. and London, 1990)

Maurice Lever, *Les Bûchers de Sodome. Histoire des 'infâmes'* (Paris, 1985)

Salvatore J. Licata and Robert P. Petersen (eds.), *The Gay Past. A collection of historical essays* (New York, 1985)

Mary Lindemann, *Medicine and Society in Early Modern Europe* (Cambridge, 1999)

Neil McKendrick, John Brewer and J. H. Plumb, *The Birth of a Consumer Society. The commercialisation of eighteenth-century England* (London, 1982)

Peter Mathias and John A. Davis (eds.), *The First Industrial Revolutions* (Oxford, 1989)

Jeffrey Merrick and Bryant T. Ragan Jr (eds.), *Homosexuality in Modern France* (New York and Oxford, 1996)

Robert Moeller (ed.), *Peasants and Lords in Modern German History* (London, 1987)

David Moon, *The Russian Peasantry 1600–1930* (London, 1999)

Rictor Norton (ed.), *Homosexuality in Eighteenth-Century England: A Sourcebook*. http://www.infopt.demon.co.uk/eighteen.htm

Rictor Norton, *Mother Clap's Molly House. The gay subculture in England 1700–1830* (London, 1992)

Sheilagh Ogilvie (ed.), *Germany. A new social and economic history*, vol. 2 *1630–1800* (London, 1996)

Sheilagh Ogilvie, 'The European economy in the eighteenth century', in T. C. W. Blanning (ed.), *The Short Oxford History of Europe: The eighteenth century* (Oxford, 2000)

Sheilagh Ogilvie and Markus Cerman (eds.), *European Proto-Industrialisation* (Cambridge, 1996)

Mark Overton, *Agricultural Revolution in England. The transformation of the agrarian economy 1500–1850* (Cambridge, 1996)

Roy Porter, *English Society in the Eighteenth Century* (London, 1982)

Roy Porter, *The Greatest Benefit to Mankind. A medical history of humanity from antiquity to the present* (London, 1997)

Roy Porter and Lesley Hall, *The Facts of Life. The creation of sexual knowledge in Britain 1650–1950* (New Haven and London, 1995)

Marc Raeff, 'Pugachev's rebellion', in Robert Forster and Jack P. Greene (eds.), *Preconditions of Revolution in Early Modern Europe* (Baltimore and London, 1970)

Julius R. Ruff, *Violence in Early Modern Europe* (Cambridge, 2001)

Eda Sagarra, *A Social History of Germany 1648–1914* (London, 1977)

R. Schofield, D. Reher and A. Bideau (eds.), *The Decline of Mortality in Europe* (Oxford, 1991)

Tom Scott (ed.), *The Peasantries of Europe from the Fourteenth to the Eighteenth Centuries* (London, 1998)

B. H. Slicher van Bath, *The Agrarian History of Western Europe 500–1850* (London, 1963)

Jan de Vries, *The Economy of Europe in an Age of Crisis 1600–1750* (Cambridge, 1976)

Merry E. Wiesner, *Women and Gender in Early Modern Europe*, 2nd edn (Cambridge, 2000)

Stuart Woolf, *The Poor in Western Europe in the Eighteenth and Nineteenth Centuries* (London, 1986)

Power

John T. Alexander, *Catherine the Great. Life and legend* (New York and Oxford, 1989)

M. S. Anderson, *Peter the Great* (London, 1978)

Michel Antoine, *Louis XV* (Paris, 1989)

Ronald G. Asch, *Nobilities in Transition 1550–1700: Courtiers and rebels in Britain and Europe* (London, 2003)

Ronald G. Asch and Heinz Duchhardt (eds.), *Der Absolutismus – ein Mythos? Strukturwandel monarchischer Herrschaft in West- und Mitteleuropa (ca. 1550–1700)* (Cologne, Weimar and Vienna, 1996)

R. Nisbet Bain, *Gustavus III and His Contemporaries, 1746–1792* (London, 1894)

Thomas Bartlett, 'Protestant nationalism in eighteenth-century Ireland', *Studies on Voltaire and the Eighteenth Century*, 335 (1995)

Derek Beales, *Enlightenment and Reform in Eighteenth-Century Europe* (London, 2005)

Derek Beales, *Joseph II, Vol. I: In the shadow of Maria Theresa, 1741–1780* (Cambridge, 1987).

William Beik, *Louis XIV and Absolutism* (Boston, Mass., 2000)

David A. Bell, *The Cult of the Nation in France. Inventing nationalism 1680–1800* (Cambridge, Mass. and London, 2001)

L. Bergeron, *France under Napoleon* (Princeton, 1981)

T. C. W. Blanning, *The Culture of Power and the Power of Culture. Old regime Europe 1660–1789* (Oxford, 2002)

T. C. W. Blanning, *The French Revolution. Class war or culture clash?* (London, 1998)

T. C. W. Blanning, *Joseph II* (London, 1994)

J. Bosher, *French Finances, 1770–1795: From business to bureaucracy* (Cambridge, 1970)

John Brewer, *The Sinews of Power: War, money and the English state 1688–1783* (New York, 1989)

John Brooke, *King George III* (London, 1972)

Peter Burke, *The Fabrication of Louis XIV* (New Haven, 1992)

John Cannon, *Aristocratic Century. The peerage of eighteenth-century England* (Cambridge, 1984)

Guy Chaussinand-Nogaret, *The French Nobility in the Eighteenth Century* (Cambridge, 1985)

J. C. D. Clark, *English Society, 1660–1832: Religion, ideology and politics during the ancien regime* (Cambridge, 2000)

J. C. D. Clark, *The Language of Liberty 1660–1832. Political discourse and social dynamics in the Anglo-American world* (Cambridge, 1994)

Linda Colley, *Britons. Forging the nation 1707–1837* (New Haven and London, 1992)

Linda Colley, 'The apotheosis of George III: loyalty, royalty and the British nation 1760–1820', *Past and Present*, 102 (1984)

James Collins, *The State in Early Modern France* (Cambridge, 1995)

Jonathan Dewald, *The European Nobility 1500–1800* (Cambridge, 1996)

P. G. M. Dickson, *Finance and Government under Maria Theresa 1740–1780*, 2 vols. (Oxford, 1987)

Simon Dixon, *Catherine the Great* (London, 2001)

Basil Dmytryshyn, *Modernisation of Russia under Peter I and Catherine II* (New York, 1974)

W. Doyle, *Venality. The sale of offices in eighteenth-century France* (Oxford, 1996)

William Doyle, *Origins of the French Revolution*, 3rd edn (Oxford, 1998)

William Doyle, *The Oxford History of the French Revolution* (Oxford, 1989)

John Dunn, *Setting the People Free. The story of democracy* (London, 2005)

Geoffrey Ellis, *Napoleon* (London, 1997)

R. J. W. Evans, 'The Habsburg Monarchy and Bohemia, 1526 to 1848', in Mark Greengrass (ed.), *Conquest and Coalescence. The shaping of the state in early modern Europe* (London, 1991)

David Fraser, *Frederick the Great: King of Prussia* (London, 2000)

François Furet, *Revolutionary France 1770–1880* (Oxford and Cambridge, Mass., 1992)

Jacques Godechot, 'Nation, patrie, nationalisme et patriotisme en France au XVIIIe siècle' *Annales historiques de la Révolution française*, 43 (1971)

William D. Godsey Jr, *Nobles and Nation in Central Europe: Free Imperial Knights in the age of revolution, 1750–1850* (Cambridge, 2004)

Michael A. R. Graves, *The Parliaments of Early Modern Europe* (London, 2001)

John Hardman, *Louis XVI* (New Haven, 1993)

Adrian Hastings, *The Construction of Nationhood. Ethnicity, religion and nationalism* (Cambridge, 1997)

Nicholas Henshall, *The Myth of Absolutism. Change and continuity in early modern European history* (London and New York, 1992)

Lindsey Hughes, *Russia in the Age of Peter the Great* (New Haven and London, 1998)

Lynn Hunt, *Politics, Culture and Class in the French Revolution* (London, 1986)

Robert E. Jones, *The Emancipation of the Russian Nobility 1762–1785* (Princeton, 1973)

Derek McKay, *The Great Elector* (London, 2001)

Isabel de Madariaga, *Russia in the Age of Catherine the Great* (New Haven and London 1981).

P. Mathias and P. O'Brien, 'Taxation in Britain and France, 1715–1810', *Journal of European Economic History* (1976)

Vincent Morley, 'Views of the past in Irish vernacular literature, 1650–1850', in Ti Blanning and Hagen Schulze (eds.), *Unity and Diversity in Europe c. 1800* (Oxford, 200

R. R. Palmer, *The Age of the Democratic Revolution. A political history of Europe an America, 1760–1800*, 2 vols. (Princeton, 1959, 1964)

Peter Paret (ed.), *Frederick the Great. A profile* (London, 1972)

Munro Price, *The Fall of the French Monarchy: Louis XVI, Marie Antoinette and the bar de Breteuil* (Basingstoke, 2002)

Donald Quataert, *The Ottoman Empire 1700–1922* (Cambridge, 2000)

Marc Raeff, *Origins of the Russian Intelligentsia: The eighteenth-century nobility* (New York, 1966)

Marc Raeff, *The Well-Ordered Police State. Social and institutional change through law in the Germanies and Russia 1600–1800* (New Haven and London, 1983)

J. Riley, *The Seven Years War and the Old Regime in France: The economic and financial toll* (Princeton, 1986)

Hans Rogger, *National Consciousness in 18th-Century Russia* (Cambridge, Mass., 1960)

Hans Rosenberg, *Bureaucracy, Aristocracy and Autocracy. The Prussian experience 1660–1815* (Boston, Mass., 1966)

Guy Rowlands, *The Dynastic State and the Army under Louis XIV. Royal service and private interest, 1661–1701* (Cambridge, 2002)

Simon Schama, *Citizens. A chronicle of the French Revolution* (New York, 1989)

Theodor Schieder, *Frederick the Great*, ed. and trans. Sabina Berkeley and H. M. Scott (London and New York, 2000)

H. M. Scott (ed.), *Enlightened Absolutism: Reform and reformers in later eighteenth-century Europe* (Basingstoke, 1990)

H. M. Scott (ed.), *The European Nobilities in the Seventeenth and Eighteenth Centuries*, 2 vols., 2nd edn (London, 2006)

Quentin Skinner, 'The state', in Terence Ball, James Farr and Russell L. Hanson (eds.), *Political Innovation and Conceptual Change* (Cambridge, 1989)

David L. Smith, *A History of the Modern British Isles, 1603–1707: The double crown* (Oxford, 1998)

Hannah Smith, *Georgian Monarchy: Politics and culture 1714–1760* (Oxford, 2006)

David Sturdy, *Louis XIV* (Basingstoke, 1998)

D. M. G. Sutherland, *France 1789–1815* (London, 1985)

Julian Swann, *Politics and the Parlement of Paris under Louis XV, 1754–1774* (Cambridge, 1995)

Julian Swann, 'Politics and the state in eighteenth-century Europe', in T. C. W. Blanning (ed.), *The Short Oxford History of Europe: The eighteenth century* (Oxford, 2000)

J. Tulard, *Napoleon. The myth of the saviour* (London, 1984)

Dale Van Kley, *The Damiens Affair and the Unravelling of the Ancien Régime 1750–1770* (Princeton, 1984)

Peter Wilson, *Absolutism in Central Europe* (London, 2000)

Richard S. Wortman, *Scenarios of Power. Myth and ceremony in Russian monarchy*, vol. I (Princeton, 1995)

Religion and culture

John Adamson, *The Princely Courts of Europe. Ritual, politics and culture under the Ancien Régime 1500–1750* (London, 1999)

Nigel Aston, *Christianity and Revolutionary Europe c. 1750–1830* (Cambridge, 2002)

Nigel Aston (ed.), *Religious Change in Europe 1650–1914* (Oxford, 1997)

Hannah Barker and Simon Burrows (eds.), *Press, Politics and the Public Sphere in Europe and North America 1760–1820* (Cambridge, 2002)

Derek Beales, *Prosperity and Plunder. European Catholic monasteries in the age of revolution, 1650–1815* (Cambridge, 2003)

Derek Beales, 'Religion and culture', in T. C. W. Blanning (ed.), *The Short Oxford History of Europe: The eighteenth century* (Oxford, 2000)

Wolfgang Behringer, *Witchcraft Persecutions in Bavaria. Popular magic, religious zealotry and reasons of state in early modern Europe* (Cambridge, 1997)

Barry Bergdoll, *European Architecture 1750–1890* (Oxford, 2000)

Ann Bermingham and John Brewer (eds.), *The Consumption of Culture 1600–1800. Image, object, text* (London and New York, 1995)

Theodore Besterman, *Voltaire*, 3rd edn (Oxford, 1976)

T. C. W. Blanning, *The Culture of Power and the Power of Culture. Old regime Eur*
1660–1789 (Oxford, 2002)

T. C. W. Blanning, 'The role of religion in counter-revolution 1789–1815', in D. E. D. Bea
and G. Best (eds.), *History, Society and the Churches* (Cambridge, 1985)

Ian Bostridge, *Witchcraft and its Transformations c. 1650–1750* (Oxford, 1997)

Nicholas Boyle, *Goethe. The poet and the Age*, vol. I *The Poetry of Desire* (Oxford, 199

Michael Brander, *Hunting and Shooting from Earliest Times to the Present Day* (Lond
1971)

Volkmar Braunbehrens, *Mozart in Vienna* (Oxford, 1991)

John Brewer, *The Pleasures of the Imagination. English culture in the eighteenth cent*
(London, 1997)

Anita Brookner, *Greuze. The rise and fall of an eighteenth-century phenomenon* (Lond
1972)

Anita Brookner, *Jacques-Louis David* (London, 1980)

Joseph Burke, *English Art 1714–1800* (London, 1976)

Peter Burke and Roy Porter (eds.), *The Social History of Language* (Cambridge, 1987)

William J. Callahan and David Higgs (eds.), *Church and Society in Catholic Europe of*
Eighteenth Century (Cambridge, 1979)

Raymond Carr, *English Fox Hunting: A history* (London, 1986)

Owen Chadwick, *The Popes and European Revolution* (Oxford, 1981)

Roger Chartier, *The Cultural Origins of the French Revolution* (Durham, N.C. and Lond
1991)

Roger Chartier, 'Print culture', in Roger Chartier (ed.), *The Culture of Print. Power and*
uses of print in early modern Europe (Cambridge, 1989)

Thomas E. Crow, *Painters and Public Life in Eighteenth-Century Paris* (New Haven a
London, 1985)

Jean Delumeau, *Catholicism between Luther and Voltaire: A new view of the Coun*
Reformation (London, 1977)

Otto Erich Deutsch, *Mozart – A Documentary Biography* (Stanford, 1965)

A. G. Dickens (ed.), *The Courts of Europe: Politics, patronage and royalty* (London, 19'

William Doyle, *Jansenism* (Basingstoke, 2000)

Jeroen Duindam, *Vienna and Versailles. The courts of Europe's dynastic rivals, 1550–1*
(Cambridge, 2003)

Cyril Ehrlich, *The Piano. A history*, rev. edn (Oxford, 1990)

Markman Ellis, *The Coffee-house: A cultural history* (London, 2004)

Lucien Febvre, 'Witchcraft: nonsense or mental revolution?', in Peter Burke (ed.), *A N*
Kind of History (London, 1973)

Orlando Figes, *Natasha's Dance. A cultural history of Russia* (London, 2002)

Martin Fitzpatrick, Peter Jones, Christa Knellwolf and Iain McCalman (eds.), *The Enligh*
ment World (London, 2004)

Elliot Forbes (ed.), *Thayer's Life of Beethoven*, rev. edn (Princeton, 1969)

Michael Forsyth, *Buildings for Music. The architect, the musician and the listener from*
seventeenth century to the present day (Cambridge, Mass., 1985)

Marc R. Foster, *Catholic Revival in the Age of the Baroque. Religious identity in south-u*
Germany, 1550–1750 (Cambridge, 2001)

Mary Fulbrook, *Piety and Politics. Religion and the rise of absolutism in England, Württ*
berg and Prussia (Cambridge, 1983)

R. Gawthrop, *Pietism and the Making of 18th-Century Prussia* (Cambridge, 1993)

Marijke Gijswijt-Hofstra, Brian P. Levack and Roy Porter, *Witchcraft and Magic in Eur*
The eighteenth and nineteenth centuries (London, 1999)

Anne Goldgar, *Impolite Learning. Conduct and community in the republic of letters 16*
1750 (New Haven and London, 1995)

Dena Goodman, *The Republic of Letters. A cultural history of the French Enlightenm*
(Ithaca and London, 1994)

Hanns Gross, *Rome in the Age of Enlightenment. The post-Tridentine syndrome and the ancien régime* (Cambridge, 1990)

Louis Hautecoeur, *Histoire de l'architecture classique en France*, vol. IV *Seconde moitié du XVIIIe siècle. Le style Louis XV (1750–1792)* (Paris, 1952)

Louis Hautecoeur, *Littérature et peinture en France du XVIIe au XXe siècle*, 2nd edn (Paris, 1963)

Louis Hautecoeur, *Rome et la renaissance de l'antiquité à la fin du XVIIIe siècle*, Bibliothèque des écoles françaises d'Athènes et de Rome, vol. 105 (Paris, 1912)

John Henry, *The Scientific Revolution and the Origins of Modern Science*, 2nd edn (Basingstoke, 2002)

Henry Russell Hitchcock, *Rococo Architecture in Southern Germany* (London, 1968)

Denis Hollier (ed.), *A New History of French Literature* (Cambridge, Mass., 1989)

Hugh Honour, *Neo-Classicism* (Harmondsworth, 1968)

Hugh Honour, *Romanticism* (London, 1979)

Holger Hoock, *The King's Artists. The Royal Academy of Arts and the politics of British culture 1760–1840* (Oxford, 2003)

J. P. Hore, *The History of the Royal Buckhounds* (London, 1893)

R. Po-Chia Hsia, *The World of Catholic Renewal 1540–1770* (Cambridge, 1998)

David Irwin, *English Neo-Classical Art. Studies in inspiration and taste* (London, 1966)

David Irwin (ed.), *Winckelmann. Writings on art* (London, 1972)

Jonathan Israel, *Radical Enlightenment. Philosophy and the making of modernity* (Oxford, 2001)

David C. Itzkowitz, *Peculiar Privilege. A social history of English fox-hunting 1753–1885* (Hassocks, 1977)

W. M. Jacob, *Lay People and Religion in the Early Eighteenth Century* (Cambridge, 1996)

Wend Graf Kalnein and Michael Levey, *Art and Architecture of the Eighteenth Century in France* (London, 1972)

Thomas Da Costa Kaufmann, *Court, Cloister and City: The art and culture of Central Europe 1450–1800* (London, 1995)

Hugh Kearney, *Science and Change 1500–1700* (London, 1971)

Lawrence Klein, *Shaftesbury and the Culture of Politeness. Moral discourse and cultural politics in early eighteenth-century England* (Cambridge, 1994)

Martin Knoll, 'Hunting in the eighteenth century: an environmental perspective', *Historical Social Research*, 29, 3 (2004)

H. C. Robbins Landon (ed.), *Haydn in England 1791–1795* (London, 1976)

James Lees-Milne, *Baroque in Italy* (London, 1959)

James Lees-Milne, *Baroque in Spain and Portugal* (London, 1960)

Michael Levey, *Painting at Court* (New York, 1971)

Michael Levey, *Rococo to Revolution: Major trends in eighteenth-century painting* (London, 1966)

Roger Longrigg, *The History of Horse Racing* (London, 1972)

John Lough, *An Introduction to Eighteenth-Century France* (London, 1960)

John Lough, *The Contributors to the* Encyclopédie (1973)

John Lough, *The* Encyclopédie (London, 1971)

Howard Loxton, *The Garden* (London, 1991)

J. McManners, *Death and Enlightenment* (Oxford, 1985)

John McManners, *Church and Society in Eighteenth-Century France*, 2 vols. (Oxford, 1998)

John McManners, *The French Revolution and the Church* (London, 1969)

Gary Marker, *Publishing, Printing and the Origins of Intellectual Life in Russia 1700–1800* (Princeton, 1985)

John Rupert Martin, *Baroque* (London, 1977)

P. G. Maxwell-Stuart, *Witchcraft in Europe and the New World 1400–1800* (Basingstoke, 2001)

James Van Horn Melton, *The Rise of the Public in Enlightenment Europe* (Cambridge, 2001)

Robin Middleton and David Watkin, *Neo-Classical and Nineteenth-Century Architecture* (New York, 1980)

Alain Montandon, *Le Roman au XVIIIe siècle en Europe* (Paris, 1999)

E. William Monter, 'Witchcraft in Geneva 1537–1662', *Journal of Modern History*, 43 (1971)

Chandra Mukerji, *Territorial Ambitions and the Gardens of Versailles* (Cambridge, 1997)

Thomas Munck, *The Enlightenment. A comparative social history 1721–1794* (London, 2000)

Malcolm Oster (ed.), *Science in Europe 1500–1800* (Basingstoke, 2002)

Dorinda Outram, *The Enlightenment*, 2nd edn (Cambridge, 2005)

R. E. Palmer, *Catholics and Unbelievers in Eighteenth-Century France* (Princeton, 1939)

Giorgio Pestelli, *The Age of Mozart and Beethoven* (Cambridge, 1984)

Nikolaus Pevsner, *Academies of Art – Past and Present* (Cambridge, 1940)

James Raven, *Judging New Wealth. Popular publishing and responses to commerce in England, 1750–1800* (Oxford, 1992)

James Raven, Helen Small and Naomi Tadmor (eds.), *The Practice and Representation of Reading in England* (Cambridge, 1996)

T. J. Reed, *The Classical Centre. Goethe and Weimar 1775–1832* (London, 1980)

Jane Ridley, *Fox-Hunting* (London, 1990)

John Robertson, *The Case for Enlightenment. Scotland and Naples 1680–1760* (Cambridge, 2005)

W. D. Robson-Scott, *The Literary Background of the Gothic Revival in Germany* (Oxford, 1965)

Gordon Rupp, *Religion in England 1688–1791* (Oxford, 1986)

R. G. Saisselin, *Taste in Eighteenth-Century France: Critical reflections on the origins of aesthetics or an apology for amateurs* (Syracuse, N. Y., 1965)

Philippe Salvadori, *La Chasse sous l'ancien régime* (Paris, 1996)

Geoffrey Scarre and John Callow, *Witchcraft and Magic in Sixteenth- and Seventeenth-Century Europe*, 2nd edn (Basingstoke, 2001)

George Ryley Scott, *The History of Cockfighting* (Hindhead, 1983)

James J. Sheehan, *German History 1770–1866* (Oxford, 1989)

Alan G. R. Smith, *Science and Society in the Sixteenth and Seventeenth Centuries* (London, 1972)

Maynard Solomon, *Beethoven* (London, 1977)

Norman Sykes, *Church and State in England in the Eighteenth Century* (Cambridge, 1934)

Richard Taruskin, *The Oxford History of Western Music*, 6 vols., vol. 2: *The Seventeenth and Eighteenth Centuries* (Oxford, 2005)

Mikulas Teich and Roy Porter (eds.), *The Enlightenment in National Context* (Cambridge, 1981)

Keith Thomas, *Religion and the Decline of Magic* (Harmondsworth, 1973)

Rolf Toman (ed.), *Baroque* (Cologne, 1998)

W. R. Ward, *Christianity under the Ancien Régime, 1648–1789* (Cambridge, 1999)

David Watkin, *A History of Western Architecture*, 2nd edn (London, 1996)

David Watkin, *The English Vision. The Picturesque in architecture, landscape and garden design* (London, 1982)

William Weber, *The Rise of Musical Classics in Eighteenth-Century England* (Oxford, 1992)

Richard S. Westfall, *Science and Religion in Seventeenth-Century England* (New Haven, 1958)

Reinhard Wittmann, 'Was there a reading revolution at the end of the eighteenth century?', in Guglielmo Cavallo and Roger Chartier (eds.), *A History of Reading in the West* (Amherst, 1999)

Neal Zaslaw (ed.), *The Classical Era. From the 1740s to the end of the eighteenth century* (London, 1989)

War and peace

Martine Acerra and Jean Meyer, *Marines et Révolution* (Rennes, 1988)

M. S. Anderson, *The Eastern Question 1774–1923. A study in international relations* (London, 1966)

M. S. Anderson, *The Rise of Modern Diplomacy 1450–1919* (London, 1993)

M. S. Anderson, *The War of the Austrian Succession, 1740–48* (London, 1995)

Lucien Bély, *Les Relations internationales XVIᵉ–XVIIIᵉ siècles*, 3rd edn (Paris, 2001)

Jeremy Black, *A Military Revolution? Military change and European society 1550–1800* (London, 1990)

Jeremy Black, *European International Relations 1648–1815* (London, 2002)

T. C. W. Blanning, *The French Revolution in Germany. Occupation and resistance in the Rhineland 1792–1802* (Oxford, 1983)

T. C. W. Blanning, *The French Revolutionary Wars 1787–1802* (London, 1996)

T. C. W. Blanning, 'The French Revolution and Europe', in Colin Lucas (ed.), *Rewriting the French Revolution* (Oxford, 1991)

T. C. W. Blanning, *The Origins of the French Revolutionary Wars* (London, 1986)

Michael Broers, *Europe under Napoleon 1799–1815* (London, 1996)

Martin Boycott Brown, *The Road to Rivoli: Napoleon's First Campaign* (London, 2001)

David Chandler, *The Campaigns of Napoleon* (London, 1966)

John Childs, *Armies and Warfare in Europe 1648–1789* (Manchester, 1982)

Stephen Conway, *The War of American Independence* (London, 1995)

Martin van Creveld, *Supplying War: Logistics from Wallenstein to Patton* (New York, 1977)

François Crouzet, 'Wars, blockade and economic change in Europe, 1792–1815', *Journal of Economic History*, 24 (1964)

Heinz Duchhardt, *'Balance of Power' und Pentarchie: internationale Beziehungen 1700–1785* (Paderborn, 1997)

Christopher Duffy, *The Army of Frederick the Great* (Newton Abbot, 1974)

Christopher Duffy, *The Army of Maria Theresa. The armed forces of Imperial Austria 1740–1780* (Newton Abbot, 1977)

Christopher Duffy, 'Rossbach', in Cyril Falls (ed.), *Great Military Battles* (London, 1964)

Christopher Duffy, *Russia's Military Way to the West: The origins and nature of Russian military power, 1700–1800* (London, 1981)

Jonathan R. Dull, *A Diplomatic History of the American Revolution* (New Haven and London, 1985)

Jonathan R. Dull, *The French Navy and American Independence: A study of arms and diplomacy, 1774–1787* (Princeton, 1975)

C. J. Esdaile, *The Wars of Napoleon* (London, 1995)

Alan Forrest, *Soldiers of the French Revolution* (Durham, N.C. and London, 1990)

Patrice Higonnet, 'The origins of the Seven Years War', *Journal of Modern History*, 40 (1968)

T. O. Lloyd, *The British Empire 1558–1995* (Oxford, 1996)

John A. Lynn, *Giant of the grand siècle: The French army, 1610–1715* (Cambridge, 1998)

John A. Lynn, 'International rivalry and warfare', in T. C. W. Blanning (ed.), *The Short Oxford History of Europe: The eighteenth century* (Oxford, 2000)

John A. Lynn, *The Wars of Louis XIV, 1667–1714* (London, 1999)

Derek McKay, *Prince Eugene of Savoy* (London, 1977)

P. J. Marshall (ed.), *The Oxford History of the British Empire: The eighteenth century* (Oxford, 1998)

P. J. Marshall, 'Europe and the rest of the world', in T. C. W. Blanning (ed.), *The Short Oxford History of Europe: The eighteenth century* (Oxford, 2000)

Geoffrey Parker, *The Military Revolution. Military innovation and the rise of the west, 1500–1800*, 2nd edn (Cambridge, 1996)

David Parrott, 'The military revolution in early modern Europe', *History Today*, 42 (December, 1992)

J. H. Parry, *Trade and Dominion: The European overseas empires in the eighteenth century* (London, 1971)

Fritz Redlich, *De praeda militari. Looting and booty, 1500–1815*, Vierteljahrschrift für Sozial- und Wirtschaftsgeschichte. Beihefte. no. 39 (Wiesbaden, 1956)

N. A. M. Rodger, *The Command of the Ocean. A naval history of Britain 1649–1815* (London, 2004)

Karl A. Roider, *Austria's Eastern Question 1700–1790* (Princeton, 1982)

Gunther Rothenberg, *The Art of Warfare in the Age of Napoleon* (London, 1977)

Paul Schroeder, *The Transformation of European Politics, 1763–1848* (Oxford, 1994)

H. M. Scott, *The Birth of a Great Power System 1740–1815* (London, 2006)

H. M. Scott, *The Emergence of the Eastern Powers, 1756–1775* (Cambridge, 2001)

H. M. Scott and D. McKay, *The Rise of the Great Powers, 1648–1815* (London, 1983)

Samuel F. Scott, *The Response of the Royal Army to the French Revolution. The role and development of the line army 1787–1793* (Oxford, 1978)

Brendan Simms, *The Impact of Napoleon. Prussian high politics, foreign policy and the crisis of the executive, 1797–1806* (Cambridge, 1997)

Peter Wilson, *German Armies: War and German politics 1648–1806* (London, 1998)

Index